JUST ONE IN A MILLION
A True Life Story

A. Ray Calhoon

JUST ONE IN A MILLION
A True Life Story

by
A. Ray Calhoon

Heart of the Lakes Publishing
Interlaken, New York
1986

Library of Congress Cataloging-in-Publication Data

Calhoon, A. Ray, 1892–
  Just one in a million.

  1. Calhoon, A. Ray, 1892–   . 2. Educators––
United States––Biography. 3. School superintendents
and principals––United States––Biography. I. Title.
II. Title: Just 1 in a million.
LA2317.C24A34 1986   370'.92'4 [B]   86–3072
ISBN 0–932334–44–X

ISBN: 0-932334-44-X
Manufactured in the United States of America

A *quality* publication by
Heart of the Lakes Publishing
Interlaken, New York 14847

Contents

1. Montana—South Dakota 1
2. Life in Iowa 23
3. Ohio 41
4. Houghton 51
5. Home in Houghton 61
6. First Year College 77
7. A Year at Work 85
8. Clarkson 97
9. Back at Houghton 107
10. Oberlin 123
11. West Park 141
12. World War I 161
13. War in France 175
14. Army of Occupation 201
15. Oneida Community Ltd. 227
16. Burlington 243
17. Minoa 257
18. Saratoga Springs 299
19. California 325
20. Middletown 347
21. Utica Free Academy 355
22. Roscoe Conkling School 385
23. Theodore Roosevelt School 413
24. Principal of Utica Free Academy 461
25. Director of Secondary Education 497
26. Scholastic and Retirement 505

To Marjorie and Dorothy
who encouraged me
to write this story.

Foreword

The events of my early life as related in this book are from my memory. For later years, I had the help from a few old letters and newspaper clippings. Since 1935, when we started our circulating family letter, I kept my contributions and I have what is much like a fifty year diary.

A reminder to the reader that this is a story of one member of a generation that was born before the turn of the century into the simple life of the "horse and buggy" days and has lived through the many mechanical and electrical inventions that changed the lives of people on the farms, in the factories and in the homes all across America.

Ours is a generation that experienced great booms and deep depression. We lived through two World Wars and two conflicts, each leaving a mark on the lives of the people of this country. We suffered the shock of the birth of atomic energy and saw how science changed transporation, communication and medicine. Then with the aid of computers saw men explore outer space. Our generation has experienced more changes than any other since the beginning of civilization. But with all its great accomplishments it has left the most serious problems that ever faced mankind. The question remains, can man learn to live with man in peace and to use the tremendous force of atomic power for good, not for destruction?

As I write about each school, I am mindful of the many fine teachers I met and in every place I had good rapport with the students. While I never made much money in education, I am now rich with the many friends I made both in and out of school. This book is not only for the members of my family but also for those many friends.

A. Ray Calhoon
Utica, New York
1986

Acknowledgments

In compiling this book I owe thanks to many people:

Dorothy Calhoon Raemsch, for giving considerable time in proof reading the manuscript and galley sheets.

Marjorie Calhoon Horton, for encouragement to write my story.

Dick Bryant, art teacher at the Utica Free Academy, for locating a picture of the Academy building as it appeared in the 1930–1960 years and for obtaining permission to use it for the cover.

Robert Igoe and Sheila Orlin, North Country Books, for reading the manuscript, recommending a publisher and handling the distribution and sales.

Cindy Myers for keyboarding the manuscript.

Walt and Mary Steesy, Heart of the Lakes Publishing, for reading and editing the work and and seeing it through to publication.

CHAPTER 1

MONTANA—SOUTH DAKOTA

Now that I am an octogenarian I have the urge to put some of my life story on paper. Like every other person, I can say my life has been unlike that of anyone else. Some day, perhaps, my grandchildren will be interested in knowing about me.

My father, Francis Elmer Calhoon, while pastor of the Wesleyan Methodist Church in College Springs, Iowa, met and married Lena Crow, the 19 year old daughter of one of the leading members of the church. Both of my parents came from pioneering families. My father's sister, Clara, still lived on the old Calhoon homestead located in the James River Valley in South Dakota. The Crow family lived for a time in South Dakota and loved to tell the story of how the younger children had been marooned for two days in a one-room school house. The teacher was given credit for saving their lives by keeping them all night, rather than letting them start home in the terrible blizzard of 1888.

Two years after my parents were married, I was born on November 12, 1892. Soon after that they moved to a church in Charles City, Iowa. Here my first sister, Leeta, was born. Here the first event in my life that I can remember took place. Sunday night services in the church were the custom in those days, and as a family we always attended. Leeta, being a baby and I only two or three years old, would stretch out on the hard church pews and sleep through the service. After one service, I remember being awakened and taken to the front of the church and told to stand there. My mother left me and returned for the baby. It was dark and rainy, so people were standing on the steps waiting for their carriages to be brought to the door. Among the group was a lone man, a stranger, and I stood staring at him. Half asleep, I began to weave and as he explained later, he thought I was going to fall. When he made a grab at me, I let out a scream that I can still hear. My mother came dashing out to see what had happened and then to console me. The poor man was very apologetic and really concerned that he had frightened me so much. But I never forgot the episode and it influenced my feelings toward strangers the rest of my life.

When I was four years old, my father decided to go to Montana to stake out a claim on a newly opened government land grant. My mother took us children back to College Springs to stay with her

1

parents until the claim could be filed and a cabin built for our family. In the spring Father sent for us to come. I do not remember the long ride on the train, but I do remember meeting a rancher at the rail head and riding in a buckboard behind a team of rather wild horses. It was some forty miles to get to Father's cabin, and since it was early spring, every little creek bed was full of running water. There were no bridges so every stream had to be forded. More than once the water was so deep that the buckboard began to float down stream while the horses struggled to keep their footing. My mother often expressed her concern not only our safety but also as to the condition of our clothes packed in a trunk tied to the back of the rig.

After a day long ride, Father welcomed us at the one room half-log, half-sod cabin he had built. The law stated that in order to obtain the land free, one had to live on it at least six months of the year. So we lived there that summer and the following winter. I recall that the cabin was in the Yellowstone River Valley west of Miles City. There was a line of willow trees that marked the banks of the river about a half mile to the north. Once in a while we saw some river men poling their flat bottom boats up the stream. It still was one of the major means of transportation for the fur trappers and river traders.

Of course, in this dry country water was essential for the family, and soon after we arrived, Father began to dig a well. He had it down about fifteen feet when it proved to be very nearly my undoing. Leaving his digging to do the evening chores, Father left the well unguarded. Unknown to him, I was playing back of the house with a little red cart that I thought was wonderful. I was walking backwards watching the wheels turn and I came around the cabin backing into the open well. I must have screamed for the next thing I knew I was looking up into the face of my mother peering down at me and yelling for help. Fortunately, there were a few inches of water in the well, and it broke my fall. Father came running, rushed down the ladder, picked me up and carried me to the top. I was examined for broken bones, but the verdict was that I just had the wind knocked out of me and a good scare. Through it all I was still clutching the little red cart.

Mother had brought some garden seeds with her from Iowa. Father plowed a patch for her to plant a garden. However, I remember how disappointed she was when the hot dry winds of the summer killed most of the plants before they could mature. The summer was so dry that the meat of a quarter of venison could be preserved by hanging it outside the cabin. The outside of the meat would dry like leather and thus keep the inside good for a long period of time.

Father had obtained a team of horses and a milk cow. So when the cow became fresh that spring we had fresh milk and butter. There was plenty of home baked bread, and with the game which was plentiful, we had good fare for growing children.

In the late summer, Father cut some wild slew grass for hay to feed the cow and horses in the coming winter. He stacked it near a small barn he had erected and for protection put a barbed wire fence around it. The country was still nearly open range for cattle, and he knew if any came near in the winter they could eat the whole stack in one night. In fact, in the middle of the winter a lone long-horned steer did come in the night, and smelling the hay walked right through the fence and helped himself. The next morning I watched out the small cabin window as Father took a pitch fork and tried to drive the steer away. But the steer charged and Father was only two jumps ahead in getting back inside the barn. He then mounted one of the horses and armed with the pitch fork drove the steer away, but not without a battle in which the horse nearly got gutted. This was an example of why it was considered fatal to be caught on foot on the open range. These long-horned steers were worse than most wild animals. It was no wonder that horse stealing was considered a capital crime in the old west.

Our cabin was small and simply furnished. At one end was a bed, beside it a small cot for me and a cradle for Leeta. Extra clothes hung along the walls. At the opposite end was a small cook stove and a homemade table. A couple of wooden benches served as chairs. An open cupboard held the dishes and cooking utensils. There were two small windows between which was the only door.

One day in early winter Leeta and I were playing with some blocks on a buffalo robe spread on the cabin floor. Father had left early that morning with the team and wagon to cut some fire wood from a grove near the river. Mother was working around the cabin when the door came open and looking up we were startled to see a big Sioux Indian framed in the doorway. The sound of his approach had been muffled by the constant wind which blew across the open country. Mother gave a little cry of surprise and in a quick motion grabbed Leeta, putting her on the bed and pushed me up beside her. In a low voice she cautioned us not to move or say a word. Her manner was such as to make us freeze like some little frightened animals. We sat there with big eyes staring at the intruder. Saying "How," the Indian raised his hand in the sign of peace and motioned to see if he could come in. Mother let him in and in sign language asked if he was hungry. He nodded, "Yes." Taking a bowl from the cupboard, she filled it with some venison stew which was usually on the back of the stove, broke off a large piece of homemade bread, and set it before him. He gulped down the stew and held up the bowl for some more. When he had finished he sat looking around the cabin. He spied Father's rifle which hung on the wall and motioned to see it. Although we had seen a few Indians at a distance when they left the reservation to hunt, none so far had come near the cabin. This brave had an antelope on the back of his pony and had come to see if he could make a trade. It had been only a few years before that the U. S. Army had forced the Indians on a reservation, and there were many stories circulating as to what they might do when they wandered off their territory. Much to Mother's relief, when he saw that he could make no trade, the Sioux silently strode out the door, mounted his pony and rode away. As the Indian left, I climbed up to a window and watched him ride away, slumped over his pinto pony. Not until she heard the creaking of the wagon as Father returned with a load of wood did she begin to weep. All these years I have felt somewhat sorry for him, once an Indian brave, now reduced to asking a white woman for a handout, forced to live on a reservation when once free to roam where he pleased, now truly riding toward the vanishing point of his people.

In the spring after the snow had gone and before the new grass began to grow, the old prairie became tinder dry, and it was easy to start a dangerous fire. One morning at daylight my folks woke me to see just such a fire. A strong west wind was blowing a line of fire down the wide valley. Flames were mounting fifty or more feet into the air carrying patches of burning grass well ahead of the line of fire. Thus new fires were being started so the fire was traveling faster than the wind. Ahead of the fire, racing for their lives were the wild animals of the prairies. A herd of antelopes alongside some black deer sped by. Jack rabbits were scooting in every direction, some so confused that they actually raced back into the fire, perishing in an attempt to escape. Coyotes and some big timber wolves were running side by side. In the face of a common danger, the whole animal kingdom was at peace with itself.

The line of fire came within a half mile of our cabin, but Father had long before taken the precaution of plowing a wide border all around the buildings. As a further precaution against a sudden change of the wind, my folks had pumped tubs and pails full of water. They also had soaked several gunny sacks to have ready to beat out a fire if it did cross the plowed ground. The main danger now was that a rabbit or some other animal would wait so long its fur would catch on fire and then in desperation would run toward the cabin setting new fires along its path. This did happen, but Father saw the jack rabbit in time, grabbed his gun, and shot it before it crossed the plowed ground. The fire roared on until a spring shower quenched it, but it left the prairie a blackened mess, dotted with the smoldering carcasses of animals too slow to escape. The picture of that prairie fire is still vivid in my memory.

After a crop failure, it became evident to my folks that the land would never be good for farming, so as soon as the claim was settled, they sold it to a rancher. This rancher bought a number of similar claims, thus keeping the land for cattle grazing. That is all this land was good for and is still so used to this date.

A man who ran a large horse ranch had recently lost his wife and asked my mother to come and keep house for his family. At the same time he gave my father a job on the ranch. This ranch house was several miles up the river valley from our cabin, but in an area where there was a number of high buttes. One Sunday after a big dinner served to the family and guests, the children in the group decided to climb one of the buttes to pick wild flowers. They took me along. I remember how "spooky" the river valley looked from the butte as a large herd of cattle had been caught in a flood a few years before and all had drowned.

4

Their skulls and bones which had long since been picked clean lay bleaching in the sun. It was spring, and while the floor of the valley was still brown, the sides of the butte showed green grass and a lot of early prairie flowers in full bloom. We climbed the steep slope and were having a great time seeing who could find the best flowers when I lost my footing. I slid and rolled clear to the bottom, yelling all the way down. The others rushed down the butte and picked me up, all scratched and dirty with a bloody nose. I was rushed back to the house and came in screaming with my clothes all covered with dirt and blood, giving the party quite a fright.

When my father left Iowa he was an ordained minister, but since there were no churches in that part of the country where he expected to take up his claim, he was given the status of missionary. One school house had been recently built in the area, and he was asked to form a Sunday School which was allowed to meet in this building. It met with considerable success. This school house became a sort of community center, and I remember being taken to an evening entertainment where I saw my first jig dance. Some of the cowboys were clever in song and dance and put on a real show.

Every child who grew up in this country was repeatedly warned about rattlesnakes. One day after returning from a Sunday service, Leeta, who was now old enough to walk and talk, was left on the back porch while Mother hurried in to start the dinner. I was in the yard when I heard Leeta call, "Come, see this." I looked up to see her standing near the screen door which had been pushed back and fastened. When I got closer I was startled to see a big rattler back of the screen hissing and striking in all directions. I yelled for Mother and when she saw the situation, she snatched Leeta out of harm's way and called for help. Leeta was saved partly by the screen door and partly due to the fact it was August and the snake was shedding its skin and thus blinded. It was a narrow escape which we never forgot.

Another snake story was one we always kidded our mother about. One afternoon she was sitting near an open window sewing, when she kept hearing a peculiar croaking sound. It persisted so she got up and went outside to see what it was. She discovered a snake near the house in the act of trying to swallow a big toad which it had captured. The toad was rather large for the snake, and every time it made an effort to get more of its meal down, the toad would give a loud croak. This was too much for Mother, and she hurried back of the house, found a hoe, and returned intending to cut off the snake's head. She got ready and made a tremendous chop. Just then the snake moved and she cut the toad in two. When we laughed at her about the episode, she always claimed she saved the toad from suffering, even if she had to end its life to do so.

While the ranch where my folks now lived and worked did have some cattle, they were primarily interested in raising and selling horses. Every so often some of the horse herd would be rounded up and the best looking yearlings cut out to begin their training. I spent many hours watching the breaking of these young horses. The first step was to lasso one, get a halter on his head, and drag him outside the corral. One end of a long rope would be attached to the halter and the other end snubbed around a post inside the barn door. To the colt, who had spent all his life running free on the open range, the looks of that dark inside of the barn was terrifying. He would set all four feet and brace as hard as he could against the pull of the rope. Now it was a case of patience for the men who were on the end of the rope inside the barn. Every time the colt would struggle and give a little, the men would take up the slack, always keeping the rope taut. This slow struggle would sometimes go on for hours before the colt would finally give up and go through the barn door. Once inside he would stand trembling, but when he saw there was no danger, he usually soon calmed down and was led into a stall. While this did seem somewhat cruel, it was far more humane than the usual bronco busting done on most cattle ranches.

Once the colt was in a stall he was left for a time until he became used to having men around. When not harmed and given food and water, it was surprising how quickly the colts tamed. The next step was to place a saddle on his back and then a bridle was introduced. Many times it was a real struggle to get one to accept the bit. Just like people, there was a big difference in the reaction of each colt to this training. Some gentled easily and soon accepted a rider on his back, while others never became anything but a bronco, one that was tough and sturdy for work, but always wiley and never to be trusted.

My father's work was largely around the barns and other buildings on the ranch, but on occasion he would be asked to join the riders. One winter morning he was asked to help round up some cattle. With my mother, I stood in the window watching. Since it was cold, all the horses were very frisky. Father was the last one to mount and before he could get a good seat, his horse reared. As it sometimes happened, the horse reared so far it went over backwards pinning Father underneath. My mother screamed; she was sure he was killed. Father was carried into the house, and it was feared that he had a broken hip. There was no doctor short of Miles City, over forty miles away, so the rancher examined Father and decided there were no broken bones, but he was laid up for weeks. It was an injury that bothered him the rest of his life. My mother was very upset; she scolded the rancher for giving Father a half-broken horse and berated Father for attempting to ride it. It was a long time before he could ride again, so he lost his job on the ranch.

The next event I can remember was being at Grandfather's house in College Springs, Iowa. I do not recall the trip to get there, and it was only recently when my sister found some old letters that my parents exchanged that I did understand just what happened. When Mother found out that she was to have another baby, she decided it was too much to stay working on the ranch in Montana and made plans to return to her parent's home. Taking Leeta and me she left Father, who decided to stay to find work he could do. Money was very tight in those days, and the only thing he could find was to cut fence posts. He contracted with a rancher who had some timber on his land for a few cents a post. This was the time when some of the land was being fenced in with barbed wire. The big cattle ranchers resisted this movement strenuously, as they wanted to keep all the land for open range. In fact, it led to almost open warfare. But since to string the wire there had to be posts, it did make a market for those who were fortunate to have some timber. The only drawback for Father was he cut posts all winter but had to wait until spring for the rancher to sell before he got any pay.

When we got to College Springs we also had problems. Grandfather's house was small. Two of my aunts and my uncle Roy, who was only two years older than me, were at home. The older children had left as soon as they could support themselves. Also, my great-grandmother had a room by herself in one end of the house. She was paying the mortgage, so they took care of her although she was over 90 at that time. The only place for us to sleep was in an attic bedroom together with my aunts. Mother paid some of our board and room, but she was not satisfied with such arrangements, especially as she was expecting. To understand the situation, I should explain more about my grand-parents. I remember Grandfather as a large bearded man, six feet tall and weighing about 200 pounds. He was a man of striking contrasts, outside the home he was a jovial man always telling jokes and kidding the ladies. At home, he was overly strict, so much so all the boys ran away from home at sixteen, and the girls left as soon as possible. He was one of the leading members of the Wesleyan church, noted for his loud singing and long prayers. He was very strict about keeping Sunday laws, but rumor had it that he could strike a sharp bargain with his neighbors on week days.

My Grandmother was a small woman but she ruled her house with a sharp tougue. She was used to living with little money and knew how to stretch food and clothing to the limit. When not busy cooking she seemed always busy sewing and kept a thimble on her finger. Her favorite way to admonish a child was to rap him on the head with that thimble. It hurt and I used to resent it.

Crowded as we were, we children spent part of our time in Great-grandmother's room. She had been a Wesleyan Methodist all her life and was a strict fundamentalist. She and any women visitors who came to see her would discuss in our presence how terrible the world was becoming. I gathered from her that all the men were drunkards and going to the dogs. All the young women were not dressing properly and were leading a loose life. She never hesitated to tell us children what we should or should not be doing. We were somewhat awed by her and didn't like her interference. For example, one Sunday afternoon Leeta

7

and I were playing with some blocks on the floor of her room. She was horrified that our mother would let us play on Sunday. "Why," she said, "when I was young we were never allowed to do anything on Sunday except go to church. We were never allowed to even touch money so the preacher never was paid until Monday."

Facing all this situation, Mother began to see if she could have an extra small room added to the house so we could have some privacy. She talked with her mother, who approved, but her father was dead set against it. He could see no reason we couldn't get along with what we had, and when she explained she needed to have a place to have the baby, he thought the couch in the living room was good enough. But Mother was persistent, and found a carpenter who agreed to add a small room for $25.00. She then sent a letter to Father explaining the situation and begged him to send the money. She ended the letter by saying, "It is impossible to think of having a baby on the couch in the living room. I would rather lay down under a sage bush where it will be quiet." Evidently her letter was effective, for Father somehow found the $25.00 and sent it to her. When she showed her father that she had the money and he wouldn't have to do anything to help build the room, he reluctantly consented.

The room was finished in March, and we thankfully moved into it. It was small, just big enough for a bed and two cots and small wash stand. Our extra clothes were hung from nails along the walls, but we were happy to have a place we could call ours. Soon after we were located, I became very ill. I always thought it was due to food. We ate with our grandparents, and their diet was different from what we had been used to. For example, they had a lot of salt pork for meat and a lot of home canned fruit. Sometimes for supper all we had was a big bowl of wild plums or gooseberries stewed up and thickened with corn starch. This with a slice of bread and butter composed the meal. Evidently it was too much acid for me.

I continued to get worse, so they sent for a doctor. By that time I couldn't keep anything on my stomach, not even water. The doctor gave me a superficial examination, mixed up some powders in a glass of water, and told me to drink it. I did, but threw it up immediately. He just shook his head, left some of the powders, and walked out. I continued to suffer. I couldn't stand any light in my eyes, so the room was kept dark, and I became so dehydrated that my tongue swelled up and I was unable to be understood. One afternoon while in a dazed condition I heard my two aunts just outside my door discussing my condition. It was evident they didn't think I was going to last and they thought my father should be sent for. Then they began to discuss what they would wear for the funeral. What I heard made me mad. I sat up, reached for the glass of water which was kept beside my cot and drank half of it. Of course, I threw it right up, but I drank some more. After two times I did keep a little down and from that moment began to get better.

Ula, my second sister, was born May 7, 1898, in our small room. The room was now so crowded that Mother made arrangements for me to go stay with my Uncle Ed who lived in a nearby town. I had only met him a time or two and had never seen his wife. When I did meet her I didn't like her. They had no children and there were none in the neighborhood, so I was alone. I didn't have anything to do and the days seemed endless. For the four weeks I was there I was utterly miserable.

After Father sold the claim and saw we could not live in Montana, he began to contact heads of the Wesleyan Church in the nearby states. This was a small denomination and most of the churches were small. Only a few were able to pay the salary of a full-time minister, especially one with a family. Then in the spring before Ula was born, he was offered the pastorate of the church in Northville, South Dakota. The salary was not large, but there was a good-sized parsonage, so Mother encouraged him to take it. She was so anxious to have a home again with the family altogether that the salary was secondary. So when the baby was about six weeks old and Mother felt strong enough to travel, she called me back to College Springs. She persuaded Aunt Nell to go with us to help with the children, and we packed our belongings and left for Northville.

Father had secured some furniture and had the house all arranged for us. We were so happy to see him and be a family again that we didn't care what the town looked like. In fact, Northville was a very small place about 15 miles south of Aberdeen. There were a few stores, a railroad station, a grain elevator, a school house, the Wesleyan Church, and a dozen or so houses. It was located in a strictly western wheat farming area. The land was flat and not a tree in sight. We soon felt at home, and I was delighted to find several boys my age to play with. Together we roamed the countryside outside the town. Most of this area was in its natural state. It had never been plowed and the native grasses were left for some of the town folks to use to graze a cow or two. In this area we could hunt gophers catching them with string snares. We watched the activities of a prairie dog town. We tried to wring the necks of the ground owls that lived with the prairie dogs, by walking around and around them, but they had the ability to look straight at you, and it was impossible to tell when they changed the direction of their heads.

We went barefooted all summer and while our feet became hard and tough, we did have trouble with thorns like those on the wild rose bushes. One time I stepped on a ground cactus and my folks spent a long time picking out the scores of sharp needles which were imbedded. But in spite of their efforts, my foot became infected, and I had to remain in the house for days while my foot was packed in a poultice to draw out the poison.

Some five miles to the east was a larger town, Millette, and two miles beyond was the Calhoon homestead. Father's sister, Clara, had married George Stelle, and they lived on this farm. The family was unusual, as there were eleven children, all girls, except the oldest, Earl, who was a young man, and being the oldest, he took over the management of the farm, especially as his father was supposed to have heart trouble. The older girls were a husky lot and when needed, they would go into the fields and do a man's work. They all could ride a horse and some were a crack shot with a rifle. I was invited to stay on this farm several times. I enjoyed it all, following Earl around the farm, riding the machinery when possible, learning to ride a horse, and being a part of the activity of the large family.

While Uncle George did very little work, he did like to hunt. Prairie chickens were plentiful, and it was not unusual to see a flock of twenty-five or more birds fly up at one time. There were many jack rabbits and the brush along the river was full of cottontails. I was thrilled when Uncle George would let me follow him on some of his trips. I think both Leeta and I were staying on this farm when my brother, Dale, was born in Northville on November 29, 1899.

Aunt Nell, who had come with us from College Springs, got a job that fall teaching in a one-room school a few miles out of Northville. She still wasn't 18 years old, which was the requirement for a teacher's certificate, but there were so few teachers available they took her anyway. As was the custom she roomed and boarded with the families of the children that were in school, but she spent a lot of her weekends with us. After that experience she was accepted as the teacher of the first three grades in the Northville school. Mother took her and one other teacher in as boarders. I entered school that fall so she was my first teacher. That presented a problem for me for at home she was Aunt Nell but in school I had to call her Miss Crow.

Since we lived near the school I went home for lunch each day. Then one day during my first week in school some of the boys in the first grade asked me to join them in a gopher hunt in a pile of railroad ties near the station. As the first grade was dismissed before the upper grades, they assured me that there was plenty of time. I was so flattered to be asked to join the gang that against my better judgment I went along. We spied a stripped gopher in the pile of ties and were so excited chasing him from one level to another we lost all sense of time. I had heard of the wrath of God in Sunday School, but it didn't mean much to me. But suddenly I looked up and saw the real wrath of God staring down at me. I heard a voice from above saying, "Ray! Come home." When I looked again I realized it was my father's face and his voice. I meekly followed him home. As soon as we were inside the door, he took me over his knee and for the first time in my life that I could remember, he gave me a good spanking. I was then told in no uncertain terms to never go anywhere without permission. I never forgot and never needed to be reminded.

At school I seemed to get along very well. I not only knew the alphabet before I entered school, but could read many words. I was a little disgusted to have to sound out all the letters of a word I already knew. I couldn't say "cat" when it was printed on the blackboard, but had to draw out "K-a-tt." This was the method then in vogue in teaching reading.

One incident happened that year in school which caused a big commotion in the community. Many of the boys in the upper grades had to work on the farm in the spring and fall and only attended school in the winter months. Consequently, many of these boys were sixteen or more years old. Since they were accustomed to doing a man's work, they resented some of the school regulations. The teachers were usually young women and the boys didn't like to be "bossed" by them. As in many schools it was forbidden to chew gum in school, but one day the son of a prominent citizen in the community was caught chewing. The teacher made him spit it out and put it on a piece of paper. Then at the end of the morning session she told him to put it back in his mouth before he could go home. When he refused, she called on the other teachers for help. They tried to force the gum into his mouth, but he was too strong for them. They then tied him in a chair with a rope. The boys in the school knew about the situation and stayed around to see what would happen. After a time when the boy didn't come out, they got together and plotted to rescue him. While one group assembled at the front door pretending to force their way in, thus drawing all the teachers to the door, a second group raised a window, crawled in, cut the prisoner loose and all escaped out the window. Of course, this created a big furor in the town, people took sides, some for and some against the teachers. My father was caught in the middle, one of the teachers was his sister-in-law, while the father of the boy was a leading member of the church. As far as I know, he never said anything about it outside the house and it finally all died down.

One experience I had at the end of my first year in school had a lasting effect on my life. Aunt Nell, my teacher, wanted to do something special the last day of school. She planned a little play to be presented by the first grade pupils in which a girl was to present her doll, supposed to be her baby, to a boy acting the part of a doctor. I was picked to play the part of the doctor. I didn't want to do it, but she appealed to my parents and they forced me to take the part. On the day of the play the parents were invited and many mothers came. I was dressed in one of Father's long black coats and across my chest was his big watch chain attached to his open faced watch. At the appropriate time I had to take out the watch and pretend to count the doll's pulse. I thought it all very foolish and when the guests laughed and applauded, I was extremely embarrassed. Then when it was over and they said how cute I was, I vowed to never be in another play. I never did, although I had chances to do so. I could be on a stage to give a speech, but never wanted to be an actor.

It was in Northville that I first became aware of being called "the minister's son." I learned the meaning of the epithet when I was warned by my mother that I must not do some things other boys did because I would disgrace my father. I was sometimes taunted by other boys to go with them on some escapade and if I did and was caught, all the neighbors would say, "How terrible for the minister's son to do such a thing. Oh well, you know they always turn out bad." It was like being branded and I had to live with it all my early life. Later in life when I met other minister's sons, they told me they had the same experience. It was a common saying that all minister's children turn out bad, but history proves otherwise.

While most of our time in Northville was on the good side, there was one dark spot. Ula, still a baby, developed a serious illness. She had frequent severe convulsions and more than once we thought she was gone. The doctors never did diagnose her trouble and gradually her condition did improve. But for several years our family life rotated around her spells. The only medicine that seemed to help was a new patent medicine then becoming popular. It was a bitter concoction which Ula hated, but it did seem to help whenever she showed signs of another spell. I know it contained a syrup so I have always wondered if her trouble was an early sign of diabetes. She did outgrow the spells, but in later life she did become a diabetic.

While we were in Northville the Spanish-American War took place. The only thing I remember was the excitement it created among us boys when we heard that a train bearing some of Teddy Roosevelt's Rough Riders coming back from the war would go through the town. We gathered at the station at the scheduled time and although late, it came and to our delight, stopped. Since many of the Riders came from the Dakotas, a number of the soldiers got off the train. They were in high spirits and made quite an impression on us boys. My mother, however, wasn't impressed. She said they were all drunk and should be ashamed.

We were used to the extreme weather patterns of the prairies, the long cold winters when it was not uncommon for the temperature to drop forty or more below zero, and then the very hot days of summer. These hot days often produced some violent thunder storms, some turning into tornadoes. These storms were called cyclones, and were extremely destructive. For protection every house had a nearby cyclone cellar, an excavation dug in the backyard, then covered over on top with boards on which was piled the dirt dug from the ground. The cellar was equipped with some old chairs, a table and a cot or two plus some food and water. More than once I can recall being aroused in the middle of the night and dragged or carried to our cyclone cellar. Lightning would be constant so the whole area would be lit up. While a lantern was taken along, it was hardly needed. The air would be filled with the roll of thunder and a low roar could be heard as the sound of the wind of the approaching storm traveled across the flat prairie. One such storm did come within a mile of the town and destroyed several farm houses.

After each of these severe storms reports reached town as to the number of buildings damaged and the toll of cattle and horses killed by lightning. Sometimes people were injured, but most had learned to take early refuge in the cyclone cellars. As more of the land became enclosed by barbed wire fences and since both cattle and horses tend to drift before a wind, in such storms they would do so until they came up against one of these fences. Lightning striking nearby would charge the fence and knock these animals cold. At times lightning would strike a horse or steer out in the open. This led to a saying that animals attract lightning. However, lightning will strike the highest point and such a lone animal would be the highest point on a treeless prairie. It was for this reason that boys were taught early to never ride or be near a horse in a thunder storm.

Part of a minister's income was the donations that church members brought his family. Whenever a farmer butchered a pig or steer he would bring some of the meat to the minister. But such gifts were not enough to support a growing family, so Father had to work outside his regular duties. One year he formed a partnership with another man in the town, and they took a venture in planting a big field of potatoes. The wheat farmers thought they were crazy and predicted the potatoes would all dry up in the hot summer weather. However, they did get a break, and there was enough rain that year so they did get a fair crop. They had the potatoes, but by the time they paid the shipping costs to get them to a market, they didn't make much on their venture.

When the big fields of wheat were ready for harvest, every able-bodied man and boy was expected to work. Father was no exception and when I was eight years old, I persuaded my mother to let me go with him. I was thrilled to get a job driving the team of the header box. In those days most of the grain was cut by a header. This was a big machine pulled by a six horse team and so designed that it went ahead of the horses cutting off the heads of the grain. Only the head containing the wheat grain was wanted, the less straw the better. As the heads were cut they fell on a revolving canvas belt which delivered them to another belt which elevated them to a header box. This box was the size of a hay wagon but built solid and drawn by a team of horses. The box was about seven feet on one side but slanted down to three feet on the opposite side. It was on the lower side that the wheat was delivered. One man rode the rig as a loader. In some cases he had a team that was trained to keep the right distance from the header and could do it alone. In most cases it required a driver to control the team. To keep the straw from covering the driver a small box was built in the front of the rig. It was enclosed on the top and three sides, open only on the front so the driver could see where to go. On the hot afternoons this box became like an oven. Usually boys were hired as drivers and paid fifty cents a day. This was the job I got.

There were a number of header boxes in line so while one was being unloaded at the threshing machine, others would be ready to keep the header moving. My job was to bring my loaded box in for unloading, climb down, and then up into the next box. The days were long starting at daylight in the morning and ending at six at night. Time was taken for a big dinner at noon and a mid-day break in the morning and afternoon for refreshments. I thought it was great to be working with the men, but some of those teams were hard to control and would nearly pull my arms off. One day I came home after an especially hot afternoon too tired to eat supper and had a fever all night. Undoubtedly, I had a heat stroke. After that my mother refused to let me go back. Anyway, the harvest season was about over and before another summer, we had moved to another area.

My father was ten years older than my mother, but while he left the usual daily upbringing of the family to her, we all knew he was the head of the house and his word was law. We were a close-knit family and both of our parents, while not permissive, did have a lot of understanding. They really loved each other, and we knew it. Any differences were settled in private. Home was a real refuge for us all. It was a place not only to get our cuts and bruises healed but also to obtain an understanding of the outside world. Of course, we all had to spend a lot of time in church, and I was just old enough to listen to my father's sermons. There was much I didn't understand, but I always liked his illustrations. One Sunday after we had been working in the harvest fields, I recall he told how he had been associated with the rough crew of drifters who followed the harvest season from the south up through the Dakotas and couldn't help hearing the foul language they used. Then he said, "While I have to hear the swearing, God keeps me from ever using such language." That remark stuck with me all my life.

It was the custom of the Wesleyan Church to move a minister every two or three years. It was a common saying that by that time he had reached the bottom of his barrel of sermons and they wanted someone new. Two of my father's brothers, Henry and Owen, lived on farms not too far from Northville, and they sent us a special invitation to visit them. When we arrived we found the reason, for they both had decided to sell their farms and with their families, move to the State of Washington. A land development company had convinced them of the wonderful opportunities in that area, and in addition, the attraction of a more moderate climate made them eager to go. They tried to talk my folks into going with them, but it didn't work. Father did buy a team of horses and a covered wagon from them. This outfit became our means of moving to our next home.

Since there were no other churches in the conference large enough to support our family, Father decided to become a farmer-preacher. Somehow he heard of a desirable place to do this about ten miles north of Watertown, South Dakota. To get there, Mother took Leeta, Ula and Dale on the train, while Father and I loaded our household goods in the covered wagon, tied our cow and heifer on back, and started cross country. The first day we went south until the road ended at the edge of a big swamp. We were informed that this swamp could be crossed in dry weather, and it would save us a lot of miles. With the help of a local farmer we tried to cross, but before we were halfway, the team and wagon began to sink deeper and deeper. We had to make a wide turn and scramble back.

The rest of the day we kept on the road, which followed the edge of the swamp until we could reach a bridge. That afternoon we met a band of men on horseback armed with rifles. They stopped us and said they were a posse looking for a murderer. This was the first time I learned the real meaning of the word. They told us that two men were working on a farm and had an argument, one shot the other, and had escaped. They asked if we had seen anyone, but although we said "No," they insisted on searching the wagon. Satisfied that the man was not hiding in the wagon, they let us proceed. All afternoon I kept nervously scanning the long grass along the swamp, but no one appeared.

It was evening before we came to a long causeway and bridge to cross what was no longer a swamp but a lake. There was a town at the other end of the bridge, and Father knew a minister who lived there so he wanted to make it for a place to stay overnight. However, it was too far for the cow and she played out. She would lie down and refuse to move. I had to get out of the wagon to go back and twist her tail to get her back on her feet. Then I had to walk back of her with a stick to keep her going. As we approached the bridge we could hear the sound of gun fire from hunters who were after the heavy migration of waterfowls. As darkness fell, these sounds mixed with the weird cries of the birds added to my fear of meeting the murderer. There was the usual talking of the Canadian geese, the quacking of the wild ducks, the lonesome cries of the loons, and the pitiful cries of some wounded fowls all of which made the night seem unearthly. Because of the condition of the cow, we were late in finding the house where we could stay. Once there we got the horses and cattle fed and were given a late supper. There was no room for us in the house, so we retired to the hay mow and rolled up in blankets. I fell asleep in a hurry; not even the squeaking of the barn mice could keep me awake.

The next two days we spent in slower travel and on the third arrived at our new house. We had covered over 100 miles. The house was a typical farmhouse, an extra building on a large farm, but not the land which Father was to work. About a mile to the west was a railroad, and we could watch the long freight trains moving the grain to market. In sight was a station, called Rawville, with a grain elevator and a single house for the operator.

This was an area of more diversified crops than I had ever seen. Besides the big fields of wheat, there were acres of oats and barley. For the first time I saw fields of flax. This was raised not only for the fiber in the stalks, but also for the seed which was ground into meal, an important stock food. The picture of these fields of flax when in bloom with its deep blue flowers waving in the constant wind resembling the waves of the open sea could never be forgotten.

There was still some areas of native grass. As a boy I watched the plow turn under the virgin prairie sod exposing the rich black earth to the view of man for the first time. Even then I felt a wave of sorrow to see man spoiling the earth which had taken centuries to form. The native grasses and flowers thus destroyed could never be replaced. Of course, it was all done because man thought he was conquering nature. It was the so-called "winning of the west."

The one-room country school that Leeta and I attended was less than a quarter of a mile from our house, so we generally went home for the noon meal. At times we carried a lunch so we would have more time to play with the other pupils. The games we played were typical of the times. Pum-pum-pull-away was the most popular then. When the big boys of the district attended, they liked crack-the-whip. This was played by having everyone take hold of hands, the largest being at one end and then on down to the smallest. All would start running in a straight line. Of course, the largest boys would be ahead, whereupon they would stop short. Due to the momentum, the rest of the line would continue forward until the force would break the hand holds and the little ones would go flying in all directions. It was great fun unless someone got hurt, which happened to Leeta one time. Being at the small end of the line, she flew the farthest. She evidently cracked her collar bone and put in a sleepless night. She was laid up for some time with considerable pain. Needless to say, our parents put a taboo on that game. The teachers in this school were young and inexperienced, and generally stayed only one year. As I was to learn later, I made little progress. However, I enjoyed the life so much in the open I didn't worry.

The weather in this country affected everyone. Winter came early and often extremely cold. Our house was out on the open prairie and caught the full blast of the arctic north winds. All the cracks around the front door and all windows were stuffed with strips of cloth, but with all that there were times when it was impossible to keep the house warm. Our winter supply of potatoes and vegetables were stored in the cellar. Barn manure was banked all around the outside of the house to protect the cellar and a lighted lantern would be kept burning to try to keep the temperature above freezing, but one winter everything froze. It was impossible to get to Watertown for supplies, so we had to live on short rations until spring. We always had a supply of sugar and flour on hand, so Mother kept us supplied in homebaked bread. Corn meal was also a staple, and with a milk cow, we never starved. The honking of the first flight of Canadian geese coming from the south heralding the return of spring was a welcome sound.

Spring was a beautiful time of the year with the new grass coming up green mixed with a perfusion of prairie flowers. Then I watched the farmers driving the teams of horses back and forth on the big fields of plowed ground planting the spring wheat. Once the wheat was up, the farmers watched the skies to see if there would be enough rain to keep the wheat growing and not dry up before it could mature. Then if there was enough moisture to get by the critical period, there remained the danger of a sudden thunder storm with hail hard enough to flatten the grain making it impossible to harvest. It was generally considered that if one could get a bumper crop every third year, he was all right.

Summers were as uncomfortably hot as the winters were cold. As a rule, the heat was a dry heat and temperatures of 100 degrees or more were livable. Once in awhile a phenomenon known as a "hot wind" would strike, and then it was unbearable. There was no relief, for any breeze felt as if it was coming from an open furnace. Then temperatures of 100 degrees caused a lot of damage. Such a wind cooked all vegetation, struck down cattle and horses and often caused fatal heat strokes with people. At such times all work in the fields had to stop and all took shelter wherever they could find it.

Following a heat wave another disaster, called a dust storm, would often strike. A high wind would pick up the dry earth and whirl it high into the air. The sun would be blotted out as if a thunder storm was approaching, but there would be no rain, only the choking dust. This dust was so fine it would sift through the cracks around the doors and windows of a house, covering the floor with a coating of gray. It would be all over the furniture and into the beds. The food would be gritty. It would be impossible to be free of the dust until the wind died down. Much of this dust was due to the plowing up of so many acres of the prairie sod. Buffalo grass and other prairie grasses had tough roots which held the soil in place even in the high winds, but once they were destroyed, the grains that were planted would not do the same. At times the growing wheat or barley would be literally blown out of the ground. After a time the western farmers began to realize that their land was in danger of being blown away and began to plant rows of trees to act as wind breaks to help save the land.

One morning I heard Father say he was taking a cow to a farm a couple of miles away to see a bull. I wanted to go with him, and he granted permission providing I could get my dishes done in time. My curiosity was aroused about the cow, and I asked Mother where calves came from. I knew instantly that I had asked the wrong question both by her manner and by her answer when she said, "You'll have to ask your father that." In my embarrassment and haste I dropped one of Mother's favorite dishes. It broke into a thousand pieces. When she saw what had happened, she burst into tears, something I seldom saw her do. I was terribly sorry and said that I would give up going, but she recovered and said, "No, it was an accident and nothing could bring the dish back." After that, I was very careful not to break another dish.

After we visited the farmer and verified that the cow was in heat and the bull served her, I was more curious than ever about calves. After a long period of silence on the way home. I finally got up my nerve to ask Father. His matter of fact explanation that the bull planted a seed inside the cow and the calf grew from that set me at ease. Any question about anything pertaining to sex was never talked about. The result was, it left a feeling of guilt. That was a mistake, for I am sure if Mother had answered my question the same way Father did, I would have thought nothing more about it.

From the time I broke the dish and Mother's reaction, I knew she wasn't feeling well. Then I knew from her appearance she was going to have another baby. To help, Mother sent for Aunt Nell to be with us for the time. One night I was aroused by a number of voices. I went back to sleep but kept waking up because lights were on in the house. In the morning we were all introduced to our new baby sister, Faye, born July 19, 1901. Father had hurried into Watertown in the night and brought back a doctor. When we got up, the doctor was eating his breakfast and Father was ready to take him back. That was the usual procedure in the country.

Father was in partnership with a local farmer in farming a large tract of land some distance from our house. Accordingly, he was away from home many of the weekdays, and then on Sunday he held services in some of the school houses around the country. I was all excited when it came time to thresh the wheat and got permission to spend the day watching. The threshing machine was run by a crew of eight or more men while the farmer had to furnish any extra help. Also, the farmer had to feed the crew while on his place. It was arranged for the crew to spend the night at our house so the wife of Father's partner came to help with the cooking. At daybreak the men were up and the women hurried to get their breakfast. I woke up and hurried into my clothes so I could leave with the men. I went with Father and helped some loading the wagon with the new wheat and driving to the elevator, but I spent most of the time watching the machines operate. Machines fascinated me.

The night before I heard the women planning the meals for the crew. For breakfast they cooked a big kettle of oatmeal and some hard boiled eggs. They thought it would take too long to fry them. Mother worried about the eggs; she wanted to be sure they were fresh. Of course, there was no refrigeration in those days and eggs would not keep long in hot weather. We had some hens and accumulated a supply of eggs. All went well until one man broke the shell of his egg only to discover a well-developed chick inside. My mother nearly passed out, but the men just laughed and kidded the man about his chicken dinner. It was a big relief when the day was over and the grain sold.

Aunt Nell never did like South Dakota and as soon as she thought Mother could get along without help, she hurried back to Iowa. She was homesick for the trees and plenty of water. We had a well but had to conserve water in the summer months as it would almost go dry. When she left, Leeta and I were pressed into helping more with the younger children and the housework. It became our duty to wash and dry the dishes. I hated it, partly because I knew it wasn't considered a man's work and partly I didn't like the greasy dish water. I used to say I couldn't enjoy my meals just thinking about doing the dishes afterwards. My mother was not one to tolerate idle hands and as soon as each child became old enough, they had to share the daily chores.

Our team of horses consisted of two grey mares. One was bred and I watched with interest the development of the foal inside the mare. One Sunday when we drove into the yard after church we could see the mare was down and giving birth. I learned then a curious fact of nature that grey mares always have black foals. Later the colt sheds and turns grey.

Only small game was left in this part of the state. The large game, such as antelope and deer, had been driven into the hills beyond the farming area. Buffalo had been slaughtered almost to extinction some 25 to 30 years before this time. A reminder was the many buffalo skulls that could be seen bleaching in the sun in the fields of grass that had not been plowed. The small game consisted of jack rabbits on the prairie and cotton tails along the streams. Prairie chickens were plentiful, and it was a thrill to hear the cocks crowing on a spring morning. At that season these birds were frequently seen in typical cock fights. So intense would they be that one could approach within a few feet before they would take alarm. It was a common sight to have one or more of these chickens run alongside the road as one drove a horse and buggy across the country. They didn't seem to be afraid if a horse was present and would follow for a hundred yards or more before dashing off into the high grass.

Watertown is noted for the number of lakes in the area, so there was an abundance of waterfowl. In the spring and again in the fall when the ducks and geese migrated there would be thousands of these birds in big flocks overhead. Many ducks stayed in this region and every body of water was full of nesting birds. In the fall the Canadian geese would spend the night on a lake and then fly inland to feed. A straw stack about a half mile from our house was one favorite place for one flock to search the straw for food. While the flock was feeding, sentries were posted to give warning if danger approached. In the open field it was impossible to get near such a flock. It was surprising how late in the fall these geese would stay if the food held out.

Not all the animals in the area were game, some were considered varmints. The most common was the coyote. Although hunted, trapped and sometimes poisoned, they still learned to live in the neighborhood of man. They would sometimes steal a chicken or turkey and therefore, were hated by the farmer's wives, but they lived mainly on rabbits and thus had a beneficial purpose in keeping the rabbit population in check. Although not plentiful, there was another smaller animal that could cause trouble. One winter morning we found one of our hens dead, and it was repeated on several mornings. There didn't seem to be any mark on the body of the hen nor was any part eaten as it would be in the case of a rat or skunk getting into the hen house. We were mystified until early one morning Father and I went out to see if we could find the culprit. I went in back of the house while Father quickly opened the door. I saw a movement and out from the underside of the house came a small white furry animal. I had never seen a weasel, but when it stopped and stood up on its hind legs staring at me with black beady eyes, I recognized it. A close inspection of the dead hen showed a dark blue mark on her throat. This was where the weasel had punctured the jugular vein and sucked out the blood. Checking we found a tiny opening between two boards so small it was hard to believe any animal could get through. But when this was closed we had no more trouble.

During this time we acquired another addition to the family, at least it seemed that way for they were part of our family life for the next seven years. For some time Father had been wanting a horse or a team that he could drive to his various preaching appointments other than the slow farm horses. He heard that a team of ponies was for sale in Watertown. We went in to see them and instantly fell in love with them. They were about the size of Indian ponies but a nice bay color with a white strip down their faces and white stockings. They were well broken to harness but showed a lot of zest. They were named "Topsy" and "Turvey." No more fitting names could have been imagined. Topsy was the more lively of the two and being the leader, was always hooked up on the right. Turvey was slower but most gentle and we soon found out we could ride her bareback. Along with the ponies Father bought a two-seated surrey, and for the first time we had a rig that would carry the whole family at one time. We were all thrilled with these ponies and I learned how to harness them, drive them and took care of them for the next several years. Topsy was not broken to ride, but after she was used to me I dared to try. After being thrown several times, I succeeded but I was the only one in the family who could ride her.

Acquiring the ponies made a big difference in the trips Father had to take. Now he could reach the distant schools where he held Sunday services and be back in the afternoon. It also cut the time for a trip to Watertown in half. These ponies would trot along for long periods of time and cover ten miles an hour. One thing I had to learn was how long to have them trot and then how long to let them walk in order to save their wind. One axiom that I learned was "if you have a long journey, start slow and then you can hurry at the end."

The reliability of the team was clearly indicated a few months after we got them. Father received word that his mother had died back on the old homestead. He wanted to go to the funeral, but there was no train out of Watertown that would get him there on time. However, there was a flag stop on a railroad that did not go into Watertown where he could catch a train and make it on time. This stop was about twelve miles from our house in a part of the country strange to me. He took me with him to drive the team back home. We got to the flag stop in plenty of time, and Father turned the team around telling me to get going as the ponies might be frightened by the train and I might not be able to control them. After I had gone less than a mile, I heard the train whistle and then the answering toot for the flag, so I knew Father got on the train all right.

I kept the ponies trotting along at a brisk pace trying to remember the road back. Not a house was in sight nor a landmark of any kind. As far as I could see in every direction it was a sea of waving grass. The country was laid out in sections so that every mile was a crossroad. Some of these roads had been traveled, but some not at all. I knew I was to go west for so many miles and turn right, but with everything looking the same I wasn't sure where to turn. I remember hearing cowboys telling about being lost and letting their horse take the lead and thus trusting them to get safely back home. So when I came to the road I thought might be the one I should turn right on but not at all sure, I decided to let the ponies have their lead. Without my consciously pulling the reins in any direction, they did turn. After some distance on this road I came to a wooden bridge over a small stream I recognized, so I knew I was on the right road. Without any trouble I was back home. I never told anyone how I was almost lost but let on that I was perfectly able to travel alone.

Before we left South Dakota an event happened which had a lasting effect on me. For some reason Mother took us children with her to stay with someone she knew in another part of the state. It was in a farming area settled by families who had migrated from Germany. These people were very industrious but had the reputation of making all their children work hard on the farms. There were tales of how some of the men would keep even the small children out of school and tie them on the seat of a plow in order to get the planting done in time.

School was in session while we were there and since we were to be there for more than two weeks, Leeta and I were sent to the country school. I shall never forget that first day. We were complete strangers and more than that, we discovered that every child in the school except us spoke German. At recess the children stood in a circle around us talking in German. We couldn't understand what they were saying but knew by their expressions they were talking about us. It was a miserable time for us. It was an experience I could never forget and all my life I had a feeling of sympathy for any child in school who was from a minority group. Unless a person has such an experience he can never know how it feels.

When I was ten years old, Father received a call to go back to College Springs, Iowa, to again be the pastor of the Wesleyan Church. Mother was especially delighted, as it was like home to her. Grandma and Grandpa Crow still lived there, so we were all glad to go. We didn't want to give up the ponies, so Father decided to drive them, a distance of over 300 miles. Our household goods were shipped by freight and the rest of us went by train. It was a long tiresome ride, caring for the small children, sleeping the best we could on a day coach, eating fried chicken with bread and butter for all our meals and grimy from the smoke from the steam engine. It was a welcome sight to see Grandpa Crow when he met us at Coin, the nearest station to College Springs.

Father planned a week to drive through but down the Missouri River Valley he ran into rainy weather. He found out what mud in that part of the country was like. It is called "gumbo," and gummy it certainly is. This mud stuck to the horses' feet and rolled up on the wheels of the buggy until they looked like drums. One mile of this was like ten miles of ordinary driving. Father was due to preach on Sunday morning and thought he had plenty of time, but it was late Saturday night before he arrived. The mud had continued right to College Springs and the poor ponies were all in. It took so much out of them it was weeks before they began to act natural.

Thus ended our life in Montana and South Dakota, and we began a new one in Iowa.

CHAPTER 2

LIFE IN IOWA

College Springs was my birth place, and I had been there for a short time when Ula was born, but I was too young to remember much about it. I knew Grandpa Crow's house was on the edge of town, and we stayed there for a few days until our household goods arrived. I soon learned that the Wesleyan Church was near the center of this small town with the parsonage next door. Within a block was the main building of Amity College. This institution was founded by an idealistic group from the east who wanted a college free from any church. They liked this area in southwest Iowa a few miles north of the Missouri state line and most important, there were several natural springs nearby, so they felt assured of an ample source of water. Hence, the name College Springs. Amity College was a very active school at this time but closed its doors about 1920. Mother was especially pleased, for with her musical ability, she joined the College chorus and other activities.

Right after we had moved into the parsonage I heard that the town band was to give a concert in the bandstand, which stood in the town square, that Saturday evening. Since it was only a short distance from our house, my folks let me go. I stood by myself watching the bandsmen assemble with their various instruments which I had never seen, when a gang of ten or more boys faced me. They were led by a boy much larger than me. He wanted to know who I was. I told him my name. "Oh, a new boy in town," he jeered. "Let's initiate him," he called to the other boys. This was something new to me, and I didn't like it. I was too dumbstruck to move. But when this big boy came near me and started to grab me, I got mad and gave him a shove. Evidently he didn't expect it and went flat on his back. With an angry shout he jumped up and came at me. He knocked me down and jumped on top of me. I had never had to fight before, wrestle maybe, but I didn't know the first thing about fighting. He started to punch me and although I was on my back, I instinctively hit back. By luck I got in one good punch and his nose began to bleed. Just then a man came along, pulled the boy off me, and told him to lay off. By that time a large crowd of boys had gathered and continued to stay to see what would happen. The boy and I stood glaring at each other and then he turned and walked away, followed by his gang. Several boys gathered around congratulating me and wanted to be friends.

The next morning in Sunday School the teacher had a hard time getting the attention of the boys. The news of my fight had traveled, and they wanted to hear all about it. The fact that I had stood up to the town bully made me a hero in their eyes. I didn't know that boy was the town bully or maybe I wouldn't have dared to do what I did. Anyway, I never had to assert myself again in that town. I never was one to start a fight nor look for one, but I had learned that time it never paid to run away from one.

Although the parsonage was near the center of the town, like most of the houses it had a rural atmosphere. There was a barn for the ponies and space for a cow. We acquired a Brown Swiss milk cow that was unique in one respect. While she had the usual four tits, only the back two had developed, but even so she gave a full pail of the richest yellow milk I ever saw. It was so rich that Mother would put it in pans and let it stand overnight and then in the morning skim off the heavy cream. Some cream was used for cooking, but most was churned into butter. I learned to milk this cow and it became one of my daily chores. We also kept a number of hens, so we had a supply of eggs and an occasional Sunday chicken dinner.

Some of my new friends invited me to go fishing with them. Unlike the dry country we had been living in, there was enough rainfall here so small streams ran the year round. One such creek was about a half mile outside the town and since we could see the belfry of the college building from any place on it, my folks let me go. The only thing we could catch was some small catfish and shiners, but we had fun. Then on one trip I had the strangest fish story to tell. While fishing, my hook caught on something big and after some work I pulled up an old earthen jug. There was a small hole in the bottom so someone had discarded it. I got my hook loose and threw the jug up on the bank. The water began to drain out of the jug and then we heard a strange splashing sound. When the sound continued, I got up to investigate and decided that there was something besides water inside the jug. I picked up a stick and broke the jug open and to everyone's amazement, out popped a good-sized catfish. He was too big to get out either through the spout or the hole in the bottom, so we reasoned that he must have gone in when small and finding a safe refuge, had stayed until he got so big he couldn't get out. He simply waited for the stream to wash food to him and grew fat in his prison. He was my prize fish for the summer.

The school in College Springs was an eight room, two-story frame building. Each grade had a room; the lower grades were on the first floor and the upper ones on the second. This was my first, and it turned out to be my only experience in a graded school. It didn't take me long to learn I was not up to grade. I did alright in reading but was lost in arithmetic. The class was doing something in division that I had never seen. I was too timid to ask the teacher, and she just assumed that I knew. By looking at an example in the textbook and watching the other pupils, I somehow made out.

24

Another thing that was new to me was special teachers in music, art and penmanship. The Palmer method of writing was new and being introduced in this school. I was able to do the push and pulls and make the circles real well, but the method never stuck. The music instruction followed a method which I have observed many times through the years. The music teacher was trying to teach us how to read music for singing. The notes she called, "do-re-mi," etc. I never learned how to tell one from another, and I never heard her explain how it was done. She evidently assumed we had been taught that in a lower grade. This is a fallacy common to many teachers in a graded school. Anyway, this teacher would call on a pupil to read the notes of a song. A few knew how, but the rest of us stumbled along and as soon as we said a wrong note, she would tell us to sit down. We were either right or wrong, but never told why we were wrong.

The room I was in was considered the hardest room in the school to discipline. Knowing this the boys in the room thought they had to maintain its reputation. I don't recall that we did anything so bad but did band together to keep the teacher upset. So when this woman teacher left in the middle of the year, the principal hired a man for the job. In short time he proved he didn't know how to control boys. He started yelling at anyone he thought out of order and giving out big threats. I had never been in trouble at school, but I thought I had to be one of the group. It was at this time that the use of a dictionary was introduced. Each pupil was issued a small desk dictionary. Some of the boys found words which had a double meaning, and it became a game to see who could find the most such words, especially if it might have a dirty meaning outside the school. The teacher found out what was going on, and he lectured us about it, threatening us with punishment if anyone turned his head around.

All was quiet for a few days, and then the boy directly back of me kept punching me. I turned my head to see what he wanted when the teacher looked up and saw me. "Come here, Ray," he shouted. I walked up to his desk and watched as he drew a half inch rubber hose out of a drawer. It was evident he had it ready to use. He grabbed me by the shoulder and began beating my back sides and legs. I stood stock still for five or six blows and then it began to really hurt. I yelled, "Stop it," and tried to twist away from him. His glasses fell on the floor and broke, and he hit me harder and harder. He sent me back to my seat, but when I sat down my thighs and legs began to throb. Just then the bell rang for recess. I went to the boy's outhouse, took down my pants and saw blood running down my legs. I was also in a state of shock. I had never been thrashed in school or at home. I told the boys who had gathered around that I was going home.

When I walked in Mother looked at me and knew something terrible had happened. She called Father, who was in his study, and I told them what had transpired. They took one look, put me to bed, and sent for the doctor. He came, examined me, and gave me some sleeping powders. It was evening before I roused and heard voices in the living room. I recognized the voice of the teacher and then I heard my mother say she wanted her children to be good, but she didn't believe in any such punishment. I knew by the tone of her voice that she was very upset.

The whole school and town was upset by the episode. The school was on my side, but the town was divided. Some thought the teacher was justified, especially as it was the minister's son. "They are always the bad ones," they said. The back of my legs and thighs were a mass of black and blue bruises, so it was over two weeks before I could sit down for any time in comfort. I never knew whether that teacher decided to leave or was asked to go because of the affair, but he was gone when I went back. A substitute finished out the year with no more trouble.

Roy Crow was Mother's youngest brother and although only two years older, was really my uncle, but we never thought of him as such. Being the youngest of seven children, he became his mother's favorite. More than once I could see how he got his way with her, who was very strict with the other children. Roy was quite a clown and loved to mimic people. He was a favorite with the young children and always made them laugh. I saw him walk into a room where there was a crying baby and without him doing a thing have the baby stop crying, look at him and start to laugh. He had some sort of magnetism which made him likable to most people. Knowing this, he could get out of all sorts of scrapes by making them seem funny. My folks understood this and didn't like my running around with him, but since it was family, they didn't think they could stop it.

He did get me into one scrape which I never forgot. The boys in the school bragged about playing hooky. It was considered one hadn't lived unless one could say he had done it at least once. One day Roy and one of his pals decided to play hooky for the afternoon and pressured me to go with them. I hesitated but they made me feel that this was a chance to prove myself a worthy member of the hooky club. So at noon, instead of going into school, we ran down the hill to Grandfather's barn and climbed a ladder to the hay mow. We kept quiet for a time, then hearing no one around, we began to talk. Soon we were bored, it wasn't the fun or excitement that I had been told about. In order to pass the time we made up a game. At the back end of the mow the hay was stacked almost to the roof, then slanting down to the bare floor in front. We would climb to the highest point, then slide down to see who could go the farthest. The floor was not made of boards but of long poles which were not nailed so they would roll under one's feet. They were safe if covered with some hay, but in sliding down I hit a bare spot and without any warning fell through. I landed on my back right behind one of the horses. The impact knocked the wind out of me, and I lay for several moments stunned and gasping for breath. Fortunately, the old horse was gentle and although he jumped, he did not kick. The boys rushed down the ladder, picked me up and brushed me off. Once on my feet I was dizzy and became sick, throwing up. After a time I felt better and declared I was going home saying I would not tell on the others. When I got home I told my mother that I came home sick, and when she saw how pale I was, she believed me. So I had no trouble getting her to write an excuse for school, but the others had to write their own. Thus, I became a member of the hooky club, but I wasn't thrilled by it and was never tempted to try it again.

Another of Roy's traits was to play practical jokes on someone. He particularly liked to scare small children. I cured him of trying to do this again in our family. One evening both of our parents had gone to a special service at the church and left us children at home. I was supposed to be old enough to care for the rest of the children for a short time. Like others, our house was heated by a stove in the living room which burned soft coal. This kind of coal would crust over and if the crust wasn't broken, the fire would give off little heat. I had a heavy iron poker in my hand breaking up the crusted fire, when the outside door which opened into the living room burst open and a hairy-like animal emitting a cry of a mountain lion jumped into the room. The children all screamed. With the poker in my hand I reacted instinctively and hit the apparent beast over its head. With a groan it collapsed on the floor, and then I recognized our buffalo robe which the Crows had borrowed. I drew it off and discovered Roy holding his head with both hands. He had come to return the robe and looking through the window, saw us children alone and thought it would be a joke to scare us. I hit him so hard that only the thickness of the robe saved him from serious injury. Anyway, he never tried anything like that again.

My last year in the College Springs school was a delight. We had a new teacher, one of a few who influenced my life in a good way. She was small, not particularly good looking, but had a personality that appealed to all the pupils. She knew how to deal with boys our age and every boy in the class fell in love with her. She introduced us to some good literature by reading a chapter from an interesting book near the end of each day. School became a place we wouldn't miss. Near the end of the year the boys got together and plotted how we would all fail the final exams so we could stay in the same room with this teacher the next year. Of course, it didn't work and then we were heartbroken when we learned she was to be married that summer.

It was due to that teacher's influence that I learned there was a school library from which I could draw books. I avidly read all the Horatio Alger and Hinty books on the shelves. I distressed Mother because she said when I got my nose in a book I was lost. I couldn't hear her call and the baby would be screaming her head off right beside me, but I wouldn't hear a thing. Intensive reading was a trait I kept all my life.

For the minister's family Sunday was the important day of the week. Actually, the day began on Saturday when everyone had to take a bath. In those days there was no such thing as a bathroom or bathtub. The

27

ritual started by heating a wash boiler full of water on the kitchen stove. A wash tub was placed on the kitchen floor and half filled with warm water. The girls came first, and then a change of water for the boys. The adults of the family came last. Clean clothes were laid out ready for Sunday morning.

Sunday was a full day. After an early breakfast followed by the daily reading from the Bible and morning prayers, the chores had to be done. Then the dressing of the children in their Sunday clothes started. The older children had to help the little ones so it was a real family affair. It often became a time of stress when I had to comb the girls' long hair. They would cry and appeal to Mother saying I was pulling their hair too hard. Probably I did, trying to hurry to get out the many snarls so we could get to Sunday School on time. The minister's family must never be late. Sunday School ran from 10 to 11 a.m., immediately followed by the morning church service. This would last over an hour, as no preacher was considered any good unless he could give at least an hour sermon. After the preaching came a testimony hour, called a class meeting. All members of the congregation were encouraged to get up and give a testimony. They would thank the Lord for what he had done for them the past week, confess what they had done wrong, and promise to do better. To us children it soon became apparent what each person would say. To us boys some of the people were humorous as they repeated every Sunday what they had done wrong, and we knew they would go out on Monday and do the same thing again. However, it was sort of a confession and they felt saved if they made the testimony.

Mother would often give her testimony and then take the small children home to start the dinner. The rest of us had to stay until the end, arriving home after 1:00 p.m., tired and starved. First, we had to change out of our Sunday clothes and help with the dinner. By the time the dinner dishes were done, it would be the middle of the afternoon, a time for relaxation. We were not allowed to play games out of doors, only take a walk if the weather was nice or lounge around the yard. Our church was very strict about Sunday observance.

Only certain books could be read on Sunday. I was guilty of making my first protest to my parents about this rule. I had been given a copy of Dickens' *Child's History of England* for Christmas. I found it very dry reading, not interesting at all to me. My folks said I could read it on Sunday, but not the books I brought from the school library. I told them the *History* was nothing but an account of wars and kings killing each other off. Evidently they must have examined the book before another week went by, for after that they never questioned my selection of books to read.

The Sunday dinner was the big meal of the week so supper was light. By seven Leeta and I were back in our Sunday clothes and ready for the Young People's service at the church. This was followed by another preaching service for everyone. The younger children would be brought to this evening service and long before it was over would be stretched out on the hard pews fast asleep. When it was over they would be half carried and half dragged home to get their clothes off and into bed. The rest would fall into bed, exhausted, glad that every day wasn't Sunday.

Half the congregation lived on farms near the town. They were generous with donations of vegetables and fresh meat, especially when they butchered in the fall. They also would send word when we might pick up windfalls of apples and other fruit. Mother was a great canner and nothing ever went to waste if she could help it. One fruit we found novel was berries from the mulberry tree. Years before some enterprising people thought they could raise silk worms and planted these trees for the worms to feed on. The venture was not successful, but the trees remained. When the fruit was ripe, people let us spread a sheet on the ground under a tree and by shaking the tree vigorously, the sheet would be covered with the black berries. They were soft and rather insipid, but when mixed with gooseberries or rhubarb made good pies.

Other than my daily chores the only work I did was to help Roy at times to care for Grandpa's small truck farm. He had a lot of vegetables, berries and fruit trees. When it was time to pick berries, I learned about chiggers. These microscopic red mites come off the leaves of berry bushes and grass and bury themselves under a person's skin. The result was welts that itched furiously. Grandpa also kept a flock of chickens, a number of ducks, and a few geese. The care of all these was left largely to his children as Grandpa worked with his team of horses wherever he could find a job. It was during one of these times that one of their sows started to give birth. Actually, she was too young to have been bred and was in serious trouble. There were few vets in those days, so most farmers had to be their own. Roy tried to help the sow, but his hand was too big. He came to our house to see if I, with a smaller hand, could help. Mother was rather skeptical about me doing anything like that, but at his pleading did consent for me to try. When I got there the sow was certainly having birth pains and was in distress. She was on her side and didn't object to our trying to help. By greasing my hand I could force it up the birth canal and feel the piglet, but when I closed my hand to get a grip on it I couldn't get my hand out. Her pelvic bones hadn't opened, and we couldn't spread them. We did all we could and after a time the pains must have ceased, for she got up, took a drink of water, and began to eat. We couldn't get near her again. She stayed on her feet for a couple of days, then died, evidently from internal infection. This taught me all I needed to know about where babies come from.

One event occurred in College Springs which had a profound effect on my later life. Aunt Nell, who had lived with us in South Dakota and taught school there, decided she needed further education. She heard about Houghton Seminary, a Wesleyan Church school, located in Houghton, New York. With a friend she had made in South Dakota, she entered the school. One of the first teachers she met was H. Clark

Bedford. During the year they started going together, and before she left at the end of the school year, he proposed marriage. She waited until after she got home before she accepted and they set the date of the wedding in November, 1902, during his Thanksgiving vacation. The wedding was in our church on a Saturday evening with Father officiating. He asked my new Uncle Clark to preach the sermon the next morning. I guess he wasn't too keen about preaching the next morning after his wedding night, but the whole family insisted. To hear a professor from a school such as Houghton was something they couldn't let pass. Since the wedding was at night, we children didn't attend but heard him at church and saw him briefly. I liked my Uncle Clark at once and for many years after.

The custom of the Wesleyan Church was for a minister to move every two years. I think my father hoped to break this pattern and stay in College Springs, but the heads of the conference did not approve. I heard some of the conversation between my parents which indicated there was a lot of politics in the church organization. There was no Bishop in the Wesleyan Church to place ministers as it is done in the Methodist Episcopal Church. However, there is a conference organization and the elected president had a lot of influence on the individual churches as to who to consider for its minister.

While College Springs was a small town, it had an abundance of churches. The largest was the United Presbyterian, next the Methodist Episcopal, then the Wesleyan Methodist and the smallest the Free Methodist. There was a strong rivalry, sometimes bitter, between the various denominations. The Wesleyans were strong fundamentalist and thought no other church could be right. My father was more liberal in his views than most of his peers and while in College Springs did what no other Wesleyan minister had ever done. He joined in some of the united church services. He gave the citywide Thanksgiving sermon in the Methodist Episcopal Church. It was one of his best and he received a number of compliments on it. Later it was published. I remember the sermon and was quite impressed and proud of him.

On another occasion he was asked to preside at a joint Sunday evening service in the Presbyterian Church. I heard him discussing with Mother how he should act when it came time for the prayer. The Wesleyans held that the minister should kneel to pray, while in the other churches he stood. I went wondering what he would do, and was rather amused when I saw him compromise by kneeling on one knee and keeping his opposite hand on top of the pulpit. Everyone seemed satisfied with his solution. I am sure that his cooperation with the other churches was one of the main reasons he was not recalled to this church.

With no call from any Wesleyan church in the conference, he accepted an offer from the Congregational Church to serve four small groups in a rural area north of Greenfield, Iowa. All the services were held in one-room school houses several miles apart. He would be in one place every fourth Sunday. In the school near our house we held Sunday School every Sunday even when he was not there.

The house we moved into was an old farmhouse, which was vacant because two farms had been combined into one. We had shipped our goods, the ponies and cow by rail, and we were once more living in the country. Along with the animals we brought we added a big flock of chickens, a few ducks and a couple of pigs. The barn was small, just room for the team and cow, so to have a shelter for the buggy, a farmer let us cut some saplings out of his woods. I thought my father was clever to erect a pole carriage house annexed to the barn. After we cut some long slew grass we were able to make a thatched roof which shed the rain fine.

After we were well settled a neighbor offered me a collie puppy. I was delighted when my parents said I could keep him. He grew into a handsome dog with a white collar around his neck, so we named him Ring. He was good company for us children, and when we roamed the countryside, Mother felt better about us with a dog along. Our house was at the top of a hill overlooking a valley through which flowed a small stream. Along the stream was a fair number of trees, and it was this area we liked to explore. On one of these trips I witnessed an unusual sight of animal behavior. As we approached the stream a rabbit jumped out of the grass with Ring in hot pursuit. The rabbit ran by a large oak tree and thinking to outwit the dog, reversed his direction and came back on the opposite side of the tree. Ring, instead of following the path of the rabbit, decided to cut on that same side of the tree. Consequently, they came face to face. It was such a surprise to both they skidded to a halt and sat looking at each other. There they sat for several seconds and then, as if by a signal, they both stood up, the rabbit hopped off in one direction, and Ring trotted back to me with a foolish look on his face.

When winter came I thought I was old enough to have a gun. I begged my folks to give me a .22 rifle for Christmas. However, Mother was against it. So I woke up on Christmas morning to find a set of steel traps as my gift. I was disappointed, but decided to do some trapping. I learned how by reading, and did fairly well. I caught several skunks and a couple of muskrats which I proudly sold for furs. Mother insisted I visit my traps every morning before school. I don't think the teacher was too happy to see me on the mornings I had a skunk to skin. My season wasn't too long as a couple of local young men considered that I was encroaching on their territory. Several times I found my traps robbed and then the traps disappeared. Anyway, I had gained some good experience and a little money.

All of the children were now of school age except Faye, the youngest. The one room school was about a mile from our house down the long hill and on the opposite bank of the stream, which was the headwaters of a river, so it was called a river. Since Father had the distant charges, he would often be gone all day in order to make pastoral calls. At times

Mother liked to go with him. She made arrangements with the teacher to let Faye stay in school with us for the day. In order to reach the school house, we had to cross a wooden bridge over the river. The floor of the bridge was made of wooden planks with cracks between each one. If one looked down, the water in the river could be seen. Faye had a horror of stepping on these cracks and insisted on stepping on each plank. The rest of us would be exasperated with her being so slow when we were all in a hurry to be on time. More than once we heard the school bell, and then we would drag her, screaming, across the bridge so we wouldn't be late. The teachers we had in this school were young girls from town who could hardly wait until Friday night to get back home. They let us know they considered us as country "hicks." We, in turn, called them "green horns." There were only a dozen pupils in the school ranging from first to seventh grade, so we did have individual attention.

For once I was the oldest and biggest boy in school, so I didn't have to prove myself as I did at College Springs. The next oldest boy came from one of the leading families in the community. He had been "boss" of the school before I came. He knew he couldn't lick me, so he took his resentment out on the smaller children. After I watched him make life miserable for some of the children, especially those from a very poor family, I took him aside and told him I didn't like what I saw and for him to lay off. For a time he did, but one day in the winter when we were sliding on the ice on the river, he pushed one of the boys from the poor family into the open water in the middle of the stream. The boy was soaked and had to go home. There was a big fuss made over the incident. The teacher quizzed me about what had happened and while I well knew, I had to tell her I did not see anyone pushed. The culprit claimed the boy had slipped into the water.

Since this boy thought I had covered for him, he became worse with the small children. After I had warned him several times and he continued, I got disgusted with him. At recess when he wouldn't promise to stop, I threw him on the ground and sat on him. When the bell rang for us to go back inside, I wouldn't let him up. I held him down until he promised to let the little kids alone. The teacher learned from the other pupils what was going on and she was wise enough not to ask us why we were late. Of course, this boy went home and told his folks how I had mistreated him, and they reported it to my father. When he asked me, I told him exactly what it was all about. I think he must have checked with the teacher, because I never heard anymore about it, and it was peaceful the rest of the time I was in that school.

Of course, the toilet facilities in those days were the usual boy's and girl's outhouses. Each day two boys would be given time to walk to the nearest farmhouse to bring back a pail of drinking water. This pail was set on a shelf in one corner of the room and a tin dipper hung nearby. Everyone used the same dipper, we didn't worry about germs then. In the cold weather the school was heated by a pot bellied stove set in the middle of the room, so we baked on one side and froze on the other. But we were all used to that at home.

One day shortly after the noon recess, we all got excited as we saw farmer after farmer driving past with the horses at full gallop. Finally one man on horseback stopped to ask the teacher to let him take our water pail. When she asked why, he said the Calhoon house was on fire. I knew my folks were away for the day, so I asked the teacher if she would excuse a boy who had ridden a pony to school that day, to ride me home. When we got there a large crowd had gathered and while the fire was in the roof of a summer kitchen built on the back of the house, a number of men were carrying furniture out of the main part of the house and piling it in the front yard. In order to get at the fire, some of the men tore off the roof near the chimney and put the fire out. Once that was done, the whole affair turned into a community gathering.

In order to be free to go on long trips, Mother had hired a young German immigrant girl to help with the housework and to be there when we got home from school. In order to do the weekly ironing, this girl had built a wood fire in the kitchen stove and was heating the irons. However, she didn't understand the use of the dampers and the chimney had overheated, thus catching the roof on fire. A few days before we had installed our first telephone. It was a rural line with a number of subscribers on it. When the girl saw the house on fire, she knew there was no neighbor within calling distance and although she didn't know how to use the phone, she did pick up the receiver. Two women were talking on the line when they heard the poor girl, so frightened, crying. They finally got her to tell her trouble and told her to hang up and they would send help. They rang an alert signal. All the women who were home heard the signal, got the news, and in turn called their men folks. These were some of the men we saw rushing by the school. This was typical of the times when neighbors rushed to help others in trouble.

I was now old enough to hire out for some farm work. The school year was arranged so there was a vacation time in the spring during the planting season and another in the fall when the corn was ready to pick. That made it possible for all the boys to be free for these critical periods. The first job I got was in the spring. It was on a large family-run farm which was different from many in that this man believed in diversified crops. He did have many acres of corn, which was the main crop in Iowa, but he planted a variety of small grains. He was also experimenting with red clover as a hay crop, something new at the time. He kept a herd of dairy cows which again was not too common, as most farmers raised beef cattle only. The milk from the cows was put through a new machine called a separator. This machine was hand operated, so it was part of the daily morning and evening chores. The fresh milk was fed into some high speed revolving discs so by centrifugal force the lighter cream separated from the heavier milk. The cream was collected and sold to a creamery to make butter. The milk was used to raise the

33

calves and the excess fed to the large number of hogs on the farm. Besides the usual number of horses, this farmer was raising mules. All these animals made a lot of chores, so the farmer's wife and teenage daughter did their share. The man and his son spent most of their time in the fields. I was hired to take over a lot of the chores, but also took a team and helped with the plowing.

It was the mules that proved to be the most interesting on this farm. The farmer's son, really a young man, taught me a lot about them. He drove one span of big strong bay mules. At first, because I was a stranger, I couldn't get near them. Gradually they became accustomed to me, and I was able to harness and drive them as well as anyone. It worked fine until one day when the weather became warm. I changed my stocking cap, which I had been wearing all winter, for a cooler hat. For some time I couldn't get near the mules. I suddenly was a stranger because I had changed my headdress. Thus, I found out the mule is a creature of strict habits; if you want to get along with them, be the same.

The most fun and excitement I had was when the young man decided to break a team of young mules. After a long patient job we got the harness on them in the barn. They were then blindfolded and led out and hooked to a wagon. As long as they were blindfolded, they stood perfectly still. He invited me to go with him, and I eagerly accepted, climbing up into the wagon behind him. When ready, he had two men slip the blindfolds off and yelled, "Hold on." When the mules could see, they stood fast for a few seconds and then seeing the driver standing back and above them and hearing a loud yell, they sprang into instant high gear. They ran with ears laid back and bellies low to the ground with no thought of direction across the big pasture. The wagon was hopping up and down over the rough ground, and we were both yelling and laughing. When the driver thought they had run far enough, he pulled on one rein until he got them headed straight for the barn. I became alarmed as it looked as if they would charge right into the side of the building. Then just before they reached the barn and still going at full speed, they suddenly set all four feet, and everything came to an abrupt stop. The back of the wagon went up a good three feet in the air, and if the driver hadn't caught me, I would have catapulted over the heads of the mules. It was then I learned one difference between a horse and a mule. A runaway horse will often go blind and charge into a fence or side of a building with serious results, but a mule never will, as he is too smart to hurt himself.

The mule is a hybrid between a donkey and a horse. They cannot reproduce, but they acquire some of the qualities of each parent. They are often considered stubborn, but it is usually a case of self-preservation. They are stronger than a horse of equal weight, will work harder, stand the heat of a summer better than a horse, but will not work themselves to death as will a horse at times. They never fully trust anyone, and it requires a special technique to handle them. They

34

always remain independent and never become friendly like a horse. I had been kicked by both a cow and a horse, but never by a mule, which was reported as being pure dynamite. One thing about it, if you work with mules, you learn to stay alert; you never sleep on the job if you want to survive.

During the summer I went with my father to work on different farms. He was considered an expert at stacking hay or grain, so he was often offered such a job. I worked with him to learn the secrets of the trade. If done properly, a stack after settling will stand straight and shed rain water so it never sinks in, thus preventing the hay from rotting. I have seen stacks after a time lean and even fall over when the stacker didn't know his job. In case of grain which had been harvested by a binder, the bundles had to be placed in a certain circular fashion and the center at all times kept higher than the outside layers. This could be tricky, especially with oats which have a very slippery straw. The things he taught me became an asset in later life.

One day while working in a hay field, a heavy black cloud appeared in the west. We hurried to get as much hay as possible loaded before the storm struck, but with only a half load had to rush to the barn for shelter. Hurriedly we unhooked the horses and got them inside just as the storm struck. Not only was there severe thunder and lightening, but hail began to fall. As the storm continued, the hail stones became larger until some were the size of golf balls. We sat in the barn door watching the storm smash its way across the open country. The farm dog had taken shelter under the hay wagon, which was left in front of the barn. Soon he was joined by a dozen chickens and then an old hen, who had stolen her nest, came leading her family to safety. Then a mother rabbit and two young ones joined the group, and finally a big skunk hurried to find shelter from the hail. Ordinarily, the dog would have chased the rabbits and skunk, but now he sat looking the other way. I had heard about natural enemies in the animal kingdom seeking shelter together in the face of a common danger, and now I was seeing it happen.

This hail storm did a tremendous amount of damage. Whole fields of corn were stripped of all leaves. Fields of wheat and oats were flattened and driven into the ground. Cattle out in the open suffered casualties— some wounded, some killed. One farmer caught on the road in open territory took refuge under his wagon only to see both of his horses knocked dead as they were hit behind the ears with the huge stones. Hundreds of window panes were smashed in the houses that were in the path of the storm. Such storms as this made farming in the west always a gamble.

One day that summer when I was with Father stacking grain, he remembered it was the date he had made to take the ponies to another farm which kept a stallion. He had decided to breed the ponies. Dale was with us that day, so he told me to take Dale and drive the ponies to the farm. He would stay and finish the stacking and ride home with a farmer who was helping on this job and lived near us. Dale and I drove to the farm with the stallion and found the man in charge waiting for us. I was then initiated into the way horses mate. After the initial test only one, Turvey, would stand for the stallion. Before the final act, the man in charge told Dale, who was then about six years old, to go up to the house and stay with his wife. After it was over we hooked the ponies back to the buggy and started home. On the way, Dale laughed because while he had to go to the house, the farmer's wife invited him to stand in the window with her and watch the whole proceedings.

It was late afternoon before we started for home, and because I thought I should, I let the ponies walk most of the way. They were slow walkers, so it was past suppertime when we arrived. Mother was in a stew because the whole family was expecting to go to the school house that evening for a box social. I had forgotten all about it. She hurried our supper, and we got there on time.

A box social was a common event in those days as a means of raising money for some non-profit organization. In this case it was for our Sunday School. The idea for such an affair was for the women and girls to put up a box lunch, then after a program, these boxes would be auctioned off to the men and boys. The highest bidder for each box would have the privilege of sharing the lunch with the donor. It was always a game for the boys to try to get the box put up by his favorite girl. The girls were not supposed to tell anyone what their box looked like, but would sometimes give her favorite boyfriend a clue. Any box which was guessed to be that of a popular girl would be bid real high. I had all of 50¢ to spend, and while I had a certain girl in mind, the only clue I had of her box was it would be tied with a red ribbon. Unfortunately for me, several boxes had red ribbons, and all went for more than my allowance. I was rather embarrassed when the box I did get was put up by a young married woman. We both got a lot of kidding.

October brought another school vacation so the boys could help pick the ripe corn. I got a job on a big farm and began a new task. In those days corn was husked by hand in the fields. After a frost the leaves of the corn plant became dry and the edges were as sharp as a razor. Heavy clothing had to be worn and scarfs tied around one's neck and ears to protect against those sharp edges. Special gloves were worn, the right one had a sharp steel knife-like tool, called a husking peg, attached to the thumb. This peg was used to open the thick husk on each ear, which was then stripped off the ear and the stem snapped free. If the corn was real dry, the stem would snap fairly easy, but if at all damp, it became tough and required a lot of strength in the wrists to break it. A husker was judged not only by the number of bushels of corn he could pick in a day, but was penalized by the number of husks he left on an ear and the number of long stems that showed. I worked with an experienced farmer, and he took two rows to my one. Long before the end of the day my wrists would be so tired I could hardly break a stem. It took a few days to harden up so I could keep up with the farmer.

Alongside the pickers would be a horse drawn wagon equipped for corn husking. The wagon box would be built up on the opposite side of the pickers to a height of three feet above normal. As the picker freed each ear, he would bank it against the high side so it would fall into the wagon box. When the wagon box was full, the team would be driven to the farm buildings and the corn shoveled into a corn crib. This was a long narrow building made of open slats so air could circulate through the corn to keep it from molding. Corn thus cribbed was the feed for the cattle and hogs raised on the farm. Excess corn could be kept until the farmer was ready to sell it on the market.

The cultural life of people who lived in the small towns and rural areas was greatly enhanced by the formation of the Chatauqua circuit. These traveling educational and entertainment groups appeared in many parts of the country and for many years it flourished in the middle west. The programs would be given under a large tent pitched in the center square of a town or on a nearby fair grounds. When on a large site, people would sometimes pitch their own tent and thus enjoy a week or two outing. The fair grounds at Clarinda, Iowa, near College Springs, was the site of one Chatauqua and one summer my grandparents decided to pitch a tent and enjoy the programs. My mother thought I should have the opportunity of attending, so she made arrangements for me to join them and Roy for a week.

To get to Clarinda, I had to go by train and had to make two changes. Father took me to Greenfield, where I boarded a train which took me to Creston on the main line west. From there I got a train for Red Oak, where I was to change to a spur line to Clarinda. I got to Red Oak alright and went into the station to ask about the train for Clarinda. "It's right out there," the station agent told me. I went outside and seeing a train standing with no one else to ask, I got on. As soon as the train started, I had an uneasy feeling that something was wrong and when the conductor took my ticket, it was confirmed when he said, "You should have got off at the last station." "I did," I replied. It turned out that I got on a train taking me back in the direction I had just come. At the first stop the conductor put me off and explained to the ticket agent what had happened and asked him to see that I got on the next train back to Red Oak. I had a long tiresome wait until after noon before a train was due. This time I made sure I got the right train for Clarinda. It was an experience I never forgot and from that time on I never got on a train unless I asked an official if it was the right one.

When I didn't show up at the expected time, my grandmother wondered what had happened. I explained that I had missed the train at Red Oak and she accepted it. I never told anyone that I made such a foolish mistake. The Chautauqua was a wonderful experience for me. While I didn't understand some of the lectures, I did enjoy the musical numbers. It was the first time I had heard or seen an orchestra perform, and I was thrilled watching the musicians play the various instruments. The week passed all too soon, and I took the trains back without any

37

trouble. I did heave a sigh of relief when I arrived at Greenfield and saw my father with the team of ponies. waiting for me.

During the summer of 1905, Aunt Nell and Uncle Clark returned to College Springs to show their first baby, Esta, to the relatives. On the way back they stopped at our house for a weekend. I knew Uncle Clark was a professor in a college, so I thought he must be very smart. But my opinion fell when I took a walk with him and Father. We went down the hill toward the river where there was an area that had never been plowed. This plot contained the native grasses of the original prairies. Uncle Clark noticed these grasses and flowers and asked the names of them. I thought how ignorant those easterners were not to know buffalo grass, red top or fox tail grass. Little did I dream how ignorant I would be about the names of trees when some years later I went east. My estimation of Uncle Clark soared when I heard him preach on Sunday at the service we held in the school house. He was a fluent speaker and always held his audience to the end. The part I remember was an illustration he used. Evidently his point was how important it was to stick to a course of action. He told of walking in the woods and coming to a cliff out of which was a trickle of water dripping. He looked down and saw that this constant dripping of the water had worn a deep hollow in the hard rock.

Again I thought he was great one evening as we all sat visiting after supper. The point of discussion was about a man they all knew and Uncle Clark was asked what he thought of such a character. "Well," he said, "he may be like a big tree my father had on his farm. It was tall, stately, and looked fine on the outside, but on examination we found it was hollow on the inside and very shaky at the butt." We all laughed, but Aunt Nell pretended she was shocked at his use of such an expresssion.

When it was time for them to leave, I drove them to the station in Greenfield. As was our custom, I started the ponies out slow for the twelve mile trip and knew I could push them near the end if necessary. Starting slow, Uncle Clark kept looking at his watch and began to protest about getting there on time. I knew the ponies and got them to the station in plenty of time, feeling rather proud.

It was during this time that church people became quite agitated when Rockefeller offered a large sum of money to a church in New York City. One faction thought it was fine, but another said it was blood money rung from the workers and the church should refuse it. To many midwesterners, any eastern tycoon was considered evil and shouldn't be in a church. I heard my folks discuss this question and while Father didn't want to take sides in the community, he knew sooner or later he would be confronted with the question. He was aware if he did take sides he would alienate about half the people. I was with him one afternoon when we met one of the leading men in the church. In the conversation as we were about to leave, the man confronted Father with the question about Rockefeller. I held my breath to see how Father would reply, then I heard him tell this story.

"Maybe," said Father, "it is like two young boys who were walking down the street past a house where a very poor old widow lived. They heard her loudly praying, pleading with the Lord to send her a loaf of bread as she was destitute and hungry. The boys thought it would be fun to play a trick on her, so they got a loaf of bread, put it on her porch, rapped on the door, and then hid behind a tree. The old lady came to the door and seeing the bread, began to thank the Lord for it. The boys then jumped out and cried 'Ha Ha, Lady, the Lord didn't put it there, we did.' 'Oh,' said the old lady, 'I don't care if you young devils did bring it, I know the Lord sent it.' " The farmer laughed and laughed, we could still hear him laughing as we got in the buggy and drove away. Evidently the story worked as the farmer spread it all around the community, and it so satisfied everyone that Father was never to face the issue again. It illustrated perfectly how a good story can often solve a problem better than a lot of debate. Later in life I tried the same method with more or less success. The main problem is to have a good story ready for every occasion.

Father's youngest brother, George, had also entered the ministry in the Wesleyan Church. He wrote that he was leaving a church located at Africa, Ohio, a rural community north of Columbus. He had decided he needed more education and was returning to Houghton Seminary to finish his requirements for ordination. When he decided to leave, he told the church officials about my father. They liked Uncle George so well they took his recommendation and sent my father an invitation to come and be their pastor. My folks talked it over. Father wanted to get back into the Wesleyan Church, but there seemed to be no immediate chance in Iowa, so the Ohio offer appeared to be his chance and he accepted the invitation.

Since we were to be in a rural community it was decided to keep the ponies. A freight car was ordered and Father took the ponies, a cow and calf with all the household furniture to Greenfield to load for the journey east. Father was to go with the car, as it was the rule of the railroad that if livestock was shipped, one man could go free to care for the stock. I went with a neighbor to help load the car and then returned to his house where Mother and the children were staying for a few days while Father went on ahead.

I had read about the Mississippi River in school and thought it would be a wonderful sight, so Mother planned our trip leaving Greenfield at the right time to cross the river in daylight. But it didn't work; the train from Greenfield broke down in the yards as it entered Creston where we were to transfer to the main line, and we sat watching the big train pull out without us. We had to wait several hours for the next train, so we crossed the Mississippi in the night.

We were now leaving my native state. It was goodby to the richest farm land in the world, the place where the tall corn grows, leaving the hot humid nights of summer when you could actually hear that corn grow. It was to forego the wild bareback rides on the ponies across the

39

open prairies. No more the chance to pick the wild rose blossoms to decorate the school house for the Children's Day program on Sunday. It was to forget the waiting until May 15th when we were allowed to take off our shoes and stockings and once again feel the hot dust of the road on our bare feet, or wiggle our toes in the cool mud of a puddle after a summer shower. It was to leave behind the pungent odors of the farm barn and the nearby hog wallow. We could no longer watch the sunny summer skies dotted with lazy white clouds or see those clouds turn into ominous thunder heads which could spell disaster. No longer in fall gather and store black walnuts to crack in winter with which to make the most delicious cake ever concocted, or in winter find a slippery elm tree and peel its under bark which made the best chewing gum ever. It was to end the chance visit to a farm when the women folks would run down a spring rooster, ring its necks, pluck the feathers, parboil it and fry it in country butter, and if the season was right, serve with heaping platters of rich yellow sweet corn, a banquet the memory of which would last a lifetime. All these and many more memories were soon to be just that, memories. We were joining the overflow from the middle west, some going to California and the west coast, while others like us were joining the ebb flow of migration back toward the east from whence our forefathers had come.

Family Picture when we moved from Iowa to Ohio, c. 1906.

CHAPTER 3

OHIO

Since we had missed our train in Iowa, we arrived in Columbus, Ohio, in the evening. Our tickets were to Lewis Center, the nearest railroad station to our new home, but there was no train until morning. As we stood huddled together in the waiting room of the big railroad station wondering what to do, we were thrilled to see Father coming toward us. When we did not arrive as planned, he guessed what had happened and had come to Columbus to meet us. He had arrived several days before with the household goods and stock and had the house all ready for us.

With all our baggage we followed him outside to a trolley station. A short wait and we boarded our first trolley car. After the long ride on the big trains, it seemed very small and gave us a rough ride north out of Columbus to Westerville. This was a town about a dozen miles from Columbus and four miles from the crossroads village called Africa, where we were to live. Father had driven the ponies to Westerville and when we arrived, we all piled into the surrey to complete our trip.

It was late when we arrived so we could see nothing of our surroundings but fell exhausted into bed, our brains still spinning as if still moving. The next morning we struggled out of bed to examine our new home. We found the parsonage to be a frame building with four bedrooms on the second floor. My parents took one room, the three girls shared another, and Dale and I had one. The fourth was reserved for Father's study. The first floor consisted of a living room, a dining room and a small bedroom off the living room, which was used for a guest room. At the back of the house an addition had been added for a kitchen. Unfortunately, it was not on the same level as the main house, but one step down. This became the cause of many falls.

To heat the house, besides the wood burning stove in the kitchen, there was a large sheet iron stove in the living room. This stove was designed to burn chunks of wood. It had a large sliding door on the top so big chunks could be dropped onto the fire. It had no grates, so it was like keeping a camp fire going. If the wood was seasoned, it gave off a lot of heat, but much of the time we had only green wood which Father and I cut from a farmer's wood lot. Such wood caused a problem, not only to keep a fire going, but it formed a pitch like tar which would run back down the stove pipe and out to ruin the wallpaper.

41

As soon as we had finished breakfast on our first day, we children rushed outside to see what it was like. From the back yard we noted that the house was located on a low bank of a wide valley. We could see in the distance a bridge which crossed a stream. Later we learned this stream was called Alum Creek, a slow, sluggish current which meandered south to the Scioto River. The wide valley contained the best farm land in the area but was subject to flooding, especially in the winter and spring and even damaging crops as late as June.

Walking around to the front yard we saw the Wesleyan Church directly across the road from the parsonage. About two-hundred yards to the north on one corner of a crossroads was the one room schoolhouse which we would attend. In sight were a half dozen houses and a small country store. This was Africa, so named, we were told, because it had been a way station on the underground railroad used by the runaway slaves before the Civil War.

Walking up the road we could see more houses on both sides of the valley, so while it was rural, it seemed more thickly settled than we had been used to. We were struck by the small size of the fields on the farms. Compared to the 160 acre wheat fields of South Dakota the 40 acre corn fields of Iowa seemed small, but now we were looking at fields of 10 acres or less. To us they seemed like gardens, but of course the nature of the land called for such plots.

In time we found the soil very different from the black loam of the west. Much of it was a yellow clay which held the water for a long time after a rain and would dry into a hard cake. While we knew mud in Iowa, this was a new kind, lasting all winter into late spring. It was bad for farm animals, clinging to their feet often causing a disease called foot rot. I winced when for the first time I saw a farmer treat his sheep for this rot by first washing the mud out of the cloven hoof and then rubbing salt into the open sore. The poor sheep would blat piteously and stumble off to lie down in pain. It seemed cruel, but had to be done. Otherwise the animal would lose a foot and possibly die.

Back of our house was a small barn. There we kept the ponies, a cow and heifer and later a sow with a litter of pigs. Since the barn was on a slope, rain water would wash down into it. The floor was mostly dirt and in spite of ditching to drain the water away, many times the floor was just mud. I felt sorry for the animals when the straw that was used for bedding became so damp, but they survived.

Drinking water for people and animals came from a well near the back door of the house. Also nearby was a cistern which collected rain water which drained off the roof. Most of the houses depended on such a cistern to provide soft water for washing clothes. Well water in this region was very hard.

Another difference we noted in Ohio was the weather. There were many more cloudy days, especially in winter. Many times when we got up in the morning the sun would be shining, only to have clouds move in by nine o'clock and stay the rest of the day. There was not much snow in the winter but a lot of drizzly rain. It did freeze and was cold enough to form solid ice on the creek. Skating on this ice was our best winter sport. The summers were not as hot as in Iowa, but the humidity was much higher, so it was uncomfortable. The long fall was the best time of the year.

There was one thing we found very confusing, the keeping of time. Actually, there were three different systems in use in this area. One was sun time, which all the farmers used. This time was determined by sunrise and sunset, so the sun was always directly overhead at noon. Then there was rail time, which was set by the railroad officials. Last was Standard Time, which was not fully established but used by the large cities. Most of our activities were regulated by local or sun time, but if one wanted to catch a train or go into Columbus, everything had to be adjusted. Also, when an event was publicized, the time system used had to be indicated.

We found that the customs and habits of the people were different from any place we had lived. This struck us children with quite a shock on the first day of school. Since the school house was so near, we were able to be home for lunch everyday. So we put away our lunch pails we had carried before. On the first morning Dale and I put on a clean pair of overalls and the girls their customary gingham dresses. When we arrived at school all the children stared at us. They were all dressed in what we called our Sunday clothes. At recess we were surrounded by other pupils making fun of our clothes. They considered what we had always worn to school as outfits to be used when working on a farm. As soon as we could get home at noon, we told Mother and she understood our embarrassment and got out our good clothes for us to put on to go back to school. Our old school clothes now became our work clothes to be worn to do the chores before and after school. It also meant that we gave up going barefoot in the summer. Others didn't do it, so as the minister's children, we had to conform to custom.

We had two different teachers in school that year. The first one was a man who had been a teacher in a large city school. Because of poor health he had moved to the country. He was an experienced and inspiring teacher, and I learned a lot from him. Part of the time I was the oldest boy in the school, but during the winter months a boy old enough to be in high school attended and this teacher taught him some algebra. Since it was in a one room school, we could always listen to others reciting, so I watched and learned a considerable amount of algebra. In the middle of the year, this man became ill and the doctor diagnosed it as TB, and he had to give up teaching.

A married middle-aged woman, a retired teacher, lived right across the road from the school, and she took over to finish out the year. Her husband was in poor health and never did any more work than to keep a flock of chickens. His hens ran loose and when school was in session, they would come across the road in the school yard looking for crumbs and crusts the pupils would throw away while eating lunch outside.

When we came out at recess it was great sport for us boys to throw stones at them to drive them back home. One day as one old hen paused on the edge of the bank which bordered the road, I let fly with a stone and hit her on the back of her head. She flopped over into the road, and when we went to investigate, we found her dead. All the boys looked at me and exclaimed, "What are you going to do?" They were scared as it was the teacher's hen. I pretended that I was real brave, picked up the hen, and took her to the back door of the teacher's house, rapped and when the husband answered, I told him exactly what had happened. I said I was sorry; I didn't intend to hit her but I did. He listened, thanked me for telling him, took the bird out to the chopping block and cut off her head with an ax. "There," he said, "we will have an unexpected chicken dinner." I felt greatly relieved and the other boys thought I was a hero. However, after that we decided to stop throwing stones at the hens. From this espisode I learned it was far better to admit to a mistake than to try to cover up.

While the woman teacher was in charge, she hired me to act as janitor of the school house. I took care of the fire in the pot bellied coal stove, which meant I had to get up early on cold mornings so the room would be warm for the morning session. I swept the floor every day after school and dusted each morning. For this I was paid a dollar a week. But that was considered good pay for a boy, as men were working on the farms or factories for a dollar a day. Besides, it was good experience for me to have the responsibility. Of course, I had the usual chores at home taking care of the ponies, cow, pigs, and some chickens. It was a busy life and time never dragged.

Since I had worked on farms before coming to Ohio, I was interested in getting a similar job during school vacations. The first opportunity came in the spring vacation, on the Jaycox farm just outside the village. This farm had a small sugar bush and the run of sap came just right, so I was offered a job of helping to collect the sap, split wood for the fire under the pans where the sap was boiled down to syrup, and after a time I attended the fires during part of the day so Mr. Jaycox could get some sleep after staying up all night. I had read about making maple sugar in the old reader we had in school in Iowa. It had a picture of men and boys gathering the sap, and I always dreamed how great it would be to do this. I was so thrilled for this chance I would have worked for nothing but Mr. Jaycox insisted on giving me fifty cents a day. Ohio is not noted for maple syrup and the season is very short, so the week's vacation just about covered the time. The important thing was that I seemed to fit into this family so well I was given a whole summer job.

As soon as school was out for the summer I moved to the Jaycox farm. The family consisted of Mr. Jaycox, a large man of 200 pounds, his wife, a small woman who had little to say, two boys, Harold and Homer, younger than I was, and a grandfather who had once run this farm. The grandfather had given over the farm to his son and lived a semi-retired life picking up produce, chickens and eggs and taking them to market in the city. He did this, in spite of protests from his family, until his health failed, and then with nothing to do, he died.

Mr. Jaycox was rather easy going, a hard worker, but he never got excited over things. He was good to his boys, letting them help when they wanted to but never insisting that they work all the time. I never heard him bawl them out if they did something wrong but would say, "I guess you didn't use your head, did you?" I knew the boys in school and wondered how it would be to live with them. I didn't need to worry, as they considered me as an older brother. I did find out that I had to be careful of what I said or did, for I heard them say several times to their mother, "Well, Ray does it."

I was surprised to find how much of the farm work in this part of the country was done by hand. For example, corn fields, which were small by Iowa standards were all gone through with a hoe after cultivation. This was necessary to control the so-called pea vine, which is really a wild morning glory vine. If this vine was not destroyed when the corn was young, it would entwine the stalk and smother the corn to death. Another example was that corn was not husked in the fields as in Iowa; the stalks were cut by hand and put into large shocks. In early winter they would be husked and the stalks used for fodder for the cows. This corn left in the fields in these shocks became a haven for countless field mice and rats. It was a great sport to have a rat terrier handy to catch the rats when the shock was disturbed.

Rats were a real plague on the farm. They infested the corn cribs and bins of grain. The winters were mild enough so they could live in the fields and all the farm buildings. Most farmers kept a rat terrier and on rainy days time would be spent in hunting rats. Dale was Homer's age and often came up to be with the boys that summer. One afternoon they took the dog into the corn crib to hunt rats. The pile of corn was low and all they had to do was move a little and out would run a rat or two. When I came in from the field, they ran to meet me and wanted me to guess how many rats they killed. I started with a dozen, but they kept saying, "Higher." When I got up to 50 I wouldn't believe them, so they led me to where they had 75 dead rats laid out in a row. We considered that to be a record for a one day hunt.

Mr. Jaycox had two teams on the farm, one a team of heavy horses used for most of the work, the second an unusual team of mules. One mule was an old large gray veteran, slow and lazy, but gentle. The other was a small black jenny, very nervous and set in her ways. Some times she was used alone, but when hooked up as a team, the driver had to be constantly prodding old Gray, as he would lay back and let Blackie do all the work. She didn't seem to mind doing the major part of the pulling in order to be with her friend, old Gray.

There were things about Blackie that everyone had to learn. When in her stall, one entered on one side only. There was a certain ritual in the

45

way she was harnessed and hooked to a wagon. When teamed with Gray, one had to go behind him, fasten the inside tug of Blackie, finish the tugs of Gray and then go around to hook the outside tug of Blackie. That was the way it was done and as long as I followed the rules, all was well. One day, however, I was in a hurry and being on Blackie's side, I thought I would hook her outside tug first and then go around and do the others. But I learned my lesson. As soon as I had hooked the one tug, Blackie began to buck and kick. She got her hind feet caught in the harness, and she never stopped until she had torn the harness off her back and into shreds. With nothing left on but her bridle and collar, she turned around and looked at me as if to say, "Young feller, don't ever try to do things different with me." I should have remembered that mules are creatures of habit, and I never forgot again as it took me two hours to repair the harness and get back to work.

When the haying season started, I found it different from Iowa where most of the hay was stacked outside, but in this climate it was put in large hay barns. As was the custom, farmers exchanged help so some men came to work with us. Although I was small and light, I could pitch hay with any of these men. One man took over the loading, but he was far from an expert and as he was going along the side hill which approached the barn, one of his loads tipped over burying him underneath. We had to hurry to dig him out before he smothered. Mr. Jaycox had seen me load, so he had me take over, and with the skill Father had taught me, I never had a spill.

I was also introduced to a hay fork and track to get the hay into the mow. To save time, Mr. Jaycox decided to use Blackie on the hay fork rope rather than unhook the team every time we came in with a load. He was setting the fork and I was driving Blackie, but if he set the fork for a full load, the weight was too much and would pull Blackie right off her feet. He told me to get on her back to hold her down, but it made no difference so he got on and with his 200 pounds, held her feet on the ground and she would pull a load as well as a team. So for the rest of the season I not only did all the loading, but set the fork to unload. Working on that farm was one of my best summers. I have fond memories of that time.

In the spring of 1907, my teacher told me that I had finished the work of the 8th grade and should plan to take the county examinations in May. These examinations were given at the county seat, which in our case was Delaware, Ohio. Father arranged to take me. All the 8th grade pupils from the rural schools in the county met at the high school in Delaware. We were ushered into the largest room I had ever seen. The exams began at 9 a.m. and lasted until 4 p.m. All the common subjects were covered and at the end I was sort of dazed to do this in one day. The man who had been the former teacher was very interested in my success, and since he lived nearby, came to go over the question papers that I was able to keep. He quizzed me about my answers and at the end told me he felt sure I had passed. Two weeks later I got a notice that I had passed all exams and therefore, completed the 8th grade.

I was the only one in the Africa school to take the exams and when I passed, I was asked to join a few pupils from other rural schools in the township for a sort of graduation program. It was held in a school at Lewis Center. My teacher had me learn a poem to give as a recitation the same as the others in the group did. Father had been asked to give a talk to the group. Father was the only one in my family to go, and he was surprised to have me get up and speak. I hadn't said anything about it at home, just assumed it was part of my school program. His talk was to encourage all of us to continue our education and to become specialists in some field. He said, "The day of the jack-of-all-trades was over." I remember his talk, but I fear I didn't follow it entirely.

Now that I had finished the 8th grade, the question arose as to how I could further my education. We were in a strictly rural area and the nearest high school was at least 15 miles away. There was no transportation for pupils in the country as there is now. None of the young people we knew in the area had ever gone to high school. The boys usually took up farming and the girls looked for a boy to marry. If I was to go to high school, I would have to go somewhere to board and room. The decision was finally brought about by our church connections.

Now that we once again lived in a church parsonage, much of our family life centered around the church. We had to attend the morning and evening services on Sunday and a mid-week prayer meeting. While this was a Wesleyan church, it was the only church for several miles around, so it was like a community church. Father liked this, as he felt he could call on any and all the people in the area. He was well-liked, and while the congregation was small, it did grow and the Sunday School increased even more. I was asked to take part in the young people's meetings, but they were not very active. Such meetings didn't appeal to the young folks, especially as the boys had the use of a horse and buggy on Sunday evenings and could take their girl for a ride. This began at an early age and most of them got married young.

It was the custom for the Wesleyan church to hold a revival service for a two week period sometime during the winter months. This was an extra chance for a boy to get out with his girl, so these services were well attended by the young people. The service consisted of some special music, a rousing sermon followed by a strong altar call, much like the Billy Graham services which are now seen on TV. The church had special traveling evangelists that came on invitation to the local churches to conduct these services, but Father was not satisfied with many of them because he didn't like their "Hell and Brimstone" style. They tried to scare people into repenting and being saved, but surveys showed too many of these folks "backslid" and were no asset to the church. Accordingly, Father preferred to hold the services himself and use a calmer approach. His method did have a more lasting effect.

One year he did use the help of a group of students from Houghton Seminary, a Wesleyan Methodist Church school, located at Houghton, New York. One member of the team was a young man named Dave

Graduation from eighth grade
Africa, Ohio
June 1907

Scott. He had a beautiful tenor voice which was very affecting in church. He stayed at our house, so we got to know him and liked him very much. He told us about Houghton, saying it was not only a school for the training of ministers and missionaries, but was also a preparatory school for college. Much of the student body was made up of boys and girls from families who like us lived in a rural area far from a high school but wanted to prepare for college. Of course, we knew some about Houghton as Uncle Clark was teaching there, but Dave Scott's description gave us a better insight. The result was when I finished the 8th grade, arrangements were made for me to go to Houghton for my high school work. I was to live with Aunt Nell and Uncle Clark and help with their small children for my room and board.

Since I was to leave home in the fall, Mother insisted late that summer that we go to Westerville and have a family group picture taken. Also, she wanted one of me alone. While there I was outfitted with some new clothes and much to my pleasure, graduated into long trousers. Also, I got a trunk and suitcase to take on my trip. I looked forward to going with mixed feelings. I wanted to go to high school, but was not keen about leaving home. Neither was I thrilled about living with Aunt Nell and helping with the housework and taking care of her two small children. But that was the condition, and I was determined to make the most of it.

During the last week in August we drove to Columbus to attend the State Fair. It was a hot humid day, and while we did enjoy seeing the big buildings full of exhibits and the prize animals, we arrived back home that evening exhausted. While that trip remained in our memory as the last one we took as a family, it also may have been a bad one. The headlines of the Columbus daily paper told the story of an epidemic of typhoid fever around that area. It may very well be where the family was exposed to the disease.

Just before it was time for me to leave, we learned that a young married couple from Ohio was going to Houghton that fall. Arrangements were made for me to join them. We took the train to Cleveland and then the night boat on Lake Erie to Buffalo. This saved a hotel bill and made a pleasant journey. From Buffalo we took the Erie Railroad to Portageville and then changed to the Pennsylvania to Houghton.

So I left home to be more or less on my own at the age of fourteen. Little did I dream that when I said goodby it would be the last time our family would be all together. Rather, I left more in the spirit of adventure.

CHAPTER 4

HOUGHTON

I arrived in Houghton on Friday evening of the week before school began. The only thing I could see when we got off the train was a small station. I walked through the village and up a long hill to get to Uncle Clark's house. The next day after getting my trunk from the station and unpacking, I had a chance to look around the village which was destined to be my home for the next seven years. The first thing I noticed was the house was on a plateau about 400 feet above a wide valley. This I learned was the Genesee River Valley. On the opposite side about a mile away was the highest hill I had ever seen. It looked like a mountain to me. In fact, this area is in the foothills of the Alleghany Mountains.

Uncle Clark's house was built on the edge of the school campus which encompassed most of the plateau. Across the street was one brick house owned by J. N. Bedford, Uncle Clark's uncle. Down the street were four houses and back of them on another street were three more. On the campus were three buildings. The first was the main school building; a large rectangular structure of red brick with a slate roof and trimmed in white facing east overlooking the Genesee River Valley. The front entrance was dominated by high stairs leading to a large portico, enclosed on either side by white banisters, and from which rose several large round white columns to support the roof and cupola which held the school bell. Just beyond the main building was another, also made of red bricks, which I learned was the girl's dormitory and about a hundred yards behind of the school building was the President's house, also made of red bricks.

When I went after my trunk I found that the road followed the brow of the plateau, then down a steep incline in front of the dormitory, crossing a bridge at the bottom over Houghton Creek and curved around to meet the main road which was dirt and followed the river through the village, running south to Caneadea and north to Fillmore. Houghton Creek, a small boisterous stream, came running down from the hills in back of Houghton, through the village, and emptied into the Genesee River.

The main part of the village was on the river flats, consisting of some twenty houses built on both sides of the road. Near the station at the south end was a country store and a small post office. On beyond just out of sight was a one-room school house. Near the north end was the Wesleyan Church and at the edge of the village was the only business, a cheese factory, a place of activity in the early morning when the farmers brought in their cans of milk and then carted away the whey, a by-product of the cheese-making to be fed to the calves the farmers were raising, even though it was not a complete food and made them potbellied.

All my life I had lived in a flat or fairly flat country, and my first reaction to the high hills was to feel hemmed in. So for the first week end I was terribly homesick; my first and only experience with the affliction. That first Saturday Aunt Nell had little for me to do, and Uncle Clark, sensing my feelings, told me to take his bicycle and go for a ride. I had never tried to ride one, but I was so glad to get away by myself I decided to ride it or bust. I followed the street away from the campus and discovered a second road down the hill, one which wound around below another plateau which I learned later was the camp meeting grounds. I came out on the main road leading toward Fillmore. Looking up from this road I saw a third way up the hill. A long flight of wooden steps had been built straight up the side of the cliff making a short-cut from the main road to the campus. I did very little riding the first afternoon, but whenever I had some free time, I took the wheel out and soon mastered it.

On my first Monday morning I went to the Seminary building to register. It was very simple, just filling out a card with name, parents' name and address, etc., then paying my tuition which I think was $25.00 per semester. The subjects were prescribed for a first year student. They were English, algebra, biology, ancient history and Latin. This was to be my first experience of having different teachers for each subject, and it seemed strange to change classrooms at the end of each period, but I soon got used to it and began to feel more grown up.

One thing happened in my algebra class, where Uncle Clark was the teacher, the first week of school that made it special. He started with the usual method of explaining positive and negative numbers by using a diagram of a thermometer. He marked the point of zero and then reading off some numbers above that point, he said, "We can call them positive numbers and mark them with a plus sign. Now, Ray, what might we call the numbers below zero?" With the knowledge I had by listening to the teacher back in Africa, I quickly answered, "Negative numbers and they can be marked with a minus sign." Uncle Clark looked real surprised and said, "That's right, I forgot there are two Rays in this class, I meant Ray Hazlett." Hazlett was repeating the subject, and Uncle Clark knew it, so called on him but I jumped in first. I liked math and after a good start did very well in that class.

At this time, Aunt Nell had two small children, Esta a little over two years old and Ward, about one. When things got organized I found she wanted me to care for Ward after school in the afternoons and part of

52

the time on Saturday and Sunday. On Saturday morning she asked me to help with the washing by running a washing machine. The machine was a manual type, consisting of a long handle on top which when pushed back and forth operated a set of gears which rotated an agitator inside the tub. I had never seen such a machine and thought it quite an invention to beat the old scrub board I had been used to. There was one source of danger, which to my consternation I discovered one morning. Ward was a toddler and followed me around a lot. That morning he stood by the machine watching the gears go around. I warned him several times not to get his fingers near the gears, but when my attention was distracted, I felt the machine suddenly pull harder and looked down to see his hand caught in the gears. He didn't make a sound but stood with his mouth wide open. I yelled and backed up the machine, thus releasing his hand. When his mother rushed into see what had happened, he began to cry. There was no doctor in Houghton, and it was afternoon before one came from Fillmore. He said one finger was broken, put on a splint and said he would be alright. I was very upset, because I thought Aunt Nell would blame me, although she said she didn't, but I blamed myself for not watching him closer.

Most of the girls in the school lived in the dormitory, but the boys had to find rooms with private families in the village. Many of these boys got their meals at the girls' dormitory. Some of them were lucky enough to get jobs waiting on tables for their board. Almost every house in the village rented one or more rooms, and Aunt Nell was no exception. Besides me, there were four or five other boys who roomed there. Two of the boys, Theo and Gail Thompson, I knew. They were from Northville, South Dakota, and were in school when I started in the first grade. The other two, Glenn Carpenter and Charlie Pierce, were among the oldest boys in school. We had the whole of the second floor and arranged it so we had one room for study. This was my introduction to regular study hours, which the school enforced from 7 to 9 pm every evening except Sunday. There was no electricity in the area, so we had to use a large kerosene lamp with a green shade for illumination. None of us were taking the same subjects, so there was little discussion during the early study hours, but near the end before going to our rooms to sleep, we would hold a "bull session." We talked about the school, the teachers and whatever was current. Of course, there was no radio and only a day old newspaper in the school library, so the news of the world was far away.

My room was a small one directly over the kitchen. A stove pipe from the kitchen stove came up through the room, so there was some heat in cold weather. Of course, along with the heat came all the odors of the cooking. There was one small window so I could air out the room before going to bed and leave the window open at night. Sometime after school started Aunt Nell took in another roomer to bunk with me. He came off a farm in Indiana and brought some of it with him. He slept in his underwear and I don't think he had taken a bath since summer. He had an aversion to fresh air and objected to having the window open at night. I offered to sleep on the front side to be near the window, but he insisted on that side. As a rule he didn't do much studying and went to bed early. One night when I was ready for bed the air in the room was so foul I opened the window a little and crawled into bed. My roommate got up and shut it. I lay for a time trying to go to sleep, but the air was so bad I couldn't, so I got up and opened the window again. Up he got and shut it and up I got and opened it. I don't remember how many times this happened until I finally won. The next morning he told Aunt Nell that he was leaving, he couldn't stand being frozen all the time. I expected she would be mad at me, but she just asked me what happend and I told her. I heard her tell Uncle Clark she wasn't sorry to have him go, as he was arrears in his rent and she didn't think he was any good.

With my school work and helping Aunt Nell I was so busy I soon got over being homesick. I was doing fine in all my subjects except Latin. Languages were always my poorest subjects, but Latin was a required subject, so I kept trying. I was getting adjusted to my new life when I had disturbing news from home. First Leeta and then Mother came down with typhoid fever. They thought they had picked it up on our trip to the state fair that summer. Father was the only one to care for them, so I offered to go home and help, but he told me to stay in school. He was afraid if I was home I would get it too. I had weekly reports and as the Christmas vacation approached, the news was better; both patients had passed the critical stage.

It was too far for me to go home for Christmas, as it was for the other roomers in the house, and so we spent more time together. The others were all older and one night decided they wanted to do something to relieve the boredom. They planned, with a few others who were also staying over the vacation, to rent a team for a sleigh ride going to Belfast and play a basketball game against the town team. I was eager to go with them, but they refused to let me go as they were breaking the school rules and they didn't want to get me involved. They did go and were called on the carpet by the Dean of Men, but since two of the boys' father, Mr. Thompson, was a big financial supporter of the school, they were let off easy. So I learned about the rules of the school.

Houghton Seminary was founded by the Wesleyan Methodist Church and since they continued to support it, the church board prescribed the rules for the student body. No student was allowed to smoke, or drink any alcoholic beverage. In fact, the deeds of all the property in the village of Houghton prohibited any liquor or beer being sold or consumed on the premises. The hours of all students were regulated, whether in the dormitory or outside. No student could leave town without permission. There was no dancing permitted on campus nor could a student attend a dance off campus. Association between boys and girls was strictly limited; they could date only at an early hour at the dorm or attend a lecture or concert in the college chapel. Dress was to be very plain; the girls could wear no jewelry nor have feathers in their hats. A few of the boys went farther than the rules and considered it sinful to wear a tie. The rule that caused the greatest reaction was that any athletic games were to be on an intramural basis only. This rule was interpreted to cover vacations as well as school time. It was broken more often than any other in the book.

All students were required to attend the daily chapel services, which were held in the auditorium on the second floor of the Seminary building. These services were mainly religious in nature, opening with a hymn followed by a prayer, then any announcements the faculty wanted to give, and concluded by a short sermon or inspirational talk by a member of the faculty. Sometimes there would be an outside speaker or a brief concert given by the music department which was a welcome change.

The seating of the students for chapel was determined by tradition. In the front row of seats were the academic freshmen, in back of them the sophomores, and so on to the back row where the few college students were permitted to sit. So my first year I started in the front row and through the years worked my way back until in the end I was proud to be in the back row.

To show that all the faculty did not agree with all the rigid rules, I quote from Uncle Clark's life history telling about his experiences when he was a member of that faculty. He writes, "In those days the discipline at Houghton was enforced by many rules pertaining to evening study hours, boy and girl relations, daily chapel attendance, and strict observance of the Sabbath, including church worship. Some of these regulations were puritanical and I chafed under them. Many of the students at Houghton were mature and why not treat them as adults? When infringement of some disciplinary rule was up for discussion in a faculty meeting, I often presented the student viewpoint. I argued that the enforcement of so many rules was not conducive to self-control on the part of students, an important factor in character building." From this it can be seen why Uncle Clark was one of the most popular yet highly respected members of the faculty in the eyes of the students as long as he taught at Houghton.

Early in my first school year something happened which played a prime importance in my future life. A few boys in the school, including the Thompsons, knew how to play a band instrument. They originated the idea of organizing a school band. They learned that J. W. Pepper Co., a manufacturer of band instruments, had a plan whereby a group sending a certain amount of money would be furnished all the instruments for a thirty piece band. It was advertised throughout the school that any boy who put up $15.00 could join the band. That was the basic fee and when the instruments came, tryouts would be conducted so the better players could get the better instruments if they wanted to pay the difference. The school agreed to pay for the big instruments, such as the bass drum and tuba, and they would be kept in the school for future use. All other instruments would belong to the player paying for it. I was anxious to join but didn't have the $15.00. I hurriedly wrote home explaining the plan and my desire to join. Evidently Mother was glad to know I was interested in music and to my delight, sent me a money order which came just before the time expired to join.

When the instruments came I was given the last choice, but being the youngest one in the group, I expected that. My instrument was an alto horn made in the shape of a French horn, but fingered with the right hand. Also, my money covered the price, so I was satisfied. I had no idea how to blow a horn so had to start from scratch. I took it to my room and I expect I drove Aunt Nell crazy at the beginning, but I persisted and before long I could play some simple tunes. By contributing 50 cents a week we were able to hire a man who lived near Short Track to give us lessons. He had the reputation of starting several successful town bands in the area, and we found him to be an excellent teacher. He conducted the band as a group but also helped each one individually. That way he learned that I was one of a few who could do the after beat which the horn part features. Thus, I became the leading horn for some time. Later I did learn other instruments, such as the tuba, and finally had a cornet before I left. Being able to play in this band meant a great deal to me then and more so later.

Soon after Christmas vacation I received the bad news from home that Father had contracted the typhoid fever. After taking care of Leeta and Mother for so long, he was very run down and Mother warned me that it might go hard on him. Again, I offered to go home but she wanted me to stay in school. Then soon after school started after the New Year, Uncle Clark got a telegram saying for me to come home and asked him to come also. We took the five o'clock train to Portageville and then to Buffalo. We arrived in Cleveland in the early hours of the morning and had to wait for a train to Lewis Center. Exhausted by the night travel and by the anxiety of not knowing how we would find Father, I fell asleep sitting on the bench in the waiting room. I was rudely jarred awake by a hurting blow at the bottom of my feet. My eyes popped open to see a big burly uniformed policeman standing over me. He wanted to know what I was doing there. I explained that I was waiting for a train. Realizing Uncle Clark wasn't in the seat beside me, I looked around and spotted him across the room pacing to keep awake. The policeman wanted to know if I was alone and I said, "No, my uncle is over there looking at us." "Well," he said, "you can't sleep here," and walked away. I often wondered what would have happened if I had been alone.

We arrived in Lewis Center just after noon and were met by one of our neighbors with a team and surrey. As we started for home, I wanted to ask what had happened but was just too stunned to do so. Finally, the man asked Uncle Clark if we had heard, and when Uncle Clark replied, "No," the man said, "he is gone, he went last night." I just sank in a huddle on the back seat of the rig. He died January 16, 1908.

When we got home, Mother greeted us and as soon as I got my overcoat off, she took me into the small bedroom downstairs where Father was laid out. I stood looking at him completely stunned. All I could think about while standing there was the words he had said to me the past summer as I was driving him to take a train to attend conference. "Son," he said, "if anything happens to me you will have to look after your mother." How little did I dream that those words would mean so much so soon. After a couple of minutes Mother left me alone and I just stood there hearing the words over and over. After a time I walked out into the living room and huddled in an old chair. I still couldn't cry. I didn't want anything to eat, but Mother insisted and to please her, I choked down a little and then felt better.

Funeral arrangements were completed and Uncle Clark was to officiate. I guess that was why Mother had asked him to come with me. The day came and the family assembled in the living room for a brief prayer service before we went to the church. We then viewed Father for the last time, only I didn't realize it was to be the last time. I knew it was the custom in a church funeral service for the people to pass by the coffin for a last look, and I thought we would do the same. But I was mistaken, the family sat in the front pew while the others filed past. All these years I have felt rather cheated; I wanted to look one more time. The church was full for the service. I have little recollection as to what was said, but I was glad Uncle Clark was there to conduct the service. As we came out of the church to take a carriage to the cemetery, I saw all the boys I knew standing on both sides looking at me to see how I was taking things. I had hold of Mother's arm and held my head high, determined I wouldn't flinch under their gaze. Father was buried under a tree in the old Africa cemetery. Later Mother had a nice stone placed to mark the spot.

After the service we had to plan our new life. I had brought my trunk home, as I expected I would have to drop out of school, but Mother thought otherwise. The next day I took Uncle Clark to the train to return to Houghton. As I was near the end of the first semester, he thought I wouldn't miss much if I stayed at home for two weeks. The church let our family stay in the parsonage until the end of summer. For this Mother led the church services on Sunday, reading from a book of sermons and sometimes giving a talk of her own. The church knew they couldn't get a new minister until the fall conference, so it worked out well for all concerned.

I was now 15 years old, the oldest of five children left to my mother with no means of support. I thought I should go to work, but at that time of year there was no opportunity in a rural area, so after getting things adjusted so the stock could be cared for, I reluctantly went back to Houghton to finish the year. The second semester had just started when I got back, and since all my subjects were year courses, I returned to the same classes trying to make up lost time.

My Grandmother Crow had come to visit Aunt Nell and had been given my room. Uncle George Calhoon had built a house at the end of the same street, so I was asked to live with his family for a time. This house was made of cement blocks, a new type in the village, so it attracted quite a lot of attention. After I was back about a week probably due to my trip and changing beds, I caught a very bad cold. I developed a raspy cough and a severe pain under my shoulder blade. I was put to bed and soaked with camphorated oil covered with flannel cloths. I was close to pneumonia, but I recovered. My cough held on until spring, but I did get back to school, having lost more time.

Before spring, I was back with Aunt Nell helping with the children. Also that spring Uncle Clark became the pastor of the Wesleyan Church in Fillmore, in addition to his teaching. That meant he was gone every Sunday, which Aunt Nell didn't like, so when the weather warmed up she decided to take the family and go with him. She asked me to go along to help with the children. The first Sunday Esta had to go to the toilet during the sermon, so Aunt Nell took her out leaving Ward with me. He didn't like the idea and squirmed away from me getting out into the aisle. I thought he would follow his mother, but instead he walked up the aisle and into the pulpit. At first Uncle Clark tried to ignore him and continue the sermon, but it soon became apparent the congregation was paying more attention to Ward than to the sermon. So Uncle Clark stopped and said, "I guess someone will have to come and take this young fellow out of here." Very much embarrassed, I got up, went into the pulpit, picked Ward up, and carried him back to our seat. I expected every minute to have him set up a howl, but to my relief he didn't and the service continued to the end.

One of the traditions at Houghton was for couples to spend Memorial Day on an all day picnic at Portage Falls park. A boy would ask a girl to go and pay her transportation while the girl would furnish a picnic lunch. Some of the students I knew were going, and I wanted to join them. I talked to Aunt Nell, and she approved my going. Since I didn't have a girl, she suggested I ask Grace Bedford, a cousin of Uncle Clark. Lynn, her brother, was my age and in several of my classes, and I became friends with the family. Grace was Lynn's younger sister and was delighted to go, and since Lynn was taking his girl, the mother approved.

It was a bright sunny morning as we took the train from Houghton to Portageville. From the Penn station we had to climb a high steep hill to the Erie station and then follow a foot walk on the high railroad bridge to the entrance of the park. From the bridge we had a view of the first two falls and the beautiful grounds surrounding them. At this time it was a private park owned by William P. Letchworth, a Buffalo man who later gave it to the state to be developed into a beautiful state park. We had a permit to enter the grounds, and while there were some trails, most of the area was in the wild state. After seeing the first and second falls, we gathered in a group for our picnic lunch. There were two members of the faculty with us to act as chaperones, and they kept us together. We then hiked along the rim of the deep canyon about a mile to the third falls. This falls proved to be the most spectacular of all. The water follows a narrow bed, rushing with tremendous force before dropping over a high cliff, then taking a ninety degree turn, forming a swift whirlpool. Anyone falling into the river would have no chance of surviving. Now all of that is safe-guarded by railings, but then we viewed it at our own risk. It turned out to be a beautiful day and while it was my first experience with a girl, it really was more of a group affair. We returned on the evening train tired but satisfied that it was worthwhile. It was the first of several such trips to follow.

Our school band had progressed so much we were asked to give a concert on the lawn in front of the school building one afternoon during commencement week. We had some chairs brought from the study hall, but discovered there were not enough to seat the whole band. The door of the study hall was locked and no one was around to let us in. We found that the door of the library was unlocked, so we barged in to pick up a few more chairs. We surprised a few faculty members in a circle in one corner of the room. We recognized some but noticed there was a stranger in their midst. We grabbed some chairs and beat a hasty retreat. Later we learned that we had interrupted a meeting of a faculty committee interviewing Dr. Luckey for the position of President of the school. The fall I entered Houghton, Professor Bond, who had been President, resigned and one of the older faculty professors, Professor McDowell, finished the year as acting President. Dr. Luckey was a distinguished scholar and when he accepted the position, he brought to the school an atmosphere of higher education which ultimately made it possible for him to obtain a charter from the State of New York, making it a four year college. I always hoped he didn't recognize me as the one who barged in on that meeting. If he did, he never mentioned it.

After commencement all the high school students stayed to take the Regents examinations. I had heard these examinations discussed in tones of almost awe. I knew I had one in biology, algebra and history. On the morning of my first Regents, I saw most of my classmates nervously walking up and down the hall with books in their hands trying to cram in the last few minutes. My impression was Regents was some kind of "third degree." When I got into the room, except for the formality of the opening, I found it was just an examination. I passed all the Regents exams and received credit for English, but failed my first year Latin. I had missed so much time in the middle of the year I was lost. It was the only time I had a failing mark in all my years of education.

Exams over, I joined a family going back to Ohio, leaving Houghton with my trunk. I wondered if I would ever see it again. Being the last part of June, the weather was perfect and the night boat trip on Lake Erie from Buffalo to Cleveland was a delight. But inside I had the uneasy feeling of wondering what was to become of our family.

CHAPTER 5

HOME IN HOUGHTON

When I got back to the hamlet of Africa, Mother and I had a talk. I learned that Father had a small life insurance policy which paid less than $1,000.00. A year before he died he had used most of his small bank account to buy some land in northern Michigan. It was supposed to be a real estate development that would pay big dividends. However, it turned out to be a failure. Mother tried to sell it, but finally had to let it go for taxes, a total loss. In those days there was no such thing as aid to a widow with children, nor would the church do anything. It was up to us to support ourselves.

I hoped I could find work again on the Jaycox farm, but Mother had already arranged for me to work for Mr. Taylor, one of the leaders of the church. His farm was about two miles from Africa across Alum Creek toward Westerville. As the haying season was about to start, I got out my working clothes and hiked to the farm. I soon found out it was nothing like the previous summer with the Jaycox family. There were two small children, a girl and a boy. I got along with them fine, and since there were few chores to do, I often played with them after supper. Years later I learned that the boy, Charles, married my cousin, Uncle George's youngest daughter. They still live on the farm near Africa.

Mr. Taylor was a very strict religious man. He was rather dour, talked very little and expected everyone to tend strictly to work. He was supposed to be very humble, but I learned there was one thing he was very proud of. On the lower part of the farm near a grove of trees he had a large plot of paw paw bushes. These bushes bear a pear-like fruit with a delicious spicy taste. He knew they would bring a good price on the market and as the time neared for them to be ripe, he worried for fear some boys would sneak in and pick them. So for a period of ten days he spent the early part of each night and all weekends guarding them with a shot gun. He finally picked them and sold them and became more relaxed after that.

We did all the haying as a two-man job and finished the last of July. I expected to keep on working and as usual walked to the farm on Sunday night. But after breakfast on Monday morning he told me I was no longer needed. I never forgave him for he saw me at church that Sunday, and he could have told me then. I felt the worst because it was impossible for me to get another job that summer, so I could not contribute any more money to our family budget. I just couldn't understand how this man, a leader in the church who knew our financial situation and more than that was supposed to be a good friend of Mother as they had sung many duets together in the church services, would cut me off from earning a few more dollars. After that experience I became rather distrustful of some church people.

It was now August, so we had to make plans to get out of the parsonage before the end of the month. Before I got home Mother had sold the ponies. She had offers to sell one, but refused as they had been together all their lives and she would not separate them. Finally, a rural mailman bought them but he only wanted one, so he sold the other. We heard later that they both died in a year. True, they were past their prime of life, but we always felt they died of broken hearts when separated. We kept the cow and chickens until the last.

When I lost my job, Mother told me how she and Aunt Nell had done some scheming. Aunt Nell told Mother there was a shortage of rooms for boys in Houghton so she thought Mother should move to Houghton and open a rooming house for boys, thus she could keep the family together and I could stay in the Seminary. She also said the old farm house on the Waldorf farm was vacant and could be rented for a small amount. Mother saw it as a way out of our dilemma and closed the deal. I went with her to Columbus and we visited a wholesale furniture store. She bought six iron bedsteads with springs and mattresses to match and ordered them shipped to Houghton the last week of August.

We packed our household goods to ship by freight, sold the cow and chickens and were ready to leave. A kind neighbor invited us to stay for a week so we could send things ahead. Another neighbor used his team and wagon to take our goods to Lewis Center railroad station. I went with him and when we arrived with the load, the station agent was furious. He berated us for not notifying him in advance so he could have ordered an empty freight car for us to put the goods in. "Now," he said, "the trainmen will have to load all this stuff on the local freight and will they curse." Then he said every single piece will have to be tagged. So I had the job of filling out the name and address on about seventy-five shipping tags and fastening them to every piece of furniture and box. Of course, this held up the man with the team, so he wasn't happy. It was an unpleasant experience.

While we were staying with the neighbor, Mother had us going back to the parsonage to clean the whole house. I thought it a lot of useless work, but she insisted, saying she didn't want anyone to say we left a dirty place. When it was time for us to leave, the man with whom we had been staying drove us to the station. We left with a sinking feeling. We had come to Ohio with high hopes and when there seemed to be such a bright future, everything had crashed and we now faced an uncertain future.

Our depression was deepened by an incident that happened as we were driving away. Just beyond the Jaycox farm the road took a bend so beyond that point we would be out of sight of the church and parsonage. Just as we got to the bend we heard Mother give a startled cry and burst into sobs. We all turned around to see what had upset her. From every house in sight we saw a woman dressed in a dust cap and apron, carrying a broom, mop and mop pail, rushing toward the parsonage. "Oh," Mother cried, "they think I left a dirty house." I was angry, not only because she was so upset, but also to think how all of us, including the youngest child, had slaved to clean the place and all to no avail. I was sitting next to the man who was driving, and although he knew that one of the women we saw was his wife, he muttered to me, "The damned old biddies. Why couldn't they have waited until we were around the bend?" As we passed the cemetery, we paused a minute to view Father's grave, saying goodbye to him and thus closing that chapter in our lives.

Since I had been back and forth to Houghton several times, I led the way from the station in Cleveland to the docks where we boarded the night boat for Buffalo. Like many others, we did not get a state room but spent the night in the large lobby, sleeping the best we could in the chairs. It turned out to be a windy night and the lake got real rough, so some of the passengers became seasick. We all stood it pretty good but didn't want any breakfast. The docks were several blocks from the railroad station, and even though we were loaded down with suitcases, baskets, coats and packages, we walked the distance. It was early morning, so there were few people around, but those who did see us probably thought we were an immigrant family struggling along, stopping every few yards to let the small children rest.

We got the morning train out of Buffalo for Wesley, a flag stop on the Buffalo and Susquehanna railroad line. This stop was about two miles west of Houghton and frequently used, as this line gave a direct ride to Buffalo. We had wired Uncle Clark when to expect us and were thankful to see him with a team and surrey waiting for us. He told us that our goods had arrived and he had them delivered to our new house. He took us directly to the house, and we spent the rest of the day setting up the beds and unpacking, relieved to have a home again.

This house was located on the top of a high hill across Houghton Creek from the school campus. It looked down on the campus, the village and the river valley. There was a road which wound around back of the hill and approached the old farmhouse and barns from the rear, but the shortest way was a path straight down the hill. Getting back was the problem. The hill was so steep steps had to be cut in the ground. The house was an old rambling wooden structure painted a barn red. The rooms had high ceilings and were very drafty and hard to heat in cold weather. The first floor had enough rooms for our living quarters, so the half dozen bedrooms on the second floor Mother expected to rent to the young men. The beds and supplies we had purchased in Columbus arrived a few days later, and we set them up, ready for business. However, our plans never worked.

63

The last week in August Uncle Clark developed typhoid fever. Mother wondered if he had picked it up when in Ohio, but that was unlikely as so much time had elapsed since he was there. Anyway, it was a disease that was quite prevalent in those years. Mother felt under some obligation to both him and Aunt Nell, so she left us children to keep house on our own and went to be his nurse. Whenever she could get away, she would come home to check on us and help stock up on food. I was ready to enter my second year in the Seminary. Leeta was ready for the eighth grade and was allowed to join a class in the basement of the Seminary building for children of the school personnel. Ula, Dale and Faye took their lunch pails and walked to the one room school just outside the village.

In back of our house the upland had all been turned into a pasture for a dairy herd. In that pasture were several large chestnut trees. After the first frost and the nuts began to fall, all of us children rushed out after school to pick them up. Other children in the village were doing the same thing, so it was a race to see who could get there first. Then one day Mother, who happened to be home for a time, informed us that Mr. Waldorf, who owned the farm, had been there and informed her that he would give us permission to gather the nuts on 50–50 basis. We were pretty mad, as everyone else was picking them up for free. However, Mother insisted that we give him half of what we got. Even so, we picked up nearly a bushel, selling them for ten cents a pound and keeping a lot to eat later.

Unfortunately, that was the last big crop of chestnuts. A blight which was destroying the chestnut trees in Pennsylvania was creeping up into New York State and in two years' time they were wiped out. It was sad to see the destruction of one of America's best trees. Not only were they valuable for the delicious nuts, but the lumber from these trees was used for furniture, building material, fence posts and firewood. Through the years efforts have been made to restore them using the nuts from a few scattered trees which survived the blight, but the saplings only grow to a certain size and the spores of the disease kill them.

The fall of 1908 was noted for many spirited political rallies for the presidential election. The school band now in its second year gained the reputation of being good and was engaged to play for a number of these rallies in nearby villages. Not only did this give us a lot of good experience, but brought us some revenue to keep the band going. It also gave us boys a chance to break the strict atmosphere of the school.

Just before school opened that fall a family by the name of Frazier had moved into the village. The father was a Wesleyan minister and he wanted his children, two boys, William and Jess, and one girl, Bonnie Jean, to attend Houghton school. He thought it was better to move there than to pay board and room for all. Will, the oldest, was of college age, but Jess was my age and in my classes. We became buddies for many years. As in many such cases Jess had to find out who was boss and after he had persisted in pestering me one day and I had told him several times to lay off, I had to take him down and sit on him; I wouldn't let him up until he promised to stop his actions and that was the first and only time in our long years as pals that we fought. It was a good thing for me that it happened then, as he soon outgrew me in height and weight and I would never have been able to throw him again. I liked Jess' father very much because he had a very common sense approach to life quite different from that of other ministers associated with the school. In fact, members of this family were to be an important part of my life for several years.

Uncle Clark was sick all fall, just able to return to teaching after Thanksgiving. Mother was now free to be at home, but troubles were not over as Dale came down with the fever. So all thoughts of taking roomers for the second semester vanished. Dale was very sick and grew weaker and weaker. Mother was up with him nights so much I had to be home as much as possible so she could get some rest during the day time. When the time came for the fever to break, Mother had me stay with her all night. As I sat watching, I thought how strange it was that four members of our family had the disease and three did not. In Uncle Clark's family, he was the only one to have it. I also wondered if I was in any way responsible for Dale getting it. When I was cleaning out the barn in Africa before we moved, I was throwing the manure out of the barn door with a heavy four tined fork. To get the manure to the top of a high pile, my fork was extending beyond the frame of the door. Dale was playing in the yard and just as I let fly with a load, he ran in front of the door. One of the four tines struck him in the head just above the temple. When I felt the impact and saw him go down, my heart stopped for several beats. He never made a sound as I picked him up and rushed to the house. I cleaned him up, washed the wound, discovering the skin had been punctured but not too deep, and doctored him the best I could. He recovered quickly and claimed he was all right, but now I wondered if germs from that dirty fork could have caused his having the fever. Just at daybreak Dale's breathing became easier and regular, and when we felt his brow, we knew the crisis had passed and the fever gone.

When Dale became ill with the typhoid fever, it was evident we were never to get any roomers and Mother wanted to leave this big house, but she had signed a lease for a year. In the spring the well water became so dirty from surface water we had to boil it, and when the landlord refused to do anything about it, she decided to break the lease and move. The house that Uncle George had built was vacant. He had left to go back to preaching and rented it to a family who had moved away. We contacted him and secured the place for a reasonable sum. We began to move some things, waiting for Dale to become strong enough to change houses. When we thought he was able, four of us boys, carried him on a cot down the hill to our new home.

This eight room concrete square house was ideal for our family. It was easy to heat in the winter and delightfully cool in the summer. It was at the very end of the street and a small stream had cut a deep ravine near the north side of the yard. This gully was lined on both sides by a grove of tall pine trees. In the grove directly opposite the house was a small enclosed plot containing the grave of Old Copperhead, an Indian who was friendly to the early settlers of the region. The pine trees not only gave off a healthy spicy odor, but the slightest breeze would start them sighing, which was very noticeable in the night. The quality of sound from the trees depended on the strength of the wind. Before a storm when the wind became strong the sound was a wail. Then the small children would become frightened as they were sure it was Old Copperhead's ghost flying about.

The lot on which the house was built was rather large, so we were able to have a good-sized garden. Besides the usual vegetables, we had some sweet corn and several bushels of potatoes. There was a good cellar under the house to store vegetables and canned goods. Also, there was a hen house on the back of the lot so we were able to have some hens to furnish fresh eggs. One feature was unusual in that the well for our drinking water was drilled in the cellar and the pump located in the cellar way. Thus, we never had to go outside for water and there was no danger of the pump freezing in the winter.

After the doctor watched Mother nurse both Uncle Clark and Dale, he told her if she wanted to do nursing he could keep her busy. At that time there were very few qualified nurses outside a hospital, so people had to depend on what are called practical nurses today. Having had experience in the past with helping women have their babies, Mother felt qualified and told the doctor she would try it. Since the rooming house didn't work, she had to do something to support the family and nursing paid more than anything else she could do. The drawback, of course, was it meant leaving us children to live alone.

The first case that Mother took nearly proved to be her last. A farmer back in the hills was sick with pneumonia and the doctor decided that unless he had some expert care, far more than the family was giving him, he was a goner. He came to see Mother and persuaded her to take the case. When she got there she found the patient in a dark room with the windows boarded up and nailed shut. The first thing she did was to ask for the boards to be taken off and the windows fixed so she could get some fresh air in the room. Instantly she met a storm of protest. They said fresh air would kill him. But Mother, in her determined way, insisted in spite of the threat of the grown boys in the family. They said if their father died they would shoot her. It was nip and tuck for a time, but Mother stood her ground and the man did recover. When she got home after that ordeal, she fell into bed and slept for hours.

For the next three years Mother was called on case after case, so she was away more of the time than at home. We children learned to care for each other and to keep house by ourselves. Leeta did most of the cooking, but we each had our daily household chores. Our meals were simple, and we depended on Mother baking a big batch of homemade bread when she could get home. Our budget allowed for very little meat, anyway, there was no butcher shop in the village, however except in bad weather in the winter, a meat cart from Fillmore would circulate through the village giving people a chance to buy fresh meat. Sometimes we would be able to get a few pork chops, but most of the time we depended on a large soup bone which we got for 10 cents. This bone with our garden vegetables would make a stew to last a week. After a time Mother gave her consent for me to send to Montgomery Ward for a cheap single barrel 12 gauge shot gun. During the fall and winter I was able to bring in rabbits and squirrels to help with our meat problem. Then one Thanksgiving morning Dale and I went hunting in a nearby woods. As I stood on the brink of a deep gully, a partridge flew up directly in front of me. It was a perfect straight shot, and I got my first bird. I went home real proud to have it for our Thanksgiving turkey.

At the beginning of my third year Jess Frazier's family moved to Bath, New York, where his father became the Chaplain of the Soldiers and Sailors Home located there. Jess had to find a room and decided as long as we were such close friends he would room with us. Since Mother was away so much, the school did not approve of the arrangement, but he kept telling them he couldn't find another room and kept right on staying. Being together gave us a chance to break the rules whenever we felt in the mood. One thing we did the most was to hike to Fillmore and then hop a freight train for a ride back home. We did it enough times that we became efficient at catching a train going 35 to 40 miles an hour. It had just enough danger in it to give some excitement as well as a relief from the boredom of school.

One night when we got back from a trip to Fillmore we ran into a bunch of younger boys who had found some long poles and were using them to rap the high windows of the girls' dorm, creating a lot of excitement. The matron made such a fuss to the dean of men about the episode that he felt he had to find out who was involved. Some of the girls claimed that Jess and I were in the group. Since Lynn Bedford, Jess and I had been caught in several escapades, we could understand why the dean took the word of the girls rather than ours. Jess and I could have proved we were not in the group, but to do so we would have had to admit to being out of town without permission. So we decided to take the punishment for something we didn't do rather than one we did do. Later in the year several of the boys in that group got religion and confessed all, telling the authorities that Jess and I were not involved. To everyone's surprise, the president of the school publicly apologized for not taking our word.

Our punishment was a week's suspension. It was in the fall and the hunting season was open, so with nothing to do Jess and I borrowed a couple of shotguns and went hunting. It was a beautiful week, the woods were at their best with fall colors, and with an abundance of gray squirrels for game we had a swell time. The gun I used was an old ten-gauge double barrel heavy shotgun. The first time I fired it I thought it was a cannon, it sounded so loud, and kicked so hard I nearly fell over backwards. It was after this that Mother let me buy a gun of my own.

Since my home was in Houghton, my life was somewhat different from the boys who were there just for the school year. To help with the family expenses I worked whenever I could find a job. Each summer I worked on a farm at least through the haying season. The first summer was on a farm near Wesley. Both the father and son who ran the farm had heart trouble, so I did all the pitching of the hay. I felt rather proud to be considered able to do a man's job, and the family treated me fine. Another place I worked was near Short Tract high above the river valley. Early mornings we could look down and watch the fog evaporate. It was too much like being isolated on a mountain, but Mother got the job for me after she had done some nursing there, so I felt I had to accept it. At these places I received a man's wages of $30.00 a month with board and room and in every case I earned it.

One summer Mother was able to take the three younger children with her so both Leeta and I got jobs. Leeta worked for a family in Fillmore, and I went to a farm directly across the river from Houghton. There was no bridge across the river at this point, but by taking off my shoes and socks I could wade across. That summer I worked harder than at any other place. Not only did I do most of the pitching of the hay in the field, but went into the hayloft to mow it away. On the hot days I would come out of the mow with my clothes wringing wet with sweat, but I was rather proud I could do a man's work with the best of them. When the month was up, I was asked to stay a few more days to help finish the work. I was glad for the extra time, but when it came time to settle up, I had my first disagreement as to my pay. I felt the extra time should be rated on a day basis, but the man claimed it was just a continuance of the month. I had to leave with a bitter feeling of not receiving just pay for my work.

I should have been forewarned because I found these people being stingy with food. It was the only farm I ever worked on where they never had fresh milk on the table to drink. They had a large dairy, but they wanted every drop to sell. I used to drink some when milking in order to be satisfied. Another example was the lady of the house served fried salt pork rolled in flour every morning for breakfast. It was too greasy for me, so I ate very little of it. One piece of the pork she served was rancid, and I couldn't touch it, but she kept right on using it. The man was getting away with it, and it took me awhile to discover how. One morning when he saw I wasn't eating any of the pork he said, "Well, Ray, we have to eat all of this meat before my old lady will get a new cut." Then when his wife's back was turned, he swept the platter clean and fed it to the dog under the table. As he did so, he gave me a big wink, but it was plain who was boss in the kitchen.

One spring when Easter recess came in March Jess and I formed a partnership to cut firewood for a man who owned a wood lot outside the village. We borrowed a cross-cut saw and an axe and by working long hours, cut a lot of wood and made some money. The weather turned real hot for March and at the end of the week Jess proposed the last afternoon that we quit early and go down to the river for a swim. The river was the place where the boys in the neighborhood had a swimming hole. In my first year at Houghton I went with the others and learned to swim. At first I had considerable difficulty as the current would carry me downstream when I tried to swim across, and the first time I tried it I had to be pulled out. We always selected a place out of sight of the road so we all went in clad in our birthday suits. No one had a swim suit, and none were sold in the area. So when Jess said "Let's go swimming," it seemed so hot I agreed. When we got to the river we tested the water, and it was very cold, but we dared each other and plunged in. For a long time we bragged to others how we went swimming in March.

Usually my work on the farms would end in early August. I would then work in the garden, and for three summers I got a job working on the camp meeting grounds. These grounds were on a plateau just above our house. It took a small crew of men to clean up the grounds and make repairs on the buildings to have things in shape for the meetings. One summer I was able to stay on during the meetings, helping in the cook tent and waiting on tables, an experience which was a big help to me in the future.

These camp meetings were a big event in the lives of the Wesleyan ministers and church leaders of western and central New York. Some would bring their families and pitch a tent for a summer outing while attending the meetings. Some would cook their own meals, but many preferred to eat with others in a large tent fitted with long tables. People bid for the chance to do the catering, running the cook tent, and hiring their own help. That is how I was able to get the job because I knew the right person. I did so well that before the summer was over I was considered the head waiter.

A director of the assembly was appointed by the camp meeting association, and he regulated the time for all events. A large bell signaled the time for all meetings and for meals. Daytime meetings were a sort of workshop and Bible study groups. The evening sessions were evangelistic with a sermon by a loud shouting preacher followed by a high-pressure altar call. At times the prayer session around the altar would last until midnight.

Sunday was the big day with preaching services all day ending with a rousing evening session. People came from miles around to attend. They came for various reasons, some came for inspiration, and some to vent their religious feelings; they were the ones who aroused the whole grounds with their shouts of "Amen and Halleluiah." Some of these folks bordered on the actions of the Holy Rollers, consequently, some people came just to see the "show."

For those of us who worked, Sunday dinner was the highlight of the week. There were hours of preparation, and it took two or three settings to accomodate the big crowd. These two weeks broke up what otherwise was a quiet and dull Houghton summer. After the meetings were over the same crew who got the grounds ready cleaned up and closed the buildings. All was then quiet until the next season rolled around.

One summer the Association granted permission for the village to hold a Fourth of July celebration on the camp grounds. The Fillmore town band was to play for the celebration, but they were without a tuba player. A year before I had taken over the tuba in the school band after others who had played it had left. The director of the Fillmore band had heard me play and recommended me for the job that day. I was given $10.00 for playing two concerts and felt real proud, not only for being praised for my ability, but for the money. That was a busy day for me, as the son of the new minister in town, who was my age, suggested that with another boy we get permission to set up a small tent and sell lemonade at the celebration. When we received a permit, we went to the proprietor of the local grocery store to see about buying the necessary ingredients for our venture. This man was a good friend of all the boys, and he not only sold us the things we needed at cost, but gave us some valuable advice. He suggested we buy only a dozen lemons and then go to the drug store and get an ounce of citric acid and mix it in a twenty gallon crock filled with water and ice. We then added enough sugar to make it taste right and with the lemons cut up in slices floating on top, it looked delicious. When ready, we put up a big sign, "All the lemonade you can drink for 5 cents." The citric made it so tart only a few people would drink more than one glass. But it attracted a lot of attention. The man at the store suggested we take along a bunch of ripe bananas and sell them one at a time rather than by the dozen. We hesitated, but decided to try it and much to our surprise, sold the whole bunch in a short time and sent for another. Bananas were not so common in those days, and the farmers who constituted the bulk of the crowd thought they were getting a real treat.

I had it understood when we made our plans that I would be given time to play with the band. We made the schedule up so the others also were given time to rest, for we found it was real work to run such a stand. When the day was over and we had cleaned up everything and counted the money, we discovered that we had cleared over $25.00 apiece. We were delighted with the results and gained some valuable experience.

With some of the money I made that day I bought some fireworks to take home. That evening after dark the younger children got a chance to shoot off some Roman candles, fire crackers and wave sprinklers in the air. It was the first time we ever had the fun of fireworks.

When the weather was good, Dale and I would go fishing in the river, usually on Saturday afternoons during the spring and early summer. The only thing we caught were suckers, but they were large ones and before hot weather were good eating. One day when we approached our favorite hole we discovered a man seated on the bank fishing. When he looked up, I recognized the father of Miss Greenberg, my Latin teacher. A year or more before he had come to live with her after his wife had died. When we first saw him he had the typical Scandinavian blond hair, but now in his seventies it was turning dark and became jet black. We were a little in awe of him, but when he saw us hesitating about disturbing him, he said, "Come on, boys, maybe you can catch some. I can't." We saw that he had a fine rod and reel, while I had an old bamboo pole and Dale a branch which I had cut from a willow tree. Our lines were tied on the end of our poles, and I had put an old bottle cork on Dale's line for a bobber. This hole was in a bend of the river where it had cut under the roots of an old tree and formed a large deep pool. So when Mr. Greenberg invited us to stay, we moved near the head of the pool so not to interfere with his line. We baited up and cast in. In a few minutes Dale had a bite, he pulled up and threw a big sucker high on the bank. Before anyone else could get a bite, Dale had four more fish. I finally got two and in less than an hour we left for home. Mr. Greenberg kept chuckling as he watched Dale pulling out the fish and as we said goodbye, he remarked how the smallest one with the cheapest pole had the best luck.

Houghton had no athletic program, but the boys in school organized some intramural games. I learned to play baseball in that way. In the summer Houghton village had a town team which played similar teams from nearby villages. Since I lived in the village, I was invited to play with the team. I usually played in right field, but could play wherever needed. One afternoon we were playing a team from Fillmore at a big old home week picnic. I was playing second base and Ray Hazlett was pitching. In the fifth inning with no score two men got on base. I was playing close to second to hold the runner on when the batter hit a line drive high above my head. I leaped high and the ball stuck in the webbing of my glove. In two steps I touched second base, which made two outs, and then whirled and threw to first, catching that runner off base, thus completing a triple play. The large crowd gave us a great hand. That play gave us the inspiration to win the game.

Houghton had no gymnasium, but a year before I entered, a group of students who were interested in playing basketball had gone to the old Seminary building which still stood on a hill about a mile from the campus and had cleaned out the auditorium, which was on the second floor, and put up baskets at both ends. There was no heat and in the very cold weather it was hard to hang onto the ball, but it was a place to play. We had a small portable kerosene stove which we put in the old office, a small room which gave us a place to dress. I took to the game readily and before I left the school was rated as one of the top players.

Another winter sport we enjoyed was skating. About a mile north of the village there was a long cove which froze over early in the season. This cove was originally an oxbow bend in the Genesee River but was cut off by the railroad when it was built years before. The main road followed the railroad, so the ends of the cove were right against the embankment of the road about 100 yards apart. So when the ice formed and before snow came, we could skate over a mile in one direction and be back almost at the starting point. When the ice was safe, boys and girls from the school would have the opportunity to enjoy some skating parties. If the girls could get permission to be out of the dormitory in the evening, we would build a big bonfire and skate together, a time for a little romancing.

There were sections of the cove that were quite shallow, and this would freeze over first. We would skate on this even when the middle was open water or at times be so thin it would give when we dared skate across it. We called this "rubber ice," and we took chances in skating over it. One time one of the heavier boys attempted it and the ice gave way, plunging him into the icy water. Every time he grabbed the edge of the ice trying to pull himself out, it gave way. We all called to him to hold still. It happened that I was the nearest to him, so I laid down flat on my stomach and began sliding out toward him. I called for someone to grab my skates and then another to form a human chain. Slowly I inched out toward him, but by the time I could grasp his hand, I was halfway in the water. I got a circus grip on his wrist and called for the others to pull us out. Once on the thick ice he slid out and was safe. He was soaked through and I was half-soaked, so we had to walk home as fast as we could. I discovered that as soon as my wet clothes froze, they protected me from the cold wind and I was comfortable.

That wasn't the only time I got wet in the winter. One night during Christmas vacation when most of the students had gone to their homes, I was reading late. I heard someone shouting. I opened the door and several voices could be heard yelling, "Fire! Fire!" Quickly putting on my winter clothing, I hurried out to follow a group of men running toward the school heating plant. This was a building containing the steam boiler to heat both the school building and the girls' dorm. It was built into the side of a high bank above Houghton Creek and from the campus appeared as a basement building. Only the roof and two small windows below the eaves showed above ground. By the time I got there smoke was pouring out of the building. The windows were broken and water was being thrown on the fire. In a short time no more fire could be seen but to be sure, President Luckey produced a lighted lantern and when the smoke had cleared, decided to enter the building to investigate. Another boy and I volunteered to go with him. We found some charred empty packing crates near the boiler, but no fire. Just then someone saw the light of the lantern that President Luckey was holding and yelled, "There's the fire," and dumped several buckets of water on our heads. Before we could stop them, we were drenched. When we were sure the fire was all out and no damage done, I started for home. It was ten degrees below zero and even though I ran, my clothes froze solid. Again, I didn't feel the cold; the ice was a perfect wind breaker.

The road that ran down the hill in front of the girls' dorm was steep enough to make excellent coasting when covered with packed snow. One winter Jess, Lynn and I decided to make a bobsled to increase the fun of coasting on this hill. We bought a two inch, twelve foot long oak plank and treated it with hot wax to prevent warping. We made two sleds, one of which was fastened rigidly to one end of the plank, and the other fitted with a large bolt running through two washers becoming the steering device for the front end. For runners we found a discarded hay rake, took off four of the steel tines, and took them to a blacksmith shop. We had these tines straightened and then fitted to the grooves we had cut in the bottom of each runner. These round steel shoes made our bobsled the fastest thing around. After a time some of the steel runners would come loose, but we learned how to use the fire in the heating plant boiler to heat them and refit them on the runners. We used the same principle that we knew was used to fit an iron tire on a wagon wheel. We put the steel runner on red hot and when in place, poured cold water on it. The metal would shrink and grip the wood real tight.

We found that the best way to increase our speed down the hill was to have our bob sled follow the same track each time. Thus, two ruts were cut and the sled would follow them like a train on a track. We purposely made our track on one side of the road so not to interfere with any regular traffic using the road. All others who were coasting understood our plan, so when we loaded the bob with six to eight passengers and then yelled, "track, track," they would give way and give us a clear run. We took turns steering and another would act as brakeman, only we didn't have any brakes. He would be the one to start the sled with a push, then hop on the back. He would also call to the passengers to lean right or left to gain speed around a curve. Spills did occur, but it was considered a black mark on the record of whoever was steering. There developed a lot of rivalry as to who had the best record.

One Saturday we were coasting and just after starting down the hill we saw President Luckey walking up the hill with a box in his arms. He was on the side of the road right in our track. We yelled, "track, track," but he didn't understand and stood still thinking we would pull into the middle of the road. In order to keep from hitting him, the steerer tried to turn but spilled the load, but not before President Luckey jumped and went over the side of the bank. We hurried to rescue him and found he had dropped the box he was carrying. The box rolled clear to the bottom of the hill, stopping just short of the water in the creek. When we got it, we learned to our dismay it contained the January Regents examination question papers. President Luckey wasn't very happy about the incident and while we tried to explain, he wasn't impressed and told us if we couldn't be more careful, we would have to stop using the hill.

Another time, when the coasting was at its best, we persuaded the matron of the dorm to let the girls, who wished to, come out on a

Saturday night and enjoy the fun. We had taken several trips down and were at the height of a good time when it came to an abrupt end. At the bottom of the hill was the bridge over Houghton Creek, so our track had to bend into the road to cross this bridge. One of the dangers of coasting at night was the possibility of a team of horses coming up the road, and if we met them head on, it would be disastrous. The understanding of all coasters was that if a team should start up the hill, those at the foot would yell, "team, team," and no one would start down until all was clear. That night when I was steering a load of girls down and had reached the half way point, a group of young boys coming up the hill began to yell, "team, team." It was dark, but I could see a black mass against the snow on the bridge which looked like a team. I could take no chances and spun the bobsled out of the track, spilling the passengers in all directions. All the girls were screaming and laughing, except one who couldn't get up. We put her on the sled and drew her up the hill. We carried her into the dorm. A first aid inspection indicated that she had either a badly sprained ankle or it was broken. The doctor from Fillmore came the next morning and diagnosed it as a fracture, putting on a cast, so she had to be on crutches for some time. We all felt very sorry for the girl and also for the rest of the girls, because the matron refused to let them out again.

The fall of 1910, Lynn's father asked me to help on his dairy farm while he was away with a threshing machine. Lynn was then the only boy at home and needed help. I moved down to the farm and we got up early each morning to milk a large herd and then after school hurried back to do chores and the night milking. This was the time of Halley's comet. It was a thrill to get out in the early morning hours before daybreak on those frosty October days and look up into the clear sky to see one of the most spectacular sights to ever appear in the heavens. To see the long tail of the comet stretch across the whole sky was breathtaking. Right then the comet was at its best. I was taking physics in school at the time, so we all were interested in the story of comets. Later that winter when the head of the comet had passed around the sun, it was expected to be visible in the evening. On the day it was expected to be first visible, four of us boys gathered in the upper floor of the school building to see if we could spot it at sunset. Looking hard, we thought we saw it as a faint image. Just then President Luckey, who was also our physics teacher, came along and asked what we saw. We announced we had seen Halley's comet, although according to the papers it wasn't due for a couple of days. He looked and said, "Maybe you have discovered a new comet." We laughed, but he continued, "There is no reason why any of you might not be the one to make such an important discovery." It was a statement that none of us ever forgot.

The fall of 1910, when I began my senior year of high school work, Mother decided that she had left us children alone too much. The doctors kept her busy going from case to case, so she would be home less and less. She decided to break up our home and put the furniture in storage. She arranged a place on a farm near Short Track for Dale to stay and go to school. She took Ula and Faye to be with her and Leeta went to the girls' dorm for a semester. Leeta was in high school and also taking piano lessons with Miss Hilpot, a music teacher at Houghton for many years. Jess and I got two connecting basement rooms in the Coleman house, which had been recently built on the street back of our house. This house was built on the side of a hill, so we had an entrance to these rooms independent of the rest of the house. Jess and I moved in at the beginning of school, then Jess was alone while I was at the Bedford farm. I returned in November for the rest of the year. Mr. Coleman was a minister who came to Houghton so his two daughters could be in school in Houghton, but in the spring he got a church and the family moved out, leaving the house for sale. He told us we could stay in the rooms free of rent and look after the place until he could sell it. The school didn't approve of our staying there and being so independent, but they couldn't find any other place for us, so we stayed. We had one problem. In the spring the roof of the house leaked so bad the water dripped down on us. We had to use pots and pails to catch the water and to move our beds in order to stay dry. This breaking up of our home was an important step in all our lives; we were never to be all together again as a family. Thus, a senior in high school, I began to live more and more an independent life.

Near the end of that year as commencement time approached, there occurred an incident that I have always regretted. Mr. Thompson, from Northville, South Dakota, had moved his family to Houghton so all of his children could be in the Seminary. Both Theus and Gail had been there for some time, but he brought his daughter, Lois, who joined my class. Jess, Lynn and I had been members of this class for the longest time, so we thought we should have the most to say about its activities. But Lois Thompson was the type who wanted to run things and since her father was influential around the school, the girls in the class followed her lead. As was the custom, the class was to go to Fillmore to have a group picure taken a few weeks before commencement. A class meeting was called to decide when to go. Lois wanted it done right away and proposed the date. Both Jess and I had ordered new suits for graduation, and they were not due for a week. We asked the class to wait the week. Actually, although I didn't want to say it, I hadn't bought a suit of clothes for a long time, and I didn't have anything good enough to wear for a picture. The class was divided, all the boys supported us but the girls voted with Lois. The result was that both Jess and I were so hurt by the action of the class neither of us showed up for the picture. So the picture of the largest class in the history of the academic department of the school up to that time was short two members.

Graduation was a very formal affair. The school had a rule that each candidate had to write and give an oration at commencement before receiving a diploma. Since our class was so large we thought so many orations would become boring. We requested that members of the class who had the ability be allowed to substitute a musical number for an oration. After much deliberation, the faculty agreed to let Lynn Bedford give a violin selection and one of the girls who had been studying piano play a solo. This change was the first in the history of the school.

For their orations most of the graduates selected topics dealing with the church or religion. I wanted to be different and in searching for a topic, I recalled how impressed I had been in reading about Clive and his work in India. So I selected *Clive of India* as the title of my oration. I felt quite proud when a number of people, including some teachers, congratulated me on my topic and delivery. Leeta had left the dorm and none of my family was able to be at my graduation. But the Frazier family came from out of town to attend and after the program was over, Jess' father took us outside and took our picture. He also gave me a four volume set of Shakespeare's plays for a graduation present, which I still treasure. I heaved a sigh of relief when it was all over, and I held my high school diploma in my hand. I was now, in June, 1911, eighteen years old and faced with the problem of what to do next.

Ray and Jess Frazier
At Graduation from Academic Department,
Houghton Seminary in 1911

CHAPTER 6

FIRST YEAR COLLEGE

At our graduation from high school, Jess Frazier, Lynn Bedford and I talked about returning to Houghton for the beginning of our college education. There were several reasons for our considering this. First, we had become close friends during our years in school, and we would like to stay together longer. Second, Houghton was the most economical place we could choose and the subjects we had taken in high school were a typical college entrance course and nothing else. Third, while Houghton was not then a chartered college and therefore, could not grant a degree, the type of work offered and standard maintained made it possible to take up to three years at Houghton and then transfer to some colleges with full credit. This came about when President Luckey made arrangements for a test trial of four advanced students to go from Houghton to Oberlin College to see if they could do an acceptable grade of college work. The four selected were Leland Boardman, Bill Frazier, Ralph Rindfuz, and Clark Bedford. They entered Oberlin in the fall of 1909. Uncle Clark moved his family to Oberlin and the others lived with them. The high grade of work that these men did so impressed the faculty at Oberlin that it opened the doors for all future students at Houghton. So when we were ready to choose a college in 1911, we knew that if we did good work at the college level in Houghton we could transfer to Oberlin to earn a degree. It was interesting to note that three of the first students who went to Oberlin on the trial basis returned to Houghton to teach after receiving their degrees.

For me it was a tough decision to make to stay in school. I liked my high school work and wanted to go on to college, but had no financial backing. For a year now our home had been broken up, and I felt Mother had more than enough to do to provide for the younger children and I should help, not be a burden. I talked with her, and it was sort of agreed that she could get along and take care of the other children, but if I decided to go to college, I would have to do it entirely on my own.

I learned that a middle-aged couple with no children had taken over the old Waldorf farm. This farmhouse was right in the village with all the tillable land on the river flats across the railroad tracks. It was a dairy farm and the herd followed the bed of Houghton Creek to reach the pasture land in the hills back of the campus. I learned the people's name was Sherwood, and the next day after graduation, I went to see them. I liked them at once, and it seemed to be mutual. When they learned my experience on farms and especially that I could milk, they hired me for the haying season at the usual rate of $30.00 per month with board and room. So I packed my things and moved right in, not knowing it was to be my home for over a year.

Jess' father had been appointed the Chaplain of the State of New York Soldiers and Sailors Home in Bath, New York. When Jess got home that summer, he got a job as attendant in the hospital of the Home. We kept in contact and as the haying season neared the end, I hinted that I would like to do something other than work on a farm. About the first of August a messenger came from the local grocery store to tell me I had a long distance telephone call. When I called the operator she connected me with Mr. Frazier. He told me that there was an opening for an attendant in the hospital and if I wanted it, he could get the job for me. He said I would have to be there by Monday and he would have to know right then. I was on the spot, as there was no chance for me to talk with the Sherwoods, but I felt it was my chance to get off the farm so I told him I would come. I returned with a sinking heart to tell the people who had been so good to me about my decision. But when I explained how I didn't know whether they wanted me longer now that the haying was done and it was a chance for me to find out about hospital work, they took it fine and then to my joy, they said if I wanted to come back for school in September, I could live with them helping with the milking and chores for my board and room. That was the break I needed to make it possible to enter my freshman year at college.

When I arrived at Bath, Mr. Frazier took me up to the hospital and introduced me to the head nurse. He had me fill out an application and put me right to work. After being outside all summer, it seemed rather strange to be inside during all the hot weather. But I looked upon it as a chance to observe something about the medical field, a career that I was considering. After a week of training by being with other attendants, I was assigned as a regular in one of the front wards of the hospital. This was considered as one of the choice jobs and some of the others who had been there for a long time resented me getting it. I didn't ask for the job and never knew why I was selected, except possibly I showed a knack for the work that others didn't have. As the attendant of a ward, I had the usual hospital tasks, such as making the beds hospital style, giving of medicines on time, keeping the room neat and clean, supervising baths, including helping a handicapped man in and out of the tub by sliding him up, not lifting, and assisting the nurse when needed. All the patients and all the staff were males, so it seemed a bit strange to work with men nurses.

The patients in my ward were all ambulatory and many could go outside and enjoy the grounds. While they were gone, it was a trick for others who had trouble holding their water to take a nap in the absentees' beds. One time a man of German descent came to complain that someone had wet his bed. I inspected and found his bed slightly damp and told him I thought it all right. "Vat," he replied, "you think I can swim?" I had to laugh and got him a dry sheet.

Besides taking care of our regular wards all the attendants had to take turns doing relief duty in various wards. One place I didn't like was the ward for mental patients. One day I was left alone in that ward with about thirty such patients with strict orders that no one was to leave the room. I kept close watch on the door, but when my attention was distracted, three of the big husky men started for the door. I got there first and told them they were not to leave. They argued, saying they were permitted to go outside. I had no previous experience with such patients, but I looked them straight in the eye and very quietly said my orders were that no one leave before the nurse in charge returned. Much to my relief, they agreed and went back to their bunks. Later I found out that I had instinctively used the right method by talking quietly to these men.

I not only was learning something about the medical care of people but also could observe psychological behavior, things which were helpful when I studied the subject later. For example, I could observe one case of split personality. This veteran would be on the Union side one day and tell about the battles he had helped win, then the next day he would be a Confederate soldier and tell how he made the Yankees run.

One thing I missed was the good food I was used to on the farm. We had our meals in the hospital when on duty, but it was institutional food, so much of it was tasteless. Separated as we were when on duty, I did not get to know the other attendants very well. I only saw Jess once in a while when our lunch time coincided. There was a little time for recreation and I had a chance to practice with the baseball team that the employees of the home maintained. Jess, who had been there all summer, made the team, but I was only a substitute. I had one Sunday off so I could go with the Frazier family on an excursion train to Binghamton, New York, to attend the encampment of the Civil War veterans. Mr. Frazier was the chaplain for that organization.

Back of the buildings of the home was a large cemetery where hundreds of soldiers were buried. One day when Jess and I were both free at the same time, we took a walk between the many rows of small uniform head stones containing the name and identification of the person buried. Suddenly Jess exclaimed, "See, I was in the Civil War." He had found a stone inscribed with the name of Frazier. While he stood looking at it, I moved a few feet and got even by saying, "So was I." I found a similar stone with the name Calhoon. One of the strange coincidences that one sometimes meets in life.

I was always glad for the experience I got working in the hospital but was relieved when the summer came to an end and Jess and I left for the trip back to Houghton. My room at the Sherwood farm looked good, and I was more than ready to milk my ten cows morning and night seven days a week and help with the other chores to pay for my board and room. Jess got a room on the hill and boarded at the girls' dorm. Lynn lived at home, but we were together starting our college life.

Like the high school classes where we had little choice, so it was with the college courses. The first year was practically prescribed. Trigonometry was the math for the first semester, and President Luckey was the teacher. We knew that math was President Luckey's field, so we looked forward to being in his class. He was a master teacher but started us out in an unusual way. He explained the work for the first day and assigned some problems for homework. At the beginning of the next session, he asked if we had any questions about the problems. We expected him to proceed as former math teachers had done, i.e., go through the problems. But when we didn't say anything, he simply remarked, "No questions?" and proceeded to explain the next day's work. By the third day of this method, we were really lost and finally had to admit we couldn't do the problems. I am sure he knew it all the time but was waiting for us to admit we were lost. Then he proceeded with a method I had never seen before nor since. He placed a problem on the board and looking at it, began to think out loud. He would say, "If I make this move so and so will happen." I am sure he purposely made some wrong moves to show what would happen. But it was a revelation to us on how to attack a problem, to think logically and to persevere until we found the solution. Using his method, we soon were making rapid progress. One day after he had solved a particularly difficult equation on the board, he stood back and gazing at it for several seconds, softly said, "Isn't that beautiful! No painting by Michelangelo could be more beautiful." It was something none of us in the class could forget. He truly was a master teacher and years later when I taught high school math I adopted some of his methods.

Another course that Houghton required in the first year of college was Freshmen Bible. Will Frazier, who had returned from Oberlin, was the teacher. He had us purchase a copy of *The Modern Readers Bible* by Moulton. It was something new to us, as it had everything arranged according to literary style. Poems such as the Psalms were put into poetic form, essays into that form, and likewise for other forms of writing. Using this Bible as a text, we were introduced to a much broader outlook on religion than the narrow concept we had been exposed to in our high school days.

No one could live in Houghton all the years I did and not be influenced one way or another by the religion they taught. I had been raised in the religious atmosphere of a Wesleyan Methodist minister's family; we had a family worship service after breakfast every morning, attended all the church services and at age twelve I had become a member of the church never thinking much about it, just assuming I was a Christian. But to my surprise, I learned that in the eyes of the strict church people of Houghton, I was not considered one unless I could testify that I had gone through an experience of confessing my sins and receiving the assurance that I had been forgiven. Then to publicly announcing that Jesus was my personal savior. This was called conversion or justification. Then to live the Christian life, one had to refrain from all forms of sin, such as lying, stealing, cheating, smoking, drinking, and premartial sex. The keeping of the Ten Commandments was not enough, for each Sunday the preacher would dwell on the sin of pride, admonishing women and girls against wearing any jewelry or decorating their hats with flowers or feathers. Some even preached against the boys wearing ties.

Then the church advocated a second step called sanctification. This was another personal experience when a person entered the state of holiness. This state of grace kept a person perfect so they never sinned. There were a number of people in the church and some students who claimed they were sanctified. We boys couldn't see any difference in their lives, but they were loud in their belief. They were the ones who shouted "Amens" during the sermon and a very few would run up and down the aisle shouting, "Halleluiah!" Coming from a home where religion was considered a personal, calm approach to life, such actions proved very puzzling to me.

After a time I did try to follow their concept of a Christian but became "turned off" when I was pressured into taking part in the prayer meetings, praying out loud and carrying on as some did. Then when Dean Bedford, Uncle Clark's brother, became the pastor of the Houghton church, I did become somewhat active. Dean had a more common sense approach to religion than the other ministers we had known, so all of us boys liked him. One time he talked to Jess, Lynn and me about our lives and he finished by saying, "You boys have the ability to do anything in life you want to do." It made a strong impression on all of us. One Sunday he asked me to lead the young people's service. After the service a number of the young people complimented me and Dean was loud in his praise. I felt good about it and probably would have continued, except Dean Bedford was soon replaced by a man who preached holiness and I did not feel comfortable, so I dropped out.

Uncle Clark was now the full time pastor of the Wesleyan Church in Fillmore, so he sold his house in Houghton and moved to the parsonage in Fillmore. He drove back and forth to continue his teaching. Consequently, I didn't see much of him or the family that year. I came more under the influence of President Luckey, Will Frazier and Leroy Fancher, my French teacher. Also, I had many contacts with people outside the church who I found to be good honest folks. In fact, the Sherwoods, where I lived all that year, never went to church, but nicer people I never knew. So in trying to find myself, I practically forgot religion and concentrated on doing good college work. One thing for which I have always been grateful was the high regard for good scholarship which Houghton taught me.

After we broke up our home in Houghton my family was so scattered that I had difficulty keeping in touch with them. While I felt more free and did not have the responsibility of heading a home, I did miss the others. So when during this year I heard from Mother telling how a doctor in Belfast, a village seven miles up the valley from Houghton, persuaded her to set up a small hospital in the village, I was delighted. This doctor had seen her work and convinced her that she could operate such a place for their mutual advantage. It would give him a place where he could take his patients to have their babies and minor operations, while for Mother a chance to do her nursing at home, and most important, have a home for the younger children. With the help of the doctor she bought some equipment for an operating room, got our furniture out of storage, rented a good-sized house on a side street, put up a sign, "Rest Home" and was in business. Ula, Dale and Faye were now in the same school, while Leeta worked outside when Mother didn't need her. It gave me a place I could call home, although I wasn't there but briefly between jobs. For several years this venture worked out fine.

Lena Calhoon and Children at Belfast in 1912.
Front, left to right: Ray, Ula, and Lena.
Back: Leeta, Dale, and Faye.

As the year progressed we boys began to feel more like college students, and we resented the many restrictions the school put on us. Late that spring we heard that the London Symphony Orchestra was playing a concert on a Saturday night in the Buffalo city auditorium. A group consisting of Lynn, Jess, Tubby Lawrence, a boy named Edgar and I talked it over about going to hear the concert. We were all members of the band but none of us had ever seen a big orchestra perform. We decided it would be useless to ask for permission, so that Saturday we hiked to Wesley and took the B&S train to Buffalo. We got rooms at the YMCA and tickets for the evening concert, using the rest of the time sightseeing. To us the concert was a thrill. I didn't understand all the music, but watching the musicians perform was an eye opener. We all felt we had enhanced our education.

The next day we did some more sightseeing, then went to the station to take the afternoon train back home. Then to our dismay we discovered that only two of us had saved enough money for a return ticket. We decided to pool our money and buy tickets for all to Hamburg, a town outside Buffalo, so we all got on the train. When we reached Hamburg we stayed on, hoping to make a deal with the conductor so we could get to Wesley, but it didn't work. When he found us on the train, he was real mad, refused to talk, and put us off at the next stop, a little village. We all had experience in riding freight trains between Houghton and Fillmore, so we figured that is how we would get home. We talked with the station agent, and he told us there would be a fast freight going through around midnight, so after he closed the station we sat around waiting. Sure enough, right on time a long freight train came rambling through. It never slowed up, traveling at a speed much faster than we were used to, so it presented a real problem to get on. Jess led the way and made it, Lynn followed and also got on. Then Tubby tried, but he was too slow, stumbled, and fell into the ditch along the track. I was next, but when I saw Tubby fall, I didn't try to hop on but ran to see if he was hurt. Edgar, who was last, also gave up and followed me. By the time we recovered Tubby, the train was gone. Some miles out of town we heard the train stop, and we took after it, but it started again before we could catch it.

Jess and Lynn stayed on the freight and got home that night. I never quite forgave them for leaving us stranded. The three of us kept on hiking to the next town. When the stores opened in the morning I used some of the little money I had left to buy something for us to eat. Then when the station agent came to open up, we told him of our plight. He was understanding and told us a local freight was due the middle of the morning and for us to get on the other side of the tracks so we could hop on when it pulled out. This we did, riding all the way to Wesley. That being a flag stop, we had to hop off while the train was going full speed. Again, Tubby had trouble and landed in the ditch but was only scratched and dirty. The three of hiked down the road to Houghton tired and hungry but glad to be safe.

When I left I told the Sherwoods what we planned to do, but when I didn't return as expected they did worry some. They said the school did ask about me, but they said they told them nothing. After getting the soot and grime washed off and some welcome food, I made it to my last class so I wasn't reported absent all day. When I got to the school building Jess and Lynn greeted me and wanted to know what had happened. They said when they found out we were not on the train which they caught they debated what to do, but decided I would take care of the others and kept on going. I wasn't too gracious with their explanation, as after all I was the one who had the money to get back home and had given it up to help the others. I felt they should have seen that none of us were hurt and not leave us stranded. From that time on Jess and I were never quite the close friends we had been all through high school.

The second episode came near the end of the school year. One warm night a bunch of us were out after study hours and feeling our oats we wanted to do something daring. Several times during the year someone had suggested creating a commotion by ringing the chapel bell in the middle of the night. So that night when someone suggested it again, we all said, "Let's do it." It was about midnight when we raised a window in the school building, went up to the top floor and found the ladder which led to the belfry. We pushed up a trap door and when all were up, closed that door thinking that by standing on it we could keep anyone from coming up. We grabbed the big wheel of the bell and began to ring it furiously. In a short time we had the whole campus and village aroused. A crowd assembled and we could hear them asking, "Where's the fire?" After all were assembled, we stopped ringing the bell and began to think how foolish we were to leave no way for an escape. It was dark but those on the ground could see someone was in the belfry. They tried to push open the trap door, but we wouldn't let them. Not until the Dean of Men, with some help, brought up a crow bar and smashed the door did they get up. We were caught and he took our names and told us to report to his office the next morning. We had to pay for a new door and received a stern lecture, indicating they didn't know what to do to us as nothing like that had ever been done before. After it was over we felt rather foolish and stupid to get ourselves in such a position. But we got it out of our systems and settled down for the rest of the year. However, we were tagged with the name "Bell Ringers" for a long time.

At the end of my first year of college, I was very undecided as to what I should do. Jess planned to return for his second year and then transfer to Oberlin for his degree. Lynn thought he would try for an engineering degree and planned to enter Clarkson College in Potsdam, New York. While deciding what I could do, the Sherwoods gave me a full-time job on the farm, indicating I could stay as long as I wished at $30.00 a month, including board and room.

CHAPTER 7

A YEAR AT WORK

During the summer of 1912 while working on the farm, I decided to drop out of college for a year and work. I didn't feel right in asking Mother for any more funds to pay for my tuition since she was undertaking the establishment of the hospital in Belfast. I knew from experience that I couldn't earn enough during the summer to take me through the year, and I was just plain tired of trying to get along with little or no money. Late in the summer I told the Sherwoods my decision and while there was no agreement made, I just kept on working on the farm.

Soon after school had started in September, Sylvester Bedford, Lynn's father, came to see me one evening. He said he heard that I was not returning to college and wanted to know if I was interested in helping him run his threshing machine that fall. Lynn was going to Clarkson College and his other son had left home, so he needed help. He had sold his dairy farm and moved into the village, but he had kept his machine and had calls for a lot of work. I said I was interested but should talk with the Sherwoods before I decided. I did and they offered me $30.00 a month for the year if I wanted to stay. So I told Mr. Bedford what they said, and since they had been so good to me, I thought I should stay. He left but was back in a hour saying he really needed me and would pay me more. I was torn between wanting to do something other than working all year on the farm or staying so as not to hurt the feelings of the Sherwoods. I talked to Mr. Sherwood and he understood why I wanted to go, but Mrs. Sherwood was real mad at Mr. Bedford for enticing me away.

The threshing outfit consisted of a small steam engine, an old threshing machine which was hand fed, a water wagon, and a team of horses. My job was to take care of the horses and keep the water wagon at least half full at all times. I was expected to do this while we were not threshing, for then I was expected to fire the steam engine. I enjoyed running the engine and keeping all the machines in top shape by oiling them everyday. I liked being out of doors during the nice fall weather and as we moved from farm to farm, we had excellent meals. Usually one day was enough at each farm, so we did a lot of moving, staying overnight at the farm where we were to thresh the next day. Saturday nights we would get back to the Bedford house for a Sunday rest, a bath and clean clothes.

Keeping the water wagon full became a problem at times. Most of the farmers refused to let us use their water wells for fear we would pump them dry, so I had to find a stream where I could get water, sometimes traveling two or three miles. Once when we were threshing on the farms on the river flats, I got stuck getting water from the Genesee River. I had to ask for a second team to help pull the wagon out of the soft mud.

Each farmer was expected to furnish enough coal to finish the job and get us to the next place. A few times they didn't have enough, so to keep the engine running I had to break up boards or split logs, anything for fuel. Just before we finished the threshing season, Lynn came home from Clarkson. Why, I never knew for sure, but he said something about being sick and getting so far behind in his work that he decided to drop out for the year. Even with Lynn being home, Mr. Bedford kept me on.

Mr. Bedford also had a corn shredder so as soon as all the grain was threshed we began to fill silos. This called for a lot more power from the steam engine so it was a full-time job for Lynn to do the firing while I continued my other jobs. Just before Thanksgiving we finished the last job and we pulled all the machinery back to Houghton for storage. I was now out of a job and on Mother's invitation, I packed my bags and left for Belfast.

When I arrived she introduced me to one of her patients. He was a man who was convalescing from an appendix operation. Of course, Mother had told him about me and when I met him, I found out he and his brother ran a portable saw mill. They had the mill set up in a large woods about ten miles north of Belfast in the hills east of Fillmore. When he learned of my experience with the steam engine, he offered me a job as fireman in his mill. He told me that they already had a first-class man for the job but every week or so he would disappear and return several days later after being on a "toot;" they were just waiting to find someone with experience so they could fire him. I liked the man and needed a job, so the following Monday we left for the mill.

The mill was a shed-like temporary structure containing a large circular saw and the train-like holder for the logs. The mill was built on a side hill so the logs which were being cut by loggers in the woods were stockpiled above the mill, making it easy to roll them down ready for the saw. Below the floor containing the saw, but open to view, were two steam boilers. The large one had been installed first, but it proved to be inadequate to furnish enough steam, so a small one was added. A large steam pipe connected the boilers to the engine which was placed under the floor directly below the saw. A belt ran from the big flywheel of the engine up to a pulley connected to the saw, thus furnishing it with the necessary power.

After my experience with the steam engine for the threshing

machine, it didn't take long for me to feel at home firing the two boilers and running the engine. The big difference was using the slabs off the logs as fuel. A mill hand using a small saw cut these slabs into three foot lengths and threw them down to me. Also, some of the sawdust came down a chute, and I was expected to use it along with the slabs for fuel. With this kind of fuel it was a constant job to keep a full head of steam.

I knew from the talk around the camp that there existed a strong rivalry between the head sawyer and the fireman. Anytime the head sawyer could increase the load on the engine and thus draw the steam down below the operating level, he would gloat and never let the fireman forget it. On the other hand, a good fireman would be determined to never let it happen. Only once did the sawyer win.

One day a bad ice storm hit the area and every log was covered with a thick coat of ice. When I tried to use the slabs I had more steam in the firebox than in the boilers. Down and down went the pressure until the head sawyer called for a shut down. The boss came down to see if he could help me. He said he had never tried it, but he had watched the old firemen use a trick when confronted with wet slabs. Instead of throwing the slabs in lengthwise as usual, he laid a row a few inches apart and then a second row at a ninety degree angle. He kept on with these alternate rows until the fire box was full of this lattice work. In a short time we had a hot fire and the steam went up to the proper pressure. With that trick and some I learned myself, I never let the steam fall, no matter how wet or poor the fuel they furnished me. Before the winter was over I felt real proud when one day the head sawyer announced before the whole crew that I had turned out to be one of the best fireman they ever had.

When I went to work all the crew was housed in a big farm house about a mile from the mill. A night watchman was hired to not only protect the place but to keep the fires going in the boilers so all was ready to run when I got there at 7 a.m. He was told to have the water at the right level in the boilers, but he proved to be unreliable and many times he would have the water level so high that I had to blow it down before starting the engine. With the water too high some would be drawn into the cylinder of the engine, causing it to knock with the danger of blowing a gasket. After this happened over and over, the boss came down one morning to check for himself after he had bawled the watchman out for not doing his duty. He glanced at the glass water gauge and not seeing any water level, he assumed that the boiler was once again too full and opened the blow-off valve. I was busy building up the fires and he kept blowing off more and more since he still didn't see any water level. Finally he tried the pet cocks and to his consternation, he found the water below the danger point. This time the watchman, instead of putting too much water in the boiler, hadn't put any in. When the boss realized the situation, he yelled to me to pull the fires, but it was too late. Some of the flues had melted. The mill had to be shut down for three days while repairs were made. I was thankful it was the boss, not me, who had made the blunder.

Soon after this episode a bunk house was completed near the mill. It was a long low building made from rough boards covered with tar paper. The first floor consisted of a kitchen at one end, a dining room furnished with long pine tables in the middle and a small lobby at the other end. The lobby was heated by a large wood burning stove and was the focal point for the crew on the cold winter evenings. A ladder extended up from the lobby to an attic which became the sleeping quarters for the men. There were no beds, only some straw ticks on the floor where we could spread our blankets. The place was cold and drafty and many times we woke up to see our blankets covered with the drifting snow.

Counting the loggers, who were cutting and dragging the logs to the mill, with the saw mill crew made a group of 15 to 20 men. They were rather a rough bunch but usually good natured and good hearted. There was no such thing as a radio nor daily newspaper, so our only contact with the outside world was when one of the bosses went to town for supplies. Evenings were spent with some card games and a lot of story telling, but the days were long and the work hard so everyone was ready for early bed. Working out of doors, with the smell of the fresh cut lumber, gave everyone a ravenous appetite. The cook was a woman of German descent who, with the help of her grown daughter, put on wonderful meals for the crew.

After we moved to the bunk house, the night watchman was dismissed. In order to get the fires going and steam up, I had to get up at least a half hour earlier than the others. I would roll out of my warm blankets, jump into my clothes, put on a heavy mackinaw, and rush down to the mill. I would rake over a few live coals left, pile on fresh wood and in a short time have pressure showing on both boilers. Banking the fires, I would run back to the bunk house ready for a breakfast of bacon and eggs and a huge pile of pancakes topped off with steaming hot coffee. I don't know when the cook slept, as she was always working around the kitchen when we went to bed, and she was always up before anyone, with breakfast ready. I was usually the first one to eat and hurried back to my boilers so everything was ready when the crew reported for work.

After Christmas deep snow fell and all transportation other than by sled came to a halt. Roads were never plowed in those days and the few automobiles in use were laid up for the winter. One Saturday the boss told me he was going to walk to Belfast as he had some business to look after and wanted to know if I wanted to go with him. It was a ten mile hike over the snow covered roads, but I was glad to get out of the camp for a day. The weather was brisk, so we kept a good pace and although we didn't leave until after supper I was home before the family went to bed. The boss was staying over, so I started back alone on Sunday night. It was clear and cold with brilliant starlight, and with the ground covered with snow, it didn't seem dark at all. When I got to the edge of the woods where the mill was located, I decided I could save about two miles by cutting through the woods to where I knew loggers had been working and follow their trail down to the mill.

I picked a spot which I thought would be the shortest distance to the mill and climbed through the barbed wire fence. I set a course which I figured would lead me to the area where the loggers were cutting. Due to the starlight and the covering of snow with no leaves on the trees, it didn't seem dark in the woods. Everything was still as I waded through the knee deep, soft snow. After some fifteen minutes I thought it strange that I hadn't found any tracks. I was sure that I had been going in a straight line and should be near the cutting. Then to my delight I ran into some footsteps in the snow. I followed them and after a time to my surprise I came to a barbed wire fence. I was on the edge of the woods, and looking for some landmark to get my bearings, I was flabbergasted to realize I was right back where I had entered the woods. They were my own footsteps I had been following. I had read that people lost in a woods had a tendency to go around in a circle and I proved it that night. I decided I had wandered enough in the woods so I got back on the road and followed it around the woods to the mill. I had learned a valuable lesson that night, one I never forgot.

Things were running along smoothly all through the month of January and into February. It was good winter weather and the loggers using the deep snow were piling up a large mound of logs before the mill. The head sawyer, depending on me to keep a good head of steam, was putting the logs through at a brisk pace while the tail sawyer was kept hopping to have the logs ready for the saw. Then one morning, without warning, disaster struck. All who worked in such a mill became used to the whine of the big saw and the pitch told how well things were going. I was busy as usual tending the fires when I suddenly heard the whine of the saw rising to a higher pitch. In a few seconds it became a high pitched scream. I looked up to see the head sawyer racing out of the mill on one direction, the tail sawyer scrambling over the top of the logs in another, while one of the mill hands went head first out of a small window.

In my physics class in high school I had studied about steam engines, so I knew they had to be controlled by a device called a governor. This device is made of two steel balls fastened to a rod which will move up and down to control a steam valve. When the engine is running these steel balls rotate according to the speed of the engine. If the engine speeds up, centrifugal force will move the balls outward, thus pulling the rod higher, cutting down the amount of steam, thus slowing the engine down. Thus, a constant speed is maintained. I also knew that if not controlled there is nothing to limit the speed of a steam engine. So when I heard the high pitch of the saw and heard the engine racing, I knew the governor must have stuck wide open. The real danger was that in a matter of seconds the speed of the flywheel on the engine or the saw or both would disintegrate due to centrifugal force. The mill hands knew this too, so they were fleeing out of danger.

I didn't dare go near the engine to close the throttle, but I knew that there was a hand screw valve in the steam line on top of the large boiler. As fast as I could I scrambled on top of the boiler and although the handle of the valve was hot, I screwed it shut as fast as possible. As soon as the steam was cut off, the engine slowed and all came to rest. My action saved the engine and the saw, but the bolts holding the engine to a concrete block were pulled loose. The mill had to be shut down until this could be repaired. The fact that I had acted to save the engine and saw made me quite a hero in the eyes of the crew.

Since the mill was to be shut down for at least three days, everyone who could, beat it for town. I went to Belfast. All winter in camp I didn't have a sign of a cold, but as soon as I got home I got a bad one keeping me in bed for a week. The boss came to see me and to tell me that their old fireman had returned and begged for his old job back. He promised to stay on the job, so they decided to give him another chance. However, he said they were setting up a new mill near Friendship, a small village on the B&S railroad toward Buffalo. He offered me the job of going with him and helping get this mill ready. We took the early milk train to Friendship, then walked to the mill site. The boss made arrangements for us to room and board at a nearby farmhouse.

A big steam boiler had been put in position and partially protected by a sort of lean-to. A large saw and other parts for the mill had been delivered but not set up. We arrived in a cold snap and I filled the boiler with just enough water to cover the flues and got a fire started. We worked all day and banked the fire for the night and returned to the farmhouse. That night was the coldest of the winter and when we woke up it was twenty below zero. The boss told the people we would not stay but wait for warmer weather. When we got to the mill, I took off my overcoat and hung it on a nail beside the boiler. We decided to build up the fire enough to get a little steam pressure, so we could blow the water out of the boiler. We didn't dare leave any in at that cold temperature. Soon after I got the fire going I heard a loud bang and looked up to see a stream of dirty water spraying against my coat. An outside pipe on the boiler had frozen during the night and burst, so when I had a little steam pressure that pipe thawed, spraying water out. There was nothing more we could do but open the blowoff valve and let all the water out. We then picked up our bags and hiked to the railroad station. My overcoat was soaked, but since it was easier to carry on than off, I slipped it on. In a couple of minutes the cold wind froze it solid. Thus, it became a perfect wind breaker and I was warm. But when we got to the station I couldn't bend my arms and had to stand near the pot bellied stove in the station waiting room until my sleeves thawed enough to get out of the coat.

When we got back to Belfast the boss left me saying he would let me know when he could use me again. In short, I was out of a job. Some of

Mother's women friends told her that with my education I should be doing something other than firing a steam boiler. There was no work in Belfast at that time of year. Some way Mother learned that a man she had known in school was a lawyer in Buffalo. She gave me a letter of introduction and sent me off to the city to see if he would help me get a job. Up to that time my life had been in the country or small town, so it was a real venture for me to go to a big city looking for work. When I arrived, I got a room at the YMCA, waiting until the next morning to see the lawyer.

As I sat in the lobby of the Y that evening reading a paper, a well-dressed young man came out of the elevator and sat down near me. No doubt, I looked the part of a young country boy coming to the city, and he knew it. After a few minutes he addressed me, asking if I was new in the city and looking for a job. I didn't want to be considered lost, so I told him I had a job lined up. He talked a few minutes more, saying he had come to the city at my age and gave me his card. He added, "If your job doesn't pan out, come and see me." He left and then I looked at his card indicating he was with the Bethlehem Steel Company located on the edge of Buffalo. I never used his card, but it did give me a good feeling for him to make the gesture, and although I had been warned about taking up with strangers, I shall always believe he was OK.

The next morning I located the office of the lawyer. I was so green I didn't know I was supposed to walk in but knocked on the closed door. I heard a voice say, "Come in," and when I opened the door, I saw a couple of secretaries seated at their desks. One asked me what I wanted, and when I said I would like to see the lawyer, she informed me that he was busy. I then produced Mother's letter. She took it and vanished, so I sat awkwardly in a chair not knowing how I should act. After about a half hour the girl came out of the inner office and gave me a letter addressed to the Buffalo Pitts Company. I thanked her and left without seeing the lawyer.

I inquired and located the office of the Buffalo Pitts plant in the industrial section of the city near the shore of Lake Erie. I knew the name of the company was familiar as the engine and threshing machine I had run carried that name. I presented my letter at the main office and after a long wait I was interviewed. He told me that they were not hiring at that time, but due to the letter from the lawyer, they could offer me a job as assistant timekeeper in the machine shop. I don't remember what the pay would be, but it sounded like a lot more than I had been getting, so I took the job.

After being introduced to the young man who was the head timekeeper in the shop, I went back to the YMCA. At my request, they gave me a list of boarding houses that they endorsed. I visited the one located nearest the plant which was run by a middle-aged widow. She had a vacant room which looked fine to me, and she assured me that there would be no trouble getting my breakfast on time so I could get to work, and she would also put up a lunch for me to carry. Then at the end of my first day I met the other boarders at dinner. Two of the group were young women teachers from the Buffalo State Teachers' College, which was nearby. It proved to be a very interesting congenial group, I was fortunate in my decision.

My work at the Buffalo Pitts plant was like entering a new world. I joined the head timekeeper and his sixteen year old helper in a small office near the main entrance to the big machine shop. All the machines were run by an overhead belt system, which made a deafening sound. It took time to get so I could understand what anyone was saying. Part of our job was to visit each machinist each day to check how much time he was putting on each order. We carried a sheet on a clipboard to make a record of what kind of work each one was doing and how much time he was taking. This was an education for me, because I had to learn the names of all the different operations such as drilling, reaming, boring, etc. I not only learned the names of the operations, but could observe something of the amount of skill required, thus storing knowledge to help in choosing what I might do in the future.

Once we had made the rounds, we carried the data back to the office to post the information in large loose bound books which contained copies of all the various orders listed by name and number. Much of the work was routine but interesting for a time, as I was learning how a factory operated. After a time I found the work very confining.

When I started this job the weather was still cold, so I took a trolley to and from work, but when spring came I often walked the mile in order to get some fresh air before going inside for the day. I found out that Buffalo was a windy city; there were times when the police would close certain streets in the downtown area. The strong wind would whirl around some of the tall buildings with such force it would literally sweep people off their feet. In early April the ice was still on the lake and the west wind coming over it kept the days cold. From the windows of the plant we could see the ice breakers attempting to break up the heavy ice in the harbor so ships from the west on the open water of the lake could dock. It was late in the spring before the trees in the parks blossomed. This is why the country around Buffalo is a good fruit area. The lake held back the blossoms until the danger of frost was past and then the warm water held back an early frost in the fall.

I found the nearest church to my rooming house was the Delaware Avenue Methodist, where Dr. Lynn Waldorf was the pastor. Dr. Waldorf later became one of the leading Methodist Bishops in New York State. His son became an outstanding football player at Syracuse University. I found him not only an inspiring preacher, but also a real leader of young people. I joined a Sunday School class of young people out of which was organized a baseball team. I was invited to join the team and since the games were played on Saturday afternoons, I had a chance to play several times. I was surprised to see Dr. Waldorf often attend these games and root for our team.

When the hot summer weather arrived, the machine shop was like an oven and our little office was almost unbearable. I started wondering how I could get some sort of vacation when one of the young fellows in my Sunday School class told me he was joining the National Guard. He said the Guard always went on a week's training at a camp outside the city and if you belonged, an employer had to let you go. The state armory was only a few blocks from my boarding house, so I went with my friend one evening to talk with the recruiter. He told us that this unit was part of a regiment that would be going to camp in two weeks, and they were anxious to bring their ranks up to quota. When they assured me that if I moved out of the city I would be dropped from the roster, I decided to sign up. A group of about twenty new recruits met every evening for the next two weeks for basic training. We learned some close order marching and the manual of arms enough to pass the inspection of the captain who would certify us for camp. I notified the company that I had joined and would be going to camp on a certain date, and they gave their consent without any fuss.

On a Monday morning my company assembled at the armory, marched to the railroad station, and took a train to Angola. After we detrained we marched about three miles to a tent camp set up on the shore of Lake Erie. The mornings were programmed for drilling and instructions, but the afternoons, unless one drew guard or K-P duty, were free for recreation. Baseball games were organized but the biggest attraction was the opportunity to swim in the lake. There was a fine sandy beach on the camp grounds, and since it was isolated, it didn't matter that we had no bathing suits.

After all the years I had spent each summer outside on a farm, it seemed good to get out again for a time. On the morning the company broke camp to return to the city, I was ordered for special guard duty. It had been a tradition for years for the soldiers to set fire to the temporary latrines just as they left. Orders had been issued the day before that any soldier setting fire to any of these buildings would be arrested and courtmartialed. I was posted at the latrine at the end of our company street with strict orders to prevent anyone setting fire to the building and to arrest anyone who tried. All went well until just before it was time to leave my post when a soldier I didn't know entered the latrine, and taking out a cigarette lighter, began to taunt me. I told him twice to lay off and leave, but he just laughed and asked me what I thought I could do. When he actually held the lighter to the tar paper which covered the frame building and it began to burn, I moved in and told him he was under arrest. Then he began to curse me and when I pulled out my bayonet and started to put it on my rifle, he ran. I yelled for the regular guard to stop him, which he did, and called the corporal of the guard. The soldier was taken away, still shouting at me. I didn't enjoy arresting the man, but I repeatedly warned him and also I knew there was an officer on horseback nearby watching the whole affair. I knew if I didn't follow orders, I would be in trouble. After it was over the officer rode up and said, "I saw all that. You did all right, but next time don't try to put your bayonet on your rifle, just use the butt of your gun if you need to."

When I got back to work on Monday morning I felt refreshed and felt ready to face the rest of the summer inside. The first news I got was that the young man who had been the head timekeeper for several years was out sick. Since the boy who had been the helper was too young to be the head, I was asked to take over the duties. It turned out that the young man had TB, so he never did get back to work. When it became apparent that I had to take over the duties of the head timekeeper, the superintendent of the machine shop told me I was expected to report early and stand by the time clock to be sure it was working and the men did not have trouble finding their time cards. To do this I had to get up a half hour earlier and since the trollies were irregular, many times I had to run to be on time. I did get a slight raise in my pay envelope, but not as much as I thought I should. One thing that was a real surprise was we were paid in gold coins, not paper money.

Early that summer I decided I would visit Niagara Falls, which I knew was near Buffalo. Then to my surprise the people who I asked as to how to get there and had lived in Buffalo all their lives, didn't know. I finally learned that there was an inter-urban trolley that ran from the center of the city to the Falls and I did make the visit. I was also asked to join a group of young people from the church to take a boat ride across the lake to Crystal Beach, a resort in Canada.

Late in August, Buffalo was celebrating the centennial of Admiral Perry's victory on Lake Erie. The battle was actually on September 10, 1813, but it was being observed at various times along the lake. The event was widely advertised and Mother wrote that Leeta and Ula had been working hard at the hospital and if I could have them, she would send them to Buffalo to see the celebration. Unfortunately, the time when they would arrive I would be with my National Guard company ready to take part in the big parade. When I asked my landlady if she would have a room for the girls, which she did, I told her about my problem. She volunteered to meet the girls at the station and take them to the parade. Since they didn't know each other, we agreed on a sign of her wearing a red rose in a certain way and I described the girls to her. It all went fine and I met them after the parade. The girls stayed a few days and had a good time.

All summer I had been thinking about what I should do another year. I had talked to Mother about my interest in medicine, and she rather encouraged me. When I was home before going to Buffalo, Leeta became ill and the doctor decided her appendix was bad and she should have it out. He had a surgeon come from Buffalo on the morning train to operate on Leeta and then take the afternoon train back. Mother had talked to the doctor about my interest in medicine, and he arranged for me to watch the operation. I then stayed with Leeta as she came out of the anesthetic, which was ether as was used in those

94

days. The surgeon was very nice to me, complimenting me on my bedside manner. He also said that if I decided to enter Buffalo Medical College, to be sure to let him know.

After much thought I decided that it was impossible for me to finance my way through medical school, so when Lynn Bedford wrote me that he was going back to Clarkson College that fall and suggested I go with him, I gave it serious thought. I liked science and math in school and with my experience with machinery, the idea of taking an engineering course enticed me. So when Mother heard this, she suggested that I come home with the girls and she would invite Lynn up to Belfast and we could talk things over. Lynn brought Grace, his sister, with him as she had decided to also go to Postdam and enter the State Teachers' College. Lynn encouraged me by saying he was sure I could get a part-time job and we could room together to save expenses. So we agreed to meet in early September and all go together.

I always felt that my year at work was valuable. I not only saved some money, but had some experiences that I never could have received from books. I had also matured a lot and the future took on a new meaning.

CHAPTER 8

CLARKSON

When I decided to go to Clarkson, I gave notice to the company in Buffalo. They were very nice about it and wished me well and told me if I ever wanted a job again to let them know. I got to Belfast in early September, but was there only a day or two to pack my clothes. I met Lynn and Grace as they boarded the train at Houghton, starting our trip to Postdam, New York. This was a small city in St. Lawrence County in the northern part of the state. We had to change trains three times, so it was evening when we arrived. We had to stay at a hotel that night but got up early the next morning to find permanent rooms. Lynn and I were lucky as the college gave us the name of a place where other Tech students were rooming close to the college. We found the house, and the people rented us a room that we could share. Once located, we met three other students. We took over the whole second floor and were able to have one room for a study room for all of us.

Grace had a little more difficulty finding a place, as she wanted a room plus a kitchen so she could get the meals for both herself and Lynn. Finally with the help of the Normal school, she found a place not too far from our house, which was really a small apartment. We were all settled for the year.

When we registered at the College, Lynn and I were both given credit for our freshman year at Houghton, so we were considered sophomores. But the courses in the Engineering College were so different from the work we had been taking we had to go into several freshman classes. With the good basic work we had at Houghton in math, I had no trouble in the second year work of college algebra and calculus. I had no trouble with college physics and enjoyed the lab work immensely, and before the end of the year I was flattered when others in the class asked me for help. College chemistry I found rather difficult as I was competing with others who had high school chemistry, which I didn't. But in the second semester when we took up qualitative analysis, I more than held my own. We had no classes in English or history, just one semester of economics which I got very little out of, as we had the poorest teacher I ever encountered in any place. Since neither of us had any kind of shop work, we had to sign up for freshman shop. Lynn selected machine shop, while I chose wood work. The first semester was devoted to carpentry, while the second took up wood turning. I found them both to be very interesting and I learned a lot which was valuable in later life.

Everyone had to take gym. I found some of the activities very difficult, as I was competing with boys who had this work in high school. Houghton had nothing of this kind so the work on the various apparatus was entirely new. I did find out that when we started playing basketball in the gym class I was better than most of the boys. Although we were not true freshman, both Lynn and I were encouraged to try out for the regular freshman basketball team. However, we soon learned that the coach was more interested in boys who had played in high school on regular teams, so we dropped out.

When I registered at the college, I put my name in for part-time work. They didn't give me much encouragement, so after waiting more than a week, I decided to look for myself. First I walked around the city to see what it was like. I found only two blocks from the college a business section which was divided into two parts separated by the Raquette River, which ran through the city. A hotel and the larger stores were on the same side of the river as the college, while across the river were several supply stores catering to the surrounding farms. On the banks of the river was a large saw mill, which got its logs from the big woods to the south. The loggers, largely French Canadians, floated these logs down the river on the spring floods. A considerable part of the population spoke French as indicated by the sign in some of the store windows, "Francais parlé ici."

After I had completed my survey, I decided to start in with the business places nearest the college. I got no response from the first few but when I came to a small restaurant I walked in and asked for the manager. Out from the kitchen came a nice looking young man. I introduced myself and told him I had just registered at Clarkson but needed a part-time job to pay my way through school. "That's interesting," he said, "I was just thinking of contacting the college to see if they knew of a student who wanted to take care of the furnace and clean up the place before we open up for breakfast." Then he added, "Would you be interested in doing this for your board?" I told him I was very interested. He introduced himself as Harry Van Ness and said he had graduated from Clarkson a few years before. He then called his wife from the kitchen and introduced me, telling her what we had said. They were recently married and together had started this restaurant. I liked them both and they seemed to like me. We talked a bit more, then Van told me to stop in after classes the next day and they would let me know about the job.

I returned to my room with my fingers crossed. I knew it would be a break for me to be able to work for all my board as that would be my biggest expense in school. I found out later that Van, as he was called by all his friends, contacted both the college and the people where I roomed to check on me. Both gave me a good recommendation so when I returned the next afternoon everything was settled for me to start the next Monday. I hurried back to my room, glowing, to tell Lynn my good luck.

The weather was still warm, so the furnace hadn't been started nor did I have the keys to open up the restaurant, but I did arrive for breakfast on Monday. I found the place humming with extra help in the kitchen, as they expected a big crowd for noon lunch since a women's church group was scheduled for a convention that day.

When I walked in right after noon to get my lunch, I found the place full of women. Every table was taken and Van, who was the only waiter, was swamped. I made my way to the kitchen where everyone was falling over each other trying to fill the orders. As soon as I could reach Van I asked "Don't you want me to help?" "Can you wait on tables?" he gasped. "Sure," I said, "I have some experience." "Grab a white coat," he said, "and help me take orders."

In a short time we had the situation under control. As it neared one o'clock Van stopped me and said, "You better grab a bite to eat before you are late for class. Thanks a million. I can handle it now." That evening when I came back for supper both Van and his wife were loud in their praise for my help. They were especially pleased to think I offered to help as they didn't expect I could wait on tables and anyway, it was not part of the bargain. Jumping in as I did, I became like one of the family on the first day. From that time on they treated me fine and I, in turn, helped run the restaurant as if it were mine.

Clarkson had a football team and before the annual game with its biggest rival, St. Lawrence University, which was close by in Canton, Lynn and I had our first experience of attending a big pep rally. This was something very different from Houghton where there was no interscholastic athletics. We got quite a thrill in being part of the student body around a big bonfire with speeches by the coaches, the captain of the team and some professors. There was no band but a lot of cheering and singing, creating excitement for the game the next day.

When Halloween approached, I learned that it had been a tradition for a long time for the Clarkson Engineers to hold a big rally around a bonfire downtown in the public square. But that year the city police decided that such a fire downtown was too dangerous and they notified the college to inform the students that no bonfire would be permitted. They announced that anyone attempting to start a fire would be arrested. Of course, this was a challenge to the students. Van, being an alumnus of the college, was interested on keeping traditions alive, so when he heard about the notice, he told me to quietly tell some of my friends to meet in the restaurant that evening.

When the group gathered, Van told us that there was an old vehicle in a vacant lot back of his building which had been made like a stage coach to be in a parade years before. It was now rotting and he had been trying for years to have it moved. He suggested that on Halloween

99

night we come to the restaurant one or two at a time. We could then carry some packing crates out of the basement door in back and load the old coach full. We could then draw it down a back alley, set it afire, and rush it out into the street to the square.

Word was passed around the college on Halloween day that something was going to happen that night and be at the public square at 9 p.m. As the time approached the police were nervously watching the large crowd of Tech men who were gathering. Those of us who were in on the plans followed them without trouble. Once the stage coach was loaded, we soaked the crates with kerosene and drew it to the edge of the street, but out of sight in the alley. On signal the students around the square started a big commotion on the opposite side. The police all rushed over to see what was going on. We then lit the fire and as soon as it was going good, we dashed out with the whole coach flaming like a torch—yelling like Indians. When we reached the center of the square we left it and dashed in all directions. The police yelled for us to stop, but we dashed for the back alleys and didn't look back. None of us went back to the restaurant, and although the police questioned Van, he kept a straight face pleading ignorance, so they never found out who did it.

In November when the deer hunting season opened, Van wanted to go but his wife was reluctant for him to go alone. Before he was married, Van had worked for a big lumber company in the woods. There he had become friends with a man who was a licensed hunting guide and had given a standing invitation to Van to come and go hunting. Van asked me if I had done any hunting and when I said "Yes, but not for deer," he asked if I would like to go with him and try it. He offered to borrow a rifle for me and would buy my license and pay all expenses.

I considered it too good an offer to refuse and made arrangements to go. We left early on a Friday morning which happened to be my birthday. After traveling some 50 miles south we turned onto a narrow woods road and continued for another five miles before we came to a small cabin. Van thought it was the guide's place, but when we knocked and called for several minutes, he wasn't sure. Just as I turned away from the door I spied a head peeking around the corner of a small shed. Then when Van called out his name a woman ventured out. It was the guide's wife, who had heard the car and was hiding until sure it wasn't a stranger. She said her husband was out guiding a party but would be home that night. She invited us into the cabin which was full of mounted deer heads, bear skins and other trophies.

Van's friend arrived about dark and they greeted each other warmly. He was polite to me, but I felt he wanted to size me up before he became too friendly. We sat down to a meal of venison steaks, which was great. All through the meal, Van and the guide did a lot of reminiscing. Then at bedtime he said he was engaged to guide a party the next day, so he couldn't take us hunting for deer but directed us to a couple of ponds not far from the cabin where we would have a chance to see one.

We were up early the next morning and were given a hot breakfast. We didn't see the guide as he had left before daybreak. The woman had also packed us a lunch and made sure we started out in the right direction. It was a bright sunny morning and soon after entering the woods, Van showed me how to load the 30–30 rifle, which I had never used, but made sure the safety was on. Then Van loaded his and raised it to his shoulder to sight it. We never knew for sure, but felt his safety wasn't on right because when he tried the trigger the gun discharged. At that we heard something go crashing through the underbrush, but if it was a deer, we couldn't see it.

After tramping about an hour we came to the small ponds the guide told us about. I sat with my back against a big tree and in the bright sunshine was quite comfortable. We stayed very quiet until noon when we met and ate our lunch. Following that we walked through another area returning to watch again. I never heard the woods so quiet, the wind was calm and not even a chipmunk was stirring. Late in the afternoon we returned to the cabin. The only shot we heard all day was the one Van made by mistake that morning.

After being out all day in the clear crisp air we were ready to turn in early. It clouded up that night, so by the time we left for home the next morning it had begun to snow. We were fortunate in picking the one beautiful day of the fall and although we didn't see a deer, it was a worthwhile experience. It was my first and only time for hunting deer.

After I was well established in my work and doing many extra things, Van asked me one day if I wanted to learn to drive his Model-T Ford car. He had the car, not only for pleasure, but also to make deliveries of ice cream to customers on Sundays. In the basement of the restaurant Van had installed an ice cream machine run by a small motor. In those days there were no large commercial companies shipping ice cream. Most people made it at home in small hand-cranked freezers. So when the people in Potsdam found out they could buy it and have it delivered to their doors, it became a growing business.

Once a week I helped make the ice cream and then it was stored in freezers to be sold in dishes in the restaurant or in bulk to be taken out. It became one of my jobs to keep the freezers packed with crushed ice and salt so the cream would not melt or become too soft. I soon became skillful at keeping it just right. I also helped make deliveries, so when offered the chance to drive the car, I was eager to learn. Van took me out a few times and taught me the fundamentals, then told me to go alone. The first time I did so, I ran into a ditch and fence before I mastered the trick of using the clutch properly. Only the old generation will remember the special skill of operating the old Model-T, but once mastered one was considered someone special. In a short time I was making all the Sunday deliveries with the car. Then in the spring Van had to tell me that the police had notified him that it was a city law that only owners of a car could drive in the city limits. At that time there was no state license bureau, so each city made its own laws.

101

Winter came early in Potsdam and stayed late. I had to get some warmer clothes to wear when I went out early in the morning to open up the restaurant. Many times it would be 40 below zero early in the morning and even with the sun shining would stay 10 below all day. I found that I had to buy a pair of heavy lined overshoes to keep my feet from freezing. Also, a heavy cap with fur ear laps was required to keep my ears from frostbite. Another danger was "snow blindness" caused by the reflection of the bright sun off the white snow. I had one case of this before I learned to wear dark glasses.

When properly dressed the winter weather was exhilarating and all winter sports were enjoyed. Across the river was a city park which had a steep hill just right for toboggan coasting. This was a chance for the Clarkson boys to invite the Normal School girls out for an evening of fun. Van told me to take his toboggan and join the others. Also the river froze over early so the first part of the winter there was some excellent skating. For some reason it seemed that only the town girls were out skating. I had met several of them in the restaurant so I was quite popular with the Engineers, as I could introduce them to these girls. Grace Bedford was about the only Normal School girl I knew and she was so busy with her school work and keeping house for Lynn that I seldom saw her.

One day one of the girl's dorms ordered a big supply of brick ice cream for a party. I delivered the order in a large freezer and left it outside the back door so it would stay frozen. When I got to my room I told the others what I had done and two of them sneaked up to the back door of the dorm and came back with two bricks. They all had a big feast and to be sociable, I ate some. The next day the joke was on me, for when I came in to lunch, Van told me that the girl's didn't use all the ice cream they ordered and he had been up to get what was left over. He also said they told him that some had been stolen. Of course, I was surprised but he was a bit suspicious, for he said, "I guess we will all have to eat the leftover," and he put a big helping on my plate. Although I was full of ice cream and could hardly look at it, I had to save face and force it down. After that I didn't want any for a long time.

During the year Van hired a young French girl to help with the cooking and to do the dish washing. In the middle of the winter a man who had worked with Van in the woods came along and said he was out of work. Van felt sorry for him and told him he could stay and help in the restaurant until he found something. I didn't like him very well but didn't say anything. After a few weeks the mother of the girl who Van had hired came to complain saying this man was bothering her daughter and if the man stayed, her daughter would leave. Van tried to smooth things over, but the girl left. A few days later the man left to apply for a job, and Van asked me to work all day Saturday. That night when he checked the cash register Van remarked to me, "This is the first time in weeks that the register and the cash has balanced." I was not surprised because his "so-called" friend, I was quite sure, had been taking money out of the register. Anyway, after that Saturday the man left for good. I never knew whether he had been asked to go, but I overheard a conversation between Van and his wife which indicated she wanted the man to leave.

In the early spring Van began to phase out the restaurant business and turn the place into a stationery store. His wife had become pregnant so wasn't able to do the cooking. To find a good dependable cook to take her place seemed impossible. Also, the restaurant business became so variable it was not paying.

A first step in making the change was to install a candy counter in the front of the restaurant. He stocked it with high grade chocolate and other candies. He showed me how to wait on the customers and told me then I could sample all the different kinds of candy but asked me to not take any outside the store. I followed his request and thought it would be wonderful to have all the candy I wanted to eat, but by the time I had sampled all the varieties, I was sick of so much sweets and rarely ate any more. I think he knew this would happen.

When we closed the restaurant I helped remove the tables and install counters and shelves along both walls. Van had ordered a stock of stationery and a number of oddities. Also he obtained the right to sell daily and Sunday newspapers from New York City and Syracuse. This put him in direct competition with a long established store on the public square. The result was a business war which led to the employees of the older store stealing our papers when they were thrown off the train. But before I left at the end of the school year, Van and the manager of the other store met and agreed on a compromise, so things settled down to a routine business.

Soon after the change-over, an incident happened which we all remembered and laughed about many times. One cold winter night a fine looking Maltese tabby cat came to the back door of the restaurant and begged to come in. No one had the heart to turn her away and after we fed her, she made herself at home. She slept in the basement where she cleaned up a growing population of mice. It soon became apparent that she was about to be a mother and as Van's wife was expecting their first baby, Van became very interested in the cat's condition.

One Saturday evening I was staying at the restaurant after supper and Van, his wife, and I were sitting in the kitchen. Tabby, the cat, jumped up in my lap and as I stroked her back, she lay contentedly purring. I saw her sides beginning to throb and as I felt of her stomach I remarked, "She is about due. I can feel the kittens kicking hard." Just then Tabby gave a cry and looked around. I looked down and discovered she was giving birth in my lap. I called for Van to get the box in which she slept, and we carried her in it down to the basement. Van, who had never seen the birth of any animal, wanted to watch and stayed with her. I went back up stairs to look after the restaurant. It was a quiet night and after a time Mrs. Van Ness decided she wasn't needed and left for home. Then just before closing time a large group of young people came in and ordered hot chocolate and sandwiches. There were too many for me to handle alone, so I had to go down and drag Van away from his delivery room experience. However, he had seen most of the kittens arrive and felt better educated to cope with his future.

Tabby had a litter of five kittens and after the restaurant closed, she moved her family into the store. One day a prominent lady of the town came into the shop to look over our supply of writing paper. She had her pet dog, a small long-haired poodle, with her. We had a sign posted, "No dogs allowed," but she was the kind who felt above any rule. While the lady was examining the paper her pet was examining the room. When he got near the back of the room where Tabby had her family, there was a big commotion. Out jumped Tabby spitting and snarling. Her eyes flashed, the hair on her back stood upright and her tail was twice its natural size. For an instant the poodle stood stock still and then sensing danger, started to turn away. At that Tabby made a high leap, landing on the dog's back and began to dig all four claws in deep. The poor dog let out howls of distress and raced for the door. I was near and snatched the door open so the poor dog could escape. Once outside Tabby released her victim and with head held high marched triumphantly back to her domain. The lady rushed out of the store frantically calling her pet and then and only then we let out our pent-up laughter. I don't believe the lady ever came back.

When I decided to go to Clarkson, Mother told me that my Great-grandmother Lowery came from St. Lawrence County and she was sure some of our cousins lived near Potsdam. She wanted me to look them up, but I had no way of traveling outside the city to find them. Anyway, I wasn't keen about finding some distant relatives I didn't know. Then one day two spinster women walked into the restaurant and asked for me. I came out of the kitchen and they introduced themselves as my cousins. Someway Mother had got their address and wrote them telling where I was and suggested they look me up. They were typical north country women who had lived all their lives in the country. After our greetings we had little to talk about. I tried to find out just how we were related but didn't get too much out of them. I offered them a cup of coffee or some ice cream, but they sternly refused. They didn't stay long, but I always remember it as one of the most awkward times I ever had. Mother would have enjoyed meeting them, but I was different.

One evening when we were eating supper we heard the fire signal at the nearby fire house. We were used to hearing the fire engine dashing out with sirens blowing, so I didn't pay any attention to it. After I had finished my work and walked toward my room, I was surprised to see the fire engine near my house. When I got there the firemen informed me that there had been a fire in the house but it was now out. I made my way in and found the fire had started around the light fixture in our room. There had been a lot of volunteer help and when I checked, I found that they had taken the drawers out of the dressers and dumped the contents out the windows. I looked in the closet and found all our clothes hanging untouched but soaked with water and plaster. The fire had burned only a small hole in the ceiling, but a lot of damage had been done by the large amount of water the firemen had pumped into the attic. Our bed clothes had been thrown out the window, so when Lynn came, we gathered everything we could find, and were able to sleep there that night. The insurance took care of our suits by cleaning and pressing them, but we lost a lot of small things.

A strange thing happened that day. Our landlady had a grand piano which she considered very valuable, so when the fire started, she asked a group of the men volunteers to carry it out of the house. They took off the legs and carried it through the front door, setting it on the front lawn with other furniture. Then when all was clear the same men picked up the piano and attempted to carry it back into the house. They tried and tried, but it would not go through the same door. Finally, they had to carry it around the house to a back door to get it inside the house. No one could figure out how they took it out so easily but couldn't get it back. It was an example of strange things that happen in times of excitement; of people doing the impossible.

One morning that spring when working in the chemistry lab with my classmates, we heard a low rumble and felt a vibration that shook the building. All the glass bottles on the lab desks began to tingle. The lab was on the ground floor, and we felt the vibrations strongest through our feet. For a few minutes we all stopped work and speculated as to what was happening. Our best conclusion was there had been a big explosion, maybe at the power plant which was outside the city. Not until we saw the headlines in the morning papers did we know we had experienced one of the strongest earthquakes that had ever occurred in the St. Lawrence Valley. None of us knew that such quakes occured in that region.

Near the end of the school year I was in the wood turning shop trying to finish a project to submit for my final exam. I had selected a blueprint of a wooden goblet to be turned out of a piece of sumac wood. This is a wood that is easy to work and has a beautiful grain that stands out when finished. I had it almost done but discovered one small rough spot left on the stem of the goblet. I put it back on the lathe and using my chisel I tried to be very careful and smooth the rough spot, but to my dismay the chisel caught, breaking the stem. I heard a grunt and looked around to see the shop instructor standing back of me and watching my disaster. "Too bad," he said, "you'll have to make something else out of it." I was surprised he didn't say more as he had the reputation of being a grouch. But I had found him to be a fine teacher, both in this shop and in drafting. The only time I ever heard him talk rough was to a student who was not trying to do good work.

After my instructor walked away I gazed at my broken goblet trying to make my own design out of the wreck. I cut off the remainder of the stem and then turned out a small wooden holder of small objects, such as collar buttons, to be placed on top of a bedroom dresser. When completed and polished, it looked real good and I was delighted to see it put on display for commencement. Later it was returned and I used it for a long time.

When our final exams were over, neither Lynn nor I had anything to stay for, so we left for home before commencement. I said my goodbyes to the Van Ness family, which now numbered three. A beautiful baby boy had arrived in early June. We had an understanding that I would return in the fall with the same arrangements. I was truly grateful to them for a wonderful year with such fine people, and for making it possible to finish a year in college with limited funds.

I had learned many things that year, both in and out of school. Yet there lurked in the back of my mind an uneasy feeling that maybe I wasn't on the right course. I just wasn't sure I wanted to be an engineer.

CHAPTER 9

BACK AT HOUGHTON

I got back to Belfast in June, too early for the haying season, thus there was little chance of getting a job on a farm. I put in some time helping at the hospital and found a dealer in grain and feed where I got an occasional job. About the first of July I heard of a farmer about a mile from the village who was inquiring about help for the haying season. I met the man and found that he did not run the typical farm, as he had no dairy herd. He said he kept only a cow or two for the family needs and he took care of them himself. I was pleased with the arrangements and we agreed on the salary.

I reported for work a week before he was ready to cut hay, so he had me picking up rocks and stones in an open field using them to build a stone fence. This land was a glacial deposit and every year the frost heaved these stones to the surface, so in order to keep the field tillable, they had to be picked up. After a year in college I was so soft that this kind of work made my back and arms so lame I could hardly move in the mornings. I gradually improved by the time we started haying until I was back in good condition.

I found this man rather strange, not inclined to talk and only gradually did I learn he had been a civil engineer. He had been in several parts of the world, including China, building railroads, but when I tried to get him to tell about his experiences, he would clam up. He now had a wife with a small baby and apparently he had bought this farm with the idea of settling down. His wife was not well, so he spent considerable time in the house helping her. To make the work easier, he had purchased a hay loader and side rake. These were new farm machines that neither of us had seen and they were delivered all apart. We had to assemble them with meager instructions! His engineering experience was a big help in getting them to work properly.

One day right after I started cutting hay, the boss came back from a trip to town with a sixteen year old boy to help. I never knew where he found the boy, but he introduced him as Heidrick, a young man from Germany. The boy could speak no English, so my one year of German back in Houghton came in handy. I knew enough of the common words so we managed to get along. There was a German-speaking family who lived on a nearby farm, so I took him over one evening to let them visit. They told me that Heidrick told them he came from the southern part of Germany and since he was near the age to be pressed into military service and his religion was against fighting, he had run away. He said there was an organization in this country who helped such boys escape and helped them get a job. However, there were some people in the community who were suspicious of him, especially as this was the summer that World War I broke out in Europe. The boy made no effort to learn English, as one would expect him to do if he planned to stay in this country, and I heard that late that summer he suddenly disappeared. It was evident that he knew nothing about farming, and I had to teach him, but he was big and strong and together we did most of the haying.

Since I was so near home and wasn't tied up with chores, I went to Belfast every weekend. I learned that there was a town band that gave concerts summer Saturday evenings. I got out my cornet, which I had bought from Lynn Bedford when I left Houghton, and started to practice. I met the director of the band and he invited me to join to play the second cornet part. It was good to be in a band again and it helped me get through the summer.

We finished the haying about the first of August, and the boss asked me to finish cultivating the corn. He had Heidrick cutting out the weeds with a hoe around the corn which the cultivator missed. The boss would work with Heidrick for an hour or so and then take off for the house. One very hot morning, each of us started taking two rows. The boss took a furious pace and for a time I kept up with him but soon decided it was foolish as no one could keep going like that all day. Heidrick was behind so I dropped back with him. When I did, the boss turned around and said, "What's the matter, Ray, can't you keep up?" The heat was so oppressive I wasn't feeling too good and his question struck me the wrong way. "Yes," I replied, "I can keep up but what's the hurry?" Then I added, "I'll be out here all day, but you won't." Sure enough, when we reached the end of the row, he laid down his hoe and went to the house. The more I thought about it the madder I got, so by the time we went in for the noon meal, I exploded. I told the boss, "Since the haying is done and you have Heidrick, it is evident you don't need me, so at the end of the week I'll take my pay and leave." He made a feeble effort to smooth things over, but I left.

The rest of the summer I worked for the feed dealer. That year there was a bumper crop of apples and about the only market for them was a cider and vinegar mill in Rochester. The dealer ordered several empty freight cars and advertised that he would give ten cents a bushel for apples. Farmers from all around brought them in by the wagon load and I loaded the cars until the railroad put an embargo on them. They said the freight yards in Rochester were full of cars loaded with apples and they were rotting before the mill could process them.

While I was considering whether I had enough money from my

summer jobs to return to Clarkson, I received a letter which changed my whole life. Van wrote to tell me that he had sold the store and therefore, would have no work for me if I returned. He said he was sorry but would help me find another job if I came back. I considered this letter a sort of omen that I was not to be an engineer and decided to return to Houghton for my third year and try to transfer to Oberlin for a degree. I would be following Jess Frazier, who would be in Oberlin for his senior year, while Lynn Bedford did return to Clarkson and became an electrical engineer. The longstanding friends were separated for good.

In May of that year, on her 16th birthday, Ula brought all her books home from school and declared she would never return. All of us, including her teachers, tried to have her stay to finish that year at least, but she hated school and had been counting the days until she could legally drop out. She announced that she would help Mother run the hospital, and it began a close relationship between the two which lasted the rest of Mother's life. Since the hospital was not busy, Leeta got a job as a housekeeper and in early September I left for Houghton.

Uncle Clark had given up being the pastor of the Fillmore Church and had returned to Houghton, buying the Dow house on the hill next to the camp grounds. He kept a couple of cows, a team of horses and cultivated a few acres of land. He also had built a double deck chicken house and kept over 200 white leghorn hens. He was shipping a crate or more of eggs weekly to New York City. He was doing all this to augment his small salary from the college to support his growing family. I knew that the year before he had given a room to a student to help with the chores. So when I decided to return to Houghton, I contacted him and he gave me that job. Part of my expenses were provided.

I returned to Houghton with a new outlook on life and school. In the two years I had been away, I had matured a lot, first finding what it was like to work outside school and then to experience an entirely different college life at Clarkson. I returned with the idea of making good grades so I would be recommended to Oberlin. I also took some pride in that I was one of the older students and felt I could be a leader in making Houghton a real college atmosphere.

In spite of the fact I had been in Houghton longer than most of the students, I was registered as a new student. Accordingly, I was invited to the reception for new students given at the beginning of each year. Out of curiosity I decided to go. There I met Willard Ballard, a transfer student from a school in Michigan. Since he was about my age, we were drawn together. After we met and compared notes, we stood looking over the crowd, especially the girls. In that group were two young ladies who stood out from the rest and when we inquired, we learned that they were new teachers. By mutual agreement we said, "Let's meet them and see if we can date them and thus avoid the rigid regulations that the school imposes on the girl students." We found out that one teacher was Miss Fitts, a piano instructor, and the other Miss Riggall, who was to be the head of a new speech department. When I met Norah Riggall that night we were mutually attracted, so it began a friendship which grew stronger during the year.

In order to qualify for an A.B. degree, I had to do some adjusting of my courses. I was ahead in math and science, but behind in liberal arts. I signed for a course in American history, one in psychology, another in ethics, and for English a course in debate. Will Frazier was the instructor in all these subjects except debate. I had known "Bill," as we used to call him, and always liked him and found him to be an excellent teacher. I liked American history and did so well in it that when Frazier became ill for two weeks in the spring, I was asked to take over his class. It was my first taste of real teaching and I am sure it affected my later life.

Besides his regular college classes, Uncle Clark was asked to teach the high school geometry class. To help with the paper work he asked me to grade the homework and test papers, paying me a small sum which I was glad to receive. I was learning more about teaching. Harold Luckey, President Luckey's youngest son, was in the class and after the second week he protested to Uncle Clark about the mark I had given him. Uncle Clark asked to see his paper and after he had checked it, he turned to Harold and said, "I think Ray has been more than fair to you. If I had graded it, I would have given you at least five points less." I am sure Harold thought he should have special consideration because he was the president's son, but Uncle Clark set him straight in a hurry. That was the only complaint I had all year.

I was really thrilled to be offered another job. President Luckey was teaching both high school and college physics that year. He knew about my record at Clarkson and asked me to be his laboratory assistant. I was very glad to do it, not only for the little money it paid, but for the experience it gave me. It gave me a little prestige, which I couldn't help but like. In the high school physics class was Ira Bowen, the younger brother of Ward Bowen who had been in my high school classes. Their father had been a prominent Wesleyan minister who had died several years before. Mrs. Bowen, his widow, had been given a teaching job in the school, so they were a well-known family. I found Ira an outstanding student in physics and after a year of college at Houghton, he transferred to Chicago University. In a short time, Dr. Millikan, the famous physicist who was then teaching at Chicago, picked Ira out of a class of two hundred students and made him his assistant. When Dr. Millikan went to California to be the president of the new Institute of Technology, he insisted that Ira go with him. Later Ira became the head of the famous Palomar Observatory. So I felt I had a small part in developing a celebrity.

After our meeting at the reception, Ballard and I made it a point to invite "Fittsy" and "Riggie," as these teachers became known, for Sunday afternoon walks. Both of these teachers lived in the girls' dorm and they were delighted for a chance to get out at least for a time. Since I was boarding at the dorm I also had the chance to be at Norah's table at times. More than that, after I took over the lab work I found that her room was only a few doors down the hall, so we saw each other frequently that way. Norah and I became more friendly, but Ballard lost interest and became interested in a coed whom he later married.

Norah, being a member of the faculty, and I, being a student, starting to date, created a lot of discussion around the school. Since I was a laboratory assistant, I felt I should have some freedom above a regular student, but Miss Grange, the Matron of the dorm, didn't think so, and she took a keen interest in our affairs. More than once when we took our Sunday afternoon walk, she would send someone to follow us and report to her where we went and what we did.

In the first weeks of school, I learned that Norah's home was in Cazenovia, New York. She had graduated from Cazenovia Seminary, a Methodist school much like Houghton Seminary, but with rules more liberal. Following her graduation from the high school department she took a year of post-graduate work, specializing in speech. Her teacher considered her so good that he recommended her to the School of Speech at Northwestern University in Evanston, Illinois. Norah's father was very strict about what the girls in the family could do, but much to everyone's surprise, he had let her go. She finished the two year course in this school, which was accepted by New York State for a teacher's certificate. Houghton was her first position. So while she was a member of the faculty, we were on a par with two years of college.

The village of Fillmore maintained a winter lecture course. One lecture was the famous *Acres of Diamonds,* given by the minister from Philadelphia. I had heard about this lecture and wanted to hear it. I talked with Ballard and he was interested, so we thought it would be nice to ask "Fittsy" and "Riggie" for a date to attend the lecture. They were both interested and accepted our offer. I arranged to take Uncle Clark's team, hoping for a sleigh ride, but had to settle for the surrey.

The night of the lecture I hooked up the team and drove down to the dorm. Ballard was waiting and the girls soon came out all bundled up but with long faces. When I inquired, they said just as they were ready to come out the door Miss Grange stopped them and told them they couldn't go with boy students in the evening unless they took a chaperone.

We stood there nonplused. Here we were, four people all over twenty-one years of age, going to a public lecture as a group, anyone of us could go by ourselves, and each of the two teachers could chaperone a group of students, but suddenly we couldn't go as a group. Also, I knew that the place had been sold out, so if we did take another teacher along, she wouldn't be able to get in.

When I heard the news, I asked, "Who says we can't go?" They told me that Miss Grange said it was an order from President Luckey. "I'm going right over and find out," I said, and walked across the campus to his house. When he came to the door, I explained our situation. All he said was, "I can't give you permission." I pointed out all the arguments, but each time he repeated, "I can't give you permission." After he said this over and over, something dawned on me. I felt he sympathized with us but was on the spot since Miss Grange had appealed to him and he felt he had to uphold her. He never said, "You can't go," and something in his manner made me feel he wouldn't blame us if we did.

I returned to the others and said, "Let's go." I never really answered their question, "How did you get his consent?" We attended the lecture and found it as great as advertised. We enjoyed our ride and time together, and not until we were ready to say good night did I tell them what President Luckey had said and how I interpreted it.

The next morning I went early to see President Luckey and told him the full story. I said, "I take the full responsibility and please do not blame anyone else." Nevertheless, both of the women were called to his office and while they were informed that I took the full responsibility, they were told it must never happen again. They were a bit concerned as it was their first job and they didn't want to get in bad, so we never tried it again.

I worked with President Luckey that year, and he never mentioned the episode to me, nor I to him. In fact, I got the impression from his attitude and a few remarks that he was not always in accord with the strict rules he had to enforce. He was really a remarkable man, a great educator, who was trying to bring a lot of various forces into line so Houghton could become a recognized college with a charter from the New York Department of Education allowing it to grant degrees. It was his dream, and he lived to see it fulfilled.

I am sure Miss Grange, as the matron of the girls' dorm, was one of his problems. She was not a member of the faculty, but she seemed to know everything that was going on and was ready to give her opinion about it. She told Norah more than once that she shouldn't associate with me. When asked why, she replied that I didn't have a good reputation in school and also wasn't a Christian. So of course Norah asked me about it. I had fun telling her about the scrapes I had during my early days and as far as Miss Grange saying I wasn't a Christian, I admit I am not her kind. Anyway, I didn't think too much of her. As an example, I knew that Red Grange, the famous football player at the University of Illinois, "the galloping ghost," was her nephew and she liked to brag about him. At the same time she was always saying how evil interscholastic sports were and Houghton should never consider them. It was an example of some of the inconsistencies that some of the Houghton people showed.

Once to get away, Uncle Clark let me take his car so I could take Norah for a Sunday afternoon drive. The car was an old Brush runabout which he had picked up cheap. It was a one-seater with no top and a small engine of only two cylinders. It would go along good on level roads, so we had fun driving along the valley. After we had stopped for a rest, I had trouble starting it again, so before we could get back it began to grow dusk. I tried to light the headlights, which burned acetylene gas, only to find the tank which was carried on the running board was empty. I didn't want to run the car in the dark without some light so there would be some warning to anyone driving a team of horses. In those days most horses were frightened by an automobile, so many times the driver of a car had to pull to the side of the road and shut off the engine to let the team pass. At times the horses had to be led past the "infernal contraption," as many farmers called them. Knowing all this, I searched in the back of the car and found a lantern which had some kerosene in it. I lit it and tied it on the front of the car, thus giving a warning but practically no light to see the road. Fortunately, we got home without meeting anyone and laughed at our lark.

Later that year Uncle Clark traded the old car and his team of horses for a Model-T Ford. Since I had learned to drive such a car in Potsdam, I was able to teach him how to drive it. These cars had no electric starters; they had to be hand cranked. One of the first lessons was to learn the proper way to grasp the handle of the crank so if the engine backfired it wouldn't break one's arm. Starting such an engine in real cold weather was a problem. One Sunday Uncle Clark had a preaching appointment in a neighboring village; he got up early to get the engine started and warmed up before he left. The temperature was below zero and try as hard as he could, he couldn't get the engine started. Frustrated and worried about getting to his appointment, he came in the house and rapped on my bedroom door, asking for help. Jumping into some clothes I hurried out to see what I could do. I first checked the gas, the carburetor and the vibrators which all seemed to be in order. I then tried to crank the engine but the oil was so stiff I couldn't spin it and just ordinary cranking did no good, so I got out the jack and raised one of the back wheels off the ground. I could now spin the whole assembly and the clutch would not have to drag through the heavy frigid oil. On the second spin the engine started and I had Uncle Clark hold the clutch in neutral while I took out the jack and he was on his way. It was just one more trick I taught him to operate that car.

In the Bedford house that year were six roomers, including me. Most of these boys had been there the previous year and according to Uncle Clark they became known as the "Bedford bad boys," because of many infractions of the school rules. I didn't change that reputation. The Bedford family which now consisted of four children lived on the first floor of the house, while the roomers took over the second floor. We arranged our rooms so one was reserved for study. One day I was in this room alone when five-year old Ethel came quietly up the stairs. This floor was off limits for the children, but she thought no one was around. I saw her start for the head of the stairs with her hand over her mouth. When she got down at the bottom I heard her mother say, "Where have

Houghton Seminary Band. I am in center front.

you been? Why didn't you answer when I called?" "I couldn't, Mamma," Ethel replied. "My hand was over my mouth." Later when I got a chance I told Aunt Nell how I saw Ethel with her hand over her mouth just as she said. Aunt Nell had to laugh and thought it was so cute she didn't scold her anymore.

One activity that I enjoyed very much that year was the revival of the school band. It had been inactive for more than a year, but there were a dozen or so men in school who could play some instrument. Since I had been a member of the original organization, they insisted that I be the leader. I had my cornet and with my recent experience of playing with the Belfast band, I accepted. The *Houghton Star* in the June, 1915 issue carried a picture of the band showing eleven members and naming me as "leader."

The band was asked to play at several school functions and the most memorable came in the late fall with the dedication of Old Copperhead's new grave. The old grave, that was near our old house, was being eroded so much that there was danger of it being washed into the gully. Some of the people in the village and in the school became interested and formed a group to move the site. They selected a place on the campus near the brow of the hill which looked out over the Genesee River Valley toward the hills beyond. A large glacial boulder was located in the hills back of the campus and that summer it was moved to mark the spot of Copperhead's new resting place. The boulder was set on a concrete base and a metal plaque was attached. The plaque is inscribed as follows:

COPPERHEAD
The Last One of
The Seneca Tribe of Indians
That Lived in the Town of
Caneadea, ·New York
was buried here.
His Wife died some years
before his death.
He died March 23, 1864.
He said he was 120 years old.

The dedication of the boulder was set for a Saturday afternoon in the late fall. President Luckey was in charge of the ceremony, and he requested the band to play for the event. Before the program began, President Luckey told me that he would be the last speaker and to have the band ready to play "America" as soon as he finished. He repeated, "Do this without any introduction." The band assembled and played a few marches as the crowd gathered. I then gave instructions to the band to have the music ready and start playing "America" on my signal. It was a cold windy afternoon, with a long opening prayer followed by remarks by several dignitaries. Everyone began to shiver before President Luckey began to speak. Then, when he spoke for about ten minutes I thought he had made a good conclusion and had the band all set to play, but he started again. This happened two or three times. The crowd was getting restless and some were leaving, so when President Luckey made a long pause, I considered it the end. I gave the signal and the band gave forth with a loud rendition of "America." The audience gave a loud applause, but I thought I saw a funny look on President Luckey's face. I didn't know until much later that I had cut off part of his speech. However, he never said a word to me about it and as the band led a snake dance around the campus, several people told me how glad they were to have the band end the speeches.

If the students in the nearby dorm ever think they hear Old Copperhead not resting peacefully in his new grave because it was not completely dedicated, they can blame me. Anyway, I lived for some time near his original, long isolated and neglected grave, and heard his spirit among the pine trees protesting his fate. Now he has been given a prominent site and his marker, "The Boulder," has been selected by the college students as the title of their annual yearbook. Certainly now his spirit should enjoy his happy hunting grounds.

That year the college was organizing a debate team to compete with a nearby school. Since I was taking a course in debate, I was selected to try out for the team. Two teams were formed and a formal debate was held with some college teachers acting as judges. I made my original presentation as a member of one team and was selected to be one of the speakers in rebuttal. However, one boy on my team thought he could make such a strong rebuttal that he pressured me into letting him take my place. My teammates were surprised and disgusted to have him take over, and it killed my chance to make the team.

I didn't feel too bad about not making the debate team, as they had to spend a lot of time during the spring vacation preparing and I had other plans in the offing. Norah had gone to her home in Cazenovia for the Christmas vacation, but for the spring recess she had been invited to visit a classmate from Northwestern who had married and lived in Buffalo. Since Norah and I had so few times to be together when we felt free, she suggested that I get away and visit friends in Buffalo at the same time. Uncle Clark was going to be on a trip during that time and expected me to look after everything, including the two hundred laying hens he kept. He was afraid that if a stranger tried to take care of them, they would stop laying, but I had done it before and all was fine, so he felt free to be away. Under those conditions I hesitated to leave, but I found the boy who had worked last year and he was willing to take over my chores. I talked with Aunt Nell about the situation and she thought it would be all right and encouraged me to go for a few days. She had met Norah and liked her very much. Also, she was sympathetic to our situation as she had been a student in Houghton when she met Uncle Clark who was a teacher, and they had dated during the year.

When the week arrived, I hired a man in the village to take us to Wesley for the B&S train to Buffalo. In the city Norah went to stay with her friend who lived on the west side, while I had made arrangements to stay with my friends, the Fagans, who lived near the center of the city. So we were properly widely separated at night, but got together everyday to visit some of the museums and art galleries, and attended matinees in the afternoons and theaters in the evenings. In Houghton we had heard theaters included with pool parlors, dance halls and saloons as places of vice that should never be visited. However, neither of us agreed with that view about the theater, so didn't feel at all guilty. After four full days we returned to Houghton to get some needed rest before school started again. Also, I had the time to see that everything was in order at the Bedford place before Uncle Clark returned. When he checked, he expressed his pleasure of finding things so good and especially pleased to find that his hens were producing more eggs per day than when he left. For Norah and me that trip to Buffalo brought us closer together than ever.

It was during this year that Mother made a big decision, to give up the hospital in Belfast and marry a man from Fillmore by the name of Arnold. There were several things that influenced her decision. First, the hospital wasn't doing the business that was anticipated and the health authorities were beginning to question her facilities. She had met Mr. Arnold some years before when nursing in Fillmore and since his wife had died, he kept seeing Mother. He offered her a home for herself and the younger children and since she had been the sole supporter of the family for seven years, a promise of such a relief seemed good. I was told just before that they had a quiet wedding, with

Uncle Clark officiating. So the hospital was closed and the equipment sold and the household goods put in storage.

Leeta went to live with them in Fillmore and got a job as telephone operator. Ula, who had left school to work in the hospital, now got a job in a millinery shop and learned how to trim ladies' hats. She became so good that the woman who operated the shop recommended her to a big hat factory in Buffalo where she went to learn the trade from the ground up. Dale and Faye were entered in the Fillmore school, so it seemed to be a good move for all. I was so busy with my own work that I didn't see much of them but with this new arrangement, I felt more on my own.

One thing I missed very much this year was a place to play basketball. For over two years Uncle Clark had been the prime mover in building a real gymnasium on the college campus. The summer before he had secured permission to tear down the old seminary building and with the help of students had done so, cleaning thousands of bricks which were piled on the campus waiting until he could raise enough funds to build. It was the following year before the building was completed, and by that time Uncle Clark had left Houghton to become the President of Central College in South Carolina. But since he had done so much to make the gym possible, the college honored him by naming it the "Bedford Gymnasium." It served its purpose for the next sixty odd years.

The college junior class consisted of about twenty members, the largest one in the history of the school up to that time. There were some fine students in that group; a few I recall such as Gertrude Graves, Harriet Meeker, Kip Babbitt, Leo Raub, Wilford Kaufman and Edna Hester. All of these and others went on to Oberlin or other colleges to obtain their degrees. Early in the year the class met, and I was elected the class president, which I considered an honor.

To celebrate our year together, the class decided to spend Memorial Day with a class picnic at Letchworth Park. Our lunch was prepared at the girls' dorm, and we took the train to Portageville. Many of us had been there before, but it was fun to take the long hike up the hill and then across the gorge on the railroad bridge, then down to visit the two upper falls, doing this as a congenial group. At noon we shared our lunch near the Indian long house and then took the long hike to the lower falls. On the way Kip Babbitt and I noticed what appeared to be a trail which followed a small stream that flowed over the side of the gorge into the river below. On the return trip after viewing the falls, Kip and I inspected this trail closer. It appeared that some people had climbed down the gorge at this point. Wanting to do something different, we dared each other to try it.

Following the trail with care we reached the bottom of the gorge and then followed the river along the rocky floor of the gorge. There was some driftwood left by the river when it was at flood stage, and several dead rabbits and a carcass of a deer, all of which apparently had fallen

117

over the edge of the cliff. When we reached a point which we figured was in front of the mansion where we had all agreed to meet at the end of the afternoon, we looked and it appeared as if someone had scaled the rocky 400 foot side of the gorge. Rather than going back to the point where we had descended, we took the dare to climb straight up. Carefully selecting good handholds and secure footsteps we made it to the top. A number of our group had assembled at this point and were amazed to see us appear over the top of the cliff.

After we had explained how we found a way to get down the side of the gorge and up again, Gertrude Graves and Harriet Meeker insisted they wanted to try it. We tried to discourage them saying how difficult it was and how much danger was involved, but they needled us into showing them the way. Again, it wasn't difficult to descend but when we got to the spot where we had climbed up, it looked impossible to help them up such a sheer cliff. We all knew this was the spot which it was rumored that the young bride who was supposed to live in the mansion had plunged to her death. But the girls were determined, so Kip went ahead to lead the way and check their handholds while I followed to make sure their feet were firmly planted. Slowly and carefully we scaled the cliff and the girls were really thrilled. Probably they are the only girls from Houghton who ever accomplished such a feat.

After the class had such a wonderful time on the day at Letchworth Park, we realized we would not be together much longer because more than half the class planned to transfer to other colleges to get their degrees and the girls suggested we have a class banquet to end the year. As class president, it became my duty to appoint committees to hold such an affair and to check to see that everything was carried out. We received permission to use one of the music rooms in the main building and a committee decorated it for the event. The food was prepared in the dorm kitchen and carried over by a few girls from the sophomore class who were asked to serve as waitresses. They were eager to do it so they could see how such a banquet was done.

We invited President and Mrs. Luckey to be our guests and the program committee arranged a nice program of the talent in the class following the meal. President Luckey, when asked to speak, praised us as pioneers in bringing a real college atmosphere to the campus. He said such an event would help him in getting a charter for the college so the junior classes in the future wouldn't have to break up but could get a degree from Houghton. Ten years later he was successful.

One of the big events at commencement time was the annual "Willard J. Houghton Oratorical Contest." Mr. Houghton had left a trust fund; the interest could be used as a first and second prize for such an affair. The money wasn't much, but the honor of winning was considered very high. Having done some debating, I got interested in speaking and thought I would try writing an oration. The rules specified that the orations would be judged 50% on composition and 50% on delivery. Professor Smith, my English instructor, encouraged me to enter the contest and since each contestant had to have a faculty sponsor, one who could act as an advisor and would approve of the contents of the oration, I asked Professor Smith to be mine. He consented and taught me more about writing than I had learned in all my classes. I had heard these contests in my years at Houghton and since most of the students who entered were studying for the ministry, the topics they selected were either about the church or religion. I wanted mine to be different and after doing some research, I found several interesting articles in the current magazines about a new form of city government called "The Commission Type of City Government." With Professor Smith's approval, I made that my topic. I then wrote what I thought was a good oration, but when I submitted it, I was told it was too long. The rules stated that it had to be under 800 words. So I cut it down and then began a series of rewriting, changing words and phrases, polishing it here and there until it was accepted. I had never realized before what writing over and over would do for a paper. In later years when English teachers would complain about the poor compositions their students wrote, I would suggest this method of teaching, but I never got much response.

After the oration was finished I began to memorize it and went to Norah, as head of the speech department, for help. I needed help, alright. She told me I was too tense and to pitch my voice lower. I didn't know what to do with my hands. I wanted to put them in my pockets, but I was told that was taboo. Since my room was near the campground auditorium, I frequently went over there and got on the stage to speak to the empty seats. There I became quite at ease, but when I tried to speak before anyone, I found it very difficult.

I wish I had kept a copy of my oration, but I can still recall some of it. I started with the statement, "Every age has its problems and every generation attempts a solution. Today the pressing problem is in the governing of our expanding cities." I then developed my theme of how the mayor-city council form of government had become corrupt in many cities. A new form of city government had been born on the "wings of a storm" in Texas. It was a plan of five commissioners who brought order out of chaos and it was so so successful that many cities were now forming this new commission type of government.

The best part of my oration was the conclusion. It went something like this: "Oh, City with your bustling noisy streets, your great factories and office buildings, your museums and art galleries, your hurrying throbbing mobs of mankind from many lands making you the center of the greatest civilization on earth; throw off your yoke of outmoded form of government, break your chains of corruption and take on a new clean type of self government." Then I waved the flag a little and ended with an appeal for help from the "God of Nations."

The night of the contest finally came. I was nervous, not only at the thought of speaking before an audience, but also I knew I was on the spot as everyone knew I had been going with Norah, consequently, they expected she had given me extra help. There were ten contestants and before going on the stage, we drew numbers for position of speaking. I drew number four, which was good since I didn't have to break the ice and it would be early enough so the audience wouldn't be bored.

The last instruction I received from Norah was, "Don't be nervous and don't worry about forgetting, just think of the first line and the rest will come to you." It was fine advice, but when we were seated on the stage and I looked at the audience, I was stagestruck. For the life of me I couldn't think of one word of my speech. Fortunately, I was not the first speaker. I pulled myself together when the first speaker started, thought of my first line and calmed down.

When I was introduced I was still nervous and pitched my voice too high, but as I proceeded and got into the middle of the oration, I could feel that I had the interest of my audience and I calmed down. Then when I began my conclusion I really sensed what capturing and holding an audience meant. I sat down to a loud applause and when I saw Aunt Nell and Uncle Clark nod to each other, I felt I must have done alright.

When the last speech was made and the judges retired to make their decision, all of us on the stage sat nervously trying to listen to a musical interlude. Finally, Professor McDowell, who was chairman of the affair, received the results. When he announced my name as the first place winner there was a loud shout from the students. When he presented me with the prize money, I thought he was sort of kidding me when he said he hoped I would continue a career in public speaking. The students in the audience took up the game by laughing and razzing me. I got so confused that I sat down before the only girl in the contest received the second prize.

The next day Professor McDowell called me into his room and apologized for embarrassing me. He said he didn't realize how his remarks would be taken and that he was serious when he said I showed a lot of ability and I should consider a career where I could use my gift of public speaking. Then during the next day or two I was drawn aside by several teachers, including Bill Frazier, wanting to know where I found that conclusion. They all said it was the best they ever heard and implied that I must have found it. I assured them all that it was original but I suspected they didn't quite believe me. One man who stopped me said he was one of the judges for the composition of the orations, and he was sure I would win first place as mine stood out far above all the others, and he too wanted to know where I got the idea for the conclusion. My answer was the same to all, and I never revealed my secret that I had got my idea from reading some of the Greek orations that I found in a book of translations in the school library.

Entering that contest, writing and delivering that oration with the successful conclusion, had a profound influence on my life. It gave me some self assurance, which I very badly needed, some confidence that maybe I did have some ability, and it gave me further inspiration to find a way to finish my college education.

On the last Sunday of the school year, Norah and I spent the afternoon on the Thayer farm. Mrs. Thayer had long been a friend of Norah and some of the other school teachers and had furnished them a place to get away for a time from the pressures of the school dorm. We had a chance to be alone for a time to say our goodbyes. She asked me to visit her that summer at Cazenovia, but I knew it was impossible as I had to earn some money if I ever expected to get to Oberlin for my senior year of college. I also said my goodbyes to the Bedfords, who were getting ready to move to South Carolina. It was to be many years before I saw them again. Having no other place to go, I packed my trunk and left for Fillmore, not expecting to stay, but needing some sort of headquarters.

CHAPTER 10

OBERLIN

As soon as I arrived in Fillmore, Mother showed me a letter she had from Dr. Sam R. Williams, the head of the Physics Department of Oberlin College. She said she had known him in her early days. How she found out he was at Oberlin, I never knew. Anyway, she had written him saying I wanted to attend Oberlin the next year but needed a part time job to put myself through. She asked him if he could help in any way. He replied that while there were a number of jobs available during the year, most, if not all, were taken by students who had been there for a time. For someone to transfer for the senior year and expect to find work was very unlikely. His suggestion was for me to come right away and take some courses in summer school. He was certain that I could find plenty of work during the summer and I would have the advantage of becoming known which would increase my chances of finding a job the rest of the year.

Although I hadn't planned on anything like Dr. Williams' suggestion, I liked the idea. The trouble was I was flat broke and didn't see how I could get to Oberlin until I earned some money. I didn't have a prospect for a job but intended to look for one at once as I had not intended to stay in Fillmore. I discussed the matter with Mother and she suggested I ask Mr. Arnold for a loan to get to Oberlin and start in the college. I had been told that he was very tight with his money, but I got up my nerve and asked him for a loan of $50.00. His reply was he wouldn't loan me the money but would help me get it from the bank. Together we went to the bank and he co-signed a bank note with me to get the money.

With $50.00 in my pocket I boarded a train for Buffalo, took the night boat to Cleveland and an interurban trolley to Oberlin. It was the reverse of my trip when I left Ohio to go to Houghton eight years before.

My introduction to Oberlin was a hungry one. I left Cleveland before lunch time expecting to arrive in Oberlin to eat. However, due to a delay I arrived well past their lunch time. I couldn't find even a lunch counter, so I bought some fruit and called that my lunch. Checking my bag I walked to the campus in the center of the town and inquired where the physics building was located. Entering the building I found

Dr. Williams in his office. I introduced myself and liked him at once. The feeling seemed to be mutual and in all the time I worked with him in his laboratory and sat in his class, my opinion never changed.

He told me he was glad I decided to come and told me that Dr. Lutz, a history professor, was going to Chicago to teach in summer school, but his wife didn't want to take their two-year old son to the city for the summer. If she could find a student who was willing to stay in her house at night, she would remain in Oberlin. He asked me if I was interested in doing so for my room. Of course I said, "Yes," as it would be a big help on my expenses for the summer. Together we went to meet Dr. Lutz and family at their home and after a brief time all arrangements were made. I was given a small room at the top of the stairs on the second floor, which was all I needed. All I had to do was to be there every night and on a few occasions baby-sit with the young boy while Mrs. Lutz attended some meetings. For my board I made arrangements to take my meals at Talcott, the one women's dorm that stayed open during the summer. A number of the men students took their meals there, so it was a chance to get acquainted with a large group of students. It wasn't long before I felt right at home.

When I registered I placed my name with the college employment bureau and in a few days they notified me of a professor who was to be away for the summer and wanted someone to mow his lawn once a week. I took the job and the news spread that I was available, so in a short time I had all the lawns I could do. Then I picked up several odd jobs, such as gardening, varnishing floors and washing windows; in fact, it was amazing how the wives of the college professors sent me to their friends with the reputation that I was a good worker and could do almost anything. None of these jobs paid very much, but all together I was able to accumulate enough to get started in the fall term.

After my transcript came from Houghton I checked with the dean to see what I needed to meet the requirements for graduation. I selected physics as my major and mathematics and chemistry as minors. I learned that included in the necessary number of hours I had to take were one semester in art appreciation and another semester in senior Bible. The Bible was usually taught by Professor King, but not given in the summer. The course in art was, so I signed up for it. Professor Martin gave this course, and he had a reputation on the campus as an expert in his field, but at times he was rather grouchy and very sarcastic. However, an incident happened soon after the class started that changed my opinion of him. The class met in the late morning in a room where the sun beat in through one window in particular. I was seated in the back of the room and Professor Martin asked me to pull the window curtain down on this window. I tried to do so, but found the curtain had been raised so high it had caught back of the roller. After several attempts with no success, I interrupted Professor Martin and told him about the difficulty. He got out of his chair and came back to the window, took hold of the cord and gave it a hard pull, but nothing happened. He then turned to me and said so all the class could hear, "You were very wise not to pull so hard as to ruin the curtain. I know a lot of people who would have wrecked it." Right then I lost any fear I might have had for him and enjoyed the class.

The area that Professor Martin had selected for this summer course was the appreciation of Italian sculpture. It centered on the life and work of Donatello, which opened up to me an entirely new world of knowledge. I am sure the people in Houghton would have been horrified to see the nude statues that we studied, but for me it opened a window of life that I could always enjoy. I know there were many generations of Oberlin students who shared my feelings.

Professor Martin was an authority in his field and his lectures were masterful, but if he saw the class was getting weary or bored, he would stop and tell some incident in his life, whether it had anything to do with the topic or not. One that he told on himself and I expect he told it to every class, was that he said his wife had a leaky faucet in the kitchen. She could not get a plumber to come for a long time and kept fussing about it. Finally, he got tired of hearing about the faucet, got a wrench and screwdriver, took the faucet apart, and replaced the washer. When finished, he turned to his wife and said, "There, any fool could have done that." "Yes, my dear," she replied, "that's why I asked you." Just to have sat in the class with such an instructor was an education in itself.

All the summer classes were held in the mornings, so my afternoons were free to work, with one exception. Dr. Williams took me under his wing and made me his assistant in doing some original research on the theory of magnetism. We spent at least one afternoon a week in a large room working on his experiment.

The apparatus that he had made for the experiment consisted of a long solenoid in the center of which was placed a quarter-inch by three-foot iron rod. This rod was demagnetized and one end placed against a fixed point, while the other end was fitted against a movable lever. Attached to the lever was a small mirror. A beam of light was shone on the mirror and the reflection was directed into the lens of a camera. This made a weightless lever which would register on the film any motion of the mirror. The camera was equipped with a crank which would turn the film and thus a dark line would show how much, if any, that the mirror moved.

To magnetize the rod an electric current was sent through the wires of the solenoid. In order to gradually change the magnetic field, a trough was placed below the solenoid and filled with an electrolyte solution. An inclined rod was placed over the top and contact was made with a device which slid along the rod and had two metal plates which dipped into the solution. Since the amount of current was directly proportional to the amount of surface exposed to the electrolyte, the current and thus, the magnetic field, could be uniformly increased.

It took two people to run the experiment, one to operate the camera and the other the slide. We took turns at each. One thing I discovered in operating the slide was that it was essential to keep a good pressure on the rod. Once I was careless and lifted the rod just a little and the 110 volt current shot through my arm. I never forgot it as my arm was almost paralyzed for a time.

The second thing I learned was not to talk while we were working. The first day after we started I made some remark about the weather, but got no response from Dr. Williams and when a second remark got no response either, I took the cue. Sometimes we would work for two hours with nothing said except the curt orders for the next move. This showed how serious Dr. Williams took the work, because outside the laboratory he was very pleasant and liked to talk.

This experiment showed that the iron rod did increase in length up to a certain point and then increasing the magnetic field had no effect. It was an experimental proof of the theory of magnetism which was then being proposed. The theory stated that a magnetic metal was composed of tiny unit magnets and as the metal became magnetized, they would all begin to point in the same direction. The unit magnets were probably the molecules of the metal and were oblong in shape, the reasoning continued, thus explaining why the rod increased in length.

Dr. Williams had the results of this experiment published in a leading scientific magazine. I was quite thrilled to have my name in the article giving me credit for help as an advanced student. Later, I also worked on another experiment with Dr. Williams, and it was also published. The article was entitled "The Determination of the Constant of a Solenoid," and it appeared in the September, 1916, issue of the *Journal of the Franklin Institute.* At the conclusion of the article was the following, "Expressions of appreciation are due Mr. Ray Calhoon, an advanced student in the department, for the valuable assistance rendered in making long tedious series of observations."

In order to have me receive college credit for my work, Dr. Williams had me research the scientific literature on everything published about magnetism. Since he had received his Doctorate degree from a university in Germany, he had all the latest scientific publications from that country. My one year of German was stretched a great deal to read these articles, but with the aid of a large German–English dictionary, I was able to extract the substance of each article. Many of the scientific words were not in the dictionary, but knowing that in the German language new words are often coined by using a number of small words to make the whole, I was able to decipher the meaning of most of them. At this time Germany was the leading country in scientific research, so for Dr. Williams to publish an important contribution in the field of magnetism was a big credit to both him and Oberlin.

A short time before the end of the summer session, Mrs. Lutz was ready to move into a new house that was built. She asked me to help pack and get things ready for the movers. I did help her move and also to settle the furniture in the new house and then she informed me that

Dr. Lutz would be home in a few days and she no longer needed me. So I was out of a room. Owen Walton, who had been in my class in Houghton and was also a transfer, was staying in a house alone while the people were away for the summer, so when he heard of my plight, he invited me to spend the rest of the summer with him.

When the summer session closed the middle of August, Talcott House also closed, so I had to find a new place to eat. I learned that some of the boys who had been working at the Martin Inn waiting on tables for their board, were leaving. I went at once to see Nate Cooke, who ran the Inn, to see if I could get a job. I only talked with him a few minutes, telling about my experience and the need of work, when he said, "Come to work tomorrow." I was there only a few days when he informed me that he needed someone who would take care of the desk at night and also serve short order snacks. He asked me if I wanted to do it and I agreed. The only drawback was I would close the hotel office at 11 p.m., take the money in a bag to my room, and then had to get it back at 6 a.m. to open the office. However, I learned a lot about running a hotel and became a good short-order cook. Nate did a lot of the cooking and was noted for his pies. I am sure I ate more pie during that four weeks than I had in all my previous life.

Even with my work at the Inn I still had time to keep up my lawns and other work. The last week before the fall term began I was given a job in the Chemistry Building. Besides unpacking a shipment of new apparatus, I varnished the student desks. Working there I had the opportunity to meet the chemistry professors, including Dr. Holmes, who was the department head. Dr. Holmes was a very dynamic man who was becoming world-wide known for his work on colloids. At first he seemed rather aloof, but when I became better acquainted, I found him to be a very warm and friendly person.

I knew that Gertrude Graves and Harriet Meeker were coming to Oberlin for their senior year, and they wrote they would arrive on the noon train on the Friday before school opened. I was completing my work of varnishing the desks that morning when Dr. Holmes came in to inspect the building. He was very generous with his praise of my work, so I had the nerve to ask if I could leave a little early to meet my friends at the station. "Of course," he said, "go at once." I did meet the train and helped the girls get their baggage to Talcott where they were to room. I introduced them to the matron and since she knew me, I felt it helped them to get a good start.

Soon, as the students began to arrive for the fall term, the whole town began to take on a different air. It was like a giant waking after a long sleep. Walton and I found a room together in a private house near the center of the campus. There were four other senior men in the same building; we took over the second floor and arranged our sleeping so we had one room free for study. I would have liked to stay at the Martin Inn waiting on tables for my board, and Nate would have liked me to stay, but he had promised others who were returning so I had to go on a substitute list.

For the fall term I registered for an advanced course in physics with Dr. Williams, for a class in Senior Bible, which was required, and one in organic chemistry with Dr. Holmes. The class in physics seemed almost like a continuation of the work I had been doing with Dr. Williams all summer. The class in Senior Bible was usually given by President King, but for some reason he gave it to Dr. Bosworth from the Theological Seminary. Dr. Bosworth was very much like William Frazier in Houghton, so I enjoyed that class very much. The text we used was *Rational Living* by President King, and each student was required to write a 1,000 word review of the book. A blank book was furnished each student so the finished products were uniform. Since this review had been a requirement for many terms, there were many former books that had been graded and returned to students around the campus. Such books were readily available either from a friend or for sale. It was common knowledge that these books were graded by hired readers, so most students didn't feel guilty for using former books as a basis for a review. Paul Fall, who had been an Oberlin graduate a year ahead of me, let me borrow his book which I used as a guide for points but put them into my own words. Paul had an A rating, but I was happy with a B. The second semester I started this course with Dr. King, and I had difficulty understanding him. I dropped out before the end of that semester, depending on the one term to meet my requirements.

I found Dr. Holmes a dynamic and interesting instructor in organic chemistry. However, I found that my one semester course in chemistry at Clarkson was too brief to give me a good foundation. I worked the hardest I ever did in any subject just to keep up with the class. I liked the lab work fine and made good progress. One day Dr. Holmes came into the lab while we were at work and interviewed each student. It gave me a chance to tell him how I was struggling. He proceeded to quiz me in detail about the experiment I was doing and then said, "Fine, keep it up, you'll master it, don't think of giving up." I felt better and kept working hard and someway got a good mark at the end. I have often wondered if knowing Dr. Holmes before school helped me, but knowing Dr. Holmes as I did, I don't think he let it influence him.

Two things which happened in the chemistry lab stick in my memory. One was when we were making acetylene gas and had to construct a burner from glass tubing to show how the gas would make a good light. When the whole class had the burners ready we lit them and started a parade around the room. Right in the midst of our demonstration Dr. Holmes walked in. Usually he was in the lab only long enough to get us started and then left us to work on our own. This time he came in unexpectedly. When he saw us he just grinned and said, "Time for the parade to end." We quietly marched back to our desks. This is one example as to why he was a popular professor on the campus and since he was known world-wide in his field, it was considered an honor to be in his class.

The second episode happened when we were doing urine analysis.

For several days buckets had been placed in the men's toilet with signs requesting contributions of urine. The buckets were brought up to the lab and samples issued to each student. There were three girls in the class with some twenty men. The girls were curious as to where the urine came from and one girl in particular who had proven to be somewhat of a pest went around the room asking about it. The fellows were rather embarrassed and put her off by saying to ask someone else. She persisted until the fellow next to me said, "If you really want to know, all of us boys contributed, but if we didn't have enough, we were going to ask you for some." She walked away redfaced but didn't bother us again the rest of the year. All the fellows who heard held their sides but waited until after class to have their laugh.

I signed up for second year French but dropped it after the first session. My one year at Houghton taken two years before was not enough preparation for such a class where they began by speaking only French in class. I also had an advanced course in physics with Dr. Williams. It was customary for the department head to teach the advanced courses, leaving the freshmen classes to instructors.

I found Oberlin quite different from either Houghton or Clarkson. There were three separate parts to the institution. First, the main part was the College of Arts and Sciences. Next was a fine Conservatory of Music, while the third was a small Theology Seminary. The College, founded in 1833, had a long history of fine traditions. One was its well known emphasis on high scholarship. It was a good thing that I had the good foundation which I received at Houghton, or I would never have been able to succeed.

Oberlin was the first College in the U.S. to admit women on an equal basis with men and grant them a degree. It was so popular with women that only the policy of the College keeping the entering class about equal numbers of men and women kept it from becoming a women's college. Also, Oberlin was very active in the anti-slavery days, and a well-established underground station for escaped slaves became famous. The college was one of the first to admit blacks for higher education, and it continued to have a number of black students.

Although the College was now an independent institution, it was in its early days under the sponsorship of the Congregational Church. Some of the rules instituted by the Church still existed. For example, there were no alcoholic beverages permitted on the campus, in fact the town was dry by local ordinance. Smoking by students was forbidden. There was no dancing permitted at social functions. Oberlin was unique among colleges as no Greek letter secret societies were allowed. In many ways these rules were similar to those at Houghton and in marked contrast to the freedom at Clarkson. However, the rules never seemed so strict as at Houghton, because there was more freedom to come and go and a good relationship existed between the sexes. There was so much activity on the campus that most of the restrictions weren't noticed.

During the year a movement was started to remove the ban against smoking. A survey taken by the faculty revealed that seventy-five percent of the men in the college did smoke at times. Personally, the ban didn't bother me, for while I had smoked during my year at work and while at Clarkson, I didn't mind going without as long as others around didn't smoke. Some few years later both the restriction against smoking and dancing were removed. The college began to change with the times, but one thing that has never changed was the ban against fraternities. Periodically attempts were made to organize these societies, but they always failed. The most notorious was the year after I graduated when the whole football team was suspended when it was learned that the members had joined a fraternity.

There was one regulation that was new to me. The college worked under an honor system which was explained by the student handbook as follows: "It required that, to an examination or test and such other work as the teacher may desire, there be appended the signed statement that help has been neither given nor received." Students were left unsupervised during a test. The system made it compulsory for a student to report any violation that he might see to the Student Honor Court. I never saw any violation and never heard of anyone else who did.

Oberlin in my time was a strong leader in intercollegiate athletics. Dr. Savage was the head of the Physical Education Department and was not only a leader in developing the right kind of teams in the college but was a leader in organizing good sportsmanship across the country. As a coach of football he made Oberlin a leader in the state. In 1914 Oberlin had a 50–50 season but as the student handbook states, "The reputation of Oberlin is such that every team in the state would rather beat her than any other college." Oberlin played Ohio State that year holding that team to 39 points and in 1915 produced another good team. It was the custom in those days for the large universities to schedule a small college team as an opener of the season. The small colleges were willing to compete because of the large fee they could get, although they never expected to win. That fall Oberlin opened the season for Cornell on October 2, in Ithaca; Cornell was then one of the strongest teams in the country. During the first half, Oberlin scored six points on a touchdown. Though Cornell won the game by a low score, it was a triumph for Oberlin as they were the only team to cross Cornell's goal line that year. It was during the following summer that the whole football team was suspended for joining a secret society. Consequently, the next season was a disaster. As an opener Oberlin played Ohio State that fall and lost 101 to 0. There were fellows on that varsity team who normally could not make a class team.

Not only did the college support a strong varsity program but also a vigorous intermural one. Dr. Savage became noted for this program. Being a transfer student, I wasn't eligible for a varsity team, but it made no difference; I was welcome to practice with the team. I did this for two reasons. First, Walton told me if I went out I would be given a suit and then could play with him on the senior class team. Second, I wanted to learn all I could about the game. I was not heavy enough to be a football player, but it made no difference to·the coaching staff, so I was treated like everyone else. After the season was underway a schedule for class games was arranged. These games were held on Saturday mornings and the seniors were glad to have an extra player. At first I played in the line but after Walton and others were injured, I was shifted to the backfield. Hence, I got a chance to learn about the various positions. These class games attracted considerable interest and the coaching staff was on the side lines to watch. I played the whole season without any bad injury. The things I learned helped me very much in getting a job after college.

When the football season opened a notice was posted inviting everyone who could play a band instrument to meet for the purpose of organizing a band to play for the games. Walton had an alto horn and I got my cornet out and we joined. It was a small outfit, but we did play before and during the home games. We were given a simple uniform and promised at least one trip out of town. This came for the Ohio State game, which was moved from Columbus to Cleveland. This game drew a large crowd and we were thrilled to play for such an event.

One incident happened during that game that made a deep impression on me. "Chick Harley" was the star of the Ohio State team. He was a triple threat man as he could kick, run or pass with superb skill. His favorite play was to fake a punt. He would stand in punt formation, holding the ball as the two opposing ends came in close and then sidestep them at the last second and take off on a long end run. In this game the first time he tried it, one of the ends on the Oberlin team was not fooled and made a beautiful open field tackle. Harley was thrown for a big loss. The crowd gave a big cheer and then as both men rose, Harley reached over and gave the Oberlin player a friendly pat of congratulations. It was such an act of good sportsmanship on the part of a star that the crowd gave him a standing ovation and the Cleveland papers made it a headline in the account of the game. Later as a coach I often told the story to instill the same spirit in my teams.

The Band had traveled to the game in a special trolley but after the game we left on our own to return. Walton and I checked our instruments at the trolley station and found a restaurant. We were more than ready because we had had an early breakfast and no time for lunch. After dinner we decided to take in a movie which was a treat for us. We selected the biggest theater in Cleveland and felt somewhat conspicious in our uniforms. But once inside we spotted several others from the band. We were honored when between pictures they flashed on the screen, "Welcome to the members of Oberlin College Band who are in the audience." We got a big round of applause.

After the football season came basketball. Again, Oberlin had a good team and again I went out for the experience. After my experience with this game at Houghton and Clarkson, I was much more at home and was kept on the squad until they made the final cut before the first varsity game. Walton and I then joined the senior class team. Walton had played on this team during his junior year and introduced me to the captain. The first game was against the freshmen and Walton started as a guard. The freshmen had a special coach and were considered very good. Near the middle of the second half with the freshmen out ahead the captain of our team called me in to substitute for Walton. I hadn't been on the floor more than a minute when I intercepted a long pass. I was a long way from our basket so I dribbled to center court. My team was so surprised to have me get the ball they were in no position to receive a pass, so I took a long shot and it swished through the basket. There was a loud cheer from the sidelines and I looked over to see the men from our rooming house watching the game. Everytime I got the ball, they began to shout, "Cal, Cal," which was my nickname all through my time at Oberlin. With my basket our team woke up and began to play good ball. I made two other long shots besides holding my man scoreless, so while we didn't win the game we had the freshmen worried. After the game the captain said, "Why didn't you tell us you were such a good player?" After that I started every game, which was rather embarrassing as I was displacing Walton and he had introduced me to the captain.

Soon after classes started I got a big break. I had placed my name with the employment office asking especially for a place to wait on tables in one of the college dormitories for my board. At that time they told me there was little chance of my getting such a job as all the houses were signed up the year before and there was a waiting list. I was therefore surprised when the office called me and said that Mrs. Grey, the matron at Lord Cottage, was mad at her waiters and had fired them all. They told me she was a difficult person to work for but suggested I go and talk with her.

Lord was one of the largest women's dormitories and the farthest from the center of the campus. As soon as I could, I hurried to meet Mrs. Grey. She was a small grandmotherly type, and in a few minutes I could tell she was very definite in her ways. But when I told her that I had some experience in waiting on tables she became interested. She said she had taken on four boys with no experience, and I would be the fifth and last if I wanted the job. Of course I did, and thanked her for the chance as it meant that my biggest expense, that for board, was solved.

The next morning Mrs. Grey had all the new waiters assemble and she gave us a lecture. She started by saying she understood that she had a reputation for being strict and she was. She insisted that everyone had to be on time. We were to be there at 7 a.m. ready to serve breakfast at 7:15, lunch at 12:15 and dinner at 6:00 p.m. Since the seniors had to attend chapel once a week in cap and gown, it became a problem at times for me to be on time at noon. Chapel was supposed to be over at

12 noon, but outside speakers would often run overtime. Then I had to take off my cap and gown, roll them under my arm, and run all the way to Lord.

Another thing Mrs. Grey said was she didn't expect any dishes to be dropped. Once would be considered an accident, but twice was a habit and you were through. Her method of having things served was unique as she had an aversion to trays. Only when small dishes, such as pudding, were served for dessert could a tray be used. The dining room was set up with tables down each side with Mrs. Grey as the permanent hostess at the table nearest the kitchen door. Women students were selected on a rotating basis to act as hostess at the other tables.

For the main course, the waiters brought in the meat, potatoes and vegetables in large dishes and the hostess served them on each plate. At the end of that course the waiters had to clear the table of all dishes, including the plates, without using a tray. Nor could one plate be stacked on another. The trick was to take at least three plates between the fingers of the left hand so they fanned out and then balance others up the extended arm. The last two could be held in the right hand. Thus, the table was cleared of from 6 to 8 plates at a time. It was quite a trick, but we soon mastered it.

At the first meeting, Mrs. Grey announced that she would not select a head waiter until she had tried us all out in that position. She said she would start us in alphabetical order and give each one a week's trial. The boy whose name began with a B took the first week and my name came next. I took the second week and she never gave the rest a chance. She never formally appointed me as head waiter, but she never changed me. Since it turned out that I was the only one in the group who had any previous experience as a waiter, they all looked to me for help. They were all perfectly willing that I keep the job as "head" as they were all a little bit afraid of Mrs. Grey.

As head I had only Mrs. Grey's table to serve while the others had two. But I had the responsibility of leading the line in when serving a course and seeing that each was in his proper place. During the meal we stood by our tables to see if anything was needed. When Mrs. Grey gave me the signal I relayed it to the others and we cleared the tables. All was done in a formal fashion and in strict order.

I got along fine with Mrs. Grey and she never found fault with my work, but she did with some of the other boys and she would dress them down like a drill sergeant. I could see why she had the reputation of being hard to work for. However, she and I seemed to have a mutual understanding and while she never complimented me, she never criticized, which was good enough for me.

Between the kitchen and the dining room was a small room where the waiters kept their white coats. They were laundered once a week, but had to be kept spotless at all times. In this room was a table where we ate our meals after finishing the serving. As long as we kept in good standing with the cook we had plenty to eat.

The cook was a black woman who presided over a large kitchen. She was an excellent cook and knew her job. The kitchen was her domain and she let everyone know it. Even Mrs. Grey spoke quietly when she visited the kitchen. As the head waiter, I was the spokesman for the others and right from the beginning I treated her with respect. The result was that we got along fine and at times when needed she would let me help with the food, but none of the others dared to touch a thing.

The cook had a young girl as a helper and when she was introduced to me as the cook's daughter, I nearly fell over, for while the cook was not a deep black, she was definitely colored, while this girl was real white. Fortunately, I kept my composure and gave the girl a warm welcome. She was very shy and never had anything to say unless spoken to. I often wondered how she felt living with the darkly colored people. Oberlin had a number of black students and the town contained many more, but both were well integrated.

On Thanksgiving day a special dinner was planned. Classes were suspended for that day only so all the students were in the dorm. Mrs. Grey ordered a four course dinner with turkey and all the fixings. The kitchen was a beehive of activity and I was given orders as to how things were to be served. After the soup came a special salad. It was the rule at a table that all had to wait until the hostess started to eat before they could begin. At one table at the far end of the room a girl who was a noted talker was the hostess. When the salad was served she was in the midst of a big story and instead of beginning to eat so the others could start, she kept on talking. So when Mrs. Grey gave me the signal to have the salad plates removed, no one at that table had touched it. When the waiter started to remove the plates the girl protested, and he came to me for instructions. I whispered to Mrs. Grey the situation, but she bluntly said, "Take the plates." She also muttered something about that fool girl. So the people at that table lost most of their salad and while the girl was quite chagrined, I don't think it ever stopped her chattering.

Everything else went fine until it came time for the dessert. The cook had prepared some homemade ice cream down in the basement. To serve this we could use some large trays. I had all the waiters assemble with their trays in the basement, and while the kitchen help dipped the cream into small dishes, each loaded his tray with the right number. At the top of the stairs was a narrow door and I cautioned each one as they started to be very careful. Taking my tray, I arranged all in order and led the way. Then as we paused for the last waiter to appear, I heard a loud crash. Putting my tray down I hurried back to see what had happened and just as I feared, this last man who was the most awkward caught his tray in the door. Tray, dishes and ice cream all crashed down the stairs to the floor of the basement.

For once the cook who would "blow up" over some minor accident, kept calm. I grabbed an extra stack of dishes and an extra scoop and helped fill them. All worked hard to get the tray loaded again. The cook, who I knew was burning inside, never said a word but kept making little clucking noises. All I could think of was a flustered mother hen. When the tray was ready I took it up the stairs myself and got the line organized. When we went in a bit late, Mrs. Grey wanted to know what had happened. I knew she must have heard the noise so I told her. However, the dinner was so good and everyone enjoyed it so much we didn't get "bawled out" as expected. The cook told me how much she appreciated my help to save the day, so our relationship became even more friendly.

Ever since I had said goodby to Norah in Houghton, we had kept up a steady correspondence. At the beginning of the summer she wrote that she was glad to be home and they had lots of company and she wished that I had been one of them. After I had told her some about my work with Dr. Williams, she wrote, "I was glad to hear about what you are doing. I don't know much about it but hope you do." After I had told her about my working while going to summer school, she wrote, "You better not try to do too much. It is too much to work night and day. If you lose your health your education will not do much good. Don't let your ambition get the best of you." I was glad for her interest in my welfare, but it didn't change my pace. I was fully committed to work and study and for once my health remained good.

After Norah returned to Houghton she kept me informed about the affairs at the school. In almost every letter she wrote how she wished I was there so we could take a walk and talk. In one letter she wrote, "I just found out that the faculty knew all about us going to Buffalo last year. I thought we had been real secret about it but the other day Miss Thurston said something about it, and I asked her how she knew, she said everyone knew it for she heard others talking about it after we had gone. Isn't that the limit; it sure is impossible to do anything they won't find out."

As the Christmas vacation approached, I found out that the whole school closed down for two weeks and Lord would be closed. If I stayed in Oberlin I would have to pay for my meals. I decided it would be as cheap for me to go to Fillmore and maybe I could see Norah in Houghton before she left for home. I wrote her about the possibility and she replied, "Yours rec'd. Your plans are alright unless the school here may be closed on Wed. Otherwise I will look for you on Thur."

As it turned out Houghton did not close on Wednesday and I got there in time to attend chapel Thursday morning with five or six other Oberlin students who were former Houghton students; we sat as a group in the rear of the room. At the close of the chapel program we created quite a sensation when we rose and gave a loud "Hi-O-Hi, Ohio, Hi-Hi-O-Hi, Oberlin." It was a big surprise to the students and they all turned around to see who dared to do such a thing. For a few seconds there was a complete silence. Then it dawned on them what it meant and they gave us a good round of applause.

135

I got a chance to see Norah for a little time and she invited me to visit her in Cazenovia after Christmas. She wanted me to meet her folks, and we could have a few days together. I told her I would come if she found it was agreeable with her folks, and she could let me know in Fillmore before Christmas Day. I wasn't keen about staying in Fillmore, but there seemed nothing else I could do. Mother and the children were glad to see me, but Mr. Arnold was very cool. Right away I could sense that things were not as rosy as had been expected. Mother had to do some nursing in order to have any money to give the younger children, while both Leeta and Ula were working to practically support themselves. But in spite of what I saw and things Mother told me, I thought things would turn out all right.

The day after Christmas I left for Cazenovia. It was the first of many visits I was to make at the Riggall home. As soon as I arrived I was made welcome by Norah's parents and I felt right at home. The Riggall house was not far from the center of the village, which had a number of attractive stores, and within easy walking distance of Cazenovia Seminary from which Norah had graduated. Like many of the houses in the village this house had been built by a retired farmer and made me think of the many farmhouses where I had stayed as a boy. There were electric lights in the village, but Mr. Riggall refused to install them in his house. He said it was just a game for the big companies to get people to wire their houses and then they would keep raising the rates. The kerosene lamps that he grew up with were good enough and he never changed.

Norah's mother was a wonderful cook and all the time I was there we had big meals. Her father had run a butcher shop in the village for many years, and although now retired, he knew good meat and wouldn't have anything else. Homemade bread and wonderful pies spoiled us for going back to institutional cooking.

Since I was at home with their kind of life style, I felt like I was part of the family. Norah said afterward that I was the only boyfriend she brought home that her family approved of. Cazenovia was noted for snow in the winter and this year was no exception. Mr. Riggall kept a horse and Norah and I enjoyed some great rides behind him in a cutter. In the evening it was warm and cozy around a big base burner stove in the living room. Norah and I thoroughly enjoyed the time together and all too soon it was time to say goodbye. It was to be a long time before I could return.

Back at Oberlin the first semester soon came to an end and I passed all my subjects with good marks. I had met all my requirements so all I had to do was pick up a few more hours and I would graduate. For the second semester I elected to take a special course in advanced mechanics with Dr. Williams. To fit it into his schedule he asked the five boys in the class if they were willing to meet on Saturday mornings. Kip Babbitt from Houghton was one member of the group and McAllister, like me a physics major, was another member. We all agreed to his request. As it turned out it was a break for me.

A couple of weeks after the semester started I was asked to teach a class in solid geometry at the Oberlin Academy. For some reason the instructor left and they needed someone right away. Since it fitted into my schedule I accepted not only for the small amount of money they paid, but for the experience. The Academy was maintained mainly as a preparatory school for college and gave an opportunity for college freshmen to make up a subject they needed for complete entrance requirements. Now that high schools across the country were expanding their range of subjects, the Academy was no longer thought necessary and this was its last year.

Dr. Williams also gave me some small jobs in his laboratory for which he could pay me a little. One thing I did was to make some large drawings for use in the physics lecture room. He was quite pleased with them and put them on display at once. Some twenty years later I visited the campus in the summer and was very surprised when I walked into the physics lecture room in Peter's Hall to see one of my drawings still in use.

One event that took place during the year was of special interest to the physics department. A loudspeaker was installed in Finney Chapel and the public was invited to listen to the first message sent over the newly completed long distance telephone lines from New York City to San Francisco, California. At the conclusion of the conversation came the sound of the surf on the coast of the Pacific Ocean. This was considered an important milestone in the history of communication.

After my visit to Cazenovia I relived my special good times with Norah and I wrote her frequently. One of my letters must have been serious as her reply was:

> Your letter certainly took me by surprise. I supposed that our friendship would mean only that to both of us. I have appreciated your friendship and am glad you have mine. I have tho't a lot about it since I rec'd your letter. In fact, I haven't been able to think of anything else. As I am able to judge at present time it doesn't seem that we can ever be more than good friends.

Her letter didn't change my feelings toward her in any way, but our letters continued on the basis of good friends. So I settled down into a routine of my many activities.

Then the last week of March I was faced with a difficult decision. Dr. Lord, the head of the college placement bureau, called me to his office and told me that the school superintendent of West Park, Ohio, was looking for a man who could teach high school math and science and also coach baseball. He wanted someone at once and was willing to take an undergraduate. The salary was extra good for the times. He offered $1,000.00 for a year and up to that time no graduate from Oberlin had been able to get that much for the first year. I hesitated, since I was teaching at the Academy and had planned on graduating in

June. But Dr. Lord thought it was such an excellent opportunity that he pressured me to meet the superintendent in the lobby of the Elyria Hotel that evening.

It was true that I was low on money and had borrowed from the College, so the thought of such a good salary was a real temptation. I talked with Dr. Williams and he encouraged me by saying I could stay in his class on Saturday mornings and could easily finish the few credits I needed in the following summer session. With his encouragement I met the superintendent and after a brief talk, he offered me the job right then. I accepted on the condition that I would be free of all obligations on Saturdays so I could continue my class with Dr. Williams.

The next few days I spent rounding up someone to take my place at the Academy, checking with Mrs. Grey to have someone take over my place as head waiter and cancelling all my classes except on Saturday. The only difficulty I had was with the lady where I roomed. She thought I should pay for the rest of the year even if I wasn't there. I was going to ask her for a reduced rate so I could stay there weekends, but she made such a fuss I didn't ask and left.

The die was cast and I left for West Park the first of April. I kept some of my ties with Oberlin by returning each Saturday as a sort of tramp. Sometimes the fellows I knew would tell me of somebody who was away for the weekend and I would move in. Otherwise I returned to West Park. Thus teaching full-time and coaching the baseball team combined with the Saturday work, the time went fast until the end of the year.

Near the end of Dr. Williams' course he informed us that according to the rules of the college he had to give us a final examination. He said he didn't want to make out such an exam for five students, so if we didn't object, he would give us an oral one. When the time came he placed an equation that pertained to our study of mechanics on the board and called on one of the group to start solving it. After he went a ways, Dr. Williams called on me. I picked it up and sailed along fine, then thinking ahead, I suddenly realized that after the step I was concluding I didn't know which way to move. Putting on a bold front, I kept going and then just as I reached my blind spot, Dr. Williams called on Babbitt to continue. "Kip" was equal to the occasion and no one ever knew how close I came to being stumped at least for a few seconds.

When commencement time came I felt a little sad to know I wouldn't get my diploma along with my class. However, I was allowed to participate in all the activities except the actual graduation. Mother had hinted that she would like to come so I invited her and Mr. Arnold to be my guests. I secured tickets for them to attend everything, and they were thrilled. I never let on how I felt, but bragged how I had a good job and would be able to pay off all my debts.

One event during the commencement week I was able to attend was the class breakfast, which was held in one of the large restaurants and considered a rather dress affair. It was customary for the members of the class to attend in couples. Walton and I agreed it would be nice to make it also a sort of Houghton affair, so he asked Harriet Meeker for a date and I asked Gertrude Graves. They were happy to accept and we called for them at Talcott. We were a bit late so when we walked in most of the tables were filled. I'll never forget the gasp that went through the room as I stood by Gertrude looking for an open table. She was always a good looking girl and with her beautiful auburn hair and "dolled up," she was really stunning. Since these girls were in the college for their senior year only, not many of the fellows had seen them. I had to laugh inside when one after another found an excuse to come to our table so they could be introduced. For once I was the envy of the men in the class. I had always liked Gertrude back in Houghton, but had been so busy that year I had seen very little of her. So we remained just good friends.

For the summer session I elected some courses in education. This was a new field for me but I knew I had to take them in order to get a State Teacher's Certificate, which was required if I expected to continue teaching. Ohio was one of the first states to require practice teaching for the certificate, and I was lucky to be able to sign up for such a course in plane geometry. My supervisor was the principal of the Oberlin High School. When I arrived on the first day for the class, I walked into the room to find a group of boys all seated, but no teacher. After some ten minutes and still no teacher, I thought maybe I was supposed to do something. I asked the boys if they had been given an assignment and when they said yes, I remarked, "Let's get started." I had them at the board putting on their solutions when the principal walked in. He looked rather surprised as I introduced myself. "Yes," he said, "I was expecting you. However, you are supposed to do so many hours of observation before you start teaching, so I will take over. Good of you to start things off." Later I did all the teaching and he observed me. I got along fine and at the end of the session he asked me if I had a job. When I said, "Yes, at West Park High School," he replied, "If you ever need another let me know." That gave me a real boost.

I learned that Leone Lilly, who I knew as a music student at Houghton, was enrolled in the Oberlin Conservatory that summer. Her parents, who lived in the mountains of northern Pennsylvania, didn't want her to be alone so far away, so they had rented a house in Oberlin. They had an extra room I rented for the summer which made it pleasant for all of us. I also got a summer job waiting tables with Nate Cooke at the Martin Inn. My board and room was taken care of and I didn't try to work otherwise as I did the first summer.

At the close of the summer session I was one of a group of about twenty seniors who had finished their requirements for a diploma. We were notified to assemble in a room in the Administration Building for a brief ceremony. President King was there to preside. The dean of men

139

was very upset when I arrived because one of my instructors had not turned in my grade and they had to send a messenger out on the golf course to find him and see if I had passed the course. The dean told me to pay my diploma fee and be ready. I had to sweat it out until the messenger returned just before the ceremony to say I was OK. My name was called and I received my diploma from President King. At last I had an A. B. degree. I walked out with mixed feelings, a little sad I didn't get it in June, but elated to know that I had succeeded.

Before I left Oberlin, Dr. Williams invited me to his house for dinner. I had been in his home several times and had always enjoyed the hospitality shown me by Dr. Williams and his wife. After dinner Mrs. Williams informed me that "Sam" always spent some time with the children after the meal and suggested I help her with the dishes. Of course, I was glad to do so and it gave her a chance to talk to me about continuing my work in physics for an advanced degree. Dr. Williams had suggested this to me several times, so I saw this invitation was one last effort to influence me. I didn't resent it at all, in fact, I was rather flattered. Mrs. Williams told me how she had waited to get married while Sam was in Germany working on his doctorate. Then she asked me outright if it was a girl that was keeping me from going on. I told her, "No, it was largely financial."

Later in the evening after the children had been put to bed, the three of us continued our talk. I told them that I had an offer from Ohio State University for a part-time lab assistant and could spend half my time taking advanced work. I said I had considered it seriously but it only paid $300.00 for a year, while I had signed a contract at West Park for $1,000.00. Also, after I talked with the President of the Board, he wrote me saying if I would stay I had a good chance of being appointed principal of the high school. I told about how I had struggled to get this far with my education and felt I should reap some of the benefits. Both of these people were very nice about the whole thing and had to admit that I had a good point. That evening has remained as one of the highlights of my days at Oberlin. Until his early death, Dr. Williams kept in contact with me showing an interest in my work. That evening two very different paths were open for me to follow and if I had selected the one for a higher degree, my life would have been very different. But I decided to go back to West Park and teaching became my future.

CHAPTER 11

WEST PARK

My life in West Park began when I left Oberlin the first of April 1916 to teach in the high school. I found the town a scattered residential suburb of Cleveland, Ohio. It was on the interurban trolley line that ran from Cleveland through Elyria and Oberlin. While the place was called West Park the post office and the trolley station were named Kamms, Ohio. The only business section consisted of a general grocery store, a small restaurant, and a little post office building. These were located on one side of the main street at the intersection of a cross town street that followed the Rocky River which flowed into Lake Erie. On the opposite corner from these buildings was a tavern, while a half block up the street was a small garage. Everything else in sight were houses.

A half mile up the main street toward Cleveland was the school. It was a small building with less than 200 students. The lower floor contained the elementary grades, while the second floor was for grades 7-12. When I reported to the school on Monday morning, the superintendent introduced me to the three women high school teachers. I found that I was to teach elementary algebra, plane geometry, chemistry, agriculture and civics. Also, I was the coach of the baseball team. There were no gym classes, but nearly every boy in the high school was on the baseball squad.

The baseball season had already started but the weather was still so cold and wet that we had very little practice before the second game on that Friday. Before the game I gave the team a little pep talk emphasizing that everyone was to hustle. I told them I expected everyone to run, no one walked around the field even when they didn't think they could make a play.

The game started with little action but in the fifth inning a long ball was hit over the head of our center fielder. To my surprise, this boy let it roll and deliberately walked after it. In the meantime, the batter was rounding the bases for a home run. I didn't say much but the next inning I sent in a substitute for the center fielder. All looked surprised at my action. I hadn't learned the names of all the boys on the team but I did note that the name of this boy was the same as the superintendent, although I didn't know they were related. Later the other boys told me that he was the superintendent's son, and they were delighted that I had

141

taken some action because he had always been favored. My action put new life into the team and considering the small number of boys in the school, we had a fair season.

On Monday morning following that game, I was called into the superintendent's office. He said his boy had come home after the game and was upset and his wife was greatly disturbed. I told him exactly what had happened, and I expected to start the boy in the next game, but I expected him to do as the others on the team. Thus, I had my first experience with school politics. For the rest of the year I had no trouble with the boy and I think the superintendent was secretly glad I could do something with his boy. Later I learned the boy's mother had always gone to bat for him all through school, so of course the boy thought he was special.

For a place to live I found a room in a single family house near the center of town. Right across the street lived a Mr. and Mrs. West, who had two women school teachers living with them. I was able to get my meals there. Mr. West ran the garage on the main street and was seldom around. He rarely ate with us, saying he was too busy to keep regular hours. Mrs. West was a semi-invalid so she had her sister, Mrs. Brewer, a widow, live with them and do the housework and cook.

Leaving college at that time of year and beginning a full-time job, I felt rather strange. I did feel somewhat important to be classed as a high school teacher, and I got good response from the students. But after all the activities in the college life, this town seemed real dull. The two young women teachers who lived at the Wests were also rather bored, and to have me come into their environment was exciting. So after we became acquainted the three of us spent many hours talking and kidding each other. Many times we lost track of time and it would be after midnight when we went to bed. Of course, the neighbors took notice and we were criticized. I received most of the blame because before I had come it had been very quiet. I should have known better, but I was young and had much to learn about being a teacher.

When I took the job it was agreed that I would be free to go back to Oberlin each Saturday to keep my class in physics. But in May the superintendent informed me that I would have to go to the County Courthouse in Cleveland on that Saturday to take a county examination in high school subjects to get a temporary teacher's certificate. He said he was sorry and had appealed to the County Superintendent to waive the requirement, but to no avail. It reminded me of taking the day-long exams at the end of eighth grade in Delaware, Ohio. So I spent the day taking an examination in high school subjects, including English, American history, elementary algebra, and either science or a language. Also, there was one in education called pedagogy. In that there were a few general questions which I attempted to answer and then wrote, "I have not as yet studied this subject." The examinations were held in a large hall filled with young people, mostly women, who were trying to qualify for a county teacher's certificate.

Since I did not have a chance to review any of the subjects, I wondered how well I would do on those I was not teaching. Two weeks later I received notice that I had qualified for my certificate so evidently I did alright.

Near the end of the school year an event took place which not only made a deep impression on me, but also influenced my future. Notice was sent to the residents of the school district that on a certain date an open meeting of the School Board would be held for a hearing of charges against the school superintendent. Of course, I went to see what it was all about. At the meeting two representatives of textbook companies appeared and charged the superintendent with buying books from them but refusing to pay for them. The superintendent claimed he had paid for them in cash, but admitted he had nothing to show for it. It came down to his word against theirs. After the hearing the case was settled, but it made such a "stink" that the superintendent resigned. I felt sorry for him and was concerned about my future as I had signed a contract for the next year and now there would be a new superintendent.

Before the end of the year, the two teachers who stayed at the West house told me they had taken an apartment for the next year where they could cook their own meals. So I made arrangements to move to the Wests where I could board and room for the next year. School was over in early June and I returned to Oberlin to finish my college work.

Walton had graduated in June and found a summer job in a big power plant in Lorain, Ohio. Near the end of my summer session he wrote me that they were looking for an oiler at this plant and suggested that I come up and apply for the job. I had about four weeks left before my school opened, so it was a good opportunity for me not only to earn some much needed money but to also gain the experience of working in a power plant. As soon as I was free I went to Lorain and met the chief engineer. I told him that I understood he was looking for an oiler to which he replied, "Can you oil?" "Sure," I said, although I had only the faintest idea as to what was required. He didn't ask me if I had any experience, but wanted to know how I had heard about the job. When I told him, he called an assistant engineer over and said, "Here's your oiler, show him the works."

The force at this plant was divided into two shifts. One group worked days for two weeks and the other nights. At the end of the two weeks they changed places. I was put on the night shift, while Walton, who had made arrangements for me to share his room, was on days. So I slept days and he used the same bed at night. The last of the summer we were both on days so we could be together evenings and enjoy the good weather by swimming in the lake.

Lorain is on Lake Erie west of Cleveland and an important port for the large ore boats. The iron ore was used by a large steel mill, and other factories made it a bustling small city. The power plant was located in the heart of the city on the lake front. It was a steam plant using coal for fuel with a battery of steam boilers belching forth a long line of black smoke from a tall chimney. Above the boiler room on the second floor were two large steam engines. These furnished the power to run the electric generators located in the basement directly below the engines. That room was like a hold on a ship with no windows or outside openings. One of my duties was to go down in this room and drain off the oil which had collected in a steam condensor. It was hot and damp in this pit with temperatures over 110 degrees and after a half hour working down there I would come up wringing wet with sweat.

Along one wall of the second floor, which was a large room with a vaulted roof at least two stories high, was a bank of electric switches, circuit breakers, meters and other devices to record and control the electric power. On another wall was a huge pendulum clock. This clock I learned was important because it was the standard time for the city. A big deep-throated whistle was blown at 7 a.m., at noon, one p.m. and 6 p.m., which regulated the life of the city.

As I was introduced to my duties, it was emphasized the importance of keeping the oil cups on the governor of the steam engine always full. A few years before a governor had run dry and stuck so the engine ran wild, causing the flywheel to disintegrate. The scars showed where the pieces of the wheel almost cut the room in half. I understood the danger perfectly after my experience in the sawmill.

Since it was the middle of the summer, there were frequent thunder storms off the lake, especially at night. Then the inside of the power plant was like a fourth of July celebration. Everytime the lightning was near the plant a circuit breaker would cut out with a blinding flash of light. Even if not near the plant, but near a line, the same thing happened. The engineer on duty would be kept busy all through the storm closing the breakers trying to put the lines back in operation. Sometimes a line would go down in a high wind and then an emergency crew had to be summoned.

On nights when things were quiet and I had finished my round of work, I would go in the office and chat with the assistant engineer. One time I asked him where he studied engineering. He said with a correspondence school and he didn't have a degree. He asked about my education and when I said I had one year in Clarkson Tech and also a major in math, he was very interested. He told me one of his difficulties was in math and he had trouble with square root, which he had to do everytime he made out his report. I quizzed him if he had any algebra. "A little," he replied. "Can you expand the binomial $(a+b)^2$?" I asked. He could and then I showed him how to use it as a formula which he could use as a guide so he need never to wonder what his next move should be. I never knew anyone to be so grateful as he was to learn this. He let me know that my job was secure as long as I wanted it.

At the end of the two week period we changed over to the day shift. My work was much the same except I didn't have to go down in the hot basement to recover the oil. In place of that I had to go to the roof and

144

charge a large condensor. This was done by a static machine and was supposed to keep a blanket of electrons above the building to ward off a lightning strike.

Another job was the blowing of the big steam whistle on time. This seemed a rather unimportant task, but I learned different. One day I was busy and looked up at the big clock to discover I had missed the one o'clock whistle. It was then almost ten minutes after the hour. I thought fast and decided it would be better to let it go rather than blow it late. I hoped people would not notice or else think they didn't hear it. Nothing was said until the following day when the chief engineer found me and asked what happened to the one o'clock whistle yesterday. He said his office was swamped with calls, mothers complained that their children were late for music lessons, men at the various factories were late getting back to their machines as they waited outside for the whistle to blow, etc. I decided to say, "There was nothing wrong with the whistle, I thought I blew it." All he said was, "Just be careful. Don't miss it again. We don't want to upset the whole town." I have told this episode many times to high school students as an example of how something on a job may seem very small but may be very important to others.

That four weeks' work was a very rewarding experience for me, and I left to return to West Park with a friendly feeling. Several weeks later on a Saturday afternoon, I entered a movie theater in Cleveland, when by chance I sat down next to a man who I was surprised to recognize as the engineer I worked with at the Lorain power plant. We greeted each other and he told me they hadn't found anyone to take my place. He reminded me how grateful he was for my help about solving square root. "I haven't been criticized once since you were there," he said.

When school opened in September, I met the new superintendent for the first time. He was much older than the previous man and we soon learned that his only experience had been in the elementary grades. Right away there developed some differences of opinion as he thought the high school should be run like an elementary school. I didn't let it bother me too much, as I was busy with five classes and coaching football. The school was far too small to support a football team, but the boys wanted to play and they had some equipment. So we had fun playing a short schedule.

I was now the only boarder at the West's house, since the women teachers had moved to their own apartment some distance away. The result was that Mr. West was home more often for meals and I became better acquainted with him. My weekends were free and after a time he invited me down to his garage. To keep busy I began to help around the shop, and seeing my interest, he let me help with some of the repairs, thus teaching me about the trade.

Gradually I learned that West was a brilliant engineer and had held some important positions with big companies in Pittsburgh, Pennsylvania. However, he had one serious weakness. Every few weeks he would go on a "toot" and no one would know where he was. He would show up days later a wreck, and his wife would put him to bed all day to get him back on his feet. The result was he had lost all his good jobs and was now struggling to keep his garage going. He had no gasoline pump, he just repaired cars. He was excellent at that work, but hated to get his hands dirty, so he was willing to teach someone like me to do the dirty work for which he would take the credit. I didn't mind as I was learning a new trade, and before long I could take an ordinary automobile engine apart, grind the valves, put in new rings, adjust the carburetor and set the timing, etc. I learned this over a period of two years with the added ability to diagnose an engine problem with considerable success.

My two women teacher friends were happy in their new apartment. One, the high school English teacher, I saw every day, and she kept me posted about how they were learning to cook and live independently. The other, a grade teacher, was from Alabama, but she had no southern accent. When I asked her about it, she said the so-called southern drawl varied from place to place in the south and in her home town it didn't exist. They often invited me over on Friday evenings to play cards but I didn't make the mistake of staying too late, so apparently things were going just fine.

When Christmas vacation came I decided to stay in town. I had no desire to go to Fillmore and Norah had written me from Houghton that she wasn't feeling well and was anxious to get home to see her family doctor. Since the two women teachers had lived with the Wests for two years, they thought they would show some of their appreciation by inviting Mr. and Mrs. West, Mrs. Brewer, and me for Christmas dinner.

The dinner was planned for 1 p.m., and we arrived to find they had the apartment all decorated for the occasion. They borrowed some chairs so we could all sit at the table, which was beautifully set. They had gone all out to make this a festive occasion.

I knew from the smell when we entered the apartment that they were having some sort of roast, but they had been very secretive about what they were going to serve. They knew, as we all did, that Mrs. Brewer was very fussy about what she ate. She did all the cooking at the Wests and even when Mr. West suggested someting like sweet breads or liver for a change, she would turn up her nose and refuse to cook them.

When we began to eat we all remarked how good everything tasted. The girls looked at each other and then asked, "Do you know what the roast is?" I had been trying to identify it. I saw by the bones it must be a small animal, but they had cut it up so we couldn't see the shape. I thought of rabbit, but it was too greasy so I said it must be a suckling pig. The girls just laughed and said, "No" to everything we guessed, but we kept eating, saying how delicious it was.

After dinner we helped with the dishes, although they protested and then enjoyed the afternoon relaxing and visiting. Finally when it began to grow dark we started to say our farewells. Then I said, "You've got to tell us what that wonderful roast was." Again they laughed and said, "We didn't think we could fool you, but if you insist, we will tell you now. It was possum." "'Possum!" we all exclaimed, "where in the world did you get it?" They told us they wanted something very special and the girl from Alabama said Opossum was the big Christmas treat down there, and she had her folks ship her one. I had never tasted one before and it never entered my mind. "Great!" we exclaimed, and then we thought of Mrs. Brewer. She had sunk into one of the living room chairs and had turned a seasick green. If it hadn't been too late, I am sure she would have thrown it up. Someone rushed to get her a glass of water and Mr. West began to kid her. After a time she recovered and before we left she admitted it was good but she would never have touched it if she had known what it was. We left thanking the girls for a beautiful time.

For some time I had been hearing disturbing news from Fillmore. Leeta and Dale were the first to pull out. They went to College Springs, Iowa, where Grandpa and Grandma Crow still lived. Dale went to school for a time and Leeta found a place to work. Then after a time, Aunt Adah, who had married a William Rannells, a farmer from Dunlap, Iowa, asked Leeta to come and help her with a family of small children. They lived on a big farm across the river from Dunlap. William had a younger brother, Arthur, and of course he and Leeta became acquainted. They started going together, and in September, 1916, they were married. Arthur ran the old Rannells homestead, a hilly farm about six miles west of Dunlap. After a short time in College Springs, Dale joined Leeta, helping on the farm while staying in school. In time this became a sort of headquarters for our family.

A short time before Christmas when I arrived at the West's, Mrs. Brewer met me at the door all smiles. She greeted me with, "I've got a surprise for you." I looked around the room expecting to see a package or special letter when from out behind the door jumped Ula. I sure was surprised and speechless for a minute, then after greeting her I asked, "What are you doing here?" The last I knew she was in Buffalo working in a hat factory learning the trade. "Come to see you," she replied. I knew things were not good in Fillmore and my first thought was she had run away from home and come to live with me. But after dinner when we had a chance to talk she explained that she was disappointed in the way she was treated at the hat factory and she didn't want to go back to Fillmore. She said after a day or two she planned to go to Africa where we had lived. One of her girlfriends had invited her to come. She also added that things were bad for Mother and I could expect something to happen at any time.

Sure enough, soon after Christmas I got a letter from Mother saying she and Faye had left Fillmore and would be in Africa with Ula. She wanted me to join them for a weekend, which I did. Then she told me she couldn't take things any longer and would never go back to Arnold. She also asked me to not let him know where she was at any time. After a short stay in Africa, all three went on to College Springs. As soon as it became known that Mother was available, she had calls from Woodbine and Dunlap for nursing jobs. Ula went to Dunlap to help Leeta, and Faye joined Dale in staying there to be in school. Once again they were all together, but under pleasant circumstances.

I had a letter from Dave Scott, the young man who had stayed with us in Africa years before and had influenced me to go to Houghton. I also was with him in school there, but now he was the pastor of the Wesleyan church in Fillmore. Mother had given him all of Father's library for which he was very grateful. He wrote that Mr. Arnold had appealed to him to have Mother come back. I also had a pathetic letter from Mr. Arnold begging me to get her to return. I answered both letters saying I could do nothing and Mother had requested me not to tell where she was.

In January I had a letter from Mother telling how Mr. Arnold had traced her through the telephone service and insisted on talking to her. She did talk and told him it was useless for him to continue as she would never go back. She told me that he was mentally unbalanced at times and she and the children were afraid of him. He finally gave up and my family settled in Dunlap for some time.

On election day in November 1916 I cast my first vote. Up to that time I had never been in one place long enough to qualify. This was the presidential election and one of the strangest in U. S. history. Woodrow Wilson was running for re-election against Charles Hughes, the Republican candidate. World War I had been active in Europe since August, 1914. However, most Americans viewed it as one of the many European conflicts. But beginning in 1915 this country began to lean toward England in its struggle against imperialistic Germany. Early that year Germany had declared the waters around Great Britain as war zone and warned ships of all other nations to stay out. This was a condition that the United States could not accept and continued to sail these waters. In May, 1915, the Lusitania, a declared passenger ship, was torpedoed and sunk with the loss of hundreds of lives. There was a loud angry protest in this country, but Wilson advocated a peaceful settlement. In the campaign of 1916, Wilson ran on a platform which stressed that he had kept us out of war.

Although my leanings were more Republican than Democratic, I did cast my first vote for Wilson. The morning after the election the head-lines of the *Cleveland Plain Dealer* declared Hughes the winner. But by the time the afternoon papers were out, it was indicated that there was some question. Actually, the country had to wait for several days to know the results. Not until the last distant election district in California returned its count was Wilson declared the winner.

During the year I had kept up my correspondence with Norah. She had gone back to teach in Houghton but kept saying she was getting tired of the place. Then I was surprised to receive this letter.

148

My Dear Ray,

I am here in St. Luke's Hospital, Utica, N.Y., where I underwent an operation Wednesday morning. I think I am getting along as well as can be expected and hope to be home in two weeks.

I rec'd the calendar Tues. morning just before I started. I was glad to receive it and thank you very much. I was sick all vacation after I came home from Houghton and seemed to get no better. Write me here as often as you can.

Sincerely,
Norah.

I was sure this letter was dictated as it didn't look like Norah's writing and for a change it was dated. The calendar she referred to was one I had sent her for Christmas. It was a problem for me to find something appropriate and I had to make a special trip into Cleveland to find it. I selected it for the picture which I thought would brighten up her dormitory room. On January 28 I had this letter:

Dear Ray;

Glad to receive your letter. I'm feeling much better now. Went for a ride yesterday and have walked down to the next house. They engaged a substitute to take my place until Feb. 1st. I expect to go back then but don't know for sure . . .

I don't know what I wrote her but in a later letter she wrote:

Dear Ray;

Your letter rec'd. What do you want to work like that for? I'm mad at you for going without your meals. Do you not remember what I told you one night in Fillmore? Why you will never live your time out if you continue like that.

I'm feeling much better now. I went into a decline for a couple of days but seem on the gain now. I wrote President Luckey that I couldn't come back before the 10th but he phoned me yesterday that the supply teacher had to leave today and seemed anxious for me to get back. . .

In February she wrote that she was back in Houghton and feeling better than before her operation. She added that it would be her last year there.

By the second term my school work had settled into a routine. Besides my classes I was coaching some boys for a speaking contest and leading a school chorus. Being such a small school nearly every student was in more than one activity, so I got to know them all very well.

Outside the school more and more attention was given to the progress of the war. In January President Wilson announced his policy

149

of "Peace without Victory." The Germans replied by declaring unlimited submarine warfare. During the next three months at least six American ships were sunk on the high seas. On April 2, 1917, President Wilson called on Congress to declare war on Germany. Four days later it passed and we were in World War I. Events began to happen fast after the declaration. Emotions ran high and two popular slogans appeared. One was "War to End War," and the other was "War for Democracy."

The war department realized they could not depend on a voluntary army so a plan for a universal draft was set up. All men between the ages of 18 and 45 were required to register. My draft board was located in Lakewood, Ohio, a few miles west of West Park. Each man was assigned a number according to the time of registration. A few weeks later a drawing of numbers took place in Washington, D. C. It was announced ahead of time that the first five percent of the numbers drawn would be called up at once. My number was in the first five percent, but before I was notified other things had transpired.

Soon after war was declared, Dr. Crile, a famous Cleveland surgeon, started organizing a hospital ambulance corps. He advertised for volunteers. I was interested as it would be the quickest way to get into active duty. I met a man who worked in Dr. Crile's hospital, and he told me that with my experience with cars he could put me through as an ambulance driver. But he added I would have to decide in a week's time.

I hesitated because I knew that Dale, who was still in the Dunlap High School, was so eager to get into action that with some others he left school and went to Omaha to join the Nebraska National Guard, which was soon taken into the regular service. Mother was very upset to have him do this, and she begged me not to go unless I had to. This was a big factor in my decision, while the other was I felt I should not break my contract with the school board and leave before the end of the year. So for the second time I had a chance to leave that school but honored my contract. The corps, one of the first to see service, left without me.

Not long after I had made this decision the contracts for the next year were out and much to my surprise I didn't receive one. I called on the superintendent to find out why. I hadn't been too happy working with him, but he had never criticized me or my work. He was very vague about things, only saying some parents complained because I had stayed out too late at night. I was real hurt since twice I had honored my contract and this was the way I was treated. So I lost my first job as a teacher.

My plans for the summer were rather upset but I didn't feel too bad as I knew I would probably be drafted soon. I must have written Norah in Houghton about my situation and suggested I might come to see her before she left, as I had a letter from her dated May 7, 1917, saying:

"It doesn't make any special difference what time you come. I tho't perhaps you would be having a vacation so you could come here when school is out and go home with me. . . Most all the fellows are leaving school to work on farms. The State gives them Regents credit if their work is passing grade up to this time. Several have gone already, 25 more got permission to leave this week, so I don't know as there will be any left by commencement time. . . Janice [a teacher friend] says her brother has enlisted. Now for goodness sake don't go unless you have to! Of course, if it was really necessary I wouldn't urge anyone not to go. A person who is educated can be influential in other ways. They are going to plow up the campus here and plant potatoes so they will have some next year."

I did not go to Houghton or Cazenovia at that time because an event happened which changed my life for the next year. Just before school was out, I was riding down to the garage one Saturday with Mr. West when he asked me what I planned to do during the summer. I told him I had no plans as I was sure I would be drafted soon. Then to my surprise he said he wanted to tell me something very confidential. He went on to tell me that a year or so before he had met a man by the name of Parsons. This man was an electrical contractor in the city and through his contacts he learned of a man who had a plan for a kerosene carburetor but didn't know how to develop it. Some place Parsons had met West and knew him to be a talented engineer. Together they had formed a partnership and bought the idea from the originator and were now ready to develop it.

At that time gasoline was selling for 25¢ or more per gallon while kerosene was a drug on the market, selling for around 5¢ per gallon. This was the reverse of the original importance of the two liquids. For many years kerosene was the most important product of crude oil, since it replaced whale oil for lighting homes. Then with the invention of the internal combustion engine gasoline became the important product. Of course, the lubricating oil which was also obtained from crude oil was very important. It made possible all of the great expansion of the machine age in America.

There was considerable interest at this time in using kerosene as the fuel in the automobile engine. There were a number of so-called kerosene carburetors invented, and they had been published in the trade magazines. However, most, if not all, of these devices depended on using gasoline to start the engine and then when the engine was real warm the driver could switch over to kerosene. This was a definite drawback, as the car would have to have two fuel tanks.

Mr. West knew my background and when I told him I had no plans for the summer, he suggested I come and work with him on the device. He was sure with my college major in physics I could contribute a lot in making the carburetor work. He had me meet Parsons who was furnishing the money in the partnership, and after a talk it was agreed that I would join in the venture. West would give me my board and room and while I would work with no salary, I would share in the profits if the device was successful. It was an oral agreement, but since I expected it would be only a short time before I had to go into service, I thought I had nothing to lose.

As soon as school was out I began to work with West. He had already assembled a crude carburetor made from parts of discarded gasoline carburetors and had it installed on an automobile engine placed on a block in one end of the garage. Everyone around the garage wondered about this setup, but he was mum about it. In order to have some privacy we built a partition, across the width of the garage including a door, creating a room for working on the carburetor. As I might have expected, West made some suggestions to develop the device, but I did all the work. It wasn't long, however, before I began to do experimenting on my own. A young fellow by the name of Harlan who had been around the garage a lot was hired to do what little repair work came in. West was becoming less and less interested in the garage and after a time closed it.

In July there developed a sort of lull in our work and time had to be given to decide which way to move, so I told West I would like to take a couple of weeks off to go to Cazenovia to see my girlfriend. He seemed a bit surprised because he didn't know I had such a friend, but readily gave his consent.

It had been over a year since I had seen Norah, and it was a delight to be with her again. She had recovered fairly well from her operation, but I could tell she was not back to normal. Admitting she had gone back to Houghton too soon she resigned her position there. When I told her about my decision to work with West and not to teach again, we both felt a bond of being free.

I spent two weeks in Cazenovia and during that time I met both of Norah's sisters and families. Nellie, the oldest of the family, had two young boys, Herbert and Carrel, and lived in Cazenovia, but her husband, George Hayes, had taken a job in Utica, New York, and they were preparing to move there. Norma, the youngest of the family, was married and lived in Fayetteville, New York. Her husband, Fred Benedict, ran a truck farm on the edge of that village. Their first child, Vera, was only a few months old. I liked these people very much and they all took me in as if I already belonged in the family. Norah and I had a wonderful time together, she telling me about what had happened during the past year in Houghton and I relating my experiences. Evidently we had an understanding of a closer relationship, because after that she began to sign her letter "With love."

On August 2, I received a letter from Norah, which in part said:

Glad to hear you got home alright. It has been terrible hot after you left. I hope you will know soon how the carburetor comes out & that your efforts will be crowned with the greatest success. I'm feeling fine now—so sorry to have been feeling so when you were here but would rather have it that way than for you not to come ... I felt lonely after you had gone but shall try to see you in October.

On August 6 she wrote:

Honest, Ray, I don't believe you could have had a good time here at all. The time seemed so short. I felt so miserable I couldn't hardly realize you had been here at all . . . Fred had to go to Syracuse for examination Wednesday. Norma is quite worried for fear he will have to go. They say they have to take married men.

But Fred was exempt on two counts, his family and his farm. Norah didn't need to worry about my not having a good time. It was true because of her condition there were many things we couldn't do, but it meant a great deal to me to be so taken in by her family. I had been separated for so long from my own family that I was beginning to feel like a stranger. Now that they had all gone farther west I felt more on my own, so Cazenovia began to feel like a second home. On August 25, Norah wrote from Granby, Connecticut, that she was there to visit Janice Griffen, the music teacher she had met in Houghton. She said she was getting a good rest, which she couldn't get at home; many friends visited them there.

Shortly my number was drawn in the draft; the Board in Lakewood notified me to be ready in early September. I immediately put in for a deferment because of my work on the kerosene carburetor. I was given a temporary deferment pending a hearing before the whole Board. However, as happened in many cases, there was some confusion and on September 29, 1917, I received notice to report at 7 a.m. on October 3 for military duty and for transportation to the army mobilization camp in Chillicothe, Ohio.

Since I had the notice of my temporary deferment, I didn't report and then on October 4, I got a letter from the draft board wanting to know why I didn't report and if not cleared with them within five days, I was subject to arrest.

Mr. West went with me and we had a session at the draft board office. He took along some of the drawings I was working on at the time and explained the importance of our device. The result was I received a notice on October 29 that I was exempt for sixty days.

Early in the fall West concluded we had done all the experimenting we could do on the patched up device and the time had come to have a complete one made. He asked me to make the drawings for a new carburetor. I had my drafting table tools which I had used at Clarkson and we built a workable drafting table in the back of the garage. I bought some paper and tracing cloth and went to work.

In October I had a letter from Owen Walton telling that he had been drafted in the first five percent and since he had no reason for deferment he was sent to Camp Sherman, Chillicothe. He met six other men from Oberlin and said they were all suffering from the cold barracks and shortage of supplies. He also said he doubted that I would be deferred much longer as they took McAllister, one of the Oberlin men who majored in physics with me at Oberlin. At the time he was doing original research work at the University of Chicago on an absorbent for poison gas which the Germans were using. The last I heard from Walton was in April when he wrote that he was in the hospital recovering from a mastoid operation. I never knew whether he got overseas or not.

I also had several letters from Dale, who spent some time in camp near Omaha, Nebraska, and then was sent to the 127th Field Artillery, located at Camp Cody, Deming, New Mexico. At first he helped train a lot of the boys to ride the horses and then in February, 1918, they took all the horses away and motorized the outfit. Later his outfit was sent to the Mexican border and remained there until October, 1918. Field artillery was one thing the French army was good at using and they were well equipped, so Dale's chances of getting across were not good.

In September I got a letter from Norah saying she and Janice were in Boston and having a wonderful time. They both had a few pupils to tutor but were spending most of the time going to concerts, visiting museums, art galleries, and the many historical sites. Then in December I heard she was in Utica with Nellie and finally back in Cazenovia in January.

My sixty day deferment would be up the last of December so I moved right along on my drafting. As soon as one set was ready West took them to a small machine shop where they made a pattern. From the pattern two castings were made and then the fittings were either made or purchased and the device assembled. One carburetor was fitted to the engine we had on the block and the other installed on a one and a half-ton truck we had purchased for this purpose.

To show how this device was different from any we knew about I will give a brief description. Actually, the device was more than a carburetor, being composed of two chambers. The bottom one was really a fire box. Kerosene or coal oil, as it was commonly called at that time, was piped into the lower chamber from the fuel tank. Inserted on one side was a heating coil which was connected to the car battery. Once a switch was turned on, this coil would get red hot and ignite the fuel. After a blaze was started the coil would be turned off. A small amount of the fuel was thus burned in this chamber but in doing so, the rest was turned into a hot gas. When the engine began to turn over, the hot gas and flame was drawn up through a series of baffle plates, which extinguished the flame. The hot gas was then drawn into an upper chamber, where it was mixed with the proper amount of air to make an explosive mixture.

Kerosene Carburetor

I helped develop this device which never went into production
due to a new process that made gasoline more readily available.
My activities in the development were considered important and
thus delayed my draft to the Army.

This part was a real carburetor and acted as it did for gasoline. Since we
were making gas from coal oil, the device was called an "oil gas
producer."

Once the device was in operation two important steps were taken.
One was to apply for a patent. My drawing, while good enough to make
the castings, did not satisfy a patent attorney, so a special draftsman
was employed. With these drawings and pictures taken, the proper
papers were filed with the Patent Bureau in Washington, D. C. Next
West and Parsons decided that a company should be formed and a
lawyer by the name of Younger was invited to join the group. He drew
up the necessary papers to form a corporation. It was named, "The Oil
Gas Producer Company." In the papers West was named the president,
Parsons the vice-president, Younger the secretary, and Calhoon the
treasurer. Then stock certificates were printed but they could not be
sold publicly until the incorporation papers were approved by the State
Commission and they approved the sale.

All this time I was busy experimenting with the producer. I had to
determine the proper rate of the flow of fuel, the correct mixture of gas
and air for maximum efficiency and get all parts to work in harmony. I

soon found that operating the producer on the truck was quite different from the stationary engine. So I spent considerable time testing on the road.

When we received word that the incorporation papers were approved, a meeting was called of all who had put money in the venture and a formal company was organized. Since I had put no money in the project but had contributed time and effort, I was voted some of the shares of stock. I still have the stock certificates as a memento of my work.

As soon as the company was legally formed, application was made to the Commission in Columbus, Ohio, for permission to sell the stock. A date was set for some members of the Commission to come to West Park to personally inspect our product. West and Younger met the members in Cleveland and took them to lunch. When he left, West told us he would bring the men out to the garage around 2 p.m. if they wanted to see the producer in operation. He took the drawings and pictures with him to show and wasn't sure whether the men would want to come outside the city or not.

A man named Marshall, an old friend of West and now out of a job because of an accident in a machine shop, had joined our group. When he left, West ordered Marshall, Harlan and me to have everything in order if the men came. Since I had both producers in working order, we sat around until 2 p.m., then 3 p.m., and when 4 p.m. came, we decided no one was coming. I felt we had wasted the whole day waiting, so I began to make some adjustments on the truck. Just then someone looked out the window and shouted, "Here comes West with a car full of men." Hurriedly I began to put things back in shape but didn't finish before they all walked in. West looked surprised to see me doing anything to the truck but didn't say anything. I quickly finished and at his suggestion I took the group over to the stationery engine and began to explain how it worked. I was careful to show the men before I attempted to start the engine, that all I was using was kerosene. They looked surprised when the engine started at once and checked to be sure it was only kerosene I was using. I had the engine connected to a generator which was hooked up to a bank of electric lights so they could see that the engine would do work.

After that demonstration they were interested in the truck. I offered to take them for a ride but they declined saying it was late and they had to get back to the city. However, they wanted to see it run so with Harlan beside me I started the engine and backed out into the street. As I passed West, he whispered, "Take it out of sight and don't come back until they have gone." So Harlan and I drove up the street until well out of sight and then parked on a side street where we could watch for West's car as he took the men back to the city.

When we got back to the garage, Marshall said they all watched us drive up the street and all was fine except once for a few seconds a puff of black smoke shot out of the exhaust. That was bad as we had

156

stressed, "no smoke," as most kerosene carburetors produced. In spite of that, Marshall said they seemed impressed and left in good spirits.

West didn't return until late evening and he came in very glum, not speaking to us. He was mad at us for not sitting still all day, but I thought otherwise. I felt we had impressed the men as they saw us at work, not just putting on an exhibition. Then in about two weeks we received word that we had been approved to sell our stock in the state. West then became very mellow and happy.

Marshall had come to work with us through an unusual circumstance. Years before he and West had worked together in Pittsburgh. Marshall had left to take a job as foreman in a big machine shop in Michigan. There was trouble in the shop and one of the men was angry with Marshall and shot him in the head. The bullet didn't kill Marshall but lodged in one side of his brain and when removed destroyed the sight of his right eye. Marshall was retired with a small pension. West heard about his condition and wrote Marshall asking him to bring his wife and join our group. The Marshalls had no children and West gave them a room in his house, so we all lived together. Mrs. Marshall was a very small person but very lively, and did much to cheer up the place. Marshall and I took to each other and I found him to be a man with good common sense and since he knew West's background, we got along fine.

As the time for my sixty day deferment approached, I was thinking about what it would mean when to my surprise I received notice of an additional sixty days. When I voiced my surprise, West told me that without my knowing or giving my consent he had gone to the draft board and told them I was indispensable for the project and asked for an extension. At first I was a little miffed as I had been planning to get in the service, but then when I heard the reports about how poor the facilities were in camp, I was glad to accept the postponement. But I told West not to ask for another deferment, as I would not accept it.

Now began a phase of the project I didn't really like. West wanted all experimental work stopped and had me put in my time demonstrating the producer for the purpose of selling stock in the company. Before I realized what was in his mind, I did take him to Oberlin to meet Dr. Williams and Dr. Holmes. Both were very interested in the project and both bought $50.00 worth of stock. West was a glib talker and had a charming personality when he wanted to show it. When he would get going and stretch the truth too far, I would cut in with, "Well, it wasn't quite as much as that." His response was always, "Well, you can't make a liar out of a man for a mile or two." The result was almost perfect. People thought he was an enthusiastic salesman, but I was the one to keep him in line. Together we sold enough stock to keep the company going. West was the only one who was taking money out of the business and only enough to keep his home going with Marshall, his wife and me as boarders.

That winter was one of the coldest on record for northern Ohio, but I was able to drive the truck at all times with little difficulty. It seemed I was the only one to master the technique of keeping the producer going at all times. There was a certain feel for the device that had to be developed.

Late that winter we received a notice that some officers from the Army Transportation Corps would be in Cleveland and wanted to see a demonstration of our device. I was elected to meet them and drive the truck. The officers were very interested in looking at the producer operate while the truck was standing, then a colonel asked me to take him for a ride. He sat beside me and wanted to see how much power the engine developed, but since there were no hills in that part of the city, he would reach over and put on the emergency brake. He would hold it until the engine would almost stall. Several times I thought he would stall the engine and if the carburetor flooded, I didn't know how long it would take to get the engine started again. But I finished the demonstration without trouble. Before the officers left they thanked us for the demonstration and said they would let us know if they wanted more information. However, we never heard from them so evidently they thought our device did not have enough power.

Working as I did at all hours, I had little chance for any social life. I missed the contacts with school activities but did see my women teacher friends once in awhile. That winter they asked me to join them in going to a dancing school in the city. I had never learned to dance, as neither Houghton or Oberlin allowed it. They confessed that they had never learned either, so we entered as beginners. At first we felt somewhat foolish and awkward, but after five sessions on Friday nights we got so we could do the waltz and two-step fairly well. I was always glad they enticed me to go because to be able to dance proved valuable to me in later life.

One time I saw in the paper that John Phillip Sousa with his famous band would appear at one of the theaters in the city for a concert. There was no way of obtaining a ticket in West Park, but I wanted to see and hear the concert so I went anyway. I got a seat in the top balcony, but even at that distance I was enthralled to watch Sousa conduct. Then after an excellent concert he closed with his famous march, "The Stars and Stripes Forever." The audience rose as one man and cheered and cheered. Everytime I hear that march played or play it in a band I can still visualize John Phillip Sousa as he led his band as no one else could.

Late that winter Parsons asked me to meet him at one of the leading hotels in the city. He said he wanted to give me a dinner to show his appreciation of my work for the company. He ordered a planked steak for two, my first experience of such a swell meal. I had a feeling that he had something else in mind and sure enough, after the dinner he asked me if I was interested in buying his share of stock in the company. He said his work as an electrical contractor had increased so much due to the war he no longer had time to keep in touch with the Producer Company. He made me such a good offer for his stock I had the feeling he decided there was little or no future for the company and he wanted out. I thanked him but told him I was not interested, first because I was sure I would be drafted soon, and second that I didn't have the money to buy his stock even at his generous offer. For a year I had been living off what I had saved during my year of teaching and now that was almost gone. We parted on friendly terms and it was the last time I ever saw him.

Sometime in March Mother wrote me that the household goods she had taken from Belfast were still in storage in Fillmore. She asked me to go to Fillmore and arrange for the goods to be sold. I knew Norah was home in Cazenovia so in early April I told West about Mother's request and that I would have to be away for a couple of weeks. I didn't tell him about going on to Cazenovia nor give him any address. I wanted to be free for a time.

I did go to Fillmore and made arrangements to have the goods sold at auction and then left for Cazenovia. It was good to see Norah who was still recovering from her operation, so we spent a quiet time for a few days. We did have some serious talks about the future which was good as it was to be the last time I would see her until after the war.

It was late at night when I got back to West Park, but as soon as I got to my room Mrs. Marshall came to greet me. She had my mail and was eager to tell me the news, but the first thing she said was, "Did you get married?" I laughed and replied, "No, do I look like it?" Why they thought I went away to get married I couldn't find out, maybe because I hadn't explained much about my going. The news that Mrs. Marshall wanted to tell me was the fact that soon after I left, a truck manufacturing company in Hartford, Connecticut, contacted West and asked him to bring the producer to their plant for a demonstration. So he took Marshall with him and they were there.

Two days later they returned, but had no results to talk about. Marshall told me it was unfortunate that I was not there as I should have been the one to go. He said neither he nor West could make the device work as well as I could. In a way I was sorry to miss the trip but glad the responsibility fell on West. I always felt he blamed me for not selling it to the army engineers. This time he had only himself to blame if the demonstration was not a success.

It was soon after this that a man in Indiana perfected the so-called "cracking process." If the news was true, and it was, the bottom fell out of the use of a kerosene carburetor. Up to this time it had certain factors in its favor: it used cheaper fuel, it would start in all kinds of weather, better than a gasoline carburetor in extreme low temperatures, and the inside of the engine was clean, no accumulation of carbon. On the other hand, there were certain drawbacks—there was an odor to kerosene that might prove objectionable to pleasure car owners and it did not develop the quick pick-up nor power of a gasoline engine.

To understand why the "cracking process" made such a difference to us, is to understand the source of gasoline and kerosene. Both of these liquids come from petroleum, a natural product composed of a mixture of several liquids. These liquids were separated by a process called "fractional distillation" at a plant called a refinery. At this plant the crude oil was heated and the most volatile liquid would boil off first and when cooled, would return to a liquid form. The first products obtained were napthaline and benzine, followed by gasoline, then kerosene, and on down to the various oils. This process is still used but the significance of the new discovery was that it gave the refineries the power to change a heavier liquid into a lighter one. Hence, they could now change kerosene, a drug on the market, into gasoline which was in demand. So the need of a kerosene carburetor was almost nil. The only use for our device left would be in a stationery engine and there was little market for that.

It was soon after I got back from Cazenovia that I received my notice from the draft board to report for induction into the army. It was post-marked April 23, 1918, and I was to report on the 27th. That left me less than a week to close up my personal affairs. I packed my trunk, just keeping the few personal things I would take to camp, and sent the trunk to Dunlap, Iowa.

Because of the turn of events that had taken place the last few weeks, I was almost happy to go. Almost all the boys of my age that I knew were already in service, so I began to feel left out. An excerpt from a letter I wrote Norah indicates my feelings at the time.

Kamms, Ohio
April 26, 1918

Dear Norah,

Tomorrow at 2 p.m. I cease to be my own boss but take orders from Uncle Sam. I enter a different world almost, not knowing where it may lead. But I go gladly that I may do a little part to preserve civilization for others and that millions unborn (may God grant my own may be included) may not be born into slavery but enjoy as much freedom as you and I have enjoyed in this country. I have been thinking considerable since I wrote last and if need be I am only too glad to go to France. There is a big chance that I go too. Will Kaufman was only in training 6–7 weeks and is on the way over. So you see they are sending them fast. [Then followed a love letter concluding with,] Must get to bed as I have a lot to do in the morning.

Love to you,
Ray

CHAPTER 12

WORLD WAR I

On April 27, 1918, I reported at the Draft Board office in Lakewood for induction. Those reporting were given a brief physical examination and then dismissed with orders to report at the courthouse in Cleveland at 8 a.m. the next morning. Each of us was given a sheet of instructions telling what to bring and what not to bring.

In addition to the few personal things I had ready, my teacher friends gave me a sewing outfit which contained needles, thread, buttons, scissors and other accessories, all tucked in pockets of olive drab cloth which could be rolled into a neat package. This proved to be a valuable gift, not only for my own comfort, but at times I was very popular with some of my buddies when they needed a tailor. Mrs. Marshall also presented me with a heavy wool sleeveless pullover sweater which she had knit. It also was olive drab and popular at the time in making up Red Cross packages for the soldiers. This sweater was extra heavy and saved me many times in cold weather. Evidently it was moth proof, as I still have it.

On the morning of the 28th I arrived at the County Courthouse to find a large group of recruits assembed on the lawn. My teacher friends joined a group of friends and relatives to see us off. At 8 o'clock we were lined up for roll call and the officer in charge asked if anyone had any military training. Along with two or three others, I raised my hand. Then he picked me and said he would divide the group into two platoons and I would be in charge of the second. Forming the men into a column of twos, the officer led the first platoon down the street toward the railroad station. At a proper interval I followed with the second platoon. On a siding was a long line of passenger cars where the officer brought us to a halt. We were given a few minutes to say our farewells to the friends and relatives who had followed us and then we were ordered aboard. My platoon filled one car and I was still considered in charge. I was then bombarded with questions by the men who were too scared to ask the officer.

The train moved south toward Columbus, Ohio, picking up more men at some of the stations along the way. At noon we were handed a box lunch, then late in the afternoon we stopped on a siding near Camp Sherman, Chillicothe. When off the train we formed a long line to march into camp. As we approached we passed near the camp hospital. All the patients who could walk were outside to greet us with shouts of "Wait until you get that shot!" or "Oh boy, are you going to have a sore arm. Cheer up, you'll get it tomorrow!" It was a typical initiation greeting and referred to the series of inoculation shots we were to receive plus vaccination for smallpox.

Once in camp we were assigned to a barrack and selected a cot. On each cot were two army blankets which we learned would be our bedding for the duration. We were also given a mess kit and had our first meal in the army.

During the next two days we were issued our uniforms and rifles. If we got a complete uniform that fit in every way we were considered very lucky. Most everyone had to take something back for exchange which wasn't easy as the men in the quartermaster corps didn't like refitting. We found that the size of things we wore in civies didn't count. For example, our shoes were fitted by placing each foot on a measuring paper and then a fifty pound bag of sand was placed on the corresponding shoulder. The spread of the bare foot under that weight determined the shoe size. We were given barrack bags to keep our extra clothing and personal things in; all our civilian clothes we had worn we had to pack in the bag or suitcase we had brought and all shipped home.

The second day we were given another physical examination and our shots started. If one had a scar from a smallpox vaccination he was passed, but my scar did not show, so I had to take it.

Once outfitted, daily drilling began. Since I had a little experience in the National Guard, the manual of arms and drill commands were easy for me. However, when I was interviewed by an officer the first day and asked if I had any previous military training, I told him my experience. Then he said, "I'll give you a little advice. Don't say anything about it. The regular officers don't think much of the Guard's training." So he put "no" on my record.

It was the third day when I began to feel the effect of the shots. The evening before when we were standing retreat, several of the men fainted and dropped on the ground. They were left unattended until the ceremony was finished. The next morning I could hardly get out of my bunk. I couldn't eat any breakfast, just drank a little coffee, and reported for sick duty. I was told to lie down for a while and it would wear off. But all that day and all night I was first burning up with a fever and then shivering with a chill. Not until the following morning could I eat anything but then I recovered fast.

The vaccination on my arm showed no sign of working for several days. At the end of a ten day period we were checked to see if the vaccination was working. If not, a second was given. At that time mine just showed a little red. When the doctor examined me he gave it a good pinch and asked, "Is that sore?" Actually it wasn't, but I didn't want a second, so I said, "Hell, yes." He just smiled but let me go. I was sure glad because for the next four weeks I had a festering sore and had to have it dressed several times.

One of the first lessons we learned in the army took place soon after we arrived. We were gathered in our barrack one evening right after mess when a sergeant walked in. He called out, "Can any of you drive a car?" Up jumped several with visions of being selected to chauffeur a general's car. I was on the point of standing up also, but something told me to be cautious. The sergeant looked over the group standing and pointed at two of the biggest and said, "Alright, you two come out and change a flat on the colonel's car." With crestfallen faces they filed out, and everyone else suppressed a laugh until they were out of hearing. That event established early in our minds the well known maxim of the army, which is "always look for a joker before you volunteer."

Mother's Day Sunday came the second week we were in camp, and it was advertised as visitor's day for parents. One of the young lads in my company was almost in tears because he had drawn KP (kitchen police) for that day and he expected his parents down from Cleveland. Since I had no one coming, I took pity on him and agreed to take his place if he would take mine later. As far as I can remember, I was never drawn, so he got the best of the bargain. But I never regretted it as he was so grateful and brought his folks around to meet me. They thanked me over and over.

The KP duty was the dirty work in the kitchen or mess hall. That day those of us on duty had to peel a bushel of potatoes, clean vegetables and anything else the cook wanted. Then after each meal we had to wash and scrub the big cooking utensils. Each one had to be spotless when inspected by the keen-eyed cook. KP was a detail shunned by all.

Camp Sherman was the base of the 83rd Division, which was made up of draftees from Ohio and Indiana. I was assigned to Company E, 330th Infantry Regiment. Right away our training began for the life of a foot soldier. Mornings were spent in close order drill and the recall sounded by the company bugler followed by mess call at noon was always a welcome sound. In the afternoons special classes were held, such as practice in the manual of arms, how to take care of a rifle, how to roll a pack, etc. We were issued the roll leggings, which had been adopted for overseas duty. These leggings had proved better to keep the feet dry in the muddy trenches on the front line. It took us some time to learn how to roll them so they would stay in place, but not so tight that they would stop the circulation when marching.

One noon we received the news that our company was to go on guard duty that night. Up to that time we had no instruction in such duty, so the whole afternoon was spent in giving us a crash program in this duty. We were supposed to learn all the twelve general rules so we could repeat them on order of the officer of the day, and also, how to conduct ourselves while on a guard post. A letter to Norah at this time tells of my experience.

Co. E 330, Inf.
Camp Sherman
May 23, '18

Dear Norah,

Well I'm in the guard house but not as a prisoner but as a guard. I was called on guard yesterday. We had Guard Mount last night at 5 p.m., which is one of the hardest and most strict ceremony of the army. We didn't pull it off any too well as we were all, except two or three, new. We then went on guard duty which is very strict altho not so strict as it will be across the pond. But, we had loaded rifles and use fixed bayonets after dark. I had post No. 2, which is the officers' quarters. I had a lot of fun halting them when they came in after taps. We are nearly dead today. It is so hot and we didn't get any sleep. I go on again at 3 o'clock until 5, then I'm through.

It is a pretty sure thing that we are going to move somewhere. We don't know where but all the company stuff is packed and part shipped. The 331st regiment left this morning and trucks are busy moving barrack bags of other companies. The whole division is likely to move.

I just got a chance to talk to our Second Lieut. awhile ago. He is the Officer of the Day. I asked him if there was any chance to be transferred into something more in my line. He told me I could make an application, get the Captain to sign it and try the ground work of the Aviation Corps, but things move very slow in the army. The best thing he thought was to go down to the automobile department tonight if I could get away and see if they needed anyone. If they did I could get a transfer much quicker that way into the Quartermasters' Department. So I'm going tonight if possible.

Before I said anything to him about this or rather the way the whole thing came about, he had us one at a time asking our general orders, the 12 we had to learn yesterday afternoon. I gave them OK. Then he asked me if I was a corporal of a squad what commands I would give when the Captain gave such and such commands. I gave them to him. He said he was glad I was catching on so fast as they had a number of non-commissioned officer vacancies to fill and I stood a good chance of getting one. That opened the way for me to ask about the other.

He also told me if I stuck to the infantry I stood a good chance of getting in another officers' training camp. He said there will probably be another somewhere. If I thought they were really going across to France right away and I could land a non-com job I would stick here. Probably I'll have to anyway.

I haven't your letter so can't answer it properly although I know just about all you said and all of some things. You must be having some fun with all those boys. Glad you found some of the teachers congenial.

164

I hope it isn't as hot there as it has been here the last few days and they have been working us hard just about the same, giving us a lot of battle formations. I told you about our shooting formation, didn't I? Making 790 hits out of 900 shots, an average of 8½ shots per minute with targets popping up at different distances, like men's heads. Shooting the Germans never dreamed of. Well, it's time to go on guard. I think of you and love you truly.

Ray

Norah was now at the Curtiss School for Boys at Brookfield, Connecticut. She took the job to finish out the year but remained for some time. It was a small private school and the boys came from wealthy families who didn't want them in a public school or in some cases, were problem boys. Most of my letters written during the war were addressed to her at this school. She kept a number of them during these many years so I can quote from them often.

Evidently, before I had written the above letter, we had been on the rifle range. Before we went we were issued identification tags, commonly called "dog tags." These were small aluminum discs on which was imprinted our name and serial number and were worn by a string around the neck. As in many cases all my life, they didn't spell my name right. The tag reads, "Alvin R. Calhoun, 2478519, US." That was another thing. All through my army days they insisted I had to give my first name, although I told them I didn't use it. But regulations were regulations. Also, just before we left for the range, we were assembled in a large hall to watch a demonstration of the proper way to fire a rifle. This manner of firing was something the army was very strict about. They were sure they had found the best possible position and everyone had to adopt it.

The day following the demonstration we marched two miles to the rifle range. We were fully equipped with rifles and full packs. Once there we pitched our pup tents. Each man carried a half tent, so selecting a buddy, the two halves were hooked together, thus making a low tent for shelter. At night we rolled up in our army blankets and slept on the ground under this tent. It was fine until it began to rain, then we learned two things: first, if we hadn't made a ditch all around the tent, water would come along the ground under us. Second, if we made a mistake and touched the inside of the canvas, water would seep through and drip on us. Since these tents were so low, we had to crawl into them. It was a real trick to keep dry when it rained, as it did several nights that week.

The first night it rained we heard a commotion and the next morning we learned that a young boy in a leaky tent became so despondent that he cut his wrist with his bayonet. Fortunately, they got him to the hospital in time to save his life. It was an indication that some of the boys who had been drafted couldn't take the training. We were on the range over Sunday and a lot of the men had expected company, but none were allowed on the range, so the morale was rather low.

The first time I fired at the target I hit the bull's eye and our lieutenant was elated. Then the instructors came along and insisted I did not have my legs spread far enough apart, which for me was uncomfortable. But in spite of that I was making a good showing until my shoulder became sore from the recoil of the rifle. Then I found the bolt of my gun was defective and stuck many times when I reloaded. That wasn't too bad when firing slow, but caused a lot of trouble when trying rapid firing.

After three days of individual firing we went into battle formation with the results I quoted in my letter. After we had the fun of firing with live ammunition on the range we returned to camp and then spent hours doing simulated aiming and firing at the various positions. This training would have been fine if we had it before we went to the range, but now was extremely boring. This was typical of a lot of things in the army where they get things backwards. However, they were pressured to give us basic training in a hurry and had to schedule companies on the range, whether they were ready or not.

Another letter to Norah headed Sunday PM, but no date, must have been written the last of May. An excerpt follows:

> The last few days have been HOT. Yesterday we drilled all morning, then in the afternoon we had a regimental parade with full packs, i.e., heavy marching order, believe me it was some hot work.
>
> Then this morning we drilled again and at 2 o'clock we had a Brigade review. 12,000 men marched with packs all ready to leave for France. The 331st and 332nd left last week, so we will undoubtedly leave this week.
>
> Our clothes were wet through with sweat when we got through with the parade. I have been putting in an hour washing clothes since. They won't let us send them to the laundry because we may leave before they would be back. I am getting quite proficient at washing in cold water.
>
> We had two nights off lately and I wish you were here. . . . I didn't get any information about the auto department of any value so decided to stick here for a time. I think I can make non-comm in a short time . . . .

It was just before Memorial Day when we got orders to leave Camp Sherman and entrain for parts unknown. Our long train was composed of Pullman cars, so we slept through the night. When we woke the next morning we peered through the early morning fog and could see the dome of a large building. As it grew lighter we determined it was the dome of the U. S. Capitol Building; we knew we were near Washington, D. C. After some switching, a new engine was attached and we started again. By watching the names of the stations along the route, we knew we were headed north on the Penn line. In the afternoon we pulled into the yards near New York City. Then came more switching and we were on the Long Island Railroad. After the heavy commuter traffic had cleared, we proceeded out of the City onto the Island. Our final stop was on a siding near a large military camp. We detrained and marched into Camp Mills, a holding station for overseas troops.

In this camp we were quartered in large tents, each holding a squad of eight men. I had been named acting corporal and was in charge of one tent, so it was a time when I became better acquainted with each man. There were three who stand out in my memory. One was a young farmer and very awkward; he was always out of step with the drill sergeant constantly yelling at him. The second was a "bum" and would get drunk every time he had a chance. The third was a very quiet type, but when I learned his past, it made a big impression on me. One afternoon after we had finished our morning drill, I started to talk with him. For once he opened up about his past life. When I found out he had been a locomotive fireman on the New York Central Railroad when drafted, I told him about my experiences with steam engines. This established a common bond of interest and we became good friends. Then to my surprise he swore me to a secrecy and told me he had served three years in the regular army. He had been with General Pershing down on the Mexican border and had taken part in raids across the border after the Mexican bandits. Having served all this time he knew more about army regulations than most of our officers. I expressed my surprise and asked why he hadn't put in for a non-comm. To me his reply was very interesting. He said that he had learned in the army never to take on responsibility and then one never got blamed if things went wrong. He said the third file in the rear rank was the best place in the whole army. It was the least conspicuous, the eyes of the platoon leader were generally on the front rank. Another thing I found out about him was he could "smell" a sergeant looking for men for a detail job a mile off. All the time I knew him he never got caught, and I couldn't help liking him for he could be trusted to do his duty and stayed out of trouble, something the rest of us had to learn before we could be called "regulars."

The weather at this time of the year was extremely hot and humid, but since we were there only until we could be shipped out, we were not worked very hard and had considerable liberty. Passes to visit New York City were issued freely, providing a man was not in trouble. I got one for a day and did some sightseeing. I had written to Jess Frazier, who was then living with his brother Bill and family in New Jersey across the river from New York. Bill came out to camp and requested permission to take me home for over Sunday. The captain gave me a pass good until nine o'clock Monday morning. It was good to see Bill Frazier, who was then the pastor of a church in New Jersey, also his wife, who I had known in Houghton when they were married. Jess was a chemist with the Corn Products Company, which had a plant nearby. We had a good weekend together.

As soon as I could I wrote to Norah at Brookfield, Connecticut, to see if she could come to New York so we could be together before I left, but it was right at the end of her school year and she couldn't get away. Parts of two letters tell about my time at this camp.

Co. E 330 Inf.
Camp Mills, N.Y.
June 9, 1918

Dearest;

Your letter written to Camp Sherman finally reached me also the one from you and Miss Griffin. I'm disappointed, of course, that you can't get away but will have to make the best of it. Now they have taken the passes away from us so we can't get out of camp nor anyone get in.

Will Frazier and his mother came over two days in succession before they got word to me, finally yesterday morning they reached me and I got a pass for the afternoon and evening. I sure was glad to see them. We called Jess and met him over in the city. He had just got over the measles, so looked a little thin. He hasn't been called yet but expects to soon . . . They all inquired about you and wanted to be remembered.

They have wished an acting corporal job on me and I have charge of a squad for a time. If I handle it OK I'll get a warrant as corporal. I'm not crazy about the job but it is a necessity step if I expect to get anything better. Keeps me on my nerve to handle a squad when some of them have been in for eight months and some of the stuff is new to me. But I find it is like anything else, self-confidence goes a long ways or as Virgil said, "They do because they think they can." . . . .

I don't know, can only guess that we move very soon. Our Brigadier General addressed the regiment this afternoon telling what he expected of us on the other side and since they have stopped all passes it looks like going across.

N. Y. City was as dark as a little country town last night. They are very excited over the U boat raids . . . Sorry not to see you but cheer up, the war can't last all our lives. Maybe we will enjoy each other that much better.

With a heart full of love,

Ray

Another brief letter headed Monday, but no date.

Dear;

Just received your letter and will send a note hastily. I'm very sorry but I may be on the water by Wednesday. Anyway our passes were taken away from us last Friday. However, I could see you at the gate if you came but even that will be denied if we leave tomorrow. We sent our barrack bags this morning so we only have our packs with us now.

We might still be in New York by Friday, if so, I'll call you Wednesday. If you don't hear from me you will know I am gone. Jess was down yesterday and spent the evening with him at the gate, sort of a little park where we can meet friends but can't take them in camp nor get out.

I feel sure it is goodby for us for sure this time. God bless you and keep you. I'll write as soon as possible when across.

With a heart full of love,

Ray.

Things happened fast after I wrote this letter. On the morning of June 11, we got orders to roll our packs. We fell in and marched to a train waiting on a siding, which took us into New York City near the docks where we could see several ocean-going steamers. Off the train we marched along the docks until we were halted by a medium sized ship. Single file we mounted a long gang plank and were mustered in by name. As we entered each one was given a card listing a bunk number. These we found were triple deckers down deep in the hold. Once we found our bunk, we parked our packs in the cramped quarters and hurried on deck to get some fresh air.

This was an old English cattle boat which had been converted into a troop transport. When we turned in at night we found there was little ventilation, as all the port holes were kept closed and it smelled worse than a cattle barn.

We were sailing at the time of the greatest U-boat activity off the coast of New York. Leaving the docks in the middle of the night, our ship joined a convoy of some 20 others outside the harbor. Since we were in real danger, we were ordered to keep our clothes on all night. We were assigned to a certain life boat and a drill was held at once to acquaint us with how to get there in the shortest time. The signal for real danger would be a blast of the ship's big steam whistle, otherwise there would be no sound nor any running lights. For a convoy of this number of ships to maneuver on a zigzag course under these conditions was a real test of the seamanship of the officers in charge of each ship.

Down in the hold where we had our bunks the air was hot and stuffy. All the ventilation was through some canvas chutes which were supposed to bring fresh air into the hold. But with hundreds of men in these close quarters trying to sleep, the air became thick before morning. After a couple of nights with nothing happening, I became so distressed trying to sleep in my clothes I decided to take a chance and take them off. Just as I fell asleep we were startled by a sharp blast of the ship's whistle. I grabbed my clothes, which I had laid out, and dressed as fast as possible. Everyone roused up ready to make for the life boats, but word was passed down to stay put. Our ship had used the whistle to warn another that had strayed off course and thus avoided a collision.

Once we were out of the harbor the ship began to pitch and roll. This was no passenger ship and had no compensating ballast to reduce the motion. I was alright the first day, but on the second I did become seasick and missed a couple of meals. There was a lot of kidding among the men as to how long a meal stayed down and how far it was to the lee side of the deck. After the second day I got my sea legs and felt fine, but some of the others were sick much longer.

About the third day out it became apparent that this old cattle boat was too slow to keep up with the convoy. Also, they didn't have enough English stokers to keep up steam in the hand-fired boilers. A call was made for volunteers from the soldiers to help fire the boilers. One man from our company did volunteer and I saw him once during the voyage and asked him how things were. "Not bad," he replied, "it was hard work," but they got good food and a ration of rum, which he liked.

Even with the extra help our ship could not keep up with the rest and was cut loose from the convoy. For days we were alone on the ocean with nothing in sight but water. To keep out of danger we went way north and the nights became real cold. It was June, but our overcoats which we were required to carry became very welcome. Even the days got windy and cold. The sun disappeared behind heavy clouds while the fog made visibility almost zero. The waves grew higher and higher. At night the old boat creaked and groaned. Many times she would roll so far we would hold our breath to see if she would ever right herself again.

After about two weeks, we were delighted to see through the fog a number of ships. The convoy was being assembled off the northern coast of Ireland. As the fog lifted we could see a number of gunboats dashing around the transports like sheep dogs trying to move the flock into safety. Later, in the morning sun the Giant Causeway on the north coast of Ireland looked beautiful. Now in formation the convoy moved into the Irish Sea, which was truly green in contrast to the deep blue of the north Atlantic. That evening we docked at Liverpool, England.

To celebrate our safe landing, the YMCA men aboard arranged a program of boxing matches to entertain the troops. It was my luck to draw a turn as corporal of the guard that night. Because of the show, the Officer of the Day had me post guards in places not ordinarily used. When it came time to take the new guards around I couldn't find some of my men. One poor soldier was left on double duty. When I had to round up my men at 3 a.m. to go on the next stand of duty, I had a hard time finding some of them. I think some gave me phony bunk numbers. I finally found enough to fill the regular posts and then at the end of two hours we were relieved and were told no more guards were needed and to prepare to disembark.

Being on duty that night I was struck with the length of daylight at that time of year. Somehow a few newspapers had come aboard and I got hold of one which I could read on deck at 11 o'clock that evening. We had been cut off from all news on the way over, so we were eager to see a paper. After a short period of darkness it became light again at 3 a.m.

I hadn't realized how far north the British Isles were.

It was announced that my company would be the first to leave the ship, so I had to hurry to grab a little breakfast, check to see that all the men on guard were relieved and roll my pack. Fortunately, some of my squad helped by having my pack ready. Just before we disembarked, we were given printed postcards that could be addressed and signed, stating we had landed safely in Europe. Nothing could be added. Each man was given one, but one man gave me his so I sent one to Mother and the other to Norah.

When we were issued our uniforms we were given two pairs of shoes. One pair was a tan dress shoe, which we had used when on leave, while the other pair was a heavy black hob nail shoe we wore for marching. We were ordered to wear the hob nail shoes when we left the ship. As we walked off the gangplank an officer was posted there to warn us about slipping on the rounded cobblestone pavement. After being used to the rolling and pitching of the ship for so many days, it seemed strange to plant our feet on solid ground. In spite of the warning, we slipped on the stones of the pavement and staggered along like a bunch of drunken sailors. The street rose sharply from the docks and we struggled all the way to the top. Once on level ground we gained our stride and marched to a waiting train.

This was our first experience with the European type of passenger cars. They open from the side into separate compartments. Each squad was assigned a compartment and with our full packs and rifles we were really crowded. Once aboard, the train started, taking us through the big factory district of Liverpool with its long streets of stone workmen's houses all built together. Once out of the city, the country was beautiful, just like the pictures we had seen of England with its small cottages surrounded with hedges.

All morning we bounced along the English railroad, listening to the shrill whistle of the funny little locomotive. Near noon we pulled into a station of a sizable city in the middle of England and we were allowed off the train to stretch our legs. The ladies of the Red Cross were there to serve us coffee and doughnuts. Continuing our journey, the train took us through the industrial cities of Middlesex district. Late in the afternoon we stopped on a siding and were ordered off. With packs and rifles we marched some two miles to an established troop camp. We were late for the regular meal but were given some coffee and sandwiches before being assigned to our quarters.

This was a tent camp but the tents were twice as large as those we had in the states. Two squads were in each tent, which had a raised board floor but no bunks. Using our blankets we made our bed on the floor, and we learned how cold the nights were in England, even in June. Everyone woke up cold in the night and complained loudly. All had tried to sleep with their clothes on, but on the second night I figured that it would be better to take off the tight clothes and fold my two blankets so as to make a sleeping bag. I found this to be very comfortable, and I told the men in my squad about it. Not only were the nights cold, but very damp. We found our clothes almost wet when we dressed in the mornings. I learned to cover mine or use them as a pillow and thus kept them dry.

There were no showers on our ship, so it had been over two weeks since we had any kind of a bath. We noticed a small stream meandering through the meadow not far from the camp. We made a request and our officers arranged for us to visit this stream to bathe and wash our clothes. After a long morning drill we had the afternoon free and we hurried to the stream. There were several deep pools, and it looked so inviting we stripped and plunged in. It was June, but that water felt like it came from the north pole. But we got a welcome bath and washed our shirts, which dried rapidly in the sun and strong breeze.

The days were beautiful with a warm sun, which came up real early to burn off the morning mist. The country was alive with flowering hedges and flower gardens. We were reminded of the famous poem which every high school freshman had to learn starting with, "What is so rare as a day in June." This camp was near a quaint little village named Hastings. One afternoon during a break from drilling our lieutenant sat us in the shade of some large trees and had one of the men who was a history teacher tell us about the Battle of Hastings and what it meant to England. It gave us a good feeling of being part of history past and present.

Every day rumors spread through the camp as to when we would leave for France. We began to feel as if we were closer to the war for in the dead of night we could hear what sounded like distant thunder but it dawned on us it was the sound of distant artillery fire on the front. One day we had a brigade review with full packs, so we were sure it wouldn't be long before we moved. Two days later we were ordered to roll our packs and be ready to move after breakfast.

Someway I had developed a "charley horse" in the back of my right ankle. I reported to the camp doctor, and he bandaged it and told me the only cure was to work it out unless I wanted to go to the military hospital. That meant I would be left behind when my company moved, and I wasn't interested in that. For the first hour every morning when I tried to walk it was sheer misery and would then be better. So when we got orders to move I gritted my teeth and fell in with my squad.

All morning we marched down a narrow English lane winding through the beautiful countryside. Little cottages enclosed with white picket fences and flowering hedges stretched out mile after mile. We marched for periods of fifty minutes and then a ten minute break. As the hours increased, so did the weight of our packs and rifles. While we did not have to keep in step, the officers encouraged us to do so. They told us it made the way easier, and I think it did. Anyway, we were sure this was no training hike. We were on the way to the coast.

After a ten mile hike we arrived in a large open park in the center of Southampton. It was the middle of the afternoon and we were hot and exhausted. As soon as possible we stretched out full length on the grass. Soon a small boy and his sister started to wander among the soldiers trying to sell some small tarts. At first no one paid any attention to them being too tired to say anything, and also few had any money to spend. Suddenly everyone froze when one man let out a loud oath and called them a filthy name. Swearing was very common in the army, and I knew a lot of the young fellows picked it up thinking it made them tough, and I wondered about their future. But when the men heard what this one man said, there was a loud roar like the growl of an angry beast. Like others, I raised up to see two big burly men start in the direction of the culprit. They were right down angry and only the fact they couldn't determine just who the man was saved him from a beating. The children were frightened and ran out of the park. Along with others I had a better feeling about the basic moral fiber of the American soldier after that incident. Also, there was a lot less use of foul language in our platoon.

Around six o'clock we formed ranks again and marched down toward the docks. At the end of the street just before the docks were some long tables laden with coffee and sandwiches. It was a welcome sight, since we had not eaten after our breakfast in camp. After eating we moved down a long wooden dock and up a gang plank onto a channel ferry boat. Like a typical ferry it had a large room midship, but only a small part of the soldiers could get inside. Most of the men stretched out on deck beside their packs. Around nine that night our boat joined a large fleet of all kinds of ships to cross the English Channel. All around the convoy were little torpedo destroyers scurrying in and out like a pack of hounds looking for the trail of a U-boat.

We thought the north Atlantic was rough, but it was mild compared to the choppy waves of the Channel. We still had our sea legs, so the rolling and pitching of the clumsy ferry boat didn't bother us too much. But the wind was strong and cold. The cabin was overcrowded and grew stuffy, so we spent the night shifting back and forth between the areas of discomfort. But there was little complaining, since we knew we were now really close to France. It was another step closer to the front.

173

CHAPTER 13

WAR IN FRANCE

In the early morning fog we spotted the coast of France and the harbor of a large port city. Little dispatch boats were dashing from ship to ship of the convoy. In time our boat maneuvered to the dock and we stepped ashore at Le Harve, France. We marched up the street to some railroad yards, where we halted beside an entirely different kind of train. Before we had always traveled in passenger coaches, but these were cattle cars marked 40–8, meaning they would hold 40 men or 8 horses. It hit us that we were really getting closer to the war.

After a time a strange looking locomotive hooked onto our string of cars and we began to move out of the city. One thing I noticed about the French engines was that they had no bells such as used in the United States. They also had high pitched whistles but never gave any warning when they were about to move. Later we learned that the conductor did not give the signal to the engineer, but it was the station master who gave the order to leave. However, the trains in France did run on the right side of a double track, not on the left as in England.

Our food on this trip was reduced to hardtack and some canned beef. When the train stopped, as it frequently did in or near a small village, some of the men took a chance and hopped off to buy some French wine. That was one thing we learned about the French trains; they seemed to stop anywhere they felt like it. Later, when we did ride some passenger trains, they would often stop for no apparent reason in the open country. That was the signal for the men to hop off and, with their backs to the train, relieve themselves. They simply stood and urinated no matter who was looking. This was a method of relieving the congestion of the single toilet, which was used by both men and women. Since our first ride was in the cattle cars in which there were no toilets, we had to follow the French style.

Late in the afternoon our train stopped on a siding and we were ordered to detrain. After a short march we came to an open sandy field near a grove of pine trees. Here we proceeded to pitch our pup tents, just as we had done on the rifle range back at Camp Sherman. Being the last of June, the weather was warm and nights not so cold as in England. The only difficulty was the soil was so sandy we found it difficult to make the tent pegs hold. If there had been a strong wind at anytime, the tents would probably have blown away.

Now that we were in France, guard duty was far more strict than before. At night not only were they using loaded rifles, but also had fixed bayonets. The first night in this camp we were awakened in the night by quite a commotion among the guards. One guard was from our platoon and in the morning we asked him what had happened. He told us he was on post at the edge of the trees and when he heard something coming toward him, he gave the usual command, "Who goes there?" He got no reply and it kept right on coming, so he reached out and stabbed it with his bayonet. There was a loud squeal, so he called for the corporal of the guard. The corporal came with a flash light and they saw a trail of blood which they followed for a few yards until they came upon a dead hedgehog. The next morning the officers of the company held a board of inquiry, calling the guard before them. They quizzed him closely about the episode and finally asked him what he really thought was coming at him. By this time he was getting disgusted with their seemingly endless questions, so he replied by saying, "I really thought it was the Officer of the Day who was testing us." It happened that this officer was the least liked in the company, and they all knew it. Anyway, his answer stopped the questions. We all got a big kick out of it.

My first letter to Norah after we made camp was headed "Somewhere in France." This would be the heading of my letters for a long time as we were not permitted to tell where we were and all letters were now censored. This letter carried no date, but it indicates it was the first from France.

Somewhere in France.

Dearest,

We are in France already and we are rather glad to land on French soil as that is sort of the ambition of everyone in the Army to go to France. We sure were welcomed by the French people. You can see it in their faces, even if they can't express it in words. We are near a little French village and I have had the opportunity to visit it several times.

I have been trying to learn over again my French and have had great fun trying to make myself understood and understanding. Was really surprised at the ability I had in doing so. I have been spending part of the afternoon brushing up on it, also getting out some French lessons as four of us with a little knowledge of French were asked to conduct some classes. We haven't started yet, and you can imagine trying to work out something with only two or three books for the whole company. However, I think we can get a good deal out of it from the fact the men are thrown in contact with the natives who speak no English.

We celebrated the Fourth by a parade in the village. Assembled

176

on the plaza was the mayor, who made a short speech and was answered by one of our officers. As we started off the French school children threw flowers in the street. Then we had the afternoon off.

I like the French climate much better than the English as it is not so damp. But I believe the English scenery is more beautiful than what we have seen in France. We haven't received any mail yet. Hope we will soon, as I am anxious to hear from you. I heard of soldiers carrying old letters around with them to read and I know what that means now, as I have your last two letters with me all the time.

The war can't end any too soon to suit me, but I'm in it to see the end or else the end of me, and I know you wouldn't have it otherwise. As I told Mother in my letter to her, so far I am as safe or safer than I was driving the car about the streets of Cleveland. So there is no cause to worry. I am wondering what your plans are for another year. Hope you are enjoying the summer. My thoughts are of you and I love you just as much even if far away in miles.

Ray

After a few days in the pup tent we moved into a village a few kilometers south. There we were quartered in the loft of what had been a large horse barn. This was a typical French village where the inhabitants clustered together in the village but farmed the surrounding land. All the men of army age were gone, so some of this land stood idle. One such field became our drill grounds. We learned that we were about ten kilometers from the city of Le Mans, and some of the men went AWOL to visit that city. Fortunately, none of my squad did this, but some of the corporals in the company had to go into the city and find their men and bring them back for punishment.

It didn't take long for us to realize we were in a foreign land. We were introduced to the metric system, as all distances were measured in meters, and we began to think in kilometers instead of miles. Time was kept on a 24 hour basis, not divided into 12 hour periods as in the U.S. and England. The unit of money was the franc, and all else in multiples of 10. The smallest coin was the sou, which corresponded to our penny, but we thought mostly in francs. We had not had a pay day since Camp Sherman, and when we did, it was all in francs. We discovered that there were several types of paper money. The only one that was accepted everywhere was put out by the Bank of France. But each city and region had their individual francs, but it was accepted only in the locality. This caused a lot of confusion and many soldiers lost the value of their money when they were transferred to other parts of the country.

One night as we stood retreat, several men in our company were called out of line to receive promotions. I had been acting corporal since before leaving Camp Sherman and had been promised the rank.

177

But I was advanced to private first class only. One of the men in my squad who had done just as little as possible was named corporal. True, he had been in the service much longer than I had, but he had never led a squad or anything else to warrant the promotion. The rest of the men in my squad set up a howl after the company was dismissed, but it did no good. The lieutenant in charge of our platoon objected to this man leading a squad, and he was given a job in the company office. I continued to lead the squad as long as I was with this outfit.

Since the French people helped us celebrate the Fourth of July, our officers thought we should respond and help them celebrate Bastille Day, a day corresponding to our Fourth. We assembled in full regimental strength and marched three kilometers to a large village. After a brief rest we paraded through the main street before a large cheering crowd. The day was very warm and by the time we started marching back to camp we were dragging. On the way something happened which I never forgot.

About halfway back to camp we reached the top of a long sloping hill. Looking down we saw the line of march give way to a two-wheel donkey cart that a farmer was driving up the road. In a short time the farmer turned into a gate leading to his house, but the line kept bending out of the road as if the cart was still there. It struck me as foolish for the men to keep going farther than necessary just because the need once existed. I thought to myself, when I get to that point, if I go straight the men behind me will follow and the whole line will become straight. Thus I would save all the men in the column behind us the extra steps.

In my position on the left side of the line when we reached the point where the line started to bend, I followed my plan and stayed straight. But it didn't work, as the men in back of me did not follow and I was left alone out of line. Just as I realized this, I saw the lieutenant in front of the platoon start to turn around. With a quick side step I got back into the bending line before he could see who it was. However, he came back along the line angrily demanding, "Who was out of line?" Everyone looked straight ahead and said nothing, so I got away with it. But I decided then never to try to reform the army. When we reached the top of the hill on the further side of the valley I glanced back and saw the column still bending around the place of the long vanished cart.

I have told this story many times to illustrate how an organization such as the army or a large corporation or school system can follow a procedure which once had a purpose and reason but the reason had long vanished, yet they waste time and effort by blindly following the practice.

A letter I wrote about this time shows how we were feeling.

178

Dear Norah;

This is a very quiet sunny afternoon. By the sounds emitted from the throats of the men lying around, one would think he was in a saw mill. I performed the always needful necessary and usually always waiting task of journeying to the mill stream to give my clothes a bath. I then sat down ready to write when came the order to "fall in for church." so we marched out to the drill field where we received a discourse by the Chaplain on "Why we love America." A very fitting subject I thought to a bunch of men whose chief subject of conversation is along that line . . . .

Things are not as bad as they might be. It is largely the way we look at it anyway. I got a letter from Dale, who is down on the border and bewailing the fact he isn't sent to France. I told him that even if we are in France we were not all at the front by any means.

There have been a number of transfers made out of our company but fortunately or unfortunately, I don't know which I haven't been included. It's all a game of chance anyway, so I've decided just to take things as they come and make the best of them until this is over. Of course, that's what we have to do anyway, but there's a lot of feeling that you decide it for yourself . . . Must close to stand retreat. Hope you are enjoying your vacation. Write often.

With love,
Ray.

The last part of July our drilling began to take on a new form. We were introduced to the use of a bayonet in close fighting, then drilled on the proper formation of a squad in approaching the enemy lines. Also we were issued gas masks. Chemical warfare was being used more and more, so all the troops at or near the front had to have these masks. We were instructed on how to put them on in a hurry whenever the alarm "gas" was given. These masks covered the face and were held in place with straps over the head. A device like a clothes pin was clamped over the nose so all breathing had to take place through the mouth. The mouth was placed over the end of a rubber tubing, which was connected to a canister filled with ingredients which absorbed the poisonous gas as one inhaled through this tube. Exhaling was done through a valve in the face mask. The whole thing was very uncomfortable, first because one had to breathe through the mouth and second, because the mask was made of rubber so perspiration quickly formed and ran down one's face. Vision was maintained through two large isinglass lenses, which unless frequently treated, would steam over so it was impossible to see.

After considerable practice with the masks, we were taken for real training at a "gas house." A group of 25–30 were ordered inside this building and the doors closed tight. An officer announced that at his signal real tear and mustard gas would be turned on in the room. At his shout of "gas" we were to don our masks and then march around the room clockwise. After marching for several minutes, the officer told us when he gave the signal we were to unmask and the door would be opened and we could rush out. Of course, it became a game of musical chairs to see who would be nearest the door when the signal was given. I was one of the unlucky ones, as I was at the farthest point from the door when we had to unmask. There was such a rush to get to the door that a jam was formed so a number of us couldn't hold our breath long enough to get outside before we got a lung full of the gas. Like others, I was sick for a time so I never forgot the odor of that gas. It also made me susceptible to all forms of gas the rest of my life.

A few days after our experience in the gas house, the whole regiment was ordered to march around a square of a kilometer on a side. We carried full packs, rifles, canteens filled with water and our gas masks at the position of "ready." This was the same as if at the front. When we reached the halfway point, a cry of "gas" went up and down the line, so we had to don our masks while in motion. It was a hot day and soon sweat was streaming down our faces inside the mask. To march with all our heavy equipment was hard enough, but to do so while breathing through our mouths inside those masks was really rugged. We had to keep them on for thirty minutes and before the time was up there were groans and wails coming from everywhere. Some of the men began to faint and fall out, but the sergeants began to rush up and down the column exhorting everyone to hold out. "Don't disgrace your outfit by quitting," they kept yelling. If it hadn't been for them, I am sure a lot of us would have quit. I was proud of my squad for we all finished on our feet.

The French lessons I referred to in my letter to Norah didn't last very long. Years later, when principal of Utica Free Academy, I was called on to make a presentation to a French teacher who was retiring. After a few introductory remarks, I surprised the teachers present at the dinner when I said, "Probably you don't know that I once taught French. It happened when I was in the army during World War I. Soon after we landed in France, the captain of my company learned that I could speak a little French. He decided that I should teach the rest of the men in our company. The company was divided into large groups which met in a big barn for French lessons. I proceeded with the greetings, such as "Bonjour, Monsieur", etc., then continued with common expressions such as "tout de suite, s'il vous plait, merci beaucoup," etc. Then when I got to the point of explaining the difference between "Madame" and "Mademoiselle," the brass decided the men knew enough French and the classes were discontinued." The teachers got a good laugh out of my story and thought I had made a good joke, but actually that was just about the way it happened.

The longer we stayed in this camp the poorer the food became. There was no refrigeration so all the meat we had was either canned or cured, such as salt pork. Like many others, I developed diarrhea, so one day I was excused from drill. Between times of running to the latrine, I lay on my bunk sweating it out. The company headquarters office was in the front part of this big barn where we were billeted. I didn't realize it before, but when everything was still I could hear everything that was said in the office through the thin partition. Half asleep, I heard the clerks reading a list of names which were to be transferred to the Second Division. I came wide awake when I heard my name added to the list. This confirmed the rumors which had been spreading that our division, the 83rd, was made a replacement outfit. It was years later when I read General Pershing's memoirs that I learned the reason for this. He told how the general of this division was not qualified to lead troops in the field, but was blocked by the politicians back in the states from removing him. Pershing got around the difficulty by leaving the general in place, but made the division a training outfit for those on the front.

When my platoon came in after drill, I told them what I had heard. So they were somewhat prepared when the next morning a long list of names was read with orders to pack and be ready to go to the Second Division. We knew this outfit was one of the most active at the front and suffered one of the highest number of casualties. To my surprise my name was not read, but I know I heard right because for some time my mail was sent to the Second Division and much later returned. This indicates how close I came to being sent into the thick of the fighting.

The reason my name was not included on that list was later that day a request was received for men to be sent to form an Army Corps headquarters. Since I had a college education my name was included with about a dozen others with similar education and told to report that afternoon for transfer. I was weak from the diarrhea, but I was so glad to get out of that camp that I packed my pack and with my rifle, hiked three kilometers to a railroad station. I don't know how it happend, but as soon as I left camp my trouble stopped.

When we arrived at the station we found another group assembled and we thought we were to join them when the station master stopped a train and put them on, but he told us we were not included. Later a truck arrived and took us to the Division Headquarters in Le Mans. There we met Lieutenant Vickery, who announced he was in charge of our detachment. The next day we boarded a train for Paris, where we changed to another line which took us south to a place called Neufchateau. Off the train we were directed to a large military barracks like those in the states. We were assigned to a Headquarters Troop of the 4th Army Corps.

The next morning at reveille it became apparent that there was considerable difficulty in assigning us to a troop. They were a cavalry

181

unit and while they had no horses, their commands were given as if they were mounted. We were trained with the army commands and the result was so confusing that the officers met and decided we were to be called a detachment and need not stand formations. The troop did the guard duty and stood all the formations required.

There was quite a large group of men coming from different outfits. All any of us knew was we were to report at this place for duty. Then we were informed that we were to organize the various offices of the 4th Army Corps, which had just been authorized. We lined up one morning and a certain number of the men were counted off and told to report to G–1, the next to G–2, and then to G–3 and so on. Of course, there were no such offices, but they were expected to organize them. All the group I was with, including Lieutenant Vickery, were told to organize a mobile U. S. Post Office. A check indicated that neither the lieutenant nor any man in our group had every worked in a post office. All we had ever done was to mail a letter, get our mail or buy a stamp. This was typical of the army at that time. Little or no effort was made to put men in places for which they were best qualified. But to the credit of the men in this army, it was amazing how they carried out their assignments with such a high degree of proficiency. Of course, men did get put in places where they couldn't do the work, but the trial and error methods had a way of curing the situation.

In our group besides Lieutenant Vickery, who was in charge, was one sergeant named Rutherford, who was considered second in command. The rest of the fifteen men were all privates. After a brief consultation between the two officers, Sergeant Rutherford called us together and the lieutenant divided us up into small groups for special assignments. One group was to look after the out-going mail, another to meet the trains and transport the mail bags, etc. He selected me to have charge of sorting all the incoming mail and assigned a younger man, Eddie Kihm, to be my assistant. For an office we were given a small empty store building. We found some empty wooden boxes and made pigeon hole racks for sorting the mail. Later we secured some tables and chairs and other equipment, but for the present we considered ourselves in business.

We had nothing to tell us of the organization of a Corps Headquarters nor were we given the names of any of the officers. From my study of history I knew a little of what it should be, so I labeled the rack with names, such as Commanding General, Chief of Staff, Surgeon General, and guessed at the rest. At no time were we ever told who these officers were. I had to learn them from the mail they received or quizzing the orderlies who came for their mail.

The first order we received from GHQ was we were to be a mobile post office assigned to the 4th Army Headquarters and would move whenever and wherever they did. We were given an official title of APO 775.

Since there was a permanent APO in town, our lieutenant got us permission to visit it in groups of two or three to learn what we could about what we should do. I was the last one to be sent. I was gone for two hours and when I stepped through the door when I got back I knew instantly that something bad had happened. I could feel the tension in the air and before I could hang up my hat the man next to the door said, "The Lieutenant wants to see you." "What happened?" I asked. He just shook his head and said, "You better report at once." Lieutenant Vickery was in the back of the room and I could tell by his face that something was very wrong. I saluted and said, very formal like, "The Lieutenant wishes to see me?" "You are damned right I want to see you," he shouted. "Where have you been?" I was completely dumbfounded and replied that I had been down at the town post office, just as he told me to go. He just grunted and added, "I'll have you understand, Calhoon, this is not a one man operation." Still puzzled, I replied, "Yes, sir," and walked away.

As soon as I could get Sergeant Rutherford aside, I asked him what it was all about. He said while I was away a small bag of mail came in and Eddie had sorted it, but he got the generals all mixed up. The Chief of Staff got complaints from the various offices and came himself and "bawled out" our lieutenant for not having things straight. No wonder the lieutenant was ready to jump on me. Poor Eddie was very upset, but I told him to forget it, that I was just lucky I hadn't made the same mistake. But I rather gloated inside, because I was the only one in the group who had figured out what to do. Neither the lieutenant nor the sergeant had helped.

APO 775. Lt. Vickery and Sgt. Rutherford are seated
in the front and I am in the back center.

After a couple of weeks or so another lieutenant was assigned to our office to be the censor of the mail going out from the men in the troop and detachments. But more important was the addition of a post office clerk by the name of Maguire to handle all stamps and money orders. He came from the Boston area and could speak French which pleased us and also being a real civil service clerk with experience in a post office, he was a big help in getting us properly organized. In a short time we became a congenial working outfit. Sergeant Rutherford was a graduate of a tech school in Steubenville, Ohio, and we became good friends. Lieutenant Vickery was a Cleveland lawyer and all the men were from Ohio. After some time I and another man were promoted to corporal, but in this group rank made little difference. By strange good luck our group stayed together all through the war and months afterwards.

Parts of two letters I wrote to Norah at this time indicate some of my feelings.

On Active Service.
Aug. 4, 1918

Dearest,

I have moved again so have missed my mail. Will take a while for it to catch up. I was notified one morning to be ready at any time to move. The next day I left with a few others and sent to Division H.Q. Then we were transferred to this place. I am now assigned to Headquarters Troop of the 4th Army Corps. My work for the present and probably for some time is in the post office.

I don't know how it ever happened I got into this. I never asked for anything and it all came as a surprise. We had no idea when we left camp where we were going.

We are in a beautiful part of France, some of the prettiest scenery I have ever seen. Makes me think a little of the country around Houghton. We are in a fair-sized town where they have real stores. Seems good after being in the back woods for so long.

I had a long letter from Mr. Marshall telling about the affairs of the Gas Producer Co. and things turned out just about the way I expected, not dead yet but doesn't look good . . .

It doesn't seem possible it is August. Am wondering where you will be this fall? Hope you have been feeling fine this summer . . .

Love,
Ray

A. P. O. 775
Am. E. F. Via N. Y.
Aug. 11, '18

My Dear,

I received two letters from you this week. One July 2 and the other telling me you would come to New York to see me. That made me sort of homesick or as near to it as I get.

I wrote you last week about my change and work in the Post Office. We have been getting organized and coming along fine. We have a lieutenant over us who doesn't know a thing about postal work so we plan our work about as we please, which suits me very much better than the infantry, which was drill-drill-drill. I was feeling pretty blue when so many of the fellows I came across with were being transferred and I was told I would be left behind. I wrote a letter about that time and you will probably recognize it by the tone of it.

I can't complain a bit here and only hope I can stick with this organization until the war is over. I hear that the report is around the states that we can tell where we are situated. I guess a few commands can but we can't. Anyway, we are a mobile P.O. so we will be moving from place to place. I can say we passed through Paris on the way here but only to change depots, so didn't see much. I sure would like the chance to visit it.

I suppose by the time you get this you will be thinking of school. Are you going back to Brookfield Center? You asked about sending something. I guess there are certain things that can be sent, not much. There isn't anything I really need, especially when one has to carry everything on one's back. We have plenty to eat and plenty tobacco . . .

> With Love,
> Ray

Although I couldn't tell at the time, we were near Neufchateau in the central part of France. Nearby was a small village which we learned was called DO-RE-MI, made famous as the birthplace of Joan De Arc. The country did resemble the hills around Houghton, although it was cut up into very small fields compared to those in the States.

After a time we learned that the personnel of an Army Corps headquarters was very diversified. The enlisted men were either in the Troop, which did the guard duty and stood formations, or in the detachments, which organized and ran the offices. There was also a body of army clerks who were not in the army but civil service employees. They wore a different uniform and were free from much of the army regulations. They were the stenographers for the officers. Then there were the numerous officers, ranging all the way from lieutenants to major generals. The high officers all had orderlies and among their other duties came to the post office for the mail. While I learned the names of the various officers by sorting their mail, I rarely saw them. They were in a different world from ours.

By early August rumors were rife that we were to move up near the front lines. Those of us in the offices had turned in our rifles, then one day we were ordered to report to the supply tent. The men were ordered to turn in their campaign hats and were issued the famous overseas cap and a steel helmet. At the time I had been sent out with a Ford light truck, which had just been assigned to our office. By the time I got back the supply tent was closed, but I didn't worry as I felt I could see them the next day. However, as a surprise we were ordered that evening to stand for inspection. Of course, I had to explain why I didn't have my cap and helmet. When we were told we were to march to the drill field to receive instructions on how to use the helmets with a gas mask and would be under fire with real gas shells, I thought I should be excused, but the officer in charge said, "No!" I would have to make the best of it.

After marching about a mile out of town, we were introduced to some trenches which had been dug to represent the front line. Soon after we were located we froze when we heard the whine of an approaching artillery shell. It exploded some yards in front of the trench and believe me, I hugged the side of the dirt trench as mud and gravel fell all around us. If any shrapnel was to fall on my old hat, that hat was not much of a protection. After several shells exploded around us, the cry of "gas" went up and down the line. Off came our head gear and on went our masks. It was real, they were live gas shells. We were out for over two hours and had a taste of what trench warfare was like. The next morning I got my cap and helmet, which I used all through the war and brought them with me when discharged.

The rumors of our moving toward the front proved true near the middle of August. The headquarters was considered fully organized and ready to assume action. Our office equipment was loaded on an army truck and all personnel were taken by train north to the city of Toul. At first we were quartered in a large factory building. This proved to be very interesting as one end of the building was still in operation with mostly women workers. All the latrines were outside the building on a long raised platform. They were used by both the men and women. There were no closed stalls, only seats separated by thin partitions and entered by a low swinging door. All were open at the top and to find a place, one had to go along the line and look over the top to find one not occupied. When the officers found out about this, they made a protest to the French and soon areas were posted for "men" and for "women." The French workers laughed at us as they could see no reason for the change.

The first night after we arrived, we found out that we were really near the front. About 10 p.m. we heard the sound of an airplane overhead, which had a different rhythm to its motor than we had been accustomed to with the American or French planes. When the anti-aircraft batteries opened up, we knew it was a German airplane. The Germans used a different firing order than the Allies used, so it was easy to tell, day or night, whether it was a friendly or enemy plane overhead. When we heard the firing we became so excited that we rushed outside to see the show. It was like a Fourth of July celebration—fireworks when the anti-aircraft shells began to explode high in the sky.

We hadn't been out in the yard very long before our officers came rushing out and ordered us back under cover. The building would not have been much protection against a direct hit of a bomb, but it did afford safety from falling shrapnel. This was the danger which the officers were concerned about and called us "fools" for being out in the open without even our helmets. Fortunately, no one was injured but the next morning when we picked up several pieces of shrapnel where we had been standing, we learned our lesson and never took such a chance again.

Toul was a fair-sized city, the railhead for supplies for the American army. The nearby front was the area that General Pershing had succeeded in getting the Allied command to agree should be taken over by the American army. Up to that time the British and French wanted the American units to be incorporated into their armies and under their command. Pershing consented to this at first until the Americans could gain some firsthand experience with veteran troops at the front. But now he insisted that it was time for the American army to act as a unit and be under the command of its officers. The allies finally agreed by giving this part of the front, which had been quiet for a long time, to Pershing to see what he could do with what they considered green troops.

One reason the Americans wanted their own front was they were not satisfied with the stalemate type of trench warfare that the British and French had adopted. Our Marines had demonstrated convincingly at the Marne how their accurate fire power could stop the German advance once they got out of the trenches. The whole American army from the lowest rank to the very top were eager to get out of the dirty trenches and try their own special type of open fighting.

After a few days our post office was assigned an empty store building near the center of the city and we were billeted on the third floor. The 4th Corps was now in active service and since we were the only APO in its area, we began one of the busiest times of our existence. We learned the priority of shipping near the front. First was ammunition, second food and third mail. Food became better and as members of the postal service, we had freedom of transportation.

Of course, the Germans were not long in learning that the American army was taking over this area and the activity was increasing day by day. Artillery fire began to increase and we were never out of the sound of the big guns, day or night. No shells struck the city but came close to the railroad yards which were on the western outskirts of the city.

Almost every night one or more German planes came over dropping bombs. They, too, were after the railhead, but often missed and hit parts of the city. The Germans were methodical and they seemed to plan their planes to be over us just after 10 p.m. when we had gone to bed. There were bomb shelters all over the city, and for the first few nights we would roll out and go to the nearest. We would wait until the "all clear" was given and then with our rest broken, return to bed. After a time we got sick of rolling out every night and reasoned that we were protected from falling shrapnel and the chances of being hit by a bomb was about the same as being struck by lightning. So we stayed in bed listening to see how close the bombs were dropping.

As the build up of our troops became greater, the bombing also increased. One night things really got hot. When a bomb dropped in the street in front of our building and shrapnel came in the open window lodging in the ceiling of our room, we decided it was time to seek shelter. A new shelter had recently been opened on our street in the basement of a large Catholic church. We had never been there, but after jumping into our clothes we hurried down to the street and when it seemed best, ran for the shelter.

The sign for the shelter was over a side door of the church and we pushed it open and then in the dark followed each other along a narrow hall and down a stairs. Opening another door, we entered a large wine cellar deep under the church building. The room was dimly lit with a few candles. When our eyes became adjusted we could see that the room was full, mostly women and children with a few old men and a couple of priests in their robes. Like all shelters the double doors kept any light from being seen from outside. That was a rule that had been impressed on all of us. No light of any kind was to be shone at night which might help the enemy planes to locate the city.

As we entered the room, an audible murmur rose from the crowd. Evidently they thought it must be real bad if the American soldiers sought shelter. It was, as the bombs kept falling closer and closer. This was not a case of the Germans missing the railhead. They were after the city. The explosions began to rock the church building and the floor vibrated like an earthquake. The sound of the anti-aircraft guns was constant. During the height of the bombardment everyone was very quiet. Only occasionally would a mother say something to still the fears of a small child. Then as the bombs receded, the people began to talk in low tones. Even the priests who had stood near the inner door and were the focus of all eyes when they crossed themselves after each close hit, now relaxed and began to converse. Mothers who had been holding their babies now relaxed and let the older ones loose. At the opposite end of the hall was a group of teenage girls gathered together on a blanket.

All the time we had remained standing near the door and were about to leave when there was a loud shout from the bevy of girls, followed a few minutes later by a burst of laughter. All the women looked at us to see if we understood what was so funny. Maguire, the postal clerk, was with us and we knew he understood French. But when we quizzed him as to what they said, he replied, "Wait until we get outside and I will tell you." All the time he kept a straight face so the women relaxed, thinking we didn't understand. When the girls made their big outburst, the old priest said something in a stern voice and they grew quiet, but we could see that they were dying with laughter inside.

As soon as the bombing stopped we left for our quarters. Once outside we surrounded Maguire to find out what the girls were laughing about. He explained that the first time the girls laughed was when one said, "Girls, do you know when that biggest bomb fell I was so scared I wet my pants." Then later, when they hooted, the girl said, "You know, girls, I told you I wet my pants after that big bomb, but now I discovered I came away in such a hurry I forgot my pants." We all thought it was a big joke and laughed about it many times. It also showed some of the psychological effects on a group of people gathered together in times of great danger.

Situated as we were, it became evident that our corps was building up in strength. We also knew what divisions were being added, as we were given the added responsibility of routing their mail. When two famous divisions, the First and the 42nd moved in, we knew that the rumors we had heard for some time must be true. The talk was that the American army was given the task of wiping out the St. Mihiel salient. This was a bulge in the front line extending south toward Toul and was a threat to cutting the railroad line from Nancy to Paris. This line was essential to the Allies to move supplies along this front. The Germans had held this salient since 1914 but had only used it as a threat. The high command had now decided it was time to wipe it out and Pershing had succeeded in having the American army under his command take on this task. Tension was building up daily in our headquarters, as it was to be the first test of the 4th Corps in action.

Then at 4 a.m. on September 8th, we were startled out of a sound sleep and came out of our bunks standing. Our building was shaking as if there was an earthquake. "The push is on," we all shouted. For an hour or so the barrage continued without any let up. We had become accustomed to the sound of the big guns both day and night but nothing like this had happened before. Following the heavy barrage which flattened the barbed wire entrenchments the Germans had erected in front of their trenches, the barrage started to move forward and the troops waiting in the front line trenches went over the top and moved quickly into German territory. Of course, through their intelligence information the Germans knew the push was coming and had pulled out their heavy artillery and some of their troops. Yet the timing came as a surprise, so there were enough troops left to give a good rear guard action.

All day we watched as motorcycle couriers brought dispatches from the front to headquarters. We had to depend on whatever information leaked out of the offices to know how successful the drive was. Word soon was circulated that things had gone better than expected. In fact, in several cases the infantry moved so fast they ran into the barrage which our artillery was expected to lay down in front of them. At the end of the first day our troops were beyond their objectives and in four days the whole St. Mihiel salient had been wiped out. This was a big victory for the American army and once out of the trenches they never returned.

When things had settled down after the drive, our post office was swamped by soldiers and officers sending souvenirs back home. Anything German that had been captured that was not too heavy was sent by parcel post. Some of the common articles were belt buckles, uniform buttons or insignias, Iron Crosses, (it seemed that practically every German soldier had one), and helmets. Also, a number of the units were receiving their first pay since being in France and many were sending some of the money home by way of postal orders. No one except Maguire, the postal clerk, was supposed to sell stamps or write postal orders, but when he became swamped and I was not busy, I asked if I could help. He said, "Yes, you weigh the packages and write the amount due on the front and I'll sell the stamps and make the change." This helped speed up the lines, but when a representative of a whole company would bring in a big batch of money orders, Maguire got so tied up that he asked me to take over the parcel post operation. We then divided the group into two lines, one for packages and one for postal orders, so things moved much faster.

All of us in the office got a big "kick" out of the fact that Maguire was a civil service employee and could ignore the army regulations of rank. When an officer would come in and see a long line and assert his rank by stepping in front, Maguire would look up and in a stern voice which everyone could hear say to the officer, "Please, get back in line. There is no rank in the post office." It was all we could do to keep a straight face when the officer with a red face would either get back at the end of the line or march haughtily out of the office. It soon became noticeable that officers from the rank of Major and up never pulled rank and no officer from the front lines, even when the men offered to let him go ahead, would take advantage. Thus, the post office was the only place in the whole army where all ranks were equal.

In spite of the important things that were happening on the nearby front, the censor of our mail would not let us write about it. So my letter written near the end of the St. Mihiel drive made no mention of it but this is what I wrote:

France,
September 11, '18

Dear Norah,
As you thought your letters came in a bunch, that is, three did and they looked good. It had been a long time since I had received

190

any from you and those I did get were written before you heard from me. . . Here I had been handling thousands of letters for other people, but none came for me until yesterday. Seven then appeared, three from you, two from Mother, one from Faye and one from Mrs. Frazier, which I was surprised to get. I wrote Jess a long time ago and she said he was already in camp, and she couldn't resist the temptation to open and read my letter. Of course, I didn't care and was glad to hear from her. She told about Jess' wedding, the first news I had of it.

Your letters are dated July 25, Aug. 7 and 8. Wish I could answer all your questions fully, as I would be glad to do if possible. I'll have to wait and tell you about it. I can answer some of them. I think I have described all the scenery, seems like that is all I've written about. The reason I didn't say more about my companions was I didn't make any close friends back in the company. We were all just friendly but I found no one to chum with, in fact, I was sort of lonesome there, but now I have found a "buddy." We are rooming together first time we have anything like privacy. His name is Rutherford, was in school in Pittsburgh, Penna. when drafted. A mightly clean cut fellow and we are enjoying each other's company while it lasts. We never know in the army how soon we may be transferred.

There is one fellow with us who is a constant joke, all the time getting in bad but always coming out OK. Here is an example, we dispatch mail every night late. One night this fellow went around the station to get a hand truck to load the mail on. He saw one with two officers sitting on it and taking them for French in the dark goes up and says, "Pardon Monsieurs, American Poste, parte tout de suite." The officers, thinking he was French, got up and said, "Oh, Hell! take the damned thing." He made off with it before they found out the difference. He had said all the French he knew but we tell him he would make a good Frenchman as he talks with his hands.

Tell your mother and folks I appreciate their remembrances. Suppose you are away from home now. I shall be glad to hear from you after your trip to Houghton . . . .

With much love,
Ray.

On September 26th I wrote again;

Just got a letter from you addressed back at Camp Mills, so I have all you mentioned. Our work has dropped off some as they have established a permanent P.O. in the town. We had a little time to ourselves and begged a baseball of the Red Cross and since we had four gloves in the detachment, we got out in the street to get some recreation. Ought to see the audience of natives we had. Every time the ball would strike the big glove and make a big noise, they would all say, "Ah." It was quite amusing.

I had a chance to go up toward the front lines several days ago. All was quiet then. I could see a line of observation balloons marking the front line. Whenever either side throws over a barrage it wakes us from sleep. Believe me the American boys can talk to them when it comes to big guns as well as in other ways . . . .

It has been cold the last few days so we have a fire in the fireplace in the room where we work. We have to rustle the wood from any place we can find it. The good news from all fronts begins to look as if Germany was beginning to crumble. Hope so, for it can't be over too soon for any of us. The grape season is on here and we can buy them in the shops and believe me, they are delicious. . . .

I am glad you had a good time at Houghton and I sure would want to be with you when you go back again. But everytime we get to talking about the end of the war someone always says, "Well, don't make any dates yet."

> With love,
> Ray.

In my letter I mentioned about going up near the front line. It came about in this way. After the St. Mihiel drive was over, our corps was reorganized. The battle tested divisions were moved north to prepare for the Battle of the Argonne. This left a number of smaller units holding the now quiet front north of Toul. It became our job to take mail to these outfits whenever possible. We used our light Ford truck, taking turns but always in pairs as a precaution. When it became my turn to be one of the two to go we were held up by the military police for a couple of days as they reported considerable shelling at that point. When we did get through we found the house which had been the company headquarters completely gone. The men were dug in where the cellar had been and came out with shouts of joy when they heard our "mail call." This was my first experience of visiting a battle field just after the fighting had stopped. The destruction was extensive, but the thing I noticed was the awful sickening odor of decaying animal and human flesh. Although this was supposed to be a quiet section, action did take place and casualties resulted. This odor was something I never read about in descriptions of battles, but to me it was one of the deepest impressions of the war. It made me feel that war is "hell" more than the massive destruction of towns I saw in France.

The Meuse-Argonne offense began on September 25 and while the 4th Corps was active in all the battles, we were much father from the action than previously. Rumors circulated daily that we were to move nearer the front. Early in October I decided to look around the shops in Toul for something I could send Norah for Christmas. I thought she would not want a war souvenir, so one afternoon Rutherford, who had the same problem, found a small shop on a side street which displayed silk goods. They did not speak English, so I had to make my limited French do. I found a silk scarf which the little sales girl kept repeating, "Tres jolie." I agreed that it was very pretty, but I said the price was too much. Actually, I didn't think so, but I knew the French loved to dicker, so we dickered until she beamed when I said I would take it. I sent it to Norah before Christmas and it was fortunate, as it was the last chance I had to shop for a long time.

All during the early part of October the American army was advancing, pushing the Germans farther back the lines of communication to our headquarters were too long. A letter to Norah tells some of what happened.

October 12, '18

Dear Norah,

As we have become settled down in our new place and things have become established again, I've time to write. We thought we had settled down in our comfortable place for the winter but we were fooled. One evening we got orders to be ready to move the next day. We packed up by noon and then waited until 6 o'clock for a truck and landed in our new place about 8 o'clock at night in the dark and not allowed any lights to unload. We spread our blankets on the floor and went to bed, supperless. However, the next morning after getting our equipment set up and ready to do business by noon, we then scouted around and found some old bunks left by some engineering outfit and proceeded to make ourselves comfortable. We haven't near as nice a place as we left but it could be worse.

We are in a little village built on a hillside. It is located very near where the front line trenches used to be and from the top of the hill we can look over what was once "no man's land," and also the territory once held by the Germans. We can hear the guns much plainer and can see the flashes at night. The Allies have sure got the Germans going now, if they can only keep it up it means "finis" to the Dutch before long.

I think I am due for a "Cross of Honor," or something as a General came around on an inspection tour and as it happened the Lieutenant and the Sergeant were both out, so it fell on me to do the honors. I had a very pleasant [visit?] with him while the other fellows that were in the office stood stiffly at attention. The way it happened was this; I had finished my work, in fact all of us were at ease waiting for the mail truck to get back, and I had just sat down to write a letter to mother when I heard someone, evidently an officer, "bawling" someone out. I glanced up to see a colonel and a general standing inside the door. The lieutenant in charge of the troop was in the hall calling someone down for not coming to attention.

I immediately called "Attention!" The lieutenant then came in

193

from the hall blustering and addressed the room at large, "How many men work here?" As no one was really in charge, the fellow nearest the door took it upon himself to answer. He stammered, "I don't know, Sir." I thought I would drop, it was the worst answer he could have made. Of course, the lieutenant blew up. He wanted to know where the officer in charge was, and being told that Lieutenant Vickery and Sergeant Rutherford were both with the truck going to the railhead to look for overseas mail, he wanted to know how much mail we handled.

I thought it about time to either make things better or worse, so I took a shot and answered him. Then he began a bombardment of questions on me; after he had run down, the General came over to my racks and looked things over, all the time fingering my letter. I expected every minute he would ask how it came I had time to write. But anyway, after I had answered every question, he finally left apparently satisfied. We all had a good laugh afterwards.

My dear, you have been asking several times if you could send me something. I don't really know what you can send in a box this size, but anyway, I'll give you an opportunity with the necessary authority. As we are allowed only one of these coupons, I had a hard time to decide whether to send it to you or Mother. (Just secured another coupon). Whatever you do, don't send a razor as the government has given us two while I started with one. I think they don't want us to start copying the French style of a moustache. Haven't heard from you in over a week. Hope to get one soon.

Love,
Ray.

The episode referred to in this letter came about in this way. The heavy fighting in the Argonne Forest had caused a lot of casualties in the units at the front. There was a call for replacements and rumors circulated that men from the various offices would be taken. Then a letter from the Chief of Staff was sent to all the offices saying that the Inspector General would visit and investigate all offices to see if men could be released for service at the front. Our lieutenant had been nervously awaiting this inspection for several days. We had not received any mail from the States for two weeks and he was sure that there was a hold up at the railhead, so he took the sergeant with him to go and investigate. That was the day the general came to inspect.

Actually, after the young lieutenant had blown off steam and the general came over to talk with me, things became very calm. When I explained to the general the various functions of the post office and he looked at my racks with the names of all the divisions and other outfits which made up our corps, he turned to his aide and said, "It looks as if they need all the men they have to do this job." Then as he turned to go he returned my salute and with a little smile said, "Keep the mail coming, it's important."

When the lieutenant returned with no mail he was in a bad mood. Then when he was told about the inspection he wanted to know all about what happened. He seemed a bit sorry not to be there but was relieved that it was over. He never thanked me for taking over, although the men told him how I had saved the day and were loud in their praise.

The little village we were in was too near the front lines to have any inhabitants. It had been a company command post but was now taken over as the corps headquarters. Many buildings had been demolished but those left became our offices. We had to be extremely careful about showing any light at night. All the outside doors were made double and only one set could be opened at a time.

The trip from Toul gave us the experience of how truck convoys moved at night. They could show no light of any kind, so each truck was protected at both front and back with heavy bumpers. Since there were frequent stops, they needed this protection. In order to keep on the road at night the drivers watched upward to keep halfway between the lines of the tall lombardy poplar trees which lined the roads in France. It was surprising how on even the darkest rainy nights the outline of these trees would show against the sky.

We were located about four kilometers from St. Mihiel, the village that gave the name to this area. We knew that the houses in this place had been under heavy shell fire and we wanted to see what it was like. We took turns, four at a time, hiking and sightseeing. All the houses, as in most parts of France, were constructed of stone and the result showed many freak things that happened. One of the few houses left standing had a hole all the way through where a shell had passed through without exploding. Another, a three-story house, was half destroyed. It was as if a giant knife had sliced it down through the middle. All the rooms on the three floors were left exposed with the furniture in that part of the house left in place.

The day I took this trip was the one and only time I got really mad at the lieutenant. He had divided us into groups to have an afternoon off so we could go and this was the last group. I cleared my desk and went outside to meet the others when they told me that the lieutenant said I was not to go. I was surprised and upset and I told them to wait a minute until I could see the lieutenant. When I confronted him and reminded him that he had given me permission to go with this last group, all he would say was, "I want you here if any mail from the States comes in." No matter what I said he kept repeating the same thing. I was sure there would be no mail that day and I was so mad I decided to go. The others were surprised I had the nerve to take off but didn't blame me. I had reminded him of the many times I had worked long hours to sort the mail and would do so again, but he remained stubborn. So I took the chance of going since I didn't think he would do anything to me for he depended on me to handle the incoming mail correctly. Also, I had put in a request for a transfer which he wouldn't approve. Anyway, no mail came that day but my relations with the lieutenant were very formal for a long time.

In a letter to Norah on October 16, I wrote:

"It has been dark and rainy the last few days and the work rather dull . . . In spite of the mist, Rutherford and I slipped out this afternoon for a little walk through the woods which are turning all colors of the rainbow. Made me think more than ever of the good times in the woods at Houghton. Wish we could take one of those strolls now "N'est ce pas?"

Then another letter;

October 17, '18

My Dear;

I was indeed glad to get a letter from you today and although I wrote you last night, I feel like answering right away. I wonder which you will get first. I am glad you had such a good time. As for worrying about it it wouldn't do us or you any good. We don't worry about ourselves, get sort of stoical and take things as they come.

I told you I tried to get a transfer from the post office into something more active but failed, so I've settled down to make the most of it . . . I took a little hike tonight, the clouds which had been hanging low for days have broken through and a bright moon is shining. The moon light nites are brilliant here. There were four of us in the party and we visited a big underground chambers and tunnels made by the Americans when they took over this sector from the French. It is a veritable underground labyrinth into the side of the hill. But it was never completed as the Americans decided it was easier to go over and take the German dugouts and trenches. We also visited the old French trenches and barbed wire entanglements . . . .

We get lots of news here at headquarters before it is published and some that is not published. There will be much to tell when the boys get back. By the way, Maude Bradford Warren was in our office the other day and we had quite a visit with her. She writes for *The Saturday Evening Post* and had an article in the September 19 issue which we got hold of, and she describes our conditions very well . . . .

Love,
Ray.

Oct. 23, '18

Dear Norah,

I received two letters from you yesterday, one telling of your father's accident and your own illness. I want to express my sympathy to you both. I can hardly imagine your father in bed. He always looked so strong and healthy, but we never know what is going to happen. I also hope your illness didn't last long.

Today was the first nice day we have had in weeks, so I climbed on the truck going into town for mail and while there had my picture taken. Don't know what it will be like as they don't give you a chance to see proofs, just make them for you and you pay for them.

Yes, I got your letters from Houghton and Pa. I am glad you had a good time. I have to laugh at the secrets Miss Grange told you. I believe that is all those folks have to do is to keep alive some of those happenings. They are always living in the past.

I think you are right about the war being over by next summer but I can't see it will be before then in spite of the good news from all fronts.

I am very much surprised to learn of my good fortune on the invention. It's all news to me. Fact is, I guess it's all dead for all the information I can get out of it. I've heard nothing since July and part of my letters have come back. I can't understand that but I think I'll soon find out what is going on . . . .

Lot of Love,
Ray.

Dear Norah;

I was glad to get your letter of Oct. 4 telling that you were better and able to teach. You see our mail is coming through much better now. I sent you a copy of the *Stars and Stripes* last week. It's the weekly paper put out by the A. E. F. Thought you might like to see it.

Today was nice and I got away for a hike this afternoon, the woods are still beautiful although the leaves are falling. I can't help but think of the times that fall in old Houghton among the hills and woods. I'll be glad to get back to the old USA. There is nothing to write about as the work is the same over and over again. But the news from the Allies looks good and the replies of Wilson are great.

Well, Dear, I am sure there is no other girl for me, these Mesdemoiselles don't interest me at all. I am anxious to get back to you.

With lots of love,
Ray

Oct. 29, '18

Dearest Norah,

Everytime the sun shines and the woods look so inviting I think of you . . . Yesterday was a good flying day and the Germans were dropping peace propaganda over our lines. We made some copies and am enclosing one so you can see how ridiculous they are. Also a copy of some of the propaganda dropped over the German lines by our men. It is a copy of a general order as to how prisoners of war are to be treated.

We see lots of German prisoners now and it's hard to describe how they look for each new bunch look different. But they are all alike in that they are glad to be taken.

We are hearing a lot about the havoc the so-called Spanish Flu is playing in the States. Hope it doesn't prove more serious. However, it doesn't seem to be local as it has hit France and England. So far we haven't had any of it in this locality.

Hope you are feeling well and enjoy your work.

Love,
Ray.

From these letters it is evident how much of the war is just monotony for many of the soldiers. But they also show we were watching the progress of the American armies with a lot of interest. About this time bets were being made around the headquarters that the Germans would surrender before Christmas. I didn't think so but should have realized that the morale of the German army was getting low by the attitude of the many prisoners being taken.

We were still at war and too near the front to relax. At night everything had to be done in the dark. One rainy night I got a good idea of what I had missed by not being sent to the 2nd Division. Soon after dark we heard the steady tramp of hob-nailed shoes going past our office. Out of curiosity I put on my slicker and went outside. A column of infantry clad in full equipment was marching by. They had been unloaded at the railhead near Toul and were now hurrying to reach their destination before daylight. Already the men were weary but all up and down the line could be heard the sharp commands, "Close up, men, close up." It was evident that the men were exhausted for often someone would stumble and even fall. All night we heard the steady tramp, tramp over the cobble stones of the village street. For a long time I kept the vision of these silent men pushing with bowed heads against the cold nasty rain. I kept thinking how so easily I could have been one of them, splashing and sliding along the muddy roads, being prodded on by their officers who in turn were being held to the orders of a tight schedule, all moving like a dark monster toward an unknown destination.

After a time I went back into our warm, dry office, for once thankful that fate had put me in the headquarters detachment. I didn't know it then but I had witnessed the last big troop movement along the front.

By November 1st rumors were flying fast that the fighting was almost over. One day the report was it was practically over, then the next came the news that the Germans refused to sign. Up and down went the spirits of the soldiers until at last came the general orders that an Armistice had been signed and all firing on both sides was to stop at the eleventh hour of the eleventh day of the eleventh month. November 11, 1918 thus became the first Armistice Day, a date soon to be named a national holiday.

We got the news early in the morning and wondered if all the front line troops would get the message in time. Then ten minutes before eleven every gun up and down the line let loose. Both sides fired every gun possible. The ground shook under the bombardment. Then at exactly 11 a.m. everything went still. It was the strangest feeling we had experienced in months. Ever since August we had been used to the sound of guns day and night. Then to have it suddenly stop was actually eerie. All afternoon we kept listening to see if someone broke the truce, but as far as we could tell there was no violation.

That evening we looked out over the now quiet front lines and for the first time could see lights. Soldiers were lighting small camp fires to keep warm. Then we saw cars and trucks using their headlights, so we put up the curtains in the office and let the light shine out onto the street. It was so quiet that night we had trouble going to sleep. There was no big celebration as took place in the states. We were so relieved to get back to a somewhat normal life we didn't need to celebrate. Every one quietly rejoiced that the war was over and in our hearts were a bit proud that we could say, "We were there."

Cochem on the Mosel River, Germany

CHAPTER 14

ARMY OF OCCUPATION

As soon as the Armistice was signed, the Germans began to pull out of France. The Allies followed them closely to see that they kept the terms of the agreement. The 4th Corps was selected to organize what became known as the Army of Occupation. By agreement the British were assigned the northern section of this army, the French the southern, and the Americans took over the central part.

We had been on the move to be near the front lines just before the end of the fighting, so we were prepared to move on short notice to keep pace with the German withdrawal. Our line of march was north and east taking us near Verdun. All our equipment was loaded on a big army truck and we added our packs and barrack bags and rode with them. Our progress was spasmodic, moving rapidly for an hour or so, then waiting for a longer time for the traffic to unsnarl.

Whenever we stopped for a time we would jump off the truck to explore the area near the road. One of the most interesting places we found was near Verdun. Although there was nothing to show above ground, we discovered some of the underground trenches and caves that the Germans had used during this long battle. We found living quarters which appeared to be real comfortable, with cots furnished with quilts and kitchenettes all ready to use. In one place there were dishes all set on a table indicating that the occupants had left in a hurry just before a meal.

The first few days we moved so fast our kitchens couldn't keep up to cook a meal so we lived on canned beef and hardtack. Then as the pace slowed, we would stop in a village which had been shot up, but where we could find some shelter. The kitchen would then be set up to give us a hot meal. We would find some place where we could do some business, but we were moving farther and farther from the railhead, so we had no incoming mail, only some official A. E. F. and army mail, which we delivered.

The weather in the last part of November became dark and colder, with a lot of misty rain. When we reached a village at night it was a scramble between the various offices to find a dry place to function. Once the only place we could find was an empty chicken house which we cleaned out to use for a temporary office. Since most of the buildings

201

were made of stone, there was little wood we could find to make a fire. Many times we had to roll up in our blankets and sleep on the ground or floor of a partially wrecked building.

Leaving the Verdun area, we turned east and crossed the border of Luxemburg. From there were two letters I wrote Norah, one included for the first time the names of places where I had been, and the second described a trip into the beautiful city of Luxemburg.

Luxemburg Nov. 24, '18

Dear Norah,

Some of the censorship rules are off so this will contain some ancient history. You will probably be surprised to see the address at the top. We have been moving for a week, not all the time but going and stopping, setting up for a day, then pack and move again.

I am going to start in and give you a brief history of my journeys since I came across. As you know, we landed in England at Liverpool, then by train to a camp near Southampton. Here we stayed for about four days and then hiked 10 miles to Southampton, then we were packed on a channel boat. We were packed like sardines, no place to sleep, then landed next morning at Le Harve. Mighty glad to see France.

We then hiked up the longest hill I ever climbed, at least it seemed that way, to another camp. We rested one day then boarded a train of box cars for where we didn't know. After a night and day of bumping along on flat wheels we detrained at a little place called, "Economy." It was there we lived in pup tents in the sand. We ate, drank and breathed sand.

After two weeks of that life we hiked about 10 kilometers to another small village called "Teloche." It was here that transfers began to be made. Our division became a depot division. I became disgusted as they planned to make a non-com out of me and keep me back to train new men. Then to my surprise came an order to move. I forgot to mention that these villages were near the city of Le Mans, so we were a long ways back.

When the order came, I had been sick and not able to drill for a time, but I was so glad to get away that I made up my pack and hiked several kilos to Regimental Headquarters. From there we were taken by truck to Le Mans.

There were twenty-five in the bunch with a lieutenant in charge. We stayed two nights and a day in Le Mans not knowing what we were to do. On the first of August we left Le Mans on a real French train. We landed in Paris late afternoon, where we transferred from one depot to another in a truck which is all we saw of Paris. We rode all night and landed in Chaumont. The next morning we changed cars and by slow process arrived at Neufchateau, noted as you know as being near the birth place of Joan of Arc. This is where we started our post office.

In a couple of weeks we moved to Toul. It was here we experienced our numerous air raids and heard the guns. We were here during the preparation of the St. Mihiel drive. After the drive we moved up to a little village near the front lines I mentioned so many times, called "Boucq." Then on to a place near St. Mihiel called "Wiomville," a place all shot up. We arrived there just before the Armistice and heard the final barrage. It was some barrage. It was there I wrote my last letter to you after my trip to St. Mihiel. I also took a trip to Mt. Sec, which I didn't have a chance to write about.

After a week at Wiomville we got orders to move. We moved in a slow convoy of trucks up through the war torn country. All we saw were trenches, barbed wire, shell holes and destroyed villages. Long after dark we arrived at our next stop, Etain, not far from Verdun. This we found to be a good-sized town, but it was shelled so badly and destroyed so much by the Germans we couldn't find a place to sleep under a roof, to say nothing of setting up an office. So we built a camp fire and slept by it. Next day we journeyed northeast to a village called Joppecourt. We cleaned out a pig pen and set up our office for a day. Again, we loaded and crossed the border into Luxemburg.

It was like passing from a desert into paradise and the welcome we got was astonishing to us. These people speak French, German and a language of their own, and are independent in spirit. But of course, they have been under the thumb of Germany. They have been prosperous with their farm products and steel mills.

We are in a little town called Esparage on the outskirts of the city of Luxemburg. The weather has been very cold, but we had no trouble in getting billets. I wouldn't take a great deal for the opportunity of being on this trip with the Army of Occupation.

This has been a rather dry citation of events, but I know you wanted me to tell you as soon as possible. If we stay here a few days as well, we may, since we are right on the heels of the Germans, I'll get a chance to write again.

I guess this will be a thankful Thanksgiving to all you back home. Have a good dinner for me. We will probably be on the move and fare on corn beef and hard tack. But we don't mind, as everyday means one nearer to getting back.

With lots of love,
Ray.

Esperange, Luxemburg Nov. 28, '18

Dear Norah,

Thanksgiving Day and we have much to be thankful for and a great deal to look forward to. All the offices are practically closed this afternoon, but it is a rainy dark afternoon. No one cares to even go over to the band concert. We had a very good dinner compared to our ordinary mess. It consisted of beefsteak, French fried potatoes, spoonful of jam, a slice of bread, two biscuits, and coffee. We sat down in the rain and mud to enjoy it. It was much better than we expected.

Our mail hasn't got to us yet, as we have to wait until the railroads are connected between France and Germany. I haven't sorted any mail for nearly a week and am getting stale without anything to do.

Three of us slipped out the other afternoon, made up our minds we would get into the city of Luxemburg, if possible. We got in alright, but hadn't been there more than five minutes when we were picked up by an M.P. He took us before the captain of the M.P.s and by running a good bluff, he let us go.

We then took in the city and it sure is a beautiful place. I sent you a picture of part of the city but it doesn't do it justice. The city is divided into two parts by a very deep narrow valley, which is like a park with winding roads, while up on the sides on terraces are quaint old buildings, like a picture in a fairy tale.

On the west side of the valley is the business section with fairly large modern stores. The east side connected by three artistic bridges is largely residential, but has the Dutchess Palace, Parliamentary Buildings, Embassies, and other public buildings. It is only a small city, about 22,000, but the whole country has only 240,000 inhabitants.

I can't describe the city and do justice to it, but I wouldn't have missed it for a good deal. Even if we ran some risk in going. The people are enthusiastic in their welcome and orders have been issued that they are to be treated as neutrals, not as enemy country as the Allies have the right to do. Of course, they are better off for not resisting as their little army of 200 men and three cannons wouldn't have stopped the Germans long and then their country would have been stripped of everything as was eastern and northern France. As it is the Germans took enough but they aren't as bad off as the French by any means.

I am glad to be with the Army of Occupation, and soon will be in Germany if orders don't change. But wonder how long they will hold us. As long as we keep moving it isn't so bad, but if we stop for a time it's hard not to get uneasy to get back and out of the army and take up life again . . . .

Love,
Ray.

The visit to the City of Luxemburg and the episode mentioned in my letter came about in this way. Bored with inactivity, three of us talked it over and decided to hike to the city. Maguire heard about it and asked us to take along some large bills and see if we could get some change. Right after the Armistice and when we started to move toward

Germany, we were issued side arms. We had long before turned in our rifles, which we didn't need, but now going into unknown territory the top figured we needed something to protect ourselves and the government property. So when we were given all this money we thought we better put on our side arms. It was rainy and without thinking, we put our slickers over our revolvers.

Arriving in the city we were struck with its beauty and crossed one of the high bridges to the business section. A display window in a large department store looked so pretty we stopped to admire it. That was a mistake, as an M.P. came up and asked us for passes. When we showed him our general passes from the post office, he said they were no good, also the city was off limits for the 4th Army Corps. As we reached for our passes, he saw our side arms under our slickers and arrested us for carrying concealed weapons. He escorted us to the M.P.'s main office. As we waited to be charged, I heard a soldier explaining to the captain in charge that he was a chaffeur for a general and had just put his car in a garage and was walking to his billet when the M.P. picked him up for being on the street after 5 p.m. I heard the captain say to the M.P. while he was obeying the general order consideration had to be given to such cases as the chauffer described. So he gave the soldier a pass to go.

That gave me an idea, so when we were brought before the captain I explained we were from the post office of the 4th Army Corps, which was then located at Esperange just outside the city and that our postal clerk had run out of change and asked us to come into the city to get some. I reached in my pocket and pulled out the roll of bills to prove my point. I also explained that we had our side arms for protection. This captain was more understanding than many such officers and believed our story. He told us to put our side arms outside our slickers and go about our business. He asked the young M.P. to wait a minute, but we left in a hurry before anyone could change his mind. We did get some change at a hotel office, the only place we could find open, and then doing a bit more sightseeing, hiked back to our office.

Right after the Armistice, George Sangster, a representative of the *Stars and Stripes,* the army official newspaper, was assigned to our group. Sangster had been a newspaper reporter before being drafted, working on several New York City papers. He was a very likeable character and knew how to make himself at home anywhere. He often turned a dull evening into a fun time by taking a newspaper, such as the Paris edition of the *Herald Tribune* and read it aloud, picking out the errors he found. His witty comments about these errors were really funny. It was also an education to us to see these errors which we would ordinarily overlook.

Sangster's job was to distribute the *Stars and Stripes* to the various outfits in our area. To do this he was given a Ford delivery truck. The trouble for him was he didn't know how to drive a car. That was typical of the army. They never asked him about that, just left it to him to solve the problem. Accordingly, he appealed to those of us in the office who could drive to help him out. Whenever possible we took turns taking him out on his trips and trying to teach him how to drive. He was a slow pupil and actually afraid of the car.

When we began to move, Sangster ran out of gas for the car and there was no place to get more. So we got a rope and tied his car to the back of the truck which contained our equipment. Then we took turns riding with him so he could practice steering. That proved to be a rugged experience for when the truck made a quick stop, as it often did, Sangster would forget where the brake pedal was and nearly run the car and its passengers under the army truck. After some time he did get some gas and then we could drive it in the convoy. One thing I tried to do was teach him how to start the engine. As the nights grew colder it became harder to start the engine in the mornings. After I had given him the necessary instructions, we made him try to start the engine by himself. But after a time he would appeal to us for help. Someone would take pity on him and leave his work and start the car.

One night I said to him, "Sangster, as long as we come out and give you a hand you are never going to learn to start that car. In the morning none of us are going to help. You just have to master it." We all agreed that we would let him sweat it out. We woke up the next morning to see the ground white with frost. We knew it would be hard to start that engine, but we all got busy in the temporary office trying to catch up on the work that had piled up while moving. Although no one said anything, I knew everyone was listening to see how Sangster made out. We heard him cranking and cranking, but nothing happened. Then came a long pause and we all expected to see Sangster coming in the door, pleading for help. Suddenly we heard the engine start with a big roar. We all rushed outside to see Sangster standing beside the car, which was running fine, grinning from ear to ear. We all shouted, "Congratulations," and gave him three cheers.

That day was my turn to ride with Sangster and after we were well on the way, I turned to him and said, "Sangster, I can't contain my curiosity any longer. Tell me how you got the engine started." "OK," he replied, "I'll tell you but no one else and don't you tell." "I promise," I said, as I was dying to know. Then he told me this story.

"When I got out of my bed roll this morning and saw all that frost on the car, I was pretty discouraged, but I knew what you said last night, so I had to give it a try. I pulled out the choke and turned the engine over a few times. Then I turned on the switch and cranked. Nothing happened, so I kept on cranking. After a while my arm gave out and I was out of breath, so I sat down on the running board to rest. As I sat there I began to think. I thought of all the steps you taught me, checking each in my mind, and then it came to me that I hadn't checked the vibrators. I got up and opened the box and they were gone. For a few seconds, I was panic stricken. I was sure someone had stolen them. Then I remembered I was afraid that might happen, so last night I took them out and put them under my bed blanket. As soon as I got them and put them in place, the car started fine." "Good for you," I exclaimed. "You have learned a valuable lesson. Something many people never learn, that when a car doesn't start as it should, they keep on cranking, not stopping to check. In order words, stop and *think.*"

I have told this episode several times in talks to students to illustrate the value of stopping to "think," especially when things are not going right. In Sangster's case it was such a valuable lesson that he rarely had to ask for help again.

Sangster's concern about having the vibrators taken was well founded. As the army moved farther away from the railhead, supplies became more scarce. Everyone who drove a car or truck was constantly on the lookout for any abandoned vehicle which could be stripped of parts. It got so that if anyone left a car unattended for five minutes or more he might very well return to find his car stripped of parts. It wasn't considered stealing as it all belonged to the army or so reasoned the men who took the parts.

Sangster never did become a good driver, so whenever he had a long trip to make he would wait until someone of us was free to go with him. As a result we got to see a lot of the country outside our post. Going with him produced a number of funny experiences.

One of the best was told by Wyttenbach, who had gone with Sangster to deliver papers to an outfit back in the mountains. On the way back Sangster was driving down a winding mountain road when they suddenly came to the edge of a small village. Wyttenbach kept telling Sangster to slow down, but he was having trouble with the brakes. In the village the street became very narrow and rounding a sharp curve, Sangster was confronted with a platoon of soldiers drawn up in formation for retreat. The street was so narrow the car couldn't get by the soldiers. When he saw the situation, Sangster panicked and not only lost his brake pedal, but pushed the clutch pedal into low and headed straight for the line of soldiers. The result was utter confusion, the soldiers broke formation jumping up against the side of the buildings which lined the street, and the lieutenant in charge of the detachment yelled and cursed. Not until he reached the end of the street and rounded another corner did Sangster get the car under control. Then he said, "Shall I stop?" "For God's sake, *No!*" yelled Wyttenbach. "Get the *Hell* out of here before that lieutenant finds out who we are." Wyttenbach nearly died laughing when he told us that story and we all joined him.

A series of letters to Norah tells of our moving into Germany.

Scheich, Germany
Dec. 3, '18

Dear Norah,

You see by this heading that I am really in Germany. We crossed the line today and are quite a ways into the country. Since

I wrote you at Luxemburg we moved up to the border at Granenmacher on the Mosselle River. We stayed there all day and got so much mail I had to work all day and evening to get it out of the way. Nearly froze doing it but was repaid by getting two letters from you, Nov. 6 and 11, after you heard the Armistice was signed. We thought the people back in the States would celebrate, too bad you got the false report to spoil the real thing.

This morning we packed up again and started up the river. It was a beautiful ride. I don't know whether I told you but I'm driving a Ford on these trips. We really don't know how to take these people yet. On the surface they seem pleasant enough, but little things come up which show they don't like us which of course is only natural. Others are afraid. They have heard such terrible things about us.

We have our office in a school building but are billeted on the other side of town in private houses. We haven't been over yet to see what it is like. Have to put on our automatics pretty soon and start out. We don't travel alone around these dark streets.

We came through Treves today. It looks like a very nice city with big steel mills. The people don't look starved and the country looks in good condition. Lots of vineyards on the mountain sides. It really is wonderful how the Germans have kept up their country. Of course, they haven't suffered any of the ravages of war. The towns and people are clean and look in good condition.

We have seen several Bosche trucks that have been left behind. They have no rubber and used steel rimmed wheels. The people tell us that the German army has to use men to pull back their supplies. anyway, they are licked and that badly.

I wish I knew when we would get started for home. We are still going east but some day our work will be done here and we can come back. We are clear out of civilization, don't know a thing that is going on, and haven't seen a newspaper for over a week. Well, everyone is ready to go to our billets so I'll have to stop. Will enclose a couple of picture cards. I wonder if you will ever get the picture I sent from Luxemburg.

Am sending you lots of love and wishing you a Merry Christmas. Will probably be about that time when you get this.

Love,
Ray.

Zell, Germany
Dec. 8, '18

Dear Norah,

I got your second letter written on Nov. 11, day before yesterday, but as we moved again yesterday I didn't get a chance to answer it.

We made the longest jump yet yesterday, about 45 miles down the Mosselle. As we had to detour because of the steep hills it made it a much longer trip. We left at 9 a.m. and pulled in about 8 p.m. I was nearly dead tired when we got in, it's such hard work driving in a convoy of trucks. It was cloudy and became dark about 3:30. The last part of the trip was along a ledge following the river. It would have been a beautiful trip in the daytime, but rather dangerous at night. It was so dark I couldn't see the truck in front of me. I didn't have any lights nor did any of the trucks.

Starting out from Schweich we left the river climbing for about 12 miles, then traveled over rolling upland country with ranges of hills or really mountains on each side. About two o'clock we began climbing one of those ranges until coming out on the summit, we looked down again on the Mosselle lying almost straight down 1500 or 2000 feet below. Even in the clouds and mist it was beautiful. By a circuitous route we got back into the valley, which was much narrower than where we left it, as it was cutting through a big range of hills. Then the road followed the river, sometimes almost at the edge of the water and then again 40-50 feet up the cliff where the road was cut out of the rocks.

Everywhere along these steep cliffs are vineyards as far as you can see, there is a forest of staves holding up the vines. These places were so steep it doesn't seem a person could crawl up and other places it looks like bare shale rock, still the grapevines are cultivated. Places were so steep the soil composed of red shale and red clay would slide off if it wasn't all terraced. It must be they have no hard rains as we do in the States for there wouldn't be any soil left.

I have to change my mind somewhat about the condition of the people. As we get farther into the country there is less for them to eat. They are really glad the Americans are coming, for they think we will bring food. I talked with the woman where we are billeted and she said they have had no coffee for four years, no milk for three years, as they use the milch cows as oxen (we noticed that). There are very few horses left. The bread is black and sour while meat is a curiosity. It was quite a sight to see the people gather around our cooks this morning as they cut up some meat. Most meat they had seen in years. Yet the people don't look starved, they dress well, have good material in their clothes.

Well, I must bring this to a close and get something to eat. I have been working all day, probably will have to after I get back but wanted to grab a few minutes to write as we move again tomorrow. I shall be glad to get the little book you mentioned . . . .

I hope your work will soon be over. I am looking into the future with impatience to get back and begin life over again. May the time be short when it can be with your help.

With love,
Ray.

Dear Norah,

I have been so busy the last two days with the mail which piled up on me while we were moving that I didn't get a chance to write. We are farther in Germany than when I last wrote, still on the Mosselle and among higher mountains. The scenery is very beautiful even at this time of the year when it is dark and rainy all the time. I'll send you a picture of the place so you will get a little idea of it.

The castle on the peak is used by the General, we are down in the town, have dry goods store for an office. The people have a little to show in the window but that is their total stock, the shelves are bare.

But the best of all we have a real place to sleep. Night before last I slept in a real bed, first time since I've been in the army and such beds as they have here. A feather bed under you and one over you. It was so soft none of us could sleep the first night.

The surprise to all of us is the way the people extend their hospitality. Every night before we go to bed they insist that we drink some wine with them and in the morning they want us to have coffee with them when we get up. Only they haven't any coffee. The first day we were here our kitchen wasn't set up so we got some coffee from the mess sergeant and they made us some. We gave them some, for which they were sure pleased.

The people are surprised at the way the Americans treat them, they believed we were wild Indians or something and believed the many stories which were told them. Many fled with the German army but are returning now when they find the Americans are here not to make war on the civilians. They are ignorant of what the German army did in Belgium and France. They think they will have to become Americans since we are now in control. They are pleased because it isn't the French who came in.

Well, so much for that. I begin to pick up the language again. I can talk to them more as I find I do better in German than I did in French. Just heard that we are going to move again soon, thought we were going to stay here for a month. No such luck when we are fixed so good.

News of the world we still have not. We heard that Wilson was on the way across. If he can do any good, hope they get it settled up soon so we can get back. While this is some trip I want to start the other way soon.

I suppose I'm too late to wish you a Merry Xmas and a Happy New Year, but I'll do it anyway.

With all my love,
Ray.

We were well established in the beautiful little city of Cochem or as the Germans called it, *Cochem-on-de-Mosel.* The city was on the east bank of the river hemmed in by mountains on both sides. The town was overshadowed by a large castle high on a cliff some 1000 feet above the river. It was one of a few castles left which was inhabitable. Our commanding General took over the castle for his headquarters. The most striking feature of the building was a huge mosaic depicting a large man wading a stream and carrying a small boy in his arms. We thought there must be a story about the picture but no one seemed to know what it was. The people had grown up in the town and saw the picture every day, but weren't concerned as to what it meant.

As I mentioned in my letter, our office was set up in a dry goods store on the main street. The people who owned the place lived on the second floor, but unable to get goods, they were out of business. The head of the family was a distinguished appearing man who had been a former member of the Reichstag. His wife was a fine looking woman and was now joined by their son who had been an officer in the Germany army but like many others, had hurried home and changed into civies so he wouldn't be taken as a prisoner of war. There was also a young woman who served as a maid and cook. Since their business was gone they could no longer pay her but she was more than glad to stay for her board and room.

We were given the whole third floor for our quarters and although it was not heated, we were very comfortable in the wonderful soft beds which we considered a luxury. As in most of the old world houses there was no inside plumbing, so we used an outside toilet in the courtyard in back of the house. Also, in the middle of the yard was a water well equipped with a hand pump. We used this pump to obtain water to wash our hands and faces in the mornings. Often we would take a swallow of the cold water to wash out our mouths. When the people saw us do this, they were horrified. They said to drink cold water in the morning would kill us. Water was for washing and cooking but like the French, wine was for drinking. Of course, this was the center of the famous Mosselle wine country. The cliffs on both sides of the river were terraced and all set with grape vines. It looked like it would take a mountain goat to reach some of these vineyards, but someway the farmers did.

Arriving as we did in early December, we were busy getting established so it was some time before we saw any of the countryside. A railroad ran along side the river and our mail came by train from Coblenz, a large city located about 15 kilos south at the junction of the Mosselle and Rhine rivers. Rail service was now established from France, so we had fairly regular delivery of mail.

Some letters I wrote as the holiday season approached tell how we felt and what we did.

Cochem, Germany
Dec. 22, '18

Dearest Norah,

Merry Xmas, Happy New Year, Hot Fourth of July, Glory Hallelujah! I got your Xmas package. Truly, Norah, I thank you very, very much for I sure did enjoy it. Everything in it was good, the candy, the nuts, first peanuts I have had, the cigars, *real cigars* and especially the book. If you want to know how to appreciate these things go without them for six months. Mine was the first box of any of the post office bunch to arrive so Rutherford, Maguire and I had a little feast last night. They said to tell you that you had very good taste in your selections and that I showed very good taste in selecting you. Also to thank you very much.

Pleadings, threats nor force would get me to bed until I had read the little book of verse you marked. It is rather hard to explain how I felt when I read it. Sometimes I laughed and sometimes I was very serious. I enjoyed it! As a rule, you know I'm not crazy about poetry, but I liked this . . . This box was a great treat, maybe I shouldn't have opened it until Xmas, but I couldn't wait. It is like the sun breaking through the clouds. Makes one feel that there is a God's country somewhere. I get so tired of these towns where you have to stop to think of the words to use if you wish to talk to anyone.

The mail is heavy now with a good number of Xmas boxes. Some of them don't come in good shape as yours. I spent nearly an hour yesterday rewrapping some so some poor fellow would get to enjoy it.

Your letter telling about the birthday cakes makes me hungry. The people here have been feeding us some Weinachtens Kuken, which tastes good to us. You asked about our feed, I'd rather not discuss it until I am out of the army.

Old Black Jack Pershing was along to visit us yesterday. He stopped on the town square and said a few words. He said he hoped to get us home soon, perhaps by way of the Rhine. We are not particular which way we go. It's the going that interests us.

I suppose you are at home tonight enjoying a good fire with snow outside, Nicht Wahr? It is black and muddy here, doesn't seem a bit like Xmas time. I was thinking of the winter I was with you during the holidays. Wish I might be there now but I am in spirit. I'll write you on Xmas day, as you asked.

With love,
Ray.

Cochem, Germany
Xmas night.

My dear Norah,

If someone had told me one year ago today that I would eat my next Christmas dinner on the banks of the Rhine, I would have considered them crazy. But such was the case. This morning I was told to go with the mail to Coblenz, which I had wanted to do ever since we got this close. I expected to get back in time for dinner, but just as I got started back I came up to a corner and saw a fellow out of old Company E. After I got through talking to him it was really too late to come back for dinner. So I thought I would chance getting a dinner with some of the troops in town. Anyway I wanted to see the city.

After wandering about for an hour we, (Wyttenbach, the driver and I) found a mess that looked good to us. We got our mess kits and got into line as if we belonged there. We got *some feed* for the army, consisting of mashed potatoes, roast pig, bread, coffee with *milk and sugar,* pie and sponge cake. The K of C handed us a piece of chocolate and cigarettes.

I noticed in several papers something about all the turkeys we were going to have. Well, they are still coming if they are for us. But we enjoyed that dinner. After dinner we heard there was to be a show at the YMCA, so we went but it was only a band concert, with cigarettes, hot chocolate and a little candy given away. It is the first time I have had anything handed out by the YM except paper. This K of C is the best.

Xmas is a great season in Germany and they tell us they can't celebrate it properly because of the shortage of food supplies. Last night we were all invited upstairs by the people who own the store. The family was all there, including the girl who works for them, and who has taken a fancy to Rutherford, which affords us considerable amusement. They invited all of us, including the lieutenant, to their Xmas tree. They had a big plate of cookies, Weinachten Kuken for each, an apple and plenty of wine. We sang some songs, including Heilige Nacht, with them. We had a very good time even though we were hampered by the difference in language. The attitude they take toward us makes me believe that these people are genuine in their friendliness.

Well, so much I had written when in came two bags of State mail, so I had to sort it. I was rewarded by two letters, one from you and one from Mother. Your letter contained the snapshots, which I enjoyed very much. . .

The people here promised that we would have snow by Xmas, so it obligingly snowed last night. This morning everything was a beautiful white. The trip down the valley to the Rhine was really beautiful. The sun just gets over the top of the mountain about 9 a.m. and then goes down on the other side of the river behind a mountain about 2 p.m. It makes the nights very long. I'm not planning on getting back before spring, but if we don't begin to move by that time I don't know what I shall do. I don't know what more to say except Happy New Year.

With lots of love,
Ray.

The fact as I told in my letter about our eating Xmas dinner with another outfit was not unusual for us. Since we were with the post office it gave us a chance to stop anywhere we happened to be at meal time and we were always welcome. Wyttenbach, who drove the truck most of the time, soon learned who had the best mess and he planned his trips accordingly. He told us the engineers always had the best meals. Wyttenbach was from a German family in Amherst, Ohio, and spoke the language very well. He was a big help to us in getting around the country. Although he seemed to have the knack of getting into all sorts of scrapes, he was such a friendly person he always came out on top. We all liked him very much.

All through the holidays I was kept busy with the mail, as the following letter shows:

Cochem, Germany
Jan. 1, 1919

Dear Norah,

New Year's Day, the beginning of another year. I wonder what things it holds in store for the world and for us in particular. It has been a week since I wrote you. I intended to write Sunday, but have been so busy with floods of mail that I didn't get to it, besides there is no news to write. The mail is coming at a very bad time for me now, gets here at 6 p.m., which means I have to work half the night getting it out. Then I have to hang around all day with practically nothing to do, but there is so much disturbance I can't write.

I took an outing today which makes up for several days. I traveled about fifty miles over the hills this morning after some mail which had gone astray. Got back, ate dinner and then took a train to Coblenz after some more mail. Got back at 6:30, too late for supper, then to work until now, almost 10 o'clock, getting the mail out. I'm rather tired but feel much better than I do when I have to stay in all day.

If it wasn't so serious it would be laughable, the questions one hears about, "When are we going home?" Now the war is over everyone is anxious to get back, still no one is ready to quit before the work is done. It really is funny the wild tales that float around. Just yesterday, for example, at least 20 men came in and in all seriousness asked me if it was true that mail to and from the States would be stopped by the 15th of January. The lieutenant censoring the mail said he saw one letter where one fellow had written that home. I used to think a small town was the worst place to start rumors, but the army beats that.

The steady rain has raised the river until it is over its banks. Today it was coming over the lower end of town. Our promised cold weather hasn't come yet. I don't believe they know what cold weather is here . . .

Love,
Ray.

Cochem, Germany
Jan. 12, '19

Dear Norah,

We have been hearing all sorts of rumors about our mail being held up and this morning we got an official notice saying for some reason not known all first class mail for the A. E. F. had for three previous weeks before January 6th been held up in New York.

Now the wildest rumors are afloat as to the reason. It is rather queer, I don't understand it, but it leaves us with no mail from overseas. All I handle now is A. E. F. mail and forwarded mail. The worst of it is I haven't heard from you for sometime, sure hope you are OK.

My cold is much better as I have been getting out of doors at least once a day for two or three hours for hikes. There isn't a road or trail around here that we haven't explored. We climbed hills up to old ruins of castles, very interesting; up trails over hills where every hundred yards is a little shrine with pictures constituting a story. All in all we are put to it to find something to make life bearable. At least we have a Y.M.C.A., which has put on a couple of shows which helps some.

I'm afraid, my dear, that this letter will sound sort of strained, in fact, it's the hardest work to write a letter. We don't see anything new, hear anything new, don't go anywhere to write about.

I have been reading the little book you sent me over and over. It strikes me different each time. I am sure anxious to get back and begin life again, for it will seem like that. I haven't any idea what I shall do, but I'm determined to make something to somewhere.

You are good on telling when things will happen, so when am I going to get back? I hope you are getting my letters and sure hope we have some coming soon. Will write anyway,

Lots of love,
Ray.

I did not mention it in my letters, but the flu was growing prevalent in the army at this time. To help us keep well, orders were issued that all office personnel should be outside for exercise for at least one or more hours a day. That is how we had the chance to explore all the area around Cochem. Most of the country was hills or mountains covered with second growth timber. Farther back beyond walking distance was a farming area. These farms were small with little peasant huts. Usually the cow barn was built as a wing of the house and the size of the manure pile which was just outside the barn door was an indication of the wealth of the farmer. In the spring and summer the women from these farms carried baskets of vegetables and chickens or eggs to a farmer's market in the town square.

To offset the boredom of the soldiers, the Y.M.C.A. organized groups to put on shows. If the talent was good enough, they would travel to other centers. A few came from the states and like others, some were good while others were terrible.

The flu got worse during the winter months. We knew there were many casualties as almost every day the military band led a funeral procession past our door on the way to the cemetery just outside the town. It was real depressing, as we thought of all those boys who had survived the war only to die on foreign soil before they could get home. Also, we didn't know but any of us might be next. We did have colds, but were fortunate that none of us got the real flu.

One bright spot was that each unit was allowed so many passes to visit Paris and in the middle of February Rutherford and I were awarded one at the same time. Being in uniform, we had free transportation on the trains and when we arrived, we got a room at the "Y," a big hotel that they had taken over for the accommodation of the many soldiers who were visiting the city. We decided the best way to see the various places of interest was to take the tours as arranged by the "Y." We visited the Louvre, where we walked miles viewing the thousands of paintings and other pieces of art which had just been returned from where they had been hidden underground during the war. We visited Notre Dame, which was very impressive both inside and out. At free times we walked the streets seeing the usual landmarks like the Eiffel Tower and the Bastille.

One day we took a train to Versailles. We were surprised to find it was not in Paris but quite a distance outside. Only part of the huge building was open but we did see the famous "Hall of Mirrors," where the peace treaty was to be signed. The walls were solid mirrors extending from floor to ceiling. The outside wall does have tall windows which look out onto the beautiful flower gardens. The ceiling is covered with beautiful fresco paintings, with most of the figures in the nude. Also, from the high ceiling hung huge chandeliers with hundreds of cut glass prisms which reflected the light like diamonds. It was all so grand that we all stood in awe gazing at such splendor. This building located on such beautiful grounds, tells, as nothing else could, the grandeur in which the French kings lived before the Revolution.

Paris is a big beautiful city and in the short time we had we were only able to hit the high spots. We returned to Cochem exhausted but happy for the chance to take the trip. Later that spring Rutherford and I were surprised to get a second pass for Paris. This time we passed up the tours and went about on our own. That way we could spend more time in the places that interested us the most. We also had the chance to visit some of the big department stores and the unique shops in the city. We didn't have much money to spend, but our expenses were not great either. Being in uniform we rode the trains and trolley cars free and the rates at the "Y" were low. Our meals were the biggest expense.

It was on this trip that Rutherford wanted to attend the famous Paris opera. I wasn't too keen about going but to please him I consented. That afternoon we were near the opera house and we stopped. We found the opera that night would be "Samson and Delila," which interested Rutherford and we got two of the cheapest tickets. After returning to our room to clean up and then out for dinner, we discovered we would be late for the opening curtain if we tried to walk. We spotted a one-horse cab waiting at the curb and we asked him to take us to the opera house. He didn't understand English, but my limited French had got us by so far. However, as I kept saying "opera," he kept shaking his head. Finally I remembered that the spelling was the same in both languages, so I started spelling it. Before I had finished he said, "Ah, Oui, O PAY RA." I had been saying it too much like English.

The cab got us to the opera house in plenty of time. Then as we saw the crowd going in, I felt rather out of place. We were dressed in our plain OD uniforms, which we had been wearing all through the war. The men we saw were in dress suits and the women in gorgeous long evening gowns. A few officers present were in dress uniform. There was nothing we could do about our dress and we had our tickets so we started in. Now we learned something new. We had been accustomed to tipping at restaurants, but now we found we had to tip everyone we met. First the doorman, who looked at our tickets, then an usher inside who directed us to a flight of stairs, and finally an usher at the top who showed us our seats.

The Paris Opera House was unlike any theater we had ever been in. Unlike the Follies, which we had attended, there were no seats on the floor, but everyone sat in boxes rising one above another. The boxes were arranged in a horseshoe shape around the stage. We were in the top box and looked down on the stage from what seemed a long distance away.

We were the first ones in this box so we took the front seats which were movable chairs. We had a good time viewing the ornate interior of the building and watching the people arriving in the boxes opposite us. Then just before the curtain went up, a French officer in dress uniform arrived with a party of men and women. There was some fast talk behind us and out of the corner of my eye I saw the officer give the usher a large bill. The usher then came to us and told us by a big volume of words and signs that we were in the wrong seats and had to move to the back of the box. We looked at our ticket stubs and as they were only for the box, not for a seat, we had to move. In order to see the

217

action on the stage we had to stand. However, the music was wonderful and we came out feeling we had done something extra by attending the Paris opera.

Back in Cochem the time hung heavy on our hands. True, we were busy at times with the mail and in many ways were better off than the men in outfits stationed in the small outlying villages. Of course, we kept track of the slow process in concluding the peace treaty. Wilson, with his plan for a League of Nations, came in for a lot of discussion.

As a rule we found the German people easy to deal with. Their family life was much the same as we knew in the States. We treated them like equals, not as conquered people as did the French and British armies. The French were especially arrogant as the deep seated hatred between these people showed in the French section of the Army of Occupation. The people in our area expressed themselves over and over how grateful they were to be in the American zone.

Spring came early and we enjoyed the beauty of the Mosselle valley when the leaves and flowers arrived. Spring also brought the thoughts of baseball and every regiment and large organization formed a team. There was no room for a baseball diamond in Cochem but a team was organized out of the headquarters troop and detachments to travel. Eddie Kihm, my assistant, was selected as a catcher and left to be with the team. I missed him but was glad he got the chance to play. I never saw him until the corps was ready to start for home.

George Sangster had a sister, Margaret, who was a magazine writer. She had been in Paris as a war correspondent for the *Christian Herald.* As a member of the press she was allowed to come into Germany to visit George. All this time there had been a strict regulation that no American soldier could fraternize with a German girl. If anyone dared walk down the street with a German woman, he was picked up by an M.P. and taken to headquarters. So when Margaret came, we decided it would be great sport to walk with her on the street and when an M.P. stopped us to have some fun with him before he learned she was American, not German. Margaret was a good sport and entered in the game. We took turns taking her for a walk and all had a good story to tell as to what happened when stopped. In one case Margaret had to show her credentials to the Captain of the M.P.'s before they would let the fellow go.

During the spring the "Y" got permission to take small groups on a tour of the castle on the mountain above Cochem. One afternoon a few of us from the post office were included. The fresco paintings on the walls and ceiling of the main hall were impressive, some of them carrying out the theme of the picture on the outside. The mirrors and chandeliers were beautiful but not, of course, as those we had seen at Versailles, but it was remarkable how well preserved this castle was; most we had seen were in ruins.

When we reached the bottom of the winding path that led up the cliff to the castle, a detail of M.P.'s met us. They herded us off the road but wouldn't answer our questions. Curious, we stood for a few minutes when a motorcade drove up and stopped. One car displayed a British flag. A number of high rank American and British officers got out of the cars, while last was a young man in a British General's uniform. He had the most spindling legs I ever saw on one of his rank. We stood in disbelief, for from the pictures we had seen in the paper, we recognized the Prince of Wales. This was Prince Edward, who later became King for a short time, making history when he abdicated the throne to marry an American divorcee. We knew this was no official visit to the Commander of the Corps, as no honor guard had been called. We heard later that the Prince was making a tour of the area to see famous places. Consequently, "our castle" took on more importance, and we were delighted we had a chance to see it.

Early in May some of us got a pass to visit Coblenz and take a boat trip on the Rhine River. It was a beautiful sunny warm day and the trip was inspiring. The boat took us several miles up the river past castles perched on high cliffs on both sides. This part of the valley was rather narrow; the river cutting through the mountains of central Germany. Near the rocks called "Lorelei" made famous by the song, the boat turned back, arriving at Coblenz at sunset. It was truly a ride like a picture postcard scene, a high spot on our dull times.

Soon after this trip we heard rumors that a lot of U. S. mail was piled up in Coblenz because the German trainmen would load only a certain number of bags at a time. Our lieutenant sent three of us to check it out and bring back any mail we found. The story was true and we loaded a mail car half full with the bags we found. The train crew was angry when we insisted that they hook this mail car on the regular night train. Since the Americans were in charge they didn't dare refuse and were mollified when we told them to drop this car at Cochem. It was real warm and in loading the car I became sweaty. Riding in this car with the doors open it was very drafty. I was so tired I lay down on top of the mail bags and fell asleep. When I woke up I was chilly and the next morning I was running a fever with a bad sore throat. Nevertheless, we had all that mail to get out and then I fell into bed for two days.

Before I had fully recovered, orders were issued that everyone was to receive a booster shot of the inoculations we had when we first entered the army. I remembered how they affected me before so I wasn't keen about getting them again, but the medics assured us they wouldn't hurt this time. It was late in the afternoon when we went as a group to get our shots. Waiting in line I began to feel rather faint, so when I got the needle I took two steps and keeled over. The next thing I knew, two of my friends were half carrying and half dragging me back to our quarters. I came to enough to help climb the stairs and fell into bed.

Later the army doctor came to see me and said if he had known I had been ill he would have excused me from the shots, but that was too late, and he advised me to stay in bed for three days. The fellows from the office brought me my meals so I had plenty to eat. The German family all expressed their concern about me and for the first and only time in the army I got real sick leave.

This is a copy of the last letter I wrote from Germany.

Cochem, Germany
May 16, '19

Dear Norah,

Rec'd your letter of May lst today, which isn't bad time at all. Well, my dear, I only know one thing, the rumor I spoke about has come true. We are really turning in our equipment preparatory to starting home.

Day before yesterday we had our first inspection and have been busy ever since getting stuff turned in and drawing what we lack. It is not definite when we start but probably about the 26th, i.e., leave Germany then. How long it will take to get on the boat I don't know. But we should be in the States by July lst.

The weather has been fine lately and the country beautiful, but just the same I shall be glad to leave it. Everyone is excited and I'm among the bunch. It just seems like the break of dawn. May the day come quick.

I shall keep you posted as to my moves, but as much as I hate to say it, you might as well not send any more letters overseas. We will be on the move, so probably I would never get it even if it got across before we start. Will let you know as soon as we leave. You can watch the sailing lists for Hdqrs. Troop and Det. 4th Army Corps to see when we leave and land. I'm the happiest I've been for months.

With lots of love,
Ray.

Things began to move rapidly after I wrote this letter. Not only was our personal equipment checked but the affairs of the office were being brought to a close. We received notice that all our overseas mail would be held in New York after a certain date and then all A.E. F. mail would stop soon after that. From this we knew for sure we were leaving.

Some time before the Corps was expected to move, the Commanding General ordered our lieutenant to provide mail service at the point of embarkation. Thus, we learned it would be St. Nazaire, France. The lieutenant named Sgt. Rutherford, Corp. Wyttenback and Corp. Calhoon to carry out this order. Maguire, the Postal Clerk, decided he would like to go with us, so the lieutenant got travel orders for the four of us.

The night before the four of us were to leave, the German family where we had been billeted all winter invited the whole office group for a farewell party. We had become friends of this family, and they said they were sorry to see us leave. Our whole group, including the two lieutenants, went up to their apartment at 9 o'clock that night. They had a big dining room table all decorated and in the middle was a big chafing dish with burning candles under it. They had filled the dish with their special Mosselle wine. The Germans liked the wine warm in contrast to the Americans who wanted it chilled. Also, on the table were plates of cookies and Kuchen (cake). After we were all seated around the table they filled our glasses with the warm wine and then began a series of toasts.

After a few toasts the warm wine began to work and the party got real gay. All differences were forgotten. We sang songs and told the people over and over how wonderful they had treated us. They in turn told us how happy they were that it was us who had come to them. A few months before we had been fighting these people, but all was forgotten that night.

Near midnight Wyttenbach announced he had to leave to meet the late mail train; we decided to end the party while all were in good spirits. No one felt like going to bed, so a bunch of us piled into the truck to ride to the station. We were still feeling high so we continued to celebrate by singing all the way. There was no mail and we continued the celebration on the way back. Ordinarily the M.P.s would have stopped us but they also were off duty. When we got in the middle of main street, Wyttenbach, who was driving, stopped the truck dead in the middle of the street. We all wanted to know why he stopped. "Well," he said, "a man has to stop the car to spit, doesn't he?" We all agreed.

The next morning as the four of us boarded the train, we were each handed a copy of a letter from General Pershing, a sort of thank you note from our Commander-in-Chief. Starting when we did, we knew we had four days to reach St. Nazaire before the rest of the corps could arrive. We talked it over and decided we needed only two days of travel time and just a few hours to carry out our orders. We talked with the train crew and found out we could get off at Luxemburg and get a train north to Brussels, Belgium. We all had an urge to see Belgium, since we had heard so much about it during the war. We knew we would be off our route and might be picked up by the M.P.s, but decided it was worth the chance.

When the train reached Luxemburg, we got off and went in the station. We had to wait for a train north, so we thought we might check our packs, which we still had to carry, and go into the city. Before we could act, a detachment of French M.P.s surrounded the station and kept everyone inside. We tried to find out why, but they would give us no information. We guessed that a special train was coming and sure enough, in about half an hour it arrived. A group of French and Belgian officers got off and formed a tight cordon around a central figure. By craning our necks we made out it was really Marshal Foch, the Supreme Commander of the Allied Troops in Europe. We recognized him from pictures we had seen in the papers. After his

221

group left, the M.P.s informed us that the city was off limits as long as the Marshal was there. So we had to bide our time.

Being in the station at Luxemburg that particular day made it possible for me to say I had seen three high ranking officers of the war. I had seen General Pershing twice, once when he addressed the troops in Cochem and again when I was near enough to touch him when he came in the hotel lobby in Paris. Then I was not far from the Prince of Wales when he visited the castle in Cochem, and now a view of Marshal Foch.

It was evening when we arrived in Brussels. We found a "Y" hotel but all rooms were taken. However, they assigned us some cots in a big ballroom where we could use our packs for the night. When we crossed the border into Belgium, we got quite a shock. As the train moved through the countryside in Germany, we could see how destitute the farmers were. The army had taken all the horses from the farmers, so they were using milch cows as oxen to work the fields. In fact, we saw one farmer who had hooked his wife alongside a cow to pull a plow. Then as soon as we crossed into Belgium we saw beautiful cultivated fields and the famous Belgian horses grazing in the pastures. It was an eye opener to us and it dawned on us that the terrible stories we had heard about how the Belgians had suffered during the war was pure propaganda. Of course, it was six months after the war was over, but unlike the destroyed villages of France, there was not a trace of anything touched in Belgium.

In order to see some of the city of Brussels, we took trolley rides in different directions away from the central square. It was a beautiful city full of huge fountains and many statues. We found out that the Brussels-Paris express train left in the early evening. After the day of sightseeing we picked up our packs and walked to the station.

When we reached the station we were faced with a dilemma. A big sign had been posted that morning saying no soldiers in uniform would be permitted on the Brussels-Paris express. Up to this time we had been riding the trains free when in uniform. We knew we had to take this train or we would be too late in Paris to get a night train to St. Nazaire. We checked and found we had enough money to buy tickets to Paris, but the ticket agent refused to sell us any. We huddled in a corner to talk over our predicament when a young Belgian officer greeted us, asking if we were in trouble. Maguire talked to him in French and explained our situation. "Very well," he said, "if you will trust me with the money, I'll buy the tickets. Then you can stand over by a side gate which I will make sure is unlocked, and you can run and jump on the train as it starts to move. Once on the train with tickets they won't stop to put you off."

We knew it was a gamble to give a stranger the money, but we were in such a jam we decided there was nothing else to do. The officer took our money and in a few minutes came back with four tickets. He then led us to a side gate of the heavy iron fence which extended all the way around the loading platform. The gate was marked "Employees Only", but the officer made sure it was unlocked. For his help we gave him fifty francs and many thanks. He saluted and said, "Merci, Au Revoir," and then left.

With our packs at ready we stood by the gate intently watching the train. We knew from experience there would be no warning bell or whistle, so when ready the train would begin to move. Also, we knew it would pick up speed very fast. When the train started to move, we pushed the gate open, sprinted across two tracks and onto the platform beside the train. The guards at the main gate saw us and shouting, ran to head us off, but we beat them. Grabbing the door of the first compartment we could reach, we yanked it open and in spite of the loud protestations of the occupants, we all piled in.

We were none too soon, because in another minute the train was moving so fast we could never have got on. Once all were inside we apologized to the people we had disturbed and filed out into the narrow aisle which ran the length of the French cars. We checked several compartments, but all were full until we came to one with only one person inside. We opened the door and saw a Belgian lieutenant. We asked if the other seats were taken and when he said, "No, please come in," we entered and made ourselves comfortable, but wondering what would happen when the conductor came along.

It was at least a half hour before the conductor opened our door and the train was traveling at full speed. When the conductor saw us he began a tirade in French, to which we only responded, "No compree." This was the common expression all the soldiers used when they didn't want to understand. We gave him the tickets, which he finally accepted and left still waving his arms.

When the train reached the Belgium-French border, all the passengers, except us, had to get off to be passed through customs. As American soldiers we were exempt. At this point a French crew took over and we wondered what kind of a reception they would give us. But they didn't come near and as the train gathered speed, we heaved a sigh of relief.

When the Belgian officer came back after the customs inspection, it was evident from his looks something bad had happened. At first he wouldn't tell us, but finally relented and said his supply of cigarettes had all been taken by the custom officials and also he had been fined for what they claimed was trying to take them into France. He was also upset because he said he had served all through the war with the French army and had met a beautiful mademoiselle. He was on the way to visit her and hoped to get married,

We felt sorry for the way he had been treated and fished in our packs and came up with some Camel cigarettes and several bags of Bull Durham tobacco with papers which had been issued to us. We insisted he take them, and his face broke into smiles, for the American tobacco was far better than the kind he had lost. Late in the night he left us thanking us over and over. In turn, we wished him the best of luck.

After rumbling over the rough tracks all night we reached Paris the next morning. We found a wash room where we could get off some of the grime which had accumulated during the long ride. Then after a quick breakfast in the railroad station, we approached an M.P. to see where we could check our packs so we could spend the day in Paris. To our surprise he informed us that the city had been declared "off limits" to American soldiers unless on business. We showed our passes and travel orders, but he said they were not enough. We saw a sign for the office of the M.P.s and found a captain in charge who relented and gave us a limited pass for the day. Rutherford and I didn't mind, as we had been there twice, but the others were a bit disappointed. After walking around and seeing what we could, we had an early dinner so we would be ready to get on the train for St. Nazaire when it was called. We were all set when it was called and hurried out to find a compartment. To our dismay we found the train packed. People had not waited but had gone out and filled the coaches before it had been called. It was a long train and we went the full length checking, but every compartment was more than full and people were standing in the aisles.

Again we went into a huddle. We knew we had to be on this train so we could be in St. Nazaire ahead of the Corps. Discussing the problem, someone had the idea to look for a mail car. We spotted several baggage cars on the front of the train, and we started checking them. Peeking in one we saw it loaded with pouches stamped U. S. Mail. "We are mailmen," we exclaimed, and with no one to stop us, we climbed in on top of the bags. We pulled the door shut and were relieved when the train began to move.

We moved the pouches around to get as comfortable as possible and slept fitfully through the night. We listened as the train made several stops during the night, but no one checked our car. We felt sure this mail was on the way to the coast for shipment out of St. Nazaire and we intended to go with it. In the early morning when the train stopped we heard a babble of voices and we thought it must be the end of the run. Opening the door ajar, we spotted the sign on the front of the station, St. Nazaire, and we slid out, joining the crowd. Our wild journey was over, we were dead tired and dirty, but never regretted taking it. We felt we deserved this extra trip and adventure.

Inside the station we found a washroom where we could clean up a bit and got a cup of coffee. We knew we had to get to a military camp outside the city and asked the first M.P. we could find how to get there. He told us there was a military bus that made regular runs between camp and city and named the corner where we could catch the bus. We walked to the corner and began to wait. By that time the sun was out real hot and we were weary. Seeing one of the sidewalk cafes which were common all over France, we walked over and sat in some vacant chairs. There were no customers at that time of day and we were not bothering anyone, but when a waiter came out to take our order, he made a fuss when we said we didn't want anything. He called the proprietor, who made a bigger fuss, telling us in French we couldn't stay there.

This was the second thing we learned about the country since the end of the war. First had been not riding certain trains, now we couldn't sit at an empty table even when no customers were around. It was evident that the great welcome the French had for us when we landed a year ago had radically changed. We were mad and refused to move until the owner called an M. P. off the corner where he was directing traffic and he told us it was now a regulation that soldiers could not use these chairs. We told him we were just from the Army of Occupation and never heard of such a rule, but he was nice about it and asked us to comply.

After waiting about an hour we got the bus, which took us to the camp. We reported and got our assigned barracks. As soon as we could we located the post office, where we were told there was no mail for the Corps nor was it likely there would be any. With nothing to do we fell into bed early, ready to meet the rest of the Corps when they arrived. After a couple of days we had our final inspection and turned in equipment; we were now down to a simple outfit. The last thing we turned in was the extra pair of shoes. We were told to turn in our brown dress shoes and keep the hob nails, but like some others I didn't want to land in Cleveland wearing hob nails, so I didn't follow orders. The quartermaster sergeant told us we couldn't get on ship unless we had the hob nail shoes, but several of us felt he was bluffing. Two days later when we checked in at the ship nothing was said about shoes.

It was the 5th day of June when we marched to the pier at St. Nazaire and we boarded the U.S. troop transport, *Alaskan*. This ship was far different from the old cattle boat that we came over on. The hold which contained our bunks was clean and well ventilated. From the first meal on board we found the food to be excellent.

It was my luck to be assigned Corporal of the guard the first night on board. That was strange, since I had been on the same duty the last night on the way over. After that duty was over I was free to enjoy the rest of the trip. The ship took a southern course; the days were sunny and warm. The sea was calm, no one got sea sick, the salt air was invigorating, and it was like being on a pleasure cruise.

One day the group of us who had been together so long were discussing what we would do once out of the army and I recall saying, "One thing I won't do is go back into teaching." Little did I know what the future was to be. Then in the early morning of June 15 we sighted the famous Statue of Liberty through the mist. A loud cheer went up from the boys on deck, they were so happy to see her.

We docked about noon and again marched to a Long Island train, which took us back to Camp Mills, which was now a receiving station for overseas troops. The first thing was to put everyone through a

225

delousing plant. This was a process of putting all our belongings and clothes in a net and sending it through a disinfectant tank, then baking it at a high temperature. While we waited for our clothes, we had the hair on our heads clipped very short and our body hair shaved. We then filed under some hot showers and were instructed to lather all over with some chemical soap. When our clothes were returned we dressed and were declared deloused, but our uniforms smelled of the disinfectant for several days.

While in camp the 4th Army Corps Troop and Detachments were assembled for a picture. I still have a copy of this picture of some 500 men as a memory of our outfit. Soon after this picture we were again put on a train for New York City. There we transferred to a long train of Pullman cars. We were now riding in style unlike anything we had done during our duty overseas. The next day we were back at Camp Sherman in Ohio. The mustering out process began at once. On the 24th of June I was given my honorable discharge. I had completed almost 15 months of service in the army, of which 13 months was overseas; and I now had three sets of stripes on my sleeves. One, the two stripe chevron, indicating my rank as Corporal, two gold stripes for the two six month periods overseas, and now an inverted gold stripe showing I was a discharged veteran. I stood in the same place where I had been inducted into service and now I was leaving with mixed feelings. I was a little more than a year older, but many years wiser in experience.

Taking stock of myself, I realized that I was 26 years old, a discharged veteran, three years out of college, with no job to go to nor any prospect of one. I was eager to get started in civilian life but rather concerned as to how I would be received. Accepting my discharge was very similar to accepting my diploma from high school and college; each marked the end of a regulated period of life and opened the door to the unknown.

CHAPTER 15

ONEIDA COMMUNITY LTD.

The final step in being mustered out of the army was receiving all my back pay and the $60.00 severance pay each soldier was given. I was told that if I wanted to wait a couple of weeks or more I could get my transportation to Iowa, which I had given as my mother's address, and then be mustered out. I decided I wanted to get out at once and anyway, I did want to go to Cleveland and see what had become of the Oil Gas Producer Company. I also thought I might be able to see Norah before going to Dunlap.

With a number of others I got a bus from camp to Chillicothe and then a train to Cleveland. I got a room at a mid-town hotel, which I knew was cheaper than the big hotels, and sent a telegram to Norah at Cazenovia asking if she was home and wanted me to come.

In the morning I made a call at the office of Mr. Younger, who had been the attorney for the Oil Gas Producer Company. He was in and when his secretary announced me, he invited me right into his private office. After the usual greetings he looked at my uniform and said, "When are you going to get out of that outfit?" I was rather taken aback, since I had been serving my country for some time in that uniform and was proud of it. The way he said "that outfit" made it sound like I was in a masquerade suit. It flashed through my mind that I hadn't seen anyone else around the hotel or on the street in uniform. When I left, the streets were full of soldiers in all types of uniforms. I was waking up to the fact that it had been over seven months since the war was over.

So when Younger asked me that question, I replied without thinking, "Tout de suite." He looked at me for several seconds and said, "I suppose that means soon?" Again I had to realize that the expressions we used so casually in the army were now out. So I said, "I'm sorry, that's what it means."

I asked him about West and the company. He told me that he was no longer connected with the company. He understood that West had sold whatever rights were left to a group of engineers in the American Multigraph Company. He heard that West had a little shop near that plant and he suggested I might go to see him. I made my visit brief and thanked him for the information. I had a feeling he was glad to see me go and not ask for help to find a job. He made no offer to help in any way.

227

When I got back on the street I was impressed more than ever with the change that had taken place. People were acting much the same as before the war. After Younger's remark about my uniform, I decided I had better change into civies as soon as possible. I found the men's clothing store where I had traded when in West Park. I remembered that the lowest priced suits were on the second floor. There I went from rack to rack, astonished at the prices I saw. Finally a clerk asked me if he could help. "Yes," I said, "where are the $25.00 suits?" He looked me all over and then said, "There are none. You must have been gone a long time." I finally picked out a light grey suit for $40.00. Then because all my clothes were in my trunk in Dunlap, I had to find a dress shirt and all accessories. It took a big part of my cash, but I had to do it.

The next morning I took a trolley to the east side of the city and found the Multigraph Company plant. At the office I was told I could find Mr. West in a small building outside. I found a sort of shed and tapped on the door. No one answered, so I tried the door and found it unlocked and pushed it open. When I stepped inside, I saw an old man look up. I gasped when I realized I was seeing West. He had lost a lot of weight and looked sick. The room was dimly lit, so I called out my name and greeted him. He squinted at me for a period and then answered as if I was a stranger. I tried to talk to him and inquired about Mrs. West. In a quavering voice he said she had died and he was now living alone.

I looked around the room and saw West had an old auto engine set on a block. Attached to the engine was one of the kerosene carburetors I had helped develop. To me it was evident that the engineers who had taken control were just giving this man who once had been a brilliant engineer a chance to play out his life. I couldn't bear to stay but a short time and wishing him good luck, I left. I now knew the Oil Gas Producer Company was dead, so it closed a chapter in my life.

The next day I got my suit and changed into civies, which seemed a bit strange after wearing a uniform for so long. When I left Camp Sherman I was given a small pamphlet which listed the names of firms in and around Cleveland that might hire returned veterans. I spent the next two days checking a number of these places and was told over and over all the places had been filled.

I kept checking the hotel desk to see if I had any messages, but without results. Later I learned that my telegram that I sent to Norah at Cazenovia could not be relayed to Connecticut where she was on vacation because the telegraph operators on the east coast were on strike. Norah's folks sent it on by mail, but then it was too late for her to contact me.

With my funds running low and not hearing from Norah, I put my uniform on and walked to the railroad station. I was tempted to take a train to Syracuse and call Cazenovia, but I didn't feel I should go to Norah's folks uninvited. Long distance phone calls were not made in those days. Finding a train about due for Chicago, I quickly decided to take it and go to Dunlap to see my family and get my trunk.

I had to stay overnight in Chicago at a cheap hotel near the station. It was cheap alright, and I woke up with a number of bedbug bites, something I had not experienced since a boy. The next morning I sent a telegram to Leeta and boarded a through train for Omaha which would stop at Dunlap on signal. It was a long hot ride, but the big fields of corn and grain with the well kept farmhouses and barns made me think I was truly back in God's country. At noon the conductor came by to tell me that a carload of my buddies was on the back of the train and at the next stop the women of the Red Cross were giving them a lunch. Since I was in uniform, he suggested I join them. I did and was glad to get some sandwiches, doughnuts and coffee. I talked with some of the men and found out that like me they were being discharged from the army and being from the west, were being sent to a camp nearer their homes.

It was evening when I got to Dunlap and I was delighted to see Dale and Faye there to meet me. We drove out to the old Rannell's farm which Art and Leeta had taken over. Dale had been discharged from the service and was now working for Art. Faye was in the Dunlap High School, but with Leeta for the vacation. Ula was working for Aunt Adah, who had a big family of children and lived with her husband, Art's brother, on a farm across the river from Dunlap. To my surprise, I found that Mother had gone to California, but it still made Leeta's place a sort of center for my family.

Everyone gave me a warm welcome and I had to catch up on the family news. I learned that Aunt Effie, who had been in California for some time, had persuaded Grandpa and Grandma Crow to sell their place in College Springs, Iowa, and move to California. They had bought a house in Richmond, where they tried to raise some garden produce to sell. But their health had failed so they couldn't keep going. Mother had been nursing in and around Dunlap, but when she learned the condition of her parents she decided to go to California and take over their place and their care. So I missed seeing her.

Art and Leeta had had their first baby, Ruth, now two years old. That was the first thing they wanted to show me when I arrived. Ruth was a beautiful child sleeping in her little bed, but as I was to learn when awake, very cute and real active. She was a farm girl and growing up with the various farm animals and was not afraid of any of them. She would walk all around a team of horses and if a cow or pig would get loose and wander into the yard, she would drive them away. I thought there was nothing she was scared of until one day I heard her screaming as she ran toward the house. I rushed to see what was after her and then had to laugh. Someone had given Leeta a bantam hen and rooster and they had family of baby chicks. Evidently the bantam rooster is different from the ordinary rooster, who never has anything to do with his chicks, for this bantam was helping to raise his family. He was very protective and would fly at anything he thought threatening his family. So when Ruth came near, this rooster ruffled up his feathers,

229

spread his wings and with a shrill cry, charged her. He really scared Ruth, and of all the animals on the farm, he was the only one she feared.

Art was driving a 1916 Buick touring car and I noticed the bearings sounded bad. I asked him if he had had them taken up recently and he replied, "No, they had never been done." I asked him if he would like me to do it while I was deciding what I should do. He thought it fine. So I spent the next week or more overhauling the engine. I not only took up the bearings, but ground the valves and put in new piston rings. When I tried it out it sounded like a new car and Art was delighted.

One day while I was under the car I saw Ruth come out to watch. I had put the bolts and nuts I had removed from the engine in a can of kerosene to get them clean. I heard Ruth give a gasp and I looked up to see her pouring the can over her head. I hurriedly crawled out and wiped her off the best I could with a rag, but had to take her to her mother for a bath. Fortunately, the kerosene didn't get in her eyes, but after that I was careful to keep things out of her reach.

As soon as I arrived in Dunlap I wrote to Norah to tell her where I was and that I was sorry not to see her. The first letter I got from her was one of regret that she couldn't reach me. She was rather peeved that she had cut her visit short and hurried back to Cazenovia, but then I didn't come. After an exchange of letters I told her unless I found a job in Iowa I would come to Cazenovia the first of August to see her. I thought it important that we get together since it had been more than a year we had been apart, and much had happened in that time. Even though we had been corresponding all through the war I felt we should be together again and see how we felt. She agreed to be home and wanted me to come.

Art had a big field of oats ready to harvest the last of July; Dale and I cut and shocked it before I left. I drove the four horse team on the binder, the last time I was to do such work. I did enjoy the farm and being footloose, I did think of staying in the west. But one evening Dale and Faye asked me to go with them to a 4–H club meeting. When I met the group and listened to their conversation, I realized I didn't belong. I had been away from their kind of life too long to feel at home.

The first of August I took the train back east for Cazenovia. I left my trunk and uniform with Leeta and traveled in the suit I bought in Cleveland. Norah met me at the station in Cazenovia and after our greetings, she said, "I thought you would be dressed as a soldier." It made me feel sorry I hadn't gone there first after getting out of the army. Norah's folks gave me a warm welcome and in no time I was made to feel like one of the family. In a way I felt a bit guilty, for I felt more at home here than I did in Dunlap. But I had been separated from my family for a long time.

The first weekend I was in Cazenovia, Ann Tooke, Norah's special friend, came home from Sherrill, New York. She was working in the office of the Oneida Community, Ltd., the makers of the famous silverware. I knew Ann, of course, as she had been in Houghton for a brief time and Norah was always talking about her. Ann asked me if I had a job and I said, "No, I was looking." She told me that the Community was establishing a research department and maybe I could get a job with them. She said it was a fine company to work for and they were going strong.

I was indeed interested, for it sounded like the type of work I wanted to get into. So on Monday morning I took the trip to Sherrill. At the personnel office I was referred to William S. Murray, the head of the new research department. I met him and gave my experience and qualifications. We seemed to like each other and he remarked that he was particularly interested in my training in physics. He said all the men in his department, including himself, were chemists and they could use my knowledge. He suggested to the employment manager that I be hired as a chemist and put on night duty. Since the factory was running both day and night shifts, a chemist on duty at night might be very valuable. On the side Murray said to me, "This is the way to get you started and later I will get you into the research department."

I was glad to accept the job as presented, even though the beginning salary was not large. It was seemingly the kind of work I was looking for and presented a future. Also, I would be near Cazenovia so I would be able to see Norah often. When I returned to Cazenovia and told of my decision, they were all very pleased. So after a couple of days with Norah, I packed my bag and left for work. I wrote Leeta and asked to have my trunk sent by express, and when it arrived I felt established.

Because the factory was running full tilt, I had trouble finding a room. The plant had a cafeteria which was always open, so I could eat there, but the only place I could find was in a rooming house where I could share a room with another man who worked day times. He slept in the bed nights, and I used it in the daytime. I considered this as a temporary arrangement until I could find better quarters.

Before I started I met very briefly the head of the laboratory, Dan Gray. He was about my age, and we liked each other at once, so throughout the time I was with the company we not only became good co-workers but personal friends. Dan had one disability, he was blind in one eye, but after one knew him a short time that was forgotten. He was a graduate of Millikin University, and had been working for this company since his graduation. He was a fine chemist and proved a big help to me as my training in that field was limited, and since I had been away from it so long, this was like starting over again.

When I walked into the lab, which was a small annex to the plating room, I found a note from Dan indicating the samples I should run and a book of instructions. After studying the book for a time I got ready to run my first samples of the plating solution, which had been gathered that afternoon. Before I got underway, one of the platers came rushing in with a sample from a "strike," which he said was not acting right and wanted me to run an analysis at once. I said, "I'll be glad to run it but it will take some time, as I am just getting organized." I set the other samples aside and began to look up the method for the new sample and was just ready to run it when the plater came back and reported that they found the trouble in an electrical connection, so they didn't need the analysis. I was relieved as I didn't feel established enough to make such a decision.

At first it seemed strange working during the night hours with a lunch break at midnight. But it wasn't my first experience as I thought of my work in the power plant in Lorain, Ohio. I soon was able to complete my work with time to spare, so I was able to move about the plant and observe the various operations. Since the Community Plate was well known, a number of tourists would stop at the plant and take a guided tour. To follow such a group through the plant and describe what they could see may be the best way I can tell about the making of silverware as I came to know it.

The first thing such a group would see were the long strips of less than ¼ inch thick nickel silver, which was the base of the plated ware. These strips were cut into the proper length for a knife, fork or spoon. These so-called blanks were taken into the stamping mill, where each piece was placed on a die and a heavy weight was dropped on it. Thus the shape of a spoon or knife handle and the tines of the fork were produced. After the stamping mill the shaped pieces were placed in a large tumbling barrel. In the barrel were small abrasive marbles. As the barrel was rotated for several hours, the rough edges and spots were polished off the pieces. From the barrel a quick inspection was made and any pieces with deep pits were either returned to the barrel or discarded into the waste boxes. The pieces passing inspection were taken to the black buff room. Here an operator held each piece against a rapidly rotating buffing wheel covered with a fine black abrasive material. When the piece was free of all scratches and pits, it was ready for the plating room.

In the plating room were long tables where the boxes from the buffing room were placed. On each side of these tables sat rows of women who with gloved hands wrapped a long copper wire around the neck of each piece. The result was a wire holding a dozen of the various types of ware. The pieces had to be wrapped so that none would touch another piece and the string was hooked to a metal bar ready for a plater. The "platers," who were some of the highest paid workers in the factory, picked up these bars with the wired pieces and first put them through a hot cleaning bath to remove any dirt or grease. After a rinse the clean pieces were hung on the cathode side of a copper strike. This was a small vat filled with a copper salt electrolyte, and the pieces were left for a few seconds at a high electric current. This left an extremely thin coating of copper on the piece. After the copper strike came a rinse and then a nickel strike. These operations were critical to form a base for the silver plating and it took an experienced plater to have it just right.

After a rinse the pieces were hung in the silver cyanide plating solution. This was a long tank filled with the electrolyte using pure silver bars as the anode and the tableware as the cathode. To make the silver plate uniform the holders were gently agitated. Everything about this process was critical. Any change in the strength of the solution or in the current would affect the results. The experienced platers were quick to detect any change in the proper rate of plating and would take steps to find out the cause. This is one reason these men were considered so valuable to the company and could demand high wages. Another reason was that the life of these platers was rarely over twenty years of service.

Cyanide is one of the deadliest poisons known and any compound of the chemical such as the double silver salt used in the plating tank were very toxic. While there were ventilating fans always in operation, a certain amount of the fumes from the tank would escape into the room. The first time I entered this room I could detect the sweetish, almond-like odor of cyanide. I was amazed to see these platers work over these vats hour after hour. They claimed they got used to it and it didn't hurt them, but the limited time of their life span indicated otherwise. The girls at the wiring tables were also affected. More than once I saw new women start to work and after an hour or so they would rush to the women's restroom to throw up. Many would quit right then, but if they stuck it out, they learned to live with the odor.

When the pieces were silver plated, they were rinsed and taken to the red buff room. Here each piece was held against a buffing wheel covered with a fine red oxide of iron. This process changed the dull whitish silver coating into the bright highly polished table silverware. These were then taken to the inspection tables, where skilled women inspectors looked for defects. The slightest fault that was detected caused the piece to be placed in the "second" box to be sold as such at the factory outlet. The perfect pieces were sent to the wrapping room, where each piece was folded in special sulfur free paper and placed in the containers to be shipped to the retail trade.

There were two grades of ware made by the company. One was called "par plate," which was a thin coating of silver and guaranteed for ten years and sold by mail order firms such as Sears, Roebuck. The main product was called "Community Plate," which had a heavier plate of silver and was guaranteed for fifty years. I personally know this guarantee was good, since we received a full set of this tableware for a wedding gift and at the time of our 50th anniversary we took the set back. The company replated it free, so it was like new.

This company had the practice of giving college students related to employees summer jobs. Bill Wettel was one of these students and had been working with Dan Gray in the laboratory. When he left at the end of the summer, I was told I would be given the day job. I was delighted at this change, but it posed a problem as I could no longer use my room. I went to the personnel office and met Charles Goodwin, the head of that department. I explained my situation and he was sympathetic but knew of no place open. He did say he would talk with his wife and maybe I could come to his house and use his son's room for a time. His boy was serving a hitch in the army but would not be home until later that year. I met Mrs. Goodwin, and she agreed to rent me the room and give me my breakfast and dinner. I could eat lunch at the plant cafeteria, so I was set for a time at least. The Goodwins had three daughters at home, the oldest worked at the plant while the others were in school. With this change I was put on a salary. I didn't have to punch a time clock and as our hours were similar. Mr. Goodwin and I walked to work almost every morning. Evenings I did some reading while the girls were doing their homework. Later I found the company had a club house for the employees, and I joined to get my exercise by playing basketball or other games.

Dan Gray was the senior chemist in the lab and when I reported, he divided the routine work between us. We worked together fine and one day after I had been there awhile, Dan said to me, "Ray, I forget you are new here. I feel I have known you all my life." Everything that was used in the process of making the silverware was tested to be sure it met the specifications. Also, such things as coal which came by the carload was tested and more than once our analysis showed such poor quality that it was refused. The main concern was with the chemicals used in the plating process.

An example of how important this was came about that year. The whole plant was thrown into a panic when all the silverware was peeling when it hit the red buff wheel. The plant engineers rushed around checking everything. They brought samples of every plating solution to the lab with the request we drop everything to check these solutions. All the platers knew that if there was over a certain amount of zinc in any salt used to make the solutions, the silver plate would not hold. Dan and I rushed the analysis and when I checked the copper solution used in the copper strike, the zinc sulfide precipitate came down like a snow storm. Our specification for this salt was to be not over .001% of zinc. I knew at once this was far more than that and evidently the source of the trouble. It was the rule of the plant that everything received by the shipping department must have a sample sent to the lab for analysis before it was given to anyone. A check showed that a barrel of the copper salt had been received and someone forgot to send a sample to the lab. When the plating department asked for the salt, it went into the solution with disastrous results. Hundreds of pieces of the tableware had to be sent to the stripping tanks to recover the silver and the flow of finished ware was stopped for days, costing the company thousands of dollars. The result of all this was that a bulletin was sent to every department with strict orders to have everything checked before it was used.

One of the products that this company had produced in its early days were steel animal traps. However, the market for these traps was declining and the silverware sales were increasing. The company decided that year to close the trap factory. That left some vacant space and we were delighted to have some of that space given to us for a new, much larger lab. The maintenance crew built it to our plans. This made it possible for Mr. Murray to expand the research department and he kept us busy with testing new materials. The company was considering using stainless steel blades in the knives, and I was given the task of testing a number of samples that various companies submitted for that purpose. I set up a series of tests using such acids that occur in foods to see which sample withstood the corrosive action best. That, plus other tests I could think of, showed a wide difference in the samples submitted. The steel that the company selected was based on my report rather than the sales pitch of the companies trying to sell their product.

In the late spring I was surprised when I was notified that I was to go with Dan Gray to the American Chemical Society convention which was to be held in St. Louis, Missouri. Mr. Murray was also going but went ahead of us. Dan and I took a Pullman to Chicago and then a day coach on the Illinois Central to St. Louis. It was too early for corn to be planted, so the country looked rather barren. To pass the time we played pitch, Dan winning most of the games.

It was a thrill for me to attend this big convention. I met a few men I knew, one in particular I was happy to see was Dr. Holmes from Oberlin. Dr. Holmes was widely known for his research on colloids and was considered an authority on the subject. His lecture on the subject proved to be one of the main attractions of the convention. He was scheduled for a room which held 200 people. I wanted to hear him and went early but just got in. Many were turned away. Colloids were the big topic of the day as they were the basis of the coming plastic industry. I got a chance to meet Dr. Holmes after his lecture and he was very cordial, especially when I told him what I was doing. He said he was so pleased to hear of his student's success. It was the last time I saw him, as he died at a rather early age.

There are several chemical industrial plants in and around St. Louis and tours to these places were arranged. I selected a trip to the Monsanto Chemical plant which was across the Mississippi River from the city. After touring the plant we came out on the banks of the river. As it was early spring, the river was at flood stage due to heavy rains and melting snow. The plant was protected by high dikes, but the mighty stream a mile wide was near the top of the dikes. The whole group I was with stood fascinated watching the silent but powerful flood flow past. There were no waves, only a series of eddies, and an occasional uprooted tree told of the speed and power of this flood. Silently watching we could feel the ground tremble under our feet, an impression of that river I can never forget.

After this convention, Murray pushed the work of the research department, giving me more of that work. Problems encountered in the plant were now referred to us for investigation. One example was trouble with the steel knife blades not coming through uniform. The engineers suspected the pyrometer which controlled the temperature of the furnace where the blades were heated, ready to be forged, was not correct. I was given a colorimeter, a device used to tell the temperature by the color. When I set up the instrument to check the furnace, I ran into something which exists in all factories. Just as soon as anyone tries to check an operation, the operators are suspicious that someone is trying to put them out of work. Even when I was careful to explain just what I was doing, I had difficulty getting any cooperation and sometimes encountered actual interference. So this job of checking the furnace which should have taken an hour or so, took me all day. I finally got enough data to make a report and the result was the installation of a new type of pyrometer which solved the problem.

A much longer task involved the knife handles. These handles are hollow, made by soldering two halves together and then the blade soldered into it. To do this the company had always used a silver solder, but with the price of silver rising, we were asked to investigate to see if a cheaper solder could be used. Murray assigned the project to me. He sent me to the library at Syracuse University to review the literature on solders as a start. There were a lot of publications on the subject, but my research showed that basically most solders were an alloy of tin and lead. To make a white solder, zinc or some white metal was added.

Back in the laboratory, I assembled the various metals and began to make various alloys to see if they would work as a solder. When I got one that I thought was worth trying, I took it to the operator of the soldering machine to test. Again, I found him very suspicious of my motives. I finally got his cooperation after I fully explained what I was doing and expressed a lot of interest in his work. When he looked at my first solder, he said it would not work because it wasn't strong enough to hold the narrow edges of the handle together. He was right as he quickly proved to me.

I went back to try again. To make the solder stronger I added nickel but had to keep the zinc fairly high to maintain a white color, otherwise it would show through when the knife was plated. After trying various combinations I did get a solder, which surprised the operator of the soldering machine because it held. In fact, it went through the black buffing alright, plated without showing through, but failed the final test when it peeled on the red buffing wheel. I wrote up a report of my project, giving complete details, and concluded with the recommendation that while the silver solder might cost more, no other one would give the same results, so to maintain the high quality of the Community Plate, it should continue to be used.

Running so many different tests in the laboratory, we had to be constantly on guard against accidents. But once in awhile one did occur. One day I started a carbon test on a steel sample, and I noticed the gas which was formed at the beginning was not coming through. I was peering along the line to see where the obstruction was, when the tube containing the solution of sodium hydroxide blew up in my face. This chemical is very caustic and will cause severe burns of the flesh if not washed off immediately. Blinded by the explosion, I groped my way to the sink and turned the water faucet wide open, sticking my head under it. Fortunately, the chemical did not get in my eyes, and I was able to wash it off my face, but I missed one drop on the lobe of one ear. That drop burned a hole almost through the lobe before I could stop it.

Following the policy of the company to hire children of employees during their summer vacation, one sixteen year old boy was assigned to our lab. He knew no chemistry, so all I could do to keep him busy, was to clean our equipment. I knew there were a lot of old bottles that had been stored under the sink. So one day when he ran out of work I suggested he get them out and see if any could be cleaned. I told him to set aside any bottles that contained any liquid and I would check them. I cautioned him about anything that was not labelled.

After he started to work I was called to the office. I got back in time to see him staggering out of the lab door with his hands over his eyes. I got a whiff of a gas which was following him out of the door. It reminded me of the tear gas which I had experienced in the war. I held my breath and dashed into the lab, raising the outside window and turning on a fan. Returning to the boy, I found him practically blinded, so I rushed him to the nurse's room for treatment. The gas was so strong it got out into part of the plant and drove some workers from their machines. Word of the mishap traveled fast and some of the head ones in the front offices came down to see what had happened. From them I learned that the company had done some plating of gas shells during the war and did have some of the liquid to test the plating. Evidently a bottle with a little of this liquid had been stored under the sink. After that experience I had all the old bottles discarded, not taking any chance of cleaning them. Two weeks later the plumbers had to open up the trap of that sink and there was enough tear gas liquid in there to drive them off the job. I never knew it was so persistent.

In the late spring Richard Goodwin, whose room I had been using, came home from the army. I thought I should look for another room then, but Richard asked me to stay. I tried to find out how Mrs. Goodwin felt about it, but she was very uncommunicative. I gradually learned that she was a direct descendant of the original Oneida Community, which had migrated from Massachusetts to form a communal society. This group had built a large house in Kenmore, adjacent to Sherrill, which still stands and is referred to as the Mansion House. In this house the families all lived together and the children were raised in one large group. They were taught to call all the women Mother and all the men Father, so they didn't know who were their real parents. Several of the officers of the company were also descendants of the original community, so the whole plant took on the air of a big family. Most of the people in Sherrill were employees of the company and the city government was run by the officers of the plant. It was a one industry town in the fullest sense. It was all fine if one fitted in with the group, but it took time to be accepted, and I was never quite sure whether or not I was accepted.

After Richard had been home a few weeks I could feel the tension of Mrs. Goodwin grow and then one morning when I came down to breakfast I found a note from Mr. Goodwin asking me to find other lodgings. I didn't know where to turn and told Dan about my situation. He said, "Don't do anything until I can talk with my landlady." He was rooming and boarding with a widow woman and her sister in a big house in Oneida, a small city two miles from Sherrill. The next day Dan gave me the news that on his recommendation his landlady would rent me an attic room. For a time I had to get my breakfast and dinner in some restaurant in Oneida, but after I became acquainted, the lady told me I could room and board with her on the same basis as Dan. That was fine, as Dan and I got along well and were now working, living and commuting at the same time. Dan had been married before I knew him, but his wife died a short time after the marriage. Before the year was over he got married again, but lived in his old room for a time. Later he bought a house in Sherrill and moved there.

In May I received announcements from both Dale and Faye of their graduation from high school. Mother was now well set in Richmond, California, and she urged Dale and Faye to come out there where she was sure they could find work and also would be able to enter the University of California in the fall as residents. They talked it over and could see no future in or around Dunlap, so they decided to go. This left Ula now helping Leeta with her growing family on the farm. Mother knew about it and she thought Ula should also come to California, but she didn't want her to travel alone. She wrote me, suggesting that I should take my vacation time coming to see her and bring Ula with me. I hadn't seen Mother since long before the war, so I thought I should go and planned accordingly.

When I got to Dunlap I found that Ula had made up her mind to go to California and begged me to take her. I checked with the station agent in Dunlap and he said it would take ten days for us to get reservations for a Pullman out of Omaha. I didn't have that much time, so I went to Omaha, found the consolidated ticket office, and was able to get an upper and lower berth on a tourist car in just two days. These tourist cars were not as fancy as a regular Pullman but good for our purpose and much cheaper.

When I got back and told Ula I had the tickets, she was delighted and eager to go. We got on the tourist car in Omaha at 10 p.m. and left sometime in the night. Many of the passengers on this car were changing as they took advantage of stopovers to sightsee, but we went straight through. After three days and nights we were happy to get off at Berkeley and have Dale and Faye meeting us there.

Mother was delighted to see us and she did her best to make us feel at home in the small house that she had taken over from her folks in the city of Richmond. My grandparents lived in a small annex, so Mother could look after them. Together they raised some garden vegetables and kept rabbits to sell for meat. This city was populated mostly by the workers in two big petroleum refineries. A large number were Mexicans and it was with them Mother found her customers. The first thing I noticed around the house was a strong rather offensive odor, which I couldn't identify. Finally I located it coming from a bunch of eucalyptus buds that Grandma had hung up to dry. She considered them to be a cure for all her ills. I knew the oil from these trees was used in liniments and as a disinfectant, but the odor from these drying buds was terrible.

As soon as I arrived, Mother began to work on me to stay, but somehow I couldn't feel at home there. The weather was so different from what I was used to in the summer. The sun was out bright every day after burning off the nightly fog which came in through the Golden Gate. There were no clouds in the sky, so the sun made it quite warm in the middle of the day. By three o'clock in the afternoon it cooled off so a coat or sweater was needed and by early evening a top-coat was required. Actually, as many tourists have learned through the years, this was about the worst time of the year to visit the bay section of California.

Both Dale and Faye had found jobs and were happy to be working. Roy Crow, my uncle who was just two years older than I and whom I had not seen since we were boys in College Springs, lived nearby. He had organized an orchestra which played for nightly dances. Dale and I went one night to hear him play. He was good, which to me was remarkable since he did not read music and played everything by ear. Ula was very glad to be with Mother again, and in time they formed a team which lasted until Mother's death, years later. I was glad to see Mother and to know that my brother and sisters were now together once more and seemingly well located, but I turned a deaf ear to the pleas of staying, saying I had a job to get back to and at the end of the week, I took the train back to Oneida.

When I got back from my trip, I found a radical change in the affairs of the company. The business recession had set in and the silverware business was one of the first to feel it. Orders for the Community Plate had stopped and only a few for par plate kept the factory operating. In contrast to the high importance of the research department of a year ago, now all funds were cut off and the department phased out. Both Dan and I were reduced from a salaried position to an hourly job and required to punch a time clock each day. All our helpers who had done the heavy and dirty work were laid off, so Dan and I had to do it ourselves. One such job was the tricky, dangerous task of dissolving the silver bars in nitric acid then adding sodium cyanide to make the plating solution. When I helped Dan do this task, I decided it was time to look for another job.

Another factor was my relationship with Norah. It had been a rather disappointing time for us, we had been so close together in distance, but so far apart in seeing each other. In our talks it seemed to me that we were far apart in getting married. In fact, I became convinced that Norah had decided to keep our relationship just as it was. Facing all this, I decided it was time for me to strike out for something better. I had been in communication with Dr. Williams in Oberlin and he informed me of an opportunity of a fellowship in physics at the University of California. I had a telegram offering me the position. That weekend I went to Cazenovia to see Norah. When I told her of the offer and that I had decided to accept it, she burst into tears. Sobbing, she said, "If you go out there, I will never see you again. Please don't go." I was surprised, as she had never shown such emotion before. We had a long talk, and we reached a sort of understanding and a new relationship when I said I would not go.

I returned to Sherrill resolved to make the best of the situation until I could find something better. There was one bit of work I did just before the end of the research department. A group of engineers were working on designing and making an automatic plating machine. A room had been given them on the second floor of the plant and the doors were kept locked. Since there was a sign posted "No Admittance," all sorts of rumors circulated as to what was behind the door. I found out when one day I was asked if I wanted to help by checking the solutions needed. First, I had to swear secrecy before I was admitted to the room. When I did I saw a long device already built whereby the tableware could be suspended in metal holders at one end and then by means of an endless chain would be carried up and down, in and out of a series of tanks to complete the whole plating process. If successful, it meant the elimination of all the women who were winding the wire around each piece and would take only a few platers to run the machine. My part of the project was to determine the proper strength of each solution in the various tanks. I was with the company only long enough to see a few trial runs and they seemed good. Some fifteen years later I took a group of science club students to tour the factory, and we saw the machine I had worked on in full operation.

After my visit and talk with Norah I did some serious thinking about my future. I talked with Mr. Murray and he told me confidentially that he was disappointed in the way things were going in the company and he had a project in mind and might leave. One thing that Norah suggested was that I should think of going back into teaching. Even though I had said I would never teach again after my experience at West Park, I began to think about it. I recalled the fact I did enjoy working with high school students and my pleasant relations with other teachers. This was in contrast to working on routine analysis shut away in a laboratory with little contact with other people. With all this in mind, I went into Syracuse and found the office of the Bardeen-Union Teachers Agency. Norah had recommended this agency to me as she had done business with them and found them the most reliable of several in the area. I talked to them and liked their attitude, so I registered, giving a resume of my credentials and the names of people for references.

As it was past the time for schools to open in September, I thought it was too late to get a position that year. But the last of the month I received a notice from the agency of a vacancy in a teaching position in the high school in Burlington, New Jersey. They wanted a man to teach high school mathematics, take charge of physical education of boys and coach football in the fall and track and baseball in the spring. I felt I was qualified to do all this, and since the salary was considerably more than I was getting, I applied. In a few days I had a letter from Mr. Smith, the Superintendent of Schools in the City of Burlington, offering me the job and enclosing a contract for me to sign. I showed the letter to Mr. Keller, who was now the head of our department. He congratulated me and told me if I desired, he would waive the usual two week's notice for leaving the company so I could go at once. I signed the contract and informed Mr. Smith that I would report the following Monday.

Again, I had reached a turning point in my life. I have always been grateful for the chance of working at the Oneida Community Ltd. I learned a lot about industrial chemistry and I have reason to believe I made some important contributions to the company. If it had not been for the business depression which occurred at this time, I might have stayed with this company for a long time. Fate was again intervening to point me toward my main lifework.

CHAPTER 16

BURLINGTON

I checked out of the Oneida Community Ltd. on a Friday afternoon. I packed my trunk and bags and took a train Saturday morning to New York. Burlington, New Jersey, was on the main line of the Pennsylvania Railroad between New York and Atlantic City, so it was easy to get a train that afternoon for my destination. Arriving late in the afternoon, I found Superintendent Smith at home and he referred me to a boarding house near the high school where a man teacher in the school stayed. I found the place and fortunately found they had a room vacant, so I moved in.

Superintendent Smith asked me to come to his house on Sunday afternoon. I expected him to tell me about my work and about the school, but all he did was to show me his collection of old guns of which he was very proud. After looking at them for a time, I tried to ask about the school, but he evaded my questions. All he would say was he was glad to have me in the system and I could check with the high school principal on Monday morning. He did add that he had come from upper New York State and was recruiting teachers from that area. He said the principal was from Seneca Falls, New York, so I should feel quite at home.

Monday morning I reported to the office of the high school. A woman was in the office, and I introduced myself saying I was to see the principal. "I am Miss Ditzell," she replied, "and I am the principal." I sort of caught my breath, as it was the first indication that I had that I was to work with a woman principal. I saw her as a middle-aged, slender, very determined person. I sized her up as one who expected to be the boss and no question about it.

All she did to greet me was to hand me a copy of my schedule. I looked at it and saw I had two classes in elementary algebra, one in intermediate algebra, one in advanced algebra, and a class in review of all high school subjects to prepare a group of girls to take a county examination for a teacher's certificate. That was a full teaching load, but I was also to do the boys' physical education program and coach football. It looked like a killing job, and I could well understand why this position had been open the third week of the school year. I learned that two men had preceded me, each staying just one week, so I was the

243

third man on the job. I was taken aback by the load they expected me to carry, but I was there and was determined to see it through for a year.

The high school building was old and had no gymnasium. There were about 200 students and about half were boys. For physical education I was expected to take all the boys outside two days a week. All I could do was to give them some calisthenics and a lot of marching. The weather was good until late fall, so we could get outside, but when the winter rains came, there was no class.

The first day I met the boys outside, I lined them up and found out they had already been divided into squads. Each year had been organized as a platoon with a leader. I asked them to keep the same organization and started them marching, bringing them into a hollow square. I wanted to talk to them, but the square was so large they couldn't hear me, so I told them to break ranks and come in closer. With that they came charging from all sides so fast I wondered if I was going to be crushed. I held up my hand and the senior platoon leader gave a sharp command, "Hold it! Give the man a chance." At that they stopped crowding and gave me their attention. I was indeed glad for the help and soon learned that this boy was a star athlete and a leader in the school. He was very mature for his age, a fine student and being on all the athletic teams was looked up to by all the boys. He became my right hand man, which I needed.

The building was small and crowded. Miss Ditzell and Superintendent Smith shared a small office, and since there was no teachers' room, all had to hang their coats in the same room. It made for a lot of confusion in the mornings, so I didn't wonder Miss Ditzell was high strung with such arrangements. The schedule she gave me showed all my classes were in different rooms. She did introduce me to a woman teacher who was in charge of a large study hall used as a home room for some fifty students and told me I was to assist. The man from my boarding house did the honors of introducing me to the other faculty members. Since the school was in full operation, it was up to me to catch up the best that I could.

The football team had played one game and lost. So the first week I helped them all I could and we had a game away that Friday. When we won 35-0, they were elated. I found they had excellent team spirit and they thought I was a real coach, so it turned out to be a fine season. The weather was good for football and I enjoyed being outside and working with the team.

Once I was established I had a chance to view the city. Burlington was one of several such cities on the Delaware River, fifteen miles above Camden and Philadelphia. Many of the red brick houses were built in the Philadelphia styles, i.e., the front right out even with the sidewalk and tight together. The only open space was in the back, not visible from the street. There were a few old colonial mansions. It was largely a commuter town for people who worked in Philadelphia. The one exception was a small steel mill located up-river from the business section of the city. The workers in this mill were mostly European immigrants who lived in company houses near the mill. These people put their children to work as soon as they were out of grade school, so as far as I knew none were in the high school.

Norah had taken a new position teaching at Pulaski, New York, a village about 50 miles north of Syracuse. Our letters that year were full of news about our experiences and activities in our respective schools. In October Norah wrote that Mary Doolittle, her life-long friend in Cazenovia, hadn't found a job teaching that she liked, but had received a notice from the Bardeen agency of a vacancy in Burlington, which she might accept. My letter in reply tells what happened.

Burlington, N.J.
Oct. 31, '20

Dear Norah,

I have been working on class books until I very nearly have writer's cramps. Nevertheless, I am going to start this before dinner. We don't have dinner until 3 o'clock on Sunday. It is a beautiful warm day and I did take an hour's walk this morning, out into the section where Mary's school is located. That brings me to the story of Mary. She will probably write about her impressions and troubles, but I'll tell you some of them.

Thursday evening when I got through working with the football team, I walked into the office and who should walk up to me but Mary. I was very surprised because I expected to hear that she had gone somewhere else. She had her bag with her and as Smith was busy, I took her to the place where he had told her she could stay.

She wasn't much impressed with the place, neither was I when I first landed, but there is something peculiar about it you sort of like after you have been here a day or two. It is built on the old Philadelphia style, so different from anything in other parts of the country. So I told her not to go too strong on first impressions.

Well, after supper I went over to find out how Mary was situated and feeling. Poor Mary, she was in an awful hole. It will take her to tell about it. I had to laugh and she did too, but it was serious also. We talked and decided the best thing to do was to see Smith about her place to live. He appreciated the situation, but didn't know of any other place.

It happened that one of the teachers, when I started out of the school with Mary, stopped her and asked if she had a place to stay. This teacher lived in town and felt sorry for the new teachers coming in. Mary told her she had a place, not as wise as she was a few hours later. So while at Smith's we found out the name of this teacher and went right over that night to see if Mary could stay over Sunday with her. But she was not in and as it was getting late, there wasn't anything to do but for Mary to stay where she was that night and see what she could do later.

Well, to make it short, Mary got up the next morning, went over to this place, early mind you, and by good fortune prevailed upon Miss Rogers to take her in for the year. It is one of the nicest places in town; she couldn't have found a better place anywhere.

If that was all of Mary's troubles it would be fine, but the school they want her to teach in is a "humdinger." She will tell you about it. I'm sorry I didn't investigate and find out about things before she came, but I didn't dream that such conditions existed in the same town... I don't know whether Mary will stay or not, depends on the treatment she receives tomorrow morning.

So since Mary didn't know whether she would be here or not, we decided to go into Philadelphia and celebrate. We took the noon train, went to the University of Pennsylvania vs. Pennsylvania State football game. It was a very exciting game, Mary sure got excited over it for which I was glad, I enjoyed it too. After the game we looked around for awhile, had dinner and then went to a show. Then home, we were tired but had a good time and could say we had been to Philadelphia. Mary is a good sport and I enjoyed being with her. Before we left, she made me promise we would go 50–50 on expenses. I didn't like it but she would not go any other way. Wish you could have been along. I had to laugh for Mary kept saying, "Now I must remember this place so when Norah comes down to see us I can take her to it." She has it all planned. Well, if she stays I sure wish you could come. If she doesn't I'd be glad to have you come, there are so many places to go to and places to visit. The traveling accommodations are good and not so expensive.

Just returned from dinner. I am in a pretty good place, very good hearted people and funny as can be. Have very good things to eat, nothing fancy but excellent cooking. My football team won a game and have one next Friday. The big game comes the 19th of November. Be a feather in my cap if we could win that.

Well, Dear, this is some long letter for me but I knew you would want to know all the details. I wish you were here so I could see you tonight. I have enjoyed your letters. Keep them coming.

With lots of love,
Ray.

The Miss Rogers referred to in the letter was Lydia Rogers, who was to play an important part in our lives that year. She and Mary liked each other at first sight, and Mary was so lucky to find such a fine place to stay. It did much to compensate for the hard school that Mary was assigned to teach at. This school was located near the steel mill and the children were from families of immigrants. Many of the parents could not speak English and the older boys took advantage of it.

Lydia lived with her father in one of the few old colonial houses in the city. It was a large house located on a spacious lawn, which made it unique. Mr. Rogers was a distinguished looking man in his seventies and had retired with plenty of means to enjoy life. His wife had died years before and Lydia stayed home to keep house for her father. This brought about one of the strangest "love stories" I ever knew.

Sure that her father would remarry if she left home, and Lydia didn't want that to happen, she made a pact with him that as long as she stayed home and kept house he would not consider it. Lydia had gone with a boy named Ghant ever since they had been together in school. They had been so close that all their friends expected them to get married as soon as they finished college. Instead, Lydia became a teacher in the Burlington schools and Ghant took a position in a bank in Philadelphia, commuting every working day. They were now past middle age and Ghant had been waiting patiently all these years for Lydia to give up and marry. He spent almost every evening and weekend with her. They were together so much that Mr. Rogers expressed it to me this way. "They have all the disadvantages of being married with none of the advantages." Since Mary was staying at the Roger's home, I was invited there often and got to know Lydia, Ghant and Mr. Rogers very well during the year.

Ghant was a member of the Burlington boat club and owned a very nice canoe, which he kept at the boat house. A few Saturdays in the spring when we could all be free at the same time Ghant arranged an all-day canoe trip on the river. Lydia and Mary fixed a picnic lunch and Ghant and I did the paddling. There were many small streams flowing into the big river and with the canoe we could explore them. These streams came out of swampy areas and were full of wildlife, and the canoe being so quiet we could see these birds and animals at close range. One thing we had to be sure about was the time for low tide, otherwise we could be stranded in the swamp grass. These trips were a wonderful relief from my strenuous work.

In the middle of the year I began to have bad headaches. I went to a doctor, who told me to stop eating meat as my stomach was upset so much. When that didn't help, he suggested it might be my eyes. I had never worn glasses, so he made an appointment with an optometrist in Philadelphia. I took an early train to get to the office in the morning. I demured when this doctor wanted to put drops in my eyes. I did not expect this, but he said he couldn't examine my eyes unless he did so. He had a room full of patients sitting in chairs waiting for the drops to work and I joined them. The room was close and very warm and when the drops began to work I couldn't see, so I got nervous. I felt faint and suddenly the floor came up to meet me. The next thing I knew I was on a couch with the doctor bending over me. I heard him say, "He's coming to now." After that as soon as I could sit up I was hurried to the chair for my examination. I had skinned my forehead and nose, which the doctor tried to patch, but for a week I looked as if I had been in a brawl and took a lot of kidding. A week later I got my glasses which I used for reading and close work. They did help and I began to feel better. It took me a long time to get used to wearing glasses; I only wore them for close work, taking them off to eat and all outdoor activities.

In our correspondence that year Norah and I did a lot of comparing the way our respective schools were run. From a few letters saved from that time it showed I wanted to make some plans leading toward marriage as soon as possible while Norah was giving all the reasons why we shouldn't. I began to think we were reaching a condition like Lydia and Ghant. Of course, Mary was writing Norah all the time to keep her informed of our activities. Years later I found one letter in which Mary had told Norah she should be proud of Ray for even though he was away from her so much, he was absolutely true to her. She said she personally knew it was so. She also advised Norah that she couldn't wait forever and not to get to the state of Lydia, for she was sure Ray would never go for that.

For the Christmas recess I did go to Cazenovia and had a week with Norah. It was a typical Cazenovia winter, with lots of snow and cold weather, which we got out and enjoyed. The next break would be at Easter and we didn't know whether our vacations would come at the same time. I knew I wouldn't return another year at the killing job in Burlington, so I contacted the Bardeen Agency and informed them of my decision. I told them I was interested in a high school principalship in central New York and hoped there might be an opening so I could have an interview at Easter time.

With the principalship in mind, I was studying the operation of the high school. I was observing Miss Ditzell to see how she operated. Actually, I didn't learn as much from her about what to do as I did what not to do. One such event took place in the homeroom. The New Jersey law required a reading of a certain number of verses from the Bible each day. So at the beginning of the day a homeroom period was scheduled to do this reading and to make any announcements needed. Since there were two of us in charge of this large room, we took turns, one reading the Bible while the other took attendance. There was usually a few minutes left after the reading before the bell rang at the end of the period. We talked it over and both of us in charge agreed that as long as the room was quiet it should remain so until the end of the period. We told the pupils it would be a good time to do some last minute preparations for the coming classes. Evidently other homeroom teachers didn't agree with us, as we could hear loud talking coming from other rooms in the building. Most of the students in our room liked our regulations, but a few didn't and appealed to Miss Ditzell. One morning she marched into our room and without saying anything to us told the pupils she understood they were required to keep quiet after the Bible reading. She announced that it was not a rule of the school and they were free to talk until the end of the period. Both of us

248

teachers were aghast that she would do such a thing and furious to have her destroy our authority. The students were just as surprised as we were at this announcement, and the result was a good lesson in peer pressure. The great majority of the students liked our rule and while the few started talking, they were so frowned on by the majority they either gave it up or talked so low they caused no disturbance.

The second event that happened in which I thought Miss Ditzell was wrong came after the start of the baseball season. One Friday afternoon we were scheduled to play a nearby military academy. We had a bus in front of the school ready to take us to the game and were waiting for the last boy to report. We saw Miss Ditzell rushing out the front door and headed for the bus. The door of the bus was open and she looked in, calling out the name of the only good pitcher I had on the team. He came to the door and Miss Ditzell told him to get off the bus, he couldn't go. I was dumbfounded because I had cleared all the names on the team. So I asked, "Why?" She said the boy's English teacher had reported that this boy had turned in his book report late. I tried to talk to her but she was adamant and we had to leave without the boy. Right then I made up my mind that I would never let an English or any other teacher have the power to decide who should play on an athletic team. It was the beginning of my philosophy that the physical education department was an important department of a high school and should be on a par with others.

My second string pitcher was only a freshman and the military team hit him all over the lot. They were a strong team and losing our senior pitcher took the heart out of my boys so by the fifth inning the other team was ahead 20–0. I had told their coach about what had happened, so he was very understanding, and at the end of the fifth inning he asked us if we wanted to continue the game for the full seven innings or stop the game then so we would be in time for the evening meal in the mess hall. We agreed to call the game and after the members of the team had changed their clothes, we marched into the dining hall, where all the cadets who were already assembled stood up and gave us a cheer. It was a gesture of good sportsmanship which did us a lot of good, something I never forgot.

Easter came early that year and I was debating whether to go to Cazenovia or not, when Mary decided for me. She found out that Norah's vacation started a few days before ours and she urged Norah to come down and visit us and then we would all go back to Cazenovia. I readily invited Norah to come and was happy when she did. She stayed with Mary, and Lydia made her very welcome. The three of us had one day to visit Philadelphia, and as soon as our school closed, we took a train for New York City.

Norah and I decided to stay for a couple of days in New York and got two rooms at the Woodstock Hotel. Mary thought we were being quite risque, staying at a hotel even though our rooms were on different floors. After dinner, the three of us took in a show and Mary took a night train for Syracuse. The next day Norah and I did some shopping and sightseeing and that night went to another Broadway theater. It was the first time since we had gone to Buffalo years before that we had such a chance to celebrate. With this good time together and the long ride up the Hudson on the train the next day, we felt closer than we ever had.

I had received two notices from the Teacher's Agency of positions open in New York State for teaching math and coaching. I thought I might investigate them while in Cazenovia, but first I went into Syracuse to talk with the agency. I told them I was more interested in a principalship. They informed me that by chance two such vacancies had just come in. One was in Manlius and the other in Minoa, where they wanted a principal who could coach. Both of these schools were near Syracuse, and I was truly interested.

Since my time was short, a young man from the agency took me to both places to meet as many of the members of the school boards as we could find. He took along my credentials and did a sales pitch on my behalf. Both schools said they would have a meeting soon and would let me know. I told them, on the side, that I would be taking a noon train out of Syracuse on the following Sunday.

After my interviews I had a strong leaning toward Minoa. I liked Jess Leonard, the president of the board, and I sensed he liked my experience in coaching. I left Cazenovia on Sunday morning without hearing from either place, so I was real surprised when I walked into the station in Syracuse to see Jess Leonard and another member of the school board. After our greetings they told me that the board had met and were unanimous in offering me a contract at $2000.00 a year. We talked a bit more about the situation and everything seemed satisfactory, so when they offered me the conract I signed it. I returned to Burlington happy with that contract in my pocket.

Spring came early in New Jersey. I left Cazenovia with patches of snow on the ground and cold winds blowing, only to arrive in balmy temperatures with fruit trees ready to bloom. Thus, the spring athletic program began at once. The schools in this area made a great deal of track meets. Dual meets were often held on school time on Friday afternoons so all the students could watch. I had very limited experience with track and field events so had to learn fast.

One of the first events on our schedule was entering a team in the big University of Pennsylvania relays. On Friday over a hundred high school teams were entered. These relays were well organized, competition was based on school size, so all were on an equal basis. Each team was notified of the time to report and if it was not there on time, it was scratched. When I got to the entering gate, I was surprised to learn no coach was allowed inside the grounds. At the gate the track officials took over and ran the meet. The only way I could see my team run was to hurry up into the stands with the other spectators.

All the races were one mile relays, so each man ran a quarter of a mile. There were six teams in each race; my team led for the first half mile, but the third runner trying to follow my instructions left the pole position too soon and lost the lead. The anchor man was the boy that I depended on so much. He tried desperately to win, but had to settle for second place. I was real proud of these boys and knew it was my lack of experience that lost first place.

We went back on Saturday to watch the college and university teams, which was a great experience, and we learned a lot. One thing that impressed me was seeing the many professional trainers selling their services; the dressing room in the gym smelled strong with the various liniments they were using for rubdowns. Some of the members of the track team were hurting with sore muscles, so I got the idea of making my own liniment to treat them. I experimented with combinations of some of the ingredients I knew were used, such as oil of wintergreen, camphor and witch hazel, then added a few of my own selection. I came up with a combination that proved very successful. I used it all the years I coached and then for family use afterwards.

The school did not have a field for the training of the track team, but I was so successful in keeping the boys in shape that their spirits were high and we entered several dual meets as well as two large ones. The first was an all day affair in a suburb of Philadelphia. It was so large that they did not have enough officials to run it and asked the coaches to act as officials. It was one good way for me to learn a lot about coaching the sport. The final meet was a county wide event and the day was declared a holiday so all students could attend. I don't remember that we took many prizes but everyone had a wonderful time, which to me was important.

My baseball team won a good number of games and were declared the county champions. Some of their success was due to my liniment. My one good pitcher developed a sore arm and after pitching for four or five innings he would be in such pain he would have to leave the game. As an experiment I rubbed his arm with the liniment between each inning and to our delight it took the pain away so he could finish the game.

New Jersey had no uniform high school examinations such as the Regents in New York State, so each teacher made up his own. For the final examination in elementary algebra I took a number of questions from some of the old Regents exams I had, to make what I considered a fair test. As an indication of the standard of the school, only fifty percent of my students passed my test. In talking with other teachers I found they had similar results. The best results I had was in the class of high school girls preparing for the teacher's examination. All of the fifteen in the class passed.

In other classes I had to adjust the marks, but I failed those who had poor marks all year and also failed the final examination. When I turned in my report I learned something else about Miss Ditzell. She wasn't pleased with my report and called my attention to one girl in particular that I had failed. I was quite sure that this girl had been handing in her homework papers all year done by someone else. I felt this because she could never answer a question in class and had a very low mark on the final exam. I explained this to Miss Ditzell, but her reply was, "You can't fail this girl, her father is one of the leading citizens in the city." To which I replied, "I'm not rating the father, just the girl, and I believe my marks are fair and final." So I learned something about school politics.

Another experience I had with a pupil taught me something which I found existed more than once. I had a boy in class who never turned in a homework assignment. Only occasionally would he answer in class. Then to my surprise he had one of the highest marks in the class. In fact, his mark was identical with a girl who was the best in the group. I couldn't help being somewhat suspicious when I recalled he sat opposite her when they took the examination. I couldn't let it pass and asked him to see me. I was very frank with him and asked how without doing anything all year he could turn in such a fine examination paper. Right away he asked if I thought he cheated. I told him I didn't want to be unfair, but he could understand my concern when he had exactly the same mark as the girl who sat next to him and I mentioned her name. Then he told me he never did any work in any class, just listened and then always passed the finals. Then to prove his point he suggested I give him another examination. I did and he scored just as high as he did on the first one. I apologized to him for being suspicious, then said if he would change his ways he could be at the top of his class. He just laughed and said he was happy to do it his way, then he added, "I like you better than any teacher I have in the school." So I was learning about pupils, teachers and principals.

The final assembly of the school was for the purpose of making awards. I felt I was the main attraction, as I had the responsibility of giving out the letters and awards for all the athletic teams for the whole year. For once I was more important than Miss Ditzell, and she showed her discomfort.

In a letter I wrote Norah I said, "I suppose Mary wrote you about how mad she was at the contract they offered her. How she tore it up and jumped all over Smith. It sure was funny to hear her tell about it." I, too, was offered a contract, which I returned saying I had signed one for a principalship in New York State. Smith congratulated me and hoped I would be successful. I had the feeling he was sort of pleased that I was not returning. Commencement ended the hardest year of my teaching experience, but I had seen it through and learned a lot.

Now that I was committed to go into the field of education, I knew I would have to take more courses to qualify for a permanent certificate. Columbia University was then the leading institution in the country for graduate work in education.

Jess Frazier still lived in Ridgefield Park, New Jersey, across the Hudson River from New York City. When he had learned that I was in

Burlington he invited me to his house for Thanksgiving recess. We had kept in contact after that, so when I told him my plans for the summer, he suggested that I stay with him and commute to Columbia. I knew Ethel, his wife, from our Houghton days, and as she was expecting their first child, she wanted to get away from the hot weather and was going to spend the summer with her parents in Hinsdale, New York. Jess said I was welcome to a room and we could share the expenses for food. I was glad to accept.

It was real hot before the end of school in Burlington and it stayed that way all summer. When I registered I worked out a schedule so I could make it on time each morning. Jess lived just a block from the station where frequent commuter trains stopped. I would get up, make a little breakfast, and rush to the station to catch a train for Weehawken. I then joined a crowd hurrying to the ferry to cross the Hudson River. Off the ferry, I would jump on a cross town trolley to 5th Avenue, where I got the subway to Morningside Heights. From the subway I would climb the stairs and walk across the campus to my 8 a.m. class. If I made all these connections, I would be in my seat just as the bell rang for the class to begin. I got a good taste of what a commuter's life was like and by the time the summer session was over I had had enough of it. Jess was working at the Corn Products Company in a plant on the New Jersey side, so he didn't have far to go. Sometimes I would get back in time to cook a dinner, but often I would stay at the University to use the library.

The weather was not only hot but very humid and since this was in the days before air conditioning, we had to live with it. I also learned about New Jersey mosquitoes. The windows were heavily screened, but some would find a way to get through. An open bottle of citronella in each open window was our only way to keep these pests away. A few weekends Jess and I did go to a beach for a swim and a baseball game or two. The last part of the summer Jess had his vacation and left to join Ethel in Hinsdale. I was left alone to finish the summer session.

I had mixed feelings about the courses in education I took. After my training in math and science these seemed rather indecisive. One class was large with over 200 students. The professor in charge divided the class into committees and appointed a chairman for each group. These groups met in the afternoon on the campus lawn and held their open air discussions with the idea of making a composite report to the whole class near the end of the summer. I was assigned on a committee to evaluate marking systems. The chairman was a young cocky school superintendent from the middle west and he wanted to rule the whole proceedings. Once the group got bogged down on a trivial point and I spoke up about it. The chairman didn't agree with my remarks and said so, but after the meeting broke up a number in the group surrounded me and said I was right and they were glad I spoke up. It was the first of several instances where I was to experience such action by groups. There are a lot of people who would rather sit and squirm than open their mouths when they don't agree with some action. Since the chairman had the authority to rate the contribution each member made, I wondered if he would report against me, but he didn't.

I also took a course in supervision given by William Burton, the co-author of the most widely read book on the subject of that time. I liked him and got a lot out of his lecture and kept his book for reference for a long time. The best course was in History of Education given by Dr. Swift. It was a medium sized class, so I got to know him better than the other instructors. After we had studied the history of education in the ancient civilizations, I got the idea of making a time chart to show the development of education in each country at the same time level. When I had it completed, I showed it to Dr. Swift. He complimented me on the idea and said he had never seen anything like it and asked if he could keep it to show other classes. I was flattered and gave it to him.

The big assignment for this course was for each student to write a history of some subject pertaining to education. Dr. Swift posted a list of suggested subjects but announced we could choose one of our own similar to his list. I selected one of my own, "Physics as an Entrance Requirement for Columbia University." A time was set to hand in our topic and then an outline of the paper which was followed by a conference on a rough draft.

In order to find the information I needed, I had to research all the old catalogues of the university. These were kept in the stacks of the big university library. I had no sooner started to look through these catalogues when an order was issued that students could no longer use the stacks unless given a pass by the head librarian. The reason given for this rule was that too many couples had been hiding in the stacks for purposes other than library work. To complete my project I went to the head librarian and explained why I needed to use the stacks. This man was a real Scotsman with a very broad accent. When I finished my explanation, he asked, "What mon are ye?" I was puzzled and asked him what he said. He repeated, "What mona are ye?" "I don't understand," I replied. "What college are you from?" he finally asked. Then when I told him I was a graduate of Oberlin College, he said, "Ah, we have an assistant librarian from Oberlin and a fine man." With that he issued me a pass. So I learned about the reputation of Oberlin and the value of being a "man" from that college.

I spent hours in the stuffy stacks going through the old catalogues and making notes. When the time came to submit our topic and outline, I simply turned in my topic with a note I was researching the catalogues. I expected to hear from Dr. Swift about my outline but nothing happened, and I just submitted my paper at the end of the session. We were told that if we wanted our papers back after they were graded, to leave a self-addressed large envelope with stamps and they would be sent. I left my envelope addressed to Cazenovia, New York.

I was in Cazenovia enjoying a brief vacation with Norah when my paper arrived. I was very pleased to see a big "A" when I opened the envelope and note signed by Dr. Swift. His writing was such a scribble I couldn't make it out. I showed it to Norah and we both worked to decipher it. Finally we agreed the first word was "Excellent". After looking at it over and over, we decided it was, "Excellent, this should be published, try *Columbia Review.*" Later I did get it typed and sent it to the magazine, but they returned it, saying it didn't fit into their plans. I never sent it any other place, so it remained unpublished. But I was pleased to have my research work recognized. I was glad to have been able to attend Teacher's College at Columbia and get the feel of that great institution, but I had no desire to return.

At the close of the summer session, I returned to Burlington to pick up my trunk. I took it to Minoa and found a place where I could board and room when school opened in September. I then went to Cazenovia for a couple of weeks' rest.

Of course, Norah was very interested in me becoming the principal of the school in Minoa and wondered what kind of place it was. I told her it was a small village near Syracuse with the grades and high school in the same building. I also knew it was a railroad town located at the east end of the big New York Central freight yards. But she wanted to know more and talked with Mr. Bailey, the school principal in Cazenovia. She knew him well, as he had been the principal in that village for many years. She was rather upset when he told her it was too bad I was going to Minoa, as it had the reputation of being one of the toughest schools in the state. He said no principal had been able to stay there more than one year and some less than that.

I had another angle about the situation from a letter that Norah wrote me while I was at Columbia. She had become a friend of Dorothy Ellis when they were both teachers in Pulaski. Dorothy's home was in Chittenango not far from Cazenovia and they saw each other often. Norah wrote,

> Dorothy went to Minoa to visit her aunt this week. Her aunt was anxious for her to take a position there. It is a 2nd and 3rd grades together. Dorothy wouldn't take two grades, but said she thought it would be fun to interview some members of the board and get some dope on my man. So she did. This man was very anxious for her to take the position and said they would give her $1,100.00. She said she wouldn't take any position at less that $1,200.00. He said we have a very good principal for next year. She said, "Who is it?" He said, "His name is Ray Calhoon. He is a graduate of Hobart (evidently he couldn't remember Houghton) and Oberlin, will take summer school at Columbia this year." Dorothy said, "That's fine, where is his home?" and he said, "I don't think it is anywhere around here. He is a very fine appearing young man. Every member of the board was very impressed with him and we are glad that we were able to get him for he was elected to the

position at Manlius, but he signed with us. We are fortunate to get him and are looking forward to a very good year. It is seldom that everyone on the board likes a principal."

Now what do you think of that?

Since I was now going to Minoa, Norah wondered what she should do. First she thought she should teach another year, but nothing good showed up. We thought we might get married at the Christmas vacation, so she asked her folks if we could live on $2,000.00. Her father said a lot of couples live on less, but her mother said, "I don't think you should get married." When Norah asked her why, she said, "Because you hate housework." All her friends told her different things so by the time I got to Cazenovia for my visit, she was still confused. Several times I heard her say if she ever decided to marry she wanted to stay home for a year first. Knowing this I may have encouraged her to let it be this year.

CHAPTER 17

MINOA

I arrived in Minoa in time to inspect the school building and meet the teachers on the opening day. I found the principal's office on the first floor just inside the front door. This floor had rooms for all the grades except the 8th. The second floor centered around a large study hall, which was also the assembly room for the high school and all outside activities. This floor had three classrooms, a small science lab and a very small room used as the library. A room for the 8th grade was separated from the others.

Near the front entrance, stairs led down to the basement floor. At one end of the basement was a low-pressure steam boiler which heated the building. The rest of the basement was divided into two levels. The top level consisted of a long runway off of which were some locker rooms and a shower room. The other part had been dug down about five feet and the sides sealed forming a smooth concrete wall. This was the gym and basketball court. Movable bleachers were at both ends of this court for spectators while others could be seated on the long runway.

The school building was a two and a half story red brick structure. It was almost square and every available space inside was used. Over the front entrance was inscribed **MINOA HIGH AND GRADED SCHOOL.**

The faculty consisted of one kindergarten, seven grade and three high school teachers. The oldest of this group both in age and in years of service was Miss O'Brien, who had taught the fifth grade in Minoa for over thirty years. The grade teachers looked to her for guidance and with my limited experience in the elementary field, I was glad to depend on her wise leadership.

At the high school level I found one teacher hired for all the English classes, one for history and Latin, one for science and math, and I was expected to take all extra classes. There were about 80 students in the high school and we spent the morning of the first day finding out what subjects they needed. We set up a schedule trying to avoid conflicts. With the limited number of teachers, the high school could offer only a general course, but it was flexible enough to meet the needs of a few pupils who wanted to enter college.

The first year I had one class in elementary algebra and one in civics. It turned out I taught the state required course in civics all the years I was in Minoa. After the first year I worked out a word list for civics, which proved very helpful to the students and I had excellent results in the Regents examination every semester. I also had to be in charge of three study halls and the physical education program.

Starting that year, I adopted a policy which I used whenever I changed schools. This policy was to have the school follow the same organizational plans they used the preceding year. Then, after I had a chance to observe the regulations, I would gradually make changes I thought best. It had been the custom of this school to have all the high school students assemble in the study hall for morning roll call. Teachers were assigned to check for absentees; the principal would be in charge to make any announcements needed before the students were sent to their first class. Once a week on Friday there would be an assembly program, including a reading from the Bible and a talk by the principal or a teacher. Sometimes special programs would be presented by students.

The regulations also called for all the high school students to meet in the study hall for dismissal at the end of the morning session. It was at one of these times in the second week of school that there came the "showdown" as to who was to be in charge of the school. Of course, I was aware of the reputation this school had, and on the first day I picked out the reason. There was one boy in the school by the name of Rex Monington, who towered over all the boys and was bigger and stronger than any of us on the faculty. It was apparent he was the one who had run the school in the past. No doubt he, along with one or two others, had carried the last principal out of the building on the last day of the previous year and dumped him on the front lawn. According to the story, this principal kept right on going, didn't even return for his hat.

At the school assemblies, Rex claimed a seat in the front row where all could see him. Thus, all the boys watched him for cues as to what they should do. By this time I had been taking in the signs and knew something would happen soon. On this day one of the smaller boys had a seat directly across from Rex, and to be ready to run home for lunch, he had brought his cap with him. He had placed it on his desk and Rex saw it. He grabbed it, throwing it on the floor right at my feet. A hush fell over the room and every teacher froze rigid. All realized this was the test, the challenge to see who would run the school. I instinctively knew that my entire future depended on how I met this situation. The experience of the teacher in the *Hoosier Schoolmaster,* which I had enjoyed reading ever since my 8th grade graduation, flashed through my mind. But this was not a story, it was real.

When the cap landed on the floor in front of me, I never made a move. But quietly I said, "Rex, pick it up." Everyone in the room stopped breathing; the atmosphere fairly crackled with the tension. Rex just sat looking at me to see what I would do. I still did not move and repeated, "Rex, pick up the cap so we all can go home for lunch." For several seconds, which seemed like hours, Rex continued to look at me and then got out of his seat, picked up the cap, and placed it back on the boy's desk. Like the air escaping from a punctured balloon, a sigh went up from the whole room. As soon as the cap hit the desk, I said, "Thank you, Rex, school dismissed." I was told later that every pupil ran all the way home to tell the news, "Rex has done what the principal asked him to do!" Thus, my reputation became established and from that day on I was in charge of the school. One of the older teachers who had been present at this episode remarked to me afterwards, "Today you showed us the power of a quiet approach, something all of us could profit by."

Soon after I got the school running smoothly, I thought of a plan whereby I could supervise the several study periods I had to assume, but at the same time do some of my office work. I explained the situation to each group of students and added that they could study just as well whether I was in the room or not. I said as long as they didn't bother me, I wouldn't bother them. I added that I had a lot of work to do and I expected they did too, so I was going to trust them to keep busy and not disturb others while I was busy in the office. I made it a point to drop in unexpectedly at times. For a time at first there were a few who took advantage of my absence, but when I surprised them a few times and had a serious talk, they fell in line with the majority.

One day a book salesman found me in my office. He had been in the school before and knew the high school department was on the second floor. He went directly up the stairs and he found the study hall in perfect order with no one in charge. He asked one of the students where he could find the principal, was told I was in the office, and he came right down. When I explained my system, he seemed very impressed and said he had heard of such plans but had never seen it in successful operation before.

By the end of the first semester I had made several changes in the high school department. The first was to set up homerooms based on the student's year in school and thus eliminate the daily assembly. I placed more responsibility in the hands of the teachers and did all I could to make the students feel like high school people, not upper grade pupils. Both the teachers and the students responded, so by the end of the year Minoa became a real high school.

With only 40 boys in the high school, I was surprised to find they had a football team. The previous year before the large boys in the school prevailed upon the board to buy some equipment, and they organized a team on their own. They already had a schedule set for the fall, so right away I became their coach. We were the smallest high school in the county league and didn't expect to win any games, but we did, and the boys had a lot of fun playing. I was surprised at the results and they gave me a lot of credit as a coach. After the second year most of the large boys were out of school and football was dropped. But it was during the second year I learned to appreciate the spirit of this school.

We had a football game scheduled with Baldwinsville, located on the other side of Syracuse. The game was on a Friday afternoon and on the way we had to detour so were late in arriving. While my team was dressing, I stood on the field talking with the principal of this high school. I remarked that I was surprised to see so many spectators in the stands. His reply made me very proud of my boys. He said, "Yes, this is one of the largest crowds of the year. We know your team is at the bottom of the league, but your boys never play like it. We have other teams come and when we get ahead, they fold and the game ceases to be interesting, but not your team. They can be down 40 to 0, but they still play as if they expected to win. Our students love it and probably you will hear them cheering as much for your team as for ours." This is the reputation that Minoa had in all sports as long as I was there.

Minoa was a railroad town located at the eastern end of the big DeWitt freight yards, the largest between New York and Buffalo. About 90% of the men in the village worked on the railroad on jobs such as engineers, firemen, conductors, brakemen, service men in the round house, and maintenance crews. The older boys in the high school often worked as call boys. Their job was to find the men assigned to a certain train and notify them when to report. This created a problem, as these boys felt grown up and sometimes felt above the school regulations. Since they associated with the railroad men who had the reputation of being rough and tough, these boys took on the same air. However, I found the men of the village were the same as any other group—some were good and some rather tough. But all were good hearted and once I became known, I found them easy to work with. One thing they had in common was being very sports minded. They supported the high school teams to the limit both at home and away.

The New York Central Railroad was a busy railroad in those days. Not only was the air filled day and night with the sounds of the freight trains moving in and out of the yards, but also with the roar of the many fast passenger trains passing through the village. The school was only a few hundred yards from the main track, so when the Lake Shore Limited or the Twentieth Century express trains rushed by, all conversation was drowned out. Teachers learned to wait until a train had passed.

The main street of the village ran north and south crossing the main line tracks. Many times the mile-long freight trains being made up in the yards would block this crossing to all traffic. There was a law which required the trainmen to cut the train and let the traffic through after a certain length of time. One of the main duties of the one village policeman was to time these trains, and he glowed when he made the brakemen cut the train. This was especially important in the mornings when children were trying to get to school on time. Actually, we had to be considerate in marking such pupils late.

Near the railroad crossing was a small lunchroom, the one grocery store in the village operated by Jess Leonard, the president of the school board, and a tiny meat market. Up the street bordering the school grounds was a hardware store run by Mr. Flanagan, treasurer of the school district. Near the corner of the street which ran in front of the school building was a garage run by a man who did a lot of handy work. On the main street was a Catholic church and on the side street the one Protestant church. Most of the houses were within easy walking distance of the school—most of the pupils went home at noon for lunch. I was able to find a place to room and board near the school, where I joined two teachers for meals. This family had a boy in high school and it worked out fine.

That fall Norah didn't find a position she wanted and remained at home. This made it possible for me to spend the first few weekends at Cazenovia. I would go on Saturday and then take a Sunday evening train on the Lehigh to Canastota and then catch a third rail interurban car to Minoa. It was fine for me as I could get away from school for a time, also Norah's mother was a wonderful cook, so I was well fed. But the most important thing was Norah and I could be together frequently for the first time in our long acquaintance since Houghton days. We did continue to write often and sometimes Norah's letters were full of uncertainty for the future.

Then at the last of September our schedule was interrupted. Ann Tooke, who was Norah's special friend in Cazenovia and who worked at the Oneida Community Ltd. when I did, married John White, the brother of Mrs. Lamb where Ann lived in Sherrill. John was a minister and teacher. Without a church, he took a position as teacher at the Silver Bay Boys' School, located at Lake George, New York. The Whites were moving to Silver Bay and since Ann was expecting their first baby soon, she asked Norah to go with them and help. Without a job, Norah decided to go.

After she arrived I got a series of letters telling how beautiful the place was at that time of the year. A quote from one letter tells how she felt.

> The president of the school invited the faculty and their friends for a boat ride all afternoon. I think it was without exception the most beautiful ride I ever took. I tho't thousand Is. beautiful, but this has thousand Is. stopped.
>
> Tomorrow morning I'm going to start at five o'clock with a party to Sunrise Point at the top of one of the mountains. How I wish you were here. I know you would just love it. I never knew anything could be so beautiful. If you were here my joy would be complete. I miss you very much . . . I'm glad you are getting along alright. Please don't get lonesome or blue.
>
> Ann and John are supremely happy here and I like him so much better than when I saw him just a little in Caz. He is so thoughtful of both of us and they seem to adore each other in a rather childlike manner. Everyone seems to like them. I like the

people in the school. Of course, it is something like Houghton on a much more elaborate plan. It's like Houghton in that they are so hemmed in and secluded and know each other so well.

In following letters Norah told more about the place and the school. She wrote how the school was supposed to have a house ready for Ann and John to move into and that was one reason Norah had gone with them to help settle the house. However, it was not ready and there was delay after delay. In the meantime, however, they were all staying in the school dorm and being served wonderful meals. All were enjoying the situation except Ann, who was worrying because her time was approaching and she was not in her house.

I was interested in what Norah told me about the school, which was a private boy's institution run by the Silver Bay Association. The tuition was very high—all the boys were from wealthy families. All students were carefully screened and they were of high scholastic ability. The association had plenty of money so they could attract teachers of high standing with higher salaries and small classes. One feature of the school was the stress on individual instruction. Norah said John worried because he felt overpaid for such a light load.

Of course, I kept Norah informed about my work and things I did. I also told her about some of the teachers. One I mentioned was Mrs. Hulburt, the 8th grade teacher. She had been in the school for several years and was the sister-in-law of Grant Goodell, the clerk of the board. I knew from the first she would be the one to inform the members of the board as to what went on in the school. But she was an excellent teacher and one who could handle the 8th graders. I got it across early that I would not show any favors to anyone and she liked that, so we grew to have mutual respect for each other. Then Norah wrote that she had heard from Dorothy Ellis and she knew Mrs. Hulburt. The report was that this teacher liked me very much and talked about me a lot. Dorothy added that I must be nice if Mrs. Hulburt thinks so, for she is very hard to please.

I learned early that my standing in the community was entirely different from anything I had experienced. Many of the parents called me professor, and although I told them that was a title used in college, they persisted. Most of the men called me prof. This new attitude was emphasized at the reception given by the WCTU for the new teachers the second week of school. At the reception was Dr. Bishop, the only medical doctor in the area, and Reverend Burnett, the pastor of the Methodist church, which was really a community Protestant church. During the evening I was talking with these two men in a corner of the room. We couldn't help noting that a group of the ladies who were serving refreshments were looking our way and laughing. Finally one of the ladies came over to us to explain why they were amused. She said they noticed the three of us together and someone remarked, "Look at that, there are the three wise men of the town in conference."

I also learned that the job of a principal in a small community was a lonely one. There was no one in a similar position to confer with. I was also the only man in the school, so I knew everything I did would be subject to criticism. I knew the boys were subjected to the language of the railroad men, which was similar to that used in the army. Personally, I was one not to swear or use dirty language, although having been in the army I knew all the words. At the beginning I let it be known that such language was not to be used around the school. I had only to drop one boy off a team to make the regulation stick.

A check on the school records showed that the standard of the school was not very high. In fact, the number of students passing the Regents examinations was well below the average of the state. In those days Regents examinations were required at the end of the 8th grade and in most of the high school subjects. I could see that one reason for the school's poor record was the big turnover in the high school faculty and the employment of a number of inexperienced teachers. At the end of the first year I recommended that one very weak teacher of English be let go and as I became more selective in hiring new teachers things improved rapidly.

As long as Norah was in Silver Bay, I stayed in town working in my office on Saturday mornings catching up on that work. On Sunday I did attend the Methodist Church service and right away Mrs. Goodell, the Sunday School Superintendent, tried to get me interested in teaching a class of high school students. I refused, explaining that my position in school had to be on a strictly impersonal basis. I didn't want to know who was in church or out; who was Catholic or Protestant. This was a viewpoint she hadn't thought about and wasn't sure she agreed with, but her husband, the clerk of the board, told her I was right.

Letters from Norah the last part of October told how Ann and John finally got into their new home. Norah was busy hanging curtains, and so forth, and acknowledged that she was rather enjoying it. "Maybe," she said, "I might become domestic after all." But our letters showed our future was still uncertain. Norah cited cases of couples she knew who had broken up after a short time, and she wanted nothing like that to happen to us if and when we did get married. She had decided she had been with Ann long enough when on November 3, I got this letter.

Wednesday, P.M.

Dear Ray;

A baby girl arrived this morning at six o'clock. I was all packed to leave, but of course that changed events. It is a nice baby, weighing 7½ pounds; Ann is getting along fine and much relieved that it is all over so soon. I witnessed the whole proceedings and the doctor handed me the baby as soon as she arrived. I was quite surprised at my calmness. The doctor asked

Mrs. Stephens if I was a nurse and when she said, "No," he said my calmness was remarkable for one not a nurse. Think of that! Ann began to be sick at 12 last night and at 1 we all got up and dressed, at 4 John phoned the doctor, he arrived at 5:30 and at 6 the baby was born.

I don't know how much longer I will stay, but a few days anyway. Somehow I felt sure that I was not going to see you this week and that was one thing that prompted me to write the card I did. I'm sorry not to be seeing you sooner but really glad to have been here, for I think Ann felt much better to have someone she knew here since she is so far from home. Better write me here, dear, as soon as you can. I do hope you are feeling alright now. If not, you better go to bed . . .

I telegraphed Nellie that I would not be there and she sent back a telegram of congratulations to Ann. I'm so glad it's a nice baby for Ann has wanted one so bad. She suffered everything for a few hours, but the doctor called it an easy birth, the easiest tho' is hard enough. It wasn't much like I imagined it tho'. The rest have had a nap this afternoon and I guess I'll try to take one now.
Lots of love, dear. Write.

N.

Norah left Silver Bay about the middle of November and I met her at Norma's house in Fayetteville. When she got back to Cazenovia, I began going there many weekends. We were together now more than ever and her letters were full of how much we meant to each other, but at the same time expressing doubts and fears of our future. Some of our personality differences began to appear. I wanted to get married, but like most men I didn't want to lose all my independence. In one letter Norah expresses her surprise when I indicated I didn't want her to go with me to buy some clothes.
On December 3, Norah wrote:

I mentioned to my folks today that I might possibly decide to get married. They seemed not to approve highly, which is just as I expected. I suppose it's only natural for our parents to wish to shield us from hardships or responsibilities. Yet we are as capable of bearing them as they have been. They think if I am not satisfied to stay at home, I ought to teach, altho' of course they said it was for me to decide and all that.

Then on December 7 this is part of a letter I received:

I have been thinking more about what you said about the ring. You have asked me to accept one several times and every time I have refused. I remember you asked me the same question last Christmas and I guess you understand why I refused. I couldn't think of accepting one at that time. I was too unhappy and undecided as to our future. Now, however, I feel much different about it. Of course, it may not seem best for us to marry soon, but however that may be, I have decided if you wish to give me one I shall be very happy to accept it. Whatever you may select remember that the setting must be small. I have told you before do not be extravagant! The fact you wish to give it to me will mean much more than the cost. You know I never went wild over expensive jewelry.

Following this letter I went to one of the leading jewelry stores in Syracuse and selected a diamond. At her suggestion and true to my own choice, I had it set in a simple setting. I knew the size and I had the very attractive gift ready for Christmas. Before then at one of our talks she was shocked when I told her how much money I had saved to get married on. I was puzzled, as she knew how I had to struggle after getting out of the army. Back in Minoa I got a very gloomy letter from her in which she said her folks pried it out of her why she went around so blue. Her father brought her out of it some by saying he knew Ray would make good, just give him a chance.

I spent the Christmas vacation in Cazenovia and on Christmas Eve presented her with the ring. For me it was a big step, but one I very much wanted to do. Also, I was beginning to feel like Cazenovia was my home. Everything must have gone fine since the first letter I had from Norah after the vacation said, "You were beautiful when you gave me the ring. It was almost too much for me."

In early January I had an important decision to make. I was invited to join the Masons. I knew Jess Leonard, Grant Goodell and other leading citizens of the community belonged. Also my district superintendent had told me one time in discussing the job that if I wanted to get ahead in school administration to join the Masons if I had the chance. I liked this man and took his advice seriously, so even if it was against my early training, I accepted the invitation. I knew Norah's father was not a Mason, but her brother, Carrell, had joined the lodge in Cazenovia and although he was now working in Washington, D. C., he kept his membership there. Also, I knew George Hayes, Nellie's husband, was active in a Utica lodge, so I felt I would be welcome. I didn't have a chance to discuss the matter with Norah, and she was kind of mad at me for not doing so.

At this time all the Masons in Minoa belonged to the lodge in Fayetteville, but they had petitioned the Grand Lodge to establish one in their home town. The lodge in Fayetteville didn't want to lose all those members so were blocking the move. As a gesture of goodwill, the men in Minoa said they would let me join in Fayetteville rather than hold me until they got a charter. So I became a sort of peace offering and joined in Fayetteville and then transferred to Minoa when they got their charter. I became an active member and enjoyed it very much. I never regretted my decision and now proudly wear my 50-year pin.

It didn't take long for me to learn that the biggest interest in Minoa was high school basketball. The football season was over in early November, and the boys wanted to start basketball practice right away, but I wanted a little time between seasons, so I told them we would start when the snow flew. The girls also had a team which I was expected to coach. They played the preliminary games using modified boy's rules. They used shorter quarters but played all over the floor in contrast to the adopted girl's rules. The girls played a very spirited game and the crowds loved the excitement. I told the girls they could start practice when the boys did. I was in the study hall one day when to my surprise the students let out a loud cheer. I looked up to see them pointing out the window and laughing. There were a few flakes of snow slowly floating down. I kept my promise and set the nights for practice.

To conserve my time I arranged for both teams to meet on the same nights. The girls came at an early hour and then the boys. The first time I met the teams I talked about the importance of fundamentals. After I had shown them the best way to hold the ball for a shot at the basket and how to put a spin on it so to get a reverse drop if the ball hit the back rim or the right spot on the backboard, I demonstrated by flipping the ball through the basket. I could see their eyes open wide, for I was the first one they ever had who could demonstrate the way things should be done. At once I was accepted as a real coach and never had any trouble starting each session by working on fundamentals. I often wonder what the attitude would have been if I had missed my shots.

The year before, the beginnings of a county-wide athletic league was started. Minoa was in the league and the boys had done very well without a coach. Then the principals and coaches of the schools in the county, except Syracuse City, met and formed a firm organization. The league was divided into two divisions, one east of Syracuse and the other west. We were in the east division with East Syracuse, Fayetteville, Manlius, and Eastwood. On the west was Solvay, Skaneateles, Marcellus and Baldwinsville. Later others were added. We were the smallest school in the league, but that didn't faze us, as the record showed.

Since our gym floor was long but narrow, I decided to introduce a zone defense. Jim Gallery was the only boy in school who was six feet tall and although he was young, I put him at center. In those days the ball was put in play with a jump at center after each basket. I also had Jim give signals as to which player he would tap the ball to if he could do so. Our first game of the season was with Solvay; and Jim, being taller than their center, was able to control the ball at each jump. The Solvay team was new and they didn't know how to cope with the signals, so it became just like a practice for us. The referee got so tired of retrieving the ball after each basket he just stood in the center of the court and let someone else pass the ball back, so all he had to do was toss it up again. The first time a Solvay player got possession of the ball, the crowd let out a groan when my boys left that player free and fell back into a three-two zone defense. They had never seen anything like it, and didn't understand, but when they saw the opposing team couldn't get the ball anywhere near the basket to shoot, they just howled.

Even when we got well ahead and I put in all the reserves, it still was a very uneven game. Actually, Solvay only made one field goal and one foul shot, so we won 89 to 3. I didn't call it a good game to be so one-sided, but the crowd loved it. As the weeks went by, Minoa kept on winning many, like the first game, one-sided victories.

Then just before the end of the season, disaster struck. After a mid-week practice session, I decided to take a shower before going to my room. When I finished I felt a slight chill and my throat felt queer. During the night I woke up with a pain in my jaw and when I looked in the mirror the next morning I saw one side of my face in front of my ear was swollen. I knew I had never had the mumps but there had been no cases reported in the school or in the village. In the morning I went to my office to clear up some pending work and sent word that I would not meet my classes that day. I walked over to Dr. Bishop's office and found him home. He looked at me and asked if I ever had the mumps and when I said no, he floored me when he said, "Well, you've got them now."

I was faced with a real problem. The McKinley's, where I stayed, had a boy in high school, so I knew they wouldn't want me around him. So I asked the doctor to arrange a room for me in a hospital. He thought that a bad solution and sent word around the village to see if anyone would take me in for the two week period. To my surprise an elderly couple named, Thomas, told the doctor to send me there, and they would give me a room and care for me. I was indeed grateful and packed a bag, moving in.

I had to let Norah know at once, since I had been with her that weekend and might have exposed her. She was very concerned as she didn't know if she had ever had them. All of her family told her she was sure to have them after being with me, but she escaped. I had daily letters from her telling me to keep warm so they wouldn't go down on me. She was told all sorts of stories about the effect on a man if they did go down. When I didn't recover right away, she called Doctor Bishop and asked if she should come down and help take care of me. When he told me, I said, "Don't let her come, she might get them." He called her back and I guess he was rather blunt, for she was mad at him. Later when she learned the facts she forgave him.

Soon after I got sick, I heard that Wershing, the captain of the basketball team, also had them. No one else on the team or in the school came down with them, so we figured Wershing and I must have got them from some referee that we had talked to.

At first I wasn't very sick, but as a precaution stayed in bed most of the time. Later when they did go down on one side, I was real miserable and glad to stay in bed to be waited on. Mrs. Thomas was a real motherly type and fussed over me, then the night I was the worst she asked, as a good Catholic, if she could say a prayer for me. I nodded my consent and shut my eyes while she prayed. I know she felt her prayer was answered, for the next morning I felt better and began to recover.

The fact that Wershing and I were sick at the same time was a blow to the basketball team. They were ready to go to Utica to appear in a sectional tournament, something new since the formation of the New York State Basketball Association. Daniel Chase, the State Supervisor of Physical Education, promoted and helped organize this association. The state was divided geographically into eight sections and the leagues already organized in these sections were invited to join the state association and take part in tournaments in order to determine a state champion. Some uniform rules were adopted with an emphasis on a minimum eligibility regulation, which was very much needed.

The following is taken from the report of the *First Annual Tournament New York State Public High School Basketball Association,* a pamphlet issued by Dan Chase, 1921–1922.

Section 5

The Central New York Section included six leagues—the Central New York League with two sections, the Onondaga County League with two sections, the Syracuse City League, and the Mohawk Valley League.

In the Central New York League, Ilion was the winner in the Eastern Section and Morrisville in the Western. For the League championship Ilion defeated Morrisville 22 to 17.

In the Onondaga County League, Minoa won the Eastern title and Marcellus the Western. In the play-off Minoa won 26 to 13.

In the Syracuse City League, Syracuse Central High School won out and Mohawk High School was victor in the Mohawk Valley League.

A two-day sectional tournament was held in Utica in which Minoa defeated Mohawk 26 to 21 and Syracuse Central defeated Ilion 32 to 16. In the finals, Syracuse Central ran away from Minoa 50 to 15.

Included in the pamphlet was a picture of each of these teams and a complete record of the year. Minoa is listed as follows:

MINOA		OPPONENT
89	Solvay	3
64	Eastwood	4
44	East Syracuse	15
41	N. Syracuse	6
37	Fayetteville	8
30	Manlius	11

25	Eastwood	22
25	East Syracuse	19
24	Solvay	21
36	Fayetteville	11
70	N. Syracuse	11
30	Manlius	19
26	Marcellus	13
26	Mohawk	21
15	Syracuse Cen.	50

This record is very unusual for such a small school and for the many one-sided games. I do not have the records of the following years, but I know they would show Minoa winning the vast majority of games. However, as other teams grew stronger, competition was closer, so no other record would look like the one above. The fact that both Wershing and I missed the tournament in Utica may have something to do with losing to Syracuse Central by such a score, but I doubt we could have won anyway. Syracuse was a big, strong team and later won the state championship in a tournament in Syracuse to become the first state champions of the Public High School Association.

Letters from Norah urged me to come to Cazenovia as soon as the doctor released me from quarantine. It was around the 10th of April when Doctor Bishop declared I was over the mumps and would not give them to anyone. However, I was so weak I didn't feel able to travel by train and knowing I was invited to go to Cazenovia, he took me in his car. I got a warm welcome and it was such a relief to be free to enjoy some spring weather. This was a busy time for Norah's father, who took daily trips around the country picking up veal calves, which he bought and dressed, shipping them to New York City. When the weather was good, I often went with him, thus being out in the open I began to recover fast. Norah's mother was an excellent cook and she filled me full at every meal. One thing I recall eating was the delicious fresh calves liver, which in those days was selling for 10 cents a pound. More than ever, I felt like Cazenovia was home.

Most of the time I spent in Cazenovia included the scheduled spring vacation from school; at the end of that time I was able to return to Minoa with considerable energy to pick up my duties. Basketball was forgotten and the boys were eager to start baseball practice. With only 40 boys in high school, it was not easy to organize a team, but we did and had a fair year in the county league games.

As the time neared for the board to consider contracts for the next year, they hinted they wanted a principal who was married. They didn't want to come right out and ask me if I planned to be married soon and did offer me a contract with a slight raise. Then at the next board meeting I was greeted by broad smiles and congratulations when I showed them the following clipping from the Cazenovia paper.

ENGAGEMENT OF MISS NORAH RIGGALL IS ANNOUNCED

At an Easter dinner given at their home on Nelson Street, Mr. and Mrs. O. M. Riggall announced the engagement of their daughter, Miss Norah Riggall, to A. Ray Calhoon of Richmond, California. The marriage will take place this summer. Mr. Calhoon is the Principal of Minoa High School.

Both Nellie and Norma and all their families were at this dinner. Family dinners at the Riggall house were well established customs on Sundays. Norah's mother was a wonderful cook and she really enjoyed feeding all these people. Included in these gatherings were not only the immediate families, but often Norah's aunts and uncles from Georgetown or Eaton would drop in unannounced. I used to think these people took advantage of the Riggalls, since they all had cars and the Riggalls did not, so they felt it was a center where they could all meet.

270

A Riggall Family Picnic

Now that we had really decided to be married, Norah began in earnest to prepare for the event. Norma was real interested and this appeared in the paper:

> Mrs. Fred Benedict and Mrs. Walter Freeborn gave a miscellaneous shower in honor of Miss Norah Riggall at the home of Mrs. Benedict in Fayetteville Saturday morning. Thirty-five guests were present and Miss Riggall received many useful and beautiful gifts.

Of course, this was one week I didn't see Norah, but I was busy with school activities. The small senior class wanted to put on a play and none of the faculty had any experience in directing such a project, so I was pressed into taking charge. I have forgotten the name of the play but it was one with few characters and could be presented on a small stage. The night the play was given we were faced with a dilemma. The plot of the play revolved around a certain object being found in a trunk in the second act. The trunk was shown to be empty in the first act and the stage manager was supposed to put it in between acts. As the play progressed, the girl who was the stage manager rushed up to me and said she forgot to put the object in the trunk. I thought fast and told her to stand by the light switches and at my signal to throw them off, thus putting the whole auditorium in darkness. Quickly I crawled out on the stage and put the object in the trunk, whispering to the actors who had stopped when the lights went off, to pick up the action as soon as the lights came on. Since, for the audience there was a brief period of blindness after looking at bright lights and having them suddenly turned off, no one saw me and the play proceeded to a successful conclusion. I often thought of all the educational courses I took, none of them ever prepared a secondary principal to meet a situation like this.

Norah wanted to be married in the month of June, and since school was not out until late in the month, we agreed on Thursday, the 29th of June, as the date. This gave me only a few days after commencement to finish all the reports required to complete the year. The teachers knew my situation and most of them cooperated to help. However, I ran into one problem which delayed us all. The state law required the principal of a school to swear that all teacher's registers were complete and balanced before a teacher could draw his last check. Grant Goodelle, the clerk of the board, held the checks until he received a note from me that the teacher's register was in order. I borrowed an adding machine from Mr. Flanagan, the school treasurer, and to my dismay I found that only a third of the registers balanced. For those that were incorrect, I called the teacher into the office and informed her the register didn't balance and to take it and find the error. These teachers were very upset and some informed me in no uncertain terms that they had never had their registers checked before and didn't believe they were wrong.

The last teacher I called in was Mrs. Hulburt, and she was furious when I told her that her register didn't balance. She said she never made a mistake and wouldn't believe the adding machine when I showed her the tapes. Finally she asked if she could take the register home to correct. I said, "Yes, but don't take long, you know I want to get away." It was a warm day and I had the window in my office open. This window was just above the front door. I heard Mrs. Hulburt stomp down the front steps and slam the front door shut. Then in a voice she was sure I would hear she greeted her friend, who was waiting, with the words, "That principal says my register doesn't balance. I wish that man would hurry up and get married and let us women alone." Years later I met Mrs. Hulburt after she had retired and asked her if she remembered the episode. She did and we had a good laugh.

The last week of school two of the younger teachers came to see me about something that indicated the changing times. After World War I, womens' styles of clothing changed radically. Skirts were shortened so it became proper to show ankles. However, the thing that caused the biggest stir was for women to start bobbing their hair. Some people called it unladylike, while others said it was immodest, disgraceful and even immoral. Many school boards passed regulations against it and discharged any teacher who dared cut her hair. The Minoa board had discussed it briefly but had taken no action. When the two teachers came to tell me that they had a confession to make before they left for the summer and said they had bobbed their hair a couple of weeks before but had rolled it in such a way it didn't show, I had to be ready with an answer. I thanked them for telling me and advised them to say nothing, as by fall the style might be so established nothing would be said. That is exactly what happened and soon all, except the very old women, followed the style. This was my first experience in how a change in style can affect school life.

Completing my reports, I closed the school doors and packed my bags, arriving in Cazenovia on Wednesday evening. I was dead tired and went to bed early to be ready for the big day. Norah had invited her former minister, Dr. Keppel, to perform the ceremony. He had retired, but lived in nearby Eaton. On Thursday morning he and his wife arrived before noon. I was wearing a grey suit when I was introduced to them. Then, before time for the ceremony, I went upstairs and changed to a blue serge suit which I had bought for the event. As we stood around before noon waiting for the guests to arrive, Mrs. Keppel found Norah and asked where the groom was. She didn't recognize me after I changed my suit. I had to laugh, but if she could have read my mind she would have known I was just as confused. Finally, the guests which were Norah's sisters and families, the same ones who had been at the engagement announcement, arrived. Of course, none of my relatives could be present, so I was the outsider who was to become one of this big family. I was happy to feel that they all liked me, and I certainly liked all of them. At last I was becoming one of a family. A copy of the report in the Cazenovia paper tells of the event.

CALHOON—RIGGALL

The marriage of Miss Norah Riggall to Mr. A. Ray Calhoon of Richmond, California, took place Thursday at noon at the home of the bride's parents, Mr. and Mrs. O. M. Riggall on Nelson Street. Dr. David Keppel of Eaton officiated.

The home was artistically decorated with ferns and roses. The ceremony was performed in the front living room beneath an arch of evergreens and roses, with a lovely background of ferns.

The bridal couple were attended by the little niece and nephew of the bride, Vera E. Benedict of Fayetteville, who acted as flower girl, and Carrel D. Hayes of Utica, as ring bearer.

During the congratulations, music was furnished by Mr. Ulrich Hutchinson and Miss Ruth Hutchinson.

After the ceremony, the wedding dinner was served in the dining room, which was decorated with branches of dark red cherries.

Both the bride and groom have been engaged in educational work for several years. During the war Mr. Calhoon served 14 months overseas with the Headquarters Co. of the 4th Army Corps.

Mr. and Mrs. Calhoon left for a trip through the Adirondacks during which time they will spend a month at Silver Bay on Lake George.

After September first they will make their home in Minoa, where Mr. Calhoon is principal of the high school.

I had made a reservation at a hotel in Albany for the night after the wedding. George Hayes was returning to Utica, so he took us to the station to catch a train for Albany. Ann White had asked us to come to Silver Bay to stay with her and the baby while John was gone for the summer session at Chicago University. Ann had the nice house on Lake George where the weather would be ideal, and she had no desire to take the baby to spend the hot summer in Chicago. Neither did she want to stay alone, so she invited us to spend our honeymoon with her. For us it was an inexpensive way for us to spend a month on the beautiful lake.

When we arrived in Albany, the papers were full of a possible strike on the railroads. We had planned to stay in the city for a few days, but we didn't want to be stranded there—after two nights we checked out of the hotel and took our bags to the railroad station. There we found utter confusion; no one seemed to know whether the strike was on or off. All the information we could get from the ticket agent was: "If the train starts for Lake George, it will get you there." There were no calls for a train, but we wandered out to the tracks and found a train all made up ready to go north, and we climbed on.

Somewhat late the train did start and we were on our way. When we got to Saratoga Springs I looked out to see all I could of the town. I was very interested for as a boy I remember hearing my folks reading aloud from the book *Samantha at Saratoga* and laughing over the episodes depicted. From the train I could see at least one of the big hotels and it looked just as I had pictured it.

We arrived in the village of Lake George just in time to catch the little steam boat that carried passengers to points along the lake up to Ticonderoga. Once the boat left the docks, the full beauty of the lake came into view. This lake has the reputation of being one of the most beautiful in North America, and seeing it, I could agree. Going north we were sandwiched between the Green Mountains of Vermont on the east and the higher Adirondacks on the west. In many places the heavy forested mountains came right down to the water's edge. Only in a few places there was a cove with a narrow shore where hotels were built and a landing dock for the boat to pick up or discharge passengers.

It was a beautiful day and for an hour we drank in the beauty of the scenery. When we docked at Silver Bay, Ann was at the dock to meet us, much relieved as she had visions of being left alone while we were stranded on the way. We carried our bags to the house which was located on the side of the mountain well above the lake. The baby was real cute and so healthy she slept every night and rarely cried allowing all to get a good night's rest.

After my strenuous year I was only too glad to do little but rest the first few days. Then as the weather was sunny but with a cool breeze almost every day, Norah and I began to explore the many trails that were marked in the area. One led to an ice cave back in the mountains. Even in the middle of the summer this cave at the bottom of a deep ravine was protected from the sun's rays so it remained full of ice.

After we had become accustomed to hiking and had explored the easy trails, we decided to start early one morning and take an all day hike to the top of the highest peak in the area, called Mt. Catamount. We were told that this trail was marked for a short distance and then became a blazed trail which had to be followed with extreme caution. Full of enthusiasm, we rose early, packed a lunch, and started along the road which followed the shore for a short distance until we came to the sign marking the beginning of the trail. For a time it was like the other trails we had followed, but less than halfway up the mountain it became a blazed trail, i.e., the only guides were chips that had been taken out of the tree trunks at various distances. I had never followed such a trail, but I had read that the fundamental rule was to never leave one blaze until you could see the next. The trees were large and the blazes showed up well, so we were able to follow the rule very easily.

As the sun rose higher, so did the trail and before long we were perspiring freely. This attracted the deer flies and we had to fight them all the way. We knew it was at least three miles to the top of the mountain and we planned to be there in time for lunch. We were making good time when we came to the edge of the timber line. We could see the rocky summit a few hundred yards above and even though there were no more blazed trees to follow, we felt secure in making the top. Without any warning we entered a patch of brush we found to be more than head high. Thinking all we had to do was keep climbing, we kept going. Then to our dismay, everyway was up or down, so we didn't know which way to travel. We had entered a sort of sunken hip on the side of the mountain, which was rather swampy; hence, no trees, just high brush. I realized that we were temporarily lost. I didn't say anything so as not to frighten Norah, but I stopped. Looking around, I spotted a little wild cherry tree growing higher than the surrounding brush. I told Norah I would climb it to get our bearings.

The tree was just big enough to climb, but as a precaution I kept my feet close to the trunk as I stepped on each branch. Cautiously, I neared the top and stuck my head out in the clear above the brush. I had a flash of a beautiful view. Down at the foot of the mountain was the blue waters of Lake George. To the west rose tier after tier of the Adirondacks, while to the east was the skyline of the Green Mountains in Vermont. "Oh," I exclaimed, "what a thrilling view. It is beauti—" With that I took all the branches off both sides of the tree and landed flat on my back on the ground. I had the wind knocked out of me, but I heard Norah scream and looked up to see her standing over me with fear in her eyes. As soon as possible I sat up and shook my head to clear my vision and then my first words came close to being my last. I blurted out, "Let's eat." "What," Norah screamed, "here we are lost in the woods and all you can think of is something to eat." It took me some time to assure her I was alright and I thought since it was noon we might as well eat our lunch and then find our way out. But it was evident that wouldn't work, and if I wanted anything to eat I had to first find our way out. So I told Norah to stand still in that same spot and I began to circle around her, calling out every few steps until as I made my circles larger, I came out of the brush almost at the same spot we had entered. Then I called to her and she came out to me.

Once we felt safe we took some string and tied it to the bushes every few feet all the way around the outside of the brush patch until we were in the open and could see the bare rock at the top. Scrambling up the face of the rock we came out to the beautiful view that I had glimpsed from the cherry tree. Looking down the three thousand feet we could see part of the village of Silver Bay and the dock from which the noon boat was just leaving. As the boat picked up speed I observed a phenomenon which I had read about in physics but had never seen. Several yards in front of the moving boat was a bow wave which precedes a fast moving object in the water. Such a wave is not visible on the surface, but in the clear water of this lake it appeared as a dark shadow moving ahead of the boat.

After reaching the top, I gathered some dry branches and made a small campfire on the bare rock so we could cook some bacon we brought to eat with our lunch. As we sat enjoying the refreshing breeze and our lunch, we kept exclaiming at some new wonderful sight we discovered in the distance. Once fully rested and making sure the campfire was entirely out, we reluctantly started for home. Following the trail back was easy and we arrived about 4 p.m. We found Ann in a stew. After we had left that morning some of her neighbors came to see her and when she told them we had left for Mt. Catamount, they filled her with stories of how many people had been lost on that mountain. One story was that a group of girls from a camp had become lost and had to spend all night in the woods. Some of the girls got so hysterical they had to be carried out. Ann told us that she was so worried that if we were not back by five o'clock she was going to call the State Troopers for help. We assured her we were alright, and to calm her fears, we never told her our experience.

After this hike I found little to do and now fully rested I became rather bored, but we had agreed to stay until John was home about the first of August. I knew Bill Frazier was now the pastor of a Congregational Church in Vergennes, Vermont; I wrote him that we would like to stop and see him on our way home. He answered inviting us to spend a weekend with him and his family. Since I had known both Bill and his wife in Houghton, I was glad to accept. When John returned home the first of August, we packed our bags and took the lake steamer to Ticonderoga, transferring to another steamer on Lake Champlain which took us to Burlington, Vermont. It was on this boat we had a few moments of embarrassment. About the middle of the afternoon a light shower developed. Since it was still very warm we decided along with other passengers to stay on deck. For protection, Norah opened her umbrella, which she was carrying but had not used on our trip. Then to our surprise when she opened it a shower of rice fell all over the deck. The passengers who were outside with us looked at her with wide grins. We thought we had got free of all such indications of being newlyweds back at the hotel in Albany, but overlooked the umbrella. We could hear Nellie and Norma giving us the laugh.

When we landed in Burlington, we walked to the railroad station and learned that there was an evening train for Vergennes. We checked our baggage and found a restaurant for dinner. When we returned to the station we found Bill looking for us. Besides being the pastor of the church in Vergennes, he was the Executive Secretary of the State Congregational Society with an office in Burlington. He was on the way home and took us with him.

The next morning Bill asked me to go with him to his office in Burlington. I helped him get out a big bunch of letters so he was free to catch a noon train back to Vergennes. After a light lunch he asked Norah and me if we would like to drive over to the Camel's Hump, a famous mountain in the Green Mountain range. Of course we were delighted for the opportunity. He drove to the base of the mountain and then we climbed to the top, following a well-marked trail. We could now say we had climbed mountains both in the Adirondacks and the Green Mountains.

On Sunday morning we went to church with the Frazier family. I really enjoyed this as I knew Bill was a good speaker and I wanted to hear him. It proved to be the last time I was to hear him, and as we took a train for Albany on Monday morning, it was the last time I was to see him and his family. Catching a train for Syracuse and then another to Cazenovia, our wedding trip was over.

It was now time for us to find a place to live in Minoa. I had made inquiries before I left but could find nothing for sale or rent at that time. Taking a day's trip to Minoa to look, we found the only place available was an upstairs apartment in the house owned by Mr. Rothballer, a member of the school board. This house was on the edge of the village about a half mile to the east of the school building. It was far from a luxury apartment. There was no inside plumbing, so we had to use an outhouse near the barn where Mr. Rothballer kept a horse which he used to peddle some garden vegetables that he raised. We had to obtain our water from a well equipped with a hand pump and carry it up the back stairs. There was a separate front door which opened to a stairs leading to a living room. This room had a large base-burner hard coal stove, the only thing that came with the apartment. Off the living room was a front bedroom and toward the back a large kitchen. Beyond that was a small room which became our guest room.

Once we closed the deal to rent the apartment, we went into Syracuse to look for some furniture. We didn't know how long we might stay in Minoa, so we didn't want to invest in expensive furniture. Following Jess Leonard's suggestion, we went to a large furniture store which was out of the high rent district. There we picked out a dining room set, two beds and dressers and a wicker living room set. We got a used cook stove through Mr. Flanagan in Minoa. We brought a kitchen table and some chairs from Cazenovia. These chairs are over a hundred years old and we still use them. Norah had some dishes given to her at her shower and the school board gave us a wedding present of Oneida Plate silverware. Carrel, Norah's brother, gave her a set of solid silverware, so we had plenty to start housekeeping.

When school started in September I was real busy but found time to help get settled in our new home. This marked the first time since I was in high school at Houghton that I had a place I could call home. It made me very happy, so I was willing to put up with almost primitive conditions to have one. Norah had grown up in Cazenovia with similar conditions, so it didn't seem as bad as it would have otherwise.

The people in Minoa were eager to meet Norah; the WCTU held a reception for us and the new teachers early that fall. Everyone was very kind and friendly, so it wasn't long before we began to feel very much a part of the community.

Since we did not have a car, our transportation had to be by trolley or train. There was a city trolley line which ended right near Jess Leonard's store, which was used by the majority of the people in the village to shop in Syracuse. The third rail line had a stop about a third of a mile south of the village, which we could ride to either Syracuse or Canastota to catch a train to Cazenovia.

Both Nellie's and Norma's husbands had cars, and I began to fuss about not having one. While my salary was just over the $2,000.00 mark, our rent was low and other expenses were not many; we began to get ahead some. We talked it over and decided to buy a Chevrolet four cylinder touring car from a friend of Norah's in Cazenovia. It was an open car so in rainy weather and in the winter we had to put on side curtains much like the old buggies had done for years. But with it we felt real proud to be able to drive on trips and especially to go to Cazenovia on a par with the rest of the families when we met for the big Sunday dinners.

One thing Norah had to learn when we started housekeeping was to cook. Her mother was a superb cook, but she never taught her girls the art. I knew how to cook all the staples, such as meat and potatoes, and it didn't take long for Norah to learn—we were in business. Mr. Rothballer gave me one end of his big garden to use and the next summer I planted my first garden since I was in Houghton. My garden did so well we had all the fresh vegetables we could use, which helped with our expenses. As both of us were over thirty when we were married, we quickly settled down like an old couple and people soon forgot we were newlyweds.

That fall was the last time the school had a football team, thus, more than ever, all looked forward to the basketball season. This was the year my team began to develop toward a peak. A big help came when a Mr. and Mrs. Thompson moved from the city into a house directly across the street from our apartment. The Thompsons had no children of their own, but had become foster parents to two boys of high school age. The first boy they took was Charles Freeman, who had entered the Minoa High School the last part of the previous year. He was now joined by Raymond Hiscock, which made two outstanding athletes. Charles was rather short, but extremely fast and could work his way through any defense. Raymond was tall and being left handed, could frustrate most guards. With the addition of these two players the second year of basketball was more successful than the first. Norah had never been too interested in the game, but when I took her with me to the games that winter, she became a real fan.

An example of how interested she became took place in a game we played in Eastwood. The referee that night was a sporting goods salesman who had sold us our uniforms. I didn't expect that to make any difference, but during the game my captain called time out and came to me to say that this referee was bothering them by telling them what to do everytime they got the ball. I noticed that he had been talking a lot during the game, but due to the crowd noise I couldn't hear what he said. So after the captain reported what was going on, I went to the referee and told him to lay off, that I would do the coaching. He didn't like what I had to say and from that time on called every little thing he could against my team. Still the game was real close and then, just a minute before time was up, the referee blew his whistle. The spectators thought it was the end of the game and rushed onto the floor. Even the players started for the dressing rooms. Then the timekeeper informed the referee and coaches there was time left. As I was busy helping to clear the floor, I felt someone pulling my sleeve. I looked around and saw it was Norah and I heard her say, "Let's go home. They don't play fair." After the game was over I told the boys what Norah had said. They considered it a good joke and repeated it many times when things were going bad.

One of the problems we encountered during the early days of the league was odd basketball courts we had to play on. Several of the schools in the league did not have school gyms; they played in town halls and other similar facilities. The court at Eastwood was over a store once used as a dance hall, but the ceiling was so low a player had to be within five feet of the basket to score. This made for a crowded and rough game under each basket. The worst place was in North Syracuse. This school had entered the league without a home court and for the first year played all their games away. Then they announced they had a court. No one went to check, and when we arrived for a game, we couldn't believe our eyes. The court they provided was an empty hay loft of a large dairy barn. It was on the second floor and the only entrance was a narrow stairs with a trap door at the top. There were no electric lights and they had installed a number of lanterns with reflectors to light the place. The hay had been removed but some still showed around the sides, while the floor was so full of dust, little puffs would show everytime a player stepped on it.

To me this was a fire trap and I was reluctant to take my team into such a place. But they said it was only temporary, as they were building a new school with a good gym and expected it to be ready for games this season. My players, who had won the league championship the previous year, were insulted to be asked to play in such a place. I told them I didn't blame them for feeling that way, but since it was a league game, I didn't want to forfeit and would send in the second team. As the game progressed it was evident that our second team was about equal to their first. Then in the second half with the score tied, I could feel that the first team players on the bench became more and more restive. With ten minutes left I turned and asked, "Anyone want to go in?" They all jumped up and I sent them in, and in the time left they ran the score way up in our favor.

Later when North Syracuse had their new building with a fine gym, the principal of the school, who was also the basketball coach, became very critical of ours. He claimed that we took unfair advantage by not calling the walls out of bounds and my players knew how to careen the ball off the wall, thus taking an unfair advantage. He took his complaint before the league and they agreed to change the time-honored rule that the home team set the ground rules, allowing the visiting team to do so. Then when his team came to play on our court, he insisted that the walls be out of bounds. This, of course, slowed the game but my team was so drilled in passing that it made little difference to them. We were ahead at half time, but I wanted to show my fellow coach up and for the only time in my career I explained to my team the situation and told them to go out and run the score up as high as possible. They did, making it a very one-sided game, but I never heard anything more about our taking unfair advantage. The league rule stood for several years, but was rarely used.

Again, we had a good year and won the league championship. The sectional tournament was held again in Utica and I was just able to go. Two weeks before the tournament I was sick with the flu and while in bed I developed a terrible pain near my rectum. The doctor examined me and discovered an abcess in the lower part of the large colon. He had me apply heat to try to have it break on the outside but after twenty-four hours of severe pain I got relief when it broke inside. The doctor now called it a fistula and said it would cause trouble. I was able to get out of bed and back to work, but it was very disagreeable since the fistula would not heal and kept running. Dr. Bishop took me on a Saturday to a surgeon at the Crouse Irving Hospital in Syracuse. He nearly killed me with his examination and then informed us that an operation was the only cure and the sooner the better. Dr. Bishop explained my situation and asked for time for me to go to Utica with my team.

I was miserable all the time but didn't say anything to the team. I did tell the board and they agreed that I should go for the operation as soon as the tournament was over. In the tournament we again drew Syracuse Central for the first game. They had the same team as the previous year and while we were stronger, we still were no match and lost the game. I persuaded the committee in charge to let us stay overnight so my boys could enjoy the whole tournament. Norah was with me and we knew that Mary Doolittle was teaching at the Country Day School, just outside of Utica, and we made arrangements to visit her at lunch. I hadn't seen her since our days at Burlington. She was the same vivacious person, and it did us both good to see her.

Following the trip to Utica, Dr. Bishop took me to the hospital early Monday morning and I was operated on that day. It was not a serious operation, but for a time I was very uncomfortable. At first I had a good time kidding with the young nurses and then one day a man from Cazenovia came in to see me. In the presence of a nurse he asked about my school and the basketball team. The next morning when the nurse came in she was very proper and sedate. I was curious and pressed her to tell why the change. She finally said, "Why didn't you tell us you are a high school principal? I would never have dared to say the things I did to my principal." Nothing I could say would bring back the atmosphere that existed before my position was known. Thus I began to learn how lonely my job was to be. Like a minister or a priest I was to be treated differently.

Soon after I was out of the hospital, the baseball season began. We had a team the first year, but with only 30 boys in the high school, it was difficult to field a team. Yet in spite of that, we had a fair season, winning 50% of our league games. Then an item appeared in the *Syracuse Herald* that spring that shows how our prospects for a good team changed.

HISCOCK, 1922 PULASKI STAR, REPORTS FOR MINOA HIGH NINE

Minoa High School's baseball prospects for the season appear bright, with the addition of Hiscock, star whirler for the Pulaski team last season, to the list of Minoa candidates and with several promising youngsters coming from the grade schools.

The Pulaski lad whose prowess was largely responsible for the winning of the 1922 county league championship by Pulaski, will have Freeman, Minoa basketball star, for catching mate. Six men who played in regular positions last year have reported for practice.

Seymour Wershing, outfielder, was elected manager for the 1923 nine yesterday afternoon, and the captaincy will be left vacant until after the first game, when Coach Calhoon will let the regular players pick their leader.

Hiscock was indeed an outstanding left-handed pitcher. He not only had exceptional speed but a fair curve and good control. Together with Freeman they became the best high school battery in the county. With Hiscock pitching we had a strong defensive team, but were weak on hitting. Consequently, most of our games ended in a one score win. A few headlines from reports in the Syracuse paper shows how this was true.

MINOA NINE HANDS DEFEAT TO EAST SYRACUSE, 1 TO 0

MINOA WINS 12–INNING CONTEST
FROM EASTWOOD HIGH SCHOOL NINE 4–3

HISCOCK STRIKES OUT 20 PLAYERS

These samples from the paper indicates that Minoa was now not only a winner in basketball but also in baseball. Every year that Hiscock pitched we won the eastern division of the county league and played the winner of the western division. These were usually played in the Syracuse professional baseball park. In one such game we were playing for the championship when the boys noticed a sign painted on the fence surrounding the outfield which read, "Any player hitting a home run over the fence at this point will receive a free suit from a leading men's clothing store in Syracuse." Late in the game with the score tied, Hiscock sent a ball over the fence at that sign. He raced around the bases and jumped up and down all the way to the bench. The crowd rose and gave him a big cheer. His home run put us ahead, but when he went back into pitch he completely lost control and couldn't get a man out. I always called this a home run that lost the game.

The second summer in Minoa we stayed at home most of the time. I planted a small garden and we enjoyed the fresh vegetables. We had several visitors, including Norma and Fred, who also brought Norah's parents for a Sunday dinner. We felt real good to think we could entertain them as a partial payment for the many meals we had at their house. Mary Doolittle spent a week with us and as always, being such a lively person, she brought a lot of sunshine into our lives. Late that summer my mother was on a trip east and came to see us for a week. It was a rather bad time, as Norah was now pregnant and at the worst of her morning sickness. We did manage to take Mother to Cazenovia so she could meet Norah's parents and see the place we had written so much about.

That summer the Gold Medal Mothers under the leadership of Mrs. Moore succeeded in getting a boulder placed on the small triangle of ground at the intersection of the two main streets of the village. A plaque placed on the boulder contained the names of the soldiers in the Minoa area who had been killed in World War I. The dedication of this monument was set for the Fourth of July, and I was asked to act as master of ceremonies. A platform was erected near the boulder and a display of flags placed in front. On the platform with me was the priest of the Catholic Church, who was to give the invocation, Jess Leonard, to represent the village officers, and Reverend Burnett, the pastor of the Methodist Church, who was selected to give the principal address. In front of the platform were Mrs. Moore and the other Gold Medal Mothers all dressed in white and standing rigidly at attention through the whole program.

I opened the program with a welcome to the crowd that had assembled and expressed my pleasure at being honored to be the master of ceremonies. I mentioned that this was the second boulder whose dedication ceremonies I had been a part of the first being for old Copperhead, and how I had mistakenly cut the speaker short by starting the band too soon. I hoped I could do better this time. I didn't intend to make it a joke, but the crowd laughed and Mrs. Moore turned around and gave me a disapproving look. I tried to redeem myself by continuing in a serious vein by describing how I had seen the destruction in the war zone of France and, when I returned, how wonderful it was to see the difference in this country, our country for which these boys had sacrificed their lives.

I then introduced the other speakers. When Reverend Burnett got up to speak, he turned to me and said, "I know you do not have a band to call on to stop me, but if I am too long, just pull my coattail." The last speaker was Mrs. Moore, and she concluded by pulling a rope to unveil the boulder. I then concluded by saying, "Let us dedicate this boulder in the name of all who gave of their time, their resources and especially to those who gave their lives to make this country and the whole world a better place in which to live. Let us in the words of Mrs. Moore indeed make this hallowed ground."

After it was over I was congratulated many times for helping to make it such a fine occasion. Jess shook my hand and said, "You gave it just the right light touch to keep the affair from becoming morbid." Even Mrs. Moore thanked me for a good job. I am sure my quoting her at the end made up for what she may have thought about my beginning.

That fall Norah's activities were considerably limited. She could no longer go with me to out-of-town games. At times she felt so bad I had to do much of the cooking and housework. After a few months she was better and we began to plan for the new member of the family in buying some furniture and baby clothes. We drew much closer watching her development as the baby grew.

Late that summer, on my recommendation, the board hired Miss Helen Gohringer to teach history and Latin. She was a resident of New Hartford, a suburb of Utica, and a graduate of Mount Holyoke College. She had no experience in teaching, but I was so impressed by her personality that I was sure she would make good. Events proved that I was right.

About the third week of school, Miss Gohringer came to my office asking for help. She had taken over a small second year class in Latin

283

and found the students woefully lacking in the fundamentals. The previous teacher had been very weak and that is why we had let her go. As she told about the situation, I thought of my own experience in Latin back in Houghton. By chance I had also read in an educational magazine an article about meeting such a situation. Putting the two together in my mind, I told her my suggestion was to start over at the beginning of the book and work out each word as to its place in grammar. I will never forget the expression that came over her face. She thanked me but as she rose from her chair and walked out of the office, I could sense her disappointment. I sat in my chair for a time thinking about it. Here, as a new teacher, she had come to her principal asking for help, and he had given her a foolish answer. I felt bad to have let her down.

As the year progressed, Miss Gohringer became more and more an important addition to the faculty. The teachers and students all liked her and she seemed happy in the job. Then at the end of the year she came to tell me about her results in Regents with her classes. She was elated because her students in second year Latin had all passed. Then she said something which made me very happy also. She said, "Do you remember how I came to you in distress at the beginning of the year about that class?" "Yes," I replied, "I certainly do." "Well," she continued, "at the time I thought your suggestion was too simple and impossible to work. I didn't see how I would be able to cover the work required by the state syllabus if I followed your plan. But after trying everything else I could think of, with no success, in desperation I resorted to your suggestion and the results showed it worked."

In all my years as a school principal this is one of a very few times that a teacher came to me for help. I had scores of teachers who came to rave about the poor preparation their students had when they came to them or complain about the pupils who were unwilling to work or tell me what should be done, but rarely to ask for real help. So the experience with Miss Gohringer stands out as one case I can point to with pride. After the first year, Miss Gohringer didn't need any help, she developed into a master teacher. Years later I was to meet her, after we had both left Minoa, in Utica where she was a social studies teacher. Later she became head of that department at Proctor High School in Utica. She was a member of an important state committee and a recognized leader in her field. I still take pride in picking her for her first year of teaching.

Because of Norah's condition, I asked to be relieved from coaching the girl's basketball team. One of the women high school teachers took charge while I supervised. The girls were disappointed and thought I was favoring the boys, but they had a successful season anyway. With all my school work, coaching and helping at home, the time went fast. Then on the morning of February 8 about 5 a.m. Norah woke me to say she was having pains. I jumped out of bed and began to get things ready for the doctor. Before six I went across the street to the Thompsons to ask if they would send one of the boys down to tell Dr. Bishop he was needed. In a few minutes I looked out to see Raymond Hiscock using his long legs to carry the message. Also, to have the doctor alert the practical nurse we had engaged to care for Norah and the baby.

The doctor arrived about six-thirty and was surprised to find things so far advanced. He and I were alone and he began to tell me what to do. In fact, I was his assistant helping through the whole affair. Norah was in pain only a short time, and it was a perfectly natural birth. Just as the baby arrived, Mrs. Thompson came in to see if we needed help and was more than surprised when the doctor handed her the baby. She had been a nurse and knew what to do. By the time our nurse arrived at 8 o'clock, everything was over and all calm.

I showed the nurse where things were and changed my clothes and left for school. I would have taken at least a half day off, but the county medical officer was due that morning to give inoculations to all the pupils against diptheria. A family with three children in school had the disease and one had died. Rather than close the school, this doctor had ordered all pupils inoculated. I knew I needed to be there to see that things ran smoothly. We had no school nurse, so the doctor brought one with him. I had everything planned and by helping the nurse prepare the pupils, the whole school was inoculated in a half day. When we finished, the doctor thanked me for my help and complimented me on having things so well planned. Then when I told him what had happened that morning before school, he looked at me in amazement. Shaking his head, he said, "you are one in a million."

One thing I became good at in this school and later as an elementary school principal was the ability to do all sorts of first aid work. I found the young pupils would often respond to me better than they did to a doctor. The pupils in Minoa were subjected to a special problem. The big steam locomotives would blow a lot of coal ash into the air covering the whole village when they started to move the long freight trains out of the yards. It always seemed to be the worst when the pupils were coming to the school in the mornings. Numbers of the children would get these tiny cinders in their eyes and would ask the teachers to remove them. The teachers were used to the task and were pretty good at it, but almost everyday they would send a stubborn case or more to the office for my help. Most of the time I would take the cinder out quickly but at times one would be imbedded and I would have to roll the eye lid back to find it. All the time I was in Minoa I never failed to remove a cinder nor did I ever have a complaint about it.

The first week of Marjorie's life seemed normal and we were proud of a perfect baby. Then trouble started. We had her in a crib right beside our bed and on Sunday morning I woke rather early and picked her up to look at her. To my consternation I saw her eyes cross and I felt her body grow rigid. She didn't make a sound but began to turn blue. I yelled for the nurse, who was in another room, and she rushed in, looked at her, and recognized a convulsion. She stripped off the baby's

285

clothes while I prepared her a bath basin full of warm water. Immersing her in the water, in a short time we saw her come out of it, but we knew there was something radically wrong. In a short time we discovered she became distressed everytime she took her bottle. She would keep the milk down for only a short time, and then would either throw it up or go into another convulsion.

Unfortunately, the nurse we had, talked Norah out of trying to nurse the baby and I have always blamed her for Marjorie's trouble. Now we had a baby crying night and day, first because she was hungry, and then very distressed when she tried to take her milk. At the end of two weeks our nurse left and we had to struggle by ourselves. Dr. Bishop did all he could but after five weeks with no success, he suggested we take her to a Dr. Smith in East Syracuse. He told us that this doctor was very good in treating weak babies. We made an appointment and went.

This doctor listened to our story and examined Marjorie. He told us he thought he could correct her trouble but he would have to be in complete charge. We agreed and I had the unpleasant task of telling Dr. Bishop our decision. I could see he was hurt, but I assured him we wanted him as our doctor for everything else. I think he was hurt by the way Dr. Smith acted, as we remained good friends with Dr. Bishop as long as we stayed in Minoa. Dr. Smith said Marjorie wasn't able to digest cow's milk without modification. He gave us a formula to follow in the preparation of her bottle. It was a combination of Mellon's food, condensed milk and fresh milk. It had to be heated over a slow fire and constantly stirred for an hour. It was a lot of work, but we were rewarded by seeing her keep her food down and she began to grow.

Late that spring Marjorie developed a cold and did a lot of crying. One day a neighbor woman dropped in to see Norah and watching Marjorie, she said, "Your baby has an earache. See how she keeps rubbing her ear." Sure enough, in a couple of days her ear began to run. When the doctor did examine her, he told us her ear drum had burst but he couldn't do anything for her. The result was she lost 75% of her hearing in that ear and by the time she grew older and we took her to a specialist, it was too late. It was a condition that has bothered her all her life.

My basketball team was winning again this season, in fact, it proved to be the best of my five years of coaching at Minoa. We won the league championship and again went to Utica for the sectional tournament. By this time Syracuse Central had lost its powerful team and Oswego High School was the winner of that league. In the tournament we defeated Oswego in a tight game the first night, and then Little Falls the second night. Thus, we became the representative of Section 3 and won the right to go to Syracuse University for the state tournament. Of course, Norah had to stay home with the baby and missed all this excitement.

After the tournament in Utica my boys were very tired. With so few reserves they had to play every game with little rest. So while we could have gone to Syracuse and stayed at a fraternity house, I thought the boys would do better if they stayed at home where they would be in their own beds and eat at home. I knew the university basketball court was much larger than any we had played on, so we tried to get permission to hold a practice on that court. The only thing we could do was to accept an invitation to skirmish the Syracuse freshman team. This gave the boys a chance to feel more at home on a large court and a chance to modify our style. After the skirmish in which we held our own with the freshman team, the Syracuse coaches were generous in their praise of my team. They were impressed by our passing game for which all my teams were noted, and also the high percentage of baskets made in shots taken.

The night the tournament opened, all the teams and coaches were invited to an early dinner given by the University. Since we were scheduled for the second game, we went to the dinner. The boys got a thrill out of meeting the other teams representing the eight sections of the state. Only the two teams which were to play the first game were missing. There was one other small school from the northern part of the state, but Minoa was the smallest in the tournament. All the others were from large schools like Syracuse Central, who had represented our section the two previous years. The draw that had been made before the tournament started placed us against Rockville Center, the winner of the Long Island section. This was a school of over 1500 students compared to ours of less than 100. But I kept telling my boys, no matter how large their school, they can only put five men on the floor at a time. Of course, I didn't mention that they had many more boys to choose from and also they would have a much stronger reserve bench.

Once the game began it was evident that our three-two zone defense bothered the other team and with my team feeling somewhat at home on the court, the game remained very close up until the last few minutes. Freeman was the fastest man on the floor and he kept us in the game by penetrating their defense and making his lay-up shots. Hiscock was bothered by the large floor and was missing his famous left-hand shots, so I coached the team to feed Freeman. Thus he became the high scorer of the game and was honored by being selected by the sports writers as a forward on the all tournament team.

We lost the game when Rockville Center got a little ahead near the end of the game and froze the ball. Our team had been using the zone defense all year and were rarely behind, hence, they didn't have the skill to change to a man to man game and get the ball. Anyway, they put up such a good fight I could feel proud of them. My only regret was that we had to draw the team that won the tournament for the first night, otherwise we had a good chance of staying in the tournament longer. But I will never forget how after the game when we were in our dressing room, the boys came over to me as I sat on a bench and said, "Don't feel too bad, Mr. Calhoon, we never could have won the tournament

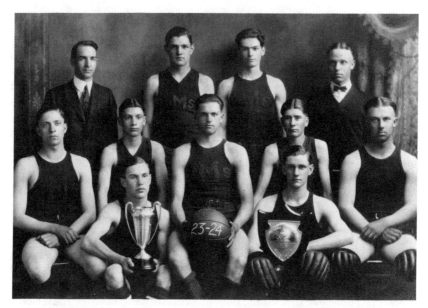

1923–1924 Championship Team from Minoa High School
Left to Right, Top Row—Manager Seymour Werching, Donald Gallery, Harold Costello. Second Row—John Sampo, John Albanese, Coach A. Ray Calhoon, Irving Schaff, Harold Platz. Lower Row—Charles Freeman, Captain Raymond Hiscock, and James Gallery.

anyway." They recognized that we were outclassed by the big schools. The marvel is that we ever were in the state tournament, probably the smallest school to ever appear.

At the close of the basketball season I was exhausted. Being up nights a lot with Marjorie didn't help, but I recovered and finished the year. In the spring I started another garden which was a good outlet for my stress. As soon as school was over, I decided to take some courses at Syracuse University, both to finish the requirements for my principal's certificate and to use the courses towards working for a Master's degree in education.

George Hayes, Nellie's husband, was an excellent trout fisherman. I heard him tell about his exploits and became interested. I asked him if he would take me with him sometime when he was up to Cazenovia to show me how to fish for these elusive creatures. He did take me out a couple of times and gave me some tips. Then Duane Joslyn, Norah's cousin who lived in Cazenovia, was good enough to take me with him to fish for the small native trout which still lived in some of the streams high in the hills around that area. So between the two I did learn and began to catch my share of trout, which Norah's mother loved to cook. But more important I found that this sport was something I could enjoy all my life. There is something about following a trout stream up through the woods which makes one forget the trials and tribulations of

288

life quicker than anything I know. All the stresses and strains which have been built up in the body are relieved, and after an hour or two of such activity, one gets a new lease on life. Only a true trout fisherman will understand about this.

Fred and Norma Benedict lived in nearby Fayetteville, so we saw them often. Fred liked to hunt in the fall, and several times we went out together. Some years before, pheasants had been introduced in New York State, and they had grown to large numbers at this time. Every fall I succeeded in getting one or more, also rabbits and squirrels gave us many meals of game. Hunting and fishing became important hobbies.

In January of the year that Marjorie was almost a year old we had one of the biggest snow storms on record in central New York. The evening it started the women of the Methodist church had a program and a good crowd was in attendance. The feature of the program was a male quartet from the Liberty Masonic Lodge of Utica, but they also asked Norah to give several readings. She had done this before and had built up quite a reputation. When the program was over and we came out of the church, everyone was surprised to see a foot of snow on the ground and the air filled with flakes. It came so silently that we had not been aware of any storm. I got Norah in the car and backed out into the street but couldn't get any farther. Finally, some of the boys gave the car a long push, and once under way I was able to just keep it going until we reached home. I had no garage, but Mr. Rothballer let me put the car in part of his barn. It took me several tries to get up the ramp and once inside, it stayed there until spring.

The next morning we woke to see over four feet of snow covering everything. All traffic was stalled, including a long New York Central passenger train just inside the village. It was over twenty-four hours before a snow plow was able to free the train. In the meantime, the dining car ran out of food and many of the women in the village baked big batches of bread to sell to the passengers.

We had depended upon daily delivery of milk from a nearby dairy farm and wondered how long we could hold out. The snow was too deep for me to try to wade to the store or to get anywhere until a path had been broken. It was three days before the dairy farmer put a box on the front runners of a bobsled and with that alone, was able to get a team of horses up our street. The snow was chest high on the horses, but by giving them frequent rest periods they were able to flounder through. We were thankful for the milk and for a path in the road, but school was closed for a week before traffic could get moving again.

On Marjorie's first birthday we had a little party of our own for her. Norah baked a cake and put one candle on it. When it came time to light the candle, she was thrilled. Then we tried to teach her how to blow it out and with our help she did. Then the next evening at supper she did something which I claimed at the time showed she was very intelligent. When we sat down at the table it was dark enough for us to turn on the electric light over the table. Marjorie looked up at the light and then began to try to blow it out just as she had the candle. We both laughed and said even if she wasn't entirely healthy, we had a smart baby.

That spring the following appeared in the Syracuse paper.

MINOA

Miss Helen Gohringer of the Minoa school, who is a student of violin at Syracuse University, broadcast several numbers at noon, Saturday, from Station WFBL, the Onondaga, Syracuse. Mrs. A. R. Calhoon, also of Minoa, was on the program for several Riley readings.

This happened as the result of Miss Gohringer using her ability to play the violin to interest a few of the high school students to form a small orchestra. She persuaded me to dig out my old cornet and we had a good time together. We did play for the school commencements, which the people thought wonderful as nothing like this had happened before. Norah had been using her talent to give readings at many programs, so she and Helen talked it over and thought it would be fun to go into Syracuse on a Saturday and see if they could get on the amateur show.

About a year before this, the man who ran the small garage in the village began assembling radios from parts. The ones he made were very good and much cheaper than the ones on the market. This was in the early years of radio broadcasing and there were only a few stations, but I was interested and had him make one for us. So when the women left for their venture, I kept the radio on to see if they did appear.

Marjorie was then over a year old, but she had been listening to her mother practice her readings ever since she was a baby. One selection by Eugene Field, "Little Boy Blue" was very sad. It told of a little boy, who at night, lined up his toy soldiers and ordered them to stand that way until he came back. But he didn't wake up and his toy soldiers were still standing, waiting for his return. Marjorie was too young to understand the words, but the pathos that Norah put into her voice affected her, so everytime Norah gave the selection she would start crying.

I was alone with Marjorie and had her lunch ready when the noon program began and I was delighted to hear the announcer say Miss Helen Gohringer and Mrs. Ray Calhoon from Minoa would present the program this noon. Marjorie had started to eat but when her mother began to speak, she stopped and looked intently at the radio, then when Norah began the "Little Boy Blue" selection, she burst out crying, just as if her mother was in the room. I thought it was a good test of how good the radio was. Both Norah and Helen were delighted to be on the radio and the few people in Minoa who heard them were thrilled.

The personnel of my basketball team, due to graduations, had changed considerably since the first year, but we were still one of the top teams in the league. This year the top competitor for the championship was the team from Eastwood High School. Eastwood was a fast growing suburb of Syracuse, and going into the final game of the season we were tied. Our last game was with them on their court. We had been hearing some disturbing rumors about their team, mainly that it was composed of dropouts and rejects from the city school who came to Eastwood just to play basketball. The game was played before a packed house with the first half ending in a tie score.

At the intermission we retired to our dressing room in the basement, where we discovered we were right next to the home team room. The wall between the rooms was so thin we could hear every word spoken in their room. We heard the Eastwood team rushing into their room shouting to each other using the most vile language I ever heard. I thought when the coach arrived such language would stop, but to our surprise it got worse, if that was possible. I had been in the army and heard a lot of swearing and dirty words, but nothing such as this. My boys looked at me in horror. They knew I never allowed a trace of such language by members of our teams or around the school. So when I saw the coach had no control, I said to the boys, "Let's get out of here." We went out into the hall away from the dressing rooms and talked things over while relaxing.

The second half was just as close as the first, then near the end my best guard nearly collapsed and I had to take him out. He had been ill and I hesitated about letting him play, but he was so eager I let him try. After we lost the game by two points, I was loudly criticized by the Minoa fans for taking him out, but they didn't know as I did that he was trembling all over when he sat down on the bench. Thus, this was the only year we did not win the league championship.

After the season was over, several of the coaches in the league put in a protest about the Eastwood team. A special meeting of the league was called and while I was not asked to sign the letter of protest, I did report what had happened when we played that team. There was so much evidence presented showing that the Eastwood team was composed of "ringers" that the league voted to expel the school from the league. The Syracuse papers made a big story out of the action and Mr. Todd, the principal, made a plea for reconsideration, claiming that he didn't know such conditions existed. But the league felt he should have known and turned down his request.

Safety rules and fire prevention were expected to be taught in the schools of the state, but there were no courses developed, so it was done mostly in school assemblies. A Syracuse fireman had developed a talk on fire prevention for high school students. To help get the attention of his audience, this man had learned some slight-of-hand tricks. He had been at the school once, and I thought he was good enough to invite back. This time he brought a stranger with him. This man stayed in the background, and I thought it rather strange I was not introduced to him. I didn't say anything but saw the man standing in the back of the room watching the show.

After the students had been dismissed and I stood watching the fireman gathering his paraphernalia, he asked in a low tone, "Did you notice the man in the rear of the room who came with me?" "Yes," I said, "who is he?" "He is my teacher of magic tricks, the great Thurston," he replied. "He didn't want anyone to know he was here so it would distract from my show, but now that it is over I'll introduce you." Of course, I was delighted to meet such a man and said so. Then to my surprise the first thing Thurston said to me was, "Did you ever think of going on the stage? I noticed when you talked to the assembly that you had the attention of every person in the room. This is the kind of personality I am constantly looking for. You have the kind of bearing which demands attention." I was taken aback by his remarks and said, "No, I never thought of such a career." His reply was, "If you ever do, here is my card, come and see me. By the way, I am appearing at the Empire Theater tonight, here are two tickets, come and enjoy the show." Norah wasn't interested, so I invited Jess Leonard and together we went and saw the performance. I was impressed with the acts, but couldn't see myself on the stage as part of such a show. But I never forgot what Thurston said about me.

In fact, I was so impressed by Thurston's remark that I used that fact all through my career. I noticed many times how effective my method was compared to others. I watched some speakers start to talk while some in the audience were conversing, and these speakers never got their audience's attention. Pausing a few seconds, or longer if necessary, until everyone has stopped talking and is looking at you, I found to be one of the most important steps in successful public speaking.

After Marjorie arrived, we spent more weekends and summers in Minoa. We often attended the community church and its active Sunday school. One of the big events was the summer Sunday school picnic. One time it was held in the suburban amusement park near Manlius. There was a baseball field which we could use and after the picnic the young fellows challenged the married men to a baseball game. I was asked to play with the married men and took over second base. Grant Goodelle had always been the pitcher for such games in the past, and for a few innings he was good. The single men were largely my high school players and soon began to hit Goodelle all over the lot. I suggested he let me try, but at first he refused. Then after the single men had a dozen or more runs, he called on me for help. The catcher of our team was a railroad engineer and very good, so I conferred with him about signals and went to work. I had a natural "in" curve, which I kept up around the shoulders of the batters. It looked easy to hit, but they were swinging their heads off, either missing or popping up to the infield. Probably nowadays my pitch would be called a "slider." Anyway, I surprised the boys and they tried to get back of the backstop to see what I was throwing. But I protested and the umpire made them get away. The boys did win, but I stopped their scoring and we had a lot of fun. After the game the boys congratulated me and wanted to know why I hadn't told them I could pitch. I thought after it was over that it was too bad now that I am too old, that I found out I might have been a good pitcher.

The school year 1925-26 started out much like the preceding ones, then conditions changed when Norah found out she was pregnant again. At first she was rather upset because we had such a time getting Marjorie started. She felt it was too soon to have another baby. On the other hand, we agreed that we had learned a lot and should be able to avoid the troubles we had experienced with Marjorie. We began to plan for the future.

I was now working toward my Master's Degree in Education by attending summer sessions at Syracuse University. This made me feel that I should be looking for a principalship of a larger school. I liked Minoa very much and I had the unusual experience of working with the same members of the school board that hired me. Yet my success with the courses I was taking in Education made me feel I was qualified for a larger school.

Things began to happen. First, two members of the Eastwood school board came to see me. They told me that the principal of the big grade school in that village was retiring at the end of the first semester. They said the principal was a woman who had been in that position for forty years, but due to ill health she wanted to retire. They said they knew of my reputation at Minoa and wanted to know if I was interested in such a position. They made me an offer much larger than I was getting and assured me that if I could be released from my contract at Minoa that the job was mine. I talked with Jess Leonard, who was still the president of the Minoa board, and he said, "Go ahead, we knew someone would be offering you a bigger job and we would have to let you go."

I thought the proposition over and talked with Norah, who left it entirely up to me. Although I felt I was better qualified to be in the secondary level, it seemed too good an offer to turn down. Then, just as I was about to sign a contract, the same two members of the Eastwood board called to say they wanted to see me at once. They came rather apologetic, saying just after they sent me the contract the principal changed her mind and wanted to stay until June. They said they had offered the contract in good faith and if I insisted, they would honor it. Under such circumstances I didn't want the job and in a way I was relieved, since I had doubts about my success in a strictly grade school. I rushed to tell Jess and fortunately the news didn't get out to the school, but the members of the board knew I would leave if given a chance.

The next thing that happened came near the end of the basketball season. On a Saturday morning, just after the night my team had won an important game clinching the title of the eastern division of the league for the fourth time, I was thinking about my record, how I had put the town on the map and how elated the school was, when I met one of the leading citizens of the village. He greeted me with, "Hello, Prof."

293

Thinking he was surely going to congratulate me on the team winning, I was all ready to express my thanks. Instead he said, "Prof., some of us men have been talking and we think there should be a coach in the school." If anyone ever fell off cloud nine, I did then with a thud. Evidently it showed in my face, for he hastened to say, "We feel you need help, you are doing too much." I knew he meant well, and I tried to recover and thanked him for thinking of my welfare, but my ego was crushed. I knew then for sure it was time for me to go, for after all my success with my teams, I would never be happy to have someone else be the coach.

Then fate stepped in. It came in the form of a letter from Ann and John White. John had left Silver Bay and was now the Assistant Minister and Director of Religious Education at the Presbyterian Church in Saratoga Springs, New York. The letter was to tell us that the principal of the Saratoga Springs High School was leaving at the end of the semester and the position was open. They suggested that I apply at once. They also said they were living in an upstairs apartment near the school and the downstairs was for rent. Ann thought it would be wonderful for us to live in the same house, and our children could grow up together. John said if I applied he would give me a good recommendation. As far as he could determine, the school had a good reputation and everything was fine.

The position sounded like it was just what I had in mind, so I sent a letter to the Superintendent of Schools, applying for the position. I explained how I knew about the position, and that he could talk with John White about me. They did contact John and asked me to come for an interview. I went on a weekend and met Charles Mosher, the superintendent, and members of the board. Things seemed fine and they offered me a contract with a starting salary of $3,000.00, which was almost a thousand more than Minoa would ever pay. I told them I would accept, providing the board at Minoa would release me so I could start on March 1.

On Tuesday, February 2, 1926, the following appeared in the *Syracuse Journal.*

CALHOON QUITS AT MINOA
TO GO TO SARATOGA SPRINGS

CLEVER COURT INSTRUCTOR HAS NEW POSITION

Has Developed Good Basketball Teams
in Past Five Years.

By Harold T. Howell

Alvin Raymond Calhoon, principal and coach of athletics at Minoa High School since 1921, resigned his position at Minoa last night at a meeting of the Minoa School Board to accept the offer as principal at the Saratoga Springs High School.

Principal Calhoon, besides his work as head of the Minoa school, has supervised athletics. His feature sport has been basketball in which Minoa High has featured for the last five years.

In basketball Minoa High has won four championships and is well on the road to a fifth with the 1925–26 court season half completed and Minoa High at the top of the county league.

When Coach Calhoon took charge of the Minoa basketball team in the season of 1921–22, Minoa High won the east section title of the county and in the playoffs beat Skaneateles for the county championship. Minoa won the county trophy in 1922–23 by again trimming Skaneateles High.

Minoa High School enjoyed its greatest year in basketball in the season of 1923–24, when Minoa defeated Solvay for the county title and entered the New York State tournament by winning over Little Falls High, Auburn High and Oswego High on successive nights in an interleague tourney at Utica. In the state championship, Minoa lost to Rockville Center from Long Island.

Last year Minoa High was defeated for the county championship by Eastwood High School. Besides basketball, Minoa has had successful and winning teams in baseball. In 1924 Minoa won the east section title, but lost the county championship to Skaneateles.

Principal Calhoon's resignation will take effect March 1. His family will move about that time to Saratoga Springs.

The Saratoga Springs School is a considerable advancement over Minoa. Minoa has an enrollment of less that 200 students, while Saratoga Springs has a student enrollment of more than 500 pupils. The Saratoga Springs faculty includes 30 teachers.

The Board of Education at Saratoga Springs has requested Mr. Calhoon to take up his duties there as soon as plans could reasonably be made for him to leave Minoa. This is due to the fact that James E. Haillegh, who has been principal at Saratoga Springs, resigned last month and his resignation took effect yesterday.

Principal Calhoon is a graduate of Oberlin College in the class of 1916. He has taught in West Park, Ohio, and Burlington, New Jersey, before coming to Minoa.

I should have been pleased with this write up and in a way I was. However, Norah had been the Minoa correspondent for this paper for more than two years, so she wrote up my resignation. When her story didn't appear she called her editor and he apologized and explained that he was overruled when the sports editor heard about my resignation, so he took the article off his desk and rewrote it for the sports page. He said he would pay Norah anyway, but it didn't make up for the things that were omitted, such as how I had raised the standard of the high school.

At the last school meeting I had given a report which showed the results of the Regents examinations over the years. I showed that the results had gone from below the state average to well above the state average in every department. I also indicated the large increase in the number of the high school graduates who were now going on to college. That they were successful was indicated when one member of the basketball team went on to medical college and later came back to Minoa to take over the practice of Dr. Bishop. Another, Lee Rising, went to Springfield College and came back to Minoa to coach and then became the principal.

The *Syracuse Post Standard* also carried a story of my leaving Minoa, and I was pleased to see this paragraph included.

> Besides playing a great brand of ball these years, Minoa was awarded the sportsmanship trophy in 1923-24 and in 1924-25.

This award was the result of Dan Chase, the head of the State Physical Education Department, who was not only instrumental in organizing the State Basketball organization, but also emphasized the need to raise the standard of good sportsmanship. The Onondaga County League decided to cooperate by not only giving a trophy to the team winning the championship, but also one of equal value to the team voted as showing the best sportsmanship. The voting was done by allowing an equal number of players on each team to cast a vote, which were sent to the league secretary in a sealed envelope.

When first proposed, some members of the league thought it would be a sort of consolation prize to the team that finished last, but the players were far wiser than some gave them credit for and it didn't turn out that way at all. So when Minoa won both the championship and the sportsmanship trophies the same two years, I was most proud of them. I felt it was a vindication of my quality of teaching. The rule was that a player could not vote for his own team and one year the secretary told me that it was a good thing my boys followed that rule because every vote in the league was for Minoa except their vote. I always felt that we refuted the well known adage, "Good guys always finish last."

Norah thought she was "due" about the middle of February, and since we were breaking up our home, it was no place for her, so on the first of February I took her to Cazenovia to be with her folks. Cazenovia had a small nursing home which also catered to maternity cases; Norah made arrangements to go there when her time came.

Before I left, the school gave me a farewell dinner in the gymnasium. I felt honored and a little embarrassed by the many kind things that were said to me and seeing the tears in the eyes of so many people. Jess Leonard represented the board and he presented to me a beautiful Illinois gold watch. It was inscribed:

I carried this watch for years and it is now among my best keepsakes. As he presented me with the watch, Jess also said some very nice things about me, some of which he put into a letter of recommendation.

To Whom it may concern;

I wish to state that I knew and worked with Mr. Calhoon for five years while he was principal of the Minoa High and Graded School.

He did a remarkable piece of work in reorganizing our school, which was at a very low standard when he came here. With his good executive ability, his tact and good judgment, together with his fine personality and knowledge of school work, also boys and girls, he raised the classic standard of our school to one above the average of the State for this class of school. He was an active worker in our community. He always kept close supervision over the school and teachers. He also kept all school records and files up in good shape, cooperating in every way with the school board and parents for the interest of the school.

His very high moral character and pleasing personality were a spendid influence with the students and won the high respect of all who knew him. We regretted much to lose him when he left for a better position.

I feel that Mr. Calhoon is well qualified for a superintendent's position and can unconditionally recommend him for same.

Respectfully yours,
(Signed) J. A. Leonard
President, School Board.

In my remarks the night of the dinner, I expressed my sorrow that Norah couldn't be present to hear all the wonderful things that were said about me. That I knew it was time for me to move, but it was hard to say goodbye to Minoa. The school had become a major part of my life. The close relationship I had with the players on both the boys' and girls' athletic teams was something I would never forget. Minoa was the place we had established our first home and where our first child was born. There is no place on earth where the people could have been kinder to us. Now in leaving, I feel that I have pointed the way, "So Minoa carry on and on."

The board found a man to take my place the middle of February and told me I could leave any time with full pay for that month. As soon as the new man came and I could show him the school, I went to Cazenovia to be with Norah. I thought Norah would go to the hospital before I had to leave for Saratoga Springs, but it wasn't to be.

297

CHAPTER 18

SARATOGA SPRINGS

On Monday morning March 1, I reported to Superintendent Mosher's office only to find he was out of town at a conference. His office was in the High School building near the front entrance and directly across the hall from the school office. I introduced myself to Mosher's secretary and she took me to my office and introduced me to Mrs. Richardson, the High School Secretary who in turn introduced me to the teachers as they arrived to sign in for the day. At the school assembly, which came later that week, I told how the first teacher I met was Miss Hayes, then the second teacher was Miss Hayes, and when the third teacher was introduced as Miss Hayes, I decided either someone was giving me a good time or else I was losing my mind. This story was only partly true, but there were three teachers in the school by the same name, Hayes, but not related. As I told the story it became a standing joke in the school.

Before I became established in my office, a telegram arrived from Cazenovia, saying Norah had given birth to a baby girl and mother and baby were doing fine. I was glad to know everything was good, but sorry I had missed the event by just a day. When Superintendent Mosher returned, he called a meeting of the faculty to formally present me. He told them about the telegram I had received. My first remark was to say while I am glad to be here, in another way I was sorry not to be in Cazenovia with my wife. They all applauded and congratulated me.

A school assembly was called for Friday morning and Superintendent Mosher introduced me to the students. It was quite a change from the study hall assembly of less than 100 students to a well equipped large auditorium filled with over 500 students and faculty. For my first talk to the students I used a play on the word *right*. I said, "There are different kinds of *right*. I did not mean *write* to get them to produce a theme in English class, nor to put inscriptions on the toilet walls which needed no decorations." I then told the story of how a famous Englishman visiting this country was asked his impression of America. His reply was, "I was struck with the people always saying "all right" to everything." I said, "It is true we use the expression a great deal, even if we do not believe everything is perfect. But the *right* I mean is R-I-G-H-T, as opposed to wrong. Doing right is the basic rule, I believe, for running a school. I do not believe in a lot of rules and regulations, for if you do right and I do right, everything will be fine. I promise you that I will do my part and I ask all of you to do yours. Just DO RIGHT."

When I finished I received a big round of applause and to my surprise, one of the boys rushed onto the stage and led the school in a high school cheer in my honor. I found out later that this was a custom of the school, but at the time I was thrilled at the gesture. That evening the *Saratogian,* the city daily newspaper, carried a report of my talk, saying I made it semi-humorous, but made my point clear. I was surprised, as I didn't know a reporter was present. It was my first experience in having my speech reported.

Since the school year was well along, I found the school well organized, so my first step was to become acquainted with the system. There were over 30 teachers on the faculty and the larger departments, such as English, history and commercial, had heads of these subjects. There were also all the subjects of a modern high school, such as homemaking, industrial arts, and physical education offered. There was a woman physical education instructor for the girls and Martin Kelly was the man instructor. Both of these instructors coached the athletic teams in their department. Mr. Beech, who taught industrial arts, was also the superintendent of buildings for the city schools.

I was informed on my first day that the Board of Education had a rule that the high school principal was to teach at least one class. Their reason for this rule was that they thought if the principal taught a class, he would remain closer to the problems of the teachers. It was news to me, but I did not protest and when I found out the former principal had been teaching a class in American History, I took it over. I thought my background in such a course at Houghton and my years of teaching civics at Minoa qualified me to do this. With good results in the Regents that June I continued teaching this subject as long as I was in Saratoga.

One problem I soon encountered came from the office of the Superintendent of Schools being in the high school building. Mr. Mosher had been in the system for several years so the teachers knew him very well. Thus, they had a tendency to take their problems directly to him, bypassing me. I blamed him for allowing this to happen, but evidently it had been a custom for a long time. I wondered if it had something to do with the former principal leaving. I tried to be diplomatic about the situation but I let it be known early I didn't like the arrangement. When a teacher told me she had the permission of Mr. Mosher to do something, I would ask her why she had gone to him and not asked me first. Many teachers got the point, but a few never cooperated.

Miss Gorman was the head of the English Department and also the Assistant Principal. She had been in the school for a long time and many teachers looked to her for guidance. She was from a real Irish family, good natured with a ready wit, but could on occasion be very outspoken. When I met her she greeted me warmly and when I said I was Scotch Irish, we hit it off at once. She agreed with me that the high school problems should be settled in the high school office, and she didn't hesitate to tell a teacher off if she learned that they had gone to the superintendent first.

As soon as school was out on Friday afternoon of the first week, I took off for Cazenovia. It was still winter and the road was almost blocked with big snowdrifts over the hills near Cazenovia. There were no snow plows then to keep the roads open, and only two ruts made by the cars to follow. So it was late at night when I arrived, but Norah's father was up looking for me. The next morning I hurried to the rest home to see Norah and the baby. Everything seemed to be fine, although Norah said she had a more difficult time than before. The baby looked fine and we both remarked about her long fingers, deciding she must be destined to be a musician.

When I returned to the house, Norah's folks quizzed me about Norah and the baby. Then, when I was so tired I took a nap after lunch, they jumped to a conclusion that something was wrong. To convince them all was well, I took Norah's mother over to see for herself. But I don't think they were fully satisfied until Norah was home from the rest home.

After spending a couple of days in a hotel when I arrived in Saratoga, I found a good rooming house where they served good meals. As soon as possible I called on Ann and John and they told me the downstairs apartment where they lived at 89 Court Street was still for rent. Ann was anxious for us to take it so she and Norah could be together. I looked it over and while the arrangements were not ideal, it was a marked improvement over what we had in Minoa. There was a large living room, a dining room with a large kitchen in back and two bedrooms in front. There was a small toilet off the kitchen, not the best location but still usable. Across the front of the house was a large porch which was to be shared by the people in both the upper and lower apartments. The whole house was heated by steam and since the boiler was in the basement, it would be my duty to service it. The apartment was furnished with electricity and running water and manufactured gas for the kitchen cooking stove. The house was owned by Mrs. Starbuck, wife of the owner of the largest department store in the city. I met her and rented the place beginning the first of April. That was the earliest Norah wanted to move with a new baby.

Coming as I did the first of March, the end of the school year came fast. I was told it was the custom for the Superintendent of Schools to select the commencement speaker and to preside at the exercise, which was held in the evening. My part was to present the class to the president of the board of education and read their names as he gave out the diplomas. I was learning that I was not number one in the system as I had been.

301

When I got to the school auditorium the night of commencement, I got a real shock. I discovered that the superintendent and all the members of the board of education were dressed in tuxedos. I had put on my dark blue serge suit, which I thought was right for the occasion. When I saw the situation I asked Mr. Mosher why he hadn't told me they dressed so formally. He replied, "In Saratoga we always wear tuxedos for anything that comes in the evening and I thought you would know." I felt rather disturbed, but when I thought about it, I decided I was right. After all, I was part of the high school and I was dressed like the boys in the class. I talked with John White about it and he agreed with me, although he said he had to buy a tuxedo after coming to Saratoga. Later I did also, but I never wore it for school functions. The result of all this was the next year the men on the board announced that they had been wanting for some time to get out of those "monkey suits" for commencement, and "if Calhoon can get away with it, so can we." After that all wore business suits. It was a change I made in Saratoga that I didn't plan.

When the summer vacation came, we decided to stay in Saratoga, first because Dorothy was so young we thought it better not to move her, and second, we were curious to see what it was like there in the summer. Ann and John were also staying, so we would not be alone. We had been told that most of the Saratogians got out of the city during the summer, renting their houses furnished to the summer visitors, especially followers of the races in August. We soon learned that Saratoga Springs was like two different cities. Most of the year it was a place of business for the surrounding farming area, then in the summer months it was a resort town. The residents who owned property depended for a large part of their income on renting their houses for large sums while they moved to camps on Saratoga Lake or places in the mountains.

Right after Memorial Day the life of the city began to take on renewed activity. Boarding houses and hotels which had been closed all winter began to open. Both men and women were hired to clean and air out the rooms, preparing for the summer trade. The first group to come arrived in June when hundreds of Jewish people from New York City came for the waters. Most of them were overweight and came to drink the water to reduce. They were typical New Yorkers, and expected to take over the sidewalks when they congregated around the drink halls, all talking at once in loud voices. They would block the walks so if one wanted to get by he either had to walk around in the street or elbow his way through the crowd. As far as I could see, neither method made the slightest difference to those people.

The Saratoga waters were a big attraction, not only to these people, but also to the many tourists. Of course we had to try them. Some were real strong and very cathartic while others were mild, and after one learned to use them, very pleasant. The water from one spring in particular was served at almost every luncheon or dinner affair in the city. The first few times I tasted this water I could drink only a few sips, but after a time I would drink it like a native.

There was one place we learned to love. It was called the valley of springs or geyser park. It was just outside the city limits and there were several of the naturally carbonated springs in this little isolated valley. One shot some twenty feet in the air, so it was called a geyser. Another called Hayes Well was walled and piped so it was easy to fill a cup to drink on the spot or fill a thermos jug to take home. There were a number of picnic tables around the park and we often enjoyed using them for a summer outing. One interesting fact developed. While the rest of us had to learn to drink the water, Dorothy, as a baby, took to it at once and drank it freely.

Saratoga Springs became famous in the early history of the country because it is one of a few places in the world where naturally carbonated springs are found. Before the white man came, the Indians had found these springs and were using them as health centers. So did the early settlers until it became a famous watering resort for the rich and famous people of our nation. Big hotels were used to house the visitors and the city grew to service them. Several commercial companies moved in to bottle the waters from different springs and sold them to cure all sorts of ailments. So greedy were some of these outfits that they didn't wait for the natural flow of a spring but began to sink pipes to pump out the water. The result was that several springs were pumped dry. Finally the state took control and now regulates all uses of the waters.

By the end of July the Jewish people had left and on the first of August the racing crowd moved in. Overnight Saratoga became a different city. All summer there had been a crew working to get the famous race track ready but now came the horse trainers, jockeys, stable boys and bookmakers, plus a flock of just plain "hangers on" who are found around every track. We felt like strangers in a strange city.

One incident happened that summer which showed what the place was like during the racing season. John White and I were sitting one evening on the front porch talking while the women were busy inside putting the children to bed. Directly across the street, but back in a grove of big maple trees, was a big brick house. We heard that this place had been rented to people from New York City. We noted that the party consisted of several men and their girlfriends. Evidently the men had come to attend the races while the women came for a good time. For a week or so we could hear them having wild parties every night until late hours. That night as we sat on the porch the girls were getting ready for the evening. The lights were on and the curtains up, so from the spot where I sat I could see one of the windows between the big trees. The young women were parading back and forth in the room dressed only in their birthday suits. One gave me a good view when she paused before a mirror to powder herself.

Knowing it was only at certain spots these windows were visible, I didn't know whether John could see what I saw or not. Since he was a minister I didn't think I should call his attention to the sight. All the time it was almost impossible for me to keep up my end of the conversation. After a time the girls got dressed and turned out the lights so the show was over. Some twenty years later when John became an assistant minister in Rochester, New York, we drove out to see them. While the women were chatting inside, John and I sat on his porch visiting about our experiences in Saratoga Springs. Finally he asked, "Do you remember sitting on the porch of our house on Court Street one summer evening?" When I replied, "Yes," he continued, "Did you by chance see what I saw through the trees that night?" Then when I said, "Yes, I saw a show but didn't know you could see it also and I had a hard time knowing what I was saying," we both had a good laugh. He said, "I couldn't even remember what we were talking about."

A few nights after that show there was a terrific fight between the men and the girls at the house. The yelling and screaming continued so loud and long that the police came to stop the noise. From what we could gather, the men had lost a lot of money at the track and they wanted the girls to cook the meals to save expenses. The girls refused as it was not part of the bargain they had made. The next day the girls packed up and left while the men were at the race track. The men stayed, but all was quiet the rest of the summer.

During the racing season the jockeys are carefully screened from the public. By chance one of the leading jockeys had rented the house next door to us that summer. I noticed he was accompanied by a husky bodyguard everytime he left the house. They never looked our way, but one morning the jockey came out the side door just as I came out a corresponding door of our house. We looked at each other and I was on the point of saying, "Good morning," when I saw the bodyguard hastily appear. I thought it better to look away and say nothing. Out of the corner of my eye I could see the guard glaring at me as I walked toward the back yard. That was the closest I ever came to meeting a jockey.

I did attend the races a few times and found it interesting to watch the horses and the crowds. I didn't know enough to do any betting, but when George and Nellie Hayes came to see us, I took him to the race track and for fun we did make some small bets, but didn't win.

Soon after I came to Saratoga, I was told by more than one person that if I wanted to succeed I should join the Presbyterian Church. The minister of this church was an outstanding person and had a lot of influence in the city. Then because John was the assistant minister of that church and was known to have suggested me for the position, it was assumed that I would join. However, the way it was said turned me against the idea. We had joined the Methodist Church in Minoa, and the board knew that, so I felt it was only right that we should have our membership transferred. The Methodist minister was about our age and we both liked him, so we became members. We became more or less active as Norah took a primary Sunday School class, and for a time I led the men's group.

When I was pressured to join the Presbyterian Church, I asked Superintendent Mosher about it, as I knew he was a member. I always remembered his reply. "Join any church you want to. Personally, I would rather be known as a good school man than a member of any particular church," he said. Soon after we were settled, we got a good laugh out of another church situation. One day while I was in school a young priest of the leading Catholic Church rang our doorbell. When Norah answered, he greeted her and asked if she was Mrs. Calhoon. When she replied, "Yes," he continued, "Father wants to know why you folks haven't been to church." Norah was surprised but said, "Oh, we belong to the Methodist Church." The young priest gasped and muttered, "I'm terribly sorry. We thought your name being Calhoon, you were Irish and surely Catholic." He apologized over and over.

The high school was large enough to have good teams in most of the sports, such as football, basketball and track. When I arrived the first of March that year, I found the basketball team playing for the league championship. It was the last game of the season and against Glens Falls, the leader in the league. Our gym was packed with an overflow crowd, so I was busy helping to control the situation. Martin Kelly was the coach and I had no intention of interfering with his job. I didn't go to the locker room at intermission thinking I might distract his efforts at coaching. Then, when our team lost the game I was openly criticized for not going down and telling them how to win. The *Saratogian* had published how successful I had been coaching basketball so some people thought I would be able to give the team the magic word. I had a talk with Kelly and let him know I had no intentions of interfering with his coaching. He had been doing a good job so I told him to just keep it up and only if he asked would I make suggestions. Nevertheless, rumors persisted that all was not well between us. This was augmented during the second season when Kelly was sick one week and asked me to take the team for an out-of-town game. In the report of this game the paper mentioned that I had charge of the team and did a perfect job. My interest in the teams remained high and I attended all home games and some away, but I told the superintendent and members of the board that I was not the coach.

I did help with the track team, since many of the meets came at the same time as a baseball game. I also introduced my liniment to the boys on the team, and it proved very popular. I was with the team on May 21, 1927, at a big track meet in Glens Falls when we heard the news that Lindbergh was flying solo over the Atlantic. Every so often bulletins would come over a loudspeaker telling of his progress. Actually, there was more interest in his flight than in the meet.

I left the meet after the races were over, but some of the field events were still in progress. It was then a tragic event took place. One of the officials for these contests was a retired physical education man from the Glens Falls schools. He had been in the system for many years and was very popular. He liked to keep in touch by helping at the home meets. Although he was quite active, he had lost much of his hearing. As the discus throwing was in progress, one of our boys released the plate just as this man, without looking, walked out on the field. Everyone yelled, but he couldn't hear them. Everyone stood paralyzed as the discus flew straight at the man, hitting him on the back of the head. He collapsed and was taken to the hospital in an ambulance, where he was pronounced dead on arrival. Everyone felt bad but agreed it was an accident and no one should tell who threw the discus. They knew he would feel bad enough without any guilt the public might put on him.

That night after I had gone to bed the phone rang, and it was a father of one of the boys on the track team. He wanted to know why his boy wasn't home yet. I replied that I didn't know but would try to find out. I tried to call Kelly, who had stayed with the team, but got no answer. By that time I had several other calls to which I could only say the bus must have broken down as there was no report of an accident.

It was late the next morning before I found out from Kelly what had caused the delay. He said after the tragic accident all the rest of the meet was called off. He got the team on the bus for home, stopping at a restaurant for a meal. They were on the road when the State Troopers stopped the bus and made them pull into the State Police station, which is on that road. The troopers ordered everyone off the bus and took them into the station. They asked each boy to tell them the name of the boy who had thrown the discus, but they all refused to answer. Kelly said he was on another part of the field and did not see the accident. The police said no one could leave until they found out the name of the boy, but the boys still refused to talk. Finally Kelly insisted on making a phone call and got in touch with the school attorney, who had to drive to the police station and take steps to have the team released. It was after 2 a.m. before the boys got to their homes, so the parents had reason to worry. The State Troopers came to my office and tried to get me to find out the name of the boy, but I refused. As far as I know, none of the boys who knew ever talked and it remained a mystery.

Dorothy proved to be a fairly healthy baby and developed fast after the first summer. After experiencing what Saratoga was like that first summer, we decided we would be like the rest of the people and get out. Norah's folks wanted us to come and stay with them. They said they missed the girls when we were so far away. Also, it would give me a chance to commute and continue my work at Syracuse University for my Master's degree. I had taken one course with Dr. Clem and was delighted to have him assigned as my advisor. Together we decided on the subjects I needed to fulfill the requirements for the degree and selected a topic for my thesis. At this time the university still required a thesis from all candidates for this degree.

It was a good summer. I attended classes in the mornings five days a week and used the early part of the afternoons to do any library work necessary. Thus, I would be back in Cazenovia by late afternoon, ready to take Norah and the girls for a swim in Cazenovia Lake. This lake is spring fed and stays cold all summer—a short dip would cool us off and "change the day." Norah's father thought we were crazy to go into such cold water, but we enjoyed it. Weekends, and sometimes in the early evening, I enjoyed some trout fishing. Chittenango Creek runs through Cazenovia, and at that time it was one of the best trout streams in the state. I caught enough nice trout to have one or more trout dinners every week. The girls loved it at Cazenovia. Their grandparents made a great deal of them, trying not to spoil them. Of course, we all enjoyed the wonderful cooking of Norah's mother. We tried to furnish our share of the food bill, but with the many fresh vegetables from Father Riggall's big garden, I doubt if we ever kept even.

This kind of summer was to be repeated as long as we stayed in Saratoga, although the last two years we insisted on living by ourselves in the old wing of the house. We felt it was too much for Mother Riggall to cook for all of us, especially after her gall bladder operation. I helped take her to the hospital in Syracuse for an emergency operation. It was a serious operation and the doctors told us she would never be strong again and would last, at best, two years. But she fooled them by living over ten years after the operation and was active until near the end.

Our old Chevy looked very shabby beside the good cars the Saratogians drove, so I began to look for something better. Fred Benedict's brother had the agency for the Hupmobile in Fayetteville and he made me a good offer on a demonstrator—I traded. It was a hard top sedan with a small trunk on the back. This '27 Hup was one of the best cars ever made, and I drove it over 150,000 miles before I gave it up. When I drove the car back to Saratoga, the school men congratulated me for my choice, so I never had to feel out of place again.

As I went through the first commencement, I discovered one fact I did not like. There was a rule that the graduates could not send out their invitations or announcements until they had passed their last examination. Since for many the last exam was on a Thursday afternoon and the graduation was on that Friday night, there was little time for them to mail their cards. I was surprised the class didn't make a fuss about it, but it had been a rule for a long time so they evidently thought there was nothing that could be done. I didn't say anything but made a survey of other schools in the area. I found we were the only school in that part of the state to have such a rule.

To bring about the desirable change, I drew up a resolution for the board to consider and gave it to Superintendent Mosher. I explained to him how I felt and also what I had learned about other schools. My resolution stated that seniors whose class marks were 75% or higher at the end of the third quarter of the year, and who were carrying the required subjects, would be graduated. Seniors who did not have 75% marks would have to pass the required examinations in order to graduate. I explained that such a plan was more fair to the good students, and they would be free to send out invitations well in advance of commencement. It did not deprive any student from qualifying and would be an incentive for seniors to maintain good school work. Superintendent Mosher thought it over and agreed to present it to the board. I was not asked to be present or answer any questions. The resolution passed, and I was notified.

The second year at Saratoga was the time the state department announced a new plan of requirements for a high school diploma. This plan was patterned after the college requirements for a major and minors. Three years of English was required but not considered a major. Majors were three years of work in such fields as history, mathematics, science, foreign language, commercial, etc. Two minors were also required, consisting of two years in any of these fields. This was a major change in the requirements for a diploma, as heretofore it had mainly been the number of credit hours.

When the new requirement was published, I was asked to appear before several organizations in the city to explain the ruling. It was evident that the people of the city were interested in knowing about the schools. As a result of my speaking, which was a new experience, I was invited to join the Lions Club. This was the newest service club in the city and composed of men my age. I did join and became an active member as long as I was in the city.

As I studied the requirements for the high school diploma, I got an idea of composing a four year report card for each student. The card was designed to show all the subjects offered in the school, grouped in the various major fields, and a place for the grade of each subject completed. Thus, a student could follow his progress toward meeting the new requirements. I had the card printed and it became very popular. I took a copy with me when I attended the secondary school principal's convention in Syracuse during Christmas vacation. I planned to show it to the Bardeen Company, who published a number of school supplies. I thought I might sell them the idea, but I found another company had a similar card on display. I was too late with a good idea, but my school benefited.

Near the end of my first full year in Saratoga we were all surprised to have Superintendent Mosher announce his resignation in order to take a position in the State Department in Albany. This posed a problem for me, as I had to decide whether to apply for his position as superintendent or remain as principal of the high school and work under a new person. The board was in no hurry to appoint a new superintendent and asked me to act as clerk of the board during the summer. This was one of the jobs the superintendent had been doing. I acted at the meeting of the board before leaving for Cazenovia and then made a special trip back for the August meeting.

It was at this meeting that one of the board members asked me if I wasn't going to apply for the superintendent's position. My answer was I was happy with my position as high school principal and felt by this time they knew me and if they offered me the position I would give it serious consideration. I was naive as I thought they would be looking for a man to fill the position, not wait and see who would apply. Anyway, I didn't feel I wanted such a job and had better stick to the place where I felt right.

The result was that late in August the board filled the position with Horace Crandall, who had been the supervising principal of the Union School at Corinth, New York. This was a small school system with both grades and high school in the same building. Actually, his experience was much the same as mine, but longer, and he was older than I was. I didn't meet him until school opened in September. I tried to make him welcome, but right away a I felt a coolness toward me. From things I heard, he was both jealous of my popularity and resentful because he thought I had been after his job. Again, it was unfortunate that his office was in the high school building where he could hear and see all that took place. It wasn't long before he let me know I should run the school as he had in the rural community. He never did understand a big active city high school. We never came to open differences, but he used a more subtle method. Since he was new, the teachers didn't go to him as they did with Mosher, but he began to call them in to quiz them about the operation of the school. I thought the school was running fine and that I had such a good standing with the board I didn't need to worry about the situation.

As long as Mosher was in Saratoga, he did all the hiring of new teachers. I was not consulted, so had no say in whom I worked with. But Crandall had a different method. Instead of consulting me directly, he would send a member of the board with a batch of applications for us to go over together and make a recommendation. I was pleased to be consulted, but thought the method strange. To show how little things can influence the choice of a teacher, I met one day with a dentist member of the board to consider applications for a mathematics teacher. In my opinion there was one applicant who stood out and I let it be known that he was my choice. However, the board member didn't agree and when I pressed him for a reason, he said, "I don't like his appearance. From his picture, it shows he is parrot mouthed, probably has poor teeth." I wanted to laugh, but I saw he was serious and had to convince him that we were looking for someone to teach, not to bite. Our selection was approved by the board and this man became a very successful teacher. Then after a couple of years his wife wrote me a sorrowful letter. She said her husband had been taken to the T. B. hospital in Oneonta, New York. She said the doctors gave them a lot of hope that he could be cured and she asked me to contact the board and request a leave of absence for two years. I made the request to the superintendent and board, but had to fight them before they would grant the request. After I left the city, he did return and some years later was elected superintendent of schools. I am sure he never knew how I had to work to save his position, but he was worth it.

I was engrossed with the many activities of the high school and it took Miss Gorman to inform me how they felt. After I went with her to an American Legion oratorical contest held in Troy, in which we had a boy competing after winning the district meet, she thanked me for being there and added, "We never had a principal who took so much interest in everything that goes on in the school."

I couldn't help but be interested in a unique experience that the City of Saratoga Springs went through these years. A group of reformers in the state became powerful enough to pressure the legislature to pass a bill outlawing all forms of gambling, including betting at a race track. When the governor signed the bill, the people in Saratoga became panicky. They were sure if no betting was allowed the races would be stopped and the city would lose its most valuable attraction. The expression was heard on all sides, "Saratoga would be a ghost town and the grass would grow in the streets."

The whole city was in a dark mood when the minister of the Baptist church, a popular figure in the city, announced that on a certain Sunday night he would hold a special service and preach on Saratoga gambling. I went early to hear him and just got inside when the doors were closed to an overflow crowd. I don't remember all he said, but I recall how impressed we all were with his common sense approach to the problem. He prophesied that the races would continue and although the church did not approve of gambling, it too would continue. He ended on a high note of optimism for the future of the city.

Actually, what he predicted came true. The races were held, the crowds came, and while no money was exchanged at the track, gambling continued. The bookies established places of business outside the track and they had runners who exchanged pieces of paper with their customers on the premises. It became a perfect example of how legislating against something will not change a social custom. Just as a few years earlier the prohibition amendment to the constitution never stopped drinking, so this law never stopped betting. This is a fundamental principle which many people never seem to understand. I found the same kind of thinking among teachers. As a principal many times I had teachers come into my office and say we should have a rule against something they didn't like. My reply was usually, "The easiest thing I can do is make rules, but a rule is no good unless it can be enforced. But more important, will it cure the root of the trouble? Let's remove the source of the trouble, then we won't need a rule." I know I never convinced some, but I found others who saw the point and agreed with me. Of course, after a few years the law against betting was repealed, and it is now legal. The Saratoga race track betting tradition lives on.

Some other activities outside the school became important in my life. One was taking a small part in the dedication of the Saratoga battlefield. The site of this important battle of the Revolutionary War was acquired by the state and ready to be opened as an historical site. An experienced director was engaged to put on a huge pageant for the dedication. He contacted the various villages and cities in the area and asked them to recruit volunteers to put on certain parts of the pageant. Saratoga Springs was selected to have a group representing a session of the Continental Congress and I was asked to join this group. We were given the period costumes to wear and were only required to meet as if in session and receive a messenger from the Boston battle grounds. The only speaking part was for someone to shout, "A horse, a horse!" as a rider appeared in the distance. The director tried several of us out for this part, including me, but my voice didn't carry well enough to suit him, so he selected another man, for which I was pleased.

The dedication was held on a Saturday near the date of Burgoyne's surrender, which was October 17, 1777. The formal program came in the morning with many state and federal dignitaries taking part. The pageant started at one o'clock and lasted all afternoon. All events took place on a broad, flat plain with a hill rising on one side to form a natural amphitheater, so the spectators had an excellent view of everything. I put on my costume and took Norah and the girls in the car early in order to get a place to park. State troopers were directing the heavy traffic and all who were in costume were given preference to park near the center stage. It was a bright sunny day and we sat on a blanket on the hillside to watch the show. It would be an hour before I was to report, so I could stay and explain to the girls what we were viewing. First, after a brief announcement over a raspy loudspeaker, came a group representing the first settlers. The people were dressed in homespun gowns and deer skins. They were driving a real team of oxen hitched to an old, two-wheeled cart, with the men, women and children walking alongside. They moved across the big stage and then others followed, representing the growth of the colonies.

The number of people involved and the scope of the pageant as it progressed was impressive and considering there was no such thing as a dress rehearsal, things moved with surprising ease. However, there were a few hitches, which to us in the pageant were amusing. First, the announcer was a prominent Saratogian and right after his opening statement, which was difficult to understand, we were startled to hear him say in a loud voice, "This is a damned poor copy, can't someone find a better one?" He was evidently talking to someone to the side and didn't realize his remarks were being broadcast.

When it came time for the Congress to meet, I left and joined the group on the front stage. We acted as if in serious discussion when a rider was seen galloping across the fields in the distance. The man selected gave forth his cry of "A horse, a horse" just as the rider approached a fence. This fence was supposed to be cut so the rider

311

could get through, but the farmer refused to have it cut. The rider was a man from Saratoga who owned a jumper, so he thought he could jump the fence and arrive on schedule. But when the horse saw it was barbed wire, he refused to jump, so after two tries the man had to dismount and crawl through the fence and walk the rest of the way.

In order to keep the various groups in the pageant moving at the right time, the director had dug some pits at key points and connected them with telephones. In the pits he had selected prompters who would relay his messages. It had rained the night before and some water had collected in these pits. Wooden racks were hastily made to put on the floor of each pit to keep the prompters' feet dry. Miss Gorman, the assistant principal of the high school, was a prompter in a pit near the center of the stage. Soon after the start of the pageant, to everyone's surprise, Miss Gorman popped up out of the ground. She was waving her arms so two of the stage hands rushed out to see what was the trouble. They looked down in the pit, then escorted her off the stage.

On Monday morning following the pageant Miss Gorman was surrounded by people asking what had happened. She explained, "You know there was some water in the bottom of the pit and I was standing on the makeshift rack. After the pageant started I heard a strange noise below my feet. I looked down and there was a snake swimming in the water. I called on the shades of St. Patrick but it did no good. I scrambled out of that place and not for all of Ireland would I go back." We all got a good laugh out of it, but I wonder what the spectators thought.

The final event was a mock battle, but it was getting late and clouding up, so we decided to leave and beat the heavy traffic. But others had the same idea, so it was slow traveling all the way home. We could hear the sounds of the guns being fired in the mock battle, but didn't mind missing it. It had been a wonderful impressive day.

I learned some valuable lessons while principal at Saratoga. One came about after John Sexton had been engaged as head of the commercial department. John came from Vermont and was not familiar with the Regents examinations required in New York State. During Regents week in January, about the middle of one morning, I heard a group of teachers who had gathered in the outer office suddenly stop their conversations when one of them called out, "Look, Dr. King is coming up the walk." There was a sudden scurrying of all, including the office secretary. I had heard some remarks about Dr. King, a prominent physician in the city. He had once been on the board of education and as such had obtained a reputation as a rough and gruff employer. I had never met the man, but walked out into the outer office to do so. A big man over six feet tall and weighing about 250 pounds strode into the office. In a loud voice he announced, "I'm Dr. King and I want to see the principal." He towered over me, but in as calm a voice as I could muster I replied, "I'm the principal. What can I do for you?" Almost shouting, he said, "I want to know why in hell my daughter was sent home and not allowed to take the Regents." I was dumbfounded, but answered, "Dr. King, I have no idea, but will find out at once." I found out it was commercial arithmetic she was supposed to take and checking the schedule, I saw Mr. Sexton was in charge of the room. Calling the room on the house phone, I asked if he was free and if so, would he come to the office. Sexton was a small man just over five feet tall and when he walked into the room and I introduced him to Dr. King, all I could think of was David and Goliath. When I asked Sexton if he had sent Ruth King home from the examination, he replied, "Yes," he said, "she had not been in his class but was coming in as a repeater and he did not have a question paper for her." All I could say was "You should have checked with me, there are ways we could have worked it out. Go back to your duties and we will talk later." I then turned to Dr. King and I said, "You see, I did not know about this but as the principal, I take full responsibility and will see that Ruth is not kept from graduating in June because of this." "That's damned decent of you," he replied, "but it's a hell of a thing to happen."

I did feel partly responsible as I should have checked Sexton's orders for copies of the examinations. I didn't realize that he would not order more than just his class size at the time. Teachers used to the system always ordered from five to ten copies extra to be sure to have enough. Of course, I had a session with Sexton and explained what he should have done and also made it emphatic that he should never make such a move without consulting me. He was a good teacher and years later he became principal of the school. I met Dr. King many times after that, especially when Ruth graduated, and we were always friendly. I never had any fear of him as the teachers seemed to have. But the important lesson I learned was if you make a mistake and are confronted, neither deny it nor try to cover it up. Admit it and make amends as much as possible. By doing so you can turn an enemy into a friend. This was a position I took in every school that I headed and I let it be known.

Miss Wells was a master English teacher in the school and while small in stature, was big in determination. Besides her teaching she was the faculty advisor for a debating team. One day she told me the team had been invited to a debate forum sponsored on the campus of a leading university. She requested permission to take the team and go. I was in favor of that but she also asked for expenses for the trip. She said the school paid for athletic teams and should do the same for debate. I agreed but told her we had no funds for such a project. I approached the superintendent, but he turned me down flat and wouldn't even suggest it to the board. So I had to tell Miss Wells it was impossible. But she found a way and the team did go. The lesson I learned was if you face a barrier that is impossible to go over, don't sit down and give up, find a way around. I called it the Wells method and I found it critical several times in my career.

Saratoga had a number of excellent teachers but to me the most outstanding was Mrs. Orra Phelps. Not only was she a master teacher in biology, but she created an interest in her students second to none. Every spring she put on a special project. She asked her pupils to search for all kinds of wild flowers and plants, which she put on display. One rule she made was, as soon as one specimen was entered, no one else was to bring in such a plant, thus teaching conservation long before the word became common. Each year I was there, one or more new plants were discovered growing in that area. She made a point of reporting such finds to the State Museum in Albany, where she became known as an expert in her field.

The last year I was in Saratoga she made an important discovery. When they began the study of fish in her class, she asked if anyone could bring in a pickerel. One boy who lived near Saratoga Lake volunteered. The next morning he presented her with his fish. She thanked him but said, "That is not a pickerel." "OK, I'll bring in another," he replied. The next morning he presented her with another, but it was like the first. When she said it was not a pickerel, the boy replied, "That is what we call them in Saratoga Lake." Mrs. Phelps asked me to look at the fish, but at that time I had done so little lake fishing I was no help. To verify her position, the class packed the fish in ice and shipped it to Albany for identification. They reported back that they couldn't identify the fish and suggested she send one to a museum in Chicago where they made a specialty of cataloging fish from all over the U. S. The boy brought in another fish and it was sent to Chicago. Late in the summer word was received that Mrs. Phelps was right, it was not a true pickerel, but they called it a hybrid between a pickerel and a great northern pike. So far as they knew, it did not exist anywhere else in the world and pronounced it a new variety honoring Mrs. Phelps by giving it her name. Unfortunately, by that time I had left, and coming during the summer vacation, this story never got the publicity it deserved.

Because of my interest and former connection with high school athletics, I was elected chairman of the North East Section of the State High School Athletic Association. It was at this time that the Association went through one of its strangest periods in its history. Dan Chase, who had been a leader in organizing the Association, retired from his office as head of the State Physical Education Department. A new man by the name of Rogers was appointed. This man had part of his education in England, and while there, he had become enamored with the so-called "Oxford Spirit" of athletics. This "spirit" claimed all games should be played for fun only, and the winners apologized to their opponents for winning.

Rogers decried the way athletics were conducted in high schools, especially the pressure put on the boys by the coaches and schools to win. Those of us who were active in the Association, knew there were violations of the adopted rules, and in some schools the coach was

314

more powerful than the principal. We also knew that many teachers complained of the pressure put on them to issue passing grades to star athletes so they could stay on a team; however we were dumbfounded by the method Rogers proposed to cure these defects. He proposed that the high school games be turned over to the members of the team and no coach or representative of the school be permitted to contact them during a game. A clever speaker, he appeared before various school administrative groups and sold his idea. Also, he forced his way with the officers of the Athletic Association.

When he called a meeting of the high school coaches in the North East Section in Albany, as chairman I decided to go. I had opposed his plan in a meeting of the secondary principals but now I wanted to see how he presented it to the coaches. He invited the coaches for a morning session to be followed by lunch and continued in the afternoon. There was a large number of coaches who accepted his invitation as the news of his idea had spread and they wanted to meet the man and give their views. Rogers opened the session with a lengthy presentation of his philosophy. It sounded like a doctor's dissertation and the audience became very restless before he finished. He then opened the meeting for questions. They came thick and fast; in a short time they had the man on the defensive. Backed into a corner, he became frustrated and seeing he was making no headway in convincing the coaches of his way of thinking, he made one of the worst "faux pas" I ever heard.

Rather angry and red in the face, the man turned on the coaches and said, "Listen, I have presented my plan to the council of school superintendents and have their approval; also to the secondary principals' association and have their endorsement [although I knew it was far from unanimous]; now I have come to you as coaches. I do not understand your attitude for you know the superintendents are more intelligent than the principals and the principals are smarter than the coaches, so I expect you to endorse the plan." If someone had opened an outside door and let in the cold winter wind, it couldn't have grown chillier in that room. I was amazed at his remark, but held myself in check. Everyone clammed up and the meeting was adjourned for lunch. It was the quietest meal I ever experienced with such a group who were usually full of conversation and stories. As soon as the lunch was over, the group dispersed and there was no afternoon session.

I never did agree with the philosophy of the new supervisor of physical education and said so on many occasions. I told the coaches and the boys on the teams in my school that while I did not agree with the rulings, we would abide by them. Under these regulations, all games were to be played with the members of the team in complete control. Neither a coach nor any representative of the school was allowed to sit on the bench once the game started. Only the captain of a team could make substitutions. It soon became evident that the players didn't like the rule as many said only members of a clique got a chance to play.

The fans didn't like it and attendance at the games fell off. Too many times an injured player stayed in the game when he should have been taken out. An example of this occurred one night at a basketball game. The coach and I were together in the stands watching when one of the players hurt his finger. We could see he was in pain and should at least be examined, but he stayed in the game. Finally the captain called "time out." I told the coach something should be done, but he felt helpless under the rules. I decided to take things into my own hands and walked out on the court. I examined the boy's finger and told him I was certain he had a fracture and to leave the game. X-rays by the doctor later confirmed my diagnosis and had he stayed in the game it might have turned into a compound fracture which could have been serious. It all added up to a situation that often happens where a so-called "cure" for an evil can produce a multitude of other problems.

As I watched the results of the new rule in operation, I prepared a paper to be given at a meeting of the North East Section. This meeting was attended by both high school principals and coaches. Some of the things I wrote were: A team representing a school should at all times abide by the rules of a game and never take unfair advantage of an opponent, but they should also play to win. They should learn to be humble in victory and gracious to the players on the team they defeat. They should remember that there is no disgrace in losing unless they have not given their best, in which case they cheat their teammates, their opponents, their friends who have come to watch, but most of all, themselves. It is the American way of playing games to always show good sportsmanship but to play to win.

The coach of a team is expected to abide by these principles. The coach is not only a teacher of the game but a leader in the right attitudes. The coach is judged, not only on how well his team plays the game, but also by the conduct of the players both on and off the field. No coach should think he is there to win by any means, nor to consider the players as puppets for him to pull the strings. His success is judged by how well he has taught his players to perform, not just to carry out his orders. It is his responsibility to safeguard the health and safety of the players. He is a certified teacher, the representative of the school and should have the authority to make decisions, especially concerning who is qualified and fit to enter a contest. This is something that should never be left to the high school players to decide in the heat of competition.

I concluded by saying the high school principal had a responsibility in all this. I noted that the schools which had the best reputation for clean athletics were those whose principal took an active interest. The principal should never leave it all to a coach nor should he let a coach run the school. Good teams and good sportsmanship develop when all work together.

As I gave my speech, I had the full attention of my audience and at the conclusion a big round of applause. Several principals complimented me by saying, "You are a living example of what you just proposed." After about three years, Rogers was removed from office and his rules went with him. However, some of the old evils never returned.

Along with other activities, I joined the YMCA, where I met a number of the younger business and professional men of the city. Two or three times a week a group met in the late afternoon for a volleyball game. I had never played the game before, but my experience with basketball made it possible for me to catch on quickly and I was honored to be selected to be on the Saratoga team taking part in a big tournament in Glens Falls. We didn't win, but had a lot of fun and I thought it increased my standing in the community.

At the end of my second year in Saratoga John White had an invitation to become the Director of Religious Education for the State of Nebraska. He accepted, and they moved to Lincoln, Nebraska, leaving us for a time alone in the house. So one of the reasons for us to go to Saratoga didn't last. I learned a lesson to never let such personal reasons be a factor in making a decision.

Of course, the girls were growing and being so near the same age, enjoyed playing together. Norah often dressed them alike, and they were often taken for twins, which they didn't like. I was home a lot more than I had been when coaching in Minoa, and I could spend many evenings with them. While Norah was doing the supper dishes I would take both of the girls on my lap and either read or tell them a story. I soon learned if I read a story which they had heard before it had to be perfect or they would correct me. To vary the program, I made up a number of stories, mostly about animals. I thought maybe they were sort of foolish, but Norah, who was listening while she worked, said they were good. I never recorded them, so they all died in mid-air.

Several times I was elected by the teachers in Saratoga to be a representative to the House of Delegates of the State Teachers Association. One year the session was held in Troy and I attended. The Association had a committee working on a plan for tenure and was to make a report at this meeting. When the president called for this report, he learned that the chairman of the committee was not present. He asked if any member was present, and a young man rose, saying he was a member but did not have a copy. The secretary produced a copy so the young man was invited to the platform to read it.

When the young man began to read, one of the most embarrassing situations developed that I ever saw in such a meeting. The word tenure was new to many teachers and it certainly was to this man. He started in by saying, "Mr. President, the committee on *te-nure* begs leave to submit the following report." Everytime he came to the word tenure, he pronounced it as if it rhymed with "manure." At first everyone listened to see if they heard right, then as the reader continued to repeat te-nure this and te-nure that, a silence fell over the auditorium. Some of the men began to shake with suppressed laughter while the women got red in the face and looked down. At last the reading was complete and the president arose and said, "What do you wish to do with this report?" An elderly, grey-haired District Superintendent, evidently from a farming area, rose and said, "Mr. President, I move that the report be spread on the minutes of the secretary and when dry, tomorrow, it be removed so we can take action." The auditorium exploded with gales of laughter. Even the women couldn't refrain. It was funny all right, but I often wondered how that young man felt when he learned what created such an outburst.

Soon after this, the legislature passed a tenure law for teachers. Like many laws, it benefited some but worked against others. The law placed all teachers who had been in a position for three or more years on tenure. They were secure in their jobs and could not be removed without a hearing. All other teachers and principals had to go through a three-year probationary period. During this time the board could fire them at any time without giving a reason.

Many school boards in the state strongly opposed the law and declared they would never give any new teacher tenure. This was the position that the Saratoga Springs board adopted. Since I had started my work at Saratoga on March 1, 1926, the board figured my probationary period would be up on March 1, 1929, and if I worked after that I would be automatically on tenure. In addition there were three teachers who had not been there for the three years. In the middle of February, I was the first to be notified. I was stunned. Other than some criticism that Crandall had made, which I didn't consider serious, I thought everything was fine.

Crandall was the one to inform me and while he pretended to be sorry, I couldn't help feel that he was pleased. Norah was sick in bed with the flu and when I couldn't sleep that night, she knew something was wrong, so I had to tell her. As soon as possible I went to see each member of the board. They would not talk; just blamed it on the superintendent and he blamed it on the board. No news of this came out, but as the time passed I prepared to clean out my desk, ready to leave. I had no hopes of finding another position at that time of the year, and with a growing family I was feeling pretty low. I remembered what the young man had called the law and I was ready to agree with him that it not only rhymed with manure, but it was just that.

318

Then just a few days before March 1, one of the board members, who was also a member of the Lions Club, and whom I thought was a good friend, came to me and said he had talked to the others and if I would give them a written resignation to take effect at the end of June, 1930, they would let me stay for that time. They said it would give me more time to find another job and they would not have to give me tenure. I thought it over and while I had no reason to resign, I knew that according to the law, even if I wanted to fight their decision I had little chance of winning. I also thought that in a year and a half I would be able to find another job or convince the board to give me tenure. So I gave them a resignation as requested with the understanding that neither of us would release any information about it before the last of the school year in 1930.

I continued on through the year, doing all I could to make the board see how successful I was. There was no hint of what had transpired and I took hope that all would end well. I spent the summer taking courses at Syracuse University, nearing the end of my requirements for the Master's degree. At that time the University still required a thesis for this degree and after consulting Dr. Clem, I chose a topic based on a survey of the junior high schools of the state on what they were doing to meet the problem of individual differences. Together we devised a long questionnaire to be sent to all such schools in the state. I wanted to send this questionnaire out while I was still the principal at Saratoga Springs, so I could use my letterhead in the covering letter. I secured a list of the junior high schools from the state department, and I mailed each a copy of the questionnaire, together with a self-addressed envelope for a reply. I received nearly a 70% reply, an unusual number which astonished the professors in the Teachers College.

During my last year the WCTU held its state convention in the city. Norah's mother, an active member, came to stay with us so she could attend the meetings. As was the custom, conventions meeting in the city invited the mayor to give a welcoming address. Perhaps he didn't want to be associated with that organization, but anyway he told them he had to be out of town. They then asked the superintendent of schools, but he also said he would be away and asked me to do the honors. It would be my first experience for such an event, but I decided to try it. Norah took the girls and her mother to be at this opening session.

Since this was to be my first, I decided I'd better write my speech and have my secretary type it. Things kept me in my office until the last minute, and seeing the first page of my speech laying on the desk, I hurriedly picked it up with a number of other pages and hurried to be on time. After I was introduced, I told the ladies that I was substituting for both the mayor and the superintendent of schools, but I was there to bid them a warm welcome to the city. I continued by saying they were such a well known organization that WCTU was almost a word in our language. To show this, I related how, when an English class in the high school was asked to write a short essay to enter a contest their organization was sponsoring, I overheard one boy whisper to another, "How do you spell WCTU?" The ladies responded with a good laugh, so I felt I had a good start. I then began to read my formal speech. When I finished the first page and turned to the next, I discovered, to my consternation, that it and all the following pages were blank. I hesitated for a second or two and then said, "I guess my secretary liked my speech so much she decided to keep it." Then I learned something very important to me. I knew what I had written and proceeded to give it as if it was extemporaneous. At once I had the attention of the whole audience, which I didn't have when reading. From that time on I never read a speech nor tried to commit one to memory. I learned I was far better off to think through what I wanted to say and then only use notes. After the session was over, both Norah and her mother said I did very well and then later, when the convention adjourned, I met the president of the organization and she thanked me for appearing and said she thought my speech was the best of any they had heard. Since I had it all typed, which I found when I got back to my office, I sent it to the State Teachers' Association Magazine, and it was published that June.

Every spring when I could get away, I did some trout fishing. I met a real estate salesman by the name of Hal who liked to fish and hunt and he invited me to go with him to the Kayaderossera Creek, a fairly large stream about ten miles west of the city. It was reported to be the best trout fishing in the area, but as such was heavily fished. When I learned to find my way around the area better, I decided to explore some of the small streams which ran into the large creek. To my delight I found these streams hardly fished at all, and several times I had my limit in a couple of hours.

It was my last year in Saratoga when I found the best of these streams. It was a very small brook coming down off the side of the mountain and flowing down through a meadow plunging over a series of falls. It looked as if years ago the limestone rock had been quarried out, leaving deep pools into which the stream fell, making these falls. Dropping my bait into these pools, I pulled out fat, 12 to 14 inch trout. It was a case of pulling them straight up as it was impossible to get down to the water's edge, therefore many wiggled off the hook, falling back into the pool. But I landed enough to have my limit.

Of course, I had to show my good catches around, but was very vague as to where I got them. Hal had been a good friend, taking me with him with his bird dog when hunting for pheasants, and also introducing me to lake fishing on Saratoga Lake where I caught my first great northern pike. Since I knew it was my last year in Saratoga, I invited him to go with me on a Saturday in early June to show him my secret place. It had rained the night before, so the conditions were just right. When he started pulling up those big trout from the deep pools, he fairly danced with excitement. He looked at my line and insisted that I was not using as heavy a sinker as I should, so to please him I took one of his and put it on my line. I was on one side of the stream and he on the other when we came to the last pool. The stream rushed down some slanting rocks, then over a fifteen foot falls. On my side it was a drop of another ten feet to the big pool below. Foolishly I dropped my line into the pool just at the edge of the falls. I felt a tug and I thought my line I was snagged on something but after pulling a few times, I felt my line moving sideways, so I knew I had hooked a big fish. After a time I worked the fish up so his head broke the surface of the water. I gasped; I had never seen such a big head on a trout and I knew it was impossible to lift him up the cliff. Letting out line, I tried to back up so I could cross the stream and get down on the opposite side where there was no steep bank, but the stream was so swift over the slippery rocks I didn't dare try it. I shouted to Hal to go down to the edge of the pool and I would try to work the line over so he could grasp it. He got down and leaned over as far as possible and just as I had the line on the edge of his finger tips, the hook broke and the heavy sinker flew up, hitting him between the eyes. I saw him fall over backwards and lie still. Thinking he was knocked out, I hurried back up the stream nearly a hundred yards to find a place I could cross. By the time I reached him, Hal was sitting up, shaking his head to clear his vision. A big "goose egg" began to form on his forehead, but he recovered. He said he was right over that fish and it was the biggest trout he ever saw.

It was over twenty years before I had a chance to return to look for that stream. I found the dirt road that led to the place and followed it right to where I remembered the stream should be, but it wasn't there. I could see the area had changed a lot in that twenty years but couldn't believe that brook would dry up. I drove back and forth trying to find the place, but it was gone.

All through the years I have had a recurring dream about that place and the big trout. In my dream I feel the warm pine-scented breeze coming down the mountain side. I sense the warm summer sun playing hide and seek with the fleecy clouds chasing their dark shadows across the valley. I hear the bobolinks calling from the pasture fence while a meadow lark erupts from the green June grass, while below in the reeds bordering the brook is the loud chatter of a convention of red winged blackbirds debating their nesting rights. In the background is the sound of the brook rushing from one falls to the next. I stand on the high cliff with my line dropping to the pool below. I feel the tug and pull the head of that monster trout to the surface, then just as my line goes limp, I wake up. We both won that day. The big trout gained his freedom and I found my "Shangri La," a priceless possession.

Not long after this I began to look for another position, but the stock market crash of 1929 brought in the big depression and jobs, even in education, disappeared seemingly overnight. While I did not lose any money in the crash, a lot of people in Saratoga did, including several of the older teachers. Many others were wiped out financially, including one of the leading attorneys in the city. The whole city was stunned when this man went to the back of the golf course and shot himself. I knew him and his family very well; he had two children in the high school. One of the most difficult things I ever had to do was to meet the wife and children after it happened.

I listed my name with the Teacher's Agency and received a notice of a few openings for a principal. I applied but was met with two sayings when I went for interviews. If the job was a bigger one than I had, they would say, "Your credentials look good, but you look too young for the job." Then if the position was in a smaller school, they would say, "You are too good for this job. You would not be satisfied to stay." I did have one job as superintendent of a school district seemingly all set, but when they interviewed some of the board members, some of them must have said something to knife me.

Unable to find another job, I talked to the superintendent and to the members of the board just before their June meeting. I asked them in light of the apparent success I had in the school to reconsider and not accept my resignation. They all promised they would think about it, but did nothing and released the news. It was like a bomb shell when it hit the school. When the paper published the reason for my resignation, many of the students wanted to go on a strike to make the board change its decision, but I talked them out of it. The teachers were upset, as they thought everything was going so fine. The editor of the *Saratogian*, a good friend of mine, said he felt guilty in not having a reporter at the board meetings to learn what was taking place.

The last weeks of school were rather hectic. Wild rumors began to circulate, some of them getting back to me. None I heard had any basis in truth, such as friction existing between me and the coach and other members of the faculty. The teachers gave me a farewell dinner to which they did not invite the superintendent. They all expressed their loyalty to me but didn't know what they could do to keep me. I tried to pass off what had happened as something that most every school administrator had to face, but it was a rather sad occasion.

As soon as commencement in June, 1930, was over, I finished my work in the office and we packed our household goods to put them in storage. Loading our car with the personal things we needed, we left for Cazenovia. I planned to continue my work at Syracuse University for my Master's degree while still looking for a new position.

After the movers took our goods for storage, I went through the whole house to see that nothing was overlooked. We had been on the road for about an hour, however, when Dorothy began to fuss because she couldn't find Betty Blue, one of her family of dolls. Norah tried to help her but to no avail. We tried to console her, saying the doll must have been packed with the goods in storage and we would find her. I couldn't see any use of going back, as I had checked and had turned in the keys. Afterwards I was sorry I didn't go back to look, for Dorothy mourned her loss all summer and the sad part is we never found her doll. What happened is a mystery and although she had a dozen or more dolls, she never got over losing one.

After leaving Saratoga, we didn't go back until the class of 1931 insisted we come to their tenth reunion. It was held at Newman's Lake House on Saratoga Lake in the evening, so Norah and I were able to go. Even though I was not there when this class graduated, they claimed me as their principal. They did not invite the superintendent and gave us a warm welcome. Mrs. Phelps was also there and she presented me with a copy of *Samantha at Saratoga,* a book I had mentioned when I first went to that school. I accepted it with many thanks and consider it a prized possession. Then in 1971 this class invited us to their 40th reunion. By this time Norah was too ill to go, but I hired a nurse to stay with her and I went. It was held in the city and I was received like an old-time friend. It was at this dinner that I received one of the finest compliments I ever had. Don Peets, a member of the class, was the toastmaster and I sat beside him. Don had gone to Canada after high school and went to college in Montreal and was now a professor of education in that city. After the dinner he leaned over and said to me, "For a long time I have wanted to tell you something; now is the chance. You meant a great deal to me when I was in high school and were the inspiration of my going into education." "Thanks," I replied, "but I don't remember doing anything special to deserve that." "No," he said, "You were just yourself."

Then in 1977 I was invited to be the guest of the Class of 1927 at their 50th reunion. DeForest Lowen was a leading member of this class and had become a Baptist minister, serving a church in Utica for several years. He had married Thelma Johnson, also a member of this class. I had worked with them both in the Council of Churches so again I got a nurse to stay with Norah and was happy to go. Again I had a warm welcome and another compliment when I said to the Lowens, "It is great of you to invite me, for after all, I was your principal only part of your high school life." Both exclaimed, "Oh, you were our principal. We never think of anyone else." I received a number of compliments after my remarks to the class after the dinner, but I have to admit that it made me feel rather old when I saw these people now grandparents and most of them retired.

The class of 1927 started a trend, and I received invitations to attend the 50th reunion of the classes of 1928, 1929 and 1931. I went to all of them. I can say that the wonderful warm reception I received from all of these classes erased any feeling of resentment that I may have had because of the treatment I received from the board in Saratoga. By their actions and things they said, they made me feel I had done a good job for the high school students and after all, I was there to serve them. I am just so happy I have lived long enough to see the results.

Norah and the 1927 Hupmobile in the California Desert

CHAPTER 19

CALIFORNIA

As soon as my mother heard that I was out of a job, she wrote suggesting we come to California for the winter. She owned a house in Richmond where she had lived with her parents until they died, but had not been able to either sell or rent it. She was now the Matron of the County Detention Home located in Martinez, the county seat. She had remarried and with her husband, Bertie Rouse, and Ula as assistants, she operated the home. This was a position for which she was well qualified due to her experience with children and nursing. She said she wanted someone to be in the vacant house and if we came, we could use it rent free.

I spent the summer working on the requirements for my degree and following up every lead in looking for a job. I did have a couple of interviews but was not successful. Facing the situation late in the summer that nothing was going to open up, we decided we would accept Mother's offer and go to California. The Hupmobile I bought while in Saratoga was in good shape and we had no misgivings about driving it across the country. It had a small trunk on the back; to carry the added baggage we would need, I bought a baggage carrier to put on the running board on one side. In this we put a camp stove and cooking outfit, which we had used on many picnics, and two large suitcases. To protect them from the weather, I bought a large piece of auto-top cover and wrapped them securely. The trunk carried our food and overnight bags. The rest of our baggage and heavy coats I packed in the space between the front and back seats. This left the back seat free for the girls to ride and take naps when tired. When packed the car was full, but there was room for Norah and the girls to move around to relieve the monotony; only I was a fixture as I did all the driving.

To be sure we had everything we needed for such a trip, we did a test run over a weekend, cooking two meals outdoors. We were ready to leave Cazenovia the first week in September. Norah's mother packed a lot of food for us to take. She didn't want us to starve on the way and Norah's father wasn't in favor of our going at all. He predicted all sorts of dire things that would happen to us on such a long trip. As a young man he had once been as far west as Illinois, where he had worked on a farm but didn't like it. Of course, Norah had been at Northwestern

University in Illinois, and I had lived in the west, thus we discounted his predictions.

We were up early on a Monday morning ready for a good start. I had packed the car the night before; all we needed to add was our overnight bags. Our emotions were mixed as we were ready to get in the car. We had been leaving Cazenovia at this time of the year many times, but this was different. We knew we would not be returning for the holidays or anytime soon. There were no tears shed, but we could see that both of Norah's parents had trouble holding them back.

After we had traveled a few miles out of town our spirits began to pick up and we began to talk about the trip as an adventure. We had no timetable to meet so we could travel as far in a day as the roads and weather warranted. Instead of going straight west on Route 20, which runs through Cazenovia, we drove south and west, taking us into the mountains of Pennsylvania. On the first day we stopped by the side of the road for lunch and later found a place where we could cook our supper. It was then we discovered our first missing item, a big meatloaf that Norah's mother had prepared for us. To keep it cool, she had put it on the cellar floor and in the excitement of starting, we all forgot it. We felt bad, as we knew she would feel terrible.

Following our supper we drove a few miles farther and found a nice looking tourist home. This was our pattern for several days, as there were no motels yet built in the east. Farther west we had to find hotels, which was not so convenient, but they were the only place we could find. This was 1930 and many of the main roads were not yet paved. Miles were graveled and many times we had to detour on dirt roads. The result was we could average only about 200 miles a day. After a time we found cooking two meals beside the road took too much time, so we learned how to limit it to one a day. But one thing we were concerned about was for the girls to keep healthy and I figured eating our own cooking would be a big factor in doing this, to keep away from restaurant meals as much as possible.

Driving through the beautiful mountain area of Pennsylvania, we crossed into Ohio. I wanted to stop at Africa, Ohio, not only to check on Father's grave, but maybe see some of the people I knew as a boy. After visiting the cemetery, I stopped at the Jaycox farm where I had worked and was delighted to find Mervin was there running the place. He gave us a warm greeting and insisted we stay overnight. I didn't know his wife, but she was very cordial and gave us a big supper. That evening Mervin called his brother, who was running another farm, and others who knew me, and they gathered for a good visit.

The next stop was St. Louis, Missouri. Faye's husband, Aldo, was a railroad dining car steward and St. Louis was now his base, and Faye had invited us to stop to see them. We knew they had two children, Lucile and John, and we arrived to find Faye in bed with a two-day old daughter, Rita. I thought we should not stay under those conditions, but she had a woman in to take charge and she informed us that we were expected and they had a room all ready. Faye said she would be disappointed if we didn't stay, so we did.

It was a Friday afternoon when we arrived and Aldo got home from his run late that night. The next morning he asked me if I would like to go to the World Series baseball game. The St. Louis Browns were playing the Philadelphia Athletics that year. Of course, I was eager to go, but didn't think we would be able to get in. Aldo was sure if we left early we could get tickets and he was right. The game wasn't very exciting, as Connie Mack and his Athletics made the Browns look like school boys, but I was thrilled to be able to say I had seen a World Series game.

After we left, Norah decided to get the children out of the house and took them all to the nearby city zoo. When I got home, Norah said she was exhausted as John, then five years old, was used to running free and she couldn't keep track of him. She was so afraid he would get lost she couldn't enjoy the trip. On Sunday, after a big dinner which Aldo cooked, he took us for a ride around the city. Faye was a good sport, enjoying her visit with us and not worrying about things.

Monday morning we left in a misty rain and by the time we were out of the city, the clouds were right down to the ground. Until about noon the visibility was near zero, then as we went north and west, the clouds lifted and finally cleared off. But now we were on dirt roads which after the rain were just mud. To help the drainage, these roads were all graded so as to be high in the center and had deep ditches on both sides. It was hard enough to keep the car on the road, but when meeting a team or another car, it took all the driving skills one had to keep the car out of the ditch.

Uncle Clark was now President of Penn College in Oskaloosa, Iowa, and Aunt Nell had written us to stop to see them. I had written her when to expect us, but due to the bad roads, we were running late. Also, we were not able to cook our meals and had to go to a restaurant. One evening Dorothy refused to drink her milk and I tasted it to find it was sour. She was sick all night, and it was nearly noon before we could start again.

Driving through northern Missouri we found a farming area with only small towns which had few or no hotels. Some of the big farm houses displayed signs for tourists and we had to resort to them. The first night we found such a place where the farmer's wife gave us a big front room on the second floor and a wonderful supper. She liked to visit and filled Norah full of stories about the life on a big farm in that region. She said they had lived through one of the hottest summers on record and insisted on showing us how they had finished the basement walls, moved a stove and some furniture down there so they could live through the hot humid time. We had a comfortable bed and I was enjoying a good sleep when about five o'clock in the morning Norah shook me awake. She said she heard the cry of a terrible wild animal and wanted to know what it could be. I listened, but at first I didn't hear anything but some roosters crowing. Then I began to shake with laughter as I heard the raucous "Hee-Haw-Hee-eeee," the morning song of a jackass. "What is it? What is it?" She kept repeating, and still laughing I tried to calm her by explaining what it was. I said, "We are in the area where they raise the famous Missouri mules and they use the jackass for breeding purposes." Only when we were at breakfast the next morning and the farm lady assured her that it was their jackass that she heard did she fully believe me.

We had planned to be in Oskaloosa in time for dinner that day, but due to the delays I saw we would not make it and called Aunt Nell to tell her. She was very understanding and said to come along and she would keep our dinner warm for us. It was dark by the time we got to the town and found the president's house. They gave us a warm welcome and wanted to fix something special for Dorothy, who still didn't feel like eating. They had just one guest room. Aunt Nell had placed chairs with boards extended between them, between our bed and the wall for a bed for the girls. I remembered this was an old custom which had been used many times when we were children. The girls were tired and went to bed early, falling to sleep while the rest of us stayed up for a time to visit. When we did retire we couldn't go to sleep because of the sound of gnawing, seemingly right in the room. I got up twice to put the light on but could see nothing. Then as it continued, I got up quietly and held my hand on the light switch and when the sound started I pushed the button and sure enough, a little mouse sat gnawing at the base of the bedroom door. I called to Aunt Nell and asked for a broom and told her why. In a few minutes Uncle Clark, clad in his pajamas, appeared at our door with two brooms. By this time the girls were awake and when they heard there was a mouse in the room, they squealed and laughed, diving under the bed clothes and peeking out to see the excitement. With the two brooms Uncle Clark and I cornered the mouse and captured him. Aunt Nell was very surprised, as she didn't believe a mouse was in the house.

Uncle Clark was busy but he did take the time to show me around the campus and to meet some of the students. It all reminded me very much of Houghton. Then on Sunday we were asked to attend the Friends Quaker Church with them. I found their service quite different from the type we were accustomed to, but very impressive. The first 20 to 30 minutes were for meditation, but if the spirit moved, anyone could stand and speak. I wasn't surprised to see Aunt Nell feel the spirit and stand up to give a five minute sermonette. After the meditation period came a more regular church service with a sermon by the minister. They did have a small reed organ, but no choir so the hymns were all sung by the congregation. It was a simple service in a plain church building, but I came away with a feeling of being in the presence of true brotherhood.

After the service we had a lunch, for Aunt Nell had invited a number of their friends to a cookout in their backyard to meet us. She was her old active self, but in the eight years since I had seen them I could see Uncle Clark had aged considerably. He had taken on this position at the beginning of the depression and like all small colleges, Penn was having serious difficulties financially. He stayed on there for four more years and then with failing health and seeing no end to the problems, he resigned and retired.

Monday we left early for a day's run to Dunlap in the western part of Iowa. Leeta was expecting us for a longer stay. To be sure of the right road to Art's farm, I stopped at Aunt Adah's farm across the river from Dunlap to ask. She was married to Will Rannells, Art's brother. We arrived in the midst of a birthday party for her youngest daughter, and she insisted that our girls come in for some ice cream and cake. They were not very keen about it, as they didn't know anyone, but we felt they had to do it. While they ate, we had a chance to visit some and she gave me the directions I needed. When we got to the top of the last hill and I looked down on the farmhouse, I felt like I was home.

For several years the Rannells farm near Dunlap, Iowa, had been sort of a center for our family. Then right after the war I had spent the summer there, so it was a welcome place where we could relax. I had brought my shotgun with me as I knew we would be here during the hunting season, and Art had a hired man picking the corn, so he could spend some time going with me. Rabbits and fox-squirrels were plentiful and now pheasants were increasing. After chasing these birds around the corn fields where it was difficult to get a shot, Art took me one day to an area which was too hilly to be farmed and was still native prairie. I had read about new hunters in South Dakota, which was the pheasant capital of the west, freezing when a big flock of these birds all flushed at one time. That day it happened to me. We were following a deep gully across the open prairie when 25 or more pheasants went up together. The roar of their wings and the sight of so many surprised me so much I stood with my mouth open, paralyzed. Art laughed and laughed, but we didn't get a bird. Another time Art took me to a big oak grove on a nearby farm and we shot at a dozen big fox-squirrels with a .22 rifle. We took turns flushing out these squirrels from their nests in the tops of the trees by banging a stick on the trunk. When the squirrel stuck his head out to see what caused the disturbance the one holding the rifle popped him through the head. So we enjoyed some squirrel and rabbit pies.

The girls were having a good time also. Eula Jean was their age and Margaret took them all to see the farm animals and gave them rides on the pony. It was the first time for our girls to ride and they were thrilled. Spot was a little terrier dog who followed the children wherever they went. He wasn't much of a farm dog but kept them good company. For some reason Art had a young calf tied up in the yard and one morning when he was ready to feed it, the girls came to watch and Eula Jean begged her father to let her ride the calf. Art picked her up and sat her on the calf, but just as she settled into place, the calf gave a big jump and he had to catch her. I stood off to one side and could see why the calf jumped. Spot was back of the calf and every time Eula Jean was seated, he would dash in and give the calf a nip on the back leg. This happened several times and Art looked around to see why the calf jumped, but each time Spot would be sitting looking perfectly innocent but his eyes were twinkling. If ever a dog could laugh, he was doing it then. Finally, I had to tell Art what was happening and spoil the fun, but to me it was a perfect example that humans are not the only animals to enjoy fun.

The depression hit the farmers hard and Art and Leeta didn't have the money to buy coal, so they were burning wood from a small wood lot on the farm, plus corn on the cob when the price fell so low it didn't pay to haul it to market. After we left we heard that the bank in Dunlap failed, and the Rannells, like a lot of others, lost all the money they had on deposit. They had a rough time for several years, but kept going because they were able to get much of their food off the farm.

I had a letter from Mother urging us to get started before we hit the snow in the mountains. Norah also heard from Ann White in Lincoln, Nebraska, wanting us to stop and visit them a few days. John was still the Director of Religious Education for the state and was traveling much of the time. Ann was left alone with their children and urged us to come.

It was only a short day's drive to Lincoln and in spite of some muddy roads, we arrived before dinner. Ann was delighted to see us, especially because we were from her home in Cazenovia and she felt rather homesick. Being alone so much she had a college boy come in twice a day to take care of her furnace. Soft coal was the fuel of that area and our bedroom was right over the furnace. The first night I could smell coal gas in the room but thought with the windows up it would clear. But when on the second night it was much worse, I had to tell Ann about it. Having had experience with soft coal, I said the boy probably was closing the damper before the early gas burned off. Ann was very upset and when the boy came the next night I heard her giving him the "devil." But my suggestion worked and after that it was all right. At the end of the week John came home, so we had a chance to see him.

We were all set to start west on Monday but couldn't when Dorothy began to have urinary trouble. Ann called her doctor and Norah talked to him. He said her trouble was due to the chemicals in the city water which came from artesian wells. He said many people had this trouble when they first came to Lincoln. He said the only treatment was to get spring water from the drug store and in a week or so it would flush her system out.

I thought it was too much for all of us to stay with Ann for an indefinite time, so I called Leeta and she suggested that I bring Marjorie and return to Dunlap until Dorothy could travel. Marjorie and I were in Dunlap for ten days impatiently waiting before Norah notified us that Dorothy was well enough to travel.

330

It was now the middle of November and the weather was growing colder. Stopping in Lincoln only long enough to pick up Norah and Dorothy, we headed west, hoping to be ahead of any snow storms. We followed the Platte River across the state and I thought of all the wagon trains that had journeyed this route years before. Stopping overnight in Scottsbluff, the next day we were out of the farming area and into the rugged hilly cattle grazing country. Soon the hill tops showed white and by the time we crossed into Colorado the ground was covered. From Fort Morgan to Denver we were driving on snow covered roads, but I didn't worry as I had been used to such conditions for several winters. In the hotel that night we had a new experience. We had always raised a window at night and knowing it had grown much colder, I only put it up an inch, but the night mountain air was so penetrating I had to get up and close it before morning. The air was so sharp it took the girls' breath away.

The next morning I debated as to whether to put on my chains in case the snow got deeper, but after talking with the garage man when I filled up with gas, he said if we were going south we should be all right. The streets of Denver were almost bare, but outside the roads were covered. In those days snowplows were only on locomotives to keep the trains running. Automobiles had to make their own tracks through the snow or they didn't move. Heading south toward Colorado Springs, I thought we would run out of the snow belt, then as we climbed toward a mountain pass, it began to snow. The road was paved, but it soon became difficult to see the edge, and I slowed down to a crawl. Suddenly I made out the form of a man standing in the road waving his arms. I stopped and then saw his car in the ditch. He asked for a lift to a gas station, which he knew was a short distance ahead, where he hoped to get help. Norah and the girls were on the back seat all covered up with blankets to keep warm, so I let the man in front with me. He said he knew this road but a gust of snow had blinded his vision and he went into the ditch. He also assured me that once over the pass everything would be all right. Once at the service station, he got out and thanked me over and over, and I in turn thanked him for the information.

Thinking we would soon be over the pass, I slowly proceded. The snow was now falling so fast it was impossible to tell if we were still climbing, and I was tensely trying to keep the car in the road. Soon I began to feel the car accelerating, so I knew we were over the crest. As the car picked up speed, I stepped on the brakes, only to find they were useless. The car had become a sled sliding down a hill.

Like a curtain rising on a theater stage, a stronger gust of wind cleared the air for a few seconds. To my consternation, I saw we were at the top of a long decline and all the way down was a jumble of cars and trucks. Some were in the ditch on both sides of the road and others crisscrossed the road at all sorts of crazy angles. In the brief view I had I could see we were in a cut with high banks on both sides and realizing my brakes would not stop the car, I spotted a small opening between two cars in the ditch and managed to steer between them, stopping with a jolt against the bank.

When I determined that all in the car were all right, I buttoned up my overcoat and stepped out of the car. First I checked the front end, which was against the bank but apparently not damaged, then went back of the car to check the road. As I did so I saw why my brakes wouldn't work—that pavement was a glare of ice. My feet went out from under me and I landed flat on my back. The snow was falling so thick I could not see down the road but could hear the voices of men. Then came a big crash up the road and dimly I could see that a big truck attempting to stop had plowed into a car in the ditch. I felt lucky I hadn't been able to stop up there but felt safer as that truck provided a shield from anything else sliding down the hill.

I decided the only way I could get out of the ditch and then control the car down the hill was to jack up the rear wheels and put on chains. All the time the wind was blowing harder and while it was about 10 above zero, it felt like 40 below. The wind went right through my clothes, as I wasn't dressed for such weather, but when I was jacking up the car and putting on the first chain I found I was panting as if it was a hot day. I wondered why, until I thought, we were more than a mile high and I wasn't used to such rarified air.

With one chain on and ready to start the other, a young fellow came along and offered to help. He had a small car which was also in the ditch and wanted to know, if we could get the cars out would I let him follow me down the hill so my car would act as a brake for his car. I agreed and with his help soon had both chains on. Every so often the wind would swirl so we could see down the road and observed that a group of men were pushing the cars aside, thereby clearing a path for traffic to move.

With my chains on I backed out of the ditch and then helped my new friend get his car out. Waiting until we could see that the way was clear I started down with the small car following. Several times I felt him hit my bumper, so I was a buffer for him. At the bottom of the hill I stopped, and learned from the men working to get cars out of the ditch, that there was a country store and gas station at the top of the hill ahead. I now let my friend go ahead so if his car wouldn't make the hill I could give him a push. Reaching the top we saw the store and pulled in amid a lot of other cars.

On top of this hill the wind was stronger, so much so that I had to help Norah walk to the door. With her safely inside, I went back and putting a blanket over their heads, I carried the girls, one at a time, to the door. I went back and took the luggage off the side of the car and placed it inside for safety. Since I had no alcohol in the radiator, I opened the petcock at the bottom to let the water drain out. I was sure if I didn't, I would have a frozen radiator in the morning.

This country store was really a large lean-to built on the side of a frame house. Once inside I saw the room was packed with over a hundred people. I took off my overcoat, which was packed with snow, and took stock of the place. Along one side of the room were shelves stocked with canned goods and other supplies. On the other side near the entrance and by the door leading into the living room of the house was a glass show case containing candy and tobacco products. Near the center of the room was a big pot-bellied stove which was already red hot trying to keep the place warm. But everytime one of the big blasts of wind hit, it seemed to go right through the walls and take all the heat with it.

The man and his wife who owned the place were trying to establish some sort of order out of the confusion which existed with such a crowd already inside and more coming all the time. When the lady saw Norah with the small girls, she invited them into her house where other mothers with children had assembled. I was so grateful for this I asked the man if there was something I could do to help. He looked at me and asked if I had ever worked in a store. When I said, "Yes," he said, "Will you take charge of the candy and cigar counter before the Mexicans take it all?" My friend heard me and told the man he would look after the grocery side.

Placing myself behind the counter, I began to sell the candy and everyone seemed to accept me as a clerk. Looking over the crowd I saw the majority were Mexicans. They were in old cars and trucks forming a caravan coming from the sugar beet fields in the northern part of the state, and while heading south had been caught in the storm. Seeing that the store was under control, the owner made a trip outside, returning a half hour later to announce that he had made arrangements for all the Mexicans to spend the night in the basement of a church which was directly across the road. It was now past the middle of the afternoon but had grown dark; he lit a lantern and escorted the Mexicans out of the door. When he returned, he told us that he found a number of their women and children in the cars and when he got them all together there were over 200 people. He said the basement would be crowded but they would be warm.

There were still some fifty people left to spend the night in the store and house. Now that the men had a chance to move around, I started doing a lot of business selling candy. The owner kept busy getting coal for the stoves and looking after the chores about the house. Once in a while he would glance our way, but he seemed assured that my friend and I had things under control. At supper time the lady of the house brought out a big kettle of homemade soup, and with the bread and cookies the men bought from the grocery side, we made a meal. The lady told us she had served the women and children inside.

As night approached the wind grew stronger. It came in gusts that shook the whole building. After the men ate, there was nothing to do but find as comfortable a place as possible and listen to the storm. Everytime a big gust of wind would hit, all eyes turned to the roof to see if it would hold. Evidently this building had been constructed with such storms in mind because the corners were not only well nailed, but large steel wires were bolted to the roof. They looked like hawsers used to tie large ships to the wharf. Even then when these blasts hit we could actually see the roof rise and strain at its fixtures.

As time wore on, the word was passed that three o'clock in the morning would be the critical time. From midnight on, all watched the hands of a clock hanging on the wall of the store slowly creep around the dial. As gust after gust struck, the thought crossed my mind that now I knew how the three little pigs felt when the big bad wolf huffed and puffed to blow their house down. Indeed the storm was like a beast of prey, tearing at the den of his intended victim. The lulls between the gusts were as if he sat back on his haunches to rest and gather strength to make another onslaught.

Just before the hands of the clock read three, we could hear a bigger than usual gust coming from the west. Like a fast express train the sound grew louder as it approached. Then it struck while all eyes were fixed on the roof. The middle of the ceiling rose a few inches and the hawsers at the corners drew taut. The whole building trembled while the timbers creaked and groaned like those of a ship tossed on a stormy sea. Finally the blast passed, receding to the east. Now everyone waited anxiously to see if the next gust would be greater or less. About three fifteen the next gust hit but it was definitely smaller and the next was relatively mild. All relaxed as we were sure the center of the storm had passed, the building had held and by morning it would be calm. Then the owner came to me and thanked me for helping and suggested I go inside the house, find my wife and children and get some rest. I was glad to do so and watched his eyes grow big when I handed over the cash drawer with all the money I collected selling the candy.

I opened the door into the living room and saw the floor covered with children and some mothers sleeping under blankets. Hearing voices in the next room, I made my way to that door. The lights were on and I saw Norah and a half dozen women seated around the dining room table. To pass the time they were busy playing the old parlor game "I went to the store and bought some A." They invited me to join but after a half hour all got so tired we could not think. I folded my arms on the table, cupped my head, and fell sound asleep.

I woke up in an hour to see daylight coming in the windows. I went out into the store and listening could hear no wind. Many of the men were putting on their overcoats ready to go out to see if they could start their cars. I followed to survey the situation. All the world was white with the new snow which was piled up in solid drifts with bare spots between. The sun was about ready to appear over the horizon to the east illuminating a wide plateau in that direction. Turning to the west, I gasped at the breath-taking beauty of the serrated peaks of the Rocky Mountains etched against a cloudless deep blue sky. I stood for a minute or so admiring the sight, but was brought back to earth by the sound of engines being started. Knowing I needed water before I could start my engine, I opened the hood and was surprised to see the engine completely buried in snow. The wind had driven the snow through the radiator into a solid mass. I had to find a screw driver in my tool kit and use it like an ice pick to uncover the spark plugs. Clearing the front end I saw an icicle had formed from the petcock I had opened to drain out the water, all the way to the ground. The cold wind had frozen the water as it drained out. The man in the store had placed a large tank on top of the stove and announced anyone needing warm water to thaw their car to help themselves. I needed that water to thaw out the pet cock and was thankful to get some. I was concerned wondering if some of the water had frozen in the radiator, but fortunately when I filled, it all was OK.

Before I could get the car ready, Norah had the girls dressed and ready to go. I explained the delay and told Norah they should come outside to see the beautiful view of the Rockies. But I got a characteristic reply when she said, "I can't see anything beautiful about this country. Let's get out of here as fast as possible."

More than half the cars had left before I was ready, but it didn't matter for before we had traveled but a few miles we caught up. The wind had swept some of the road bare, but also had piled it into hard drifts in other spots. Every so often the leading cars would get stuck in one of these drifts and only by a dozen or so men pushing would they get through. Often they would have to push several cars through before a track would be made so others could follow. This happened all the way to Colorado Springs, which we reached past noon. We found a restaurant, and, half-starved, recouped with a good lunch. There was no place to find out road conditions, so all we could do was to ask everyone who might know. The best information we could learn was that no cars were coming from the south so the roads must be plugged. We found a hotel where we could get a room and I took an afternoon nap. That evening when we were eating in the restaurant a lady approached Norah and asked which way we were traveling. When we said west, she said, "I see you stay in the hotel. Why don't you go to a motel. They are much easier to get in and out and cheaper." But Norah had a fear that the rooms in a motel would be cold and damp and wasn't ready to try them.

It was two days before we had any news that the roads south were open. We talked it over and decided it would be better for Norah to take the girls and go by train to Trinidad, Colorado, which should be out of the snowbelt. We felt it was too risky to have the girls out in the cold for a long time which might happen if the roads were bad. The hotel made a reservation for them at a hotel in Trinidad, and I took them to the railroad station to catch a morning train south.

I had the chains on the car and I figured I could get through if anyone could and should cover the 125 miles to Trinidad by night at least. The road out of Colorado Springs was much the same as it was coming in; part of the road had been swept bare, then drifts which had

335

been opened for one way traffic. So I made it to Pueblo, a distance of 50 miles with no trouble. Then proceeding south out of that city I noticed there was no traffic coming from the south, which made me wonder. The middle of the afternoon I caught up to a long line of cars stopped. Looking ahead and back I counted 50 cars in line. All had been following two ruts in the snow, which had been getting deeper. Word was passed along the line that the lead car was stuck in a deep drift so no one could move.

Not far from the road was a ranch house and the rancher was out with a team of horses drawing hay to some of his cattle. A couple of men from the stalled cars walked over to see if he would use his team to pull the lead car through the drift so as to make a path the others could follow. He was not eager to try, but when they said they would collect a dollar a car if it worked, he consented. A collection of over $50.00 was taken and given to the rancher before he would try. His team was big and strong, breaking a path for two miles to where the road was bare again. The line of cars slowly followed the path and each driver waved his thanks to the rancher who stood with his team by the open road.

For several miles everything was fine then the caravan once more came to a halt. The road dipped into a ravine and the wind had piled it full of hard packed snow. Off to the side of the road a few yards the ground looked almost bare. The lead car pulled off to this spot and others followed. But when they tried to climb the opposite bank they found it too steep. Several cars tried, but their engines would stall before they could reach the top. Soon there was a large pack of cars massed at the base of this bank. It looked like a wagon-train camp.

I joined a group of men gathered to discuss the situation. Some of the younger men volunteered to stand halfway up the bank and give a car a shove when the engine started to stall. They picked out a few of the smaller cars to try and for most it worked. Then, since I had chains on, they suggested I try it. With a little help I made the top only to be disappointed for even with my chains I couldn't make it back to the road.

It was dark and everyone was tired and cold. Small children were crying with hunger and cold, and I was relieved to know my girls were not here but safe and warm. With nothing that anyone could think of to do, all crawled back into their cars and wrapped themselves in blankets to wait out the night. Then about ten o'clock we heard the sound of tractors off to the south. Headlights appeared and two caterpillar tractors pulled up near our cars on top of the bank. The operators got out and told us they were from a work force of the telephone company located in Walsenburg, a small city located halfway between Pueblo and Trinidad. Someway they learned of our plight and had volunteered to see if they could help. They said they would hook onto a couple of cars and drag them through the snow so as to make a track others could follow.

Along with the telephone workers came a man who introduced himself as the Commissioner of Public Works in Walsenburg. He came to make a survey of the situation counting the number of cars and estimating the number of people. He did not return with the tractors but declared he would ride with someone who would follow the tracks of the tractors and see if they could make it. He noticed I was the only one at the top of the bank who had on chains and was alone, so he suggested I try it and he would ride with me. He was a big burly man wearing a fur coat, which made him look like a polar bear. As we moved into the road and began to follow the tracks the tractors had made, he remarked about my sturdy Hupmobile and my ability to maneuver it through the snow. Several times the bottom of my car touched the snow and I had to back up to get a fresh start to break through a drift. We were making slow progress when some two or three miles from the city I hit a real deep drift and was stuck. The Commissioner got out and tried to shove, but I only got in deeper. Then my engine stalled and to my surprise when I stepped on the starter, nothing happened. Driving so long in low gear with the headlights on, the battery had gone dead.

Now that I was really stuck, the Commissioner said he would walk the rest of the way to the city and send out a tractor to pull me out. To make it easier to walk he took off the heavy fur coat and left it, telling me to give it to the telephone worker when he arrived. I wrapped myself in a blanket and watched him disappear up the road. I figured it would take him an hour or more to reach the city, so I just relaxed. The sounds from the city traveled over the snow covered plain as they do over open water and I could hear the tractors as they moved about and the shouts of men, although I couldn't understand what was said. I waited until after midnight when the sounds from the city ceased and the lights went out. Then I knew there would be no tractor coming to my rescue. To stretch my cramped legs, I opened the door and stepped out of the car. I knew the sky was clear, but I gasped at the brilliant heavenly view that greeted my eyes. Never before nor since have I ever seen such a myriad of stars. They were not just twinkling but bursting like a Fourth of July sparkler. For a minute it seemed I could hear them, but all was calm. It was as if I had stepped into the hushed atmosphere of a cathedral. The tune of "Stille Nacht, Holy Night," came rushing through my mind, the words were mixed German and English, but it seemed to make sense. I thought it could have been on such a night as this that Christ was born.

As I gazed I began to pick out the constellations, first the Big Dipper with its pointers indicating a bright North Star. Then came Orion with his belt and sword, followed by Cassiopeia and the Pleaides. There was no moon, but the Milky Way formed a bright arch holding up the dome of the heavenly cathedral, making the night seem bright. I saw Sirius flashing its red and green lights as if controlling the celestial traffic. Several of the planets were lined up across the sky, including red Mars, easy to identify, and I thought others were Jupiter and Saturn. Venus, a morning star, hung near the eastern horizon bright as a young moon.

Oblivious to both cold and time, I stood gazing up into the sight of a universe that existed beyond my dreams. I was alone but did not feel lonely nor afraid. Suddenly the silence was shattered by a "Yip, yip, hiiiiiii" of a lonely coyote. In a minute came an answer in the distance, and soon a chorus of the spine tingling howls of these wild prairie wolves. It was as if a discord had been sounded on a cathedral organ, but I had to admit that these animals were part of the wild west and therefore, part of the universe. Their howls might sound like a discord to me, but it was music to them.

Brought out of my reverie, I realized how cold it was and thoroughly chilled, I crept back inside my car. Wrapping myself in a blanket, I still shivered and wished the engine was on to give some heat. Without much hope I leaned forward and turned on the ignition switch and stepped on the starter, when to my delight the battery had revived and took hold. The engine started and I sat listening to it purr and giving me the welcome heat.

Disgusted to think the commissioner had forgotten me, I let the engine warm up good and decided to work my own way out of trouble, and started to rock the car back and forth. I was careful not to stall the engine again but began to gain a few inches, then a foot, then a yard until I broke out of the grasp of that drift. In order to save my battery I did not turn on my lights, but there was ample light from the stars to see the tracks the tractors had made. Slowly I crawled across the plain, working through several drifts, and when I reached the bottom of the steep incline that rose from the plain to the plateau on which the city was located, I turned on my lights. When I reached the top a half dozen men who were seated around a bonfire rose and stood in my path. They wanted to know where I came from and if there were others coming. I answered, "As far as I know I am the only one, but I made it on my own, and here is the commissioner's fur coat which he left with me." They were the telephone crew who were waiting for daylight to resume the rescue work. They took the coat and promised to give it to the commissioner and directed me to a hotel in the center of the city which was keeping its lobby open for stranded travelers.

When I entered the lobby, I saw it was crowded, for all traffic from the south had been stalled there for days. Among the crowd I saw my friend of the previous days and he greeted me and explained he got there because his small car was selected by the tractor operators to drag. When he found out I had made it on my own, he told it to others and I was surrounded, all plying me with questions about the roads.

My friend suggested that as soon as it was light we start south together, so if we ran into trouble we could help each other. I agreed but I did want to get a cup of coffee at least and to find a phone to call Norah. It was nearly seven o'clock by the time I reached the clerk at the hotel where I knew Norah was, and I thought he sounded quite relieved when I told him who was calling. He connected me with Norah's room and when she heard my voice, she burst out crying. I assured her I was all right, and she calmed down but said she hadn't slept all night, calling the office every hour to see if they had heard anything. I told her the road south was open and I should be in Trinidad about noon and would tell her all that had happened.

At daybreak my friend and I were the first cars to leave the city for the south in days. With my chains on I led the way. We found the road bare part of the time, then drifted over, but I was able to get through all, breaking the way for the other car to follow. The farther we went the better the road and before we got to Trinidad my friend who wanted to drive faster than I did pulled by and with a shout of thanks and a wave took off. I never saw him again.

I arrived at the hotel about 11 o'clock and found Norah all packed ready to leave. I hadn't had a meal since leaving Colorado Springs the day before, so I persuaded her to give me a chance to wash and have an early lunch before starting. As we ate, I told her about my experience and she told me how worried she had been. She said when it came bedtime and I hadn't arrived nor any word from me, she began to weep. The girls tried to comfort her by saying, "Don't cry, Mommie, Daddy will be all right. He knows how to take care of himself."

After lunch I loaded the car and we started for the Raton Pass. I had been hearing all the way that once over the pass we would be out of the snow belt and all would be fine. It wasn't far to this mountain pass and as we climbed there was less and less snow. By the time we started down I stopped and took off my chains and never had to use them again on our trip. Now that we were out of trouble I said we could consider it all as an adventure which we could tell our friends about. But Norah said it was a disaster and didn't want to talk about it. So I dropped the subject and began to talk about the rest of our journey.

While I never talked about it, the time I spent stranded on the high plains of Colorado affected me deeply. The view I had of the beauty, the grandeur and the immensity of the universe made a lasting imprint on the photography of my mind. Also, the nearness I felt to his handiwork made me feel closer to the Creator. Although the stars at times might be blotted out by nature's storm clouds or dimmed by the lights and smog of man-made cities, I knew they were there. I had seen them in all their glory and stood among them. Knowing this gave me the confidence I needed to face the problems of life I would meet in the future.

Now that Norah felt safe, we stopped early. With two nights and days in a row without sleep, I was exhausted and fell into bed asleep before the rest were undressed. The next morning I was refreshed and ready to travel. From Raton we went south into New Mexico until we met Route 40, the main road west. The weather was good, but the roads were not. Long stretches of these roads were under construction and detours were often for miles into desert country, deep sand and dusty.

We crossed the line into Arizona on Thanksgiving Day and just before noon we saw a sign pointing to the famous Petrified Forest National Park. As it was only a few miles off our road we followed the sign. Actually we came into the park by a back door entrance but were soon in an area where the ground was covered with chunks of the beautiful petrified wood. Pieces ranged all the way from small pebbles up to logs three feet in diameter. Since it was noon, we decided to eat our lunch, which we usually carried with us, using one of the logs as a table. Being a holiday we were alone, and it was as if we had discovered this strange place ourselves. So powerful was the effect of seeing all the remains of a once thriving forest millions of years ago, we un-consciously talked in hushed tones. I wanted very much to take a few samples, but there were signs posted all along the road warning people not to pick up anything. The sun shone bright but there was a cool breeze which would have made it an ideal day for hiking, but after our lunch which we called our Thanksgiving dinner in the Petrified forest, we got in the car and drove slowly along to see all we could. I did take some pictures of Norah and the girls perched on top of a big log. A copy of that picture hangs in my study and looking at it, I can relive that day.

Petrified Forest, Arizona—Thanksgiving Day 1930
Dorothy, Norah and Marjorie

After a mile or so we were out of the area of the petrified wood, then a little farther along I was surprised to see pieces along both sides of the road. After we rounded a curve I laughed as I saw why. We were confronted by a huge sign saying all cars must stop to register at the Ranger's office and cars were subject to search for any petrified specimens. It was clear that when people had seen that sign they had thrown out all specimens they had picked up.

When we reached the ranger station, I got out to register and the ranger on duty wanted to know if we had seen his buddy on duty in the park. "No, we were absolutely alone, a unique experience." "He must have gone for his Thanksgiving dinner," he said. Then he asked, "Did you pick up any samples?" I answered, "No, I wanted to but saw the signs. But it looks as if others unloaded by the side of the road before they got here." He laughed, "Right, they do it all the time." He didn't offer to look in my car and it was only that night when I helped the girls take off their coats that I discovered each had a small pebble in her pocket. I had to forgive them since neither could read the signs.

When we got to Flagstaff, we discovered there was no hotel, only motels. When we used one we found that what the woman in Colorado Springs told us was true. We found the rooms clean and warm and the convenience of driving right up the door was great. No longer did I have to drag our overnight baggage through a hotel lobby. We also found many of the rooms had kitchenettes so we could cook our meals. From that time on we never went to a hotel, making our trip more pleasant.

I had planned to stay over a day in Flagstaff and visit the Grand Canyon, but when I inquired about the trip, the ranger on duty discouraged me. He said the canyon had been full of smoke (fog) for over a week and no one could tell when it would clear. We passed it by.

When we crossed the California state line we were confronted by a big sign saying, "Two miles to car inspection stop. All cars and trucks must stop." This sign was repeated every half mile until we came to a drive-out with a large platform manned by state troopers. When I pulled in, the first question they asked me was, "Do you have any fruit in the car?" I answered, "No, why?" They informed us that no fruit could be brought into the state as it might bring a disease to their fruit crops. They said they would have to inspect all our baggage and to put all on the platform and open each one. They also wanted to know where we were going and did we know anyone. When I said we were on the way to see my mother in Martinez, they said no more.

I wasn't happy about unloading all our baggage but had two suit cases out and open when we heard a car coming from the east at a high rate of speed. Everyone looked up to see a woman with a big picture hat driving an open car. It was evident she had no intention of stopping, so all the troopers jumped up, whistles blew, one shot his revolver in the air, and one ran for his motorcycle. He caught the woman and forced her to come back. All this time the troopers were so intent on watching the woman they forgot all about me. I hurriedly shut the cases I had opened, put them back in the car and drove off. Nobody said a word so we got by without being inspected.

We crossed the Mojave Desert and headed for Los Angeles. Ethel Bryner had been a student at Houghton when we both were there, and she had corresponded with Norah off and on through the years. She had been married but was now divorced and living alone in North Hollywood. She wanted us to stop and see her and said we could use her bungalow while she was working days. We found her house in the evening and she gave us a warm welcome and for three days we had a delightful time, getting some rest, catching up on some needed laundry, and enjoying trips around the city she took us on. I knew that Ira Bowen from Houghton was at the California Institute of Technology in Pasadena and being so close, I decided one morning to try to see him. By the time I found the place and the building in which he had an office, it was nearly 11 a.m. His name was on a door marked Assistant President. I walked in and told his secretary who I was and she called him on the phone. She turned and said, "Go right in." I hadn't seen him since he was a high school student at Houghton and I was very impressed to see a distinguished looking gentleman seated in a beautiful big office.

Ira gave me a warm welcome and insisted that I go to lunch with him. Afterwards he took me on a tour of the college campus explaining some of the research work he was doing. I couldn't help feeling a bit of pride in knowing I had a very minor role in the early education of this man who was becoming an important scientist.

Leaving Los Angeles I decided to follow the coast route, which was disappointing as much of the time we were in the coast mountains with winding roads and little view of the ocean. Many of the cities and towns in California have Spanish names, and I had to learn how to pronounce them. People would look at me with blank stares when I would pronounce a name as it would be in French instead of Spanish. We stayed overnight in San Jose, where I learned J was pronounced H, so it is San Hose. I thought it would be an easy drive to Martinez the next day, but the road took us through so many cities like Oakland, Berkeley and Richmond it was late evening before we reached the Bay country toward Martinez. It was dark as we drove down a narrow winding canyon road. It seemed endless and with no buildings on either side, I thought I must be on the wrong road when suddenly we came out of the canyon into the edge of the city. In just a few blocks we spotted the sign of the County Detention Home. It was near their bedtime, but Mother and Ula greeted us with open arms. Being late, we did little visiting that night.

We were given a room on the second floor in the girls' wing of the building. The next day we had a chance to talk and learn about the situation. Mother had been appointed the Matron of this home for children under the jurisdiction of the Children's Court. Also, it served as a home for children picked up by the police until the court could act. There were two wings to the building, one for boys and one for girls. At the front entrance was a reception room and above that the living quarters for the staff. Ula was the assistant matron and did most of the cooking. She was a wonderful cook and we enjoyed that to the fullest after our long journey. Mother's new husband, Bertie, was a helper and did a lot of the maintenance work as well as supervising the boys.

Mother still had her empty house in Richmond and was glad to have us take it over for the winter. After a few days of visiting we packed up our things and moved into this large frame house. It was more than we needed and to conserve heat, we closed off part of it. We were right in the heart of the city and a block from San Francisco Bay. We were near a big oil refinery and when the wind blew in from the bay, as it did at times, the fumes were stifling. Otherwise, we were comfortable and settled down to see what the winter was like in California. It was the rainy season and we found out when it rained, it poured. It grew cold after Christmas and there would be ice on the puddles along the road. But spring came early and the sun was out every day after the rainy season, bringing out the beautiful California poppies and fruit tree blossoms.

As soon as we were settled, Marjorie entered the first grade and Dorothy the kindergarten in a nearby school. The majority of the children in this school came from Mexican families, but they were well behaved and the school was well run. The girls found there were some expressions and words used in the school they did not understand. For example, when Norah visited the school one day, the teacher said to her, "It's too bad your girls don't eat their porridge." "What do you mean?" asked Norah. "Well," replied the teacher, "When we ask the children in the morning who ate their porridge this morning, everyone but your girls put up their hands." "What do you mean, porridge?" asked Norah. "Why, oatmeal or mush for breakfast," replied the teacher. "Of course they eat oatmeal every morning, but they never heard it called porridge," said Norah.

Not knowing what the future might hold, I decided to enroll in the University of California in nearby Berkeley for the second semester. Thinking I might do some teaching again, I decided on some graduate work in physics. I was assigned a Dr. Swift as my advisor, and when I met him, I was surprised to see the same man I had in Columbia when I took history of education. When I told him I had been in his class and what I did, he said he remembered me, although I wasn't sure. Anyway, he was nice to me. I explained what I wanted and he recommended some courses. One was in relativity, which when I attended the first session, I found was way over my head. He then changed me to a course on light. The best course I ever took anywhere was with Dr. Lawrence, the inventor of the famous cyclotron, in the history of physics. This man opened up a new world to me in a delightful interesting manner. I would have liked to have been able to know him personally, but in a class of over 100 students that was not possible.

In the course on light I was fortunate to be assigned a young man as a partner in the lab, who was a graduate of the university and very agreeable to work with. He knew his way around and took me one day to see the cyclotron, explaining how it worked. Little did I realize then how important this device was to become. Also, this friend told me as a graduate student I had the privilege of monitoring any of the undergraduate lectures. I took advantage of this to attend a number of the freshmen lectures. It was an education to see how such classes of 200 students were conducted. It proved to be a good semester of work.

Everytime I saw Mother she urged me to get a job and stay in California. I did put my name in the placement bureau at the University and joined a teacher's agency. I also applied at various industrial companies around the area for a position as an industrial chemist. To be sure I could take a job as a teacher, I applied and got a California Teacher's Certificate. But the depression was in full force and there were few jobs open. Then with an influx of people from outside the state coming to seek employment, there developed a slogan, "California for the Californians." I was an outsider, and they let me know it.

At Easter time Mother invited us to come and spend a few days with her, but Dale, who was teaching in the high school at Grass Valley had asked me to spend part of his vacation with him. We worked it out by Norah taking the girls and going to Martinez while I went to Grass Valley. I knew that this town was in the foothills of the mountains and the location of the famous Empire Gold Mine. I was delighted to not only be able to spend some time with Dale but also to see this part of the country. I arrived in Grass Valley on a Saturday afternoon and after Dale greeted me, he said we were invited to his girl's home for dinner. His girl was Marian McGuire, a teacher in the same school where they met and became good friends. On the way Dale informed me they were now engaged and would be married in June. Marian came from a very interesting family dating back to the days of the gold rush. Her father was a retired gold miner who had advanced to supervisor. He had many stories to tell about the mines, especially about "high grading," a term used by miners in sneaking out small pieces of rock rich in free gold. He hesitated, but Dale persuaded him in showing some of the high grade rock he had collected through the years.

After church on Easter Sunday Dale took me for a ride around the countryside, which was full of abandoned sites of small gold mines. On a road along one of the mountain streams we saw dozens of men patiently panning for gold. These were men out of work due to the depression and Dale said once they knew how, they could pan enough gold in a day to at least be able to eat. We stopped at one place along the stream and got out to walk a little. Out of curiousity I picked up several stones and when I turned one over, it showed tiny flakes of gold. For a minute I thought maybe I should turn gold prospector.

On Monday Dale took me to visit the Empire mine. We did not go down into the mine, which was over a mile deep, but watched the rock which had been blasted loose come up to the crushers mounted high above ground. This gold bearing rock was crushed and ground into fine dust, which was washed down through long troughs which had a layer of mercury on the bottom. The free gold, being heavier than the rock dust, would sink to the bottom where it was caught by the mercury and formed an amalgam of gold. When saturated with the gold, this amalgam was transfered to a large retort, where it was heated to vaporize the mercury and leave the gold free. The mercury would be condensed and used over again. I was glad of the chance to see the mine in operation, for a few years later it was closed.

The end of the classes at the university came before the public schools closed, so I had a little free time. Mother knew this, so she schemed to get Norah and me to run the Home while she and Bert took a week's vacation. We were a little reluctant about doing it, but since Ula would be there, we consented. There were only a few children in the home at the time, mostly boys, so I was busy supervising them. The girls were still in school in Richmond, so I drove them back and forth each day. While Mother was away I decided I had to tell her that I was convinced that I would not be able to get a job in California and should return to New York, where I was known, as soon as the girls were out of school. Mother was disappointed, as she aimed to keep us near her, but when she saw I was determined she said no more.

The day the girls finished school Mother sprung a surprise. She said she still had a couple of days left of her vacation time and she had always wanted to visit Yosemite National Park but never could get anyone to take her. She said she wanted to do something special for Norah and me before we left, and if I would drive she would pay all our expenses for the three of us to spend a couple of days in the park. Ula volunteered to take care of our girls and run the home with Bert so we could go. It was too good a chance to pass up, and we arranged to go.

When we got to the park and registered, we were told that the hotel and all cabins were full, so we had to settle for a tent. Mother was disappointed, as she wanted to do this trip in style, but we didn't care as it would seem more like an outing. The tent was furnished with cots and plenty of blankets, which we needed as the nights were cold this high in the mountains. After dinner the first evening we gathered with all the other tourists to watch the daily fire fall. On top of the three thousand foot cliff which forms one side of the valley park workers had built a big bonfire. Then as darkness fell, one of the rangers at the base of the cliff gave forth the famous Indian Love Call and then shouted, "Let the fire fall." At that the men at the top started pushing the burning wood over the side. It was spectacular, resembling the high water falls that dominates the valley, but it was fire, not water.

The next morning we decided to take the trail to the Yosemite Falls. As we climbed, the view became more and more spectacular, but halfway up Mother gave up, saying she would stay and enjoy the view while we finished the climb. The trail did become steeper and at times went under small falls where we got wet, but when we reached the top the view was breath-taking, well worth the climb. Coming back down the trail, we found Mother joined by other women who found the climb too much, and they were having a grand time visiting.

The next morning as we left the park we took a winding road up the south side of the canyon. At the lookout point near the top I took a picture which we later had enlarged and framed. It hangs on my study wall where I can relive that gorgeous view. I have on occasion used this picture as an example of how difficult it is to communicate. I have shown this picture to friends who have never been west or seen high mountains and their reaction is, "It's a nice picture." In no way does it convey the great heights or depths which are evident to one who has been there.

From Yosemite we drove south into the big Sequoia tree area. Among these giants is the famous General Grant tree, which has a road cut through its trunk. After two wonderful days we started back to Martinez, which seemed hot and tame after that beautiful trip. California has some of the most spectacular scenery in the world, but at such long distances apart it is difficult to see all of it.

After the trip it only took us a brief time to pack the car and start back east. It was summer weather when we left but as soon as we drove up the mountains it was spring again with the golden California poppies covering the hillsides. In Donner Pass the snow was piled higher than the car on both sides of the road. We went over the pass into the plains states where spring planting was in full force.

We arrived back in Dunlap just before Memorial Day, and Art and Leeta insisted we stay over the weekend, and not travel on a holiday. After a good visit with the Rannell families, we hurried along, making few stops. As we topped the last hill looking down over Cazenovia Lake, we all heaved a sigh of relief and exclaimed, "What a beautiful sight."

Norah's folks welcomed us with delight. Mother Riggall told us that Grandpa was up night after night when he heard a car, thinking it might be us returning. He had done all the worrying for us all. Now he could rest at night and so could we. We had been to California and back and had seen a lot of the United States, a year we would never forget.

CHAPTER 20

MIDDLETOWN

As soon as we were unpacked and settled in Cazenovia, I went into Syracuse to call at the Teacher's Agency where I had received fine service before. I wanted them to know I was back in New York State and interested in a position as a high school principal but would take a job teaching science and mathematics. I also called on Dr. Clem at the university to make arrangements to work on my thesis during the summer. I was told that the completion and acceptance of my thesis was all I needed to fulfill the requirements for a Master's degree.

At the time the Teacher's Agency had no openings but were sure something would develop before the end of the summer. With that encouragement I settled down to a routine of writing in the mornings and enjoying life in the afternoons. I spent some time fishing, some in taking the family swimming in the lake and some in taking Norah's folks on short trips. They were interested in visiting places where they had lived in their early days, such as Riggall Hill in nearby Georgetown where Norah's father was born and lived as a boy. The most interesting place was historic Muller Hill, where the Riggalls had lived for a short time when first married, in the old mansion built by the mysterious Frenchman. They told how the house was built like a fort with walls three feet thick. The house had burned down several years before but the foundation was still in place and the grounds showed how it had been landscaped, including part of the moat which had guarded the house.

After several trips to the university library to look for material, I was informed by Dr. Clem that he and his wife would be away for a couple of weeks on a vacation trip, and if I would come in each day to check on their apartment, I could use his personal library. This was a break for me! He had a fine library of books on the junior high school and it saved me hours of time.

One day while in the library in Syracuse I met a book salesman I knew and when he found I was still looking for a position, he told me the high school in North Tonawanda was looking for a principal. He claimed he knew the superintendent and board members very well and if I followed his directions and said just what he told me to say, I would have the job. I sent a letter of application, explaining how I knew the position was open and received a time for an interview. I drove out, met the superintendent and then waited my turn with others to meet the board. I did just what the salesman told me to do, but I didn't feel comfortable. I didn't get the job and in thinking about it, I decided I would never try to follow someone else's instructions again. It had to be me talking.

That was the only opening for a principalship I heard of all summer. After a year out of work our funds were getting low and I began to be concerned. I knew we could stay in Cazenovia with Norah's folks, but I would never feel right. I also knew I was not alone in being out of work, as many of my classmates in Oberlin were walking the streets, especially those I knew who had gone into industrial chemistry. World War veterans were marching on Washington demanding help for jobs. The depression was near its worst point.

Then just two weeks before school was to open I received a notice from the Teacher's Agency of a job in the high school in Middletown. They wanted a man to teach high school mathematics and assist in coaching football. It sounded like the job I had in Burlington, New Jersey, ten years before. I contacted the superintendent of schools in Middletown at once, and in a week received a contract to sign. The salary was much less than I had received in Saratoga, but that was expected in those times. Before I signed, I thought I should see the place and talk with the high school principal. Norah and I drove down; I wanted her to go along to look for a place to live.

I met the superintendent and after a brief talk, he made arrangements for me to see Dr. Wilson, the high school principal. I found the high school building was very old and Dr. Wilson a white haired, typical classical schoolmaster. He explained that I would have a full load of high school math classes plus being an assistant to the football coach during that season. I could see it would be a heavy load, but everything else looked all right—I signed the contract.

We had only a short time to find a place to live and went to a real estate office, which the superintendent recommended, to see if they had a house we could rent. The only place they had was a half house, not too desirable, but it was only a block from an elementary school for the girls to attend and within walking distance for me to the high school. We signed for a year's rental and made arrangements with a moving company to get our household goods out of storage in Saratoga Springs and have them ready for Friday before school opened. We drove back to Cazenovia to pack our car again and get ready to leave, but this time with a good feeling.

I found the Middletown High School different from any school I had been in. I was right about Dr. Wilson; he was a real classical scholar and wanted the school to be like an old fashioned academy. Most of the organization of the school was conducted by committees of teachers, while a lot of the things I had done as a principal were carried on by the assistant principal. He was a man about my age and had been a teacher

348

in the Utica Free Academy in Utica before coming to Middletown. We got along very well and I learned about the school from him. I rarely saw Dr. Wilson, but neither did anyone else; he spent most of his time in his private office getting reports from the assistant principal.

I was assigned two classes in elementary algebra, one in intermediate algebra, and one in advanced algebra first semester, with an additional class the second semester after the football season was over. All the classes were large, some 39 students, except advanced algebra, which had about a dozen students, but it caused me the most work, as I had never taught it.

I was told early that all teachers had to take turns keeping a detention room after school hours and a weekly schedule would be posted on the office bulletin board. It was the talk of the school that this was an assignment that no teacher was to miss. I never learned what the penalty was for missing, but no one wanted to find out. When my time came, I waited in my room for the students who were assigned detention to report. I had notified the football coach why I would be late for practice.

When the students reported I noticed they didn't bring any books or work with them, so I sent them back for such material. They looked surprised, but returned with work and I announced that I had plenty of work to do and probably they did too; if they didn't bother me, I wouldn't bother them. They settled right down and everything was fine.

The next day I received a notice to report to Dr. Wilson. Wondering what it was all about, I reported at my free period. He greeted me by saying, "You had the detention room yesterday?" "Yes," I replied. "I understand you had the pupils get their books." "Yes, they came with nothing to do," I said. "That is the point," he said, "that is their punishment to have to sit for an hour with nothing to do." "That is new to me," I said. "No one told me of the rule." "It is my method," he said. "Did you ever have to sit and watch the hands of the clock slowly crawl around the dial while your friends are out having a good time? That is why they are not to have their books and get all their homework done." The next time I had the detention room, I complied with the rule, but I noticed each time it was mostly the same students. The question rose in my mind as to what the detention was curing.

The football coach had been in the school for several years and had the reputation of putting out good teams. Another teacher of math in the school and I acted as assistants. I never felt football was my strongest coaching ability, but I was selected to take over the second team for its games. The coach found out I was good at treating injuries and he soon depended on me to look after injured players. The weather that fall was good and I enjoyed being outside working with the teams.

In order to meet some people in the city we began to attend the Methodist church. I was asked to take a high school Sunday School class, but refused for the same reason I had given before. But for a time I did head a small class of young women composed of teachers and business people. Norah did help with the primary department, as she had done in Saratoga.

I had one unforgettable experience at this church. One Sunday night during the winter I was asked to be one of two speakers at a layman's day service. The first speaker was the lay leader of the church and he gave what I called a typical Methodist sermon. It was nothing but a group of platitudes which every church goer had heard over and over. As always I wanted to be different and decided to talk about science and religion, which was very much in the news at the time. It happened that Thomas Edison had died a few days before and I mentioned the fact that it was reported that on his dying bed, Edison had claimed he saw a bright light which he thought indicated a future life. Church people had played this up because Edison had been an agnostic all his active life. I then went on to show some of the things that both science and Christians agreed upon and ended by saying there should be no conflict as both were seeking the truth.

After the service was over, the editor of the city daily paper rushed up to me and congratulated me on a fine talk. He asked if he could have a copy that he could use in his paper. I said I did not have a copy as I used only a few notes which he was welcome to take. A few others in the congregation spoke to me; I walked out into the cold night air rather glowing. Having been out of circulation for some time, I thought maybe I hadn't lost all my touch. I fell in behind two elderly ladies who had been at the service. Evidently hard of hearing, they were discussing the service in such loud tones I couldn't help hearing all they said. One said, "Wasn't Mr. —, the layman, wonderful. He made such a fine talk but that other man [meaning me] was terrible. I couldn't understand what he was trying to say. He made no sense to me." Right away I came off cloud nine and back to earth. The next day the editor had a long article in the paper giving me credit.

Norah was not at this service as Marjorie was sick in bed. She had come home from school sick and developed a fever. The next morning she was covered with a rash and when we called a doctor, he pronounced it scarlet fever and posted a quarantine sign on our front door. He also told me since I was a teacher I would not be allowed to stay in the house. I didn't know the next door neighbors very well, but when I explained my situation, they rented me a room to use for a couple of weeks. Due to the metropolitan atmosphere in the neighborhood, no one paid any attention to what I did, so I went in and out of our back door for my meals. Then after a couple of nights I slept on a cot downstairs so Norah was not left alone. I didn't go near Marjorie's room and she was not very sick; at the end of two weeks things were back to normal. We learned that there were several cases of this fever in the school and we expected Dorothy to also get it, especially as she had been with Marjorie, but she escaped.

I found some good men teachers in the high school and became friendly with them. One was the math teacher and assistant coach, so I knew him best. Another was a biology teacher by the name of Moon and I learned he was the author of a biology textbook used widely in the state and nation. He never bragged or even mentioned his publicity, but was always one of the group. These two with others had formed a rifle club and when the football season was over, asked me to join. Outside the city they had located a deep ravine and spent many Saturday afternoons in this protected spot target shooting. They were generous in letting me use their guns, so all I had to do was buy the ammunition. When they found out I was able to make some good scores, they invited me to join their rifle team to compete against other such teams in the area. The winters in this part of the state were open most of the time with very little snow, so we enjoyed being outside for this activity.

On March 1st of the year, 1932, the whole world was shocked by the news of the kidnapping of the infant son of Charles Lindbergh. Lindbergh had become a national hero after his famous flight over the Atlantic and for such a thing to happen was unbelievable. All the activities of the school seemed to stop that day. Both the teachers and students were just going through the motions, as this happened not too far from Middletown. The next day while in charge of a large study hall I sat at the desk on a raised platform. I felt the urge to put down some of my thoughts in the form of a poem. I would write a line or two, then stare off into space trying to think of the next line. At the end of the period a boy in the room, who had been on the football team, came up and said, "Mr. Calhoon, you looked as if you were writing a poem." That was the first time I knew there was supposed to be a poetic look.

As spring arrived I began to wonder about the next year. I had notified the Teacher's Agency to put me on the active list, as I was not entirely satisfied with my position in Middletown. Then when the contracts came out, I received one which was for teaching only, which made it $300.00 less in salary. I asked Mr. Wilson the reason and he said the board was cutting the school budget and had eliminated the coaching job. I was given thirty days to return the contract, and I held off as long as possible, signing only when no other job appeared in sight.

Then as it often happens, right after I signed the contract I received a notice from the Bardeen Agency of a position in the Science Department at Utica Free Academy in Utica, New York. Before I could act, I received the following letter:

                                                        April 22, 1932.

Mr. A. R. Calhoon
Middletown High School
Middletown, New York.

Dear Mr. Calhoon:

On June 9, 1930 you filed a personal application in this office for a position in our Science Department. Now we need another man in Physics and Chemistry for the school year opening September next and the other day notified Bardeen's Teacher Agency concerning the matter. On April nineteenth they mailed your credentials to this office.

We have several fine applicants for the position and it occurred to me that you might like to know about it. Fortunately, or otherwise, Utica Free Academy has reached the point where it is the largest high school in the state outside of New York City, it having thirty-nine hundred and fifty students registered for September. A result of this growth is that we must have in our Science Department six men to teach nothing but Physics and Chemistry. The salary for this position ranges from $2100.00 to $2900.00. Eight years of teaching experience in good high schools gives one the maximum salary. It so happens that it seemed wise for the teachers of the city to contribute to the cost of the city expenses 5.2% of their salary. This plan is now being used and will continue to be used from September to December 1932, inclusive, and possibly longer. All teachers in the system have agreed to do this.

We have told all the applicants for the science position that, if they make a personal application, it should be done on a school day between the hours of 8:30 A.M. and 1:00 P.M. as that is the time when the upper classmen are in the building. If you care to have your name included with that of the other applicants, we shall be glad to know it. My opinion, however, is that the greatest consideration will be given to those who make a personal application. If interested in the matter, please be prompt with your reply.

                              Yours sincerely,
                              E. S. Babcock, Principal.

When I received this letter, I saw Superintendent Burdick and he agreed to let me have the following Friday off so I could go to Utica and apply in person. I then wrote Mr. Babcock informing him when I would be there. To be sure of being on time, I left after school on Thursday and stayed overnight on the way. On Friday morning I reported to the office of the Academy expecting to see Mr. Babcock, but I was told to first see Mr. Burdick, the head of the Science Department, on the third floor. I found him in his office and we had a good talk. He said he knew Superintendent Burdick, of Middletown, and while they had the same name, they were not related. I was shown the laboratories and the layout of the department, which to me had the atmosphere of a small college. At the end of an hour, Mr. Burdick took me down to the main office to meet Principal Babcock. At first he impressed me as a typical classical school master like Mr. Wilson at Middletown, but after we talked I was impressed by his wider viewpoint of things. I told them both that I was interested in teaching both Physics and Chemistry, and they seemed impressed by my experience as industrial chemist at Oneida Ltd. I left with the feeling I had a good chance for the position. Then followed an exchange of correspondence.

May 3, 1932.

Dear Mr. Calhoon:

The next meeting of the Board of Education will be held on Tuesday evening, May tenth, on which occasion we hope to have elected a teacher of Physics and Chemistry. Our first choice is you and the salary concerned in your case would be our maximum, $2900.00. You, of course, will remember the fact mentioned to you the other day that at present all teachers are contributing 5.2% of their salaries toward the expenses of Utica city government.

I wish you would ascertain immediately if, in case you were elected to a position here Tuesday evening, your board would without question of doubt release you. I do not care to nominate anyone for the position who could not be released from his present contract or who, for any reason, is not free to accept the place here. I shall be in Albany the latter three days of this week and on my return late Saturday afternoon, may I have a definite reply from you?

Sincerely yours,
E. S. Babcock

May 4, 1932.

Dear Mr. Babcock:

I have your letter of May 3 and I certainly am very pleased to know that you have selected me as the first choice.

I have talked with Superintendent Burdick about this position, and he has assured me that if I am offered the Utica position that I will be released from my present position.

I recall your statement in regard to the plan of contributing 5.2% of the salary to city expenses and of course I shall be willing to do the same as other teachers in this matter.

I wish to thank you for your letter and shall anxiously await the decision.

Very truly yours,
A. R. Calhoon.

May 11, 1932.

Dear Mr. Calhoon:

At a meeting of the Board of Education held last evening, you were elected a teacher of Physics and Chemistry at our maximum salary of $2900.00. You will soon receive your contract from the Superintendent's office. I am pleased to know that you are to be with us next year.

Sincerely yours,
E. S. Babcock.

After this letter I waited for over a week and when I did not hear from the superintendent or get a contract to sign, I wrote to inquire about it. I received, what I learned later was a characteristic answer from the superintendent's office, saying that I should not have been concerned about the contract as it was official since it had been published in the Utica papers. In time I got the contract and returned it signed, then wrote Mr. Babcock.

May 22, 1932.

Dear Mr. Babcock:

I was much pleased to receive your letter informing me that I had been elected for the science position. I waited for over a week for the arrival of the contract. Then I wrote to ask about it and finally received it late last week. I have returned it signed and have received my release from this position.

I am looking forward with a great deal of pleasure to work in the Academy next year.

Very truly yours,
A. R. Calhoon.

At the end of the school year we once more put our household goods in storage until we could find a house in Utica. Of course, we wrote Nellie about coming to Utica and she was delighted. She had seen my name in the paper but didn't know what it meant until she heard from us. We left Middletown for Cazenovia to spend the summer, but with no regrets as I felt the year had been a stepping stone on the way back to better things in my field of education.

CHAPTER 21

UTICA FREE ACADEMY

After we were settled in Cazenovia, I went into Syracuse to check at the University about submitting my thesis which was almost completed. When I got there I received a jolt. I found the old dean of the School of Education had retired and a new man, Dr. Ganders, was appointed. My work for the Master's degree had been spread out over several summer sessions, but the old dean had told me I could take my time in submitting my thesis. But when I met Dr. Ganders and he looked over my record, he said some of my courses were over five years old and could not be considered. When I told him I had an understanding about this, he wanted to know if I had it in writing. I did not and even when Dr. Clem tried to support me, Dr. Ganders would not change his conditions. This meant I had lost one whole summer of work and would have to spend this summer in school to qualify. I went home so mad I was ready to throw the whole thing out the window and went fishing for two days.

While at the trout stream, I began to cool down and started to think maybe I was foolish to throw it all away, since I was so near the end, and perhaps I had better go back. Although I was a week late, on Monday I went back to the University to register. It was then I found some new requirements had been added. One was a course in thesis writing, even though I had mine practically finished. Another required course was educational psychology, which I had not taken. This course was given by Dr. Ganders, and even after my difficulty with him, I signed up. I have to give him credit, for he never held anything I said to him against me, nor did he ever mention it. On my part I found him to be an excellent teacher who challenged one's thinking.

There were about twenty-five graduate students in this class, and one incident happened we all remember. This was the time that Hitler was taking over Europe and the professors in the universities were loud in their protests. One day Dr. Ganders began to talk about Hitler and among other things he mentioned was how Hitler was advocating the selection of mates so as to breed a superior race in Germany. The idea of selected breeding of human beings was new to us and the whole class sat in shocked silence. Dr. Ganders paused and looked at us. "Hasn't anyone anything to say?" he asked, "What about it, Calhoon?" I was

355

caught by surprise and came forth with the first thing that crossed my mind. Dr. Ganders had asked if the Germans did this should we also do it to meet the challenge. My reply was in answer to this when I said, "In order to do anything like that, I guess we would have to change our religion." I saw a funny look come over his face, and he said, "Yes, I understand the Christian religion puts a premium on the individual." He then turned to another topic. After the class was over and we were outside the room, I was surrounded by the men in the class and one said, "Gee, that was a beautiful answer you gave Prof. You sure put him in his place." "What do you mean?" I asked. "You know he claims to be an atheist," they said. "What?" I almost shouted, "I can't believe it. It's unbelievable that a professor in Syracuse University would be an agnostic or atheist." "It's true," they said. All I had was their word; I never found out.

Anyway, after that Dr. Gander's attitude toward me changed. He began to treat me more like another teacher rather than just a student in the class. Others noticed it and began to speak up in class, something they said they didn't dare to do before. But Dr. Ganders liked it and we had a number of heated discussions. It proved to be one of the best courses I took in the graduate school and when I got an "A," I was delighted. I forgave Dr. Ganders for making me take the extra summer of work.

I met with Dr. Clem several times to go over my thesis. When it met with his approval, he made the arrangements to have the required copies typed and made ready to submit to a committee. Near the end of the summer a committee of professors was named to read my thesis and then give me a two-hour oral examination. They quizzed me in detail about the findings I reported and a number of other things. The front page of my thesis was as follows:

HOW THE JUNIOR HIGH SCHOOLS OF NEW YORK STATE
ARE MEETING THE PROBLEM OF INDIVIDUAL DIFFERENCES
by
A. Ray Calhoon
A. B. Oberlin College, Oberlin, Ohio, 1916
Thesis
Submitted in partial fulfillment of the requirements for the degree of
Master of Arts in the graduate school of
Syracuse University
August 1932
Approved by: Orlie M. Clem

Dr. Smith, who taught the course on thesis writing, was a member of my examination committee and he told me after it was over that my thesis was as good or better than many he had seen that were submitted for a doctor's degree. Later Dr. Clem condensed my work and it was published the following year, in the November, 1933, issue of *Educational Administration and Supervision,* under both our names. After the publication of my thesis, I was invited to join the Educational

Research Association of New York State. I did join and enjoyed my membership for several years.

A week after my examination I was notified that I was accepted for the Master's degree. Then I was really surprised to be told I had been elected to the Phi Beta Kappa, Honorary Society. If I accepted and paid the initiation fee, I would be given my "key." I never knew this honor was given for graduate work and I never worked for it which made it a special thrill. I did join and wore my key with a lot of pride for a long time.

When the summer session was over, Norah and I took a trip to Utica to look for a house. The best we could find was a bungalow at 1911 Briar Avenue. Although it seemed small, we decided to take it. George Hayes had been in business in Utica for years, so I asked him for a reliable moving company to get our goods out of storage in Middletown and have them in Utica right after Labor Day. He had a moving company who owed him for tires, by giving them the business they could pay the bill and we got our household goods delivered on time—all benefited.

The house was located in South Utica about six blocks from Hughes school, where the girls would go, and about a mile from the Academy. So again we were all within walking distance from our schools. It took me about 20 minutes to walk the distance, but during the depression many of the faculty and hundreds of the students thought nothing of walking. It was several years later when almost all the teachers thought they had to drive a car to work and many of the students began to drive a car or take the bus; only those who lived within a few blocks thought they could walk. Since there was no parking area at the school at that time, this became a problem which took years to solve.

Utica Free Academy was indeed a large school, both in size of student body and in the building, which covered a city block and was three and one half stories high. It was built in the days when ceilings were made high and it was a test of endurance to climb to the third floor where the science department was located. My first impression of the department being like that of a small college was increased when I was introduced to the teachers. General science and biology were taught by women while three men, Roy Perkins, Howard Hart and Ken Watkins taught chemistry only. Joe Dudleston taught physics only, while Mr. Burdick, the department head, taught both chemistry and physics. I was slated to teach both subjects and the first year I had three classes in chemistry and one in physics. The physics presented no problem, but chemistry had changed a lot since I had studied it; I had to work hard to keep ahead of the students the first year. I learned that all the teachers in this department had been teaching their subjects for several years so in that way outranked me, but I was the only one who had any experience in industrial chemistry and that gave me a feeling of confidence.

357

The registration in the science classes continued to grow—in January another chemistry teacher was added. His name was Larry Dresser and his home, as well as his wife's, was in Eaton. Being near Cazenovia, they knew many people that we did and they became two of our best friends, both in and out of school. Larry was a graduate of Colgate and had a doctor's degree in chemistry from Cornell. We both learned early the strange attitude the teachers in the Academy had about advanced degrees. My diploma for my master's had been mailed to the Academy by Syracuse University. I was called to the office to say I had a package and when I opened it and saw my diploma, I proudly showed it around. I was struck with the cold reception I received. No one congratulated me and then I overheard sly remarks about how foolish it was to spend the time and money to get an advanced degree; no one got any more salary for it. So when Larry came, Mr. Burdick advised him to say nothing about having a doctor's degree, as too many looked down on it. It was nearly twenty years later before this attitude changed and then only because the salary schedule recognized advanced work by paying more money.

The years 1932 and 1933 were in the deep depression and while we were fortunate to be on a salary which was always paid on time, we were affected by the conditions around us. Our expenses had been such that we had only a small bank account but were concerned when many banks were failing. Then when Roosevelt was elected and took office in March, 1933, the first thing he did was to order all banks closed. We had only a few dollars on hand but did get by. Later when WPA went into effect, the city celebrated with a big parade down Genesee Street in which all the men teachers joined city office workers and others.

All the classes in science were large, only the fact there were places for just 36 students in the chemistry lab kept those classes to that size. (Nowadays science teachers claim they can't teach over 20 in a class.) Besides the four classes which included a double period of laboratory twice a week, I had one period of study hall duty. This study hall was the largest in the building, seating 70 pupils. I made a practice of taking a lot of paperwork with me into this study hall. I announced at the beginning that I had a lot of work to do and no doubt they did also. If they didn't bother me, I wouldn't bother them. I had a seating chart of the room so I could report to the office any absentees. Of course, after my announcement some one or two had to start a disturbance to see what would happen. From the seating chart I was able to call the name of the offender and make him conspicuous before the whole room. It only took a few such occasions to get my system across.

It was a surprise to many students to learn that I was different from many teachers. I had observed some of these teachers walking up and down the aisles checking to see that everyone was studying. The first few days I noticed a few boys who sat and did nothing, waiting for me to say something. I pretended I didn't see them and after a time when nothing was said, they would look around the room seeing others all busy and when they got bored, they would open their books and get busy. My method spread around the school and while some teachers were critical, several students came to me and asked if they could transfer to my room. They said they heard that people studied in my room and they couldn't where they were. My reply was that I would be glad to have them, but they had to get a transfer from their dean. A few did and were happy to be admitted.

Mr. Burdick was not only the head of the science department and teaching two classes, but was also the dean of the junior class. This was before school counselors were introduced. The result was that he was so busy he had very little time for supervision. He turned me loose to carry on my work in my own way. A few weeks after I started I asked Howard Hart where I could find a certain piece of apparatus. He told me and then remarked, "Gee, Ray, we forget you are new here, you fit in so well it seems like you have always been here." That remark made me feel good, as I knew these men were a close knit group. Not only had they been working together for some time, but all except Mr. Burdick were graduates of Hamilton College. Principal Babcock was also from Hamilton, and it was well known that he had pulled as many men as possible to be on the faculty. To him any other college was inferior, and he openly tried to steer the best boy students in the Academy toward Hamilton. For his loyalty the college awarded him with an honorary doctor's degree.

I found the men in the department friendly and very cooperative. It was more like a college faculty atmosphere than any high school I had known. I felt it took my best efforts just to keep up with such a group. High marks in a Regents examination meant a great deal in winning a state scholarship, so it was not unusual to have students in the second semester in physics and chemistry try to raise their marks. One example was a boy in Dudleston's class trying to raise a mark of 99 in physics. When Dudleston rated his regents paper he only gave him 95. The boy appealed, claiming the answer he had on a certain problem was as correct as the one Dudleston had used. To settle the question they appealed to me. I checked it and saw the question was rather ambiguous, so several answers might be considered correct. Dudleston finally agreed and gave the boy 100, which was not changed in Albany.

One advantage we had in the Academy was getting together in agreeing on the answers of a Regents examination. Also, to be fair to the students, all papers we had rated less than 10 points below the passing mark we took to Mr. Burdick for his rating. After one of these sessions, Burdick remarked to me, "You know, you and I mark more alike than anyone else I know." I felt this was high praise as both Burdick and Dudleston spent part of each summer reviewing Regents papers at the State Department.

The arrangement of the rooms in the science department was such that no teacher had one for himself. The result was that we all had to move from room to room according to what class came next. This meant that when we wanted certain apparatus for a demonstration we had to bring it with us. There was a stock room where we could collect our material and have it more or less ready. As a rule I would just gather my material and then set it up as I talked. One day Ken Watkins saw me do this and he asked, "Don't you go through your demonstration before class?" "No," I replied. "I use it as a teaching device." "That's great," he said. "When I came here Burdick made me set up any demonstration I expected to do the next day and go through it before him."

Later I had a discussion about this with Burdick and he said he would never go before a class until he had tried out all his apparatus to be sure it worked. He said he thought he would lose face with the class if everything didn't work perfectly. I told him my idea was entirely different; I didn't worry about it not working for if it didn't, I considered it a beautiful chance to do some teaching in finding out why. Anyway, while he may not have agreed with my method, he never suggested that I had to change it.

I did have a problem with Dudleston and during my second year it came to a head. We both had to use a certain room for Physics 2 and his class was just ahead of mine. There was a long demonstration desk in the front of the room and Dudleston, who had the habit of using a lot of apparatus for each class, would walk out and leave it all in my way. At times I would have to clear a place to even put my book down. I spoke to him about it, but he would forget and the next week would be the same. I mentioned it to Mr. Burdick, but he didn't want to make an issue of it. Then one day a near tragedy took place. This room had a large switch board with outlets for both 110 and 220 volt currents. There were two heavy insulated extension cords that could be plugged into the board. There was an unwritten rule that extension cords were never to be left plugged into the board.

We were studying electric currents in my class and there was one boy who repeatedly interrupted to ask what would happen if one took hold of the ends of these cords when it was plugged into the 220 volt current. He seemed to have an obsession about this, and I tried to explain that what happened depended on a number of factors, such as how much moisture was on the hands, how firmly the cord was grasped, and the resistance of the person's body. I added it might throw the person, thus breaking the hold, or it might paralyze the person's hands so he could not let go and be electrocuted. Then I always finished by saying, "DON'T EVER TRY IT."

One day I walked into the room to be greeted by a deadly silence. I instantly knew something had happened, because usually there was a buzz of conversation. I glanced around the room and noted that the extension cords were plugged into the 220 volt circuit. The room remained silent, so I picked out a boy in the front row and asked, "What happened?" Naming the boy who had been asking about the 220 volts, he said, "Arthur took hold of the cords which were plugged in and it picked him up, throwing him over two rows of seats." I looked at the boy and he was white. He claimed he was all right, but I insisted he come with me to the school nurse's room. When I explained what happened, she made him lie down on the couch in her room. At the end of the hour when he seemed to be all right, she let him go. It was lucky it threw him, otherwise it could have been fatal. Needless to say, he never asked the question again.

I quizzed the class carefully and they all agreed that the cords were plugged in when they came into the room. With that knowledge I reported the incident to Mr. Burdick. Evidently he gave Dudleston a good talking to because, after that, half of the desk was cleared for me and the extension cords were put out of sight.

The Utica school system was based on half year promotions. Consequently, we had to have final examinations in all classes at the end of each semester. To make out separate examinations for as many as three classes in the same subject was a big task. Also in my study in education I was intrigued with the idea of making examinations hard enough to test the very best students, yet fair enough to make it possible for the normal student to pass. I began to make out examinations in both chemistry and physics based on that idea. I formed them similar to a standardized test, starting with easy questions and then increasing the difficulty to test the best in a class. I worked until I had forms A, B and C which I could use over and over. After three semesters I had enough data to give me a good correlation of the mark a student got on the test and what he would do in a Regents examination. I also used the method of scoring the answer papers and then turning these scores into percentages based on the normal curve, a method I found more satisfactory than the method used by the Regents of assigning a value to each question. I also was sure my tests were hard enough to challenge the best students, as in six years only one boy made a perfect score.

When we located on Briar Avenue in Utica, Marjorie and Dorothy entered the John F. Hughes grade school. They had to walk six blocks and climb about 100 steps to reach the front entrance, but they made no fuss about it. This was the largest grade school in the city and was considered the best. Like the other large grade schools in the city, it included grades kindergarten through the eighth. Later when the registration in the Academy became larger, Hughes kept its pupils for the ninth year. Utica was the only city in the state that did not have a junior high school in its system.

The girls liked the school and were doing fine when late that fall Dorothy became ill and broke out in a rash. I looked at her and decided it was scarlet fever. She had escaped it in Middletown but picked it up in Hughes school where there were a few cases. Dr. Harold Pender had been the family physician for the Hayes family for several years, so we called him to see if he would be ours. When he consented, he came to see Dorothy, confirming it was scarlet fever. He told us he would have to quarantine the house and I would have to leave for two weeks if I wanted to continue teaching. I contacted Nellie and she offered me a cot at the end of a hall to use and she would board me for the time. She was glad to get the extra money as George had lost his agency with the Kelly Springfield Tire Company and was struggling to run a downtown parking garage. They had to give up their nice house on Boyce Avenue and had moved into a cheap apartment near the garage. The depression had hit them as it had many small business people.

I checked with Norah every day and brought her the groceries. I didn't dare stay as I had in Middletown, as this was a different community and I couldn't afford to take a chance of losing my good job. Dorothy was much sicker than Marjorie had been, and Norah did call me for help near the end when Dorothy became hysterical.

It was while I was staying at the Hayes house I saw my first shovel board game. For several years I had heard George tell about playing the game. He and both boys, Herbert and Carrel, were members of the Elk's club team. One night they hurried their supper to go to the club for a league game. I was interested in seeing the game but thought it was in a private club and thought I would not be able to get in. But as we talked and I showed my interest, Nellie asked if I wanted to go with the boys and I jumped at the chance when George said it would be okay.

Outside of Utica I had never heard of this game, much less seen it played. I found the game is played on a polished board thirty feet long and 18 inches wide, placed on legs waist high. Two players from each of two team play at a time. They are stationed at each end of the board and are given four weights to slide alternately with their opponent. The weights are made of cast steel and are cylindrical in shape about 3 inches in diameter and 2 inches high. They are beveled slightly on the bottom and polished so they will slide easily. They are marked "A" and "B" so each player can identify his weight. The game is to see which weights can be slid and stopped nearest the end of the board and not have the weights knocked off by an opponent. A line is marked eight inches from the end of the the board and all weights of one player which are outside this line but nearest to the end of the board count one each, weights inside the line count two points each, and a weight hanging over the end is called a "chipper" and counts three points. The team that scores 21 points first wins the game. The game requires a lot of skill and is a true game since there is both offense and defense.

This game was very popular in Utica and I learned that besides the city league in which the Hayes' played, there was a church league and a Masonic league. After I affiliated with Liberty Lodge and could use the Masonic club rooms, I learned to play shovel board. I first joined the Masonic league, then the Central Methodist Church team, and for a time the American Legion team in the city league. I picked up the game rapidly and was soon considered one of the top players in the city. After World War II the game began to die out. Many of the older players were gone, and the younger men became interested in bowling. During the height of interest Herbert Hayes joined the Central Church team when his former team from Christ Reformed Church was disbanded. Each week the Utica papers reported results of all league games and one such report follows:

> Herb Hayes and Ray Calhoon of the Central Methodist entry in the Protestant Church Shovelboard League came within one point of equaling the all time high for a two-man team when they piled up a total of 27 points in their match with Trinity Episcopal.
>
> According to oldtimers, the record is 28 points compiled a few years ago. The match between Central and Trinity Episcopal was a free-scoring affair, with two games running to 24 points and another to 23 points.

The Academy had large technical and industrial arts departments, in which all the instructors were men. It was the custom for these men to gather in the boiler room after lunch to enjoy a smoke. It was the only place in the building where smoking was allowed. Men from other departments who were free at the same time used to join this group and though I did not smoke during school hours, I used to meet with all these men. It was there I became acquainted with Floyd Trieble, the head of the English department, and Ralph Ginther, who taught speech and coached the school plays.

Both Trieble and Ginther, along with some others, played golf and after I became well acquainted, they invited me to join them. I had only tried to play the game a few times in Sherrill, but never really learned. But I was interested and bought a bag and a minimum number of clubs and joined them on Saturday mornings. Valley View is the municipal course and has the reputation of being one of the finest in its class. The yearly fee for a resident of Utica was only $10.00, so I joined and kept my membership for the next forty years. Trieble taught me as much as anyone did, and after a time I got to be a fair player. He was known as the "old master," and few of the men in the Academy ever beat him, yet when some of us duffers made a bad shot it never disturbed him.

Trieble also liked to hunt and fish and we went out together many times. He was a fine trout fisherman and knew the streams around Utica, so I was delighted to go with him. He could outfish me, but in hunting I was a better shot, so we balanced each other. Ours was a good friendship that lasted for years.

At the beginning of each school year the boiler room gang had to tell about their fishing trips. Bill Beavan, an industrial arts instructor, was considered to be the best fisherman in the group and he usually had the biggest fish story to tell. One fall after everyone else had told his experience I told mine.

On the last Sunday of August, just before the end of the trout season, my wife's family gathered for an annual picnic in honor of her father's birthday. Usually it was held on the lawn of her home in Cazenovia, but this time they decided to go to Delphi Falls, a beautiful spot about five miles west of Cazenovia. Although it is a small stream, the falls are about 100 feet high and are surrounded by a wooded area. A year or so before, someone had tried to make a resort park of the place but it was not a success and was now abandoned. Some of the outdoor fireplaces and picnic tables were left so it was an ideal spot for us. Besides our family, Norah's parents, Norma and family were there, making a group of a dozen people. Using one of the fireplaces we cooked a lot of sweet corn, hot dogs and hamburgers, and there were pies, cakes and a big watermelon for dessert. The out of doors made us hungry on this perfect day and we had a big feast.

For a time after we finished eating all we could do was sit and visit. Then the children wanted some exercise and went down to the stream and began to wade in the shallow water. I stood up and remarked, "I know there used to be trout in this brook and I wonder if there are any left?" I had my fly rod in the trunk and a couple of old flies. Putting my rod together and slipping on my boots, I walked up to the foot of the falls where the water had formed a wide deep pool. I had put on one loop of my leader an old rather large brown fly and on the end a black gnat.

Casting out my line a few times to gain distance, I let the flies hit the water just outside the falls. It must have been a perfect cast for while I only felt the slightest sign of a strike, my line started moving up stream and then across the pool toward an overhanging rock ledge. I knew then I had a fish and carefully put on enough pressure to turn my catch just before he went under the rocks. Back and forth the fish went from one side of the pool to the other. Each time I gathered in a little more line. The western sun high over the top of the falls cast a single shaft of light through the trees which covered the cliff, striking the center of the pool. When I got the fish to shoot through this beam I got my first sight of what I had and my eyes opened wide when I saw the size of that trout. I also let out a gasp as I saw a smaller fish following. I didn't know then that he was also hooked.

Out of the corner of my eye I saw my girls with Melva, their cousin, lined up on the bank with their cameras pointing at me. I thought, "What a shame, they want to take a picture of me catching a trout but I'll never be able to land this big one." When they realized I had hold of a fish they began to yell and scream so the whole family jumped up and rushed down to the bank of the stream to see the excitement. Using all the skill I had learned in lake fishing, I gradually worked my catch into some backwater near the bank and Fred, my brother-in-law, reached down and pulled up my line, gasping, "My Gawd," as he held up to view an 18-inch brown trout and then on the end a fat 10-inch one. It was hard to believe such a trout would be in this small stream, but there they were and I have pictures to prove it.

As I finished telling the story, I said, "The point is, if you are going

The famous double fish!

to make a big catch, get your audience all assembled with cameras beforehand so you can prove your story." All the men in the boiler room shouted, "You win the prize. You beat Bill Beaven this year."

Every time I had my classes in the chemistry lab I smelled gas and reported it to Mr. Burdick but neither he nor the others smelled it and just thought I was fussy. But the second winter I began to feel run down and wondered if I was getting too much of this manufactured coal gas which I knew contained a high percent of carbon monoxide, a deadly poison. Also that winter I often smelled gas in our cellar and called the gas company, but they found no leaks. I continued to feel worse and finally collapsed. Dr. Pender came and thought I had the flu and treated me for it. Then when I felt some better he wanted me to come to his office for tests. I asked Carrel Hayes to take me down to the doctor's office and although rather shaky, got dressed. Carrel walked me to the door and when I hit the fresh air I fainted away. I learned later that this was a typical reaction for workers around the gas plant who breathed too much of the gas. Norah and Carrel got me back into bed and called the doctor. He was busy with people in his office, but sent his brother, a doctor who had just started a practice in Utica. By the time he came I was half conscious, he checked my pulse and elevated the foot of my bed to keep the blood in my head. Then he gave me a shot which affected me in such a way that my legs began to tremble. I couldn't control them and I thought I was on the way out. It was over an hour before I began to feel as if I might live.

When I did get to Dr. Pender's office and he gave me some blood tests, he remarked, "You act as if you had been gassed." I told him about the chemistry lab and about smelling gas at home. He was sure then by breathing a small amount of gas over a long period of time I was affected more than by a big dose at one time. When I was able to get back to work I reported what the doctor said to Mr. Burdick. I got him to come into the lab and I showed him that over 75% of the pet cocks over the students' desks leaked enough gas to show a flame when a match was held near them. I convinced him that this was bad and he tried to get the school to replace them, but they claimed there was no money in the budget for this. Finally he took enough money from the student lab fees and bought new pet cocks and the maintenance men did consent to do the work. This was my first introduction to how much red tape is involved in a big city school system.

When spring came and the frost was out of the ground, I smelled gas in front of the house and when the leaves which had just started to show on the hedge near the sidewalk began to die, I called the gas company again and convinced them there must be a leak. The crew then punched a hole through the pavement and touched a match to it, and a flame three feet high shot into the air. They then got busy and found a big leak under the street and repaired it. Evidently the gas from that leak had been seeping through the ground all winter into our cellar. With that and the gas I had got in school, it really floored me. Maybe because I had been gassed in the war I was more sensitive than others; but after the repairs were made I was all right.

We lived in the bungalow at 1911 Briar Avenue for two years. As the girls grew larger, we felt very crowded and began to look for a larger house. It happened at that time Rocco Lopardo, the head of the math department at the Academy who owned the house at 1907 Briar Avenue, separated from his wife. She took their boy and moved to Florida. Roc didn't want to live alone in this house and was glad to rent it to us. It just filled our needs, with a living room, dining room and a kitchen on the first floor. Three bedrooms and a bath on the second floor, plus a small room in front ideal for a study, were perfect.

I didn't want to buy a house until I was sure of tenure, so I was glad to rent, but when Roc got behind in his mortgage payments because he had lost money in the stock market, he offered to sell us the house if we would take over the mortgage, and we made the deal. It has been our home ever since.

When we moved to Utica we didn't hurry to find a church to attend. The largest Methodist Church was Central, a downtown church, over a mile from our house. Dorothy Greene lived on our street and was a classmate of Dorothy's at Hughes School, and she invited the girls to go with her to Sunday School at the First Presbyterian Church, which was within walking distance. We let them go and Norah and I didn't go anywhere for a time. Mr. Burdick was an active member of

Central and early that first winter he asked me to coach their basketball team. In that way I got acquainted with the young men in the church and since we had been members of the Methodist Church, we decided to join. When we did the girls didn't feel right in going to another church, so they also joined. After coaching for a couple of years I became interested in the shovel board team and played with them until the league folded years later.

Norah became active as head of the primary department of the Sunday School. She wrote and directed some plays for the small children to give on Children's Day, which were very successful. She did this while our girls were at that age, but when they were old enough to be in the upper grades she told the minister she was resigning. He tried to have her continue, but when she told him how many years it had been since she was in a church service, he had to agree it was time for a change.

In April of 1935, I had a letter from Mrs. Leonard in Minoa saying the school board was placing a bronze tablet in the school in honor of Miss Katherine O'Brien, who was the fifth grade teacher when I was there and had been in that same position for over 50 years. I considered her a master teacher and she was respected and loved by hundreds of her former pupils. She taught until she was over 80 years old and almost died in service when she fell, breaking a hip, while supervising her class at recess time on the playgrounds. The committee in charge of the ceremony asked me to speak at the dedication on May 25, 1935. They invited me because Miss O'Brien always spoke of me as one of the best principals she knew and also considered me a good friend. I gladly accepted the invitation and Norah went with me. The committee complimented me on my brief speech and said if only Miss O'Brien could have heard it she would have been so proud. It also gave us a chance to see a number of our friends from Minoa who we always considered special.

Since I was free from attending summer school after I got my master's degree, I began to enjoy the summer vacations. I found plenty to do, planting a small garden, playing golf, trout fishing with Trieble and taking frequent trips to Cazenovia. At that time the Gas and Electric Company maintained a public picnic area near Trenton Falls on West Canada Creek about a dozen miles north of Utica. The grounds were equipped with fireplaces and tables, so it was an ideal place to cook an outdoor supper on a hot summer day and we took advantage of it many times. A few years later it was closed because of vandalism.

Right after school closed in 1935, I received a message from Ula saying Mother was critically ill and if I wanted to see her, I should come as soon as possible. I knew Mother had undergone an operation for cancer but didn't know she was so bad. Norah and I talked it over and we decided I should go. Rather than leave Norah and the girls alone in Utica, we decided to drive the old car as far as Dunlap and they could spend the time there on the farm while I went on to California. We packed in a hurry and took off in the old Hup, which now had almost 150,000 miles on it, but still was a sturdy car.

After a short visit with Leeta and Art in Dunlap, Norah decided she didn't want to stay but we would all drive through to Martinez. Art thought we were taking a big chance with such an old car, but I thought if we didn't drive fast we could make it. On this trip we stayed at motels, which had grown more numerous than on our previous trip and were still very reasonable. To make better time we did not cook our meals but bought food that we could eat for lunch on the road and ate in restaurants mornings and nights. Thus we made good time without driving fast. Arriving in Martinez we found Mother in bed and suffering. She had been operated on for cancer but had waited too long and it had gone all through her system. Ula was taking care of her as well as running the detention home. She did this until near the end when she engaged a trained nurse to take over.

Not knowing how long we would stay, we rented a furnished apartment on a weekly basis. I spent part of each day with Mother trying to relieve Ula. It was a very depressing time watching her suffer and knowing there was nothing we could do but make her as comfortable as possible. It was also a dreary time for Norah and the girls, for even though the sun shone bright every day, there was nothing for them to do but walk the streets.

When it got past the first week in August with no change in sight, I told Ula we would have to start back. She understood and thanked us over and over for coming. I notified Dale when we were leaving and he and Marian met us in Nevada City that afternoon, so we had a brief visit before we left California. It had been a depressing summer, but after a day on the road I realized I had done all that I could do and began to regain my spirits. Rather than lose the whole summer for the girls, we decided to go north and visit the Yellowstone National Park. Mother had told me that her cousin, George Crow, was one of the rangers in this park and if we went there to look him up.

When we got home to Utica, I wrote a six page letter telling of our trip and sent it to Leeta and asked her to send it along to Ula and have it passed on to Dale and Faye. Thus began the start of our family letter, which we have kept going for all these years. The following are some of the highlights of that letter.

At the gate to the Park we learned that the best chance of finding housekeeping cabins was at Old Faithful. I asked the ranger if he knew George Crow and he said, "Yes, slightly." He said Crow was stationed at Mammoth Springs at the other end of the park. It was 30 miles from this entrance to Old Faithful, so we hurried along to get there before all the cabins were taken. The night before, the rangers had closed the gates early because they could not provide accommodations for more tourists. We looked all we could as we drove along, passing the cascades of the Firehole River and then coming first to the lower geyser basin and then into the upper basin. We could see some of the hot springs and steam rising from some of the geyser spouts. Then as we came in sight of Old Faithful Inn we drove close to Castle geyser and it erupted for us. We exclaimed about it, but didn't get excited for we said, "When we get our cabin we will come back this afternoon and see them all." Little did we know that it is a rare sight to see some of these geysers erupt and Castle was one of them. Anyway, we saw it and had to congratulate ourselves later when we learned the facts.

We located the office for the cabins and when Norah went in, she found there was only one solid cabin left. After we had met a bear on the road coming in, she insisted on a solid cabin. She wasn't taking any chance on one which was part canvas. When she signed for the cabin, she learned that we had to rent the bed clothes with a deposit of $1.50.

While we were attempting to get our accomodations straightened out, I discovered there was no fuel in the cabin. I wanted the girls to find Norah and have her check on that. They refused to go. They said there were bears around and they weren't going anywhere. I said, "Oh, there are no bears around in the daytime, just at night to look for garbage." So to assure them I took them by the hand and started around the side of the cabin. Right there we met an old bear and two cubs. It startled me, I wasn't expecting to see them. I exclaimed, "Heavens! There are three." "Where?" Dorothy shouted, and as I glanced down at her I saw her eyes fairly popping out of her head and she was poised on her toes ready to do a hundred yard dash. I grabbed her hand and we beat a hasty retreat into the cabin.

When Norah got back, the girls were all excited to tell her about the bears and Dorothy looked out the small window in the back of the cabin to show her. Just then one of the cubs saw her and looking for a handout climbed up the side of the cabin, looking Dorothy right in the face. Dorothy let out a yell, falling over backwards on the bed, and lay so still that Norah thought she had heart failure. Afterwards we all had a good laugh about it.

We saw bears all over the park. That night we watched about 25 bears of all sizes come out of the woods to feed at the garbage dump. There was a crowd of a thousand or more people to see the sight. They were protected by a strong wire fence and four armed guards. In spite of frequent warnings, people were careless and there were several cases of bad maulings reported that summer.

After a hasty lunch we started out to visit the geyser basin. Of course, we saw Old Faithful as it erupts about every 65 minutes,

"It's Old Giant!"

throwing a stream of water and steam some 150 feet into the air, a beautiful sight. There are scores of small geysers throwing streams of water from a few inches to several feet into the air at various times. The colored pools were also beautiful. Norah had a sore foot and we had to explore and then return to the car and tell her about the sights and suggest the ones she should see. One pool is famous for cleaning a handkerchief. I saw others doing it so I tossed mine in. The current took it down out of sight and then in a few minutes it returned all washed and white. As I was doing this a strong wind came up, causing a dust storm, so the girls ran to the car. When I showed them my handkerchief they wanted to see it done. With them I went back and threw it in the pool again. It went down all right, but never came back. It seems it won't work more than once and as far as I know, the handkerchief is still there.

I can't begin to describe all the peculiar formations and hundreds of pools and boiling springs. We spent the whole afternoon viewing them. About 5 o'clock we were getting hungry and stopped at a store to get some things to cook. We noticed a lot of people outside running by all excited. I stepped out to see what was going on. At a distance I saw a big stream of water and steam high in the air. I heard someone call out, "It's Old Giant!" I called the folks out and we jumped in the car to follow the crowd. Sure enough, Old Giant was going full force with a stream at least 200 feet high. It also lasted almost an hour, while most geysers last only a few minutes. Again, we didn't know how lucky we were. After watching a while and taking some pictures we returned to the store, where they told us that Old Giant had erupted only three times that summer. This was the fourth time and we were there at the right time. Some people had been there for weeks and had never seen it. One group of women we met had waited in vain for weeks and that day decided to take a trip to another part of the park, and when we told them what we had seen, they burst into tears.

The next day we started to go around the loop taking in the many sights . . . When we got to Mammoth Springs I inquired about George Crow. They told me he was at the fishing bridge with a party. We had passed that on the way and saw a large crowd fishing off this bridge over the Yellowstone River. I did call his wife on the phone to please Mother.

The next day we left the park at the east gate. We dropped down from 9000 feet to 4000 feet in a short distance and the temperature rose accordingly. The cars coming up the steep grade were steaming and we saw one bunch of college girls pushing their old Model T Ford up the road. It was a beautiful mountain road, but it made Norah shiver to look down from the dizzy heights.

The letter continued to tell of our trip back east. We stopped in the Black Hills of South Dakota and watched the men working on the heads of the Presidents on Mount Rushmore. We detoured into the Bad Lands, which proved to be beautiful. Back at Niagara Falls we stayed overnight so we could see the display of lights on the falls after dark. The next day we called on Aunt Nell and Uncle Clark in West Webster near Rochester. They had retired to a small fruit farm and had a lot of grapes ready for market. He told us he had sold them by the ton to the Welch Grape Juice Company. They would not sell them to make wine even for a bigger price. We only stayed for a brief visit, the girls were very tired and we had promised them we would get back to Cazenovia that night. We did and all felt a sense of relief. With a few small repairs the old car had brought us safely back the second time across the United States.

Mother died just after school had started on the 4th of September. I have always been glad that we were able to see her that summer. She had led an active life and could feel proud that under adverse circumstances she held the family together for a time and lived to see all her children grow up and be on their own. In many ways she was a remarkable woman. She came from sturdy pioneer stock, having lived in her early years on the frontier of South Dakota. There her family survived droughts, grasshoppers, tornadoes and the blizzard of 1888. Finally after two successive crop failures they gave up and moved back to College Springs, Iowa, which became the headquarters of the family for many years.

After marrying a country minister whose largest salary was $500.00 a year, she worked at times to help support a growing family. A natural born nurse, she became noted for caring for mothers at birth time. Many times she did the whole process before a country doctor could arrive. After becoming a widow at too early an age, she held the family of five young children together by earning a living doing nursing. The

371

doctors in the area called on her frequently to take charge of their most difficult cases. In the sick room she was in complete command, she gave the patient confidence and her hand on the fevered brow of a delirious child would quiet him faster than the doctor's medicine.

I have always been grateful to her for encouraging me to stay in school when she could so easily have asked me to find work and help support the family. She taught me to be responsible for my actions. When at times I was resentful for some of the arbitrary rules at Houghton, she would say, "Son, if you get in trouble in school you will have to get yourself out. I can't help you."

I had not lived with her for over twenty years and our family had been scattered ever since I was sixteen years old. Nevertheless, Mother remained a focal point to keep us in touch. To all she typified the spirit of a true pioneer woman and left us an inheritance of meeting the problems of life with a determination to succeed.

Once the girls were well established in Hughes school, Marjorie began to take piano lessons with a private teacher. After she had to break up their home, Nellie Hayes asked us to take her piano to keep and use, and the girls practice on it. Marjorie was doing very well when one day she announced she wanted to play the harp. Where she got the idea I never knew, but she was very persistent. We made some inquiries and learned that Roosevelt Jones, a noted pianist in the city, had played the Irish harp at one time. We contacted him and he agreed to bring his Irish harp to our house and let her try it.

The Irish harp is small with strings like a concert harp but not as many octaves and no pedals. Sharps and flats are produced by changing frets near the top of the strings, one string at a time. These frets can be set according to the key of a selection, then changed during the playing if accidentals occur.

Jones was surprised at how quickly Marjorie adapted to the instrument, however, he suggested that we let him give her a few lessons and see how she progressed before we thought of buying a harp. The day he came to give Marjorie her first lesson and was ready to leave, Dorothy went to her mother and with tears in her eyes wanted to know when she was going to have a lesson. Jones was so touched he sat right down and had her start. He reported that she, too, was ready for lessons.

The Clark Music Company in Syracuse was the headquarters for harps in central New York. We took the girls to this store to see about renting or buying a used Irish harp. The salesman referred us to Mrs. Rice, who was engaged by the store to look after the harps and give lessons to beginners. When we told her that the girls had taken a few lessons, she asked them to play for her and she agreed that they showed talent and advised us to rent a harp with the proviso that the rent would apply on the purchase of a harp if they continued to show progress. We made a deal, taking a harp home with us and arranging for them to have lessons on Saturday mornings with Mrs. Rice.

It was one of the most important decisions we ever made and influenced our lives for several years. Now my Saturday mornings were programmed as Mrs. Rice insisted that at least one parent had to be present at each lesson. I was the one selected and she explained that I was to listen so I could help the girls between lessons. Also, I had to learn how to tune the harp as they were too young to do it.

The word soon spread that the Calhoon girls were harpists in a city where there was no one else. They were invited to play on programs for P. T. A.'s, church organizations and other functions. At first they could only play a few simple numbers, but the novelty was enough to make them important. Mrs. Rice didn't approve of their playing on programs so soon, but I couldn't see the harm as it gave them an extra incentive to practice. When the *Utica Observer-Dispatch* published an article about them with a picture, they became more popular and I was kept busy taking them with the harp to various functions. One of the biggest was at a meeting of the Eastern Star Lodge in New Hartford when they had a visitation of State and National officers. It was one of the few places they received an honorarium for playing.

After a year Mrs. Rice let them try playing on a concert size harp. She told us she was recommending that we make the change. In April 1938 we turned in the Irish harp toward the purchase of a concert harp which the company delivered to our house. It was a while before they felt ready with the large harp to play anywhere, but when they did I was confronted with the problem of transporting it. By experimenting I found out that by taking the back seat out of my car I could just fit the harp in at an angle. At first I thought I had to have someone help me, but after a time I learned to do it alone.

For a time Mrs. Rice continued with the lessons, but I became dissatisfied with her attitude and when I heard her scolding them one day for not practicing more, I cancelled the lessons. One thing I wanted was for them to enjoy playing and if it got to a point where they had to give up all school and church activities to spend all their time practicing as if they were professionals, I wanted another teacher.

We heard that a Mrs. Zoller in Herkimer was a harpist and gave lessons. We contacted her and she agreed to take the girls for a time. But she didn't appeal to them and they made little progress. Miss Grace Weymer, a well known harpist, was the head of that department at Syracuse University. When I found out that I had to take some extension courses on Saturdays at the university, I got an appointment with Miss Weymer and told her about the girls and asked if it was possible for her to take them as special students. She suggested I bring them in the next Saturday and have them play for her and then she would make a decision. This I did, and she expressed her surprise at their ability and said she would take them. She also told me on the side that my analysis of their different styles was exactly right. It turned out to be a beautiful arrangement, and they both began to make real progress. They were almost heartbroken when Miss Weymer

announced she was to be married and was leaving Syracuse. They felt highly honored to be invited to her wedding. By this time the girls were nearly out of high school, so she was their last teacher for a long time.

I never regretted using the money we spent for the harp and all the lessons, nor the time I devoted to transporting the girls with the harp. At the time it set them up in their school and in the city as something special. In 1939, my last year as a teacher in the Academy, Marjorie was ready to enter the ninth year in January. Due to the crowded conditions at UFA, Hughes school was keeping these pupils. Marjorie wanted to get to UFA so she could play the harp in the school orchestra. I told Superintendent DeCamp about it, and he readily gave her a permit to transfer.

I took the harp down to the Academy several times for her to practice with the orchestra, but it didn't work. She couldn't read the music fast enough to keep up with the others and Miss Lally, who was then directing the orchestra, didn't have the patience to wait for her. She dropped out of the orchestra, but joined the music club where she could play solos. Her first appearance almost turned out to be a disaster. I had taken the harp down in the morning and placed it on the stage of the auditorium. Marjorie had a free period at the end of the day so she went to the auditorium to practice before she was to be on the program. I had just finished my last class when Marjorie met me with a long face. Almost in tears she told me that Miss Lally had gone into the auditorium and tried to check the harp so it would be in tune, but she had never tuned a harp and had it all off. They both wanted me to come down and see if I could get it back in tune. It took me the whole period to get it ready. In spite of being nervous over Miss Lally's interference, Marjorie did very well and the club gave her a big ovation. After that she played several times, but Miss Lally never tried to tune it again.

In 1936 Proctor High School was opened on the east side of the city. The population of this area is predominantly Italian and Rollin Thompson, who was the principal at Roscoe Conkling grammar school in the same area, was appointed the principal. I had known Thompson since the days I was coaching basketball at Minoa, as he was in charge of the tournaments that were held in Utica. Through the years we became good friends. Since Proctor would draw over a thousand students out of the Academy, it would reduce the size of the faculty, so teachers in the Academy were given a chance to transfer to the new school. Larry Dresser, who was the last one in the science department, made the request and he was accepted, being appointed the head of the science department, a position he held until his retirement. Reducing the number of students made it no longer necessary to have the double session, so the Academy returned to a normal school day.

The technical department in the Academy continued to grow larger, and one of its requirements was that all the students in that department had to complete a course in physics to graduate. The result was that a large percent of my classes in physics were boys from the technical department. I had an interesting experience with one such class composed of these boys. Regents examinations were required of all students taking physics and as the time approached, I became concerned about these boys passing. All of these boys had studied electricity in their shop courses and were real cocky when we studied that in physics, but they were doing little in other parts of the course. Finally I spoke to some of them privately and they replied, "Don't worry, Mr. Calhoon. We have checked the past Regents examinations and there are enough questions on them on electricity for us to get a passing grade and we know all about it." I then checked the examinations in the Regents review book and found out what they said was true. However, I tried to warn them that the next examination might not be the same. Then it happened. Someone in Albany noticed the same thing and that year the questions on electricity were cut down to 30 points. The result for this class was disastrous. Almost all of these papers I had to mark at 30 to 50 percent, while the passing grade was 65 percent.

Most of these boys were seniors and if they didn't have a passing grade in physics they would not graduate. I felt the Regents were unfair in cutting the questions on electricity so radically, but I couldn't change their marks, so I did the next best thing to be sure they could graduate. I raised their class marks high enough so the average passed them. The physics examination came on Thursday afternoon and Principal Babcock insisted that all senior marks had to be ready by Friday afternoon so he could have the list of graduates ready for the Sunday paper. I had a lot of senior papers to grade and worked late into the night to have my report in on time. Exhausted, I was sleeping late on Saturday morning when the phone rang. It was Babcock's secretary and she said Mr. Babcock wanted to see me in his office right away.

I got dressed and hurried down to the Academy wondering what was up. When I reported, Mr. Babcock greeted me by saying his attention had been called to the high class marks I had given many of the boys in my class. I explained the situation and said I had done it so these boys could graduate. Mr. Babcock told me if I thought the examination was not fair I should have raised the marks on it, not the class marks. I replied that there was a good chance that these papers would be called to Albany and I wanted my marks correct. Then I added that I believed the class marks were my prerogative and I didn't intend to change them. I walked out of the office wondering what would happen. Anyway all these boys graduated and I never heard anymore about it. I did wonder who the "nosy" person was who reported my marks.

I couldn't help wondering what my standing would be with Mr. Babcock after that incident, but it wasn't long before I found out. The faculty was divided into several committees to finish the work at the end of each semester. Half-year promotions were established in the city system, so the end of each semester was like the end of the year in most school systems. Each committee had a chairman, who was responsible to see that the work of his group was properly done and completed. Dr. Phelps, a Latin teacher of many years, was the chairman of the program committee and I was assigned to his committee. This committee worked in the physics laboratory, which was where I had my desk. Dr. Phelps was noted as sort of a grouch and he was very strict about how the work should be done. He personally would check out the cards for each member of the committee to work on and no one else was to touch anything until he gave his approval. Then after a couple of years working with him and since it was my room where he left the cards, much to everyone's surprise he let me check out the cards so things moved much faster.

As I learned the process that this committee was doing, I saw certain things that disturbed me greatly. In fact, some were outright wrong. One day when Dr. Phelps was in a good mood, I spoke to him about it. He gave me an answer which is so characteristic of people who

376

work in a large system for a long time. He said, "I know what we are doing is wrong, but it has been done that way for many years and at my age I don't want to start changing things."

I was considering asking for a transfer to another committee when Dr. Babcock called me to his office and asked me to be the chairman of the Regents committee. I was surprised but delighted and readily accepted. When the news spread, I was congratulated by the teachers on all sides, as it was considered the most important chairmanship in the Academy. An excerpt from my family letter tells about my appointment:

> The Regents committee has to look after all the 4000 and over answer papers, count, check and recount them. Also make up the report and get them ready to ship to Albany. I selected as far as possible my own helpers and had fine cooperation. I didn't have to do much of the work myself but had to be there early and late, plan the work for others and assume the responsibility. I didn't mind as I had been through it many times.

These were the days when all students had to take the Regents examinations and they were given in most subjects.

Soon after I came to the Academy I was invited to join a group of the men on the faculty who were interested in some recreation during the winter months. The Academy had no gymnasium, but the large grammar schools did, and we were granted the use of one of these after school hours. Two or three times a week we met and played volleyball, then after the game was over, several of us would spend some time with a basketball shooting baskets. The Academy basketball team had to play their games in the Rutger Street Armory and while they were fairly good, they did not attract much of a crowd. These were the days when the athletic association had to finance the teams and only football with its rivalry with Rome Free Academy dating back to 1892 drew big crowds and made any money. It was several years later that the Board of Education began to subsidize the athletic programs.

Fran Klein had just joined the technical faculty and was very interested in sports. Based on his knowledge of the number of men on the faculty who had played basketball, he conceived the idea of a varsity, faculty game, which should create a lot of interest and raise some money for the association. The *Utica Observer-Dispatch* of March 20, 1936 carried the pictures of the men on the faculty who would play and a story of the game for the following night. It read in part:

> Interest is naturally at fever heat at UFA with the faculty taking plenty of kidding on its chances with the varsity. It may be a close game, for such aces as Ken Edkins, Charles Murmane, Ed Butler, Fran Klein and Austin Bell, who make up the faculty's starting team, are sure to cause trouble.
>
> Reserves on the faculty squad will include Calhoon, Roberts,

Duddleston, Wildes, Burdick, Reusswig, Ringland, Perkins, Nixon, Hart, Palmiter, Morrell, Daymont and Prindle . . .

Klein, who is serving as general chairman aided by Harold Meeker, student chairman, starred in three sports at UFA . . . Later he went to Irving Prep and Clarkson, where he was captain of the baseball team.

Ray Calhoon starred in basketball at Oberlin College and then coached Minoa High School to the Onondaga County championship four times in five years. In 1924 his team won the Central New York title.

Roy Perkins was a star miler in college and Howard Hart shone in football, while Wally Nixon played both football and baseball at Syracuse University. Austin Bell is another UFA graduate who went to Oswego State to shine in three sports. Ed Butler attended UFA and Clinton High, playing football and basketball . . .

The UFA varsity will probably start Ray Tritten and Bob Meeker at forwards, Vin Eichler at center and Bernie Grestle and Chambrone at guards, with O'Hearn, Mackennon, O'Toole, Ascroft and Kowalaska reserves.

When we walked onto the court the night of the game, we were surprised to see the armory packed to the rafters. No such crowd had been at the basketball games in years. Before the game Fran Klein, with coach Edkins, had given the varsity a talk. They told the boys they would undoubtedly win but to keep the game interesting, try not to get more than ten points ahead until the last few minutes and then pour it on. None of the faculty players were told of this.

The game started with Edkins at center opposite Eichler and Murmane, who was to start at forward was ill, so I was selected. I was shorter than most of the other players, so I didn't try to rebound under the basket but kept outside and several times was able to retrieve a free ball. From that position I popped in three quick baskets. Up to that time my guard hadn't paid much attention to me, but when he saw I could shoot, he followed me closely. Then everytime I got the ball and started to shoot, he hacked me across my arms. However, the officials caught him almost every time and I proceeded to give the boys on the varsity a lesson in foul shooting, a skill that they had been notoriously weak in all season. I only missed one foul shot all night.

After the game progressed there was a lot of substituting so everyone could get in the game. The varsity followed the game plan and the score stayed fairly close and the crowd loved it. I had been in and out of the game several times when with about five minutes left one of the faculty men got hit on the nose and had to leave the game. I was called back in to finish the game. I didn't look at the score but knew the varsity was ahead and with little time left they began to try to increase the difference. But as it so often happens in such cases, they couldn't

378

buy a basket. The faculty was making a basket now and then and after each point the crowd would raise the roof. For once the students were rooting for the teachers. After one of the missed baskets by the varsity, there was a free ball, which both Edkins and Eichler went after. Eichler didn't want to rough up his coach, so he let Edkins get it. By that time my old legs were giving out and I was through running from one end of the court to another, so I was standing alone near mid-court. Edkins saw me and shot a long pass, which I took and made a quick pivot. Out of the corner of my eye I saw my guard bearing down on me and decided I had been hacked enough for one night. I took a quick dribble and let go one of my high arch shots from the middle of the court. There was a sudden hush as the ball sped through the air and when it swished through the basket, a roar which really raised the roof came from the crowd. Then before the ball could be retrieved the gun went off, sounding the end of the game. As the roar of the crowd continued, I looked up at the scoreboard and realized what my basket had done. It tied the score.

No one wanted to play the five minutes overtime, so it was agreed that the team which made the first two points would win the game. Like an anti-climax to a short story, the jump at center produced another free ball, which Edkins and Eichler both went after. This time disregarding his coach, Eichler came up with the ball and no longer trusting his teammates, he followed my example and shot a long basket, thus ending the game. The crowd let out a loud groan. Afterwards, Edkins said he let Eichler freely shoot as he was sure he wouldn't make a basket. He had never made a long shot all season.

Eichler was in one of my physics classes at the time and on Monday after the game, I walked in the classroom to hear the boys buzzing about it. I was greeted by applause and one boy with admiration in his voice said, "Boy, you can shoot." Just then Eichler walked in and the boys all good naturedly booed him. From that time on there was a noticeable difference in the attitude of my classes. I had taken on a new dimension. I was no longer just a teacher. Before I did have a few problems in discipline, but from that time on there was none. Eichler not only was a basketball player, but a star football player in the Academy and went on to Cornell University to become an All American football player.

In 1938 it became known that the principal, Dr. Babcock, had reached the retirement age of 70 and the board insisted he retire in June. A number of the teachers in the Academy who had worked with Dr. Babcock for a long time thought no one could take his place and put on a drive to petition the board to let him stay longer. A meeting of the Academy Teacher's Association was called, and this group made a number of speeches advocating that we all sign a petition asking the board to reconsider. It was evident that some teachers were not in favor of this action, but were reluctant to say anything. Finally I rose and spoke, saying I was not opposed to passing a resolution requesting the board to reconsider but I questioned the wisdom of asking the teachers to sign a petition. I made the point that one could not tell what interpretation the board might make on such signatures. It might be especially bad for the teachers who were still on probation and wanted to get on tenure. When a vote was taken, the majority favored my position. After the meeting a number of the teachers surrounded me thanking me for speaking as I did. One of the oldest teachers remarked, "We never had anyone on the faculty before who analyzed a situation for us as you did. We all thank you for it."

Mr. Burdick was an active candidate for the principalship. He had been in the Academy since 1926 as a science teacher, department head and for a few years had taken on the additional duties as dean of the junior class. He was the most logical member of the faculty for the position, but the board was divided as to whether to take someone from the system or go outside. Finally, they decided to make him acting principal for a year and then make a decision.

Mr. Burdick worked hard at the job. He wanted to convince the board to give him the full principalship and he did. He had ideas of making changes but didn't want to move too fast. However, one he made right away pertained to me. For several years Ken Edkins, besides being a social studies teacher, was the coach of football and basketball at the Academy. As coach, he also had all the duties of a business manager for the athletic association. The job was too much for one person, but as long as Dr. Babcock was principal, nothing was done. With all his good qualities I was surprised to find that Babcock was not interested in school athletics, in fact, he was opposed to them, considering them a waste of time and not properly belonging to a first class educational institution. UFA was the only large high school in the state without a gymnasium and I couldn't believe my ears when I heard him on more than one occasion brag about it.

Mr. Burdick knew about the athletic situation and one of the first things he did was have the board approve me as the treasurer of the athletic association. I was given an extra $100.00 to take over from Edkins all the duties of a business manager. I hired the ticket sellers and collectors at the gate, obtaining off-duty policeman to be at the games and other details.

When I took over I found that records were not up to date and that there were a lot of outstanding bills from several years back. So the first thing I did was to make an appointment with the manager of the sporting goods store where most of the bills originated and we went over the records. Many of these bills did not show what was purchased and several were duplicates. Football was the big sport and well supported, so most of the money to support the program came from these games. At the end of the season I was able to pay a number of the old bills, much to the delight of the merchants. In order to maintain a businesslike order, I set up a system of using purchase orders for all supplies. Things began to take shape, Edkins was delighted, as he had more time for coaching, the board was pleased as they had been hearing rumors of the association being in the red, and while I wasn't able to pay off all the debts in one year, I came close. Several years later the attendance of the games fell off so much the school could no longer finance the athletic program and the board had to support the program.

Being the chairman of the Regents committee and now the business manager of the athletic association, I was more prominent in the Academy. I began to have visions of becoming a vice-principal. Then near the end of the 1939 school year Mr. Burdick talked to me about becoming a vocational guidance counselor. It was at this time the position of a school counselor was being promoted by the State Department. I was interested but I found out I would have to take extra courses in order to qualify. While this was in the talking stage other things happened to change my future.

At a city-wide teacher's meeting, Superintendent DeCamp made a statement that if he had an opening for a school principal, he knew of no one in the Utica system who could qualify. As soon as I could after this meeting I got an appointment with Superintendent DeCamp and informed him that not only could I qualify for a principalship, I had had ten years of experience as such before coming to Utica. It was then I learned that all my credentials were at the Academy. For years Dr. Babcock had the sole decision of selecting teachers at UFA, which had been a bone of contention between these two men. Now that Dr. Babcock had retired, the superintendent and the board changed this procedure. Superintendent DeCamp listened to me and said he was glad to know about my experience, and to furnish him with my credentials.

It was soon after this interview that there was a meeting of the Peda Gamma, an organization of the wives of the men teachers in the Academy. Norah had joined soon after we came to Utica and this year she was elected president. There was considerable music talent among the members of this group, and Norah proposed that they use this talent by putting on an evening program at the Munson-Williams auditorium and inviting the husbands to attend. The group agreed and invitations were sent to all the men with a special one to Superintendent DeCamp.

The night of the meeting the men turned out in good numbers and all were surprised to see Superintendent DeCamp among them. He had rarely ever considered attending such an event. He sat on the back row of chairs with a group of technical men and when Norah opened the meeting with some words of greetings to the men, I heard him ask in undertones, "Who is that woman?" I was three rows in front of him but could hear him plainly. One of the men whispered, "That's Ray Calhoon's wife." DeCamp never learned how to whisper and in a voice that could be heard halfway across the room, I heard him say, "By God, she's good! She knows how to run a meeting."

After the meeting, which turned out to be a big success, Norah sent Superintendent DeCamp a thank you note for attending. He was very pleased as he slyly told me, so I later told her she got me my next job. A few days later while I was teaching a physics class I saw my classroom door open a crack and looking to see why, I saw Superintendent DeCamp beckoning me to come outside. When I stepped into the hall, without any preliminary, and in his gruff way, he asked, "How would you like to go to Roscoe Conkling School as principal next year?" For a few seconds I was stumped, then I said, "I really don't know, Mr. DeCamp, my work has been mostly in the secondary field. What I would like to do is become an assistant principal here in the Academy with the chance of one day becoming principal." "That will never work," he said. "The board will never approve an assistant principal. The only way to ever become a principal here is to go out and prove yourself as a successful principal of a grade school." I still hesitated and he said, "Think it over and talk it over with your wife this weekend and I'll be back on Monday for your answer." When I told Norah she was very neutral and said it was my decision and she would be satisfied with whatever I did.

On Monday morning DeCamp again appeared at my door and when I went outside, he asked for my decision. I replied, "I have thought it over and if you want me as principal of Conkling school, I will be happy to accept." "Good," he said, "there is a board meeting this week and I will put it through. In the meantime, don't say anything about it." I thanked him and returned to my class where I had a hard time picking up the discussion. My mind was full of thoughts about what the future would hold.

Superintendent DeCamp told Mr. Burdick not to put me on the schedule for the next year, and when the copies came out with my name scratched, the teachers wanted to know what it meant. I had to pretend I didn't know. Then when a committee of the Academy Teachers Association wanted to nominate me for president the next year, I had to tell them, "No, I might not be in the Academy another year."

That Saturday I walked down to the Academy to catch up on my athletic work, when I was called to the office. I was told Superintendent DeCamp wanted me see me in his office as soon as possible. One of the office people offered to drive me downtown to the administration building. When I arrived Superintendent DeCamp congratulated me on being elected as principal of Roscoe Conkling School. Burt Hawkes, who had been the principal at Conkling since Rollin Thompson had been moved to Proctor High School, was being transfered to Kernan School. Superintendent DeCamp told me I was a free agent and could go over to Conkling and spend whatever time I needed to take over the job.

The news of these changes broke in the Utica papers on June 15. They stated my salary would be $3200.00 a year, an increase of $300.00, and would increase each year for a time. I received a lot of congratulations from the UFA teachers, although some said they regretted my leaving. A number of my students wished me well and one Italian boy in my class remarked, "Mr. Calhoon, I am glad you are going to my old school. I know you will be successful, but there is one thing I can tell you which may help. The children in that school think of the principal as a father." I found out he was right and it helped me in adjusting to that community.

It seemed strange that I had been in the school system for seven years, but only knew two of the elementary principals. Vincent Brown, the principal at Hughes I knew not only because the girls were there, but also because he was a leader at Central Church. Burt Hawkes and Cliff Stanton I had met, but the women principals I did not know at all. Then when the principals and supervisors club invited Norah and me to their picnic that June and we met these people, we both came away wondering what kind of folks I was going to be associated with. They seemed so different from the Academy faculty it seemed like another world. I wondered if I had made the right decision.

CHAPTER 22

ROSCOE CONKLING SCHOOL

As soon as I was officially notified of my appointment as principal of Conkling school, I submitted my credentials to the Department of Certification in Albany to obtain an Elementary School Principal's certificate. I knew the State Department of Education had made a number of changes since I had been a principal, but with a Master's degree in education I didn't expect any difficulty. I received a letter from Albany acknowledging my application and indicating I had plenty of credits and after a review I would receive my certificate.

In June I made a couple of trips to Conkling to see Burt Hawkes. He showed me around the building and briefed me on where the records and supplies were kept. I met Mrs. Durkee, the school secretary, and a few of the teachers. When school closed, Hawkes gave me the keys to the building and wished me luck. He also made a remark which was characteristic of him when he said, "Of course you will need a lot of help in getting started, so be free to call on me." Later I found out he was really hurt when he found out I was able to successfully take over the school without asking for his help. I did spend a few hours in the building that summer just getting acquainted with things and also met the head custodian, a man I found to be exceptionally cooperative. I did look for some copies of publications from the State Department which would indicate the content of the various subjects taught in the elementary schools, but I found nothing.

In the middle of the summer I got a copy of a letter sent to Superintendent DeCamp stating that I did not qualify for an Elementary Principal's certificate and to do so I would have to take several hours of work in subjects labeled elementary. I was stunned and took a trip to Albany to confer with the head of the bureau of certification. I found the head was a woman who was very arbitrary and would not bend at all, even when I showed her I had been a principal of an elementary school at Minoa. I asked her about the letter I had and she said when she wrote that she didn't realize that Conkling was an elementary school and most of my credits were in the secondary level, which didn't count as the state now drew a definite line between the two fields.

This all seemed very strange, as I had a Teacher's Life Certificate which entitled me to teach any subject in any school in the state. I could qualify for a supervisor's certificate in science, a high school principal's certificate or be approved as a superintendent of schools, but was not eligible for an elementary school principal's certificate.

It was now too late to take any work that summer, so when I returned from Albany I saw Superintendent DeCamp. I told him of my trip and what they said and asked him what I should do. "Don't worry," he said, "I want you as principal of Conkling and I will take care of the legal part."

This was the time of the World's Fair in New York City and since I was free, we decided to take the girls and see it. We drove down and found a tourist home in Flushing on Long Island. The lady of the house advised us to leave our car and take a bus which ran right in front of the house and would take us directly to the entrance of the grounds. We caught an early bus and in ten minutes were on the grounds. The morning was fairly cool—so we walked around seeing all the sights we could until our feet gave out. One of the main attractions was the General Motors Building, but everytime we looked there were long lines of people waiting to get in. Late in the afternoon when we were tired out from walking we did join the line and after an hour we got inside. We were relieved to be able to sit down on a rotating platform, which carried us around the center of the building. A loudspeaker kept telling us what we were seeing. It was an engineer's vision of the future roads and methods of transportation. It was a glimpse of what is now the network of turnpikes and high-speed roads across the country, but then only a dream.

We did visit several of the buildings and exhibits maintained by the various countries of the world and many were beautiful and impressive. The largest of these was from Russia and I was very impressed. We had been hearing for years how backward that country was, but after seeing the exhibits and pictures of what had been done in that country, I came out saying, "If half of what we have seen is true, we had better look out for Russia in the future." That was in 1939 and what I felt then, came true.

Eating on the fair grounds was a problem until we learned that the restaurants maintained by some of the foreign countries to advertise their products were the most reasonable. We were tired, but on the first day we stayed for the evening fireworks, which were spectacular. After two days we decided we had had all of the fair we could take and drove into New York City on the third morning. I drove around the city awhile to show the girls what it was like and then decided to visit Radio City. We took the guided tour of the building and were given a chance to observe a half hour program. Following that the girls were thrilled to see Rudy Vallee going through a rehearsal for his regular Thursday radio show.

We left the city about 4:00 p.m. and due to the new parkway system of roads, were in Westchester County in a short time. The girls spotted a sign indicating that the next exit was for Sleepy Hollow Cemetery. They had been reading about it in school and insisted they had to see it. I relented and turned off into one of the strangest experiences we ever had on a trip. When we got to the entrance of the cemetery there was a big truck parked to one side of the iron gate and a group of workmen standing idly by. As I drove in I thought they looked at me in a funny way but didn't say anything. We drove around for a time and the girls got out of the car to read some of the inscriptions on the headstones. I thought it a bit strange that we didn't see anyone else, but thought it was because it was late afternoon and when I looked at my watch, I announced it was time we left to find a place to eat.

When we reached the gate where we had entered we faced a dilemma. Not only was the gate closed but securely padlocked. We were stunned and sat for a few minutes in silence with thoughts of spending the night in the cemetery. We were in the 1936 Buick which I had bought after I was sure of being on tenure, the first of a long line of Buick cars I was to own through all these years, so we were comfortable, but for once we had nothing to eat or drink with us. When I had collected my thoughts I mumbled, "Well, see what a mess you gals got us into, but there must be someway out of this place." I started driving around the outside of the grounds following the high iron fence that enclosed the place. There was another gate, but it too was locked. Then I recalled seeing a house at the top of the hill which seemed to be on the grounds, and I wondered if it was a caretaker's house. I made for it, intending to ask how we could get out. However, when we came in sight of the house there was no one around, but I saw the garage door was open with no car inside, so I figured whoever lived there was away. There was a stretch of grass about fifty yards wide between us and a driveway which curved around in front of the house. I stepped on the accelerator and shot across the grass onto the gravel driveway. Following this road down a hill, much to our relief, we saw an open gate which took us out to a side road. When we drove by the main entrance I looked and saw a sign which read, "Gate open from 9 A.M. to 5 P.M." The big truck had hidden this sign from our view when we drove in. Once we were safely out we could laugh at our predicament, but at the time it wasn't funny. Back on the main road we found a place to eat. Discovering we had spent all our money, we got back in the car and drove home that night. It was one of the best trips we were to experience together.

School opened the day after Labor Day with a meeting in the morning of all the principals and supervisors with the superintendent, where I was formally introduced as the new principal of Conkling. In the afternoon I had my first meeting with the faculty of Conkling. There were 35 classroom teachers for grades K-8. There was also a special teacher for each of the departments of art, music, homemaking, industrial arts and two, a man and a woman, for physical education. The school had an enrollment of over 900 pupils, making it one of the largest grade schools in upstate New York. Located on Mohawk Street in east Utica, 90% of the children came from Italian families. Many of the parents came from the old country and spoke little or no English. It was a different community from anything I had ever experienced, but I didn't let it bother me as I considered them just people like everyone else.

One of the first persons I met outside the school was Mrs. Tucci. She lived next to the school and all the children seemed to know her. After the first meeting of a very active PTA in which she was a leader, she greeted me and said, "I see you have some difficulty with the Italian names. Let me help you, just pronounce all the vowels." She was right and it was a big help for me. She was a rare motherly type of person who had the knack of being helpful without intruding.

One thing that bothered me was the loud voices the women used. The first time a group of mothers met to arrange for a PTA meeting they gathered in the homemaking room on the basement floor. While they were working they began to visit, all talking at once, each trying to shout over the commotion. They became so loud they could be heard all through the building, and since school was in session, I went down to see if I could calm them down. I opened the door and had to shout, "Ladies, please can you keep your voices down as we are trying to run a school." They all took it good naturedly, and it was evident that they were not aware how loud they talked. This happened everytime they met and after the first few times all I had to do was to open the door. The first person to see me would shout, "Here's Mr. Calhoon, we have to keep quiet." They would all giggle, but never got mad. For a time at least they would be quiet.

It was characteristic of these people to put a lot of enthusiasm into whatever they did. The children in the school were the same and often had to be restrained. As evidence of how accustomed the children were to loud talking, I noticed that if I spoke to one of them in an ordinary tone they wouldn't hear me. Once in talking to a boy who was in trouble I asked him what his mother said. "Oh," he replied, "she yelled at me." There were two or three Italian teachers on the faculty and I heard them shouting in class. After a time when I knew them better, I spoke to them about it. They seemed surprised and said they didn't realize how they sounded. One remarked, "I don't think the children will hear me if I don't talk loud."

The first few days in the school I felt I had plunged into a new world. I had been dealing with pupils of high school age so long I had forgotten how little people acted. I found the teachers well qualified and seemed to know what was expected at each grade level. I had a lot to learn about the curriculum of the elementary grades. In high school I was accustomed to seeing a syllabus for each subject, but when I asked for such a publication in Albany I was told there was none. I was given some bulletins which dealt with generalities, but only in arithmetic could I find any help in learning what should be covered in each grade.

I concluded that the textbook was the guide most elementary teachers used.

Since I had to take work at an approved school in the field of elementary education, I decided the best place for Saturday classes was at Syracuse University. After I started I soon learned why the State Department of Education wanted the principals in the elementary schools educated in that field. There was a new philosophy developing at this level, it was an emphasis on the child, not on subjects. This concept led to various new plans, such as doing away with rigid grade promotions, more individual instruction and finally to social promotion.

Burt Hawkes had left a well organized school and as was my custom, I let everything run as usual until I could study the system before making any changes. One thing I learned through my classes at Syracuse was that some of the methods and curriculum used in the Utica schools were out of date compared to other school systems. For example, in one course I was taking at the University we were asked to submit a typical teacher program. Since I had on file in the office a copy of each teacher's program which they were required to submit at the beginning of each term, I thought I would copy the shortest, a first grade program. At the next session of the class I was asked to put a copy of the plan I had brought on the board. Included in the program was a daily period of 15 minutes for writing. Did I get panned! The teachers in the class from other schools around the state were horrified. "What," they exclaimed, "writing in the first grade? That has gone out of the curriculum years ago."

This was the beginning of my finding out what a hold the supervisors in Utica had on the system. Miss McCalmont was the supervisor of writing and was an advocate of the old Palmer method of cursive writing. I had been introduced to it when a boy in the College Springs School. It had survived through the years by a few disciples like Miss McCalmont, but was dropped by the majority of schools in the country. All the teachers in the elementary grades were trained by Miss McCalmont to teach this method, and she was strict in enforcing her way. It was true that under supervision pupils could turn out beautiful samples of this kind of writing, and every year some of this work was put on display for the Board of Education and the public to see. However, it had been my observation in the high school that very few kept this method when they were free. But Miss McCalmont was a clever saleswoman, and she had so many convinced that her method was right that no principal dared to oppose her.

The second thing I found was that certain supervisors were not above taking advantage of a new principal. One day Mrs. Hughes, the music supervisor, called and wanted to talk to Miss McHugo, the school music teacher. Mrs. Durkee answered the phone in the outer office and told Mrs. Hughes that Miss McHugo was in class and couldn't be called to the phone. Mrs. Hughes asked to talk to me and I took it in my office, not knowing what had transpired. Since Mrs. Hughes said it was urgent for her to talk to Miss McHugo, I left the office and found her in the auditorium rehearsing the school choir. I told her Mrs. Hughes insisted on talking to her and I would stay until she returned. When I returned to the office I found Mrs. Durkee furious and she exploded, "Don't you know that it is a school rule that a teacher is never called out of a class to talk on the phone?" "No," I replied, "no one ever told me of such a rule, but it is a good one and I shall follow it in the future." It was evident that Mrs. Hughes had taken advantage of me being new to get her own way. In time I found there were a number of unwritten rules in the system which one was supposed to observe. Being new I played the game of enforcing the ones I agreed with, but claimed ignorance of the ones I didn't like.

I didn't like it at all for Mrs. Hughes to take advantage of me, but I kept still, waiting for the chance to get even. In the meantime, Superintendent DeCamp came to see me one day and after talking in the office for a time, he asked me to walk out into the hall. There out of hearing of anyone he started to talk by saying, "I want you to get a good start so I am warning you that some of the supervisors will take advantage of you if they can." He went on to give me a good assessment of the ability and character of each one. In time I found out all he told me was true and I was grateful for his help in dealing with these people.

In my study of supervision at Syracuse University I knew there was a question that existed as to who had charge of a teacher, the principal of the school or the supervisor when she taught that subject. Now I was confronted with such a situation. When looking over the programs of the teachers I discovered that certain ones in the lower grades did not teach their pupils music, while others did. When I inquired about this, I was told that Mrs. Hughes did not approve of their ability to teach music, so she had them send their pupils to a teacher of whom she did approve. They in turn sent their pupils to the first teacher for instruction in reading. I didn't like the idea but waited until the end of the semester to say anything. Then things played right into my hands. Mrs. Hughes issued a bulletin stating that all teachers employed from grade 1 through 4 would teach music in their own rooms. From grade 5 through 8 the pupils would be taught by the music teacher assigned to that building. I was delighted when I read this bulletin and informed the teachers who had been exchanging pupils in the lower grades that they would no longer do so. "What will we do?" these teachers asked. "Mrs. Hughes says we can't teach music." My answer was, "You were hired to teach this grade and if you can't teach it, you'd better apply for a different grade." The teachers who had been doing double time in music were delighted, as they never did like sending their pupils to another teacher for reading. The news of my ruling spread rapidly through the school and bets were made that I would never make it stick.

A few days later there was a meeting of the Principals and Supervisors Club. When the meeting was over and we were standing enjoying a few refreshments Mrs. Hughes made a beeline for me. She had heard of my ruling and was furious. "You can't do that," she almost shouted. "Those teachers can't teach music." I reminded her of the bulletin she had sent out and said I was just following it. "But," she persisted, "those teachers are the exception and I have always had that understood." This was a test of who had the control of the teachers in a school, and I intended to have a showdown if necessary. Mrs. Hughes continued to bluster in front of me, blocking me everytime I tried to get around her, but it did no good. She knew I had the advantage as I had her rule in writing, and I felt I was even with her for putting one over on me the first of the year. When my decision held, my prestige in the school took a big leap upward, and it was echoed through the whole system.

Of all the supervisors, Mrs. Hughes was the most difficult to work with. She was a dictator of the teachers in her department and they knew if they didn't please her their lives were made miserable. If possible, she would get them out of the system. I knew full well that after winning on the matter of the teachers in the lower grades she would look for a way to get even. It came in the middle of the second year. I received a note from her that Miss McHugo would be transferred to Roosevelt School at the beginning of the second term, and Miss Wood, the music teacher at Roosevelt, would come to Conkling.

Right away I got a call from Cliff Stanton, the principal at Roosevelt, very upset to have these teachers moved. Miss Wood had been a fixture at Roosevelt for many years and the school didn't want to lose her, nor did she want to leave. Before I made any commitment, I talked with Miss McHugo and asked her if she wanted to make the transfer. Her reply was while it might be considered a promotion, she had made no request to leave and was happy to stay at Conkling. It looked very much like this was a scheme of Mrs. Hughes to get even with both Stanton and me, since both of us had opposed some of her plans in the past. Together we got an appointment with Superintendent DeCamp and told him the situation, emphasizing that we and the teachers were very much opposed to the move. He replied that frankly he was on our side, but Mrs. Hughes was a "devil" to deal with. He asked us if we were willing to meet with her in his office and talk it over. We agreed and he set a date. When Stanton and I arrived for the meeting, Mrs. Hughes did not show up. Another date was set and again she failed to come, sending word she was ill. Then as the time drew near for the change to be made, the superintendent set another date for a Saturday morning. Again Mrs. Hughes failed to show, so the superintendent called her and when she said she was too ill to come to the office, he announced we would come to her apartment. She protested, but he was firm and said we were on the way. When we got to the door, DeCamp said, "I wonder if she will let us in." She did and we found her in a dressing gown with her hair all disheveled and without makeup, so she did look ill. Then when the superintendent informed her that both Stanton and Calhoon were opposed to the transfer of the two music teachers, she flew into a regular tirade. She raved like a demented person, using language I couldn't believe and wouldn't repeat. It became the worse scene I ever experienced. But through it all Stanton and I refused to be intimidated and held our positions. Since the superintendent had to approve all transfers, DeCamp told us when we were outside, "If you men will support me no matter what some member of the board says, I will not approve the transfer." We both agreed and no transfer was made. A few days later I was in the outer office of the superintendent and he saw me. He came out and said to Miss Lewis, his secretary, "I want you to meet one of the bravest men I know." The surprise of this affair came the next time I met Mrs. Hughes. She greeted me like an old friend. Later she made all the arrangements for Marjorie and Dorothy to try out for a Curran scholarship in music by playing their harp. This was a scholarship given each year by a musical club to the best high school musicians in the area and considered a high honor. They did not win, but it was a good experience and I couldn't help being grateful to Mrs. Hughes for her gesture. From that time on as long as I was an elementary principal in the system I never had trouble with Mrs. Hughes.

My second experience with a supervisor came in the field of art. Miss Sheldon was the supervisor and extremely conservative. I learned this through Frank Bugental, the art teacher in Conkling, when he told me how he was criticized for letting the boys in his classes draw pictures of cars or airplanes instead of a vase of flowers which was supposed to be required. He explained how much better his discipline was when he let pupils work on something they liked. Near the end of the year, Superintendent DeCamp asked me about Frank and said he was up for tenure, but Miss Sheldon refused to recommend him. I told DeCamp that I rated Frank very high, both as an art teacher and a person. I told him how he had volunteered to draw a picture on the blackboard in each classroom in the building of the most lifelike looking Santa Claus I ever saw. DeCamp asked me if I would give him a letter recommending Frank for tenure, which I did, and it went through the board in spite of Miss Sheldon's opposition.

One thing I had to get used to as a principal was that I had very little to say about a choice of teachers or other personnel in my school. Mrs. Durkee had been the school secretary for a long time, although as I soon learned she had few qualifications for the position. The first few reports she turned in were full of errors and when I called her attention to them, she always replied, "That's the first mistake I ever made." After hearing this over and over, I gave up and made the corrections myself. She had one habit which made me cringe when she answered the phone with a "yeah." I soon learned that she wasn't the only one in the system to do that. To my amazement I heard some of the older women principals use the same expression. With all her shortcomings, Mrs. Durkee was good-hearted, was fine with the pupils and teachers, and knew the community so well I came to depend on her in many ways.

Barely two weeks into the school session, I was to learn how I could be involved in the affairs of the families of the children in the school. One mid-morning I happened to glance out the window of my office which looked out over the playground to the houses on the street opposite the grounds. From one of these houses I saw a woman run out the front door screaming and tearing her hair. I asked Mrs. Durkee if she knew who lived there, and she passed it off by saying, "It is probably that retarded girl who lives on that street." But when I saw a crowd begin to gather I was certain something had happened. There was a crew of painters working on that side of the building and I saw one of them walking over to see what had caused the commotion. When he returned I went down to ask him. He said he was told that a man had just blown the top of his head off with a shot gun and his wife had found him. She was the one I had seen in hysterics. I hurried back and asked Mrs. Durkee if there were any children in school in that house. When I told her what had happened, she got busy and found there was a seventh grade girl and a fifth grade boy there. I had her contact the teachers and have these children report to the office at once. We caught them just before the noon dismissal time. When the girl walked into the outer office, she glanced out the window and could see the crowd. I saw her body stiffen, and she wanted to know what was happening. When the boy arrived I told them their father had an accident and I would walk home with them. It was an agonizing walk, because I couldn't tell them what I had heard and they were almost paralyzed with the unknown. I felt a deep grief for them and once more relived my journey home when my father died.

When we got to the edge of the crowd I asked a woman if she knew where the children's mother was. She pointed to the house next door when a woman came out and greeted the children. She turned to me and said, "I am their aunt and will take them to their mother." Then she added, "You are the new principal, aren't you? It is so very kind of you to bring the children home. The doctor is now with the mother and she is under sedation, but I will care for the children. Thank you so very much." I left to go home for lunch, but I was so "shook up" I couldn't eat.

Miss Panzone was the school nurse and coming from an Italian family, she understood the children so well I came to depend on her. However, she was in the school only part of the time, and it seemed the worst accidents happened when she was in another school. The city hospital was on Mohawk Street, directly across from the school building. Since a large number of the people in this area were on welfare, all the cases that were beyond first aid that I brought in, when the nurse wasn't there, they took as a matter of course. One recess time I saw some boys carrying a boy into the building. I met them in the nurse's room and one look at the position of his foot told me he had a broken leg. "What happened?" I asked. They were all eager to tell me and talked together. I finally got them calmed down and asked one boy to tell me. He said, "We were playing cackle and he got hurt." "What's cackle?" I asked. "Cackle, that is the game Mr. Hawkes taught us. You know, when one boy runs the rest run after him and catch him by the legs and throw him down and all the others jump on top." "I guess you mean tackle," I said. "That is what they do in football, but they are dressed for it. I guess you better not play that game anymore." "All right, Mr. Calhoon," they all shouted in unison, and that ended that game.

I knew that the injury was serious, so I made the boy as comfortable as possible and called Dr. Mahady, the head of the school medical department. By chance he was in his office and came right up. He confirmed my diagnosis and called the city hospital for help with a stretcher. I followed the boy to the hospital and by this time I had been there so many times I was accepted as one of the staff. I helped get the boy ready for an X-ray and went with him into the room, then helped set his leg, staying with him until his mother came.

After my many trips with children to the hospital, I could understand why the hospital preferred not to have the parents present when treating an accident case. Time after time I would stand by the child while the doctor sewed up a nasty cut and with the real young ones would hold their hands to calm their fears, but they never made a peep. If possible the parents would be notified when I took a child to the hospital and when the mother appeared, the child would burst into tears. Often the mother would join the child in tears, creating an emotional scene. If the mother did not come, I would take the child home and the loud crying took place there.

An unusual case developed when a teacher sent a boy to me saying he complained of something in his eye. I examined him, but at first could see nothing. But when he said he could still feel something, I turned his head so I looked in a cross light. It looked like a tiny chip had been sliced off the front of the cornea. When I quizzed him, he told me a boy had thrown something and hit him in the eye on the playground at recess. I knew this was not a case for the hospital, so I called Dr. Farrell, a leading eye doctor in the city. I explained my situation and asked if I brought the boy to his office, would he look at the eye. He agreed and after his examination he said, "You are right. A piece has been peeled off the front of the cornea. The temptation is to operate, but many times nature has a way of doing a better job, so I will give him some drops to relieve the irritation and tell his parents to wait a week, then bring him back and I will know better what should be done."

I had Mrs. Durkee notify the boy's mother that I had taken him to the doctor and would bring him home. When we arrived we were greeted not only by the mother but two grandparents, a couple of aunts and several children. The minute we got inside the door, they all screamed, "What happened?" When they calmed down so I could be heard I explained what the doctor said, that there was a piece cut off the front of his eye. At once they all wanted to see, using their fingers to pry open his eyelids. I had to step in and use main force to protect the poor boy. Then one of the aunts asked him who did it. "Tony," he answered in a low voice. "You mean my Tony?" screamed the woman, and when he nodded his head, she yelled, "Mon Dieu, I'll kill him." Sensing a family fight ensuing, I got out as soon as possible.

Thinking of the possibilities that might develop from this case, I walked out on the playground to see if I could find what had been thrown. That summer a heavy wire fence had been put around the grounds, and I picked up a small piece of a link that had been cut, leaving a razor sharp edge. It was likely this was the object the boy had thrown. I shuddered to think how close this came to being a major tragedy for just the smallest change in direction could have cut the eyeball open. It was a relief to learn that the doctor was right when he said nature could heal, and it did.

The teachers in the school had told me about the close family ties that prevailed in the Italian community. This was especially true if the parents or grandparents had come recently from the old country. I also learned how important the oldest boy in a family was; in fact, all boys were rated above their sisters. I had first hand evidence of this when a mother of a third grade boy, who had been in trouble in school many times, called to ask me to stop at her house after school one day. When I got to the door I was met by the mother, who ushered me into the living room. I gasped when I was confronted by a big family circle, consisting of four grandparents, three aunts, some brothers and sisters, and a cousin of the boy. In the center of the room seated on a low stool was the boy, who I could see was just beaming at the attention he was receiving.

None of the grandparents spoke English, so all that was said had to be translated. The mother thanked me for coming and stated she wanted to see why the teacher picked on her boy in school. He was such a good boy at home they could not believe he was bad in school. All the group nodded their heads and all took turns in saying the same thing in various ways. It was evident I would get nowhere in such a setting, so when I finally got a chance to speak, I said, "I am glad to hear this boy is such a good boy at home. I will tell his teacher and I am sure if he is like that at school there will be no more trouble." The mother thanked me, but I could see the boy's expression change and he looked rather crestfallen. This was not the way he expected things to turn out. He wanted everything blamed on the teacher.

When I got outside, I thought, "Never again will I be trapped like that." In the future anyone who wants to see me will come to my office where I can meet them on my grounds, not theirs. It became my policy that I held to with only a very few exceptions.

As a principal I not only had to deal with the problems of pupils and teachers, but those of the building. Conkling was twenty years old and had met all the state regulations in force at that time. One of these regulations stated that each classroom must have so many cubic feet of fresh air per minute. The engineers who got this adopted evidently never checked to see what effect this amount of air flowing would have on the teacher and pupils in a room. In fact, it created such a draft that the State Department was flooded with protests after these schools were built. I had learned in my studies at the university that this regulation had been modified to cut down on the flow of air. The teachers in Conkling had complained about this for years, but the superintendent of buildings refused to make any change, just told them to dress warmer. But when I got a copy of the new regulation and showed it to him, he sent the school electrician to cut down on the speed of the big ventilating fan, which helped a great deal.

When the real cold weather of the winter came, I was told about another problem. The teachers on the second floor said the halls were so cold the pupils had to put on coats to go to the toilets. This seemed strange, as the halls on the first floor were very comfortable. The first chance I had on a cold morning I went up to the second floor to check. I found what the teachers had told me was true. I walked to the end of the hall and put my hand near the glass of the outside window. I could feel the cold air coming in all around the panes of glass. Going back to the middle of the building, I stood pondering why such a condition prevailed when I noticed the sound of the big fan which was expected to recirculate the air through the building sounding as if it was crying for air. I then noticed that at the end of each stairway fire doors had been installed and these doors were closed. I walked over and opened one set. Right away the fan stopped whining and in five minutes the hall was nice and warm. This was a good example of contrary regulations. The fan had been installed to recirculate the air through all the halls of the buildings, but someone in the past has misinterpreted the use of the fire doors, which were intended to be closed at night, but had them closed in the daytime. These doors were so airtight they prevented the air from circulating.

As soon as I solved the problem I went down to the boiler room to find Pat, the head custodian. Pat was a big good natured Irishman, well liked by everyone and did his best to please people. He had his men keep the building clean, but he had his limitations in making any necessary change. I asked him to come to the top floor and showed him what I had learned. He was happy and relieved, as he always thought the teachers blamed him for the cold halls. We blocked the doors open and I informed the teachers not to close these doors and dismissed the monitors who had been appointed to close the doors at the beginning of each day.

During the depression years the board had approved a plan of engaging a crew of painters to work on the old schools. This was the year to paint Conkling. In the fall they worked outside, but when the cold weather came they planned to come inside. They wanted to start with the auditorium and asked what color I wanted it. I was glad to know I had a choice and told them I liked the shade of green on the auditorium at Proctor High School. They obtained some of that paint, but before they started they tried out a patch on the wall. It was then I learned something about paint. The difference in the light makes a big difference in the looks. The paint from Proctor didn't look the same and was not satisfactory. The painters then mixed a number of different shades until they got one we all liked.

When the painters started on the auditorium, they announced they probably would not have it done before Christmas. This presented a problem, as the school had always used the stage to put on their annual programs. I called a meeting of the teachers and after much discussion it was decided that the kindergarten and grades 1–4 would use the gymnasium for their program and the upper grades would use the stage even if the auditorium was not finished. The teachers in the lower grades rose to the occasion and put on an outstanding program of group dancing, action songs and group singing. Superintendent DeCamp was invited to this program and he came bringing Miss Lewis, his secretary. After it was over they congratulated us all saying it was the best they ever attended.

One thing happened when the lower grades were filing into the gym for a dress rehearsal that made a deep impression on me. I was in the hall watching the classes move into the gym according to a plan I had designed, when there was a delay. I moved up near the door to see what was holding up the line when I paused beside the line of kindergarten pupils. Looking ahead I felt a tiny hand creep slyly into mine. I looked down into the face of a beautiful little kindergarten girl with the merriest brown eyes I ever saw. She gave me a wistful shy smile as if asking for friendship and understanding. By this time I knew better than to say anything or I would have every little girl in line rushing to grasp my hand, so I returned her smile and gave her hand a friendly squeeze. But that little "minx" did something to me; I could never forget that look and I could never be mean to the little people she represented. There came a few times when it was necessary to punish a child, but only when they knew they deserved it; usually a good straight talk was all that was needed in dealing with these pupils.

When the auditorium was ready for use, Louis Scalise, a violin teacher in the community requested its use to give a concert by the Utica Junior Symphony orchestra. This was a group he had organized to give his students as well as others from the grades and high schools in the area a chance to help their musical education by playing with others. Permission was granted, and it was so successful that it became an annual event for many years. When I met Mr. Scalise I liked him very much, not only for his musical ability, but for his fine personality.

After I saw his first concert I asked him about the possibility of using a harp. He was interested and Marjorie joined the orchestra. Since I had to transport the harp, I sat through most of the rehearsals. Scalise was a good conductor and a fine teacher, plus he had the patience to work with young players. Marjorie got along fine, something she was never able to do in the UFA orchestra. Being so closely connected with the orchestra, I was selected to be on the board of directors, a position I held for over ten years. When Marjorie left for college, Dorothy took over the harp to play in this orchestra. In that way both girls got some favorable publicity and met a number of the future musicians of the city. Mr. Scalise kept this organization going for many years until his death, when Philip, his son, took over as director.

As a rule there was little trouble with absentees at Conkling. Most of the children liked school and the parents wanted their children to get the best possible education; when the children from a large family were out a lot, I began to investigate. I asked the attendance officer to check, and she reported that the father claimed his children didn't have clothes so they could attend. I found the family on welfare and called that office. From them I got quite a different story. They told me a long story of how the father of these children had been working for the Public Works Administration, but claimed he had a hernia so he couldn't work. He was sent to the hospital for an operation, but he claimed it didn't cure his condition. His wife died, leaving him with six children, and while he was supposed to be recuperating, he had gone down into Pennsylvania to visit and had met a widow with five children and married her. He brought her and the children back with him, so now there were eleven children of school age in the family. The welfare office read me a long list of clothes they had furnished these children and sent me a list of what they had issued the last month, which looked like an inventory of a small clothing store.

With this information I wrote the father of the children to come to my office and explain why his children were not in school. Two days later a big overweight Italian man walked into my office and said he had my letter and was there to explain his actions. He proceeded to give a long tirade about the treatment he had received from the PWA, the city hospital and the welfare people. I had been looking at him while he ranted and I saw he was dressed in a clean white shirt with a tie. His overcoat and the suit he was wearing were clearly of better material and must have cost more than I could afford. When he finally ran down, I told him I had a list of the many clothes the children had received from the welfare people, so I didn't believe they were destitute of clothes and couldn't be in school. "Oh," he said, "the things they sent this month are for Sunday. I expect them all to have two of everything, one for school and one for Sunday. There is no reason they can't have them. Uncle Sam has millions." By this time my blood pressure was rising and at his last remark I half rose out of my chair and looking straight at him I said, "Do you know who Uncle Sam is? I am part of him and I am working every day, not only to support my family but helping to pay for yours while you sit around." I started to say, "On your fat behind," but I didn't. I then finished by saying, "I want you to get those children in school or you and I are going to see another part of Uncle Sam, called Children's Court." With that he jumped out of his chair saying, "All right, Mr. Calhoon, all right." He fairly flew out of the office and the next day all the children were in school with no more trouble.

When I told the attendance officer about my interview and the result, she said, "You probably said the magic word when you mentioned the court. All of us who have been on this case have a strong suspicion that this man is in the country illegally and a court investigation is the last thing he wants." I will always remember his expression, "Uncle Sam has millions." It represents what too many people think when they want government aid. They do not stop to think who "Uncle Sam" is.

Not only was the school expected to care for a pupil who had an accident during school hours, but also if hurt on the way to or from school. At times children came to school too sick to stay or became sick during the session, and as many parents did not have phones, it was up to me to take them home. In that way I got an insight into the way these people lived. Few of these people used the front door, so I would have to ask the child which door to gain entrance. I found there were two general conditions that prevailed. In one the inside matched the rundown looks of the outside, so I knew this family was struggling. In the other, once I pushed past the garbage pails and other refuse on the back steps and rapped on an inside door, I would be ushered into a fine looking living room. The furniture looked new and modern, and when I could see into the kitchen there would be all modern appliances. These people knew the assessors only looked at the outside of a house, so they were content to have it look shabby to keep their taxes low. But in all cases I found a warm welcome and expressions of appreciation for bringing their children home.

I found that not only did the children look to the school for help, but sometimes it was a parent. One day just after the noon recess a young distracted mother came bursting into my office. "Mr. Calhoon," she said, "what am I going to do? Johnny will not eat his lunch. I have done everything I know, but day after day he will not eat." The mother's hair was flying and she was out of breath, dragging her six-year old son by the hand to get him to school on time. I looked to see a small harassed girl who was trying to meet the problems of parenthood. I looked down at the boy and he was looking up at his mother in rapture. I could read his mind as he was thinking, "Boy, have I got her going." When the mother stopped, I said quietly to the boy, "Take this note to your teacher so you will not be marked late, and stay in your room." "Oh," the mother exclaimed, "he will starve." I replied, "No, he won't, if he didn't eat his lunch it is a sign that he isn't hungry." The boy hesitated, so I repeated, "Go to your room. I want to talk to your mother." Rather crestfallen, he left.

I had a good talk with the mother. I learned that he did have some money to buy candy, which he probably ate between meals, also that his playmates came calling for him while he was at the lunch table. So I suggested that for a time she did not give him money for candy and also tell his friends that they were not to come before a certain time. I suggested that she get his lunch ready and sit down to eat with him and eat. If he didn't touch his plate not to say a word, and "when he sees it doesn't bother you when he doesn't eat, he will eat." Evidently my suggestions worked, as I heard no more about this trouble and the boy stayed in school, so I was sure he didn't starve.

While the painters were painting the classrooms, they unwittingly caused a lot of trouble. One day Miss McHugo informed me that a boy who was renting a trombone from the school band had lost his instrument. She said Mrs. Hughes was very upset and would probably call me. She did and was very excited, for she was sure the boy or his brothers had sold or pawned the instrument and wanted me to call the police. "Anyway," she said, "you are the principal of the school and therefore responsible." "Wait a minute," I replied. "You and Miss McHugo decided who got the instrument. I had nothing to do with it. So while I will do all I can to find the trombone, I am in no way responsible."

I had the boy come to the office so I could quiz him. He claimed he left school with the instrument, but when he got home he didn't have it. I asked him to retrace his steps and it came out that he did stop on the way home to play. I guessed that he had put the case down while he played and forgot about it until he reached home. He returned to look for it, but it had disappeared. To check further, I decided to go to his house and see his mother. In the meantime, I learned that the boy's father and two of his older brothers had been in prison for theft. That was why Mrs. Hughes was so sure they had sold the instrument.

On the way home one day after school hours I located the boy's house and as usual went to a side door. When I rapped, the door opened a crack and a woman with the ugliest face I ever saw peeked out. All I could think of was someone in a Halloween mask. Her hair was unkempt, her clothes dirty, one eye was closed, and her nose looked as if it had been flattened by a blow. I told her who I was and asked if I might ask her a question. She opened the door a bit wider and I involuntarily took a step backwards as the stench that came out of that room was overpowering. When I told the woman her boy had lost the trombone and wondered if she knew about it, I heard a voice from inside say, "What is it, Mom? What does the man want?" The woman mumbled something and a young man came to the door. He opened the door wider and I had a view of what might have been a stage setting for the *Grapes of Wrath*. In the middle of the room was a table holding two wine bottles. With their chairs tilted back were two young men with their hats on and their feet propped on the table. To one side was a kitchen stove, the only other piece of furniture in sight. Then to my amazement a little girl who I recognized as a second grader in our school walked across the back of the room. I talked with the young man at the door for a few minutes and was satisfied they were of no help.

I came away far more concerned about seeing that little girl in that house than I was about the trombone. The first chance I had I talked with the welfare people and the family service. Both said they were acquainted with the family and knew the condition, but as long as the child showed no evidence of abuse, the court would not consider taking her out of the home.

The next day two of the boys I had seen in the kitchen came to see me. They said the family was concerned about the lost trombone but didn't know where it could be. They informed me that they were both out of jail on parole and if reported to the police, they would be in serious trouble. I assured them I would not report them unless I had some evidence of theft and asked them to help find the instrument. They thanked me and said they would do all they could to help.

This situation lasted for two weeks with Miss McHugo frantic as Mrs. Hughes was after her all the time. Then one afternoon just as I was ready to leave the office, one of the painters came in carrying an instrument case. He wanted to know if it belonged to someone in the school. I opened it and there was the missing trombone. "Where in the world did you find it?" I asked. "On the teacher's desk in the hall outside the room we have been painting. It was covered with a drop cloth we had put over everything," he replied. The next morning I called the boy to the office and he identified it as his. When I told him where it was found, he recalled that he had returned to the building when he started to play and put it on that desk. So the case was solved, but Mrs. Hughes took the instrument away from the boy. I still worried about the little girl, but she was in school every day, seemingly all right as long as I was in Conkling.

One morning a seventh grade girl came to my office with a request that she be excused from school so she could visit her mother who had been taken to the hospital. I knew the girl, as she was frequently out of school, and an investigation revealed that the mother kept her home to look after a baby whenever she could get a part-time job. The family lived only a few houses down the street from the school and had received some notoriety as a story had been in the paper about the visiting nurse finding the baby ill. When taken to the hospital, an examination showed the baby's body with many sores, which were diagnosed as coming from rat bites. The father had abandoned the family, so the mother was left with several children to live on welfare. This girl was the oldest and had always shown a strong affection for her mother. I wasn't surprised at her request, but I explained that if I did excuse her the hospital would not let her in. She was very persistent and when I repeated, "No," she reluctantly went back to her room.

About an hour later a teacher asked me to come to her room as she had a problem. When I got there she stepped out into the hall to tell me a girl in the class claimed she had swallowed a safety pin and since the school nurse was not in the building, she didn't know what to do. I asked her the name of the girl, and when she told me, I said, "Oh, oh." It was the girl who wanted to be excused. I went into the room and talked to the girl and the pupils around her. Several said they saw her have the pin in her mouth and no one could find it now. The girl insisted she had swallowed it, so I had her come to the office. She told me the name of their doctor, and I was fortunate enough to get him on the phone. I told him about the situation and asked for his advice. He said, "I am just about ready to go to the hospital. Have the girl ready at the front door, and I will pick her up in ten minutes. I'll take her and have her fluoroscoped to see if she did swallow the pin."

The next morning when the girl was out of school, I called the doctor to find out about her. He reported that he took her to the hospital and had her fluoroscoped, but no pin showed. She still insisted that she had swallowed the pin, so he took an X-ray. That didn't show anything, either, so he told her she could go home. She then became hysterical and so to relieve her mind he gave her a dose of castor oil and put her in a bed in the room with her mother. "So," I said, "she won out after all." "What do you mean?" he asked. I told him about her persistence in going to see her mother, to which he replied, "It's a damned good thing I didn't know or I would have given her something far worse than castor oil." I have used this story several times to illustrate how persistence succeeds.

During my second year at Conkling another episode occurred that I call my Cinderella story. Gloria, a large seventh grade girl, had become a real problem. I knew about her because she was absent so much, and I had the attendance officer check several times. She reported that Gloria lived with her father and stepmother, whom she resented, and had run away from home several times. Once when she was gone for two days the police found her one night curled up in a corner of an empty warehouse, asleep.

I was debating in my mind what could be done about this problem when a group of girls came into my office at morning recess time to tell me that a lady with a baby was outside and wanted to see me. I told them to tell the lady to bring the baby and come in. In a few minutes a very attractive young woman entered the office leading a two-year old boy. She introduced herself and said she had come to see Gloria. "Oh," I said, "you are Gloria's mother. I am glad to see you, for I have been wanting to talk with you for sometime."

"I came," she announced, "because I had a quarter on the kitchen table to pay the milkman and it disappeared, so I think Gloria took it." I was surprised that she had walked all the way to the school to find a quarter, but I said, "I will have Gloria come to the office." As we waited I began a visit with the woman. She seemed very nice and spoke very well, telling me she was a graduate of Proctor H. S. but did not go to

402

Conkling. As we talked, it was hard for me to believe the stories I had heard about her.

When Gloria entered the office the contrast between the two couldn't have been greater. Gloria was stockily built, while the stepmother was small and rather petite. Gloria had on a skirt and white blouse which was torn at one shoulder so the sleeve hung down over her hand. The skirt was stiff with dirt and looked as if it would stand by itself. Her heavy black hair was uncombed and matted. She had a round face, which might have made her good looking except there was an ugly red scar running from the corner of one eye down across the cheek to the corner of her mouth. I had been told that this scar had come from a scratch which the stepmother had given her when the woman had flown into a rage because she thought Gloria had tipped a high chair over with the baby in it. The scratch had become infected and would disfigure Gloria for life.

In contrast to Gloria's appearance, the stepmother was dressed in a beautiful tailored suit. Her hair was well groomed, hanging in attractive black curls. The little boy, who was roaming around the office, was clothed in a fine snow suit.

The minute that Gloria entered the office and saw her stepmother she stiffened and stood as if on guard. When asked about the quarter, she said she saw it on the table and it was there when she left for school. I watched both as the conversation went on, and I could see the wide gap between them. Gloria was rather sullen, and while the woman had appeared so nice, I could see her black eyes snap at times, so I thought she could be a spitfire.

When it was evident that there was no solution to the missing quarter, I dismissed Gloria to return to her room. After she left I turned to the woman and said, "That girl needs help. If something isn't done, you are going to lose her." She looked at me for a minute and then began to pour out her story. She said she had grown up in a large Italian family and after finishing high school tried unsuccessfully to find a job so she could leave home. She met this older man who offered her a home if she would marry him. He had a good cottage home, but his wife had died, leaving him with a young daughter. It was a case of mutual benefit, rather than love, which led to the marriage. The girl knew about Gloria, but the man assured her that there would be no problem. However, Gloria had been running the house after her mother had died, and resented someone else coming in to take over. Then when the baby arrived, friction increased, leading to the present situation.

The woman talked so long, at times in tears, that I began to wonder how to end the session. In the meantime the little boy was restless and finally stood in the middle of my office making a puddle on the floor like a puppy dog, which both of us ignored. Finally when I got a chance to talk I mentioned about our trouble with Gloria in school, telling about her ear condition of eczema, which had gone into her ear causing an extremely offensive odor. It was so bad at times the teacher had to send her outside, as the other pupils became nauseated. Then I mentioned her clothes, which certainly needed attention. The stepmother told me the girl had a room of her own and was expected to care for her clothes, also had medicine to treat her ear, but was careless. "Good," I said, "you have tried other things. Why don't you keep Gloria home for a day or two and help her with her hair and ear." Then pausing for a minute and looking at her, I continued, "You say your husband gives you money to run the house and for clothes, but when you try to talk to him about your problem with Gloria he walks out and spends the evening at a tavern with his friends. I can see you know how to dress very well, your outfit is very becoming. So after you get Gloria cleaned up, why don't you take her downtown and buy a couple of nice dresses for her. Let her, with your guidance, choose what she wants. Try making her more of a partner rather than a daughter and see what happens. Also, if you work together maybe you can work on the "old man" and get his help to form a better family life." I rose from my chair in order to get her started out of the office. She got up, took the boy by the hand, and without another word, walked pensively out the door.

Gloria was absent from school for two days, then on the third day, right after the noon dismissal, a teacher came dashing into the office. "Mr. Calhoon," she exclaimed, "come to the front window and look out. You'll never believe it unless you see it." With her I hurried to the front of the building, where a group of teachers were gathered all talking excitedly as they looked out the window. They made room for me and I looked out to see a large group of girls gathered around Gloria. It was evident that she was the center of attraction. She was a changed person with her black hair all combed and tied with a colored ribbon and dressed in a new flowered print dress they could all envy. Then all together they went down the street chattering and laughing, a great contrast to before, as Gloria usually went by herself, an outcast. "So it's Cinderella," I remarked. The teachers who knew nothing of my interview were flabbergasted by the change. They began to make bets as to how long it would last. Some said a day and the longest gave it a week. But they all lost, for as long as I was in Conkling the clock never struck twelve for this Cinderella. I have to think that my giving that young mother a sympathetic ear and some friendly advice changed the lives of this family.

Sometimes in school, just as in life outside, there arises a problem which has no right or wrong answer. One such case arose one May morning when a sixth grade teacher, after taking her class to gym, stopped in my office. She had a distressed look on her face and said, "Mr. Calhoon, I had something happen in my room this morning which I don't know how to handle. I want your advice," and at my request she told this story.

At the beginning of each morning session I have allowed the

404

pupils an opportunity to tell anything of interest that may have happened to them recently. (Sort of a show and tell session which was very popular at the time.) That morning a boy, (I'll call him Tony) raised his hand, waving it frantically. He was bursting with news and when given permission to speak, he exploded with "Miss—I got my new suit for confirmation last Sunday. Do you know how I got it?" Not waiting for an answer, he continued, "Last week my father got a part time job and he came home with a five dollar bill, which he said was for my suit. So on Saturday morning he took me downtown to a big clothing store. We went to the boy's department and saw three long racks full of boy's suits. One rack was marked $5.00, one $7.50, and the third $10.00. We started looking at the $5.00 rack but didn't find anything we liked. A clerk came to help, but we still didn't find anything suitable. The clerk left to help another customer and my father started looking on the $7.50 rack. He found one that was just what we wanted, so when the clerk wasn't looking he slipped that suit off its rack and put it on the $5.00 one. The clerk came back and asked if we had found anything, and my father said yes, that there was one if it fits. I tried it on and it was just my size, so father gave the clerk $5.00 and he didn't notice the difference, so I got my suit."

"Mr. Calhoon, what should I have done? What should I do?" asked the distressed teacher." "This sure is a good one," I replied. "Before I answer, let me ask what did you do." "I was so surprised I was completely floored," she replied. "I looked at the boy and his eyes were brimming with admiration at how clever he thought his father had been. I just couldn't destroy that father in front of the boy's class. But I could also see the eyes of all his classmates fastened on me to see what I would say." I hesitated a minute and then said, "I'm glad you got a suit, Tony. Now it's time for arithmetic, everybody get out your book and let's get to work."

"I would say you did just fine," I said. "Children that age are pretty wise and it may be your attitude told them you didn't approve of what the father did, and they may set the boy straight. However, if you feel that you should do more, I suggest you find a story which teaches that honesty is the best policy and read it to the class. Let the pupils discuss it, but you want to be prepared with an answer if someone asks about Tony's father."

I was so intrigued by this episode that I decided to use it as a basis for a discussion with groups of teachers and perhaps parents. To do so, I made out a sheet using a new method being introduced into educational circles of stating a problem, then following it with a series of possible answers which the student is asked to rank in order from the best to the poorest. I listed five things the teacher should do, ranging from "the teacher should tell the boy at once that his father did wrong," to "the teacher should do nothing." I had copies made and I tried it out on several groups of teachers, giving them five minutes to rank the answers without any discussion. I collected a total of 100 answer sheets from teachers, ranging from kindergarten to senior high school.

I also tried it out on a small group of mothers who had children in school. The results were very interesting; more than 99% of the teachers felt that something should be done, although they varied widely in their choice, some indicating something that they thought better than what I had selected. On the other hand, 75% of the mothers indicated that the teacher should do nothing. While this was in no way a scientific survey, it did show a wide difference of opinion between the teachers and the parents as to what should be done in a classroom when a moral question arises.

The next Christmas the upper grades produced an unforgettable program. The teachers decided to put on a play and selected one called, *Dust of the Road.* All the special teachers were asked to help and true to the spirit of cooperation that existed at Conkling, they responded to the fullest. I was asked to help with the stage lighting. The play was a simple story of a little beggar boy dressed in rags being spurned by all he met as he journeyed along the dusty road. Finally he wandered into a cathedral. For this scene the industrial arts boys had constructed a large window frame and the art pupils had filled in the many openings with colored cellophane strips. With a flood light back of it the resemblance to a church window was perfect.

While the beggar boy stood gazing at all the splendor of the cathedral, the school choir off to one side filled the room with Christmas carols. Then at a fixed time I switched off all the stage lights so for 30 seconds everything was in darkness. Two teachers rushed onto the stage and changed the boy's clothes to a long white gown. With dark curly hair and big brown eyes, and in his costume, he did look angelic. Now as the choir started singing "Silent Night" I slowly dimmed the lights, leaving the boy in the bright spot. An audible but subdued sigh went up from the audience. When the choir finished the carol, the stage curtains were closed and I turned on the house lights. Then the unexpected happened. These children who would applaud with enthusiasm everything that took place on the stage didn't make a sound. Only a big sigh seemed to go through the auditorium. When I stepped out to watch the pupils move back to their rooms, I could see how deeply they had been affected. It was if they had been to a church service and had had a deep religious experience, something that neither the teachers nor I had anticipated.

I was the last person to become a principal in the city, so I was surprised to be elected president of the Principals and Supervisors Club. This was both a professional and a social organization meeting monthly for a program. This proved to be a critical time in the city school system. The school budget was then under the control of the city government and since these were in the depression years, the city was in financial difficulty. To reduce the school budget, the board of education was asked to eliminate all supervisory positions. There had been at times considerable friction between the principals and certain supervisors, but most of the principals recognized the value of the supervisors and didn't want them all fired.

The principals met in a closed session and after a long discussion made me the chairman of a committee to visit the president of the board and propose that the supervisors be retained, using the so-called Milwaukee plan. Most all city systems had the problem of a certain amount of friction between principals and supervisors, and Milwaukee had devised a plan to eliminate this condition. I had read about this plan in my studies, and when I explained it, the principals all endorsed it. In this plan the supervisors were considered experts in their field and as such, could be called by a principal of a building to come in to remedy any problem which occurred in that field. Otherwise they were not to visit a school and principals would be in charge of all teachers in the building. Dr. Platner was the president of the board, a position he held for many years, and was very influential in its decisions. He met with my committee and we explained our position, going over our proposed plan. He was interested and asked us to send him a letter stating our request for retaining the supervisors and our plan of doing so. This we did, but the board passed a resolution to retain the supervisors with no mention of our plan. So the supervisors who did not know of our efforts were more cocky than ever.

For many years the Utica school system had required uniform examinations be given at the end of each term in all grades above the first. Many teachers and some principals felt that these examinations should be eliminated. The reasons given were that the teachers were too restricted and many were drilling only for these tests. Teachers knew they were being rated on the results they got and the pressure was so great that in some cases teachers were known to do questionable things in order to report good results. The superintendent was asked to survey other cities in the state to learn how they made promotions from grade to grade. His reply was he didn't value questionaires too highly but would appoint a committee to visit cities about the size of Utica and gather firsthand information. The committee consisted of Cliff Stanton from Roosevelt, Burt Hawkes from Kernan, Hugh Shelton from Seymour, and me from Conkling. A day later the superintendent called me and said, "I want you to be the chairman of the committee." I demurred, saying the others had been principals in the system longer than I had and they might be jealous. Then in his characteristic way he gruffly answered, "If I didn't want you to be the chairman, I wouldn't have asked you. You are it."

The superintendent prepared the way for us by contacting the superintendent of the cities we were to visit. We took two full days going first to Amsterdam, Schenectady and Albany. The second trip was to Oneonta, Binghamton and Owego. We met and talked with supervisors, assistant superintendents, and others, and learned that

407

everyone of these cities had discontinued final examinations in the first six grades sometime ago. The superintendent was right; we gained a lot by talking directly to these administrators. After the visits I wrote up a report with the recommendation that Utica follow suit and discontinue these examinations. We all signed the report with the result that beginning with the second grade these examinations were phased out, one year at a time.

The summer of 1940 we rented a camp on Bradley Lake. The Dressers had built a camp on this lake and we had visited them several times. We liked the place so much we decided to spend a couple of weeks there. I was in summer school in Syracuse, but it was a short drive, and I could spend the afternoons and evenings at the lake, a real relief. An excerpt from the family letter tells about being upset when at camp.

> Norah and I had just pulled in from Syracuse one afternoon when we met Carrel Hayes coming out. He had come to tell us that his father, George, had just died. He had been sick for a long time but was up and around. That day he went down to the garage and sent Carrel home for dinner. Everyone thought he was feeling much better, since he hadn't worked for some time. When Carrel got back about 1 p.m., he found the whole place full of exhaust fumes and his father on the rear seat of a car with the engine still running. Carrel called the emergency squad, but it was too late. Norah had to leave camp and come into the city to stay with Nellie. I took the day off for the funeral. It was terribly hot and Nellie collapsed at the funeral—so we had a strenuous time.

That summer I bought a new Buick sedan, one of the best cars the company ever made. The girls were thinking of college and wanted to visit some campuses. One trip was to Fredericksburg, Virginia, where Marjorie was thinking of Mary Washington College, and the other to Poughkeepsie, New York, so Dorothy could see Vassar college where she was thinking of applying. Both places were beautiful, but at the time I didn't see how either could go, but that was something for the future.

Late one afternoon in January, 1941, Superintendent DeCamp called me and said he wanted to congratulate me. "Thanks, but for what?" I answered. "If you haven't heard you will when you get home," was all he would say. When I got home Dorothy announced that her picture would be in the evening paper. "For what?" I asked, but she just laughed and all she would say was, "You'll see." When the paper came, it had a big picture of Dorothy standing before a school blackboard with chalk in hand and on the board she had written, "Civics - 100%; General Science - 100%; Algebra - 100%; Latin - 100%; English - 94%. Following the picture was an article about Dorothy achieving this remarkable record, including the fact that she played the harp and being elected the editor-in-chief of the *Hughes Herald,* the school paper.

This was most remarkable, as these marks were made on the 9-1 semester examinations, which were given to the freshmen at UFA. It set a record at Hughes, which has never been equaled.

Dorothy's record was the more surprising, as all through the grade school she had been excused from final examinations due to her high class ratings. This time she was worried sick about taking these examinations, so I had as good talk with her beforehand. I told her to stop fretting, as she had to get used to taking examinations in high school and anyone who did good work during the year didn't need to fear an examination. So she surprised everyone, including her teachers, and I think herself. After we saw the paper, Dorothy told us how she learned about her marks. At the final assembly of each semester, Mr. Brown, the principal, always handed out certificates to pupils who had high marks, with special recognition if they had a 100 in an examination. The day of the assembly Mr. Brown called one after another to the stage to receive a certificate. Dorothy said she sat there getting madder and madder as she witnessed her classmates receiving certificates, and she knew she was a good as they were but she wasn't called. Then came the climax. Mr. Brown announced there was one final person to be recognized and called Dorothy to the stage. He handed her one certificate and then another, waiting each time for the applause. Before he got to the last one the pupils were all on the edge of their seats, and at the end gave her a standing ovation. As proof that such things do make an impression on students, I met a lady in a funeral parlor over thirty years later, and she greeted me by saying she knew Dorothy in Hughes as the girl who got all those 100 marks. After that experience Dorothy got over much of her fear of examinations, although she was always a bit nervous just as any good student will be.

In May, 1941, Superintendent DeCamp resigned. He would have liked to stay longer but he had reached the retirement age and the board wanted him out. He had been in the position for 24 years and was one of the last of the old time school administrators who ran the schools. The board was eager to have someone new, as they thought they would have more control in operating the school system.

The teachers association planned a big dinner honoring DeCamp, and I was asked to head the ticket committee. The dinner was held in the Hotel Utica with the ballroom full. Besides several speeches honoring him, the teachers presented him with a check of $800.00. He was so overcome he actually cried. I was happy when it was over and my accounts checked. DeCamp on the surface was rather rough and gruff, but inside he had a kind heart. He had been a good friend to me, helping me get started right as an elementary principal. He was a fair speaker, noted for his story telling; not a brilliant educator but a good executive, knowing how to pick good educators and give them the responsibility to run a school. The whole tone of the system changed after he left.

There was a lot of speculation as to who the new superintendent would be. I knew Mr. Burdick had applied but since he had been the principal at UFA only three years, no one was sure the board would consider him. Then the May 8, 1941, issue of the *Utica Observer-Dispatch* came out with a big article about Mr. Burdick being elected the superintendent of schools by the board on the previous night. It carried a big picture of him and one of Cliff Stanton, who was appointed the new principal at UFA. My picture was also included with the statement that I was being transfered from Conkling to Roosevelt School as principal. Rocco Lopardo, who had been the head of the math department at UFA for many years, was to be the new principal at Conkling.

Another article in the paper told the salaries that prevailed at the time. Superintendent DeCamp retired with a salary of $7500.00, but Mr. Burdick was to start at $6000.00. Stanton would receive $4400.00 at UFA, while I was to take his place at Roosevelt at $3500.00. Lopardo would start at Conkling at $3300.00. These figures show what a change has taken place in the past 40 years. Now a beginning teacher with no experience receives more than any of us did at that time.

The faculty at Conkling gave Norah and me a big farewell dinner. They seemed sincere when they said they were sorry to have me leave. I was torn between wanting to stay after just getting to know the community and the school, and with such a friendly faculty to work with, or taking a new position which was considered a promotion. Actually, I didn't have anything to say about it. I was just notified of my transfer.

From the family letter of July, 1941, there were two items of interest:

Last Monday night Uncle Clark and Aunt Nell stopped and stayed overnight on their way to Vermont. They have sold their place near Rochester and are going to Middlebury to live on Ward's place. They expect to build a small house this summer. Uncle Clark was laid up with sciatica but is much better now. They were lucky to be able to sell now just when they had to.

Another interesting thing that happened was a trip to Saratoga Springs for a reunion of the high school class of 1931. They wrote me and asked me to be there on a Thursday night to be their speaker. I wrote that I didn't see how I could make it. They wrote right back urging me to come and before I could answer, they called me long distance. They insisted that I come, so Norah and I left in the afternoon and arrived at Newman's on Saratoga Lake at 6 p.m. We had a grand time. They were exceedingly nice to us, and in spite of the fact that the superintendent was there, they let it be known what they thought of me. We arrived home about 2 a.m., tired but the trip was worth it.

The middle of that summer Dale sent word that he and Marian would be coming to Detroit to pick up a new car from the factory. He said if we would meet them in Niagara Falls, they would come that far east. The girls wanted to take a trip and since Nellie had never been to the Falls, we invited her to join us and sent word to Dale to come. We met in the evening and had a chance to see the Falls at night with the colored lights illuminating the water. After a morning of sightseeing, we left for Houghton. Dale wanted to see our old house and the town once more.

Marian drove the new car, taking Norah and Nellie with her, while Dale got in the front seat of my car so we could visit. Marjorie and Dorothy were on the back seat listening to us talk. After a time the girls began to giggle and finally burst into gales of laughter. "What's so funny?" we asked. "Oh, you're so funny," they both exclaimed. "You sound just alike." When we stopped to think it was funny, for here we were, two brothers who had been separated since boyhood having seen each other only three times in thirty years, yet having the same thoughts. In fact, it happened many times one of us would start a sentence and the other would finish it.

We arrived at Houghton in the middle of the afternoon and spent some time seeing our old house, the college buildings and the village, which except for a few new houses had changed little since we left. In our thoughts we lived over again the struggle we had in those days of the past. Leaving Houghton we went south until we hit Route 17 where we said our goodbyes. Dale and Marian headed back west while we turned east.

Since we were on a trip, the girls begged to go south into Maryland and Virginia so they could see some real plantations. We did and on the way back followed the famous Blue Ridge Skyline Drive. At first it was disappointing, as a mist hid the view, but by noon we were rewarded with some beautiful sights. Back home we now felt ready for school to open.

CHAPTER 23

THEODORE ROOSEVELT SCHOOL

Near the end of the school year, I met with Cliff Stanton to be introduced to the school building and learn where the records and supplies were kept. Then after school was over, keys were exchanged. I did the same with Lopardo, who was coming to Conkling. Roosevelt was a much older building than Conkling and quite different. Conkling had been built as a unit at one time, while Roosevelt was constructed in three stages. The center of the building was the old square brick construction originally called School No. 20. As the school population grew, two wings had been added.

The enrollment was not quite as large as it was at Conkling, but still it was one of the largest schools in the city. Roosevelt was located in the Corn Hill section of the city where the population was very heterogeneous, while Conkling had been very homogenous. The pupils in the school were typically American, coming from families with all types of heritages and backgrounds.

I had met many of the teachers in this school at various meetings in the past two years, so on the opening day that fall they were not total strangers. They gave me a warm welcome and I felt at home right away. After the faculty meeting adjourned, I got a real surprise when a 4th grade teacher stopped me and said, "Welcome to Roosevelt, Mr. Calhoon. You will find this an easy job, as we don't really need a principal. The teachers have been running this school for a long time." I was rather taken aback, but thanked her for the information. I never told Stanton what she said. The irony of this came about two weeks later when this teacher got in a jam with a parent of one of her pupils and came running to me for help. I was tempted to remind her of what she had said but refrained and helped her out of the difficulty. Time proved that she had voiced her own opinion, not the opinion of others on the faculty.

In October when school was well underway, Aunt Nell invited us all to a housewarming party she was giving on a weekend for the new house that Ward had built for them. We drove up on a Saturday, going through the Adirondacks to see the last of the colored leaves. It was cold with snow on the high peaks, but beautiful scenery. The new house was a small cottage just a short distance from Ward's big farm house. We arrived in the late afternoon and were given rooms with Ward. The party was planned for that evening, and there were friends from the town as well as from Middlebury College, where Ward was the head of the music department.

When the crowd began to thin out late in the evening, Ward sidled up to me and asked if I read the *Saturday Evening Post.* When I said yes, he continued, "Do you read the Earthworm Tractor stories?" Again, I said, "Yes, they are very good." In a half whisper he said, "You are standing right beside Upson, the author." I thought he was kidding until he introduced me. Right away Upson wanted to know if I had read his story in the current issue of the *Post.* When I replied that I had, he wanted to know if I had trouble understanding it. He said he had been receiving letters from readers who claimed he had a tractor going to the bottom of a lake but did not tell how it got into the lake. I told him I had missed it on the first reading, but I had gone back to check and then it was plain.

Norah heard us discussing the story and hurried to get the girls, who had become bored and gone to their room at the farmhouse. They came rushing back, eager to meet a real author. When Aunt Nell introduced Marjorie, she mentioned that she was a writer and had some poems published in an anthology which was on the table. Upson picked up the book with the remark that he wanted to be by himself when he read poetry and found a corner where he could read. When he finished, he congratulated Marjorie on her writing and told her to continue. As we drove home on Sunday afternoon we had fun talking over the events and agreed it had been one of our most enjoyable trips.

Back at school, I continued to learn more about the teachers and the organization. I found the esprit de corps at Roosevelt different from that at Conkling, where the faculty thought as a unit, while here the teachers tended to form groups according to the grades they taught due to the design of the building. The State Department of Education had for some time been critical of the way the Utica System had organized the 7th and 8th grades. The state claimed that these grades belonged to the secondary level, but Utica was treating them as elementary grades. The state informed the Utica Administration that if they wanted to draw money for these pupils at a secondary level, a change had to be made. Stanton, who had been a high school teacher before he became a principal, understood the secondary level organization and had done a good job. The work had been departmentalized and qualified teachers appointed for the various subjects. One of the features of a junior high school program was providing for clubs, and a period had been provided for their activity.

True to my policy when going to a new school, I let everything run as before until I could study the situation. Not until my second year did there appear any change that should be made. In talking with the junior high teachers, they suggested a change in the club program. They said that requiring all pupils to belong to a club defeated the purpose of a club and asked me to change the regulation. After I studied the situation, I agreed with them and the period was kept for the clubs, but on a voluntary basis. Pupils not interested in any club could spend the time in study.

I liked the plan that had been adopted in the school system for the promotion in the 7th and 8th grades. Since the pupils went to different teachers, it became a group decision as to who was to be promoted. Each teacher gave a grade in the subject they taught, and if all the grades were passing, there was no question about passing. As a rule, failing in one subject was permitted, but if it occurred in more than one, a session with all the teachers and the principal was held to make a decision. These sessions also had a lot of good side effects in that a better understanding of our goals and policies became evident.

The large kindergarten room was directly across the hall from my private office. This teacher had the reputation of being one of the best in the city, but she was now nearing retirement age and in my judgment was entirely too rigid in her methods. It had been the custom at the beginning of each semester when a new group of pupils entered for one of the special teachers to help with registration. They would check the birth certificates, make out the registration forms and send the children with their mothers or whoever brought them to the kindergarten teacher. This teacher would receive the children and tell the mother to go home. Some children would be all right, but others would become frightened and begin to cry. When one cried, others would become upset and join in, thus causing a lot of confusion.

At the beginning of my second year, the crying seemed to be louder than usual. It bothered me so much I decided to investigate. As soon as I stepped inside the door, a cute little girl with tears streaming down her cheeks ran up to me and pleaded, "Doctor, Doctor, can I go home?" I took her by the hand and in a calm voice tried to reassure her as we walked around the room looking at the pictures on the walls. Then I came upon a little boy huddled in a corner. He was hiding his face and when I leaned over to take him by the hand, I discovered he was trembling all over. To me he was like a frightened animal caught in a cage. I talked to him and got him on his feet, so together the three of us continued around the room. I tried to turn their attention away from being left alone. When I got them calmed down, I showed them that my office was right across the hall, and I would be there if they needed help. The little girl was all right, but for weeks that boy would not go into the kindergarten room until he looked to see me in my office.

After this experience, I decided this method was all wrong; it was no way to introduce them to school life, which we wanted to be a happy one. So the next term I set up a different method. I had special teachers in the hall at a table to meet the new pupils and their mothers. These teachers would check the birth certificates to be sure the child was the right age and fill out the registration form and tell the person to take the papers and the child to see me in my office. I did this so the children could meet me in a quiet atmosphere and dispel any fears they might have about meeting the principal of the school. It also gave me a chance to talk with both the child and mother together, creating a relationship I found very valuable in the future. When I saw all was in order, I would tell the mother to take the papers into the kindergarten room where she would meet the teacher and give her the papers. Then I added, "If your child wants to stay, fine, but if they are apprehensive, walk around the room so they can see what it is like, and then take them home."

When I informed the kindergarten teacher of the new method she said, "Oh, you can't do that, the law says the child has to be in attendance under instruction so many minutes to be counted present." To which I replied, "Let me worry about counting them. Anyway, how much instruction were they getting the first day under the old method?" I watched the first day of the new method and saw the children who came with older children and expected to go home with them did stay contentedly, but most went home with their mothers. The payoff came the next day when these pupils came back eager to begin school, and there was not a bit of crying.

Of course, the teacher told Miss Anderson, the kindergarten supervisor, about what I had done and she came to see me. She was a little peeved that I had not consulted her, but when she saw how well the plan worked, she couldn't say much. Anyway, as I had supported her on several changes she had proposed, we remained good friends. The news of my plan spread to other schools, and I heard later all had adopted the same or similar plans. This was an example of how the school can get so wrapped up in rules and regulations that they forget about using some common sense.

On Sunday, December 7, 1941, Norah and I decided to pay a call on Herbert Hayes, who had sprung a surprise and gotten married. It was done quietly with no announced wedding and celebration. He and his bride had just moved into an apartment, so we thought we should see them. When we got there, the radio was on real loud and the first thing Herb said to me was, "Have you heard the radio?" "No, why?" I replied. Then he announced that they were broadcasting about the raid the Japanese were making on Pearl Harbor. I listened with him a few minutes and saw that it was no time for a visit, and we hurried home. We turned on our radio listening in disbelief to the account of death and destruction taking place. There was no doubt that we were once again at war.

World War II made a big difference on our lives, as it did with everyone living at the time. It affected the school, as it did every institution. Soon we were selling savings stamps and bonds on a weekly basis. Every teacher was involved, but I was responsible for all the stamps and money collected. Some schools turned this task over to the school secretary, but I couldn't. Miss Kelly had been the secretary for a long time and in some ways was good, but she informed me she could not count money, saying she would have a nervous breakdown seeing all that money when she had so little. From her attitude I decided it was best not to trust her and did it all myself.

Miss Kelly was often late in getting to the office, but one morning when an hour went by I called the hotel where she stayed. I asked about her and soon got a return call from the bellboy. He gave me an account as if reading a detective story. He very dramatically told me how he went up to Miss Kelly's room, knocked, but got no response. He then found the housekeeper and with a pass key, they opened the door to see Miss Kelly on the floor. He said she was alive but unconscious. "What should we do," he inquired. I called Dr. Mahaday, the school doctor, and I met him at the hotel. The doctor examined her and ordered an ambulance. It was determined that she had had a stroke and was paralyzed on one side; she was never able to work again.

For a time I had several temporary secretaries. One was a graduate of the Business College of Syracuse University. She reported, expecting to take over the job, and from her credentials I thought she would be fine. The first morning I dictated a short letter for her to type, but when she left that night she only had it half done. She then told me she would only stay a week; she said she couldn't work under such conditions. She was used to starting a task and finishing it, but here she was constantly interrupted by the telephone or teachers or pupils.

The next substitute was a small girl with a hunch back. She was good in every way, very efficient with the office work and well liked by pupils and teachers. When I said I would help her in getting the supplies off the shelves in the stockroom, she informed me in a firm voice that she needed no help. She finished out the year and I wanted to keep her permanently, but the District School Clerk informed me that she lived outside the city so she couldn't keep the position.

The next fall Mrs. Bugental, who had been the school secretary at Brandegee School for several years, was transferred to Roosevelt. Just the year before she had married Frank Bugental, the art teacher at Conkling, the one whom I had helped save his tenure. Mrs. Bugental knew her job, and I could depend on her accuracy. Also, she was well liked by the pupils, the teachers and the parents. I discovered she had one trait which was rather common among people in similar positions. She could appear to be extremely busy when doing nothing. However, we got along fine and she was there until after I left the school.

Soon after the war started, rationing of gasoline and sugar was put into effect. The ration board asked the schools to issue the coupons. The superintendent called a meeting of the school principals to go over the process that was to be followed. Each school was to serve the people in its district. School was held in session for the mornings only, giving the teachers the time to work afternoons and evenings for a week to issue the coupons. I had the responsibility of organizing the procedure and keeping track of all the coupons, which became more valuable than money. Most of the teachers found it refreshing to do this extra work and felt they were helping with the war effort. Also, they liked the chance to meet so many of the parents in the school district. There were a few difficulties and because some of the instructions were not clear, I had to make some rulings of my own. In fact, the ration board had not decided on some situations. Later when the rulings did come out, I was pleased to find what I had done conformed with them. I heard that some schools were not so fortunate and had to recall some coupons.

An excerpt from our family letter tells about these items:

We have been through some great times at school; first the sugar rationing, which was a lot of work. We had to hold school in the mornings and then were on duty from 1 to 5 and then 7 to 10 for three days. I had a system worked out which the Utica paper was kind enough to praise in a write up. Marjorie and Dorothy came over several times to help out. We made over 7,000 books in my school and when it was over, everyone was about dead. The last night as the crowd dropped off, I asked the home arts teacher and a helper to prepare some coffee, etc. Norah came over and we had a little party. The girls made up some songs about the event and the teachers sang them. They proved so popular that every teacher wanted a copy to take home.

Then before we recovered from that week we had to do the gas rationing. The making out of these cards was easy enough, but the arguments, discussions and questions were ten times as bad. Of course, I was the final "court of appeals" in my school, and I had some tough customers to handle. The worst part was due to the fact that the ration board didn't know the answers as to who should have the X cards until we were halfway through. Consequently, they reversed some of their first decisions. At first I had to depend on my judgment. Fortunately, my decisions were very much in keeping with the final decisions of the board.

The teachers in the school decided when they got through that the "kids" in school weren't so dumb after all, after dealing with the public. You could tell very soon when asking people how far they drove to work whether they were stretching the distance or trying to tell the truth. After the papers and the radio came out saying that people who made false statements would be prosecuted, a number of the people came back and asked for lower cards, turning in the ones they had.

There was a lot of hard feelings about the gas cards. In the sugar rationing, people were very decent about it, as everybody was in the same boat, but with gas I knew there would be trouble because as soon as you begin to classify people and give some unlimited privileges and cut off others, you are in trouble. Then there were people not convinced that rationing was necessary.

Dorothy gave a speech in school about the funny things that happened during the sugar rationing. She told of one woman who brought a large bowl under her arm. The woman thought she was going to get her allowance of sugar right then. Also, each one was asked if there was anyone in the family who was physically handicapped. One woman replied, "Well, my husband is in jail for life."

The first winter at Roosevelt, I was informed of a serious heating problem. During the cold weather none of the rooms in the wing used by the 7th and 8th grades could be kept warm. On cold days the room temperature would only be 40 degrees in the morning and stay below 60 all day. This wing had been in operation for sixteen years and the teachers said it had been the same every winter. So I did some checking. First I found that in each coat room which bordered each room there was a ventilating shaft leading to the roof. At the base of the coat room door was a grill which was supposed to take the warm air from the classroom and circulate it around the coats and then up to the roof. However, I noticed that these grills had been covered with cardboard to stop the flow of air. The teachers told me that instead of the air going up the shaft cold air came down, and if they didn't cover the grill, it made it freezing in the room. I checked it out and found they were right. Also, I could follow this cold air down the stairs like a cascade of water, and on into the boiler room. It was evident that when the boilers were going full blast they were drawing the needed air down these shafts.

For fuel the school was burning hard coal, and I knew the boilers required a lot of air. All this air was coming from the interior of the building and thus creating a heating problem. To change this I suggested to John Dillon, the superintendent of buildings, that a duct be run from a window in the back of the boilers so the air needed would come in directly from outside. When the custodians heard about my proposal, they exploded. They said if that window was open, they would freeze. Nothing I could say would convince them that all the cold air would stay in the bottom of the pit and then into the fire boxes, and where they sat when not shoveling coal, some seven feet above the pit, would be warmer than now.

Dillon thought my plan worth trying and had the maintenance crew start a shaft, but before it was half done, I made another discovery. One morning when the outside temperature was below zero, the teachers in these rooms reported that they were so cold that the pupils couldn't stand it, even with their overcoats on. I went up again to check. Each room was heated by a long steam radiator along the outside wall. Back of the radiator was a fan to force air around the radiator and allow the supposedly heated air to flow into the room. I walked over and checked this radiator. The end where the steam entered was hot, but when I looked at the end where the condensed steam returned to the boilers, I saw it was covered with frost. The air coming through the radiator was very cold. Checking farther I discovered that the fan was drawing air directly from the outside; there was no way to control the system so as to recirculate the air in the room.

419

After school on the day I made this discovery I went down to the Administration Building to find Dillon. I told him of what I had found and said I had a suggestion as how to cure the situation. Typically, he sat and listened when I said I thought the radiators could be pulled a few inches out from the wall so a short duct with holes in the sides could be installed, then together with a damper, the outside air could be cut off and the inside air recirculated until the room was warm. He looked at me and said, "You are crazy." It wasn't the first time that I had run into the general notion that a school principal didn't know anything outside a classroom. I left him with the remark, "Something has to be done and soon."

About a week later I saw through the open door of my office a group of men going up the stairs. Wondering who was coming into the building without checking in the office, I hurried after them. At the top of the stairs I saw these men gathered near the radiator in the first room they came to. The class was in session, but they had barged in without saying a word to me or the teacher. When I entered I saw it was Dillon, the steam fitter, the tin smith and a stranger. I got there just in time to hear the stranger say, "That outfit is all wrong for this climate. It should never have been installed. It was made for the deep south." Dillon then asked, "What can we do?" "Take it out and put in the right one," was the reply. "What will it cost?" asked Dillon. "$200.00 each," said the man. "Can't do it. We don't have that kind of money in the budget," replied Dillon.

There was a long pause and Dillon introduced me as the principal of the school to the stranger, who said he was an engineer from the factory where they made these radiators. After Dillon had said there was no money to replace the outfit, I stepped forward and explained the plan I had told Dillon. The engineer studied for a couple of minutes and said to Dillon, "I think it might very well work. Why don't you try it on one and if it works, you can then do it in all the rooms."

Dillon then asked the maintenance men if they could do it, and they agreed it could be done. The next morning they appeared ready to work, so I arranged for the class to move until they were finished. In less than a week it was evident that the change was a success so the men continued around the whole wing. For the first time since they had been built these rooms were comfortable.

The payoff came the following winter, when one morning I walked into the boiler room and met a group of maintenance men gathered waiting for orders. They greeted me and one asked, "How are the rooms this winter?" "Fine! I haven't had one complaint all winter," I replied. "Isn't it wonderful how we thought how to cure the trouble," he said. I looked at all of them and seeing a satisfied expression on their faces, I said "Yep," and walked on. As I left I thought one criterion of a good administrator is the ability to make suggestions and plant ideas, then if they are successful let the people who do the work take the credit. Later I added a corollary; if you are the head of an organization that gets things done and makes progress, the public will give you the credit no matter who originates the ideas or does the work.

In June, 1942, Marjorie was one of the seniors in the annual oration contest at UFA. She was given honorable mention, which we thought good, but she was rather disappointed as she wanted to win. However, a number of people congratulated her and told her she should have been first. On June 24 she graduated from UFA with honors, although she missed out on a state scholarship because she was ill when she took the Regents in English 4. Anyway, she didn't plan to use it as she had made up her mind to go to Mary Washington College in Fredericksburg, Virginia.

In order to help with my expenses to send Marjorie to college, I tried to get a summer job. Each place I applied was not interested in hiring for a few weeks. Then I heard that Hamilton College, which is located in Clinton, New York, 12 miles south of Utica, was looking for a physics teacher. The college had contracted to give preflight courses to candidates in flight training at Utica Air field. An excerpt from the family letter tells what happened:

> I telephoned the college and was very disappointed to learn that they had just taken a man for the position. It seems the people they asked thought of me as a principal instead of a physics teacher. Well, to make it short, the man they selected took one look at the job and ran. He said he wasn't qualified to do it. That night the dean of the college called to see if I was still interested and if so, "come over and see them." I did and that night took the class. It was an evening class of one hour for four weeks. There were 40 boys in the class. The catch was there was no textbook for them. In fact, no one knew exactly what I was supposed to give them, so I wrote a course for them which the college duplicated. I am happy to say all of them passed the examination, which was given by Washington.

With the war going on, it was a problem for Marjorie to get to college. With the gas rationing I couldn't get enough to take her, therefore the only way was by train. She found out there was another girl from Utica going to the same place and they planned to go together. They got there after several delays, riding in coaches crowded with soldiers.

A few weeks before Christmas I had a pathetic letter from Marjorie telling how disappointed she was with the college. All the wonderful things she had read about in the college literature were either not given or else too expensive for her to take, such as horseback riding, golf, etc. More importantly, she found out what everyone had tried to tell her before she decided to go there; that the standard of work was low, not even up to what she had been accustomed to at UFA. Because of the war, the college had not taken any vacations, so they were to finish the first semester before Christmas.

Marjorie begged me to see if I could get her into Houghton College for the second semester. I wrote President Paine at Houghton and he said they would accept her as a transfer with full credit. So she brought her trunk home for Christmas and in January I took her to Houghton. There she found a much higher standard of work. She was able to get into Ray Hazlett's class in English and liked him very much, so much so that she decided to stay in Houghton for the next year, then transfer to the School of Journalism at Syracuse University.

With Marjorie in college and Dorothy planning to go, I was wondering about a summer job near the end of the school year in June, 1943, when I got a call from the Utica Radiator Company. They told me that they were preparing to do some casting of magnesium metal for parts of an aeroplane for the U. S. Air Corps. In order to qualify, they had to have a chemical laboratory to test the metal. They wanted to know if I knew any high school girls who had taken chemistry that might be interested in working in their lab. I told them I had not been teaching for some time and was out of touch with such students. Then I added, "I have had experience in industrial chemistry. Would you be interested in me for the summer?" They asked me to come down to the plant after school and talk with them. I did and met William Murray, the president of the company, and a young man named Joe Marotta, a metallurgist. When I told them of my work at the Oneida Community, they wouldn't let me out of the plant until I signed up to start work as soon as possible. They wanted me to help plan the layout of a laboratory and then to train the girls they were hiring. The only drawback was they said they had to tell me that the government had frozen all wages so the best they could pay was $1.00 per hour. But I was intrigued with the prospect of the job, so I was glad to accept the position.

I was feeling good about the prospects for the summer when on a Sunday morning just before the last week of school I had a strange pain in my abdomen. I went to school on Monday, but I didn't feel good, so I called Dr. Pender's office and got an appointment for after school that afternoon. I told the doctor about the pain and he put me on the table to examine my abdomen. He found the tender spot and informed me that I had a bad appendix and to make plans to have it out as soon as school was over. I told him of my job for the summer, but he just shook his head. Then on Wednesday morning I was so dizzy I couldn't get out of bed. Norah called Dr. Pender and he came at noon. He checked me again and announced, "We won't fool with this any longer. I'll make arrangements at the hospital and you get over there this afternoon. I'll stop on my way home for dinner and take out that appendix."

This happened at the worst time of the year for me, coming the last week of school with all the reports that a principal had to complete, the final assembly on that Friday, and a faculty dinner that night. But I had no choice. All engagements had to be cancelled and I would have to depend on Mrs. Bugental to complete the reports. I had to send word to the Utica Radiator that it would be at least two weeks before I would be ready to work. They were gracious enough to send word for me not to worry and take my time to recuperate.

While I was in the hospital, Dr. Pender decided that I was anemic. This was just after liver had been declared a cure for this condition. Up to this time calves liver had been selling for 10 cents a pound, mainly for cat food, but after this discovery the price jumped to a dollar a pound. The doctor left an order to give me a liver shot. That morning a new nurse came into my room carrying a tray with the longest needle I ever saw. Gaily she announced it was time for my liver shot. "Where do I get it, in my arm?" I asked. "Are you kidding," she replied. "Roll over, bottoms up." I rolled over and as she was filling the syringe, I began to visit with her. Like the other young nurses who had been in my room I asked what high school she had been graduated from. "UFA," she replied. "Good," I said, "I used to teach chemistry at UFA and had a number of girls in my classes who were going into nursing. Who did you have for chemistry?" There was a long pause and then in a strained voice she replied, "Mr. W—, is he a friend of yours?" Because of the change in her voice I twisted my head around to look at her. Gone was her nice smile. Her mouth was in a straight line with her lips pressed tightly together, and there was an evil glint in her eye. By that time she had my right buttock exposed and was posed holding that needle like a dagger. I knew I had said the wrong thing, but I was caught and buried my face in the pillow as I answered her question, muttering, "Yes, I worked with him a long time." "Aha," she explained, "So you are a friend of his. Boy! I hated that guy. I wish I had him here right now; I'd give it to him like this." Wham! She buried that needle clear to the bone. It hurt, but I wouldn't give her the satisfaction of making a peep. After that I made a remarkable recovery and was discharged from the hospital the next day, so I never saw that nurse again.

It was the 10th of July before I felt able to even go down to the radiator plant. I only stayed two hours, but in that time I was briefed on the situation. This company had been making iron radiators for many years, but now due to the war they were unable to obtain enough iron to continue. Since they had the equipment and the experience in casting metal, they had secured a contract from the U.S. Air Corps to cast magnesium alloy parts for war planes. However, they had to promise to set up a chemical laboratory so every heat could be analyzed to be certain that it met specifications.

A new laboratory was being constructed on the second floor over the main offices under the guidance of John Mott, a retired Bureau of Standards chemist. He had come out of retirement only because he was persuaded by the company to help in their efforts to win the war. They had also hired five girls to work in the lab, but none of these people had any experience in industrial chemistry. I was told my first task would be to train these girls in doing routine analysis. We were all under the supervision of Joe, the metallurgist, but he was too busy in the plant to spend time in the lab to train anyone. John Mott admitted he was no teacher and was delighted to have me take on this task.

Due to my weakened condition after the operation, it was a week before I could stay a full day. By that time I had a grasp on what was the biggest problem. Magnesium was a new metal to be used in casting but desirable for aeroplanes because of its light weight and strength. No textbook contained any method of analysis nor did a search of the literature produce any help. John had obtained from the Bureau of Standards a detailed method of magnesium analysis, which was long and involved as it covered all the elements that might be present. Since his experience had been with the Bureau, he thought we should use its method, so I started the girls on it.

This method took three days to run a sample, and I told Joe that was too long to be practical. He suggested I start immediately to work out a shorter method. I started by eliminating the work to determine the rare metals which I was sure would not affect the alloy even if present in minute quantities. I concentrated on the metals which did make a difference, such as aluminum, iron, manganese, copper and silicon. Before the end of the summer I had a method which I could run and cut the time from three days to three hours. John was skeptical of my method, but after I showed him that I could match the results I obtained with those the girls had with the long method, he relented. He told me to go ahead and teach my method to the girls and see if they could get the same results. Just before Labor Day when I had to leave for school, he called me over to his desk and I almost had to laugh when he said, "Calhoon, it hurts my soul to say this, but I am convinced your method is all right and we are going to adopt it. It will be called the Calhoon method." I was very pleased and replied, "Thanks, but be absolutely sure, once in awhile have one of the girls check by using both methods."

When I left, John asked me to come down on Saturdays and school vacations to help with any problems that might arise. So for the next two years I spent almost every day school was not in session in the laboratory. Problems kept cropping up, since new alloys were being introduced. One such alloy contained considerable copper, and it was a problem to get it into a solution. Sulfuric acid had to be used and if added too fast, the copper in the alloy would form a small ball which became coated with a skin that was impervious to any acid. It took me some time to find out how to dissolve this alloy, and I then wrote it up for the girls to follow. It was only a day or so later I got a distressed call from John asking me to come down after school to wave my magic wand to put that alloy into solution, as none of them could. I did go and by selecting the best girl in the group, I succeeded in getting her to do the trick.

During these war years good help was very much in demand. Women and girls who had never worked were getting good jobs. Many did fine work, but a few did not qualify. We knew of one such case when the management came up to the lab one day very much upset. They had received notice from the Air Corps that a whole carload of castings was refused because they didn't meet specifications. We were on the spot but when we checked our records, that shipment was all right. We asked to see the report that went with the shipment and noticed at once all the numbers had been copied one line off. When the office manager found the stenographer who had copied the report and asked why she had not checked it before sending it in, she indignantly replied that she was a graduate of the commercial department of a certain high school and didn't need to check. Then she added, "If you don't like my work, I quit." The office let her go and notified the Air Corps of the mistake, so the castings were accepted.

Among the girls we had in the laboratory only one did not measure up to our high standards. The second summer I was there John called me aside and said he was quite sure one of the girls was cheating by looking back on previous records and reporting what she found on that heat number instead of running the analysis. He asked me what we should do to find out for sure. I suggested we set a trap by giving all the girls a sample of a certain heat for which we knew the analysis, but listing each sample with a different number of a heat which had been run. To explain, all the bars of the alloy that came on a shipment were given a heat number and were analyzed before any castings were made, then the castings were checked to be sure nothing had changed in the heating process. When the results of our trap were turned in, every girl but one had the right analysis and that one had reported the numbers on the heat number we had given her. When John confronted her, she admitted her guilt and said she was quitting before she was fired. It was hard to believe a girl would do such a thing, especially as we had told the girls many times how important it was to be certain of the right analysis. We explained that just a slight difference in the amount of any metal in an alloy can change its characteristics. The life of an air pilot might very well depend on our analysis.

William Murray was the president and general manager of the Utica Radiator Corporation and after my interview with him when I was hired, I had little contact with him, but I was always aware of him as his influence was felt throughout the plant. It was not a large factory, so most everyone knew the management. It was rather strange as this was the second William Murray that I had worked for. The first was William S. Murray at the Oneida Community, who had left to organize the Indium Company in Utica. William C. Murray was the head of the Utica Radiator Corporation.

Bill Murray, as he was often called, lived in a big house on the Parkway in the elite section of the city, so it was evident that he had plenty of money, but at the plant he was just one of the workers. He had the rare ability to be an excellent executive who ran a successful business but at the same time was well liked in the plant. He was a leading citizen in the city and after retiring from the firm, became head of the Munson-Williams-Proctor Institute and Art Center. After a full

CONSTANT ANALYSES of the magnesium alloys are made in the plant's laboratory. Making such an analysis are Miss Mary Jane Pellettieri, 800 Kossuth, laboratory technician, and A. Ray Calhoun, 1907 Briar, research chemist who is also principal of Roosevelt School. X-ray equipment also is used to study the metal.

From the Utica Observer-Dispatch of October 8, 1944.

page article appeared in the Sunday edition of the *Utica Observer-Dispatch* telling about the work with magnesium at the Radiator Co., he was asked to speak at various organizations. I also gained some notoriety from this article, as it showed a picture of me in the laboratory showing one of the girls how to run a sample. The caption under the picture said I was the chemist at the plant and also the principal of Roosevelt School.

One night the men's club at Central Church invited Mr. Murray to be the guest speaker. He saw me at one of the tables and when he was introduced, he told the group of my work and said I should be the speaker, as I knew more about the magnesium alloys than he did. Mr. Burdick was at this dinner meeting and after the adjournment, I introduced him to Murray as my other boss. They talked a minute about my working in both the school system and at the plant, then Murray said in front of me to Burdick, "If the time ever comes you don't want Ray, let me know. We will take him at once. He is a good man." Burdick was taken by surprise and didn't know what to say, so I laughed and remarked, "That is some recommendation." In the years after the war I met Mr. Murray many times and he always gave me a friendly greeting.

Cliff Stanton was an active member of the Utica Exchange Club and soon after I went to Roosevelt, he invited me to join. I was interested and he put my name through; in a short time I was an active member. This was a service club consisting of business and professional men from the greater Utica area. They met once a week on Thursday at the Hotel Utica. At each meeting after the lunch there would be a half hour program, usually a guest speaker. One day the vice president of the Radiator Corp., was the guest speaker, and when he rose to speak about the casting of magnesium, he said he felt a bit foolish as here was "Ray Calhoon who knows a great deal more about the subject than I do." At the end of his remarks there was time for questions from the club members. My stature in the club grew that day because every question that was asked which was technical he referred to me. A few days later I was surprised to learn that the management of the plant held a meeting to discuss some of the answers I had given. Luckily for me Joe produced a copy of his metallurgist magazine with an article which supported my answers. From that time on I could feel a new respect for my services around the offices.

Of course, school was in operation all this time, and an item from the family letter of December, 1943, tells some of the problems:

> After Labor Day school started with a rush, and it has been a rush ever since. With stamp and bond sales, rationing again which was another headache, a child center now attached to my building, salvage drives, clothing collections for children overseas, air raid drills and many other interruptions, school "Ain't what it used to be."
>
> Just now we are going through a siege of grippe. So many teachers are out that we can't get substitutes. Norah has been teaching as a sub for a week. I had one report who hadn't taught in 20 years. She lasted just one day. Another left for lunch at 11:30 and didn't return until 1:30. She thought it was terrible when I told her what the hours were. She came with the popular idea so many have that teachers have an easy job.
>
> We took Marjorie back to Houghton in the car this fall. I saved enough gas so I could do it. There are no trains to Houghton

anymore, and she couldn't take a trunk by bus. Both Marjorie and Dorothy worked all summer, so we are a working family.

Some excerpts from the family letter of 1944 tell of our further activities. It starts in April.

The minister of our church asked Dorothy to play her harp as an introduction for the Easter service next Sunday. He announced it this morning, so she has something to work for.

I had an SOS call from the plant to help with aluminum analysis. The magnesium casting slowed down so now they want to start aluminum casting. There are some kinks in the analysis of some of its alloys.

Easter Sunday! This is the first warm day we have had, grand for Easter. We had to go to church early to get Dorothy and her harp there on time. She did very well. Dorothy and I then went to Cazenovia to get Norah. Her folks are better and will try to get along by themselves. It is good to have Norah back home.

June. I worked at the plant every Saturday until the 20th of May when we drove to Houghton to get Marjorie. We had a time loading her stuff. Don't see how she had accumulated so much, but she is transferring to Syracuse University next fall so we had to bring it all. Had a blowout of one tire on the way home. That makes a big problem, as I have to wait until I can get a purchase certificate to get another. All tires are rationed and very hard to get.

Now commencement is over. Dorothy graduated from UFA on the 28th. She was fourth in standing in a class of 350, which is small due to the war. She says if she had known she was so near the top she would have worked to be first. I think she could have done it. Anyway, she got a prize for the highest girl in science. She won a State Scholarship. She had the highest mark in UFA on a state scholarship examination which is new this year. She was fourth in the county on this examination.

Dorothy decided on Vassar for college next year. I told her I didn't see how I could afford to send her there. She went out and got three more scholarships. One from the AAUW in the city, one from the Mohawk Valley Vassar Club, and one from the college. Actually, in many ways she did better than the girl who was selected the valedictorian. Also, she had a picture in the Sunday paper with a good write-up.

It was this June that Mr. Brown resigned as Principal of Hughes school. He was very upset when the board asked him how much longer he expected to stay and gave them his resignation right then. Along with others I applied for the position, but to most everyone's surprise, Rocco Lopardo was appointed. I had seen the members of the board and they all said I was the best qualified, but didn't vote for me.

Anyway, I wasn't disappointed, as I liked my job at Roosevelt.

Norah's mother died in May, 1945, so the girls, Nellie, Norah and Norma, had to take turns staying with their father. That summer he became very difficult to manage, so two of them had to stay at a time. I spent a number of weekends helping them. He died that fall after school began.

I was working at the plant when the news of the atomic bomb being dropped in Hiroshima was received. Since the war in Europe was over in May, we knew our part in the war effort would soon be over. Then on V.J. day all the employees were called into a mass meeting and informed that the plant would be closed for a time until it could be reorganized for post war operations. I fully expected that would be the end of my services and said something to Mr. Murray about leaving. He said, "No, we want you to stay and help with our plans for the future."

Early that summer I looked up from my work in the lab to see Mr. Murray showing Harold Francis, one of the technical teachers at UFA, through the plant. I said, "Hello," to Harold and he greeted me by saying, "I didn't know you worked here." A little while later Mr. Murray came back and asked me if I knew Harold well. "Yes," I replied, and he told me that Harold was applying for a job in the engineering department. I in turn told him that Harold was an outstanding teacher at UFA and if they could get him, they were fortunate. Harold did get the job and when I had a chance to talk with him, he said he was tired of the way things were going at the Academy and wanted to get back in industry.

When the war ended the lab was closed and I was transferred to the engineering department. My first assignment was to do some mechanical designing. I told them I was not a draftsman, but they insisted I could do it. The work I had at Clarkson came back to me, and I was set up in a small room near the pattern shop. I was given a board and all the tools that a draftsman would need and was soon in deep. The company was bidding on making some small castings for several firms, and I was asked to make the working drawings and determine the weight of each from the drawings. If it hadn't been for the help Harold gave me, I could never have done it. But he never said a word, and I got the credit.

For some time I was very busy and then would follow several days of doing nothing while the management was holding meetings deciding what to do with the designs. Before the summer was over I became terribly bored and was glad to get back to my schoolwork.

Dorothy had a summer job at the General Electric Company in Syracuse, thus she was home only on weekends. Marjorie worked in the Utica Public Library, a job she liked so much she was almost sorry to leave for college. As a junior in the school of journalism, she was made an assistant editor of the *Syracuse Daily Orange,* the University's daily newspaper. She was in complete charge of several issues and had some editorials published which received some very favorable comments. She was getting some very valuable experience which helped her in the future.

Marjorie graduated from Syracuse University in June, 1946. She received a degree from the college of Arts and Science, as well as one from the School of Journalism, both with honors. Norah and I attended the graduation and one person seemed almost lost in the big numbers, but she was there and we could be proud of her. As soon as she got home, she began to worry about a job. She applied at the Utica papers, but they turned her down with the excuse that she asked for too much money. She ran an ad in the New York State Newspaper Bulletin and had several replies. I told her the only way to decide was to visit each place and I agreed to take her. The first place we went was to Geneseo, New York. She liked the editor and the place and was ready to settle right there, but I told her she better complete her appointments so she would be sure. We visited six places, but Geneseo was her first choice, and when she received notice she could have the job, she was delighted. She was to be the assistant editor on a weekly paper which covered the city and the county. After school opened in the fall, she found that a girl she knew from Utica was attending the State Teachers College in Geneseo and then she felt more at home.

During all this time I was carrying on my full time duties as a school principal. Some changes were taking place in the system, for one of which I was partly responsible. The city-wide examinations were being phased out, but it hadn't reached the fifth grade. I was appointed chairman of the committee for arithmetic examinations. It was customary for the chairman to ask teachers to submit questions to be used and then add some to make up a balanced test. On the day the math exams were held, the teacher of the 5-2 class came storming into my office. "Who," she demanded, "had charge of this examination?" "I did," I replied. "What's wrong?" "There is a problem on it with fractions," she exclaimed. "Yes," I said, "I know the fractions ½ and ⅓ are taught in the fifth grade, so what is wrong?" "Not in 5-2, only in 5-1," she said. Then she claimed that these fractions were introduced in the first half of the fifth grade textbook but never used in the second half. That was hard for me to believe, but when I checked I found she was right. This was not the first time I had noticed what I called a flaw in too much of our teaching. Too often things are taught and then never used again. When I notified the superintendent of the defect I had discovered in the textbook, he said it was time to make a change and named me chairman of a committee to select a new one. When the salesman from the company that published the old book called on me, I told him what I had discovered and he said, "Yes, we knew it and expected to have it thrown out long ago. Utica is the last place in the state to use that series." These books had been used for nearly twenty years and no one had made a fuss about them until I came along. My committee met and after reviewing the many books on the market, we selected one for the superintendent to recommend to the board and it was approved.

Shortly before Superintendent DeCamp retired, the supervisor of kindergarten and primary grades retired. Miss Ruth Anderson was appointed to fill the position. Miss Anderson came into the system with all new ideas in teaching these grades. She believed in the philosophy which I had been hearing in all my courses in elementary education, i.e., we should be teaching children, not subjects. This was in direct contrast to the former supervisor, who was very rigid about teaching subjects. For example, I was told by more than one teacher in the first grade that they were told on what page they should be each week and if this supervisor stepped into a room and found the teacher on a different page, there was "Hell" to pay. Whether the pupils were ready for that page or not made no difference. This was the kind of policy that was being replaced.

One observation that I had made in watching the children in the kindergarten was the wide difference in their ability. This was not due to age entirely, and it became more evident when they went to the first grade. Some were ready and eager to begin the reading program, while others were not. I talked it over with Miss Anderson and together we planned a modified reading class for those pupils who gave evidence of not being ready for the regular program. To make sure that these pupils were fairly classified, I insisted that there should be more than one criteria used. I decided on four independent criteria for making the selection: the chronological age; the rating of the kindergarten teacher; the I. Q., as determined by the school psychologist; the result of a reading readiness test which had just come on the market. I stated that if all four factors agreed, we were sure where to place the child; if three of the four agreed, we were reasonably sure; but if two were one way and two the other, we would disregard all factors and place the child in a regular class. We also made our plan flexible so adjustments could be made during the year. The expectation was the modified first grade class would take three semesters to cover the usual two.

When the selection was made for the modified class, I sent a letter to each home of the child explaining the plan and the reason for it. As expected, I had mothers come in to see me with fire in their eyes. They informed me in no uncertain terms that their child was just as smart as others. Why were they held back? I was prepared and would put on a little act. I would get out all the records of the child and lay them on my desk and study them like a doctor reviewing test results. I would explain that this class was organized to prevent these pupils from suffering the tragedy of failing. I would tell them that reading is a skill, and if the child is not ready for any reason to learn that skill, great harm can be done. I would then ask the mother if she had older children. Many did and I would ask, "Did all your children walk at the same age or talk at the same age?" They would agree that they didn't and I would say, "Why do we expect all children to be ready to read at the same age?" By this time I could see the attitude of the mother beginning to change and I would assure her that we were interested in the welfare of the child. I would emphasize that the school was trying to avoid having the child face an impossible task thereby establishing a mental block that could handicap his reading ability all the rest of his life. Then when I told the mother that at any time the child showed he was ready to go into a regular class, he would be transferred at once, I could see a definite change in attitude. Many left, expressing an interest in the program and would thank me for showing such interest in their child.

Reading was the most talked about program in the elementary grades. To gain a better understanding of the subject, I enrolled in a course at Syracuse. After that I felt more at ease when discussing the various plans and problems of reading with other principals and teachers. An interesting case developed in a second grade class taught by Miss Casale. She had been transferred to Roosevelt and it didn't take me long to rate her a master teacher, so when she came to me for help one day, I took immediate notice.

She told me that she had a boy in her class who read most of his words backwards and she didn't know how to cure him. I had read of such cases but had never encountered one, so I asked to sit in on a reading session so I could observe. It was evident that what she had reported was true, so after school we discussed the problem. She had taken more courses in reading than I had, but admitted this was her first experience with such a case and didn't know how to cope with it. I suggested as a first step we contact the parents and acquaint them with the problem and ask for an eye examination. The parents were cooperative and after an examination, got the report that showed this boy had one very dominant eye. It was so strong that the weak eye was deteriorating rapidly. Once fitted with corrective lenses, his reading began to improve. We didn't realize at the time that we had hit on a situation which several years later was declared a new discovery in medical circles. Two years later Miss Casale was promoted to a reading specialist in the school system, and I lost an excellent teacher. I was happy for her to get the promotion, and we had a fine working relationship for several years.

Another unusual case developed in Miss Farley's first grade room. Miss Farley was the oldest teacher in the school and was now teaching grandchildren of some of her former pupils. She was considered one of the best teachers in the system, and parents would do their best to have their children placed in her room. I rated her as one of the best teachers I ever knew. It was a pleasure to step into her room and observe the quiet activity of the class. All the children would be busy and their expressions told they were enjoying their work. Miss Farley bragged that she never sent a class to the second grade teacher unless they had read halfway through the second reader. So when she came to me one day to report a bad situation, I took instant notice. She said one girl in her class was showing signs of a nervous breakdown. At every reading session this girl would begin to shake all over and couldn't speak a word. Knowing Miss Farley, I felt sure the trouble was outside the school.

I got in contact with the girl's mother and asked her to come to my office for a conference. When she came, she brought her husband. The contrast between the two was striking. She was a little young-looking girl weighing less than 100 pounds, while he was a big husky older man weighing around 300 pounds. I asked them to be seated and explained what Miss Farley had observed and expressed our concern for the welfare of the child. Before I could finish the father broke in to tell me in a loud voice that he was seeing to it that his girl could read. He told how he had purchased a first grade reader and every night after supper he had the girl get the book and start to work. He said she couldn't go to bed until he knew she could read all of the page they were working on at school. "By God," he said, "I'm going to see that she can read as good as anyone in that room."

It was evident what his domineering method was doing to the child, and when he finished I pulled no punches in telling him what a cruel thing he was doing. I went on to say the teaching of reading was a skill and Miss Farley was the very best in the system. School was the place to teach reading and by forcing the child to spend her evenings on it was creating a mental block that was creating serious physical conditions. I got real serious when I said this was child cruelty and if continued, the girl would land in the state hospital. Before I was through, the mother was in tears and I gathered she did not approve of the program, but the man was such a domineering type that she didn't dare interfere. However, I could see he was affected by the tears and evidently impressed by my strong talk. The last thing I said was, "If you want your child to succeed in school and save her from a complete nervous breakdown, put that book away and after school and in the evening let her play. In any case, don't mention reading for a long time. Let Miss Farley take over, and if things don't improve soon, I'll let you know and we will have another conference." At the end of two weeks Miss Farley reported that there was a marked improvement, and I heard no more about the problem. It was a perfect example of a parent with the best intentions but poor judgment interfering with the school program.

Under Miss Anderson's supervision not only were the modified grades promoted, but all the primary grades grouped the children according to reading ability. Many schools were adopting movable seats for these grades and while Miss Anderson advocated such a change, she could make little impression on the superintendent or board. It happened at this time the enrollment in the first grade increased so much at Roosevelt that we needed another teacher. There was a vacant room near the auditorium from which all the seats had been removed. So since the board thought this would be a temporary situation, they approved, using movable seats. The teacher they hired for this position came with all the modern concepts of elementary

433

teaching. She was a tiny person but very dynamic and was delighted with the movable seats. She changed the arrangement frequently which created a problem. The first developed when the teacher informed me that her room hadn't been swept in three days. It was hard for me to believe, as it was the duty of the janitors to sweep every room every day after school was over. I checked the room and it certainly was dirty, so I went to Mr. Lawler, the head custodian, to find out why it hadn't been swept. He informed me that the men refused to sweep unless all the seats were arranged in a straight line. The teacher had been in the habit of arranging the seats in a pattern she planned for the next morning, which was not in a straight line as were the fixed seats.

I called a meeting of the janitors and tried to explain the purpose of the movable seats. They responded in hot terms indicating the teacher was crazy, and they refused to go into her room. I tried to talk quietly to them, but when I saw I was getting nowhere, I got stern. I told them it was time for them to understand something; they were paid to do a job, which included sweeping all the rooms every day. It was not their business to tell a teacher how to run her room. I was the one to do that, and I approved of her method. "From now on, I want that room swept every day. If you need to move the seats, all right, but just put them back as you found them." I guess the men were surprised to see me get tough and mean what I said, for after that the room was clean.

The second episode concerning this teacher came about when Miss McCalmont, the writing supervisor, visited that room one morning. I heard about it when Miss McCalmont came rushing into my office with her hands clenched and her face white as a sheet. I could see she was beside herself as she blurted out, "Mr. Calhoon, do you know what is going on in that teacher's room? I walked in to find the children sitting in a circle so half of them were facing the window. When I spoke to her about it, she told me it wasn't any of my business." This, of course, referred to an old rule long ago established in schools that all children must be seated so the light comes over their left shoulders and never facing a window. But with movable seats this rule was discounted, since the pupils were never left in one place for many minutes. Also, it had been noted that people not in a classroom spent lots of time looking out a window. When I looked at Miss McCalmont, I could hardly keep a straight face as I was so amused to think of that little mite of a girl standing up to a supervisor. But I did and said, "I am sorry you feel insulted, but after all the teacher was right. It wasn't your place to criticize her method of seating. Anyway, if you were to check her room a while later, you would find the pupils in a different pattern, so there is no harm done." Miss McCalmont stamped out of the office and I don't think she ever went back to that room again, which is just as well, since that teacher was horrified to learn that she had to teach the Palmer method of writing to her first grade pupils. I lost an excellent teacher when at the end of the year she left to become a supervisor in the Catholic Schools of the Syracuse Diocese.

When I learned in my studies in Syracuse that the manuscript method of writing was being taught in almost all the schools in the state, I made an effort to find out why. I found there were two good reasons. First, the pupils learned to write by the "script" method in a very short time. To their delight, they were able to write short notes to take home in just a few weeks, while with the old cursive method they were lucky to do so by the end of the year. The second and most important reason was the fact the letters were formed so much like the printed page it helped them to read much faster.

In most schools the script writing was done in the first grade and usually up to the middle of the second, when the pupils with little difficulty changed over to the cursive method. In some schools they never changed as I knew from some transfer students I had in my classes at the Academy. It was certainly much easier to read than the cursive writing of the students coming from the Utica schools trained in the Palmer method, but who, once on their own, forgot it.

I was convinced that we should be teaching the script writing in the first two grades and began to talk with the teachers about it. All the younger teachers were for the change, but the older ones were opposed. When Miss McCalmont heard about my promoting the change, she fought it. I talked with Superintendent Burdick, telling him of what I had learned, and after two years I got him to rule that if 50% or more of the teachers in a building wanted to change, it could be done. It took me two years after the ruling to convert a majority of the teachers in Roosevelt to make the change. Once Roosevelt made the change, other schools followed and when Miss McCalmont saw what was happening, she made a complete face about, announcing she would instruct the teachers in the script method. She was a clever person.

Near the end of the first year that we made the change, I was delighted to have Miss Farley come to me and say, "Mr. Calhoon, I have something to tell you. You know I opposed the adoption of the script method right up to the end." "Yes, I know but that was your privilege," I replied. Then she continued, "I have come to tell you that I found everything you said about the method was true, and I have been delighted with the results. I want you to know how happy I am that you had us make the change." This was a rare thing for a teacher to do, and it made me consider her a better teacher than ever.

The attendance record at Roosevelt was about average, but it did not satisfy me. The system had attendance officers, and each one was assigned certain schools. They were expected to call at the office each morning to check the attendance cards that came from each room to see if there were pupils out long enough to check on. I made a practice of going over the cards first and then giving the officer the names I wanted checked. By chance I learned that one of the officers would take the list to her office in the administration building and call all the names she could find in the phone book and then was taking credit for a visit. I put a stop to this by giving her only the names which I knew did not have a phone. I took the time to call the others myself. In this way I became better acquainted with the parents and they in turn appreciated a call from me rather than the attendance officer.

There was one thing about school attendance which prevailed in most school systems that bothered me a great deal. It was what I called the schools being guilty of teaching dishonesty. Parents knew that if they kept a child out of school other than for illness or impassable roads it would be marked as an illegal absence and the child would be made feel he had committed a sin. But if in such a case they wrote a note saying the child was ill, nothing would be said. Both the parent and the child knew it was not the truth, but it was a way to keep the school happy, which to me made the school one of the guilty parties. I felt so strong about this that at a meeting of the school PTA I gave a speech about it. I told the parents I wanted them to be honest about an absence, tell the truth and let me decide how to mark it. I could do this because the state department had recently modified its regulation giving the school some discretion and for a good reason could mark an absence with an F [family] rather than illegal. I had a good reaction to my talk, and some of the mothers kidded me, saying they were going to try me out.

I didn't have long to wait, for in about a week I got a note which said, "I heard what you said at the PTA meeting, so I am writing the truth. Yesterday my husband had a promotion to be Chief of the Utica Fire Department and a number of our friends came in last night for a celebration. They stayed so late the children got very little sleep, so I thought it best to let them sleep this morning rather than send them to school." It was an honest note which I liked, and I instructed the teachers involved to mark the absence in the register with an "F". The word spread through the community, and it established a wonderful relationship between the parents and the school, which I cherished.

My habit of calling the homes in case of absence produced one of the strangest stories I ever knew. I noticed a third grade girl had been marked absent for the third day; I called the mother. The mother claimed we must be wrong; that the girl had been in school every day. I told the mother I would check it out and call her back. I went to the girl's room and checked with the teacher and the pupils in the room, and they were all sure the girl had not been in school. When I called back, the mother was real excited and said she would investigate. Right after the noon recess, the mother appeared in my office with the girl. After my call the mother got to thinking about the girl getting ready for school each morning and then appearing for lunch each day as if in school, so she played it smart. When the girl appeared for lunch, nothing was said but the mother decided to watch. She heard the outside door close, but in a few minutes it was quietly opened and the girl slid back into the inside and into the coat closet near the door. This is what the girl had been doing for the three days, staying in the closet until she heard the voices of the children coming from school at noon and night and then sliding outside as if she had been in school.

Neither the mother nor I could get the girl to give a reason for not wanting to be in school. I told the mother to leave the girl with me, thinking after a time I could get her to talk, but with no results. After a time I took her to her room, telling the teacher to say nothing and I would talk with her later. Then right after recess the teacher sent word that the girl had disappeared. I thought she had probably run home, so I called her mother. She called back saying she had searched the house and she wasn't there. I quizzed the girls in her room, who said she had gone to the girl's toilet with them but didn't come back. This room was in the basement, and I knew there were a few vacant rooms nearby, so I got the custodians to help and we made a thorough search. She was not in any of the rooms and then I remembered at the extreme back of the basement there was an old flight of stairs which were no longer used. Taking a flashlight, I peered back of these stairs, and I noticed a hole in the wall where it had never been finished. I saw a child's shoe in this opening. Trying to pick it up, I discovered there was something in it. Pulling hard, I dragged the little girl out of this sort of cave which she had discovered and crawled into for a hideout.

Since the girl's clothes were all dirty, I called the mother and sent the child home. The next morning the mother again brought the girl to school and again I said to leave her with me. I let her sit in a chair in my office for a time, thinking after she had relaxed I could get her to talk. I watched her out of the corner of my eye, but she remained rigid. Suddenly she sprang out of her chair and ran like a deer out into the hall, making for the front door. I didn't want her to get away, so I jumped out of my chair and rushed out the back door of my office, hoping to catch her before she got outside. But she was too quick and reached the door before I could catch her and she pushed the door open, ready to run. However, she had long hair and the wind blew it out straight behind her, so I reached out and grasped it, bringing her to a halt. I often wondered later what the neighbors thought if they chanced to see me.

Once I stopped the girl, I got her back inside and closed the door, but she refused to walk and sank down on the floor in a heap. The only way I could get her back to the office was to pick her up and carry her. When I did so her body was tense and stiff, then halfway up the stairs a strange thing happened. She went completely limp. I took her into the office and sat her on a chair. I could see that she had changed, but I still couldn't get her to tell why she hated school. She did answer a few questions and consented to go back to her room. When I took her in, I said on the side to the teacher, "Don't say a word. Just act as if nothing had happened." The teacher was wise and followed my instructions, then to the surprise of everyone, the girl stayed in school all year.

I never did learn what caused that little girl to seemingly fear school, but I wondered if the older children had told her stories about the principal, how he would eat her or something. Then when I picked her up and showed only kindness, her fear vanished and her attitude changed. It was weeks later when Miss Farley surprised me by saying, "I saw you pick up that little girl and carry her into your office. I suppose it is because you have girls of your own that you knew how to do that, but in all my years I never saw any principal do such a thing." I never told her or anyone why I did it.

After the atomic bomb had been dropped on the cities in Japan to end World War II, everyone was intrigued as to how the bomb was made. Only a few scientists knew, and there was great secrecy about it. In the spring of 1947 a series of meetings were scheduled across the country to acquaint the public with some aspects of the bomb and also to arouse public opinion to bring pressure on Congress to appoint a commission to control this new force. One such meeting was scheduled for Colgate University. Invitations were sent to civic and professional organizations in Central New York asking for one or two representatives for this conference. The Utica Exchange Club received one of these invitations and the officers, knowing of my background in science, asked me to go. There was a fee which covered lunch and a dinner at the Colgate Inn and the club said they would cover all my expenses.

The first session was to start at 9 a.m. on a Saturday at the Colgate Inn in Hamilton, New York. I drove over and registered in time to hear the first speaker. Using diagrams, he explained how the atomic force was released, so for the first time I began to understand some of the mystery. This speaker was followed by a panel of atomic scientists, including Dr. Hugh C. Wolfe, Department of Physics, City College of New York; Dr. R. R. Wilson, Cornell University, President Federation of Atomic Scientists; Harry A. Winne, Atomic Engineer, General Electric Company, and Dr. A. J. Coale, Secretary, Commission on Social Aspects of Atomic Energy. These men emphasized the importance of the public knowing about the bomb and its tremendous power. They also talked about the social and moral aspects of having the bomb. Over and over they stressed the fact that if other countries learned how to make such a bomb there would be no defense except the fear of retaliation. They brought the discussion to a close by telling about the good possibilities of using atomic energy in medicine and as a source of energy to produce electric power.

The first session lasted all morning, stopping in time so tables could be set up for lunch. Following the lunch, two speakers continued the themes presented by the panel. Before time for the dinner there was a short rest period which everyone needed. Dinner was served in the main dining room of the Inn and other scientists were introduced. It was announced that at eight o'clock a meeting would be held in the Colgate Chapel which would be open to the public. At the dinner a request was made for volunteers to give a ride to Utica for some of the guest speakers. Since I was alone, I volunteered to take three with me.

438

As I walked into the lobby of the chapel that evening, I saw a display of a number of pamphlets and books on atomic energy. Some were free and others for sale. I wanted all the material I could get for further study, so I picked up all the free material I could find and bought some, including the much discussed Smyth report. With the literature in my hands, I walked into the chapel to find a seat. I spotted one right beside one of the scientists who had been on the panel that morning. I asked if the seat was taken and he shook his head and invited me to sit beside him. He saw the material I was holding and asked where I got it. I told him in the lobby and when he noticed the Smyth report, he asked if he could look at it. I gave it to him and he leafed through it and with a sly smile as he returned it, said, "Talk about secrecy. This report has it all." I knew then what I had was authentic.

The chapel was full for the evening session and the speaker gave a sort of review of what we had been hearing all day. At the close I located the three men who wanted a ride to Utica. In that hour drive these men, who were experts in the atomic science field, never stopped talking. Two of them had been in San Francisco as representatives to the founding of the United Nations. They told of many interesting things that took place, including the many difficulties, especially those created by the Russians. I left two of the men at the Hotel Utica and the third at the railroad station. I got home after midnight and fell into bed, but so supersaturated with all the things I had heard I couldn't go to sleep for hours. Just before I did fall asleep I made up my mind I would put together a talk about this new force but put it in non-scientific language so the ordinary person could understand what it meant.

It happened I was the program chairman for the meeting of the Exchange Club the following Thursday. It was Easter week, and I had invited a minister who had visited the Holy Land as the guest speaker. Before I introduced him I gave a brief report of my attending the conference at Colgate. As it happened, my remarks fit the story the minister told perfectly. Just before the meeting closed one of the members stood up and moved that Ray Calhoon be given a whole program to talk more about the atomic bomb and energy.

To give such a talk I needed some diagrams to explain where this tremendous energy came from. I remembered that the previous year the school had subscribed to a weekly world map for the social studies teachers. These maps were now out of date, but had not been discarded. I checked and the back of each map was blank and perfect for my diagrams. Also, the maps could be rolled up and were mounted on a collapsible stand, so it could all be transported easily.

It was two weeks later when I gave my talk. Armed with the charts, I tried to explain the source of the atomic energy without using too many scientific terms. I showed Einstein's equation, $E = mc^2$, to show how such tremendous power could come from the tiny atom. I told of the frightening consequences of letting this force loose in the world, how the scientists had released a force that could be used for the good of all mankind, but also could destroy civilization and man himself.

After my talk, which was limited in time, many of the men remained to congratulate me on the speech and to ask questions. One was Irv Evans, a leader in the club and a man I had come to admire. "Ray," he said, "that was a good speech. But while you were speaking I didn't understand one damned thing you were talking about. However, when you finished, I found out I knew more than I did before." I laughed and replied, "You have given me a new definition of education."

After my presentation to the Exchange club, the news spread that I had something special and I began to receive invitations to speak before other organizations. To round out my talk where I was not limited to a short time, I wrote the following conclusion.

Man has not reached his present stage of civilization by a steady incline but by sudden surges in various fields of endeavor. He reached his highest point of political science three thousand years ago in ancient Greece. No country has yet reached the plane of pure democracy which the Greeks contributed to human ideals. The highest concept of religion was attained two thousand years ago and man has looked back at that event ever since. The Elizabethan age produced a Shakespeare and there is none to compare. Today the surge is in the field of science.

Were I an artist I would like to draw a picture representing civilization as a giant form of a man scaling a high cliff. At the foot of this cliff would be the dark stinking jungle out of which man has ascended. As a talus slope at the base would be the rubble of all previous civilizations. Civilizations which had attempted to climb the cliff but each in turn had slipped and crashed. After each crash man had somehow rose to climb at yet another place.

The giant is now near the top, but I would see him so exhausted that he has practically lost control of his limbs. His left arm representing science is extended high above his head with a strong hold at the very top. The plateau which the man is striving to reach is not flat but gently rising in the distance. On the plateau are all the luxuries that science can offer. Gone are the burdens from the backs of men. The vast energies of the universe are harnessed to conquer famine, floods, and pestilences. Swift is transportation and communication. This would not be an idle life for man but one of ever striving to make it better. A life with time to cultivate the arts and literature and the time to think through his philosophy, the true meaning of life itself. And then when man has lived out his full span he can lie down upon his couch to enter his eternal sleep free from a bed of pain and disease.

So near the top is civilization that he can see all this but his head is turned down to the right. For his right hand of political government has lost its grip on the rocks. It has grasped frantically at every projection and crevice until the rock is worn bare and now in desperation has seized the atomic bomb from science threatening to blast a new handhold ignorant that the blast will blow all civilization back into the jungle below, may even annihilate the chance for man to ever rise again.

The eyes of the giant are turned to inspect his footholds. His left foot of religion is firmly planted, but so bound around with vines of tradition that it seems helpless to raise the body. His right leg of education is drawn up with bent knee digging out a new foothold, the education of the masses. But it too is struggling with the vines of special privilege and tradition, which are holding it back.

Over the face of the man are mixed emotions. In his eyes is the fear and horror of falling. The mouth is drawn with the determination to make the last desperate effort to scale the cliff. Over all is an expression of pleading to all the innermost forces of courage and spiritual values which had brought man to his high level above the jungle.

Yes, the scientists want the man in the street to know what a great responsibility is thrust upon him. It is for him to decide whether this energy shall be used for an abundant life or for an instrument of destruction, which may blast him from the face of the earth.

As I reread my speech today, I am impressed as to how timely it all continues to be. The problems created over forty years ago when the atomic bomb was dropped have not been solved. In fact, due to the making of the hydrogen bomb and the widespread knowledge of how to produce these weapons of destruction, the problem has increased.

One place I was able to give the full speech was at a meeting of the Men's Club in Central Church. It created a lot of interest and discussion. Russell Brown was the minister of the church, and he was present, listening intently. I knew it was his habit to use people's names in his sermons, so I was prepared to hear him say something about me. Sure enough, the next Sunday about halfway through his sermon he began to talk about the atomic bomb. I just knew what was coming and began to shake with silent laughter. Norah gave me a poke and wanted to know what was the matter with me. "Here it comes," I whispered, just before Reverend Brown said, "I don't care if Professor Calhoon says there is no defense against the bomb. I know there is, the power of Almighty God."

After the service he greeted me by saying, "I hope you didn't mind being quoted." "Not at all," I replied. Then he continued, "That was a great speech you gave at the Men's Club and it made me think more than anything I ever heard."

For more than two years I was one of the most popular speakers in the city. I appeared before both men's and women's organizations as well as mixed groups. Educational and scientific organizations were interested in the scientific aspects of the talk, while the women liked the conclusion best. I could tell this by the questions and comments from the audience at the conclusion of the talk.

One memorable incident grew out of my study of atomic energy. Seldon Gerrish was not only the head of the visual education department in the Utica public school system, but also the head of an organization called the Educational Film Exchange. Seldon and his wife had the vision of having the schools in Utica and the area form a sort of co-op and set up a film library from which they could all draw, thus forming a source of material far greater than any one school system could afford. For several years I was elected to the board of directors of this exchange and had become acquainted with much of the equipment used in the field of visual education. Not only did the Gerrish's run the library, but Seldon maintained a shop to repair films and projectors and became well known in the city. He was often asked to run a projector for various meetings and when he had a conflict, he would call on me for help. One evening he called to tell me that he had a late call to run a slide projector for a meeting of the Tri-County Medical Association at the Hotel Utica, but he was already engaged and would I take the call. I was free and consented to do it.

When I arrived at the hotel I found the ballroom full of doctors who had just finished their dinner. There was a large turnout for the program was to be a lecture with slides about the damage to people who had survived the blast of the bomb that fell on Hiroshima. The pictures had been taken by Japanese doctors and were now loaned to medical schools in the United States for their use, *only*. The medical college of Syracuse University had received the slides and two doctors from the college were to give the lecture. A large screen was already set up on the stage and a table for the projector was in the back of the room. I was at this table when the doctors from Syracuse rushed in late and put the projector and slides in front of me, with a hurried statement that they would have a brief introduction and then be ready with the slides.

I opened the case and took out the projector and was surprised with a new one I had never seen. Anyway, I hooked it up and got it ready, all but having it in focus by the time the doctors called for the first slide. I sort of held my breath while I got it in focus, wondering if the rest of it would work. Fortunately, it did. It only took a few pictures to see why these slides were not released to the public. Many were gruesome. The two doctors took turns explaining the slides, while the audience was deathly quiet as they listened and viewed the grisly condition of these innocent victims.

After the lecture was over, I began to put away the projector and arrange the slides, when I noticed some of the audience going to the platform to ask questions of the two doctors and some coming toward me. The first to arrive greeted me by saying, "Doctor, what about this?" referring to some phase of atomic energy. I told them I was not a doctor, but I could answer the question. In fact, after listening to the lecture I felt sure I knew more about the scientific aspects of the bomb than the doctors did; not, of course, the medical terms. After I had answered the first question they came thick and fast, so much so I stopped saying I was not a doctor, just answered the questions. By the time I had put the equipment away, I looked up to see I was attracting a crowd five times the size of that on the stage. Then on the outskirts I spotted Dr. Pender, my doctor, grinning as he listened to me being called doctor and answering the questions. After the crowd had left, the doctors from Syracuse picked up the projector and slides with a curt "Thanks," never saying anything about the crowd around me which they must have noticed. As I walked through the lobby to leave the hotel, I was stopped by Dr. Pender, who was talking with a group of doctors. He introduced me and then asked, "How did you like being a doctor for the evening?" "Fine," I replied, "I tried to tell them I wasn't a doctor, but they wouldn't listen. I suppose since I was showing the slides they thought I was one of the group from Syracuse." Then he flattered me by saying, "Doctor or not, you were answering the questions better than they did."

In June 1947, Dorothy graduated from Vassar. Like many colleges, Vassar followed a "war schedule" and had covered four years of the usual curriculum in three. Dale and Marian and daughter, Maridale, were here at the time and drove their car, while Norah, Nellie and I took ours to attend the graduation. The weather was beautiful, so we enjoyed the many events which were held outside. The graduation ceremonies were in the chapel and only Norah and I could get in. I couldn't help but feel proud when Dorothy received her diploma, having accomplished what I thought was impossible. It was the custom at Vassar for the girls to furnish their rooms, so when they graduated there was a lot of activity selling their used furniture. Dorothy sold all except a couch, which could be turned into a daybed. For some reason she wanted to keep it and prevailed on me to take it home. Dale and I struggled to put it on the top of my car, and I dodged the showers all the way to Utica to get it home dry.

After graduation Dorothy got a job as a chemist in the Medical College at Syracuse University. Except when she was busy with an experiment which had to be carried through the weekend, she could be home on Sundays. While the girls were in college, their harp had been idle at home. Dorothy became interested in playing it again and took it with her. The next year she came home to play in a concert with the Junior Symphony Orchestra. Later she joined the Syracuse Community Symphony Orchestra and played several concerts with them.

For several years we had been visiting the Dressers at their camp on Bradley Brook Lake. On the dirt road leading to their camp was a small valley coming down from the high hill where we could drive the car off the road and we could enjoy a picnic. It was the only spot on the north side of the lake where this could be done. We did it so many times we began to think of it as ours, a place not only to have a picnic but where the family could enjoy the swimming while I rented a boat and went fishing.

Then in late summer of 1947 a man fron Endicott bought the Cook farm which included the pasture land all along the north side of the lake. He wasn't interested in farming but was a promoter and began to lay out the land into lots to sell for camps. The Cook farm was Bea Dresser's old home, and as long as her father was alive, he would not allow any camps to be built on the farm except the ones built by Mr. Yale, his friend, and the Dressers, where he gave them the land.

When we heard what was going on and saw the stakes marking the lots, Norah began to fuss, wanting me to buy the lot which we had been using as a picnic ground. I met the promoter and bought a lot with 60 feet of lake front and 100 feet deep, which included half the valley and some side hill. Once we had the lot, Norah and Dorothy insisted we should build a camp. I demurred, saying I was not a carpenter nor did I have the money to hire one. However, when Dorothy was home she and I drew a set of plans for what we thought would be a good camp building. I knew the owner of the Cazenovia Lumber Co., as he was a classmate of Norah's in the Cazenovia Seminary, and I took my plans to him to figure the cost of the lumber. We had plans for a building 20x16 feet, but the price for the lumber came to more than I could afford, so we cut it down to 16x16 feet.

Knowing Fred Benedict had been doing some carpentry work on his house in Chittenango, I talked with him and he agreed to work three days a week to help me build. I told him I expected to pay him and we agreed on terms. So as soon as my vacation started in the summer of 1948, I began to lay a foundation of concrete blocks. I was on the last layer when I got a message that Leeta and Ula had arrived unexpectedly in Utica. I hurried to put the last block in place so there would be at least two weeks for it to set before we started to build.

The girls had come as far as Buffalo on a special bus tour, then by train to Utica. I was sorry not to be home when they arrived, but our next door neighbors invited them in while they tried to call me. They were here for a week, so I could take them out to the lake and show them our site. Their special bus was to leave Buffalo; so I took them there by way of Niagara Falls. It was a nice day and we left the car outside the park, walking along to view the Falls. I saw a small cloud forming over the Falls, but it looked so tiny I wasn't concerned. Then without warning it began to sprinkle and in a minute turned into a downpour. There was no shelter nearby and I told the women to stand under a big tree while I ran to get the car. Before I could return they were soaked. There was no place to change and we started for Buffalo; within a mile we were in sunshine so hot it dried them in a few minutes. Reaching the bus station in plenty of time, they thanked me for bringing them, but I was sorry to have treated them to such a shower bath.

In July I had the lumber delivered to the campsite and Fred and I began to build. When we started, Fred said to me, "I like to swing the hammer but not to plan, so I will depend on you to give directions." I was taken aback, as I thought he had the experience and could count on him. However, I found that my woodwork at Clarkson years before came in handy, and we got along fine. As we approached the time to put up the rafters, Fred said, "Do you know how to cut a rafter?" "No," I replied, "I was depending on you." We both laughed, for without knowing it we both had been worrying about cutting them so they would lie flat on the plate. Our work had attracted a couple of kibittzers, two old timers who had nothing to do but come around each day to watch us. Both were great talkers, which bothered us, but since they had bragged about what they had done, I greeted the first one to appear that day by asking, "Do you know how to cut a rafter?" "Oh, sure," he replied. "Good," I said, "there is one, how about laying one out for us." I was busy and had my back turned. I didn't hear anything for several minutes, and when I turned around I burst out laughing; the man was way down the road walking away as fast as he could go. When the second man appeared I greeted him with the same question. He said he knew how, but was too busy to cut one. We never saw either of them again all summer.

When we were ready for the rafters, I told Fred I wanted a ⅓ pitch, so we held up two of the 2×6 rafters. I had ordered 2×6 instead of the usual 2×4 in order to prevent any chance of heavy snow caving in the roof as it had done on so many camps the previous winter. We marked where the two rafters intersected and cut them, then while Fred held one I marked the bottom at the plate. Much to our delight when we cut it and held it in place, it lay perfectly flat on the plate. The rest was easy as we used that as a guide to mark the rest.

As we kept building we were impressed on how close the manager of the lumber yard in Cazenovia figured the amount we needed. For example, when we were about three fourths finished laying the floor, Fred was sure we didn't have enough. I didn't think so, either, but said we would keep on using what we had and when we ran out, I would go to Cazenovia and get what we needed. Then to our surprise we had enough with one piece about a foot long which we had discarded because of a bad spot. Everything else came out the same way.

By the end of August the camp was completed enough so we could stay in it. On Labor Day weekend both the girls were home and we celebrated by staying at the lake where we could enjoy fishing and swimming and the new camp. During the summer we had strangers come and park in the vacant lot and picnic where we used to. We decided if we wanted to have any privacy we would have to buy that lot, also. I met the promoter and bought it just before he sold it to another party; we now had the whole valley and the only place a car could be driven in off the road. Then the next summer I enclosed the double lot with a wire fence to keep the cows and strangers out.

I now had something to keep me busy every summer and something I could enjoy. I bought some knotty pine and built a kitchen cabinet with cupboards below and put in a sink. Many people, when they saw it, thought we had bought the cabinet and had it installed. The next two

Our Camp at Bradley Brook Lake

years a lot of new camps were added around the lake, so the rural electrification company ran a line from the road to our camps. I went to Sears and bought the supplies to wire the camp. Some of the campers had trouble passing inspection, but when I notified the company I was ready, the men came and took a quick look and made the connection. They ran a 220 volt line to the cabin—Norah was delighted when we got an electric stove to use. We brought extra furniture from the house in Utica, including the couch which Dorothy brought from Vassar. We had two small bedrooms, a fairly large living room, and dining room and kitchen combined. The only thing we lacked was running water and an inside toilet, so I built a comfortable outhouse in the edge of the woods on the back part of the lot which we used. I said we should have some feeling of real camping!

For fishing I bought a 12-foot row boat, which seemed perfectly all right for several years. But as more camps were added, people came who had boats with outboard motors. I felt I had to have one in self-defense. The girls grew up learning how to row a boat and to fish and Dorothy became quite an expert. Later I had the pleasure of teaching my grandsons who also became first class fishermen. For the next twenty years this camp became an important part of our lives, a place of relaxation and a place where we could entertain company.

After being a member of Central Church for several years, I was elected to the official board. Most of the members of this board had been serving for many years, so as a new member for the first several sessions, I just listened and said nothing. Then one night a proposition was presented which I didn't think right and expressed my opinion. However, the chairman of the board advocated it very strongly and to my surprise, was supported by the minister, both stating it was the expedient thing to do. When the question was put to a vote, the majority voted in favor, a number didn't vote either way, and everyone almost fell out of their chairs when I came out with a lone strong "no." After the session was over two of the younger men stopped me and congratulated me on my stand. Then they told me that it had been the custom for years for members to only vote "yes" if they agreed with a motion, but if they disagreed, they kept still. I had set a precedent and from now on they were going to follow my example. They did, and the character of the meetings changed.

Being more active in the church, I was appointed chairman of the music committee. Russell Johnson, who later became the president of the Oneida National Bank, was then the director of the church choir. One of my first duties as chairman of the music committee was to work with Johnson to obtain a new church organist. Together we arranged a meeting with Mrs. Fague, one of the best organists in the area and persuaded her to come to Central. For years she was one of the key members of the church staff.

Probably my most important contribution came when the congregation voted to renovate the interior of the building. As chairman of the music committee, I was automatically a member of the renovation committee. The church organ had been in poor condition for a long time and before the war a committee had given a contract to the Estes Organ Company in Vermont to build a new organ. Before they could start, the government tied up all materials they needed so nothing was done. The renovation committee wanted the organ rebuilt at the same time the other work was done and asked me to have my committee proceed. I contacted the Estes Company, but they refused to do the work at the same price they had contracted to do it before the war. We offered to renegotiate, but they refused. I consulted the church attorney who said we could sue the company but doubted we would gain anything satisfactory. He advised me to notify the company that since they would neither do the work according to the contract nor renegotiate, we considered the contract null and void.

When we heard nothing from the Estes Company, the committee prepared new specifications and advertised for bids. At the beginning I knew nothing about the construction of a pipe organ, but with the help of one of the leading organists in the city who I knew very well, I learned fast. The low bidder for the job was the Buhl Organ Company in Utica. On investigation we learned that they had built several good organs in the area and being a local firm, we let them have the contract. They agreed to use all the old pipes that were servicable to save us money. When finished the result was one of the finest organs in the area.

447

When the work started on the organ and the old large pipes which covered the right side of the front of the auditorium were removed, it was discovered they had been hiding two beautiful gothic arches. When the architect in charge of doing the renovating saw these arches, he advised us to have all the organ pipes put inside the organ loft and keep these arches exposed. The committee agreed, and it added to the beauty of the sanctuary.

While I was a member of the renovation committee, something happened which I could never forget. A memorial stained glass window was planned for the front of the sanctuary high above the altar. When the design for the window, which was a copy of the famous painting of Christ in the Garden of Gethsemane was ready, a special meeting of the committee was called late one afternoon to approve it. I was a little late in arriving and found the rest of the committee in session. They had viewed the drawing and the colors and had all agreed it was beautiful. They were ready to approve it but waited for me. I looked at the design and while at the first glance it seemed perfect, something struck me as out of harmony in the design. I stood looking at it intently as the others waited impatiently to take a vote. Then just before a motion was made for approval, I realized what was wrong. When I pointed it out all saw it, including the architect who promised to have it corrected. With that understanding, it was approved and to this day is one of the highlights of the church.

As I left that meeting I began to think how my pointing out a defect in the design changed the view for all who heard. I couldn't help thinking how this is like what we do to people. People will think of someone as such a fine person until someone comes out with, "Yes, but I knew him or her when so and so happened." Right away that person's reputation could be damaged. I have used this episode as an illustration of why I advised young people going into teaching not to take a position in their hometown. I told them we are all human and tend to make mistakes, especially at the beginning of a profession, but if we make them outside our hometown, we usually can leave them there. But if you make the same mistake in your home school, someone is sure to remember it and keep reminding you and others of it, and it may even ruin your career.

In April, 1948, I was elected second vice-president of the Exchange Club. My duty was to find members to serve as program chairman for each month of the following year. I was lucky and secured a group early. A man by the name of Dudley was elected president for the year. He was fairly new but was such a "go getter" that the nominating committee thought he would be a big booster of the club. He had served a year as first vice-president but had never been called on to conduct a meeting. After he became president and got up to preside at his meeting, he got stage struck and panicked. We all felt sorry for him but not a word of criticism was uttered since we all thought he would get over it. However, he was so upset he resigned from the club. Rex

Stratton was the first vice-president and was moved to the presidency. For the time being I was considered both first and second vice-president. The club did not hold luncheon meetings during July and August and the only activity was an annual outing and picnic at Sylvan Beach at a member's camp.

As the time for the picnic approached I thought I better check to see if all arrangements had been made. I called the Niagara Mohawk company where I knew Rex was an engineer and was surprised to have the operator say Stratton was no longer with the company. She asked if I would speak with someone else. I said, "No, I wanted to talk to Rex about the Exchange Club picnic." "Oh," she said, "you better call Ray Calhoon about that." "Fine," I replied, "this is Ray Calhoon and he doesn't know anything either." I did reach the secretary of the club and learned that everything was in order. This outing was one of the highlights of the year for the club. The members came to have fun; playing games, swimming and a lot of "horseplay," finishing with a big feed. At a previous outing I had volunteered to cook the sweet corn, and it turned out so good I was drafted to repeat each year. After the meal the board of directors met and then informed me that Rex had resigned after leaving the city and asked me to serve as president for the rest of the year. I became the only man to hold three offices in the club at the same time, the only time in the history of the club such a thing happened. For over thirty years I was an active member of this service club, making many wonderful friends and contacts in the city I would not otherwise have had the opportunity to meet.

While Mr. Burdick was superintendent of schools he tried to upgrade the educational status of the administrators and teachers by inviting prominent educators to our professional meetings. One man he invited was a professor of education in a western university who had published a book entitled, *Every Teacher a Reading Teacher*. The meeting was held in the UFA auditorium, but Mr. Burdick called a meeting of the supervisors and principals an hour early so we could talk with the man informally. After the man was introduced, he spent a half hour expanding on his theory. It was like a typical college professor's lecture, and as I listened it seemed like a theory with little to support it. When he finished, Mr. Burdick said there was time for questions. There were a few, then Rocco Lopardo spoke up saying, "Do I understand you to say that you do not believe in special reading teachers, that it is better to have every teacher a reading teacher?" "Yes," the man replied, then looking all around the group, "Don't you all agree?" My mouth was open and I was surprised to hear a loud, "No," come out of it. Everyone looked shocked to think I had the nerve to disagree with such an expert.

Mr. Burdick also looked surprised and glancing at the clock said, "Mr. Calhoon, you have three minutes to defend your position." I was ready, as all the time the man had been talking I was thinking of how I disagreed. So I started by saying, "Reading is a skill and as such is

449

better taught by someone who understands that and has had training in teaching it. A survey in the schools in Utica shows that where there is a special reading teacher the reading scores of the pupils are the highest. For example, at Roosevelt year after year the I.Q. ratings are in the middle of the other schools in the city, but at the same time the reading scores in the 7th grade are at the top of all others. I believe this is due to the fact that I have one teacher who has taken courses in how to teach reading, and I have worked out the program so all the junior high pupils can go to her for such a class. Other teachers in this department are good in their fields, but they admit they are not reading teachers." Then I concluded by saying, "Too often when something is left for everybody's business it all too soon becomes nobody's business."

Following our meeting we adjourned to the auditorium where the professor gave his lecture to the teachers. Listening, I felt he lacked some of the enthusiasm he had had when he talked to the administrators, and I felt a little guilty, but at the same time I felt justified in letting him know all of us didn't agree with his philosophy. Lopardo evidently did, and I was to pay for that later.

With all my outside activities I still was busy running a school. Changes were taking place, and I had to keep abreast of them. For years school pupils had to buy their books and Grant's Book Store downtown in Utica had a monopoly in this area. They not only sold new books but did a big business in buying and selling used books. For sometime parents had been complaining about how little they could get for a used book but had to pay so much for another. These complaints reached the school board in such volume that they decided to take action by passing a resolution that schools could set up a rental system of furnishing books to the pupils. Each school was free to set up its own system. After consulting with some representative parents who were enthusiastic about such a plan, I decided to inaugurate a rental system. I estimated that a book would last on the average two years, so I set the rental fee at one fourth of the price of the book per semester. I designed an order sheet for each pupil to fill out and it was easy for a teacher to issue the books and collect the money.

I stamped each book with the name of the school and inscribed a code number inside the front cover so a pupil could be held responsible for returning the right book at the end of a semester. I tried to establish a system that would be as simple as possible to operate, but at the same time make it possible to account for all books and money. Once the system was established, pupils, teachers and parents were happy. It made a lot more work for me as I was responsible for about 4,000 books and also handling several thousand dollars to keep the system operating. The money part bothered me, as I had known too many school administrators who had been in trouble over book money. However, the system I devised passed the inspection of the state auditors and I felt it was all worth the effort for the good of the school.

Social promotion had been started in the first grade several years ago and had now worked its way up to the junior high school level. I considered the teachers at this level the best in the city, but when they had pupils sent to their rooms who were reading at a first or second grade level, they became frustrated. I held several sessions with this group to discuss the matter, and we decided to try grouping these pupils according to their ability. I used the same idea I had used in placing pupils in the modified first grade, and we established a modified junior high school course.

Discipline at Roosevelt was not a serious problem, but it did exist at times. One thing I learned was that physical defects are often the basis of discipline problems. One case was a second grade boy who would howl like a monkey at times upsetting the room and driving the teacher to distraction when she couldn't control him. She appealed to me and by checking with his family doctor, I learned that the boy's testicles had never come down properly, causing these outbursts. One boy got out of hand in the seventh grade and I decided to take him to Children's Court. In doing so, I learned a lesson. For the hearing I had prepared a detailed history of this boy's actions and all the things we had tried to remedy the case but were unsuccessful. To my surprise the court judge talked to him as if it was his first offense. I learned then why boys who had been in this court just laughed if I threatened to send them to court if they didn't behave. They knew from experience that nothing would happen for a long time and maybe never. After that I decided to handle the cases myself.

One day Superintendent Burdick called me and asked if we would take an eighth grade boy who had been suspended from two other schools in Utica, the last being Kemble school, where he had thrown a temper tantrum and walked through a new glass front door. My reply was I would talk to the junior high school teachers and if they were willing, we would take him. I explained that it was my policy to never place a problem case with a teacher unless I had first talked with her and we agreed on such a move. After I had a session with these teachers, and they all agreed to try the boy, I notified Superintendent Burdick and the next morning the mother brought the boy to my office. As I made out the registration form, I was quietly sizing up the boy. It was evident the mother had no control over the boy, who was large for his age and looked at everyone with a defiant air. I just asked the few questions needed to register him and announced I would take him to his room. I thought he looked rather surprised as if he had expected a lecture. All was fine for a few days, then Miss McRitchie, one of the best in that department, told me about an incident that happened with the boy. She had a class all lined up in the hall waiting for the bell to ring when she heard a disturbance. She turned around to see this boy out of line and bothering others. She walked back and told the boy to get back in line. He just grinned at her, so she told him again. The boy still didn't move and said, "Don't tell me what to do, I've got a temper." Miss

451

McRitchie said she faced him eye to eye and said, "Young man, I'll have you know that I've got a temper, too, and I don't think you want to see it." With that the boy got into line and we finished the year without trouble. Soon after school was out for the summer I picked up the evening paper and saw an item about a boy going beserk in a tavern down the valley who had smashed everything in sight. The state police had picked him up, and he was being held for trial. It was our problem boy.

Then a strange thing developed when I was in Dr. Pender's office a few days later. As we often did we had a discussion on problem cases and he asked me if I had read about the boy down the valley going beserk. I said, "Yes, I did." Then he told me he had been called to give the boy a physical examination and he found that the boy had the lowest sugar in his blood of anyone he ever knew. Dr. Pender was real surprised when I told him that we had that boy in school for several weeks. We both agreed that it might be that his physical condition produced those outbreaks and maybe many of our problem cases in school could be traced to physical maladjustments.

Snowball throwing around a school was, and always will be, a problem. Every year right after the first snowfall I would make the rounds of all the rooms in the school. I did this rather than call an assembly because I could pitch my talk to each year level. My talk was always the same, telling the boys how I knew it is fun to throw snowballs, but they must be careful whom they threw at, and never throw at the doors and windows of a building. I told the boys to go over on a vacant lot, build a snow fort, and have fun with a snowball fight. Some of the teachers thought I was wrong to suggest this; I should tell them not to throw snowballs at all, but the men teachers agreed with what I had said.

One day just after I had made my rounds right after the noon dismissal a girl came into my office crying. She said a group of boys had thrown snowballs at her just as she went out the front door. One hit her in the face and broke her glasses. She knew two of the boys and gave me their names, so I told her to find out what it would cost to repair the glasses and I would see that the boys paid for it. When she had the information, I called the two boys into the office and they named two more who were in the group. When I had them all together, I talked to them real stern, reminding them that they had done just what I had told them not to do, and adding they were lucky that the girl was not injured, so the least they could do was pay for the repair of the glasses. They all admitted they had done wrong and were willing to bring $2.00 each to pay for the damage.

After the boys went home and reported, my phone line was hot. Each mother wanted to know if her boy was the one to throw the snowball which broke the glasses. If not, they should not be made to pay. To each I replied, "I don't know which boy threw the snowball that knocked off the glasses, but I do know that your boy was in the group. This was right after I had warned all the boys not to do this, so he was disobeying my orders. You can be thankful the girl's eye was not cut and her parents had not called in the police." The mother who made the biggest fuss was the president of the school PTA. She wanted to know if the school didn't carry insurance to cover such cases. I said, "No, and you are missing an important point. I don't want you to pay for his share of the damage, make him pay. Also, this is a chance to teach him that he has to be responsible for his actions." All the boys brought their money and the case was settled.

It was interesting that this happened soon after a meeting of the PTA where there had been a lot of discussion about discipline in the school. The president had been one of the most outspoken about discipline and said something should be done! Now when it was her boy she fit the statement I often made, "Parents want strict discipline in the school, but don't touch my child!"

This episode indicated the growing feeling about insurance. We were aware that some schools were being sued by parents saying a teacher had not treated an injured child right. The school nurse was on duty in the school only half the time, so at a faculty meeting I talked about this situation and told the teachers I was placing a record book in the nurse's room, and anytime they treated a child to make a full accounting in that book, indicating the nature of the injury and what treatment they gave. I said this might not stop a suit, but it would help in any defense that might be needed. Of course, this made the teachers afraid to treat a child, so when the nurse was not there I got the cases. But in all these years I had only one complaint about my treatment; one mother didn't like the bandage I used.

One of the most persistent and annoying thing we had to deal with in Roosevelt school was pediculosis (head lice). There were certain families who had trouble every winter. All teachers, even in the eighth grade, had to hold daily inspections to keep a check on the situation. If the teacher suspected trouble, she would send the pupil to the nurse, who if she found lice or nits would send the child home with a printed notice telling the parent what to do. If the nurse wasn't in, the child would be sent to me. I became quite an expert in inspecting the girl's long hair, but sometimes when the child got home I would get an angry phone call from the mother saying they never had lice and it was only dandruff, not nits, I saw in the hair. There was one large family who lived on the outskirts of the city and these girls were notorious repeaters. I had met the mother at a PTA meeting, and she was what I had visualized her to be, a very large, happy-go-lucky woman. Yet she was concerned about the situation and always tried to cooperate. One day after the girls had been sent home repeatedly she called me and said, "Mr. Calhoon, do you know anyway I can get rid of these nits?" I have tried everything the drug store has suggested and bought their products, but none work." I thought a minute and said, "I never tried it, but I suggest you take a cloth and saturate it with alcohol, put the cloth between your fingers and run it down over a small strand of hair." I knew the nits were held on the hair by a sort of natural glue, and I thought alcohol might dissolve it. In a couple of days this mother called me and exclaimed, "Mr. Calhoon, I could kiss you. Your suggestion worked like magic." In a short time she had all the children clean and no more trouble for the rest of the year.

Children entering the school for the first time showed many different reactions as well as the parents who brought them. One day a young mother brought her first grade boy as a late entry. School was in session, so I made out the registration form and escorted her and the boy to his room. As we walked down the hall I could sense the pride this mother had in her son and out of the corner of my mouth, I whispered, "Your first?" She nodded her head as she glanced down at her boy marching along like a soldier. As I called the teacher to the door to receive her new pupil, the mother reached down to kiss her boy goodbye. But he turned his head away, his action plainly saying, "I'm too old for such sissy stuff." I introduced the boy to the teacher, and he marched into the room with head held high. As the door closed, the poor little mother leaned against the wall and burst into tears. She suddenly realized her boy was no longer her darling baby.

Every school principal has some experience with children who on occasion will stretch the truth. In talking with parents about this, I tell them I never say the children lie, but they may be telling things in a way to put themselves in a good light. One morning a young mother who had a boy in the second grade room came to see me. It was evident she had spent some time in dressing so as to make a good impression. She came to make a complaint about her boy's teacher. She said her boy came home everyday saying he couldn't do his work in school because the teacher treated the pupils so bad. He said the children were all afraid of the teacher because she slapped them so much. I expressed my surprise, as this teacher had been in the school for many years and was considered one of the best. I said this was the first time I ever had a complaint about her and suggested we see the teacher and see what she had to say. "Oh, no," the mother hastily said, "I don't want my boy to know I came to school. Anyway, if the teacher finds out that I complained, she will take it out on my boy." This is an opinion that is commonly held by parents and in some cases it does have a basis of truth.

I told the mother I passed that room many times a day, and I never heard any disturbance, but I would investigate and if at the end of a week she was not satisfied, to come back and we would go farther. With that assurance, she started to leave, but at the door she turned and asked, "When are the report cards out?" "They were out last week," I replied, "didn't your boy get his?" When she said "no", I rose from my chair and said, "Let's go and find out about it."

When we reached the door of the room, I said, "You stand aside so no one will see you, and I'll call the teacher out." When the teacher was outside, I introduced the mother and asked why her boy didn't get his report card. "Oh, but he did," said the teacher and stepped back into the room, returning with the card and holding it out so the mother could see it had been signed with her name. I never saw anyone so crushed. All the time she had been telling me how this teacher treated the children she had said over and over it must be true, because her boy never lied. Now she was confronted with the evidence that her boy had forged her name. Her angel had just fallen out of heaven. I could see it was almost more than she could bear, and I thought the kindest thing I could do was to walk away and let her finish the talk with the teacher. From my office I watched her slowly walk down the hall toward the door, her shoulders shaking in sobs. Needless to day, I never had any more complaints from her.

One thing I found rather frustrating in the Utica system was the fact that as the principal of the school I was held responsible for its success, but rarely did I have a chance to select a teacher or drop one who was not competent. Only once in my career did I help get a man physical education teacher out of the system when I refused to recommend him for tenure. This was a man whose character made him undesirable for a teacher. The superintendent did all the hiring and placing of teachers, usually without consulting a principal. It was my policy to trust the teachers I worked with, and the vast majority responded to that trust. However, like any group of people there were a few who did not conform. This was illustrated by a substitute teacher who was sent to finish out the year for a second grade teacher who had been taken ill.

This second grade teacher started right away complaining about things in her room. Then she was in my office several times a week fussing about her pupils, reporting one boy in particular who she couldn't stand. This woman had a very strict voice which irritated me and I guessed it may have done the same to her pupils. It all came to a head when one day she marched into my office and demanded that the boy she had trouble with be transferred. I tried to calm her down by explaining that it was my policy to never transfer a pupil to another teacher except in extreme situations. I said if I honored every request I had from a parent or teacher I would be transferring the equivalent of one classroom each semester. But my explanation did no good, so she declared that if I didn't move the boy out of her room, she would leave. This then involved another policy I had adopted—never let a problem go to a higher authority if possible. Solve the problem yourself in some way, for if it goes to the superintendent or board and you are not supported, your authority in the school becomes almost nil. Even if you are supported, your reputation as an administrator is diminished. I didn't want this teacher to leave and have the matter go to the superintendent, so I asked her to hold on for a day or two and I would see what was best to do. I contacted the mother of the boy and we had a frank talk. Then I acquainted the other second grade teacher with the situation and had her assent to take the boy if I thought best. After careful consideration, including the welfare of the boy, I made the change.

Two weeks after this there was a PTA meeting, which was held in the school auditorium. When the meeting adjourned, there was a rush to get out the door to get to the homemaking room for refreshments. I was caught in this jam and I heard the voice of that second grade teacher back of me. The quality of her voice was such there could be no question as to her identity. In a loud voice I heard her call out, "Oh, Mrs. B—, it's so nice to see you, how is Jimmy?" "Good," replied the mother in a low voice. Then the teacher continued, "I miss him very much, he was such a good boy. I don't know why Mr. Calhoon moved him out of my room." I couldn't believe my ears and as soon as I could turn, I looked back right into her face. She stopped short in mid-sentence and her face turned all colors of the rainbow. I didn't say a word but noticed the mother with her head bowed and a little smile in the corner of her mouth. I noticed the teacher did not attend the social hour, and she avoided me for days. Neither did I have any more complaints from her that year.

Once I had established the new method of entering kindergarten pupils I rarely had a problem. One did develop with a boy who lived right next door to the school building and entered in the January term. For years he had watched the children at play during recess and sometimes had joined them, going back home when they returned to their rooms. He was a big husky strong boy and was used to playing rough games. His teacher was one of the older rigid type, and when this boy entered and was asked to sit around in a circle with the other pupils while the teacher read a simple story, he was disenchanted and marched out the door to go home. The mother would bring him back but he wouldn't stay. Once the teacher tried to stop him, but he was so strong he pulled her finger out of joint. The teacher who had been in the system for many years would never admit a failure, but after several days of this going on, the mother marched the boy into my office and explained the situation. She announced she wanted the boy in school and gave me permission to do whatever I needed to do to keep him there.

The mother left the boy with me and after I had talked to him explaining what he was supposed to do, I took him back to his room. I was familiar with this teacher's methods, so I had a good idea why the boy did not want to stay, but I waited a while to watch his reactions. As long as I was in the room, nothing happened, but I had a feeling it wouldn't last so I picked up one of the little kindergarten chairs and took it out into the hall, where I could sit right in front of the door. Just as I expected, in about five minutes the door burst open and my football player came charging out. He came so fast he couldn't dodge and slammed into my outstretched arms. I caught him and bent him over my knees, giving him several good spats on his seat. He never made a peep, but fought like a wildcat. It was all I could do to hold him, but after a few spats I felt his body go limp. I stood him on his feet and said, "Now, let's go back into your room and you stay there." I marched him into the room, put him in front of his chair, and commanded, "Sit." He did, and I went back into the hall. It was near the time for the kindergarten dismissal, so I waited and was there so he could see me when he came out. I guess he must have thought I was always there, for after that he stayed in the room. Both the teacher and the mother were very pleased, although I doubt the boy was.

Of course, I had violated an unwritten school rule which was usually stated, "One never spanks a kindergarten child." When the teacher saw me do it, she reported me to Miss Anderson, the supervisor, who came up to see me. She pretended she was horrified, but when I asked her what she would have done under the circumstances, she admitted she didn't know. Anyway, I had suported her in many of the changes she had made in the system, so she couldn't say much.

Another unusual and serious case developed in the kindergarten my last year in Roosevelt. This teacher had been in the school for many years and for a long time considered the best kindergarten teacher in the city. Now she was almost ready to retire and in my opinion had become so set in her ways I did not think she was one of the best. She bragged many times that she could handle any situation, so I was surprised when one day she called on me for help.

When I walked into the room, I noticed a little girl standing alone in the middle of the floor. Her whole body appeared stiff and the teacher told me that the child had frozen in that position for a long time and she had to admit she didn't know what to do. I examined the girl and found out I could put her arms in any position and they would stay that way. It was as if she had become a mechanical doll. I tried to see if I could get her onto a chair, but all I could do was to bend her knees so she was in a sitting position but not touching the chair. I removed the chair and she remained in the same position.

I decided the child was in a "catatonic state," something I had read about but never seen. I told the teacher to go on with her program and pay no attention to the child; and when she came to, not to say a word. I tried to find out what triggered the spell, but got no satisfactory answer. As time went on there were some repetitions of this condition, much to this teacher's frustration, as she had met a situation she couldn't control, something which she considered spoiling her reputation. In time the child outgrew the problem.

Soon after the war the State Department of Education came out with a plan of granting a high school equivalency diploma. It was for young people who had dropped out of school and were now 21 years or older who could pass an equivalency examination. The diploma they received helped them to obtain a better job. Horace Griffith, Assistant Superintendent, was in charge of these examinations in Utica. He was also in charge of night school, and when he saw a high percentage of the people trying the examinations and failing, he decided to set up classes in the night school program to prepare for these examinations. He said he had noticed that a number of these people would pass the English, social studies and even math, but take one look at the science and give up. The rule set by the state was that a candidate had to have a passing mark in all these subjects to obtain a diploma.

Griffiths came to me to see if I would take a night school class in science to help these people. I told him I was interested and could I see a copy of an examination to find out what kind of questions were asked. His answer was "no, the exams could not be shown." I thought it over and decided the best approach was to teach the vocabulary of science much like learning a new language. When I met the class I told them what I planned, and they agreed that was the big problem they had, for when they saw the questions they couldn't answer because they didn't know what the words meant. I was real delighted when every member of my class passed the next examination. I repeated the class for three years with such excellent results that other cities sent representatives to Utica to see how so many of those who tried the examination were passing.

In the spring of 1950, Cliff Stanton announced he would retire as principal of Utica Free Academy in June. I was interested in the position, but before I made any move I saw Roy Perkins, who had been the assistant principal for several years. I considered him a good friend, and I wanted to know if he intended to apply for the position. If so, I didn't want to run against him. He was very pleased to have me ask and assured me he was not applying. In fact, he said he did not have the qualifications to obtain a secondary principal's certificate.

With that knowledge I applied at once. I had enjoyed being an elementary principal most of the time, but someway I never felt satisfied. Most of my training and experience had been on the secondary level and I wanted to get back as a high school principal again. I talked with Superintendent Burdick and he encouraged me to apply and would be glad to recommend me, but warned me at the same time that the board wanted to make their decision, so I would have to see each member of the board and sell myself.

After I filed my application with all my credentials and a list of my experience, I started making appointments to see each board member. Dr. Natiella, a dentist, was the president of the board, so I made a point of seeing him first. He was very cordial as I knew him very well. His wife was an active member of the Roosevelt PTA and his children had been pupils in the school. As we discussed the position and my qualifications, he surprised me by saying, "I always remember how you treated me when I came to your school to inspect the Child Day Care Center during the war. I came at your lunch hour, but you took me to see the room and introduced me to all the people working there. You spent your time to show me everything." "Of course," I said, "didn't everyone do that?" "No," he replied, "when I went to other schools they would say the center is down the hall and I would have to find it myself." That was hard to believe, but it was a good example of how a little courtesy may pay off in the future.

Mrs. MacMackin was the only woman on the board and I knew her quite well outside the board through several civic organizations, also Norah's sister, Nellie, was a special friend of the family. But when I saw her she greeted me by saying she had a candidate and would not vote for me. After we had talked awhile, she gave the name of her man. I told her I appreciated her telling me how she felt but must remind her that her man was a good friend of mine since we had worked together, but he had only been a principal of one elementary school, while I had been a principal of four different schools, two of them high schools.

The last member I saw was Richard Balch, who was the only businessman on the board, being the president of a company making fishing tackle. Just before I met him, Superintendent Burdick suggested that I might have a better chance by taking the position as acting principal as he had done years before. I wasn't interested in that idea at all. My interview with Balch was in his office and the first thing he said to me was, "Why do you want this job? You have a good position where you are; why change?" I answered by saying, "There are two reasons; one, I do have a good job but most of my educational studies have been at the secondary level and much of my expeience has been in high schools. Second, the principalship of the Academy is considered one of the top positions in the city and a man likes to go as far as possible before he retires."

Then I said to him, "I want to tell you something which I want someone on the board to know, and you being a businessman, I believe will understand. It has been suggested to me that I take the position as acting principal. I am not interested in that at all. There are a number of teachers in the Academy who were teaching when I taught there, and I need the full authority of a principal to deal with them. If the board doesn't think my qualifications and experience are sufficient to appoint me as a full-time principal, I don't want the job." He looked me straight in the eye while I was talking and asked, "Whose idea was that?" "I don't know," I replied. He sort of grunted and remarked, "I'll bet I do." His desk was in the corner of a large room and when I rose to leave, he continued to look at me intently. I could feel his eyes on me as I walked the long distance to the door.

When I finished the interviews I had no definite commitment for me and one against me. So the night the board met to make a decision, I waited with mixed feelings to hear the news. About 10 p.m. the phone rang and a voice said, "This is Folsom, the clerk of the board, and I want to be the first to congratulate you on being appointed principal of Utica Free Academy." I knew Folsom very well, both in the school system and also as a prominent member of Central Church, and he had sneaked out of the meeting to give me the news.

459

The news of my appointment was in the morning paper and on the radio, so all the teachers knew about it. Mrs. Bugental was the first to greet me and with tears in her eyes added her congratulations. Soon the office was full of teachers expressing their regrets to have me leave but adding their congratulations for such a promotion. When the office cleared I looked for Mrs. Bugental, but she had disappeared. She was gone so long I began to worry as she had never done anything like it before. Then by chance I found her hiding in the dark stock room, weeping. I knew we had a wonderful working relationship for the past years but didn't think she would take my leaving so hard. She said she just couldn't bear to think of coming to work and have someone else in my office. She was a good secretary, and I would have been glad to have taken her with me, but the civil service rules prevented it.

The last week of school in June the faculty planned a big farewell dinner for Norah and me. It happened that Ula and Faye were coming east to visit and were arriving the same day as the dinner. I asked the committee if I could bring them as my guests, but they said "No, bring them as our guests." It turned out to be a beautiful evening, and Ula and Faye were thrilled to be there, while I was happy to have them see how I was treated. In a way I was sorry to leave Roosevelt, for I was saying farewell to a fine group of teachers, most of whom I could call real friends. I always felt a good relationship with the pupils of the school and to this day I meet many of them who will greet me by saying, "You were my principal at Roosevelt."

CHAPTER 24

PRINCIPAL OF UTICA FREE ACADEMY

The week after school closed, I spent some time with Cliff Stanton in the Academy office. He wanted to get away as soon as possible; he briefed me on the things he thought necessary and turned the keys over at the end of the week. After he left I stood alone in the office and thought how eleven years before I had told Superintendent DeCamp that some day I wanted to be the principal of the Academy. I had followed his advice and spent those years being a successful school principal and now I had reached my goal.

The office at the Academy was kept open all summer. There were four secretaries who took turns working while the others were on vacation. While the principal was not paid during the summer recess, I found it wise to spend considerable time in the office. Since we were staying out at camp, I drove back and forth, spending half of most days in the office getting acquainted with details. By the time school opened in September I felt quite settled.

Utica Free Academy was then one of the largest public high schools in the state outside of New York City. It had a student body of 2500 students and a faculty of 130. As I had been a teacher in the Academy, I was familiar with the building and the organization. I admit that I was a bit nervous when I met the faculty for the first time the afternoon of the first day. I knew it would be critical, as there were a number of teachers in the group who would remember me as a fellow teacher, and I couldn't help but wonder how they would take me as the principal. After the usual greetings I said I knew I was following some very fine principals. I had known three of them very well, having taught under Babcock and Burdick and followed Stanton at Roosevelt. I considered them all to be excellent administrators, and I would build on their foundations. However, I wanted it understood that while I admired each of these men, I could not be like any of them. I would be myself. I closed by saying it was my policy to have everything run as before until I could study the situation and then, and only then, would I propose any changes. After the meeting a number of the teachers gave me some warm personal greetings and some told me that they never heard so many, both men and women, express their pleasure with my remarks. It looked like I was away with a good start.

461

The office at the Academy consisted of three rooms; the largest called the outer office, was the entrance from the hall, contained the teachers' mail boxes and had a long counter where the teachers signed in at the beginning of the day. Near the entrance was the switchboard for the telephone system and the operator acted as the information clerk. Two of the secretaries had desks in the back of this room. One was the attendance clerk keeping the records for the whole school. This was a unique system which had been devised in the early days of the school and never changed. The State Department did not approve of the system, claiming that each homeroom teacher should keep a register, but the school disregarded their protest. The other secretary ran the duplicating machine, putting out the daily bulletin which went to every teacher in the building. She also did general office work, which I often assigned.

The telephone system was different from any I knew in any school in the state. Some years before, Bell Telephone had installed this system, which included a phone in every room with an outside connection possible. This was a privilege which most teachers appreciated and were careful not to abuse, but a few did and at one time the superintendent threatened to have it changed. With all the house calls in the building and the outside service, it was the busiest exchange in the city. Keeping a good operator on the job proved to be a problem.

The inner office contained the school safe and files for the pupils' records. Mrs. Churchill, who was considered the secretary to the principal, had her desk in this room. A small corner of this room had been partitioned off, which was the principal's private office. I had known Mrs. Churchill for many years, mostly when she was Miss Lewis, Superintendent DeCamp's private secretary. When Mr. Burdick became superintendent, he wanted his own secretary, and Miss Lewis was transfered to the Academy. Soon after that she married Walter Churchill, a teacher of auto mechanics in the Academy. Knowing past history, I wondered how she would react to me being her "boss." But I didn't need to worry, for from the very beginning without anything being said, she indicated she understood her position and never tried to assume authority. She was a clever person and if possible would pass off work to another secretary, but when she had to do the job she could put out a lot of excellent work in a short time. Actually, I soon established a fine working relationship with all the office personnel.

The biggest change I found in the Academy since I had been there as a teacher was the addition of one of the finest gymnasiums in the state. Len Wilbur, the sports editor of the Utica daily papers, spearheaded a drive to pressure the board of educatin to build a gymnasium at the Academy. Bonds were issued and the building was started just before World War II broke out. During the war all building was stopped; for years only the foundation showed. After the war contracts were renegotiated and the gym was finished. The main floor was large enough for a full sized basketball court with bleachers seating 2500 spectators. The bleachers were retractable and with folding doors the whole gym could be divided into three parts so both the boys' and girls' classes could be held at the same time during the day. This addition made the Academy a full comprehensive high school.

The physical education department was fully staffed with Fred Collins as head and two more men and two women teachers. Fred was also the basketball coach and after I had been at the Academy a year, he told me on the side that he had been a player on the Oswego basketball team that Minoa defeated in Utica on the way to the state finals when I was coaching there. We had a different relationship now of course, but we soon learned that our ideas of physical education and team sports were the same; we got along fine.

For years Ken Edkins had been a teacher of social studies in the Academy, but also had been the coach of football and basketball. When the gym was added and had a full staff, Bill Boyle, the supervisor of physical education, pressed to have the teachers in his department be the coaches. Superintendent Burdick endorsed the plan and Edkins was relieved of all coaching but retained his position as teacher. Bernie Gretsel, a former UFA football player but with no coaching experience, was appointed head coach of football. He took over the same year I came to the Academy as principal and inherited a squad of green players. That fall marked the opening of the Rome Free Academy's new stadium. The football game between Rome and Utica dated back to 1891, the oldest athletic rivalry in the state. This annual game had always been held to end the season but because of the special occasion of opening the stadium, Rome requested UFA to be their opponent. We felt honored to be asked but with a green team and a new coach, it was almost a disaster for us. None of our players had ever seen a football field lighted at night and when they ran out onto the field and saw the big crowd, they became stage struck. They could do nothing right the first half, settled down a little better in the second half, but lost 47-0. The rest of the season was no better—they lost every game.

My observations during the first year indicated that the school organization was much the same as when I taught there. The committees of teachers that functioned at the end of each semester were the same and doing the same things. For example, I was surprised to walk into the room where the Regents committee was working and see the signs that I had made over a dozen years before when I was chairman of this group. I also learned that the same complaints and bickering by some teachers still continued. I felt this was due to the fact that so many teachers had been assigned to a certain committee and never changed. They often had the erroneous idea that their committee was the only one that did any work. Having worked on more than one committee, I knew this was not true, so I decided the only way to cure this situation was to change the personnel of each committee a little at a time. Beginning with the second semester of the second year, I switched one-third of each committee, leaving enough to carry on the continuity of the work, but introducing some teachers to a new line of work. By the time each teacher had worked on two or more committees, all complaints stopped. By that time they learned what I knew; everyone worked on each committee and all were important.

Of all the committees the work of the program group remained the most unsatisfactory. I thought of several revisions and decided to try one proposed by several teachers. Their suggestion was to have the homeroom teacher make out the program for the students in that room. Their argument was that this teacher knew the students better than anyone else and therefore knew what was the best for them. I held a meeting of the teachers involved, and the majority agreed to try it. The result was most did an excellent job, but there were a few who did such a poor job the plan didn't work. Then as we moved into more ability grouping, this work became so involved I decided the only solution was to have it done in my office where I could supervise it. I relieved Mrs. Churchill of some work and gave her the task of making out the program cards. Whenever possible I worked with her and the result was that we started each semester with far less confusion than previously.

Most of the teachers accepted me as principal without question. I did have one who had been in the school for some years inform me on the first day of school that she had some special privileges granted by Mr. Burdick. I listened and promptly forgot what she said, as this was contrary to my policy. I intended to treat everyone the same. Only once did I have a showdown with a teacher. It came about when one of the teachers who was teaching in the Academy when I was there as a teacher deliberately and openly refused to follow one of my directives. I knew she was rather a firebrand and when I called her into my office to explain, she proved it. She informed me that she was not working for Ray Calhoon, but for the Board of Education. When she ran down, I reminded her "That I was appointed by the Board of Education as principal of this school and if they think teachers are free to ignore a reasonable request given by the principal, I would like to know it. Suppose we go together and see the president of the board and see what he says." With that I put my hand on the telephone and continued, "I'll call him now for an appointment." She looked real surprised and in a calm voice said it wouldn't be necessary. I had called her bluff and she knew it. From that time on my authority was never questioned and there was no more trouble of this nature.

The wave of social promotions which I had encountered at Roosevelt reached the high school the same time that I did. Before I suggested any method to comply with this situation, I decided to let the teachers in the high school experience what it was like to have some of these pupils in their classes. In a short time I heard plenty from the teachers of the freshman classes, especially those in English and social studies, who were dumbfounded to find such students entering the Academy. As I had learned, there was practically no communication between the high

464

schools and the grade schools in the Utica school system. Up to this time pupils who entered the high school had been a selected group, consisting of only those who could pass the citywide eighth grade examinations. I had to explain to the faculty that this was no longer true, the high school was now a common school in that it was for all the children of all the people, and they had to stay until past the legal age of 16 to drop out.

I had sessions with the department heads and counselors, and they agreed to my plan of modified classes to accommodate these pupils. We started with a class in English to try out my method. Looking over the teachers in that department I selected Miss Hand as having the maturity and personality to handle such a group. I had a talk with her, explaining the situation and what might be done to meet this problem. Some of the teachers thought I was wrong in selecting such a good English teacher for this kind of work, but after my talk with Miss Hand she consented to try.

To select the students for such a class, I used the same method I had devised at Roosevelt, i.e., I took four unrelated criteria to make sure of my selection. The first modified class consisted of boys and only an experienced teacher could hope to cope with the discipline problems that were certain to develop. I told Miss hand that from my observation these pupils had spent most of their school life sitting in the back of the room. They rarely took part in class work and as long as they kept quiet and stayed out of trouble, they were ignored but passed along to the next grade. I felt this was wrong and we should find out what they could do and help them with that. There was no thought of them completing any goal in English and no rating of the teacher for failures. Miss Hand reported that it took her several weeks to convince these pupils that they should do something; they never had.

At the end of the first month Miss Hand reported her experience. In order to get them to do something she asked each one to bring a short clipping from the daily paper and read it before the class and explain why they thought it interesting. The next day when she called for this report boy after boy said they didn't have anything. She asked each one to report after school. After the class was dismissed, one boy lingered and when all the rest were out of the room, he said, "Miss Hand, I didn't want to say I didn't have an article, but I can't read." Miss Hand said, "I was startled, looking up at this good looking six-foot boy standing there with tears in his eyes, admitting he couldn't read. I asked him to sit down and gave him a quick test and found out it was true. I found a short item in the sports page of a paper and read it to him. I gave the clipping to him and told him to remember what it said and he could stand up and say it so no one need know he wasn't reading."

The boy did as suggested and was so grateful to Miss Hand that all her discipline problems, which were beginning to be many, vanished. This boy was the largest in the group and from that day on if anyone stepped out of line, all he had to do was to look at the offender and everything straightened out at once. "I never knew what he did outside the classroom, but he sure had things under control for me in my room," laughed Miss Hand.

My friend, Floyd Trieble, who had been head of the English department in the Academy for many years, had retired in the forties and now Ralph Ginther, who took his place, retired just before I became principal. Superintendent Burdick had hired a man by the name of Walter Eddington to be the new head. Eddington proved to be a strong character, sometimes too overpowering and had to be curbed, but he knew his work and had good ideas about his department. Ted Reusswig, as head of the counselors in the city, had made a survey indicating that the greatest weakness of the local high schools in preparing students for success in college was in the field of English. To remedy this condition in the Academy, Eddington proposed that all the top students who were potential college material be grouped in special fourth year English classes. I concurred and Eddington took these classes and gave them the "works." To many of these students it was the first time they had to extend themselves, heretofore being the brightest in a class where they could be at the top with little effort. After a couple of years reports from UFA graduates who had gone to college came back saying they had a good start in their college classes because of the training they had in our special groups.

With the success in grouping in English, I thought it time to expand to the social studies department, but I ran into opposition with Miss Nelson, who was now head of this department. I had known Miss Nelson in my teaching days in the Academy as a master teacher and very strict in her classes. Now promoted to be the head, she carried the same firm methods with her teachers. She was very jealous of her department and fought any attempt to make a change. There developed a feud between her and the counselors who wanted some consideration given to students who wanted to take other subjects rather than so many social studies classes. Even when the state changed the requirements from four years to three years of social studies for a Regents diploma, she refused to change in the Academy.

The issue became so intense that I called a meeting of all concerned to see if we could work out a compromise. It was of no avail; compromise was never in the vocabulary of Miss Nelson. She bragged that she was a descendant of Lord Nelson of British fame, and she gloated that she was just as stubborn as he had been. I listened to both sides in a stormy session and when it was evident nothing could be worked out as a compromise, it was left to me to make a ruling. I had to give her credit, for after I ruled against her, she took it like a soldier. She said, "Mr. Principal, I will follow your instructions but will never agree with you." She always called me Mr. Principal, never by my name.

Miss Nelson had one disconcerting habit. My office closed at 5 p.m., and I liked to leave on time but ever so often at five minutes before five she would come to the office to see me. She always had a long discourse to give, and I learned by experience never to interrupt, for if I did, she would go right back to the beginning and start all over. I learned to listen to her story and when she finally came to the end, I would say, "I will consider what you have said." If I tried to discuss it with her, I would never get home for supper.

The third year I was at the Academy Miss Nelson was stricken with a serious illness. With Norah I went to see her in the hospital and she looked so bad I felt she would never get out. The doctors told her that her bones had grown so soft she would never be able to walk again, but she wouldn't listen. She ordered the nurses to bring her a walker and by sheer grit she got out of bed and on her feet. Using the walker for a time she got out of the hospital and by using a cane came back to school. Everyone who knew her attributed it to pure determination that she was able to be back, but unfortunately her illness affected her mind so she became very difficult to work with. She became entangled with the board over the salary schedule for department heads in the high schools, and when the teachers in her department refused to support her, she became embittered and retired. She refused to attend a dinner the socials studies teachers gave her at her retirement, but it united the group in such a way it made it easier for Frank Mason to become the new head.

True to her indomitable character, Miss Nelson went back to Syracuse University and worked for a doctor's degree, which she obtained. She then worked for her church helping to establish church related nursing homes all over the country. Up until the year she died she always sent me a Christmas card, even when I didn't know her address to respond. She truly was an unforgettable character.

There were four counselors in the Academy, two men and two women. Each counselor would take an entering class and stay with them until they graduated. Working closely with them I came to know each very well. I considered Art Wildes the best of the group, and he was also the faculty advisor of the student council. He had the rare ability to work with high school students and guide their enthusiasm in the right directions. I came to depend on him in many ways.

It happened that Roger Murphy was the counselor for my first graduating class in June, 1951. The *Utica Observer-Disptach* always published a list of the graduates of UFA in the Sunday edition before commencement. The paper had set up a tentative list, but they expected the principal to revise it on Saturday morning, thus making it official. On Friday afternoon I checked with Murphy to see if his list of graduates would be ready on time when to my surprise I found him working on a large list of uncertain seniors. He was in so deep I went back after supper to work with him. It was two o'clock in the morning before we had the list ready. I vowed, "never again," and set in motion a different method so we would have the list ready in plenty of time.

In the main I got along with the counselors fine, but there was one point on which we did not agree. They felt they should have nothing to do with discipline. I claimed they should know the students in their group who were in trouble and as counselors could straighten out a situation before it got serious. I felt this way because ninety percent of the cases involved both the students and teachers. Two things happened to bring us together on this issue. First, a transcript being sent to a college for a student came to my desk for signature. This student was a notorious trouble maker in the school, but the counselor had given him a glowing recommendation. After that I insisted that every transcript go over my desk. Most of the time I just looked at them, but it gave me a chance to see what was being said about a student and could add something if I felt it should be included.

The second thing which changed the situation came about when Mr. Perkins was out for several weeks due to illness. I had to take over his work but found it impossible to handle all the discipline cases as he had been doing. I held a meeting of the counselors and convinced them to have all first offender cases sent to them. An exception would be a major offense or if a group of students was involved. The counselors agreed to give it a try and after a few weeks agreed with me that the change worked to the benefit of all.

Mr. Perkins and I worked out an understanding so far as discipline cases were concerned. With his years of experience in handling such cases, Mr. Perkins could settle the majority of troubles. Only when he had reached his limit with a student did he refer to me. By that time he would arrange an appointment with me to meet the student with at least one parent. Because of experience with Children's Court, I made up my mind that I would never treat these cases as if it was the first offense. At the beginning of such a conference Mr. Perkins would present a written review of all the times the culprit had been in trouble and what he had done. After listening to the record and if the student was 16 years or older, I would say, "All right, let's find out if you want to stay in school." Often the parent would interrupt by saying, "Oh! He has to stay in school and get an education." To which I would reply, "No, since he or she is over 16 they can drop out. You want him to stay. We want him to stay, but I want to know what he wants. We have a fine school with some excellent teachers who are ready to help, but none of us can do anything unless he wants to learn. Right now he isn't learning and what is worse, he is keeping others from learning. My advice is, unless he is ready to follow the simple rules we have and settle down to business, let him turn in his books and go out and find a job. Let him see for himself what it is like to work for a living."

Many of the parents were aghast to hear a high school principal talk like that. But it was an eye opener to the student. I am sure it was the first time they had ever been faced with an opportunity to make a decision of their own. Usually I would end the session by saying, "All right, you take your child home and talk it over. If tomorrow morning he comes in and convinces me that he really wants to stay in school and means business, fine, but he has to convince me." Most of the time they would be back with a new outlook on life and would change for the better. A few would drop out and then be back the next semester after finding out for themselves what everyone tried to tell them, that they couldn't find a decent job without a high school diploma.

One case that I recall illustrates our method. One day Mr. Perkins brought a boy with his father to see me. When Roy began to read the list of what the boy had been doing, the father interrupted by saying, "I don't think you men know how to deal with a boy. Why don't you try so and so." At each suggestion Perkins would reply, "We have done that several times." Finally I broke in and asked the man what he did. "I'm a locomotive engineer on the New York Central Railroad," he proudly replied. He was a large robust man and looked like some of the engineers I had known in Minoa. "Fine," I said, "let me ask you something. Suppose Mr. Perkins and I came down to the railroad yards and climbed up into your cab. Suppose we told you you were doing everything wrong by pulling the wrong levers, what would you say? Never mind, don't answer. A few years ago I was principal of Minoa High School and I knew a lot of railroad men, so I know what you would say and the language you would probably use to say it. Let me remind you that Mr. Perkins and I have dealt with literally hundreds of cases. Now, just as we respect your ability to run your locomotive, I think you should give us credit for knowing our job." Again, I went through the routine of asking the boy what he wanted to do, and finished by telling the father to take the boy home and talk it over. Evidently I made an impression on both the boy and his father, for the next morning the boy appeared with an entirely different attitude and became a good school citizen, graduating with honors.

A second case developed when a principal of a Central High School some distance from Utica called to inform me that a group of boys from UFA were apprehended in his building racing through the halls and disrupting classes. They got the number of the license plate on the car they were driving and gave me the name of the owner. I expressed my regret that any student in the Academy would do such a thing and was glad he could give me the name of one boy so I could take action.

I notified Mr. Perkins and by calling the driver of the car in, obtained the names of all the group. I considered the boy with the car the worst offender and he admitted he persuaded the others to go along. The father of this boy was notified and came with him the next day. I had checked the record of the boy and noticed that he was a senior with a fair record until a month or so before this happened and now his grades were dropping, so much so his graduation was in jeopardy. As I began to question the boy, his father volunteered the information that the boy had just reached the age where he could own a car. The father didn't approve of him having a car now, but his mother did and helped him buy one. The boy was so thrilled that he was spending all his time with the car and no one could control him. "In that case," I said, "let's find out something." I had already explained to the boy I considered him to be the worst offender, so I turned to him and asked, "Do you want to stay in school and graduate?" When he replied, "Yes," I continued, "Since you apparently can't control your time and your grades have dropped so fast you are in danger, let's see how bad you want to graduate. I'll help you by having you bring in your license plates off the car tomorrow morning, and I will put them in a sealed envelope with your name on it so if anything should happen to me you can claim them. I will put the envelope in our safe and the day you finish your last examination, you come to the office and I will return your plates." I glanced at the father and he was so red in the face I thought he might have apoplexy, but he didn't say a word. The next morning the boy appeared with the plates and I did just as proposed. The boy was bright enough, so in the three weeks left he pulled his grades up and graduated. When he came for his plates I congratulated him and asked if he thought it was all worthwhile. He agreed it was and thanked me for bringing him into line. The day after commencement I noticed a short item in the paper that the State Troopers had arrested a driver on the Thruway going over a hundred miles an hour. It was this boy, who still hadn't learned how to control himself.

I found one system going on in the Academy which I didn't like. How long it had been in operation I never knew, but someone had introduced a detention room plan. Any teacher could assign any number of periods of detention after the regular dismissal. It was much like the system I had observed in Middletown, I didn't like it then and when I investigated it here at UFA it wasn't any better. I let it run for a year, then I talked to the faculty committee about it. This was a committee established by Stanton representing each department with an elected teacher. The teachers thought in this way they could present their views directly to the administration and not go through the department heads. They seemed to think it was more democratic. The idea did have some merit, but as I looked over the minutes of the meetings of this committee, I could see little progress. The same points had been raised over and over with no solutions.

However, this committee did give me a chance to express my views about the detention system. After some discussion they asked me to present the problem to the whole faculty. This I did, telling them that my investigation indicated that 90% of the cases in the detention room came from a small number of the teachers. Since all teachers had to take turns keeping this room, a lot were doing the dirty work for a few. Also, I found students in the room who had so many days of detention assigned there were not enough days left in the year to match. Clearly, assigning these detentions was not curing the problem. I likened it to a parking violation, one could pay the fine and keep right on doing the same thing. I said, "In my opinion, we are missing the important thing. We are not curing whatever the student is doing wrong, we just feel relieved by assigning detention periods."

470

I waited a month before I made my final decision. During that time I let the teachers talk it over among themselves. I sounded out a few and learned that a good number were in favor of eliminating the detention room, so I announced beginning the next fall there would be no such rooms. Some of the younger teachers exclaimed, "What are we going to do with no more detentions?" "I didn't say no more detentions. You can keep all you want to, but you are on your own." The ones who had made a crutch of the room felt hurt, but it changed the atmosphere of the whole school.

The fifties marked a decided change in the structure of the high school in America. First was the impact of social promotion and the influence of such educators as Conant of Harvard with his book on the comprehensive high school and the change in standards for a diploma. The Academy had existed for years with little change. It was organized with departments that functioned much like small states independent and sometimes jealous of others. They had a tendency to be more concerned with their own importance than with the welfare of the students who had to exist in many departments. I knew from my previous experience and talking with the present teachers there had never been any discussion by a principal in regard to how the school was to meet the coming changes. For years all the teachers who had joined the faculty were those with considerable experience, but now the superintendent was hiring teachers with little or no experience. With this in mind I decided it was time for me as principal to spend some time at each faculty meeting in discussing some of the problems we were facing. By doing this before the whole group I wanted to see if I could bring the teachers to think of the welfare of the whole school, not just their own class or department.

To start my program, by invitation I gave a condensed version of my talk on atomic energy. It was well received, but I could see the looks of surprise on the faces of some of the older teachers as this was a new kind of faculty meeting they had never experienced. My next theme was the problem of meeting the conditions of a common school where we had to meet the needs of students expecting to go to college and at the same time give the rest of the students good training to find a job. The next talk was on meeting discipline problems. This raised quite a lot of discussion among the teachers when I remarked that many times we created our own problems. I did not mention names, but I said I knew some teachers who set the stage for trouble. "For example," I said, "if there is something you don't want done in your room, don't announce to the class that if someone does this thing such and such will be the penalty. If you do, you can be sure someone will try to see if you intend to enforce the penalty." I got quite a reaction with this statement, some nodding their heads in agreement, but others audibly protesting. Evidently I did make an impression, as years later a group of retired teachers "kidded" me about my talking about setting the stage.

Another time I talked about assigning a penalty that could not be

471

enforced. I told the teachers if they got in trouble with a student or parent when assigning a reasonable penalty, I would support them to the fullest, but not if it was out of line with the age of a high school student. In such a case I would expect them to admit a mistake or find a way out of the situation. I said this because a few days before this I had a large senior boy appeal to me because his teacher had told him he had to sit on the floor in a corner of the room. The boy explained if he did he would be ridiculed forever by other boys in the class. The teacher was a man who had been in the Academy for years, was in fact, in his last year before retirement. When I called him into the office and informed him that the boy had appealed, and I didn't think the penalty was right for a high school senior, he exclaimed, "What shall I do? If I don't enforce my order, I will lose all the respect of the students in the class." This is a statement I had heard many times by teachers who had put themselves in a similar position. My answer to the man was, "I am not going to tell you what to do, but if I was in your place, I would see the boy privately and tell him if he promised not to repeat what he did, you would not enforce the penalty. Then announce to the class what you did." The surprising thing to me was that a teacher of so many years would put himself in such a position, but it was an indication of the changing times.

Near the end of my first year as principal of UFA, Superintendent Burdick announced his retirement in June. I was now faced with the same situation I had encountered in Saratoga Springs. I had just become established as a high school principal, a position I liked, but would now have to work with a new superintendent. I thought some of applying for the superintendent's position, but decided I didn't want it. The board let it be known that they were considering going outside the system to fill the position, but to the surprise of many they elected Rocco Lopardo. Of course, I knew him very well, as he had been the head of the math department in the Academy when I taught there. He had followed me at Conkling as principal and was now in Hughes school, so we worked together and shared many problems. There were some things in Lopardo's background that made me wonder how we might get along. Years before when we were at the Academy, Lopardo had openly declared he expected to be the principal when Babcock retired. They were both graduates of Hamilton College, so he thought he had an inside track. When Burdick was appointed, Lopardo was very upset and decided then to follow my example and go for an elementary school principalship. Then he lost out again when I was appointed at UFA, and I knew he always wanted that job. Now he was to be the superintendent, and I couldn't help wondering what our relationship would be.

It wasn't long before I found out. The school counselors of Central New York had formed an association and Art Wildes, as president, invited the organization to hold their annual meeting in the little theater at UFA. Since the meeting was in Utica, both Lopardo and I were invited to attend. The theme of the meeting was to gain a better understanding between the counselors and the admission officers of the colleges. A number of such officers from the area colleges were invited.

Near the end of the morning session the question arose as to what a school should do with a request for a transcript to be sent to a college when the school could not recommend the student. After some discussion I was asked to give my views. I said our policy was to honor every request for a transcript, but if we felt the student wasn't qualified to do college work, we left the line for recommendation blank. I also stated we wanted to be fair to both the student and the admission officer, as there might be other factors the college would consider besides our ratings.

As I spoke I could see a number of heads nodding in agreement, but I had hardly finished when Lopardo jumped to his feet. In his characteristic bombastic way he shouted, "That is the worst answer I ever heard. I would think a lot of you would be on your feet protesting such a position. If the school can't recommend a student, they should not send a transcript." I was in the back of the room, and person after person turned around to see how I was taking such a blast. I sat with a blank look on my face just letting him rave. As soon as Lopardo paused, the chairman announced that lunch was ready in the cafeteria and they would have to adjourn until 2 p.m. Everyone stood up and I was surrounded by people who assured me over and over that I was right and some wanted to know how I could work with such a superintendent. When Lopardo didn't show up for the afternoon session, a good meeting resulted.

Another example of how different Lopardo and I were in our thinking came about in the spring. Bill Carney, the director of the UFA band, came into my office very upset. He said the superintendent had just called him and gave him an order to have the Academy band out at 4 p.m. on Friday afternoon to play for a parade organized by city hall to display some new street cleaning equipment they had just purchased. Carney tried to explain that this was no time for the band to parade, as it was the night of their annual concert, but Lopardo would not listen. I was also upset to hear about this, not only because it was an unreasonable order, but also because the superintendent bypassed me as head of the school. I picked up the phone and succeeded in getting Lopardo at once. I told him that Carney was in my office and repeated what he had been told, continuing with the fact that I felt it as wrong to expect the band to play for a parade just before their concert. Lopardo cut me off by saying, "I promised the mayor that the UFA band would play for this parade, and I expect them to respond, after all, I am number one in the system."

After I had hung up the phone, I turned to Carney and said, "You heard me protest, but I got nowhere, so tell the members of the band if they cannot be present for both the parade and the concert, to forget the

473

parade. I suggest that you use only the drums when the parade moves and just play an easy march when the parade stops. This will help the brass players keep their lip for the concert." Evidently Carney took my advice, as the paper reporting the news of the parade commented that the UFA band made a good showing, but only played when the parade stopped.

This episode is a good example of playing the old army game. You never refuse to obey an order, but there are many ways of not carrying out the intent. In my years of dealing with teachers, I tried to avoid giving a direct order. I put things in the form of a request and then worked to gain the cooperation of the people involved to carry it out. It was a way of avoiding the feeling of people working under orders.

One of the most dramatic episodes occurred during Lopardo's second year in office. Some way he heard that Miss Nelson was not following the state syllabus in social studies. I knew it and had talked to her about it and had accepted her reasons for not doing so. Since the students in her department had such high ratings in the Regents examinations, I saw no reason to have her change. Lopardo kept at me about this, so I finally said, "Why don't you come up and talk to her?" I had the feeling that was what he wanted to do and jumped at my suggestion. I made the arrangements for them to meet in my office.

They were both very prompt and when we were seated, I opened the discussion with a few words about the purpose of our meeting. I knew the session would be stormy because when Lopardo was head of the math department and Miss Nelson was the head of the social studies department, the whole school knew about some of their violent differences. Now that he was the superintendent, Lopardo felt he was in a position to tell Miss Nelson what she should do. He told her she was wrong in not following the state syllabus, and he expected her to do so. She and I both knew that a syllabus was a guide, not a dictum, and furthermore she did not propose to let anyone, not even the superintendent, tell her how to run her department. Soon they both began to interrupt each other and in a short time it developed into a shouting match. I sat back in my chair and let them go. In fact, I was rather enjoying seeing Lopardo, who had been telling me what I should do, now meeting his match. After a time they both ran out of breath and like two roosters in a fight, sat glaring at each other. I decided it was time to end the meeting and with a few words dismissed Miss Nelson. Lopardo stalked out of the office and I followed to see if the secretaries, who couldn't help hearing the shouting, were still around or had fled.

I think I was the winner of this session because after a few days Lopardo apologized for creating such a scene in my office and never again made suggestions on how I should run my school. Miss Nelson never apologized, but it was apparent that she considered me in a new light as the principal of the Academy.

With the fine gymnasium at the academy, basketball was rapidly taking over the interest that football once held. Fred Collins was the coach and produced some fine teams. We got along fine together as we held the same ideals of good sportsmanship. I enjoyed sitting on the bench with the team, as I attended all the home games and many away. The only thing I ever said was "Go get the first basket." when the team first took the court to begin a game. I did this because after watching hundreds of games I noticed that it was a better than a fifty percent bet that the team making the first basket became the winner. The spectators near the bench heard me say this, and soon they made it a rallying cry.

All the indoor sports were now under our direct control, but for the outdoor sports, football, baseball and track, the teams had to travel a mile to Murmane field in south Utica. The management of this field was set up in a rather strange way. Years before the land had been given to the city as a recreational park, with the proviso that the city would maintain the park in good condition, but the use of the faciities was given entirely to Utica Free Academy. So for years it was considered to be the athletic field for UFA. By tacit agreement the field was used solely by the Academy teams during the school year, then during the summer recess it was given over to the city recreation department.

For a time this arrangement worked fine, but the city was not keeping up its part of the agreement. The club house which was used by the teams was in such bad condition as it was unsafe to use; the dressing rooms had no heat and the showers were useless. The condition became so bad that there was a public demand to city hall to do something. I was asked by the superintendent to come down to his office and meet with him and the board's attorney to talk over our position. Before I went I located in the old school safe a copy of the deed when the land was transferred to the city and stating the conditions, so I was prepared. When I got to the administration building and met with the superintendent and the attorney, I learned that a meeting had been arranged within the hour with the mayor of the city in his office. To my surprise the superintendent said the attorney and I would go as the school's representatives. The superintendent then told me that the mayor had informed him that if the Academy would relinquish all claims to the field, the city would take over and do all the repairs needed. They would agree to let the Academy use the field, but it would be under the city's control. Both the superintendent and the attorney worked on me to accept this agreement, and when I refused to agree, they couldn't seem to understand. It was time for the attorney and me to leave for the City Hall which at that time was only a few blocks up Genesee Street and all the way the attorney kept at me to change my mind.

When we reached the mayor's office, his secretary told us to go right into his private office as he was expecting us. Then as we stepped inside I caught my breath. I had expected to see the mayor, but the room was full with the heads of all the city departments. The mayor greeted us and invited us to sit down. He then proceeded to lay out the trouble that existed at Murmane Field and his proposal to have it remedied by the city acquiring the park, but letting the Academy use it.

My reply was the Academy would not give up its rights to the field. If the city took it over, then we would have to compete with all the other organizations in the city for its use and would never be sure when the teams could practice nor be able to schedule games in advance. I finished by saying I did not think the city had lived up to its agreement when they accepted the land as a park, since they had allowed the club house to deteriorate so much. Then to my surprise the attorney, who had counseled me all the way over to let the city have the field, suddenly changed and strongly supported my position. After some further discussion the meeting broke up when the mayor announced he was having an ordinance prepared to have the club house renovated. I was rather mad at the mayor for trying to bluff me out of my rights and madder still at the superintendent for supporting him and leaving me to stand alone to protect the rights of the Academy. Whatever they had cooked up together I spiked for the time being. Years later after I had retired, this same situation arose again.

Most all the time I had good relationships with the physical education staff. Only once did I have trouble when a new man was given the job of coaching football and he used a player who had been declared ineligible. I had a showdown with him about his violation of my position on good sportsmanship and the reputation the Academy had built up through the years. Now a new problem arose, when the women on the staff began to advocate eliminating the cheerleading squads. It developed that a movement had started across the state by some women physical education teachers that it was degrading for high school girls to perform as cheerleaders. This movement became so strong that the state supervisor of these teachers held a series of meetings around the state to discuss this problem. One of these meetings was held at Proctor High School and along with the women teachers, the principals of the area high schools were invited to attend. I joined a few principals who decided to go, trying to be inconspicuous by sitting in the back of the room. There was a big turnout of women physical education teachers, and it became apparent the most important matter for discussion was the cheerleading problem. Listening to the discussion I determined that a small group of these teachers were very strongly in favor of girls not being used as cheerleaders, a small group were in favor of retaining them, while the majority were undecided. Fred Collins had informed me that the two women on his staff were against girl cheerleading squads, so I wasn't surprised when they both spoke in favor of the movement. After a lengthy discussion, the supervisor who acted as chairman of the meeting said she would like to hear what the principals had to say. While I had not met her, she knew I was present and called on me first. I started by saying I had listened with interest to the discussion and I tried to evaluate the views that had been expressed, but I considered cheerleading as an accepted part of the athletic contests. I felt the girls who were on these squads were an important part of the program. In no way did I consider them playing an inferior part. By leading the group cheering they were helping not only the team but also controlling the crowd. More than once I have seen them jump to their feet to quiet an angry group of spectators. I can say I believe the girls are doing a real service to the school and to eliminate their activity would be a great loss. All the other principals present supported my position.

After the meeting adjourned the state supervisor rushed to meet me and said she wanted to thank me for my response and then she added, "You must have a fine school." "I think so," I replied, "but why do you say so?" Her response was, "I travel all over the state and anytime I find a school where the teachers are not afraid to express their opinions, even when contrary to those of the principal, I find an outstanding school." "Aren't teachers always free to express their opinions?" I asked. "By no means," she replied. "In fact, in most schools they would never have dared to take a position as your teachers did today in the presence of their principal." I laughed and said, "Well, my teachers are free to express their opinions, but I don't have to always agree with them." As indicated by this meeting, only a small number of teachers supported this movement and it died out—cheerleading continued.

One thing happened which sent a shockwave through the whole school system, not only because of what was done but by the way it was done. Lopardo remembered the meeting we had with the professor, who advocated every teacher a reading teacher, and no need of special teachers of reading. He sold the idea to the board and one night in a meeting they passed a resolution firing all the special reading teachers by putting them back in regular classrooms and eliminating the position of the reading supervisor. They did this without warning and the first the teachers involved knew about the action taken was reading it in the morning newspaper, something I considered reprehensible.

Mrs. LaLonde had been the special reading teacher in the Academy for some time. Students who entered the school with reading disabilities were put in a class where she did excellent work in helping them. When the news broke of the action of the board, she came to me asking what her status would be. She also showed me a letter which she had received from Superintendent Burdick when he was in office, stating if she went to Temple University for a summer taking their course in teaching pupils with reading problems and worked with such students in the Academy, her salary would be increased $200.00 a year. This she had done and besides teaching some classes in English, she did the special work.

I had no instructions from the superintendent as to her status, so I called him. Lopardo informed me she was included in the resolution and would have to give up her special class in reading and return to a full time English teacher. I then told him about the letter she had, but he said that was from a former superintendent and was no longer binding. I also tried to tell him how much her services were needed in the Academy, but he wouldn't listen. Mrs. LaLonde heard all I said and when I hung up the phone, I shook my head. I then said, "If you want to take the letter to your lawyer and he goes to court, I will be glad to help all I can." She said she wouldn't do anything as her arthritis was developing so fast she would soon be crippled so that she would have to retire. However, for the two years she had left she did help a number of students on her own time. Thus, the school administration with one blow eliminated a much needed program which Superintendent Burdick had worked hard to build.

Ralph Steiger, supervisor of the reading program in the city schools, left to teach in a southern university. Several of the teachers who had taken extra courses to become special reading instructors left the system. One of them whom I considered a master teacher when we were together at Roosevelt, was Miss Casale, became the reading supervisor of the schools in the nearby city of Rome. The Utica school staff lost a number of fine, talented people but the biggest losers were the many children in the city with reading problems who needed the expert help.

It was during these years that the student council initiated the idea of the school adopting a name for the athletic teams. For years sports writers of the newspapers had been calling them the "Utes," which many felt was no longer appropriate since Proctor was also a Utica high school. The council opened the idea to the whole school passing out slips for students and teachers to submit names to be considered. After some thought I felt that since UFA was the largest high school in upstate New York, the name "Titan" would be fitting. Since the slips were not signed, I put mine in with the hundreds submitted. After a committee of the student council had screened the names and had narrowed the choice down to about 25, they asked Mr. Wildes, the faculty advisor, and me to join them in making the final selection. The majority of the names suggested were either names of animals or Indian tribes. The committee felt these were similar to those used by nearby schools and they wanted something distinctive. Someone spotted my slip with the name Titan on it and mentioned that it stood alone. There was more discussion and when I was asked how I liked it, I replied, "Good, it is the name of a race of giant semi-gods in Greek Mythology. They were instrumental in putting Zeus on the throne of the Greek gods and were noted for helping mankind. Since UFA is the largest high school in up-state New York, I think it would be a fitting choice." A vote was taken and the name Titan was adopted. At the next assembly the president of the student council announced the choice to the whole student body. He asked me to explain why the committee selected the name. The newspapers were notified and the sports writers began to use the name, which became popular. While during the suceeding years the size of the school has diminished, the name still remains. I don't think anyone knew that I was the one to suggest the name.

Both Marjorie and Dorothy made some important changes during these years. While working at the medical college in Syracuse, Dorothy kept up with the harp. She was good enough to be the harpist for the Syracuse Community Orchestra, playing in their concerts. She became so interested in the harp she applied and was accepted as a student of Salzedo at his famous harp colony in Camden, Maine. Together with Norah and Mary Jane, a friend she had worked with in Syracuse, Dorothy spent the summer in Camden, renting a cottage by the sea. Gaining so much from her study with Salzedo, she decided to resign her position as chemist and applied for entrance at the Oberlin Conservatory of Music. Since Miss Weymer had left Syracuse University, their harp department had folded, but Oberlin maintained a harp section. I took Dorothy and her harp to Oberlin and helped her to find a room. She planned to get a degree in music. But after one semester she became dissatisfied and came home with her harp.

Soon after she returned home, Dorothy drove up to Tupper Lake to see Bruce Raemsch, a young man she had met in Syracuse. He had been a student in the Medical College but had to leave when he contracted TB. He was now in the Tupper Lake sanitorium but was soon to be discharged as cured. Dorothy returned from her visit to announce that she and Bruce planned to be married in the spring. We had met Bruce once when Dorothy brought him out to camp and liked him very much but couldn't help wondering about his health. We could see that Dorothy had made up her mind, so we went along, enjoying having her home the rest of the winter.

She wanted a church wedding and after a conference with Mr. Roy, the minister at Central Church, the date was set for April 9, 1955. This was the Saturday before Easter Sunday; the church was all decorated for that day and very beautiful. It turned out to be a warm spring day and a wonderful occasion. I will never forget my mixed feelings as I walked down the aisle to the strains of the wedding march with her arm on mine. Here was the little girl I had held on my lap telling bed time stories, and had helped nurse her through sickness, watched her excel in grade and high school, then largely through her own efforts enter and graduate from Vassar, one of the highest standing colleges in the country. She had secured an important position as a chemist, became an accomplished harpist, now as she held my arm, I could feel the self-assured young woman she had become. I could rejoice with her that she had found such a fine young man. He had been seriously handicapped, but now recovered, had the courage to start a new career. I felt certain they would have a good life together.

During this time Marjorie had been a successful associate editor of the paper in Geneseo, New York. She had written a number of editorials which had attracted the attention of a radio station in Rochester and had been read over the air. She had received the

479

congratulations of a number of people on her creative writing, so much so, she decided that was a field she wanted to pursue. She felt she had progressed as far as she could in that position and it was time to make a break. I hated to have her give up a good job, but if she was determined to pursue her ambition to do creative writing, now was the time to leave. After checking many college catalogues, she selected Boston University. She applied and was accepted in the graduate school to work on a Master's degree in English. She thought she could do this in a year but soon found out as so much of her undergraduate work was done in journalism that she lacked many of the fundamentals. It took her two summer sessions and a full year before she could pass the comprehensive examination and get her M.A. degree in English.

One of the summer sessions Marjorie took was at the University of Montana in Missoula. She flew out and then kept writing glowing accounts of the wonderful scenery around that area. In the middle of the summer she suggested we drive out to see the country and she could come back with us. Since I had never seen the western part of Montana, I decided to take a couple of weeks out of the summer and go. She was right, that part of the state is beautiful, so different from the eastern part that I remembered as a boy. With the car we were able to visit many of the points of interest around Missoula and then after Marjorie finished her last class, we took off for Glacier National Park.

We got a housekeeping cabin in the park in time to drive around in the afternoon to see some of the nearby scenery. The road ran along what looked like a beautiful trout stream and knowing I didn't need a fishing license in the park, I announced I was going to try it the next morning. That evening we attended a session by one of the park rangers telling about the park and the many trails which the visitors could follow, most of them marked with signs of the flowers and plants along the path. So when I left for the trout stream, Norah and Marj decided to go with me and follow a nearby nature trail. I found the stream was fed by one of the glaciers and the water like liquid ice—I didn't get a strike, but I had the pleasure of trying.

When I returned to the car and met the women, they had a big story to tell me. They said after they had gone along the trail for a half mile enjoying the many wild flowers and plants, they were confronted by a big sign which read, "Caution, from this point on bears may be encountered on the trail." As they were reading the sign they saw a woman seated on a stump. She greeted them by saying she was not going any farther as her nephew who was with her had been bitten by a bear during the night. As they talked, the woman told how she was from California and her young nephew was from the east and spending the summer with her so they could travel around the country. They had a camper but that night the boy had insisted he was going to sleep in his sleeping bag on the ground. About midnight he was aroused and saw a big black bear standing over him. Instinctively he threw up one arm and the bear grabbed it. The aunt heard him yell and looking out saw the bear. Grabbing the only thing at hand, a broom, she rushed out and drove the bear away. Following the directions that all campers were given, they reported the incident to the Rangers, who insisted they had to take the boy to their headquarters to be examined by a doctor. The bite was not bad, so the bear was not considered vicious.

After the woman said her nephew was from the east, Norah replied, "We are from the east, where does he live?" Norah and Marj both gasped when the woman replied, "He lives in Utica, New York, and will be going to a huge high school next fall. I think they call it UFA." Then the woman got her surprise when Norah said, "We live in Utica and my husband is the principal of UFA. I am sure he would like to meet your nephew." I met the women as they were coming out of the woods and heard this story, but the boy did not return before we left for an afternoon trip, so I did not see him.

The highlight of our trip was the sky line drive up near the glaciers. The road was cut in the side of the mountains with breathtaking views. When we reached the top of the divide, we saw a ranger station with a lot of cars parked around it. We stopped and learned that a ranger had formed a party to guide over the mountain to view "Lost Lake." Marjorie wanted to join the party, but I felt it was too much for Norah to keep up at that high altitude, so we told her to go along and we would follow part way, at a leisurely pace. The sky was a brilliant blue with no sign of a cloud and the sun shone with intense rays. The trail led up close to one of the glaciers, and we stopped to walk on the ice in August. About halfway up the trail we met the party coming back, and Marj enticed us to continue because the view of the lake was so magnificent and she could show us the way.

More than satisfied with our hike, we returned to the car and started back to our cabin. On the way Marj said she was getting sick and lay down on the back seat and then when we stopped at a supply store to get some meat for supper, she told us to hurry, as she was getting very nauseated. Norah and I ate our supper, but she was too sick to look at food. About midnight I woke up terribly nauseated and rushed to the bathroom, vomiting and stricken with diarrhea. At first we thought it was some kind of food poisoning, but since Norah had eaten the same things we had and was not affected, we ruled that out. After thinking, I decided it was the so-called mountain sickness, which is really radiation sickness. We had stayed in the strong sunshine at high altitude on that trail too long. Marj was sick first because she had been bareheaded. I had on a cap, which shaded my eyes but did not protect the back of my head. Norah had escaped because she was protected by wearing a broad brimmed straw hat. For 24 hours Marj and I were so weak we could hardly get out of bed and could not eat a thing. When she saw our condition, Norah hurried to the camp office and made arrangements for us to keep the cabin another day. The following day we felt we had to leave, and Marj, who was sick first, got over it first and thought she could drive until I recovered. It was a week before we felt normal, an experience we never forgot.

481

On the way home we met Dorothy and Bruce in Des Moines, Iowa. They were on the way to Oregon. Bruce had to give up being a medical scientist and had enrolled in the University of Oregon, as the first step in becoming an anthropologist. They had stopped in to see Margaret and Don Wetter, and we were there in time to join them at a dinner party one night. Margaret is my niece, Leeta's youngest daughter, while Don, her husband, was a high school principal in Des Moines. So we had lots to talk about. The next day Dorothy and Bruce left for the west to be gone for a year, while we continued on east, with Marj to finish at Boston University.

As we were driving on the way home one day while talking over our trip, Norah asked me if I was going to tell about the boy and the bear when school opened. "No," I replied, "boys of that age are often sensitive and he may not want it known. If he tells it I shall verifiy the story." Then in the second week of school one of the English teachers came into my office, laughing. "I've got a good one to tell you," she said. "I gave an assignment to my freshman class to write a story of some interesting event they had during the summer. One boy with a vivid imagination wrote that he was in Glacier National Park with his aunt this summer and while sleeping on the ground in his sleeping bag was bitten by a bear. He added that Mr. Calhoon, the principal of UFA, was there at the time. HA! HA!" I looked at her and said, "What's so funny? It's all true." "Why, Mr. Calhoon," she exclaimed, "I didn't know you had been out of the city other than to your camp this summer." She asked again if it was true and when I assured her it was, she walked out, shaking her head and I heard her muttering something about "truth being stranger than fiction."

After Marjorie got her degree from Boston, she was out of a job for a time. She did answer an ad in the publisher's magazine, which sounded glowing, about a job on a paper in Georgia, but after she was there for a few months found it impossible and came home. Then the placement bureau of Boston University notified her of a teaching position in journalism at Vermont Junior College in Montpelier, Vermont. I took her up for an interview and although the position was for a year only, she liked it so well she accepted. At the end of the year when the regular teacher returned from a year of absence, the college liked her so much they gave her a position teaching English. She was happy because this is what she had prepared for.

While at Boston University, Marjorie met a young man in one of her classes who liked her. After she went to Vermont he called on her most every weekend. Then she surprised us by saying she was bringing William Horton home with her at Christmas vacation and they wanted to get married. She told us Bill was an ordained Unitarian minister and had served several churches in the New England district, but the salaries were so low he had taken a full time job with the U. S. Army Corps of Engineers as a writer for flood control projects in that area.

482

So Marjorie and Bill arrived before Christmas and the wedding took place in the chapel in Central Church on December 22, 1956. After a short trip they both returned to their jobs. Then before the end of the school year Marjorie announced that she was pregnant. The school insisted that she finish out the year even if she didn't feel good. That summer she and Bill found an apartment in Framingham, Massachusetts, and on October 12 Billy, our first grandson, was born. A year later Jon added to a growing family. Their apartment became too small and I helped them buy a house in nearby Marlboro, where they still live. At first Marjorie stayed home to care for the babies, but later in order to help with the rising cost of living, she did work on the local newspaper. Much later after Holly and Heidi came along and all were old enough to care for themselves, Marjorie began teaching in Framingham State College. She finally reached the goal she had set years before.

In 1956 Lopardo decided to retire. I happened to be at the board meeting when his resignation was read. A member of the board quickly moved that it be accepted and that Theodore Reusswig be appointed as superintendent to take his place. The president of the board ruled his motion was out of order, as it contained two items. The board did accept Lopardo's resignation and went into a closed session to consider a new superintendent. I thought of applying for the position, but from the motion which had been presented, it was evident that the board had already decided.

Reusswig had been a teacher in the technical department at UFA when I taught science there. He became a high school counselor, then head of counselors and pupil personnel with an office in the Administration Building. About this time Mr. Folsom, who had been clerk of the board for many years, had a fatal heart attack. Three clerks followed and none were competent, so the school finances were in a mess. Knowing Reusswig was a graduate engineer, the board asked him to take over the position, and he soon had things in order. He made such an impression the board did not consider anyone else for the position of superintendent. This was following a trend all over the country, whereby superintendents of schools were no longer considered as educational leaders but more as business managers.

Reusswig became the third superintendent since I had become principal of UFA. I knew him very well, having worked with him in all his positions and had played golf with him many times. I knew he was a good organizer, but I felt he lacked one essential, he had never been a principal of a school. His idea of running a system was to issue orders without consulting anyone to see if they were practical. He let it be known right at the beginning of his term that previous friendships were never to be considered. I never expected to use that in my dealings but was surprised to have him be so blunt about it. But now that I had tenure in my position, I didn't let his attitude bother me.

The first evidence of his way of doing things came about in 1957, right after Sputnik burst on the scene. Before that he had publicly announced he was opposed to any ability grouping and condemned what I had been doing in the Academy. Then the State Department became all excited after Sputnik and said the schools were not doing enough for the bright pupils and should group at once. Reusswig did an "about face" and ordered all pupils in grades 7 through 12 to be grouped at once. The brightest pupils were to be placed in classes to be called "A groups." I tried to tell him we had been doing this in subjects where there were large numbers, but I didn't think it practical in subjects with small numbers. He wouldn't listen and ordered it done in every subject. The result was that all the good responses I had established in some departments, such as English, were destroyed. Teachers resented being ordered to do something they were not convinced was right.

The appearance of Sputnik in the sky sent a shock wave of fear across the country. Everywhere talk was heard that the next move by the Russians would be to send a space ship over the country and drop bombs on military bases and nearby cities. Civil Defense teams were hurriedly formed and the state ordered all schools to organize air raid drills. Each school was given the opportunity to make its own plans for such drills, but basically at a prescribed signal all pupils and others in the building should move into a hall away from any window or door. Also, it was recommended that all should assemble in the basement of the building. After some thought I decided that it was not practical to crowd 3,000 students and teachers into the basement floor. I thought mobility was more important, making it possible to move people away from the direction of an expected blast. I talked with the men counselors and they agreed to be in charge of the two upper floors, while I could stand in the center of the main floor to issue orders. I called an assembly of the whole school to explain how the air drill would be conducted. I emphasized the seriousness of the situation and how important it was for everyone to be perfectly quiet once they were in place so orders could be transmitted. I told them instead of using the fire bells, the signal for the air raid drill would be short rings of the corridor bells, then one long ring for the "all clear" signal.

The assembly was held in the morning and that afternoon we held the first drill. The result was astounding. In less than a minute the nearly 3,000 students, teachers and school personnel on duty were in the halls and completely silent. The building suddenly became as quiet as midnight. It was as if there wasn't a soul in the place. It was almost eerie. As soon as the men in charge of each floor reported, "all in order", I had the "all clear" signal given before the spell could be broken. The strange thing was every drill we conducted proved to be the same. Every member of the faculty was as impressed as I was with the response and from bits of conversation I overheard, I gathered the teachers were floored by the unexpected control I had over the student body.

Dr. Steele, the head of the physics department at Utica College, was appointed chief of a radiological team in the civil defense organization. To obtain a place where he could train the members of his team, he asked me if they could use the basement of the Academy on a Sunday morning. I made the arrangements and on the day they met I was there to greet them. When Dr. Steele learned of my background in science and of my knowledge of atomic energy, he asked me to be a member of his team. I was glad for the opportunity and was an active member as long as the organization existed.

To give the team some experience with active radioactive material, Dr. Steele had secured a shipment of some radioactive cobalt from Oak Ridge laboratory. The amount was only the size of a fifty cent piece, but so powerful it had to be shipped in a lead container weighing over 300 pounds. This container was unloaded with a crane and opened just inside the basement door. With a three-foot pair of tongs, Dr. Steele removed the piece of cobalt, placing it under one of a series of empty coffee cans which had been placed around one of the basement rooms. Cobalt itself is harmless, but when radiated by uranium, as this had been, it became lethal. One half of the team using geiger counters and a walkie talkie circled around the room, sending their readings to the other half of the team in a distant room where they could construct a map pinpointing the can under which the cobalt was hiding. I was excited to be part of the team and have the experience of working with real live radioactive material.

A few days after this I had a visit by a team of men who were inspecting bomb shelters and schools to see if they were holding air raid drills. When they checked my plan, they said I was not following instructions. They claimed I should have all the students go to the basement. When I tried to explain my reason for not doing so, they told me I didn't understand how serious the bomb could be. I let them go on trying to overcome my ignorance until they ran down. Then I rather set them back by saying there was nothing they could tell me about the effects of a bomb, as I had studied atomic energy and had given lectures about the bomb and was now a member of the radiological team. I informed them I thought my plan of the air raid drills was correct and I expected to stand by it; if they wanted to report me, to go ahead. They left, shaking their heads, but I never heard anything about it.

One of the constant problems in most high schools is to keep the walls in both the boy's and girl's toilets free from writings and drawings. I worked with the custodians on this problem by telling them the best way to control the situation was to remove any writing as soon as it appeared. Anything on the walls invited more to be added. When I returned to UFA as principal, Charley Jones was still the head custodian, as he was when I taught there. He was an unusual character for this job, good looking, a gentleman toward everyone, respected by teachers, students and most of all, by his staff. He was by far the best I ever worked with as a custodian, and I never had a complaint about the building not being clean, so when I suggested his men check the toilets whenever possible and remove any writing, it was done. But Charley reached the retirement age during my second year.

Thomas Carville was transferred from Hughes School to replace Charley Jones. Carville was the father of a large family and I had known some of his boys as students in the Academy where they had made good names for themselves. But right from the start I could see a big difference between the two men. Carville didn't have the personality to work harmoniously with his staff, some of whom resented anyone coming from the outside. I began to get complaints from the teachers about the service they received, and I got no cooperation in keeping the toilets clean. Some of the complaints reached Reusswig's ears, and he came to inspect things. At first he tried to blame me, but I showed him copies of memorandums I had given Carville about the conditions I found and asked him to see that things were cleaned. A week later Reusswig inspected the toilets again and finding no change, called me to tell Carville unless those rooms were cleaned at once and kept clean, he was fired. I didn't like the idea of being a messenger boy, but had no choice. When I delivered the message, Carville just laughed. The custodians had organized a union, so they felt free of being fired.

Since conditions did not improve, Reusswig called me and the school attorney to his office. They quizzed me about Carville's work in general, and I had to admit it was not satisfactory. For example, after I had given him a written notice to have the gym set up for an assembly the next morning he forgot all about it and the high school boys had to do the work. Reusswig and the attorney both thought there was enough evidence to support the superintendent in relieving Carville from duty and bringing him before the board for firing. I had my doubts that it would hold, since they had a union to deal with, but they went ahead anyway.

The hearing was conducted like a court trial with the school attorney acting as the prosecution, while Carville was defended by a lawyer engaged by the union.

The hearing took place in the evening at the Administration Building and the newspapers made a big story out of it. They carried a picture of me in the witness chair saying I was the chief witness for the prosecution. The board, at the conclusion, voted to uphold the superintendent and declared Carville fired, but the union took the case to court and the board was overruled and ordered Carville be reinstated with all back pay. It was a clear case of how the organizing of school personnel was to change the whole structure of school systems in the future.

My relationship with the city police while at the Academy proved to be very different from what I experienced at Roosevelt. Years before a directive had been issued by the superintendent stating that the police or detectives from that department could question a pupil during school time if it was done in the presence of the principal or teacher. I objected to such a rule, saying nothing like this should be done unless it had something to do with the school. However, I followed the directive until one day two detectives came to my office a few minutes before the noon recess and asked to see a boy. I had the boy come to the office and they began to question him about something which had occurred in the neighborhood, but not connected with the school. Before they had finished the noon bell sounded, and they said they didn't want to hold me up, so they would take the boy home before they took him downtown for further questioning. I agreed on the condition they take the boy home so the mother would know where he was. They promised to do this. Just as I sat down to lunch, my phone rang and it was the boy's mother, wanting to know where he was since he didn't come home for lunch. I explained what had happened and let her know how the detectives had lied to me, and I would follow it up. I called the head of the detective bureau and let him know that I was good and mad at his men for pulling such a deal and told him not to bother sending any more detectives to my school, as I would not let them interview another pupil, unless it had something to do with the school. After that I was never bothered again. Incidently, these two men who lied to me were caught in the investigation of the police department by a special prosecutor sent by the state and along with others, were convicted of taking bribes and sent to prison.

After this affair the police department was reorganized and one officer was appointed to handle all problems concerning children of school age. After a series of thefts in the gym locker room, the gym teachers thought they had a suspect so I called the police department for help. To my surprise Joe Piccola walked into my office. I recognized him as the policeman who had been in my first science class I had for preparing for the equivalency diploma. He greeted me warmly and eager to tell me that through my help he got his diploma and with that was now promoted to be head of the youth bureau of the police department. I called the suspect into my office and was impressed by the way Piccola conducted the questioning session. He had a quiet way of approaching a suspect, giving them the idea he was there to be of help if they were in trouble and taking plenty of time to get the young person to talk. It was surprising how many times once the suspect began to talk they would let something slip which would give away who was the guilty party. I also learned from him how important it was to take a suspect to the scene of the crime. Several times I saw a person once confronted with the scene, break down and admit everything. I learned a lot from Piccola, and he said he learned much from me, so working together through several years we were able to straighten out a number of cases without taking anyone to court. That was his primary purpose, and I fully agreed.

Unfortunately, Piccola became too popular and because of jealousy in the police department, he was relieved of his position. Rather than go back as a regular officer, Joe resigned and took a job as security guard at Utica College. Later, because of his popularity, he was asked to run for sheriff of Oneida County and was elected. He held that office for several terms until he retired. One day after his retirement I met him and his wife at a shopping center. I was somewhat embarrassed when he introduced me to his wife as the man who had inspired him to continue his education so he could hold the jobs he did and also the finest gentlemen he ever worked with.

Using the Piccola method, I was able to solve a baffling case. Mr. Perkins came into my office one day very agitated, reporting a series of mysterious fires breaking out in some lockers. At first I thought I should call the fire department, but before I did, Frank Mason, a social studies teacher, rushed in to report that after his last class he smelled smoke and traced it to a smoldering fire in one of the student's desks. He put the fire out, then noticed a small capsule, which he gave to me. I looked at it and as I held it between my thumb and finger I realized something was happening and exclaimed, "This thing is hot!" I dropped it into the wastebasket where it burst into flames.

Convinced we had a firebug in our midst, I got the name of the student who had last used the desk where Frank had found the capsule. It was a boy, and I sent for him to come to the office. When he arrived, I observed a slight, pale rather nervous individual who was very reluctant to talk. In a quiet voice I asked about his school work and if he was in Mr. Mason's class. All I got was monosyllables until I mentioned that someone was starting fires in the building and how dangerous that could be, when to my surprise he interrupted by saying, "I know how to make a firebomb." Once he started he continued to tell how he had experimented with chemicals and found those that would ignite. I told him that I had been a chemistry teacher and knew about these chemicals and how we had to be careful in using them. While he didn't admit bringing the capsules into the school, I was certain he was the boy and after we agreed that he would not experiment anymore, I let him go. My decision to wait and see if there were any more fires, rather than prosecute the boy, was because I believed it was better for the school to help set a student straight than to punish, paid off as there was no more trouble.

Fads come and go among high school students and a crazy one developed at the Academy. Boys started rolling pennies across the floor in a study hall to bother the teacher in charge. They got their pleasure when a teacher raved at them, but the fun stopped when some of the wiser teachers picked up the pennies and collected them in a bottle so all could see what they were gaining. Then a group took the fad outside and thought it smart to bother a policeman by throwing a penny in the street in front of him and shouting, "dirty copper."

At the same time this was taking place, a number of boys who had cars were picking up girls at the noon hour and taking them for a ride around the neighborhood. Not content to just take a ride, they were driving at high speeds and using a "cut out" on the exhaust pipes to make a loud noise. A few of these boys were in school, but most were former students who knew some of the girls in school. I began to get calls from people in the area, especially from mothers with small children. To each caller I said that I was disturbed also, and if they would give me the license number of a car, I would take action. When things continued to get worse I asked the Chief of Police to send some motorcycle police to patrol the area and stop these cars before someone was seriously injured. He agreed and then a new wrinkle developed. If the police stopped a car near the building, two or three hundred students would gather around and razz them. After watching this for a couple of days, Mr. Perkins came to me and said something should be done to stop such actions. I agreed and sent out a notice for a special assembly, the only one I had while at the Academy to discuss discipline. I made the assembly short, but spoke firmly about the throwing of the pennies at the police and seriously about the cars speeding around the area. I ended by saying, "I am the one who requested the police to patrol the area and if any of you get in bad with the police, you will be in bad with me."

The next morning a crisis was reached. A group of ten boys from north Utica got off the bus on Genesee Street and started walking over Hobart Street toward the Academy. Two motorcycle policemen rode by and as they passed, some of the boys threw pennies toward them. One policeman was hit in the eye. Fed up with such action, the police whirled around and lined the boys up against the corner store wall and sent for the paddy wagon. They took them all to the police headquarters and booked all but two who were under 16. Enough of the students saw the episode, so the news spread rapidly through the school. When I heard about it, I called the police station and got the names of the boys who were booked. In each case, I asked one question, "Are you in bad with the police?" When they answered, "Yes," I reminded them of what I had said in the assembly and told them they were suspended until clear with the police. I had them turn in their books and go home.

It wasn't long before my telephone was hot. Every parent who called wanted to know if it was their boy who threw the penny that hit the policeman. To each I replied, "I don't know, but your boy was in the group and I had just warned the students in the assembly that if they got in bad with the police, they would be in bad with me. Unless some boy tells me he was the one who threw the penny, I will consider all in the group equally guilty." One couple came with their lawyer to protest my action and the mother said she knew her boy didn't throw the penny as he had never been in trouble in school, and I should take him back at once. I just repeated my position and the lawyer turned to the parents and said, "I know Mr. Calhoon very well, and he means what he says. I think he knows best and my advice to you is to accept his decision." After they left I felt rather bad if this was the first time this boy was in trouble, so I called the grade school where he had been before entering the Academy. I asked if they knew the boy and they did. Then I said,

"His mother says he has never been in trouble in school, how about it?" They just "hooted." They told me that the mother was the most noted in the school as she had been in the school at least once a month trying to get her boy out of trouble. After that I ceased being sorry for any of the group.

Before I left the office that afternoon, Reusswig appeared. He said he had been beseiged all day with calls from parents and some board members. He wanted to know just what had happened, so I explained it all to him. He listened, then said, "You can't suspend a student for more than five days, so you will have to change that part. Also, I do not approve of your action in taking the books from the boys." I could see by his attitude that he didn't approve of my way of handling the situation. It made me feel how narrow the position of a principal can be. Several times Reusswig had needled me about the discipline in the Academy, but now that I had taken action, he was ready to criticize me. It confirmed a feeling that I had in my mind for some time that he thought I was too independent and he would like to get me out so he could appoint someone who would be under his control.

I did send a letter to the parents of each boy saying the suspension was for five days or less if the police cleared the case and also they could have their books. Only two of them came for their books. That noon when a large crowd of students gathered around a car the police had stopped, three boys were arrested for harrassment. I got their names and suspended them also.

The city papers made a big story out of this affair, so the city attorney hurried to get the case into the city court. At the time set, I went down to see what would happen and found a large crowd of parents and relatives packing the courtroom. I was near the door waiting to see if I could get inside when the policemen who made the arrests appeared. A shout went up from the crowd, and I couldn't believe my ears at the foul language that was hurled at the police. The women were worse than the men, and I was surprised the police took it.

The city attorney saw me and invited me to sit at his table as a "friend of the court." When the court opened, the first witness called was the policeman who was hit in the eye. He described the incident and then when the defense attorney asked him which boy threw the coin, he admitted he didn't know. At that the judge interrupted and asked the policeman which boy threw the penny, and when he said he didn't know, the judge turned to the prosecuting attorney and chided him by saying, "You know better than to bring a case in against a group. Case dismissed."

The case of the boys taken in for harrassment was dropped, so all the boys came in the office and picked up their books. I didn't say a word to any of them, just nodded. Then that noon the payoff came. During the first lunch period I heard one of the secretaries in the outer office fairly shout, "Will you look at this." Everyone jumped up to look out the front windows, including me. I couldn't believe my eyes. The police had stopped a car right in front of the building and where before there had been two hundred or more students gathered around, there was now not a single one in sight. Clearly the action I had taken had traveled around the school and the students were convinced I meant business. I had to think that by not being bound by legal rules I could act against a group and get results. The fad of throwing pennies stopped and in a few days the racing cars disappeared. The police were called off the patroling of the area, and things reverted to normal.

Discipline was not the only thing a principal had to deal with; although at times it seemed the most important, there were other things I felt equally important. Once in discussing problems of a school with a very wise teacher, she made the observation, "One of the reasons you are such a good principal is you know how to communicate with the students. It's a rare gift." One case that I recall may illustrate this point. Right after school closed one afternoon a tall senior boy asked to see me. When he came into the office I could see he was furious at something. He came to appeal to me because he said his teacher had penalized him for something he didn't do. He had tried to tell her he didn't do it, but she insisted he did. "No one believes me," he said. "I do," I quietly remarked. He stopped short and looked in surprise at me. "What did you say?" he asked. "If you say you didn't do it, I believe you," I replied. Then I continued, "If you will keep it confidential, I'll tell you it happened to me once in high school." I then related enough of my story to show how sometimes it is better to take the punishment for something we didn't do rather than admit something we did do. Then I said, "I'll bet you have done things and got away with it, so why don't you just consider this punishment for some of them." I could see his attitude changing and after he pondered my suggestion for a minute or so, I continued by saying, "If you feel that you should get even with your teacher, just go back and quietly take your seat, then if she says anything, answer politely and be as nice as I know you can be, then watch her reactions." A little smile broke over his face and he walked out of the office with his head held high. Two days later this teacher came into my office and wanted to know what I had said to that boy. She said he had been sullen, resentful and almost defiant, but when he came back he was as nice and polite as could be. "I never saw such a change in a person, what's your magic word?" she asked. To which I replied, "If I told you, it would no longer be magic." Then after talking a few minutes, she turned to leave and I said, "Do you suppose it possible maybe the boy didn't do what you thought he did?" She left shaking her head, a wiser teacher I hoped.

One time when I was talking before a group of teachers who expected one day to become principals, I remarked that one of the important things a principal has to learn is how to say "no" without saying "no." Then I told this story to illustrate my point. One fall, a boy and a girl came from one of the parochial schools in the city with high ambitions. They had been leaders in their school and let it be known they expected to be in the Academy. During their first term they came to see me with a copy of a play which they had written and wanted permission to produce it on the stage in the auditorium. I told them Miss Gates was in charge of all plays and they should see her. They told me they had been to her and she sent them to me. I said to myself, "Ha, passing the buck" but to them I said "Leave the copy with me and I will read it tonight and you come back tomorrow and we will see." A quick look at the play showed it was nothing fit for a high school, the students would hoot it right off the stage.

I could see they had put a lot of work into the script and I hated to say no, so when they returned I told them I read the play and one thing I noted was it would be very difficult to stage, such as having angels floating down from above. Their reply was, "Oh, we know how to do it." Then I continued, "You know no show gets on Broadway without first being tried out to find out audience reactions, so before you go any farther why don't you ask your English teacher to give you a chance to read part of the play and see how your fellow students react. They did, and as I expected, the response was such I never heard anymore about the play. However, I have to give these two students a lot of credit. The girl fulfilled her ambitiion by having a leading part in the senior class play, while the boy became a politician and was elected president of the student council.

It was only after the gym was built that it was possible to hold an assembly where the whole student body could be present. The students were seated in the bleachers while those taking part in the program were seated on the main floor. This was quite a contrast to an auditorium where the speaker was on a stage above the audience. Actually, the conduct of the students was better under these conditions than in the auditorium. I wondered about this and finally concluded it was because the students seated on the bleachers felt more exposed to their actions than they did seated in the auditorium back of another person. For a speaker it was a unique experience for now the audience was above and one could no longer look down on an audience but had to look up.

Each year there were certain regular programs held here such as pep rallies for football and basketball games, introducing new members of the National Honor Society, awarding of school letters and prizes given at the end of the year. At most of these events I was asked to speak. Out of the many speeches I gave during these years there were two that made the greatest impact. One was at a pep rally for the basketball team which was going to Syracuse to play in the finals for the championship of Central New York. It happened the semi-finals were held at Colgate University, and I rode in the bus with the team. There had been an ice storm, so when we reached the hill out of Oriskany Falls, the road was blocked with cars which could not make the hill. Since this was the way to my camp, I told the driver to back up to the village and I would direct him along a road by Oriskany Creek, thus avoiding the hill. He did and

492

we reached Colgate just in time for the team to dress for the game.

Since Utica was in the Mohawk River Valley, and Vernon-Verona-Sherill High School, our opponent at Colgate was near Oneida, and West Genesee High School who was to be our opponent in Syracuse was in Onondaga County, I used these Indian tribe names to represent the schools in my talk at the assembly rally. I started by saying how our team representing the Mohawk Indians went to attack the Oneida Tribe at Colgate. How the Oneida prayed to their gods who caused the north wind to blow, covering the trail with ice and snow, so we could not reach their wigwams from the front, but we found a way to reach them from the back and took their scalps. Now we are challenged by the Onondagas to meet their braves in battle. I know we can depend on our braves, such as "Dead Eye Dick" and "Sure Shot Metzger," and I went on to name others on the team. I never had such a response from the students and faculty as I did after that speech. Time and time I was stopped in the halls by people to tell me what a clever and inspiring speech it was. The irony was the team lost the game in Syracuse, so we had to admit we lost our scalps. It was a bitter defeat for both the coach and me, as it was the best team the Academy had had in years and we counted on them so much.

Probably the most outstanding organization in the Academy was the A Cappella Choir. This choir had been established years before by Miss Lally and was now carried on by one of her former pupils, Mrs. Charlotte Williams. It had a statewide reputation for being one of the best in the country. They were invited to sing before many groups, including once at the annual banquet of the Secondary School Principal's convention. One year they were included in the CBS nationwide broadcast of best choirs on their Christmastime programs.

Mrs. Williams had charge of the annual Christmas assembly which consisted mostly of selections by the choir and the school orchestra, but each year she insisted I should give a short talk. It happened that the year of Sputnik, the superintendent of schools and two board members from a large school near Albany came to interview Edward Hacker, the director of our band and orchestra, right at the time of our assembly, so I invited them to be our guests. As usual, the program was too long, but Mrs. Williams insisted on introducing me. I tried to be brief, but the point that I made was: ever since the Star of Bethlehem had appeared, certain men had tried to blot it out. Now a new attempt was being made by a manmade star, called Sputnik. If these men succeed, they would not only destroy the Star of the East, but all it stands for, including events such as the wonderful assembly that we have enjoyed this morning. But we can be thankful the Star of Bethlehem still shines and we pledge our lives to keep it there. After the assembly was over, the guests came to thank me for inviting them and said they enjoyed the music but wanted to congratulate me on my remarks. They kept repeating, "What you said was so timely and it was evident the deep impression you made on the audience." Many teachers told me how the students returned to their rooms in the most thoughtful mood they could remember.

When I was about to leave the Academy, Miss Gates, the speech instructor, told me she always had her class in speech analyze my assembly talks. I sort of gasped as I had never given a thought to such a thing. She added that she had the present class write a critique of all the talks they had heard me give, and would I like to see what they had said. My answer was yes, so she gave me the bunch of papers. I read them with interest and one boy summed up what most had said. He wrote, "I have noticed that Mr. Calhoon never starts to speak until he has the attention of every person in the room. Many times I have seen some kids fooling around when others are speaking, but always stop when Mr. Calhoon speaks, and I don't think it is just because he is the principal. I have heard him now for almost four years, and I never heard him repeat a talk. He always had something new and interesting to say even when it was the same kind of assembly." I felt highly complimented by these students.

At commencement time, as the principal, I had a prominent place in the activities. At the exercises I was not only the Master of Ceremonies, but was expected to give a short talk to the class before they received their diplomas. Before my first commencement I spent some time thinking about what I should say. In the past I had listened to Mr. Babcock's rather lengthy flowery talks, which I knew he thought were very literary. Mr. Burdick's were shorter, but sounded like a sermon. Stanton's were even shorter, but mostly platitudes. I wanted mine to be different. For the Class of 1951, I started with the usual words of congratulations and then I said,

> As you stand before me today, ready to go forth as citizens of this city, I ask you to take with you the oath that the young men of old Athens swore to when they became citizens of that nation. The oath is:

> "We will never bring disgrace to our city by any act of dishonesty or cowardice, nor ever desert our suffering comrades in our ranks; we will fight for the ideals and sacred things of the city, both alone and with many, we will revere and obey the city's laws and do our best to incite a like respect and reverence in those about us; we will strive unceasingly to quicken the public's sense of civic duty; and thus, in all ways strive to transmit this city not only not less but greater, better and more beautiful than it was transmitted to us."

I received a lot of compliments on my talk by parents of the graduates and by the teachers who called me "the orator of the day." This set a pattern for my future talks.

For the Class of 1954, I concluded my talk by quoting the verse that I had written for their yearbook which had the theme "Time."

Thoughts, deeds, plans and dreams
Include that space of eternity, which
Mystically shapes our destiny and
Ever spins our web of fate to the tick of
an eternal clock called TIME.

When I finished and turned to go to my seat, the commencement speaker grasped my hand and said, "That was a wonderful bit of literature you just gave." I was flattered and more so when this class at their 20th reunion had this verse prominently displayed on the printed program.

All my commencement talks contained something original and I did feel highly complimented when Lopardo, who considered himself to be a good orator, told me after he retired that he enjoyed my talks more than any he had ever heard.

In January of 1958, Reusswig came to see me in my office. He said the State Education Department was pressuring him to do something about the organization of the Utica school system. The city was drawing state compensation for the students in the 7th and 8th grades as secondary school students, but the system was not treating them as such. He said he had talked with the state department and with the Utica board, and they had agreed that the problem could be solved if a director of secondary education was appointed whose main job would be to see that all grades from 7 through 12 were properly organized. He surprised me when he said, "I have come to offer you that position. With your education and experience in both the grade and high schools as principal, you are the best qualified in the system for such a job."

For a minute or more I sat thinking about such a proposition, I couldn't stop a thought that crossed my mind, "He has found a way to get me out of this office." But what I did say was a word of surprise and thanks for offering me the position, but I told him I expected to retire in two or three years, so maybe he should consider someone else. He replied that two years would be fine and he wanted me to come down to the administration building on March 1 when he would have an office ready for me. I said I would rather finish out the year at the Academy, but he had it all planned to have Roy Perkins be the acting principal for the rest of that year, and in my position I would be able to oversee things. I still hesitated, as I wanted to retire from the Academy, but it was a chance to take a higher position and the way Reusswig put things, I felt rather pressured into taking it. I was happy to have Roy Perkins have the chance to be principal for the short time, so I consented to leave.

CHAPTER 25

DIRECTOR OF SECONDARY EDUCATION

I left Utica Free Academy with mixed feelings. I felt I was at the height of my career as a principal and could retire in a couple of years at that level. On the other hand, to be named as the first Director of Secondary Education in the history of Utica seemed like too good an opportunity to pass up. The teachers at the Academy talked about having a dinner in my honor, but coming at that time of year they couldn't find a time when all were free, so I told them to wait until the usual dinner at the end of the year when they honored all teachers who were retiring. This they did and presented me with a special gift at that time.

An indication of how the students felt came as a surprise just before I left. As was my custom, I sat on the bench with the players at the last basketball game of the season. The team won the game and as the gun sounded ending the game, the whole squad rushed to the bench, picked me up, and carried me off the floor on their shoulders. The crowd in the bleachers rose and cheered. As the players put me down they chanted, "Goodbye! You have been the best principal ever."

Soon after I accepted the position, Reusswig called a meeting of the principals of the grade schools that had the 7th and 8th grades and the two high schools. He outlined some of the things he wanted done and as director, it would be part of my duty to see that all the mandates of the state were followed. From this time on this group would be known as secondary school principals. I had been a fellow principal with all these people, so I wondered how they would take my appointment. But I had always had good relations with them, and they congratulated me warmly. If there was any resentment, I never knew it.

The first of March I reported to the Administration Building. Since there was no precedent to follow, I wondered what I was expected to do first. Reusswig had promised me an office, but it wasn't ready so he gave me a desk in a back room on the second floor away from everyone. The room had been used as a storage place for scores of back copies of educational magazines and Reusswig asked me to go through them, cutting out any articles that were worth saving and discarding the rest. The morning I arrived all the supervisors who had offices in the building, together with the clerks and secretaries, drifted in to give me a welcome and then left me alone.

The contrast from the busy Academy office where people were constantly moving in and out, telephones ringing and typewriters clicking was almost unbearable. I felt isolated and began to think I had made a mistake. When the news broke that I was leaving the Academy, I had a number of prominent citizens of the city ask me, "What is Reusswig trying to do by moving you out of the Academy?" It was an indication that people of Utica considered the principalship of the Academy the highest educational position in the city. I tried to explain that this was a promotion, but many did not consider it as such.

For two weeks I worked at the old magazines and finished them just as it was announced that my office was ready. It was just inside the front door on the first floor and right across the hall from the superintendent's office. It was fitted with a nice desk, conference table, book case, telephone and my name plate on the door. Once established, I held an open house for the principals and supervisors. Norah had a beautiful basket of flowers delivered for the occasion and I began to feel important and looked forward to making something of my job.

In the fall of 1959, Miss Emily Carroll was appointed Director of Elementary Education and she was given a part of my office. I had known Miss Carroll for a long time, first as an art teacher at Roosevelt when I was the principal. She left to become an elementary school principal: we had worked together and found that we had much the same philosophy of education. Our desks were in opposite ends of the large room and we had no conflicts; we also were given a secretary to share. Once established, both of us spent considerable time visiting schools, so only for short periods were we both in the office at the same time.

Reusswig had hired two young girls right out of college without any experience or courses in education to teach in Kernan school. The 7th grade is hard enough anywhere, but especially difficult in Kernan. Reusswig told me both girls were in trouble and ready to quit and wanted me to see them to see if I could save the day. I did go to observe and talked with them, but they were hopeless. One girl said she thought all she had to do was make the assignments and the pupils would do them. She had no concept of all the things a teacher had to do. The other teacher had a class in math and when the pupils couldn't do a certain problem, she tried to solve it on the board but failed, which with pupils of that grade is fatal. So at the end of that week they both left.

After that Reusswig informed me I was to interview and screen all candidates for teachers at the secondary level. The drawback was he insisted on seeing everyone I planned to recommend and many times he was not available when they came. The second year I had 17 positions to fill, a record number, but I managed to secure some fine teachers. One was a breakthrough by placing the first black teacher in the Utica public school system. I had quite a discussion with Reusswig about where she should be placed. He thought she should go to a school like Hughes where there were no black pupils, while I held she should go to Kernan where there was a large number of such pupils. I claimed she would be a good influence in the school and an inspiration to the black pupils when they could see one of their race elevated to the teaching profession. For once I won the argument and I never observed a better regulated classroom or better teaching. She was accepted by the other teachers in the school on an equal basis and a barrier was broken.

During the first year I was spending considerable time in visiting the grade schools and going over the organization to see what changes were necessary to meet the state requirements. As I expected, Hughes and Roosevelt were well organized and did not need changes, but all the others did. I tried to be diplomatic about the situation by suggesting gradual changes so not to stir up resentment by the teachers involved. I had to take a chance on this, as I knew Reusswig would not approve if he knew how I was handling the situation as he was the type to order all changes to be made at once. But my method was gaining for me a lot of respect when it could have been easily a lot of resentment.

During these years Marjorie and Dorothy were living almost equidistant from Utica. So we took turns going to see them. After the year in Oregon where Bruce got his Master's degree, he applied and was accepted at the University of Pennsylvania. He wanted to go there as Pennsylvania was noted for its department of anthropology which was headed by Loren Eiseley, the world famous anthropologist. Bruce started working for his Doctor's degree in the department of American Civilization.

While Bruce was studying, Dorothy had to work and got a job as chemist at Smith, Kline & French, one of the leading pharmaceutical firms in the country. One Saturday this company held an open house for the families of employees. I made arrangements to get away on Friday so we could see Dorothy that night and be able to visit the firm the next morning. The plant was roped off so visitors could follow a tour through the various departments. When we came to the research department, we asked a guard on duty if Dorothy was around. When we told him who we were, he lifted the rope and let us under, directing us to her office. She showed us around the lab where she spent part of her time and the library where she did research work. We also met her fellow chemists and the head of the department. Bruce, who took us from their apartment to the plant, was delighted to see the place because he had never been in the plant, and I was especially thrilled, telling her she didn't have a job, it was a real position.

Bruce finished his resident requirements in June, 1958, and started looking for a job while completing his thesis. They both liked the west so much they hoped to find a position that way, but nothing opened up, so he took a position teaching science at the Pennsylvania Military College in Chester. They found an apartment in Chester and moved near the college. Dorothy announced she had worked long enough to help Bruce through the University, and it was his turn now. Anyway, they decided it was time to start a family. In August, 1959, we were invited to come to Chester once more to welcome Dorothy home from the hospital with our third grandson, Rob, a strong healthy baby.

In February, 1959, the board granted me permission to attend the National Secondary Principals Convention held in Philadelphia. I enjoyed every minute of the four day session, as in all the years I had been a high school principal I had never had a chance to attend this annual event. I used to feel rather resentful as all the other high school principals around Utica were sent by their school districts, but Utica would never do so. The big theme of this meeting was ability grouping. I attended some workshops on methods and was able to make some contributions. Dorothy came in one day from Chester and took Norah shopping while I was busy and we all had a good time. I got so much out of this convention, I put in to go the next year, but it was turned down.

Since my position was a new one in the city, I was asked to speak at a number of the school PTA meetings. This gave me a chance to explain the proper organization of the secondary grades and also to show how the high school had changed from an institution that could select its students to one that was a common school, i.e., a school for all the children of all the people. One week the Exchange Club asked me to speak about my new position and invited all the secondary principals as guests. This talk was well covered by the press, so I was getting my message across.

The most interesting experience I encountered at a PTA meeting came at Jefferson School in north Utica. This was a 6th grade school but for some time the parents in the district were pressuring the superintendent and board to leave the 7th and 8th grade pupils in that school rather than have them walk the long distance to Seymour. The PTA asked the superintendent to attend this meeting and explain why this couldn't be done. He didn't want to go, and told me that this was my department and I should go.

When I was introduced and began to speak, I became aware of a very hostile audience. This was a new experience for me, and feeling the tension in the room, I condensed my remarks, just outlining the requirements the state put on a school to maintain the secondary grades. I then stopped to give the audience a chance to ask questions. It became evident that one woman who sat in the front row was the prime leader of the movement, and she plied me with questions. I was ready with answers then came the surprise when she remarked, "In the midwest where I came from they did so and so." "That is interesting," I replied, "I also come from the midwest. Where did you live?" "In Iowa," she said. "Really, I was born and went to school in Iowa," I said. I could see she was getting interested and the climax came when it turned out she was born and lived near Clarinda, only a few miles from College Springs, my birth place.

The audience got a good laugh out of our revelations and right away the whole atmosphere changed. The woman broke up the meeting when she announced, "I can now see Mr. Calhoon's position makes sense." The social hour that followed was a very friendly affair. The next morning Reusswig met me in the hall and wanted to know how I had made out at the PTA meeting. My response was, "Fine, I learned how to win over a hostile audience, just be born in the right place." I then told him about the meeting, which evidently stopped the movement, as nothing more was said.

In 1959 I made a survey of the results of the "A" groups in all my schools. I wrote up my findings and put in into a booklet with copies going to all the principals, supervisors, the superintendent and members of the board. It was the first time anything like this had been done in the school system, and I received a number of complimentary comments about it. The Sunday edition of the *Utica Observer-Dispatch* gave it a big article.

It was at this time the Utica-Rome section of the Institute of Radio Engineers became active, and they wanted to do something to bring teachers in the public schools up-to-date on the many changes taking place in science and mathematics. They approached Superintendent Reusswig and while he approved the idea, he turned the whole project over to me. I worked with these engineers and some from the General Electric plant in Utica to develop a plan. A plan was formed to give a series of lectures on Tuesday nights for ten weeks at the Kernan School auditorium. I submitted the plan to the board, and they endorsed it, giving teachers who attended all lectures points for credit toward a salary increase. The result was that 80 teachers signed up and completed the course.

Some of the topics presented were contemporary chemistry, bacteriology, physics, electronics, nuclear energy, satellites, space and others. All the speakers were specialists in their fields, so their presentations were really on a graduate level. Much of the material was over the heads of a lot of the teachers, but it did give them an overview of the great changes that were taking place affecting the present world.

At the end of the lecture series, the committee of engineers put on a dinner for the teachers who attended and invited Reusswig and me as special guests. I was asked to speak at the dinner, mainly giving thanks to the Institute for bringing us such outstanding specialists to give the lectures. Then I was somewhat embarrassed by the excessive praise I received by both the engineers and the teachers for heading the project. I was sorry for this, as I felt a tinge of jealousy on the part of Reusswig right after this.

Gradually my work with the principals was progressing in bringing them together, but one perplexing problem remained. Checking with the schools I found there was no uniformity in the way promotions were made in the 7th and 8th grades. I brought this up for discussion several times at my meetings with the principals, and while they agreed there should be some uniformity, they remained far apart on their thinking. I believed in the community school and didn't want to destroy that, but since these schools were feeding the high school with students, I felt there should be a common method. After talking with the various principals I felt I had a good understanding of each one's philosophy on this question. With all this in mind, I drew up a plan which was a compromise between the extreme views and had it duplicated to present to the group in the spring meeting. I left a copy with the superintendent a week before this meeting. A few days before the time of the meeting he informed me he wanted to attend. He didn't say a word about the plan, so I made no comment about it.

When we were all assembled, I opened the meeting and announced that the superintendent had requested the opportunity to be with us. I then briefly outlined the problem of promotion policies and how important it was to the high schools. I announced that I had worked out a plan which I was submitting for consideration. I then passed a copy for each to read. For a time all was quiet as each one studied my plan, then before anyone made a response, Reusswig spoke up and said, "I do not approve of this plan. I know some of you would not follow it." Everyone looked up astonished at his outburst. I was dumbfounded. Here he had a copy of the plan for a week and hadn't said a word to me about it but waited for this meeting to give his disapproval. I was so upset I couldn't say a word but picked up my copy and put it in my pocket. I then turned to another subject and Reusswig left.

Our meeting was very short and while no one said anything to me, it was evident to all that the superintendent had pulled the rug out from under me. Whatever his motive he had succeeded in destroying all the authority I had built for my position. I was so furious I couldn't eat my lunch and sat at my desk for a long time, considering whether to confront Reusswig and have it out with him or say nothing, just resign. Since I was near the end of the two year period which I had promised when I took the job and seeing no chance of accomplishing anything under such conditions, I decided it best to retire. I wrote my resignation to take effect on July 1, 1960. After Reusswig read it, he asked me if there was anything about the position I didn't like. I'll admit I didn't tell the whole truth. I simply said after 43 years in education, I thought it was time to retire. I did add that before this position I had always been associated with a particular school, but now I felt sort of lost. I knew anything else I might say would not change him, so I thought it best to leave without any disagreement. When the news of my retirement was published, I was deluged with both congratulations on my retirement and regrets that I was leaving. Many said they thought I was too young to retire. I had to believe the personnel at the Administration Building were sincere when they said they hated to have me leave. In early June the Principals and Supervisors Club held a luncheon in my honor. The papers published a picture of me being presented with a model of a

A model of a satellite was presented at my retirment.

satellite. Besides saying some very nice things about me, they composed a couple of parodies, which they had fun singing. A few verses follow:

> Down at Lizzie, 13 Lizzie*
> Is a man named Ray Calhoon
> He is busy, oh so busy
> Every mornin', night and noon.

> You may find him in the classroom-
> Explaining how atoms split,
> Or consulting with the school heads,
> What'll they do when he quits?

> Finds new teachers, buy equipment,
> Selects textbooks, plans the schedules-
> Thus, the time does quickly pass.

> School days, school days
> Not the one room school days
> Physics and math and chemistry
> 7th through 12th is his specialty
> Split the atom, parse the verb
> Explain the theorem, define the word,
> With Mr. Calhoon the schools O.K.
> As he guides us along the way.

*Administration building, 13 Elizabeth St.

These verses seemed to best describe how these people felt about me and my work. I couldn't help feeling touched by the honor thus bestowed upon me by this group of which I had been a member for twenty years. A few days later an editorial appeared in the Utica paper; part of it follows:

> Mr. Calhoon has been in the Utica system almost 30 years. His activities covered grade school principalships and that of the Utica Free Academy. At this time he retires after 43 years in education here and elsewhere. He is director of secondary education. It was a mark of the respect his associates have for him that he was chosen to undertake the new duty as American schools began to answer the challenge of what some called the competition from Russia.
>
> In addition to his duties as an educator, Mr. Calhoon took part in civic affairs and had a big part in training people for special work during World War II.
>
> Ray Calhoon may leave the school system for a well earned rest and take with him the high respect of those who know his earnestness, sincerity and integrity—but what he contributed to the community will remain with us and for that we can be very content.

The last day of June I cleaned out my desk, packed my personal things and said goodbye to the people in the offices. Actually, some shed real tears. I was surprised to see how in a period of two and a half years I had made such an impression. It would take a while to realize that I would no longer be answering to a school bell.

CHAPTER 26

SCHOLASTIC AND RETIREMENT

The summer after I retired I spent part of the time painting my house and the rest of the time enjoying the camp. I knew I would feel strange to be at home when school opened in the fall, so we thought the best thing to do was to take a trip. We contacted Ula and she agreed to come to Dunlap, Iowa, where we could meet her at Leeta's for a family reunion. We found September a good time to travel, but were surprised to find the motels full due to so many retired people traveling after Labor Day.

The weather was beautiful all the way and continued into Iowa. With Ula we visited the farms that belonged to our relatives, greeted at each place with a big farm dinner. Art and Leeta had retired from the old farm and moved into the village. Francis, their oldest son, had taken over the farm and we enjoyed seeing it again. To keep active, Art had laid out a miniature golf course on a vacant lot across the street from his house and we enjoyed it to the fullest. Francis came in and we played a couple of rounds of golf on the Dunlap course. We had such a good time I forgot about school.

Ray, Faye, Ula and Leeta at Dunlap, Iowa in 1960.

505

In early 1961, Marjorie's boys, Jon and Billy came to stay with us when she went to the hospital to have our first granddaughter, Holly. She did not arrive until March 18 so the boys were here with us several weeks. It was the first evening they were here that one of our family jokes developed. We were at the dinner table when Norah fixed three-year-old Jon's plate with meat, potatoes and gravy. But Jon just sat looking at it and kept repeating, "Butter! Butter!" Norah tried to tell him to start eating, but to no avail. Finally Billy said, "He wants butter on his potato." Norah explained that he had gravy and didn't need butter, but it didn't make any difference.

I hated to interfere, but also thought it was too bad to have trouble on the first day, so when his grandmother wasn't looking, I slipped a little butter on top of his potato. I watched out of the corner of my eye to see what would happen and then had to smile. When Norah thought I wasn't looking she did the same thing. All smiles, Jon looked down on his plate and shouted, "Aha! Two butters!" We both got a good laugh out of it and for years whenever anyone in the family got a reward for doing something special, we would greet them with "Ha! Two butters."

The boys coming to stay with us was the beginning of a series of such events. As the grandchildren grew older they took turns coming to visit during their summer vacations. In 1967 Holly came to stay while Marjorie went to the hospital when Heidi was born. She was here at the time of her sixth birthday and so we gave her a little party which she always remembered.

One summer when the boys were five and six years old, Marj came with them to spend her vacation. We spent a lot of time at camp and the boys wanted to learn how to fish. One Sunday Dorothy came with her two boys, Robby and Jay, who were about the same age. All of the boys wanted to fish so I took them down on the dock and had them take turns holding a pole. The rock bass were hitting, but they couldn't hook them, so I would bait the hook and throw it out. When I got a strike I would hook the fish, hand the pole to a boy and watch the fun. When the boy felt the fish tug on the line, he would let out a yell and all the rest of the boys would begin to scream. With all the excitement I made each one pull the fish onto the shore so they could say they caught a fish.

Billy was the oldest and he wanted to catch his own fish, so I baited the hook and let him throw it out. In a few minutes he got a strike and managed to hook a 12 inch rock bass. I had them using an old fly rod and such a fish put up a real battle. I wouldn't help him other than tell him what to do. When the bass jumped out of the water a couple of times, all the boys were screaming at the top of their voices, while Billy was in tears with excitement, but he landed his fish. The women who had been up in the camp came down to the dock to see what all the excitement was about. Billy rushed up to the group and exclaimed, "Oh, Grandma, we all caught a fish. Jonny got one so big, (holding his hands about six inches apart) but I got one like this," and he threw out his arms as wide as they would go. This was his beginning of a true fisherman. All through his years in grade and high school he demonstrated his ability by winning several prizes in fishing contests. He was and still is an outdoorsman.

In August, 1961, V. G. Brown called me to see if I was interested in taking over his job as the representative of *Scholastic Magazines* in Central New York State. I knew he had done this for several years after he retired and liked it, but now he said it was too much for him to travel. I was interested as after a year of being free I thought of looking for a part time job, not only to be active, but I needed to earn some extra money to keep up with rising inflation. Mr. Brown said Jeff Watkins, the District Manager, was at his house and if I was interested, he could come right over to see me. I invited Watkins to come so I could talk about the job. It was about 4 p.m. when he arrived, and Jeff was such a dynamic person he was going strong telling about the company and its products at six o'clock. I invited him to take "pot luck" supper with us, but he declined and since by that time I had told him I would take the job, he said he would leave, stop at a fast food place to eat, then go back to Mr. Brown's house and pick up all the supplies he had and bring them to me.

He left a contract for me to look over and if satisfactory, I was to mail it to him at his office in New York City. The contract named me as the official representative of *Scholastic Magazines and Book Service* for six counties in central New York. I was to call on the schools in these counties presenting the books and magazines to the teachers, help adjust any difficulties that the schools had with the magazines, etc. Orders were usually sent into the main office by mail, so I could do what was commonly considered "soft selling." I liked this aspect, as I didn't consider myself a pressure salesman. One important activity was exhibiting the books and magazines at the various teacher's conferences. This proved to be the feature I enjoyed best.

The company representatives were considered outside salesmen, i.e. self-employed, and I was free to call on the schools as I wished. Consequently, I planned my trips to conserve the distance I traveled each day. I also planned my trips to the schools up north to be in October when the leaves were at their peak of color. I always took my camera with me and accumulated scores of beautiful colored slides taken on these trips. On all day trips Norah often went with me and we soon learned all the best places to stop for a picnic lunch. Trying to find a restaurant was time consuming and in the central schools noon was a good time to see teachers. It proved to be a very different type of work from what I had been used to in a classroom or an office, but I liked traveling and enjoyed meeting the many new people in these schools. I always put in what I considered to be a good day's work for the company, but I liked the freedom of planning my time. The fact that every year I worked for the company my sales increased, indicating I must have done all right.

507

Every year the district Manager held a conference meeting for all the representatives in his area, which consisted of the New England States, New York and Pennsylvania. These meetings were held in different cities in the area or sometimes in a resort hotel. The first one for me was in Albany and Norah was invited to go with me. It was her first experience at such an affair, so being free while we had our workshops and being a guest at all the fancy meals, she had a wonderful time. That was the only time she was invited as a guest, but by paying her expenses I often took her.

After two years Jeff was promoted to a position in the main office in New York and Jim Young took his place. Jim came to see me in Utica and I liked him at once. He was a very different type from Jeff, not the Fifth Avenue type salesman at all. I invited him to our house for dinner, and we had a chance to discuss many things, finding our ideas were much the same. As long as I was with the company I considered him more than just a boss; he was a good friend.

In 1968 the company, which from its beginning had been a family owned business, decided to go public and list their stock on the market. They gave each representative an opportunity to buy a certain number of shares before it became public. I did buy my allotted number, which I kept long after I retired from the company. At the same time they announced that from this time on all employees had to retire at age 65. However, the rule did not apply to those in service. I had to laugh, because if that rule had been in effect I would never have been offered the job. Jeff told me the company would not hire any more retired people as representatives, so I was lucky to get in when I did.

During these years I made a lot of new friends. After the first year I was invited to join the New York State Educational Salesman's Association. I found the men in this organization an exceptionally fine group. They held two business meetings a year, one at Christmas time and the other in the summer. I was surprised to see these meetings conducted better than some of the educational groups I had witnessed. This organization made the arrangements for the exhibits at the various educational conventions. If for no other reason it paid to belong to be sure of a space to set up my exhibit.

The highlight of the year was the summer meeting of the bookmen. It was held at some country club where all who wished could play golf all day and end with a good dinner followed by the business meeting. I was not a great golfer but I did enjoy playing and found others who were in the same class. My association with the salesmen's group was one of the highlights of these years.

Many of the principals of the schools where I called knew my background and after talking with them about Scholastic materials for a time, the conversation would often turn to educational problems. Some would say, "You were a school administrator for a long time; you must know all the answers." To which I would usually reply, "From my experience I know all the questions but I am still looking for the answers."

I also had people say to me, "Your job must be easy for you since you were in schoolwork for so long." To which I would reply, "Don't you believe it. I am now on the other side of the desk. There are schools where I cannot get beyond the office to see a teacher, even when I have known the principal for many years. The only advantage I may have is I know the language so I can communicate better, but I receive no favors." On the other hand, I was making some very fine contacts and after the first few visits I was well received in most schools. One thing in my favor was the material that Scholastic produced was of the highest quality, so I never felt I had to apologize for talking to anyone about it. Actually, once I could get it into the hands of a teacher, it sold itself. I found the company good to work for and as my sales increased every year, the company seemed to appreciate me; at least I know Jim Young did.

As I was free to adjust my time, we were able to take several trips during these years. One was a trip to Dunlap, where we met Ula once more. We were there during the World Series, and it was fun to watch the games with Ula. I knew she was a football fan but after retiring, she became interested in all sports. We had a wonderful week together with Leeta and Art, and it proved to be the last time we were to see Ula, so we were glad we took the time to go.

Another trip we took was at Christmas time to visit Aunt Nell in St. Petersburg, Florida. Some years before Ward had helped Uncle Clark and Aunt Nell move out of the cold winters in Vermont to the warm climate of Florida. He helped them buy a house, but Uncle Clark had died and left Aunt Nell alone with the house. She knew she couldn't keep it by herself and had written me suggesting we retire to Florida and we could live together so she could keep the house. I knew her well enough to know that we could not do anything like that, but I called her to see if she would like us to come down for Christmas. She was delighted, so we took off on short notice. I knew Floyd Treible spent his winters in Winter Park and we planned to stop to see him on the way down. By chance we found a motel very near where Floyd had a rented cabin. We had a visit after dinner that night, and he persuaded me to stay over so we could play golf. I had my clubs, hoping I might have a chance to play at least once while in Florida. To play with him once again after the many times we had enjoyed the game in Utica was a real treat, but in order to do so, I had to get up at 6 a.m. as that was the time he played with two other retired men. I was out of practice, so it took me a few holes to get going, but then I showed them all how it should be done. It was a beautiful morning and a great experience.

It was late afternoon when we found Aunt Nell's house on the causeway in central St. Petersburg. The first few days were warm and we enjoyed walking around the neighborhood viewing the beautiful houses and flowers. We also took Aunt Nell to see a number of her friends, which she appreciated as she had no transportation. One day we drove to Clearwater to see Lynn Bedford, whom I hadn't seen since we were in Clarkson together. Lynn had retired on disability after he had both legs removed several years before, but it was amazing the things he could do from his wheelchair. We met his wife and she took us through their beautiful home. Then Lynn insisted on taking us on a drive to see the beauty spots of the area. I'll admit I was a bit nervous to ride with someone who had no legs, but he had a car especially equipped that could be controlled by his hands and he was a good driver.

Aunt Nell had invited some friends for Christmas dinner and to my surprise, it was a couple I had known back in Houghton. I bought the turkey and helped get the dinner which turned out to be wonderful as Aunt Nell was a good cook, and seeing the guests made it special. On Sunday Aunt Nell wanted us to go with her to the big Pasadena Methodist Church, where she and Uncle Clark had joined. But it was so popular that in order to get into the auditorium we had to go to Sunday School where we would be given a ticket. This was a new experience for us, but we had to do it. Afterwards I was glad we did because the church was beautiful and while it seated over 2,000, there was an overflow crowd outside in their cars listening to the service over loudspeakers. Aunt Nell said the minister was a fine speaker and she was right; it was a memorable day.

A couple of days after Christmas the weather changed as a north wind brought a freeze. Most of the flowers were spoiled and when I went out in the morning and saw the top of my car all white with frost, I decided it was time to leave. On the way back we ran into some very cold winds in the Carolinas, and Norah picked up a bad cold which put her in bed when we reached home. We had now visited Florida both in the summer and in the winter giving us a chance to judge if we wanted to live there. Our decision was it was a nice place to visit, but for us, not a place to live.

In the summer of 1965 Dorothy wrote that Bruce was invited to Oneonta for an interview for a position at Hartwick College. She said they would stay overnight in a motel in Oneonta before the interview and then come on to Utica. We were excited to hear this, and when they arrived they were both elated. Bruce reported that the position, teaching anthropology and being an assistant curator at the Yager Museum, was just what he wanted so when they offered him a contract, he signed it. The next day they left the boys with us and drove back to Oneonta to look for a house. After spending all day with real estate agencies, they could not find a suitable house for sale or rent and finally contracted for a house to be built in a new area in West Oneonta.

While the house was under construction they spent the summer with us. When it was finished they had a beautiful home in a nice neighborhood. Of course we were delighted to have them nearby and located in a beautiful part of New York State. They were happy to get away from the smog and dampness of the Philadelphia area.

After Bruce got established in his new position, he learned that there

510

were a number of old Indian village sites in the area, and he took his classes on several field trips to explore them. Later he secured some Federal funds to pay students in the summer to do some digging in a couple of sites along the Susquehanna River flats near Oneonta. The results were very gratifying, as the students found a large number of artifacts and Bruce received some good publicity.

All the published literature by the anthropologists stated the earliest man had been in America was 10 to 15 thousand years ago. Bruce became skeptical when he found some artifacts in a gravel pit near West Oneonta which the geologists dated as between 15 and 30 thousand years old. When he published his findings it raised a storm of opposition. But it did focus attention on his work in that area.

The schools of Oneonta were in my district; when I planned to visit them I took Norah along to spend the day with Dorothy. One time in early June the public schools were in session but the college had been closed for a few weeks. Bruce had his group well organized and was on a site outside the city limits. I wanted to visit the site as I had heard much about such a dig but had never seen one, so late in the afternoon I picked up Norah and with Dorothy as a guide, we drove out to see Bruce. We had to drive through a big corn field across the flats until we came to the site near the banks of the Susquehanna River. Like pictures I had seen of such places, the site was all staked out in squares with letters to designate the position of a dig. The students worked in pairs digging in pits of varying depth. Judging from the amount of dirt heaped near one pit, I thought it was one of the deepest. Looking down I saw two college girls working away in the gravel about 15 feet down. I called down and asked if they were finding anything. "No," they replied in discouraging tones. They added they were well below the 15 thousand year level of gravel, where all the literature said to stop, but Bruce wasn't satisfied and kept them digging. Before I walked away I said, "Listen, I brought my camera and I want you to find something so I can take your picture." "Too bad," was their reply, "we are too far down to find anything."

I walked around to visit other pits, when Bruce blew his referee whistle and announced in a loud voice, "Five minutes to closing time. Clean your tools and get ready to leave." His voice had hardly died out when the two girls who I had talked to came bouncing up out of their pit screaming at the top of their lungs. I thought they must have dug into a wild animal den or a snake pit, then as everyone stared in their direction, one of the girls held her hand high over her head and shouted, "Look! See what I found!" In her hand was a perfect projectile point. Grasping my camera I hurried over to take her picture, but when she showed the artifact she found her hand was trembling so violently I couldn't get a picture. By that time Bruce had arrived and seeing my trouble said, "Donna, what is the matter?" "Oh, Dr. Raemsch, I'm so excited I am trembling all over," was her reply. Finally, with her holding the point against her body I did get a good picture. It was a perfect example of what a thrill it is to these people working on a dig to find something of significance. These girls knew that to unearth such an artifact at this low level was very strong evidence in favor of Bruce's theory that man was in America long before the 15 thousand year period. After this visit and keeping in touch with Bruce about his work, I often wished I was years younger becuase I would have really enjoyed such work.

The year 1966 marked the 50th reunion of my class at Oberlin. For once I was free to attend a reunion, so Norah and I went. It turned out to be an enjoyable experience. I had taken my golf clubs and got up early on Saturday morning to join an alumni golf tournament. It was a beautiful morning, Owen Walton, my classmate, was there also, and wanted to play with me but was scheduled to give an invocation at the dedication of the new King building that morning, so had to pass it up. I found a younger man from Chicago who was alone, and we teamed up for a fine round of golf. That night the class of 1966 and 1916 had a joint dinner. It was arranged so members of each class were at each table. Norah fell in love with the four young men who were members of the class of 1966 who were at our table. During the conversation there developed a discussion of the students protesting the actions of the president of the college. These were the years of college student unrest, and Oberlin was no exception. Turning to me, one boy asked, "What did your class protest against?" By the way he asked the question it was evident that they thought that college protesting was a normal way of life.

While we were in Oberlin we got a call from Bruce telling us that Dorothy was in the hospital with a new baby they had named Carol. We expected to be home before this happened but were glad to hear all was fine. Then in February of 1967 Holly came to stay with us while Marjorie went to the hospital for Heidi. This marked the end of the girls' families and gave us the perfect number of seven grandchildren. We could now watch them grow and develop. We made it possible for each to come and stay with us, and it became sort of a game to see which could stay the longest. At first it seemed strange to be called Grandpa, but after a time I rather enjoyed it. While they were all different individuals, I found I could relate to each and we enjoyed a mutual relationship which was good.

In the spring of 1969 Jim Young stopped in Utica to see me and told me that he was forced by the company to inform me that I had to retire as a representative of Scholastic at the close of the school year. The company had gone public with their stock and one condition they had to meet was a 65 year old retirement for all employees. They found I was eleven years over that retirement age, so they had no choice. Jim said he tried to keep me, as I had done such an excellent job, but was overruled. In a way I was sorry to leave the job, but I expected it and also Norah was beginning to fail, so she could no longer travel with me and I knew I would have to quit soon and take care of her.

The decade of the 70's was the time when I became a housekeeper, cook and nurse. The first sign of Norah's trouble came in a series of falls. In spite of my watching her, I had to pick her up off the floor, checking each time to see that she had no broken bones. She also became very forgetful and more than once I had trouble finding valuable things, such as checks, which she would hide and forget where she put them. In July of 1971 she had her first recognizable stroke. The doctor diagnosed her condition as a case of arteriosclerosis and told me what to expect.

For a time I was able to get Norah in the car to take short rides, including a monthly trip to the doctor's office, but after a time that became impossible. I had to give up going to camp and for two years it stood empty. I had several inquiries about selling it and when I saw how fast it was deteriorating, I decided it was best to do so. I notified all who had shown an interest in the camp that I would be there on a certain Saturday afternoon to show the camp. I hired a nurse to stay with Norah and met the people there on time. I was surprised at the number who came as the word had spread, and many whom I had not notified lined up to see the camp. Everyone raved about what a beautiful camp it was inside, and while the first two parties who saw it thought the price I had set was reasonable, they said they couldn't afford it. The third party asked for a week to decide, which I gave, and then the following week closed the deal. I had my lawyer draw up a deed and received cash, which I divided with my girls. I felt as if I had lost part of me when I handed over the keys for I had built the place and we had many happy years of summer vacations there, but conditions at home made it necessary to let it go.

As Norah's condition became worse, I had to give up most of my outside activities. One that I did not give up was being a member of the Ziyara Temple Band. I had been a member since 1954 and became real active in 1964 when I volunteered to become the band librarian. I did so to keep the director when he threatened to quit because he found the job was taking too much of his time. I didn't realize what a job I had undertaken. For over forty years the music that belonged to the band had never been catalogued and I found it all jumbled together in a large cupboard on the fourth floor of the Masonic temple. With some help I sorted out over 400 selections and got them organized in some filing cabinets which I purchased and had them all listed in a card file. For the next ten years I took charge of all the music for every parade and concert the band played. In 1965 I was elected the president of the band and for a year I had a dual responsibility.

I knew that the year 1971 marked the 50th anniversary of the founding of the Ziyara Band and I thought some recognition of this should be given. With the knowledge of the officers of the band, I undertook the project of writing the history of the band during these 50 years. Leaving Norah for short periods of time, I spent time in the Shrine office doing research in their records. Mrs. Adams and her

I played the Alto Horn in Ziyara Band and marched in the second row. This picture was from a visit to Herkimer in June 1957.

daughter, Carolyn, who had been a student in the Academy when I was the principal, were the office staff and they gave me free access to all the material I needed. My history included the organization of the band in 1921 with the names of all the charter members. It continued with the various concerts it gave and a description of the many cities where they paraded at the Imperial Sessions. At some of these, including New York City, Washington, Montreal and Chicago, I had been with the band. When I had finished the 25 page history, Mrs. Adams, who was the active editor of the *Bugle,* Ziyara's monthly magazine, asked to see it and was so impressed she made it into a serial of three issues. It became an instant "hit." The band members were delighted with the publicity and the many compliments they received from the Shriners and others. As a result of all this, the band was made the special guests at the fall ceremonial dinner. The Divan of the Temple had printed my history in a gold covered booklet and gave each member of the band a copy as a memento of the event. I was seated at the head table and introduced as the author of the history and presented with a plaque which was inscribed:

PRESENTED TO
A. RAY CALHOON
IN APPRECIATION
OF HIS DEVOTION
TO THE ZIYARA BAND.

In June 1972, Marjorie and Dorothy, with their families, came on a Sunday to celebrate our 50th wedding anniversary. Norah was able to be at the table and enjoyed all the attention. With all the grandchildren present, it made quite a crowd, but the girls insisted on bringing all the food so I could relax and enjoy the occasion. It was to be the last time we were all together as a family group.

Before this reunion, Marjorie and family had made an annual visit for Thanksgiving. I would have a big turkey and the children delighted

50th Wedding Anniversary—June 29, 1972

in helping stuff the bird and get it ready for the oven. I learned that people, especially children, have a better time when they go visiting if you let them help rather than do everything for them or they get bored. Heidi, the youngest, when she went to bed on Wednesday night would say to me, "Are you going to have pancakes for breakfast?" She thought that was a big treat and I did bake them so everyone was full but still were ready for the big Thanksgiving dinner. One weekend as the Hortons had the car all packed ready to start home, Heidi announced to her mother, "I'm not going." "But you have to go back to school," her mother replied. "I don't care, I'm staying here," said Heidi and looking at me, she continued, "You're a good cook." I walked over and gave her a big hug which solved the problem. As the children grew older and got into high school, they became interested in their own activities and came to see us only in the summer.

From time to time we had other visitors, including some of my relatives from the west. In 1973 my cousin, Bernice Bedford Conley, from California came with her husband and stopped overnight. She was working on the genealogy of the Crow family and had asked me for help in looking up some leads in this area. We had a good visit, talking about her work, which she finished some months later. It is an excellent piece of writing and a complete history of my mother's family. Later Margaret and Don Wetter from Des Moines, Iowa, dropped in unexpectedly. Don was then a principal of a high school in Des Moines and had been to a convention in Washington, D. C., so we had much to talk about.

Barbara White Geiger, the daughter of Ann Tooke White, Norah's best friend in Cazenovia, moved to Oneida with her husband, who was a minister. Every few weeks they would stop when he was calling on someone in his church who was in a Utica hospital. Then in 1979 Barbara said they would be alone for Christmas and wanted me to come to their house for dinner. I explained it was impossible to get anyone to stay with Norah on that day and invited them to come here for dinner. They accepted and I had roast chicken with all the fixings, which they said was excellent. Of course, Norah was a patient in bed and all these people marveled how I could cook such good meals while caring for her. Anyway, the word spread to others in my family so my reputation grew.

In 1970 Bob Esrich, my next door neighbor, retired from the New York Central Railroad. He knew I had been playing golf from time to time and asked if he could join me. I was delighted as we teamed up to go early in the morning playing nine holes, and I would be back in time to care for Norah. We played about the same game, so it was a wonderful outing for both of us. Then in 1978 Bob had a heart attack, spending some time in the hospital. The doctor thought he was much better and encouraged him to try golf again. We went out a couple of times, but he tired so much he gave it up. Then in August he collapsed and his wife called an ambulance but he did not make it to the hospital. After that I gave up golf.

Another reason for giving up golf was my left knee went bad. The doctor thought it was arthritis and maybe it was some, but the biggest factor was when lifting Norah one time she started to slip and I threw my knee under her and tore a ligament. For weeks I was in pain. At first it was excruciating to get up and down the stairs, but I had to grit my teeth and do it. I wore an elastic bandage which helped some and the fact I had to keep using it probably proved to be a good thing. If I had sat down, it probably would have become permanently stiff.

In the middle of the summer while my knee was slowly improving, I was going down the stairs one morning with my arms full of laundry when my foot slipped and I went head first down the rest of the way. I landed in a heap at the bottom, crashing into the telephone stand. When I got my breath back I found the telephone on top of me. My first thought was, "Well, if I can't get up, at least I have the phone to call for help." I untangled my legs, thinking of my knee which I examined and found it unharmed. After I sat up and shook my head to clear my vision, I got up and went about my work. In the evening my right knee, which had been my good one, began to stiffen, but it didn't seem bad so I went to bed. Then at two o'clock I woke up with a terrific pain in that knee. I got up, hobbled to the bathroom, applied some liniment, took some aspirin, and with a hot water bottle went back to bed. I didn't sleep much but was able to get out of bed and drove to the drug store to get another elastic bandage. A couple of days later I met my neighbor at the back fence and told him about my experience. "Now," I said, "I have both knees bandaged so I don't know which one to limp on." His quick response was, "Boy, you've got a real problem." When I told my doctor about my knee, he said such a delayed reaction was not unusual.

During the 70's the high school classes for which when I was their principal began to hold their 25, 40, 45 and 50 year reunions. I felt honored to be invited as a special guest at so many of these events. While the UFA classes were holding their 25th reunions, I felt it was a record to be invited to the 50th reunions of the classes of '27, '28 and '29 at Saratoga Springs High School. In every case I received a warm welcome and when asked to make some remarks, I tried to follow Dr. Ehresman's advice. One day when he was here to see Norah I told him I was asked to speak at one of these reunions and was wracking my brain as to what to say. His advice was, "Don't try to be profound, make it pithy and not too long." From the response I received after each time I talked, I found his advice had been very beneficial.

After the class of '27 reunion in Saratoga, I received a letter of thanks which said in part, "What a great thing you did for all of us by coming and speaking as you did . . . it really sparked the occasion and you fulfilled our expectations perfectly. Your presence and bearing made our high school memories a good feeling for us. You were one I could honestly say that we believed in; you never failed us."

Then at the end of the program at one of the UFA class reunions the president of the class, after thanking me for my speech, introduced me to his wife, who was not from Utica. She greeted me by saying, "I am so glad to really meet you. That was a wonderful speech, for years I have heard talk about Mr. Calhoon and now I know why." These are samples of the affection and awards I received, which more than compensated for the higher salaries I never got while working in education.

One thing that helped me through some frustrating years was maintaining my league bowling. I took up the game after I retired in 1961, when I was invited to substitute in the Utica Teacher's Bowling League. At first I worried about keeping my ball on the lane, but after a time I improved enough to be concerned about putting the ball in the pocket. I never have been a great bowler, but I did have a few 200 games and once in a while a total of 500 or more. There were only eight teams in the league when I joined, but it has now grown to eighteen. Each team is composed of three women and one man. Many of the women are better bowlers than the men and it has become a very competitive league. But this has kept me in contact with a number of teachers who are still working, plus a few like me who have retired.

The biggest event for me in the league took place in November, 1977. Someway the officers found out that it was the month of my 85th birthday. As we were bowling that week the president of the league came on the loud speaker ordering all bowling to stop and members to gather near the lunch counter for a meeting. I knew there was a meeting overdue, so I thought this was it. As I approached the crowd, which had gathered, two men took me by the arms and escorted me through the

"He's still knocking them down"
proclaimed the headline on November 13, 1985 the day following the bowling party for his 93rd birthday. Ray Calhoon keeps a 130 average stated the Utica Observer-Dispatch.

crowd. When I turned the corner of the alcove which contained the lunch counter, I gasped, for I was confronted by a huge cake big enough to serve 80 people. It was highly decorated with an inscription, "Happy Birthday A. Ray," and a big "85" in the middle. I was completely surprised, as no one had breathed a word of it to me. I was also presented with a plaque which read:

TO
A. RAY CALHOON
U.T.B.L'S
FAVORITE
BOWLER
WITH OUR LOVE
1977

When I was presented with the plaque I made a brief response, thanking the league for the gift and telling what a surprise they had given me. I added they should not think by honoring me that I would be an easy opponent. After we were served the cake and coffee, one teacher remarked, "Your speech was fine. You couldn't have done better if you had weeks to think about it." They had invited a photographer and a reporter from the Utica paper, so I had a big "write-up" with the picture.

To my further surprise the league repeated the party the next November. When I told the officers I thought one party on my 85th was enough for a lifetime, they replied, "Oh, we had so much fun we decided to make it an annual affair." This they did and on my 89th year they included the camera crew from the TV station. Also, on that year I bowled a 509 on my birthday with the Senior Men's League, which I had joined several years before. All this gave me quite a lot of publicity, but the important fact was I was making and keeping a lot of good friends which kept me going through some difficult years.

In 1975 Dr. Ehresman started coming to the house to see Norah. I was asked many times how I got a doctor to make a house call. I told them Dr. Ehresman did make such calls for his old patients and also he was one of my best students in my physics class when I taught at UFA. So he was more than just a doctor for us. When Norah became a complete bed patient, the doctor and I had frequent discussions about the human brain and the strange results that occurred when the supply of blood was cut off from a portion of it. I often thought about what a marvelous part of the body the brain is. Not only does it store a great amount of information, but also retains the feelings and emotions of our past experiences which can be recalled. It also has the ability to connect facts, reason, think through problems, and invent new ideas while meeting the events of our daily lives.

I watched the deterioration that took place in Norah as more and more of the blood supply was cut off. First the loss of memory, and the slow fading of the knowledge of the outside world.

One example of this trend was shown by the way Norah read. To keep her busy in bed, I gave her books to read, but had to stop it when I discovered she was underlining everything on a page with a black pencil. After that I gave her magazines, which could be discarded. Soon she began to read everything out loud. Then I noticed she was repeating a paragraph, then the same sentence, and finally the same line.

During her last years Norah gave up reading but did something else very strange. Looking at the design on the bed spread, she would spell words. Some were very difficult words but she would spell them correctly. I told the doctor about this, but he was rather skeptical until she demonstrated it for him several times. He stood in amazement. He said of all the old people he had treated, he never heard anything like it.

After Norah became a bed patient, I had to care for her just like a baby. When the doctor checked her each month he would shake his head saying, "It is strange how her vital signs are so good, but her mental condition grows so much worse." Dorothy came often enough

Norah Riggall Calhoon

so she could adjust to the change, but Marjorie came only in the summer and wasn't prepared. She brought Holly and Heidi during the summer of 1979 for a brief visit. They arrived at night, then in the morning while I was busy in the kitchen, they all went in to see Norah. In a few minutes Marj came down the stairs weeping. "She doesn't know me or the girls," she sobbed. "How do you stand it?"

My friends had asked me that question many times. My answer was based on a talk I had with the doctor after Norah's first stroke. In describing what I could expect, if I was to care for her he said, "From now on your relationship will be different." To which I responded, "Yes, I know from now on she will be my patient." He looked at me and said, "I couldn't have said it better." That is how I stood it.

Everytime the doctor came he asked, "How is she eating?" Until the first of June I could always say, "Very good." Then after a large stroke she did not eat for three days. She also slept during the daytime, something she never did before, even when she kept me awake all night by constantly talking. I knew she was getting close to the end and when the doctor came, he confirmed it.

Each day she ate less and grew much weaker. I hoped she might last until the 18th for her 90th birthday. Also, Marjorie was a delegate from her church to a conference in Alberquerque, New Mexico, and would be gone for a week. I didn't want to spoil her plans.

The doctor and I had agreed that she would not go to the hospital and be put on a machine but we would let her go peacefully in her own bed. On the 24th she drifted into a semi-coma. I alerted both girls. Then in the early morning hours of June 26, 1980, her loud and labored breathing woke me from my sleep and I knew the end was near.

> Numbed, I sat on the side of the bed
> Sensing the presence of the Angel of Death
> First hovering, then touching and fled.
> Listening to the silence that followed.
> Time passed, how long I do not know.
> Slowly the thought crossed my mind,
> I have now seen the Alpha and Omega of life.
> First, the gasp of a new born babe
> Sucking in its initial breath
> And now the choking of the old
> When all breathing stopped.
> These mark the beginning and the end
> Of the greastest mystery of all
> LIFE that exists between.

Her body had outlived her mind by a considerable time, but for the record her days were eight beyond her 90th birthday and three short of our 58th wedding anniversary. While waiting to get hold of the doctor I pondered the long life we had together. I thought of the unusual chain of circumstances that led to our meeting in the first place. How for a school year we enjoyed so many good times together and saw each other almost every day. Then our paths separated and for the next nine years we lived independent lives. For long periods we were far apart, not able to see each other. Yet, neither of us found anyone else and when we were brought back near each other again, we decided to be married. This made a big difference to me for the first time since I was 16 years old, I had a place to call home.

I remembered how she gave up her career as a teacher to become a devoted homemaker, wife and mother. After the girls were born, her chief interest was in their welfare. While she did have some outside activities, it was only after the girls left home for college and a life of their own that she became real active in some women's organizations. In those years she made a host of friends, most of whom she outlived.

After we were married it was always our life. She never complained when during the depression we had a rough time. Many times our bank balance was down to almost zero, but she trusted me to make the right decisions even when we had to move. I was thankful I could repay her some by caring for her during the last ten years, and she could enter her eternal sleep free of pain. Now my life would be different.

As the doctor was leaving after he came to verify my report, he turned to me and said, "Well, you saw it through to the end. There were times I didn't think you could. You never need to have any regrets. You did everything anyone could do and more. Now get some rest."

I called the undertaker and while waiting for him, I called the girls. I asked Dorothy to come and help with the arrangements. The undertaker was prompt and since it was early Thursday morning, he agreed we could get a notice in the afternoon paper so we could have the calling hours on Friday afternoon and evening, with the funeral on Saturday morning. I had an obituary all ready, which he said was fine, and he would proceed to follow my wishes. I included in the obituary the fact that Norah was a direct descendant of Stephen Hopkins, the 14th signer of the Mayflower Compact. She was also a relative of Elisha and Samuel Paine, who gave the land for the campus of Colgate University. This was something of which she was rather proud but rarely talked about. In fact, we had been married several years before I knew it.

Rob came with Dorothy late that morning and right after lunch we all went to the funeral parlor to make all the arrangements. When Norah and I had decided we would probably stay in Utica the rest of our time, we selected and bought a cemetery lot. Later, when Norah was confined to her bed, I had selected a monument and it had been set, so all that was ready. When Dorothy was satisfied that everything was set for the following days, she was ready to go back home. Then Rob announced that he would stay with me. I said it wasn't necessary, but he insisted. I was grateful to him, for it did help me get through the first night.

Dorothy and family were here early for the calling hours on Friday afternoon, but Marjorie and her family didn't make it until about 2:30. I had a supper planned for all before going to the funeral parlor in the evening. Also, we found a place for everyone to sleep except Dorothy and Bruce, who decided it would be better for them to go to a nearby motel. Bill, who was in Arizona, and Jay, who was in California, were the only ones of the family missing.

Dr. Mingledorf, the minister of Central Church, officiated at the funeral and all thought he was very good. I asked Bruce, Bill, Rob and Jon to act as bearers. When we left for the cemetery, none of the friends who attended the funeral went with us, so it became a real family affair, which pleased me very much. After the funeral, Dorothy and family left in the afternoon, but Marjorie and her family stayed over until Sunday. That was good, as it gave me a chance to adjust to a different life.

Norah was the last of her family and mine was growing smaller. Soon after the last time we had been in Dunlap, Iowa, Arthur, Leeta's husband, had died. Then after several years of being an invalid, Aldo, Fay's husband, died in 1977. Dale had gone through a tragic experience when Marian, his wife, was found dead in her home. Then in September of 1980, after suffering for many years with diabetes with periods of being in and out of the hospital, Ula had a massive stroke and died. She was the first to break our family of brothers and sisters. Ula never married and since she was the middle child of the family, we all looked to her to keep us together. She remembered everyone's birthday and anniversary. We so missed her, but we continued keeping our family letter going.

My brother Dale visited in 1982.

In March, 1979, Aunt Nell had died on her 98th birthday. For several years she had been in a nursing home in Des Moines, Iowa. Knowing how she loved to receive mail, I wrote her several times a year, to which she replied with long letters telling her philosophy of life and true to the Crow family trait, telling me what I should do. I read these parts of her letters with a smile. After my surprise birthday party at the bowling lanes on my 85th year, I wrote her all the details. She replied saying what a thrill she got out of hearing about the party. She closed her letter by saying, "I want to ask you a question. After all the years you spent in education as teacher, coach, elementary school principal, high school principal, and director and now that you have retired, you have become a housekeeper, nurse, do your laundry, cook, bake, have a garden, do canning, make pickles, and now you say you are a bowler; how can one man do so many things?"

I answered by telling about an episode which happened to me and she told me later that she got a chuckle everytime she thought about it. I wrote saying she asked how I could do so many things. You could have added a few more, such as in my younger days I worked on farms in four different states, was in the army in World War I, worked my way through high school and college by doing all sorts of jobs. After the war I was an industrial chemist, draftsman and my last paying job was a traveling salesman. How I could do all these things I can best explain by telling this story.

When I became a full time housekeeper, I thought I had to keep up with my neighbors and do some spring house cleaning. When I took down the kitchen window curtains, they started to fall apart, so I knew I needed new ones. It happened that Grant's store had mailed a sales flyer in which was pictured some curtains like I wanted at a reduced price. I took a trip to the store, walked in, found the curtain display, but they were not the ones I wanted. I could not find a clerk to ask, and was about to appeal to the cashier when a little, young, black haired girl came dancing out of a back room. She rushed up to me and asked if she could help. "Yes," I said, "I'm looking for these curtains on sale," pulling out a copy of the ad from my pocket. "Oh," she said, "Those are all gone, but we have these at the same price." The ones she indicated were not what I had in mind but were so much cheaper than anything else on display I decided to get them. Then I began my education about curtains, when I asked if these would cover the whole window. "No," she replied, "you need the valance to cover the top." These I discovered cost twice as much as the curtains, but I wanted to do it right so I said, "I'll take two of them." Grabbing a couple of packages off a shelf, the clerk thrust them at me and said, "Pay the cashier."

I looked down at the cellophane covered packages and while they seemed to match the curtains, I discovered one was marked a dollar more than the other. I looked at the shelf where the girl got the packages, but it was empty. So I stood holding them, waiting for the clerk to be free after dashing off to wait on another customer. After a time she came back and wanted to know if I wanted something else. I held out the two packages and started to explain the difference, but before I could finish she grabbed them, exclaiming "Somebody goofed." She ran back into the stock room and came out with two alike. "Thanks," I said, "I didn't want to get home and find I had different sizes." Looking up at me with a serious expression, she said, "Gee! You are a smart man."

So you see, Aunt Nell, I wrote, that is why I could do so many different things. I am a smart man. The clerk in Grant's store told me so. But after all, I am "JUST ONE IN A MILLION."